Limited Edition of 750 copies

C000294805

A
HISTORY OF
WEST BROMWICH

BY

FREDERICK Wm. HACKWOOD

F.R.Hist.Soc., M.S. (Salt) Arch, Soc.

AUTHOR OF:–
"SOME RECORDS OF SMETHWICK"
"HANDSWORTH: OLD AND NEW"
"HISTORY OF TIPTON"

REPRINTED FROM 'MIDLAND SUN'
OF
April 7th 1894 – August 31st 1895

EDITED BY ALAN A. VERNON

Brewin Books

First published as a Limited Edition
and Printed by the
"B'ham News" and Printing Co., Ltd.,
28, John Bright St. 1895.

This edition of 750 numbered copies published by
Brewin Books Ltd., Studley, Warwickshire, B80 7DL, 2001

© Introduction – Alan A. Vernon 2001.
All rights reserved.

The editor's rights have been asserted.

British Library Cataloguing in Publication Data
A catalogue record for this book is available from
The British Library

ISBN 1 85858 206 7

Made and Printed in Great Britain by
Warwick Printing Company Ltd.
Theatre Street, Warwick CV34 4DR.

Dedicated to Right Honourable The Baroness Boothroyd of Sandwell who was formerly M.P. for West Bromwich for 27 years.

Published in a limited edition
of 750 copies

No: **326**

FREDERICK WILLIAM HACKWOOD

F. W. Hackwood was born to Enoch and Sarah Hackwood on the 18th April 1851 at 69 High Street East, Wednesbury. His father, Enoch was a tailor, the family had settled in Wednesbury in the middle of the 18th century, the Hackwoods originally came from Stoke-on-Trent.

In 1868 he was admitted to St. Peter's Teachers Training College, Saltley and in 1871 he was appointed headmaster of St. Bartholomew's Church Schools at Wednesbury. In 1878 he was Headmaster of Dudley Road Board School, Birmingham and in 1888 he became Headmaster of Soho Road Board School also in Birmingham where he stayed until 1916 when he retired.

In 1874 he married Sarah Phoebe Simkin and they had two children, a son, Harold and a daughter, Louisa. He lived with his family at Comberford Lodge, Bridge Street, Wednesbury, until a subterranean fire at a neighbouring colliery forced them to leave the house and move to Handsworth. During the course of his life Frederick Hackwood wrote 28 books about Staffordshire and the Black Country, 'A History of West Bromwich' being one of them, and was published in 1895. Apart from writing on local history, he wrote books on a variety of other subjects including Natural History, Education, Church Lessons, Biography, Marriage, Sport and Food.

In addition to being a teacher and an author he was also a magistrate, a town councillor, a footballer, and the founder of several clubs and societies and was involved in creating open spaces like parks, allotments and re-afforestation of reclaimed colliery waste areas.

The last years of his life were spent at 2 Veronica Road, Balham near to his son, where he died on the 4th December 1926 aged 75 years.

PREFACE.

This History, in its reprinted form, is now presented to the local reader for what it is worth. It is known to possess some inaccuracies and not a few shortcomings, as must ever be the case with any work published from week to week in the columns of a periodical paper. (This particular work ran uninterruptedly for no less than 74 weeks, or 17 months). The Author, however, claims to have kept faith with his readers in producing a History which in its style has been popular enough to be readable by the average newspaper subscriber; special care having been taken to avoid the old-fashioned system of compiling a History which is merely a collection of isolated facts, a list of names and dates, and all the dry bones of ancient records thrown promiscuously together, without due regard to their correlation and actual hearing upon each other. As to those portions dealing with recorded ancient history, of course nothing could be attempted beyond the re-adjustment of the accents. And where lists have unavoidably crept in, they have been preserved solely for their undoubted value as references. There has certainly been no attempt to embalm genealogies, or to enshrine family greatness. And while nothing essential has been overlooked or omitted, no one single portion has been allowed to throw the others out of perspective. Impartially has every phase and feature received its just and proper treatment: of West Bromwich the history has been slowly traced from the obscure Traditional, to facts. Territorial, both Manorial and Parochial; through its progress Ecclesiastical (Roman, Anglican, and Non-conforming) and also its progress Educational; in its development Social, Political, and Municipal; bringing it onward right to its Present Day maturity, and not making the common mistake of leaving off at the date when modern newspapers came in. Only has the narrative turned aside at the very rarest intervals, when neighbouring localities have thrown the influence of their contiguity too powerfully upon the life-story of West Bromwich—such as its closely related borderlands of Barr, Oscott, Handsworth, Halesowen, Wednesbury, etc., etc. F.W.H.

Wednesbury,
  Sept., 1896.

ACKNOWLEDGEMENTS

I wish to thank the following for their help and assistance in republishing this volume. Firstly, to Alan Brewin, in agreeing to my suggestion to make this book available once more to a wider public. Stan Wilkins, Chairman of West Bromwich Local History Society, Sandwell Community History and Archives Service at Smethwick Library, West Bromwich Central Library staff. Finally the people of West Bromwich who have seen and lived through all the changes in their town.

BOOKS BY F. W. HACKWOOD.

Notes of Lessons on Moral Subjects.   1883.
Darlaston.   1887.
History of Tipton, in Staffordshire.   1891.
A History of West Bromwich.   1895.
Some Records of Smethwick.   1896
Sedgley Researches.   1898
Handsworth Old and New.   1908
Annals of Willenhall.   1908
Oldbury and Round About.   1915
The Story of the Black Country.   1892
Chronicles of Cannock Chase.   1903
Staffordshire Curiosities and Antiquities.   1905
Staffordshire Stories.   1906
The Birmingham Midlands.   1906
Staffordshire Worthies.   1911
Staffordshire Sketches.   1916
Staffordshire Customs, Superstitions and Folklore.   1924
Staffordshire Glimpes.   1925
Staffordshire Miscellany.   1927.   [posthumously]
Through the Midlands.   1905
Westward of the Wash.   1906
Story of the Shire.   1921
Olden Warwickshire.   1921
Notes of Lessons on Kindness to Animals.   1892
The Practical Method of Class Management.   1896
Natural History Reference Notes.   1897
Notes of Lessons on the Church Service.   1897
New Object Lessons [Animal Life]   1898
Chatty Object Lessons in Nature Knowledge.   1900
The Good Old Times.   1910
Old English Sports.   1907
Inns, Ales and Drinking Customs of Old England.   1909
Good Cheer, The Romance of Food and Feasting.   1911
William Hone, His Life and Times.   1912
Life of Lord Kitchener.   1913
Dragons and Dragon Slayers.   1923
The Bridal Book. The Lore, History and Philosphy of Love, Courtship and
     Marriage   1923
Wednesbury Papers   1884
Wednesbury Workshops   1889
Olden Wednesbury   1899
Religious Wednesbury   1900
Odd Chapters in the History of Wednesbury   1920
Wednesbury Notes & Queries. 3 Vols.   1902.
Wednesbury Ancient & Modern.   1902.
Pocket Guide to Wednesbury.   1908.
Christ Lore

INTRODUCTION

When 'A History of West Bromwich' was compiled in 1895 by Frederick Hackwood from articles originally written for the B'ham News and Printing Co., Ltd., this Black Country town, like its neighbours was an area that administered its own affairs and this remained its status, unlike neighbouring towns it became swallowed up and part of the Metropolitan Borough of Sandwell.

The changes that have taken place over the intervening one hundred years have enabled West Bromwich to grow from a 'barren waste land' into a town of increasing importance.

The earliest historical reference to West Bromwich dates back to 1086 and the compilation of the 'Domesday Book', before that date it does not appear to have had a separate existence, its sparse population leaving no trace of their human history, apart from it's name, 'Bromwich', a village where you find broom growing, eventually becoming West Bromwich by the 14th century.

Like many Black Country towns West Bromwich was originally a rural community, with an iron and nail-making industry developing from small beginnings. There is evidence of local metal manufacturing by the early 16th century producing buckles, rings and bridle bits.

Nail-making continued to be important to the workers of West Bromwich providing employment until the early part of the 19th century, eventually being replaced by factory made products.

Apart from these items other trades and skills were developed e.g. gun and pistol locks, steel bayonets, spring balances, buttons, watch chains, hat-pins and sword-hilts.

By the end of the 18th century a foundry industry became established, producing light and heavy cast ironmongery and with this growth in the foundry trade, came a growth in the use of wrought iron and an increase in the number of blacksmiths and forges, these were used in the production of items for the construction and railway industry which in turn demanded boiler and engine making and structural ironwork for bridge building.

West Bromwich continued to grow in the type and range of products it made and at one time it was producing its own coal and ironstone. The manufacturers were successful because they were prepared to diversify, a lesson learnt too late by many modern manufacturing companies.

If we are to learn anything from reading 'A History of West Bromwich' it is that West Bromwich as a town has a history worth repeating and it continues today to make its mark for present and future generations.

A. A. Vernon.   November 2001
A & B Books.   ©

CONTENTS

A
HISTORY OF
WEST BROMWICH

1.—Introductory. The Development of West Bromwich.

West Bromwich may not infelicitously be called the Chicago of the Midlands, for fewer English towns have risen so rapidly into the front rank of municipal life. The beginning of the century found it a mere straggling village; at the close it stands revealed as a County Borough of some considerable size, dignity, and importance. This rapid development would seem to be the outcome of that restless activity and enterprising spirit, which after being the secret of their own private commercial successes, its prominent men have carried with them into the public life of the place. Tracing this civic growth to its very earliest sources, there would appear to be little doubt that the first impetus to the corporate prosperity of West Bromwich was given when this parish was selected as the centre of a Poor Law Union. In 1834 the Poor Law Amendment Act constituted West Bromwich a "union," uniting together for Poor Law administrative purposes the parishes of West Bromwich, Wednesbury, Oldbury, Handsworth, and Warley. But although for more than 20 years afterwards no union workhouse had as yet been erected, to be peopled with its aggregation of the pauper population of four other parishes; and though the higher orders of officialdom had as yet to be introduced, the great fact was accomplished for West Bromwich, which would eventually force its name and existence into prominence, it was constituted a Union, and upon it, as such, the Local Government Department in London focussed all its papers, documents, and correspondence, Whether from the Poor Law Commissioners, the Poor Law Board. or the Local Government Board (as the same central authority in London was successively designated), the whole of its dealings with this district in respect of matters of local government came to, or through, West Bromwich. A brief check to the town's self-development may possibly have been given when, in 1868, it was included within the parliamentary borough of Wednesbury. But in 1882 renewed vigour was put into the public life of the place by its incorporation as a municipal borough; in 1885 the new borough was freed from the parliamentary fetters of Wednesbury, and became a parliamentary constituency of itself, while the consummation of all its greatness came in with the year 1890, when it became an independent "county," self-contained for all the purposes of local independence and unrestricted self-government. The Union Workhouse in Hallam Street, West Bromwich, was opened in 1858, when the paupers of the five parishes were concentrated there, as it was said, for their better care and supervision, and for the cheaper and more effective administration of the Poor Law. The small parish workhouses at Wednesbury, and the other places, were finally closed. But that the preference of one parish was to the prejudice of the others may be inferred when we consider that at West Bromwich the Poor Law is now administered for a united population of about 130,000, and in being so draws money from an area, whose rateable value is about half a million sterling. But let us go back a few steps in the development of the life politic of this parish. At the commencement of this century West Bromwich took its proper part in a great national movement. It would appear that early in the Tudor period corn-lands were enclosed as pastures to keep in the sheep, reared in vast numbers for the rapidly-growing staple trade in wool. For instance, in February, 1516, no less than 60 acres were enclosed in Rushall parish. But the nineteenth century finds another enclosure movement in progress—common, and wastes being enclosed to provide corn-lands for the rapidly increasing population—an increase stimulated by the inventions of the steam engine and multiplying machinery of all kinds. Hence the attention directed to the extensive waste lands existing in West Bromwich at that time which were situated, too, in a neighbourhood which was quickly becoming a great and populous industrial centre. West Bromwich consisted largely of part of a wide elevated heath, which commencing at what is still known as "The Heath," stretched away to the east and to the south, finishing at Birmingham Heath, near to Winson Green. Remnants of this heath land may still be seen almost in their pristine state of wildness at The Summit, Smethwick, and near the Railway Station at Handsworth. The highest point of this tableland is reached near the top of Thynne Street, which is 569 feet above sea level—Liverpool mean watermark. Hill Top is at an elevation of 520 feet, the old Parish Church 507 feet,* while the Birmingham Road, near The Woodman Inn, attains 550 feet. The lowest point is the Old Forge Mills which is only 347 feet. In the name *Sandwell* we obtain a fair idea of the nature of the land—a sandy subsoil—and the prevalence of hard sandstone rock. Under the new red sandstone and at a great depth the coal has been found in recent years; at Sandwell Colliery it is some 300 yards below, while at Hamstead Colliery it is nearly 500 yards down. The parish first began to emerge from its rural state of village life, when in 1802 an Act was obtained for enclosing these waste lands, which were estimated to comprise an area of 387 acres. The Commissioners appointed to carry out the provisions of the Enclosure Act were Messrs. John Chamberlain, Richard Fowler, and Thomas Green, gentlemen. In dealing with the common fields, common pastures, waste lands, and commons within the manor, they were required to make public carriage roads, which were to be at least 40 feet wide, exclusive of ditches 4 feet wide, while the turnpike road, which was a main coach road between London and Holyhead, was to be 60 feet wide. For the repair of the roads the Commissioners were to assign two acres for the provision of stone, gravel, etc. In the hedges along the roadside no trees were to be planted at a less distance from each other than 50 yards. To the lord of the manor was reserved the right of mining under these waste lands for coal, iron, etc., and for the erection of all necessary works in this connection. How far this Act was useful may be judged best from the "History of West Bromwich," written in 1836 by Joseph Reeves, who says (p. 155) "We have seen a once barren waste land enclosed, ploughed, sown, harrowed and where formerly stones, weeds, thistles gorse, fern, and pools overspread the soil, there have we seen the corn waving to and fro, there have we gazed at the flowers that decked the beautiful parterre, and at the cattle grazing in the verdant pastures, we have seen these enclosed fields marked into streets, and these streets in great part filled with horses, and these houses with inhabitants. We have seen more than this, in the place where the coney inhabited we have a magnificent church and five dissenting chapels, We have also some princely edifies, and many good shops where one can buy all kinds of things as cheap as in Birmingham. The situation of the common being on rising ground with plenty of excellent soft water, and the great Holyhead Road also passing through it, have induced many respectable families to settle in the place. There can thus be little doubt that the development of coaching towards the close of the last century had also something to do with the rise of West Bromwich. Before 1752 the "coach" road from Shrewsbury to

---

* Wednesbury Old Church stands 537 feet above sea level.

London missed West Bromwich, as it kept the Watling Street to Brownhills, and then proceeded via Castle Bromwich and Coventry. In that year the Shrewsbury and London "Caravan" was brought through Wolverhampton to Birmingham, performing the whole journey in four days, and stopping the first night in Birmingham. The good road here thus gradually attracted the traffic from Shrewsbury to London through Wolverhampton and Birmingham till 154 miles was Performed by the "Wonder" in sixteen hours. With regard to the traffic from London to Holyhead, that also missed West Bromwich till 1779; as previously, after leaving Coventry, it proceeded via Coleshill, Lichfield, and Chester. Ultimately the Irish traffic was also attracted through West Bromwich by the vigorous efforts of the Shrewsbury hotel keepers. Chester was missed, and the Welsh Hills were crossed till in 1810 the coach over Hill Top with the Holyhead mails performed the $276\frac{1}{2}$ miles in $40\frac{1}{2}$ hours. This route was through Oxford, but when it was shortened, by going through St. Alban's, to 261 miles, the Post Office timed the journey to be done in 26 hours 55 minutes, and the coldest spot on the whole of the journey was said to be Hill Top. There were seven coachmen employed for this entire length from end to end. It must be borne in mind that previous to 1784 there were no "mail" coaches—there were only heavy "slow" coaches the mail-bag being conveyed by post "boys"' on horseback. In 1784 lightly-built quick travelling coaches were substituted, and the post "boys" ceased travelling through West Bromwich and everywhere else. In 1785 the mail coaches were exempted from tolls. Toll gates stood till a quarter of a century ago at Holloway Bank, at Sandwell Road, and at Three Mile Oak. A coach running between London and Birmingham would have had to pay as much as £1,428 a year in tolls.

Such is the picture of West Bromwich in the first stage of its urban growth, in that period just anterior to the introduction of railways, and while horse-coaching was still in vogue. Presently we will turn our gaze upon the same place as it existed long ago, centuries back in the dim days before the Doomsday Book.

Enumerated in proper order we thus get four great causes contributing to the development of West Bromwich: (1) The attraction of the main coaching traffic between the capital and Holyhead; (2) the cheap construction through the parish of a very fine highway, which quickly becomes a new centre of commercial life; (3) the formation of a union to which gravitates much of the local government of four other surrounding parishes, and (4) the very late discovery of valuable coal seams just as those in the adjacent Black Country parishes were worked out.

II.—The Period of Legendary History.

Unfortunately for the outset of our history West Bromwich seems to have had no separate existence during the more remote stages of the nation's early development. The place as a distinct entity—that is, as the fixed habitation and settled home of certain members of the human family—is unknown or at least unnamed, during those dim and distant centuries away back behind the Norman Conquest. The very earliest historical reference to West Bromwich dates back only to 1086. While, therefore the national chronicles are running steadily onwards through the respective periods of the Ancient Briton, of the civilising Roman, and possibly of the Anglo-Saxon, we are left to imagine that the primeval solitudes of West Bromwich were but occasionally invaded by the straggling hunter, and that the place itself remained an unbroken wilderness to a comparatively late period, and that it was for the most part high, dry, bleak, and to a degree uninviting in its nature. If its history during this remote period remains a blank, what has been lost? Outside the region of sentiment, positively nothing! For of the majority of those more favoured towns, whose people do claim for them a higher antiquity it will be found that much of the boasted history of such places resolves itself, when closely and carefully examined, into mere legend and unreliable tradition. Accepting for West Bromwich the position that at this time it possessed no independent existence, and therefore had no human history, it may not be altogether unprofitable to glance at some of the reputed "history" of those surrounding localities, in which that of West Bromwich is more or less involved. And the obscurity and the haziness of it all will be at once apparent. The whole farrago will prove to be little more than fables of giants and such equally mythological personages. Let us test the history of the most ancient settlements of the immediate vicinity.

Barr Beacon is 750 feet above sea level. Dr. Plot supposes that Barr Beacon was the residence of the Arch-Druid in early British times, and that the contiguous wilds received their denomination *Cyl*, "a temple," or *Coel* "an omen, or beacon," from which we thus get a British derivation *Coelfine* signifying "stones of omen" for the "Coldfield" of Sutton. Taking into account the proximity of the two places it is quite possible on the other hand that *Col* may signify "a sharp hill," and Bar "a summit." According to Salmon, a writer of the last century, there were round the Beacon Hill "lines" on one side "enclosing a large camp in form of a half moon." Other ancient remains at Barr consist of large stones (by some said to be of Druidical signification) and a few mounds. One mound north of Aldridge Church is supposed to be the burial place of a great chief. In 1824 there were discovered at Lower Stonall, and forwarded to the Society of Antiquaries, the following remains:—

A British sword or *cleddyf*.

A British dagger, or *cleddyfan*.

Three *Celts* or battle-axes, the bwyelbawan of the Britons.

There were also lance-butts, a rod of office, sword pommels, etc. The metal was an alloy of copper and tin—the same compound sometimes used by the Romans for armour, but not for their weapons such as they used in Britain. The Anglo-Saxons also knew the use of steel, so that little doubt is left as to there remains being British. Here (and possibly even at West Bromwich) dwelt some of the Cornavii tribe, in clusters of beehive-like huts, embowered in the woods, as did others of the same Cornavian Britons on Maney Hill, Walsall Hill, Wednesbury Hill, and all other ancient hill settlements. On each summit was a stone altar surrounded by the usual concentric circles of large stones, in which the Druids practised their astrological studies, and performed their cruel rites. After the earlier period of lurid offerings and human sacrifices, perhaps the less bloodthirsty sway of the Bards succeeded for a short time, when under the same sacred oaks the gentler forms of the *gorsed* or convocation were observed—the Bards laying the sword of peace on the high altar, and reciting their poems in the midst of the upright stones. Then came the Roman occupation of Briton. Watling Street, running between Dover, and Chester passed near Barr. This road was crossed at Wall near Lichfield by the Icknield Street, which running through Harborne, Birmingham, and Handsworth, crosses the Tame at Perry Barr, and runs on through Sutton in a perfectly straight line. The river Tame indubitably obtained its name during the period of the Ancient Briton—Tame being a British word signifying "overflowing." With the invasion of the Saxons a new epoch sets in, the British flying before the fierce onslaught of the barbarian hosts, and giving place to the new comers; those of any substance taking with them their portable possessions in the chariots of war (for which roads had always led down from such hill forts as Wednesbury and Barr), and the flight of which would now be facilitated northwards and westwards by the great Roman roads, as at Wall (Etocetum) near Lichfield. Thus briefly summarising the British and Roman periods, we pass on rapidly to review our local history under the

Anglo-Saxons. The midland kingdom of the Saxon heptarchy was Mercia. One of its greatest kings, Offa, is said to have lent his name to the hundred of Offlow; hut this is doubtful. Offa's usual place of residence was Tamworth, at which town he had a mint, and coins struck at Tamworth are still extant. It is not unlikely that Sutton acquired its name from the feet of its being the "south town," or royal hunting station south of Tamworth; for when not engaged in war these Saxon kings and their great nobles indulged largely in the pleasures of the chase. In those times there frequently broke from the coverts of Sutton forests, or the wilds of Cannock Chase, the wolf, the boar, and the red deer, whose pursuit was easier to the eager huntsman across the wide heath of Bromwich and over the sandy stretches of Handsworth, than through the tangle of the dense woodlands. *Cannock* is said to have derived its name from the Danish monarch Canute, whose favourite hunting-place it became. Of Danish influence upon the Midlands there are yet many traces easily recognisable. Whether the boats of the marauding Norsemen ever penetrated these upper reaches of the Tame is extremely doubtful. At Nottingham, which they took, and at Derby, whose name is of Danish derivation, and yet again nearer at Croxall, where they certainly did land from the narrowest of streams, we have positive records of the Northmen's near presence and warlike activities. One writer has said that "Old Barr Beacon might often have reddened the midnight with its warning glare in reply to the bale-fire on Cannock Chase," and has suggested that the recesses of Sutton Woods may have hidden the weary limb of many a Saxon fugitive driven out by the fierce Northman. But by the late period at which the Dane occupied this midland district, be it remembered that he, too, had begun to come under the softening influences of the Christian religion. King Offa; jealous of the kingdom of Kent, had succeeded in getting from the Pope permission to make Lichfield an archiepiscopal See like that of Canterbury. A succeeding Pope soon after annulled the concession, and Lichfield remained a small town throughout the entire Saxon period. After the Conquest, when it was ordained that bishops should quit the villages and reside in cities, the bishops of Lichfield migrated to Chester, and afterwards to Coventry. But to return to the Danes, and their influence on the Midlands. About the year 943 the Danish King, Olave from Ireland, headed the Northumbrians, penetrated as far south as Tamworth, stormed that town, and after much slaughter carried it, and gave it up to pillage. After another fearful battle at Leicester terms were arranged, and Mercia got a little rest from bloodshed. The attempt of Ethelred the Unready to buy off the Danes only served to whet their appetite for more plunder. Then the massacre of the Danes in 1002 was both equally foolish and feeble. This incapable monarch placed Mercia under the rule of his mean and profligate son-in-law, Edric Streone, who was most unpopular with the Mercian nobles. In the civil war there was no cohesion among the Saxon nobles—one shire would not support another. The Danes conquered sixteen counties, and obtained payment of £48,000, *i.e.*, the price of 771,056 acres of arable land. The King then ordered the people of Mercia to take the field against the foe instead of gathering in their harvests. The perfidious Edric Streone went over to the enemy and the King had to fly to Normandy, leaving Sweyn, the Danish King, master of the situation in England. During this period of bloodshed, treachery, and invasion (A.D. 1002) the only places of safety for the harried populations of this locality would be in the fortified towns. Allusion has been made to the fact that Sutton derived its name from its relative position to Tamworth; this was because Tamworth had been made a stronghold, and fortified against the Danes in 913. In the same system of defence Wednesbury (or "Eddesbury") had been fortified in the year 916; and in a similar manner to the one already given, Aston (or *Eastown*) derived its name from the relationship of its position towards Wednesbury. This scheme of Midland defence which characterised the government of Mercia by Ethelfleda (daughter of Alfred the Great) had consisted of the erection of five forts—four of them forming a quadrilateral, and the fifth, a central rallying point. The inner fort was Wednesbury; while the four corner strongholds were Bridgnorth, Stafford, Tamworth, and Warwick. The cause of these precautions was the liability of Mercia to attack from two sides—the Welsh on the west (faced by the line of Stafford and Bridgnorth), and the Danes on the east (faced by the line of Tamworth and Warwick.) The fierceness of these turbulent times scarcely abated between the years 1002 and 1017, at which later date Canute the Dane ruled in England, and as has been suggested, lent his name to Cannock Chase. What was the further amount of Danish influence brought to bear upon this Midland district? The base and treacherous Edric Streone was confirmed in his vice-royalty of Mercia. Coventry was included in the government of Leofric the Earl of Chester, and husband of the Lady Godiva. While Leofric aided the restoration of the Saxon royal line in the person of Edward the Confessor, the despicable Edric perished in a quarrel with Canute; his body was thrown in the Thames, and his head nailed up over the highest gate in London. His nephew in after years was known as the insolent Earl Godwin.

Sutton was held not only by this family of Leofric, but by that of the ancient Earls of Warwick whose family tree is more legendary than historical (so far our history has been general in its nature, and reliable in its facts. But now to descend to the particular—and the doubtful.) The pedigree of this famous family begins with one Arthgal, one of the Knights of King Arthur's Round Table. The syllable "Arth" signifies bear; this animal appeared on his ensign, and has been the badge of the Earls of Warwick ever since. His successor was the valiant Mowidius. He in single combat slew a giant who to encounter him had torn up by the roots a young tree and stripped it of its branches. For this achievement the ragged staff was added to the shield. It is thus tradition accounts for the "bear and ragged staff" as the heraldic device of the Earls of Warwick. In the reigns of Alfred and Edward the Elder, and about the time of Ethelfleda the Earl of Warwick was one Rohun, another famous warrior. His only child, Felicia, married Guy, son of Siward, baron of Wallingford. In right of his wife this Guy became Earl of Warwick. King Athelstan was in Winchester and at his wit's end, because the Danes having ravaged the land, their leader, the great Giant Colbrand, had offered to rest his claim to the Crown on the result of a single combat. Sir Guy was supposed to be on a pilgrimage to the Holy Land, when the King received a message that a palmer; in performance of his vows to the church, desired to undertake the encounter with the insolent foe. So the combat was arranged; the King and his trembling people looked on from the walls of Winchester, while the Danes surveyed the meeting from their encampments. The giant came forth so heavily armoured that his charger could scarcely bear his weight, while in front of him was sent out a wagon laden with fearsome weapons. Almost at the first stroke the giant struck off the head of his opponent's horse; the alert palmer regained his feet and made a cut at his antagonist's crest, but could reach only to his shoulder. In the fury of the fray the monster happened once to drop his ponderous iron-bossed club, when the palmer instantly seized the opportunity to chop off his hand as he reached to recover it. The fight continued furiously till sunset when Colbrand fainting at last from loss of blood, the champion of the English cut off his head. The palmer refused all honours, and it was only in confidence that he revealed to the King that he was Sir Guy of Warwick. Repairing to Warwick, but still unknown, he received for three days the alms of his sorrowing countess, whose daily practice it was to feed thirteen poor persons. (She mourned not only an absent lord, but her beloved son, Reynburn, had been stolen by strangers and carried off to Muscovy, and in search of whom their true and faithful knight, Sir Heraud de Ardenne had set off.) Retiring to a cell in the rock, now known as Guy's Cliff, he lived as a hermit for two years and then feeling the approach of death sent his wedding-ring to his loving wife, who buried him with all honours in the year 929. The recovered son, Reynburn, inherited the earldom: for, although carried away in childhood, he maintained the family reputation in Russia by performing many deeds of valour there, and on his return to England had been honoured with the hand of Leonette, the beautiful daughter of King Athelstan. Such is the legendary story of Guy of Warwick. Of his successors little need be said. Reynburn died at Venice and was succeed by the devout Weyth the Humid; then came Ufa the Humid, followed by Walgeat, who was deprived of his lands for oppression in 1006. Soon after the whole of this midland district was laid waste by Canute. The earldom is afterwards found in an hereditary successor, Wigod, who married a sister of Leofric, Earl of Mercia. Then came Alwine. or, as he is called in Domesday Book, Alwinus. To Alwinus succeeded Turchill, the first Englishman to copy the Normans in using a surname. He called himself De Eardene, from Arden, the woodland district in which he lived. Turchill gradually lost his lands, and the family greatness fades away after this (to be traced only in the history of Peddimore one of their 48 manors), although Alwinus had once been designated *vice-comes*; perhaps because he had exercised the power of his uncle, the Earl of Mercia.

Leaving Barr and Sutton, and going over to the other side of West Bromwich, the ancient chronicles of Dudley would be found equally musty, and savouring as strongly of the fictitious. Here, in all his glory, we find a mythical Dodo. Heading a genealogical tree of the barons of Dudley, he is depicted in armour, studded with gold, over which he wears a scarlet robe edged with ermine. On his head is a ducal crown of gold. Over is a scroll, reading:— "Dudd Earle of Coventry, Sommerie, and Arden, had by his wife, daughter of Edmund Ironside, King of England, Athelstan who built the Castell of Dudley." Not satisfied with attributing all this to a fabulous personage, the topographer Cooke, writing at the beginning of the present century, says that Wednesbury Church "Was built in the year 711, by Dud or Dudo, lord of Dudley, at which time he was lord of the manor of Wednesbury; and about four years after built the castle of Dudley." After this West Bromwich may he considered fortunate in having escaped the inventions of the monkish chronicler and his parchment nebulosities.

III.—The Domesday Survey of West Bromwich (a.d. 1086).

While Wednesbury had risen to importance during the Saxon period, West Bromwich has no record earlier than Domesday Book. And till recently it was believed that no mention of the place was to be found even in this great national land register.

The Domesday Book, compiled by order of William the Conqueror, 1085-6, was so-called because it was presumed to be a record so exact as to settle the land question in England as fairly and as finally as all things would be settled at domesday. From a study of its pages it is possible to glean a very fair insight into the condition of the country at that remote period.

Although not directly recorded, it may be inferred that Staffordshire was thinly populated, miserably, stocked, and so normally poor as to be unable to bear ordinary taxation. Between the Conquest in 1066, and the date of the Survey of the county 1086, there had been twenty years of extraordinary troubles and depressions. In every part of the count, the Commissioners had to report the existence of isolated estates which they designated *terræ vastæ*, that is, lands "waste," or "unoccupied." This portion of the old Saxon Kingdom of Mercia was in a state of chronic poverty and unproductiveness unparalleled by any other part of the Norman's new dominions.

West Bromwich is in the Hundred of Offlow. The boundaries of this Hundred, and, indeed, of all the other Hundreds of Staffordshire, remain still practically what they were in the 11th century. It may, however, be necessary to mention the few rectifications of frontier that have taken place. (1) A post Domesday change between Offlow and Cuddlestone was caused by the enlargement of the royal Forest of Cannock. A tract of forest originally appurtenant to Lichfield (or more correctly, its outlying members Norton Canes and Little Wyrley) was absorbed into the Royal Forest, and thus transferred from Offlow to Cuddleston Hundred in which was the vill or township of Cannock. (2) Two Derbyshire Manors of Edingale have since Domesday been *mised* into Offlow Hundred and consequently into Staffordshire. Exclusive of Edingale, Offlow contains more than one-fifth of Staffordshire, or about 165,000 acres. Of these nearly 20,000 acres cannot be definitely assigned to any particular Manor by the Domesday Book reckoning; and these unaccounted acres include:—

Bentley. 1,650 acres, perhaps appurtenant to Willenhall.

Darlaston (near Wednesbury), 2,551 acres.

West Bromwich, 5,719 acres, no doubt one of Fitz-Ansculph's Manors.

This William Fitz-Ansculph was a great Norman baron, and a favourite of the Conqueror. He became the proud possessor of nearly one hundred English manors— among them Dudley, Birmingham, and without doubt the intervening one of West Bromwich. It is highly probable that the rotulet (or loose roll) on which the Domesday Commissioners made their entry of the survey of West Bromwich, became wrongly classified after it had been sent in to the King's Exchequer. In this Government office the return, after being examined, checked, registered, and duly noted in every way, should have been codified with those of the same Hundred. It would appear, however, that the West Bromwich return by some means found itself allocated according to tenure—that is to say, instead of being arranged in its proper Hundred, it was placed amongst the other holdings of Fitz-Anculph in the same Domesday Circuit, and as the same Commissioners had made returns of his holdings in Northamptonshire, by some clerical carelessness West Bromwich is actually returned under the heading of that county. Hence it was that, till the recent researches of the Rev. R. W. Eyton, it was believed that Domesday Book contained no record of West Bromwich. The lately discovered entry informs us that the manor had previously been held in Saxon times, during the late reign of Edward the Confessor, by one Brictuin. That in 1086 it is held directly of the King by William Fitz-Anculph as tenant-in-chief, but is underheld of him by by sub-tenant Radulphus. That there are three hides (360 acres) with three carucates or ploughed lands, and a wood of 720 acres. the whole valued at 40 shillings a year. The population is returned as 13, consisting of 10 villains or dwellers in the vill (village) and three bordarii or cotters with allotments under ten acres each, and who worked certain days in each week for the Lord of the Manor, The Domesday name, by which the place has been identified in the returns of the County of Northampton, is Bromwic. No satisfactory reason has yet been forthcoming as to why and when the name was first prefaced by the word West. One reason assigned is manifestly absurd; namely, that the town was so called because it lay west of the residence of the lord of the manor. To give any weight to this contention it would be necessary to identify the particular lord and the exact locality of his manor-house. Another suggestion is that it was so called to distinguish it from Castle Bromwich, and that in fact it is really West Birmingham, or West Bromwichham; the ancient pronunciation of the name of the Midland capital, did actually more nearly approximate the vulgar "Brummagem" than the present classic manner of styling it. Again it may be objected that West Bromwich is inclined more to the north than to the west of Birmingham, although Castle Bromwich may be more directly to its east. However, there is more warrant for this assumption, as towns have very frequently been named, as indeed we still continue to name our streets, according to their relative positions. For instance, on the authority of no less an historian than *Dugdale*, Aston took its designation from Wednesbury under similar circumstances. He says (writing about 1660)—"Aston originally ESTONE, *i.e.*, the Town East of Wordsbury (Wednesbury) a town of some note in Saxon times."

Coming back to a direct reference to our subject, we find one in an old road-guide book called BRITANNIA DEPICTA, published in 1753; speaking of the road from Birmingham to Shrewsbury, it says that the old way *via* Dudley and Bridgnorth "is now disused," while a better one "in respect of goodness and shortness" is to be found after leaving Birmingham —"the new road breaks off on the left acutely and passes *W. Bermingham.*" Evidently this is the High Street of West Bromwich, passing over Hill Top and through Wednesbury to Wolverhampton. This quotation is evidently copied from OWEN AND BOWEN'S ROAD BOOK of the year 1731. The old road after leaving Birmingham passed through Oldbury towards Dudley and Wenlock. The main road from Birmingham to Wolverhampton passed through Great Bridge and Ocker Hill. The present route through Wednesbury was first turnpiked in 1727, and afterwards improved by Telford, the engineer, in 1816, and again in 1826. Reeves ventures to fix the addition of the word *West* to the name as first made about the year 1180. The terminal *Wich*, or *wic* he rightly interprets to mean in the Saxon "a village." As to the stem of the word, which is common to the names *Bromwich*, and *Bromwycham* (Birmingham), he also rightly conjectures it to be derived from the plant "Broom," which no doubt grew in great profusion throughout the locality. The probability is that the Middle English prefix West was added about the fourteenth century, to distinguish it from the other Bromwichs.

The surmise of Reeves that West Bromwich was first constituted a "parish " in A.D. 643 may or may not be true. There is no one to gainsay the assertion. The settled feet now is that the place constituted a Saxon "manor" early in the eleventh century.

Reeves says England was first divided into parishes by Archbishop Honorins, about the year 630. This ecclesiastical area of jurisdiction is also claimed as the work of Theodore, Primate of England from 669 to 690. Now if Theodore of Tarsus possessed not this local influence so far as West Bromwich is concerned there is conjectural probability that he did possess indirect influence on the industrial development of the neighbouring Black Country. He it was who first introduced Greek art in the sacred objects of metallic construction. But the metallurgical skill of the Danish Goths, who, with the Mercians shared this Midland district, was not confined to the fashioning, brazing, and riveting of the softer metals of gold, silver, and bronze, as practised by the Byzantian artificers; the people who had built the warships of the Saxons and the Danes were more expert as blacksmiths, and their swords were often things of such great beauty that they gave them names of affection, and handed them down to their successors as sacred heirlooms. Such people as these, finding themselves in a country rich with iron ore, could not have been slow to use it; and the influence of the Church in the Staffordshire coal-field, if not wielded by Theodore himself, was probably exercised by St. Chad under his countenance and encouragement for this busy prelate came from the North, where religion and art flourished side by side, and he was not likely to be slow to take every natural advantage of the place. That ironworking was actually carried on at some such remote period we have evidence in the existence of "Dane shafts" at the Delves, in Wednesbury, the very name of the locality pointing to mining operations, and in the remains of ancient workings on Cannock Chase we might trace resemblances to the old bloomeries of Loch Maree in Scotland.

*   *   *   *   *   *   *

Quoting further from Reeves' HISTORY OF WEST BROMWICH, we may here add three items of interest not pertaining strictly to the parish itself, but which throw some light on the early history of the adjacent locality. The quotations are:—

(1)—WEDNESBURY A ROMAN STATION. —In October, 1817, some workmen, employed by Mr. Jackson, of Wednesbury, dug up some old Roman Coins of the Emperors Nero, Vespasian Trajan, &c. From this circumstance I am led to believe that Wednesbury was once a Roman Station. ... Besides the great Roman roads there are many others in Britain of less note, some of which extend from Staffordshire in different directions.— [The Portway Road is one, if it is not an ancient British trackway (through Darlaston, Moseley Hole, Wednesfield and Peartree) to Chester.]

(2.)—CHRISTIANITY INTRODUCED HERE.—Staffordshire belonged to the Kingdom of Mercia, established A.D. 585. Mercia owed its conversion from Paganism, to a woman, Alchflida, the wife of Peada, and who was the daughter of Oswy, King of Northumbria, about the year 656.

(3.)—WEDNESBURY CASTLE.—Wednesbury Church was originally a Castle, and was founded by Dudo, lord of the Manor, about the year 711: it was *repaired* by Ethelfleda about A.D. 913, and was converted into a Church about the reign of Henry II.

IV.—WIGMORE, A BATTLEFIELD; ANCIENT BOUNDARY TREES, &C.

The heaths skirting Sutton Chase extended over the high ridge of Barr Beacon, but were perhaps separated from the rolling wilds of Cannock Chase by the enclosures of ancient Aldridge. West Bromwich Heath was but an outlying portion on this other side, with a population of only 13 in the year 1086.

The oppression, however, of the Normans at the Conquest cannot now be adequately estimated. In the last chapter we saw something of the poverty of this Midland locality. Depopulated towns, and lands left untilled, brought more curses than mere famine— desolation reigned supreme in many parts. Along the line of the great Icknield Street— running through Harborne, along Hunter's Lane, Handsworth, and straight through Sutton Park—neither house nor village arose along the whole length of its course between Perry Bridge and the village of Chesterfield.

In the nineteenth year of the Conqueror's reign a Danish Invasion was expected. Among the measures taken to prepare for this emergency the yoke of military tenure was forced upon the nation. It was thus we got the record of the military resources of West Bromwich, together with these of every inch of available land besides, in 1085-6.

Another precaution of the Conqueror was to watch the attitude of the English Danes, that is, of those Danes who had long settled in England. In Mercia or at least in Staffordshire, we find the Danish Chief Turchill, Earl of Warwick (mentioned in Chapter II), popularly elected to the office of Sheriff in the year 1068. This office of *Vice-comes* was then held for life, and the holder of it in this case was no doubt watched by the King with a jealous eye: his estates gradually dwindled away! Thus every element for stirring scenes in history-making seems to have existed, and yet historial record attaching directly to West Bromwich is practically a blank. The reason is that the place was dominated so entirely by surrounding localities of greater importance. Whether or not West Bromwich was formed into a parish at the first creation of these ecclesiastical divisions by Archbishop Theodore, in the year 680 will never be decided. Its impoverishment at the Domesday survey was no worse than that existing generally in the whole of the County of Stafford. But that the parochial boundaries were far from what they now are, is more than probable: and the proffered suggestion is, that the present parish grew out of the original manor.

Of its close connection with ancient Wednesbury two instances may be given. Two battles were fought at Wednesbury. In the year 560 a great Saxon chief named Ceawlin, who had four years previously shown his prowess by inflicting a great defeat upon the Britons near Banbury, succeeded to the throne of Wessex. He afterwards "reduced a multitude of cities and took immense spoils," fighting with his brother Cuthwin against the Britons of the West and South. The SAXON CHRONICAL fixes the date about 591, calls the place Wodnesbeorg, and states that Ceawlin was succeeded by his nephew Ceolric. Then on the testimony of ETHELWERD'S CHRONICAL, written in the 10th century, "Anno 592: There was a great slaughter on both sides at a place called *Wodnesbyrig*, so that Ceawlin was put to flight and died in one more year. " Corroboration of this is found in the text of FLORENCE. the scribe of Worcester, who, writing towards the close of the eleventh century, says under the same date: "A battle was fought at a place called *Wodnesbeorh*, that is 'Woden's Mount,' in which there was a great slaughter and Ceawlin was driven from his kingdom." Now this battle is not to be confounded with one fought by the same king against Ethelbert, the first Christian king of Kent in the year 568, at Wimbledon in Surrey. The exact site of this battle was, perhaps, Wigmore, which is in the parish now called West Bromwich, but which at that remote period would take its name from Wednesbury, the nearest point important enough to bear a distinctive name known to the Saxon chroniclers.

If Wigmore was not the site of this battle, there is another ancient slaughtering which may have taken place here. On the authority of the "Anglo-Saxon Chronicle" and the other scribes, a second Battle of Wednesbury took place in the year 715. This was an undecided conflict at "Wothnesbeorghe," between Ina, King of Wessex, and Ceolrid, King of Mercia. Henry of Huntingdon, a later scribe, says in his chronicle of 1135, that after the battle of *Wonebirih*, in 715, Ceolred died the year following and was buried at Lichfield.

The reasons assigned for believing Wigmore to be the actual locality of one of these battles are:—(1) The word Wigmore in Anglo Saxon signifies "a battle field." (2) This valley lying to the east of Wednesbury and within sight of its fortified mount, is a location likely to be selected by a military commander for giving battle; and (3) tradition has long pointed out Wigmore as the spot "where a battle was fought."

Dr. Willmore, in his "History of Walsall" (p. 29) says: Very grave doubts have, however, been thrown upon the locality of these battles (those of A.D. 592 and A.D. 715) and Guest and with him Green, are unanimous in assigning Wansborough in Wiltshire as identical with Wodnesbeorg. That some unrecorded action did, however take place is probable from the fact that the ancient name of the plain lying to the east of Wednesbury is Wigmore which is Anglo-Saxon for "the battle-field."

So far, then, in tracing our history, our researches have shown West Bromwich a Saxon Manor in the 11th century, occupied in the Conqueror's reign by Radulphus, and in the Confessor's time by Brictuin. Yet was it of so small importance that it was completely overshadowed by those more ancient places Sutton, Barr, Cannock, Dudley, and Wednesbury; and with regard to the last-named, it is manifest that the present boundaries between the two places did not then prevail. This conclusion will be further strengthened by the next point now to be recorded.

The other connection between the two parishes during the early period of their history is discoverable in the fact that a part of West Bromwich derives its name from that of a family who held the manor of Wednesbury between the years 1180 and 1420. The Heronvilles, lords of Wednesbury apparently held lands in West Bromwich, situated at *Harvill's Hawthorn*. About 1530 the place was known as *Hervill's Oke*, a corruption of *Heronville's Oak*; but as soon after this all the oaks in these parishes began rapidly to disappear, owing to their extensive use as charcoal for the smelting of the local iron-ore, the presumption is that "Hawthorn" was substituted for "Oak" in this place-name.

Oaks, from their hardy, sturdy, and long-lived nature, were of considerable importance in olden times. As marking a boundary, or measuring a distance, we have an instance in the place-name *Three Mile Oak*, on the opposite or southern side of West Bromwich. In religious rites they were of great and sacred import, both in the Druidical and in the Christian religions; as exemplified in the name *Gospel Oak*. The *Shire Oak* is a name of probably a thousand years' standing, indicated by a tree twice that age. All oaks had disappeared from Wednesbury before the devouring furnace of the iron-smelter by the end of the last century. In West Bromwich they have naturally lingered longer, as the use of coal was substituted for that of carbonised wood just before the iron trade had pushed itself over the northern and eastern boundaries of this parish. The only spot where, within living memory, Wednesbury people could readily gather acorns, was over the boundary, and into West Bromwich parish, along Crankhall Lane.

According to the county history of NIGHTINGALE the remains of some large oaks have been dug up in Rotton Meadow on the Walsall boundary, near to Wednesbury. Dr. Willmore in his HISTORY OF WALSALL surmises that this locality was a sacred spot in the time of the Druidical observances of the Ancient Britons. At the present time it is believed that not a single oak tree, beyond perhaps a mere sapling is to be found growing within the confines of Wedneshury parish. Such is the devastating effect upon these sturdy trees of the sulphurous fumes belched forth from the myriads of furnaces and chimney stacks. West Bromwich is more fortunate in possessing a green borderland, at least, upon one side, where its vegetation is still free from the ravages of the chemical manufacturer and the irons-melter. Their nearer proximity would prove even now more blighting than the actual presence of the charcoal burner of olden times; and his demands averaged a consumption of 120 acres of wood per annum for each single iron furnace in operation.

There was printed in the "Notes and Queries" column of a Birmingham Weekly (April 16th, 1887), a strange record of the discovery of gigantic forest trees at Handsworth and at Wednesbury, accompanied by the surmise that the said trees were either "of antedeluvian growth," or else "planted by the Danes during their occupation"—truly a remarkable alternative in speculation!

In a later chapter we may also note the possibility of the existence of a Saxon Church in West Bromwich, but so far as the pre-Norman period is concerned there is nothing else to chronicle.

V.—BROMWICH, A PART OF THE BARONY OF DUDLEY: ITS DESCENT FROM THE FAMILY OF FITZANSCULPH TO THE PAGANELS (1066—1194).

The lapse of a century after the Norman's national survey found Bromwich still a solitude, its silence scarcely broken by the score, or less, of inhabitants who were then to be found widely scattered over its 5,000 or 6,000 acres. The place yet lingered in its state of pristine wildness. Across the wide expanse of its wind-swept plateau broom and heather, ling and fern prevailed and flourished in all-pervading luxuriance; except only where surface-scratchings revealed the presence of man or of beast, or disclosed the agency of weather and water; and there the sandy and gravelly nature of its dry soil at once declared itself, lending a somewhat bareness of aspect to the whole scene. Not that it presented the appearance of an arid waste; for both its eastern and its western flanks lent a welcome relief to the landscape by framing it deeply and recessfully in the verdant foliage of primeval woodland.

Such was the aspect presented to the eye by this fragment of the great barony of Dudley; which while adding to the acreage of the "terræ Normanorum" was too insignificant in value and in military strength to have made it an acquisition of any importance. No doubt the roads across it were mere trackways, as they passed over the common land; or were else tangled bridle-paths as they intersected the woods. The most frequented of these paths was the one from Birmingham, and the other southern manors of the barony, leading up to the great feudal castle at Dudley.

With other parts of the estate, this vast barony had descended from the great Fitzansculph, that favoured follower of the Conqueror, to another Norman family, by the marriage of his daughter and sole heir with a Paganel or Paynel.

This family, who now came to exercise jurisdiction over Bromwich, have been styled " the noble family of the Beaumonts, ancient Earls of Leicester, surnamed Paganell." The extensive barony of Dudley acquired by them through marriage, comprised 25 Staffordshire manors, 14 more in Worcestershire, and 7 in Warwickshire, all lying within a few miles of the castle; to say nothing of 45 others held in more distant counties.

Fulke Paganel, the feudal baron of Dudley, was a younger son of William Paganel, lord of Moutiers Hubert in Normandy, who died about the same time as the Conqueror. William's eldest brother, Ralph was already settled in England, at Drax, in Yorkshire. Fulke was succeeded in the lordship of Dudley by his son Ralph, who married a daughter of the Lord Ferrars, who founded Tutbury.

As to the actual occupier at this time—the one who dwelt upon and had a direct interest in the soil of Bromwich in succession to Brictuin and to Radulphus—this is an identity we cannot now hope to discover. The last-named was most probably a Norman. The territorial magnates of such high standing as the head of Norman families of Fitzansculph and Paganel, thought little of dispossessing Saxon landowners, and replacing them with followers of their own. In the neighbouring manor of Birmingham, for instance, the holder of the land there was a follower and creature of the Paganels, styled their "dapifer," which literally signifies a *feast-bearer*, and no doubt indicates that he was a kind of steward, among whose duties, not the least important one, was the superintendence of the service of his lord's meals on state occasions. The holder of Bromwich Manor may possibly have held even a less honourable post in the stately household of the great Baron of Dudley.

VI. —Some Local Place-Names, and their meanings.

Almost on the threshold of our historical investigations we have been compelled to recognise the importance of place-names, and the bearing they have upon the story of the locality they indicate. For instance we have already become acquainted with the etymology of the names *West Bromwich, Sutton, Aston, Barr, Wigmore, Tame,* &c.

Hidden under the common and familiar names of towns, villages, and localities lie many a quaint and curious fact of ancient history, or many a fanciful descriptiveness of natural features. But the reader must be wary or he will be sometimes asked to accept in the way of etymological derivation much that is often more fanciful than historical. Here, then, it may not be out of place to try to trace the etymology of a few other local names in the immediate vicinity.

STAFFORD, which gives its name to the County, may have been named in allusion to the *staff* or pole fixed in the water (of the river Sowe) to show where it was *ford*able.

OFFLEY, which is the name of the Hundred, may derive its name from that of the Saxon king, Offa (who built the great dyke to keep out the Welsh); with the terminal *ley*, derived from the A. S. *leag*—"a meadow." The Hundred of Offlow, like all five of the Staffordshire Hundreds, is divided into two divisions—"North" and "South"—with some 30 or 40 parishes in each. The former comprises the eastern corner of the County near Burton-on-Trent, &c.

BIRMINGHAM.—There is one objection to the assumption that the name Birmingham was ever in some such form as *Bromwycham* (see chapter III.), and having a common derivation with West Bromwich from the word "broom." The probabilities are that Birmingham really is the *ham* or "home" of the *Birmings*, or "sons of Birm." The name *Bromwycham* is an impossible Saxon name, and although it has been spelt thus (some records of Hales Owen Abbey, 1497), it must have been a corruption on the part of the writer.

BLOXWICH.—The first syllable is said to have been originally the English *blac*— "black"—*wich* as before, signifying "village." This would be the same etymology as that of *Black Lake* or *Blake Lake*.

ROWLEY REGIS.—The *ley*, as before, and *Row* from the Anglo Saxon *Ruh*—"rough"— that is "ragged" or "uneven." *Regis*, signifies "of the King," because the place was once part of the royal domain.

WIGMORE is said to have been anciently *Wigcynga-mere*, meaning "the pool of victory." Just below Wigmore flows the Tame, forming the boundary of the parish; close by the stream has been diverted, possibly to form a mill pool. A farm called Jone Mill, stood here, and the adjacent bridge is called *Jone Bridge*.

BARR.—According to Flavel Edmunds the name of *Great Barr*, in Staffordshire, is traced readily to *Bar*—"a bar, fence, or gate." The derivation from *Bar*, "a summit" (as given chapter II.) is far more probable.

HAMSTEAD.—Is perhaps from *Ham*—"a home or village", and *stead* A.S. equivalent to the German *stadt*—"a town."

HANDSWORTH.—The first syllable is said to be the proper name of the original Saxon owner *Hondes*; while *worth* is the Anglo-Saxon *weorthig*, meaning "farm, estate, hall, court, manor, or mansion,"

SMETHWICK is said to get its name from *smeth* or *smithy* from "smith," a word still pronounced "smeth" in Scotland. EDMUNDS gives as an example of such derivation "Smethwick in Staffordshire—smith's village." But it is possibly (and probably) derived from the Anglo-Saxon *smethe*—"smooth" (that is, not hilly). Smethwick is not a parish of itself; It is a hamlet or chapelry appurtenant to the ancient parish of Harborne. So little known was this district or part of the parish at the beginning of the present century, that it very readily acquired the nickname of *French Walls*, which was given to the best known centre of it—the locality around the site of Muntz's Metal Works. Here were so extensively manufactured gun-barrels and other munitions of war, which went out so largely to sustain the long-continued fights of the Napoleonic campaigns, that the place was said to have been of as much defensive utility as "walls" round France—whence the fanciful name *French Walls* was given to the place.

WARLEY WIGORN.—Warley may be derived from *War* or *Weare*—"weir." or "an enclosure on a stream", and *ley*, as before. WIGORN signifies "of Worcester," to which county it belonged. Worcester was anciently written *Wigera-ceastre*. It is easy to see that *ceastre* is *castra*, "a camp," or Roman station, but it is difficult to explain *Wigera*. One writer says the word was originally *Wicci*, the name of a people, another authority goes further, and says it was originally *Hwyce*, a name of a people so called because they dwelt on the "windings " of the River Severn—deriving the meaning from its signification of "winding."

WARLEY, SALOP, was formerly (with Hales Owen) a detached portion of the Brimstree Hundred of Shropshire. West Bromwich Union includes a part of Worcestershire still— a case of overlapping boundaries.

OLDBURY.—From *burh* or *bury* as in WEDNESBURY; and *Old*—"a wold, or wild uncultivated land." Or the name may indicate the antiquity of the place as a *burh*; from *Old* or *Eald*, signifying "old"; the Saxons so naming it because they found traces of its occupation before their time. Ironworking around OLDBURY and SMETHWICK probably dates from either the British or Roman period.

DUDLEY.—This is often interpreted as *Dodda-lege*, or *Dodda's land*; from *Dudo*, the mythical founder of the castle, and *ley*—"a meadow."

SEDGLEY.—The English *secg* or *sedge*, indicated the watery site of the ley or meadow in which grew the *sedges*.

STONE CROSS.—During times of pestilence and plague, people in trafficking with each other, were afraid to come into actual contact, to obviate which certain meeting places were used, often a broad, flat stone. Here money, dipped in vinegar, would be paid down and received by the creditor when the payer had retired to a safe distance. Plague-stricken men fixed upon such places as Stone Cross to transact their worldly business at such times when mortal fear possessed their souls. Stone Cross in those ancient times was on the highway between Wednesbury and Birmingham and Coventry. Mrs. Willett's in her HISTORY (*p. 191*), says there was a stone cross there in early times which was used for reading the Gospel during the perambulation of the parish boundaries on Rogation Days. She quotes from the HISTORY OF SHENSTONE, "I have seen one of the stone pillars in the road between Walsall and West Bromwich. They are of polished stone, much like those upon which dials are placed, but vastly higher." The pedestal was in existence at the end of the last century; and in pre-reformation times no doubt there was here set up a gaudily-painted wayside crucifix, at which every passer-by muttered a prayer or made a genuflection. There is far more probability that it was a wayside cross, rather than a market cross, which is the theory Mrs. Willetts seems to favour.

SPON LANE.—If *Spon* is not the proper name of some person, but an ancient place-name it must be derived from *Spona*, "a chip or splinter of wood," as applied generally to fragments of the true cross. Many Spanish towns are designated *Vera Cruz*, that is, TRUE CROSS. But Reeves (p. 157) gives *Spon* as the name of a family who lived in some large house in the locality about the year 1700, and who also gave their names to such localities as *Spon Coppice* and *Spon Meadow*.

SAM'S LANE, on the same authority, was so called from a man named Samuel Partridge, who lived there about 1780. Other personal names, according to Reeves, gave the place-names *Ryder's Green*, *Cole's Lane* (from one Daniel Cole), *Ireland Green* (Ireland lived a century before Reeves), *Taylor's Lane* (from a schoolmaster), and *Sawter's Lane* (originally Shorthouse's Lane), *Witton Lane* (from a Dissenting minister). *Carter's Green* is evidently of similar derivation. But who was Carter? May he not have been the John Carter, High Constable of the Hundred, who in 1647 directed inquiry into the seizure of all goods and cattle during the war times of the previous six years? This important warrant was dated from "Wednesburri, April 20th" of that year. The same writer also derives *Camp Bank* from Cromwell's (? Earl of Denbigh's) earthworks, and the adjacent *Cross Guns* from the shooting of a deserter there at the same time. *Monk Meadow* he mentions as a field in the three continuous parishes of West Bromwich, Handsworth, and Smethwick, left by the Whorwood family towards the support of a school. *Over-End*, he says, was waste land enclosed about 1690 or 1700;

while *Old End* was so-named from the collection of old huts and hovels there. *Virgin's End* got its name from the three virgin daughters of one John Ward, who kept an ale house there. These latter names, which all included the word "End," denote the naming of an entire locality when houses began to be first erected there, but were not put up in sufficient numbers as to gain a designation for each particular lane, road, or street, in that "end" of the parish. Similarly in Wednesbury we find Hall End, Oakeswell End, &c., &e

Of natural features, which have lent their names to the formation of place-names, mention has already been made of Harvills Hawthorn and Three Mile Oak while the name Bromwich itself is borrowed from the plant "broom." In the same way the place known as *Ling* may be connected with the heath of that variety; *Lyndon* may be derived from the "lime tree" or "linden," as may also Lyne Purl the "purl" or "stream" under the "lindens', the nature of the land in Marsh Lane makes that name quite self-explanatory.

As we have said, there is often a wealth of meaning to be found in a place-name. How one may be sent off, however on a false scent when deriving local place names is easily illustrated by turning to two authorities for enlightenment on the origin of the names TIPTON and SWAN VILLAGE. TIPTON is generally believed to be derived from *Tib-ing-ton*, the "town" of the "ings" (or family) of the Saxon chieftain "Tib," who settled there. (See HISTORY OF TIPTON, chapter I.) But an accepted authority may mislead us by suggesting that the name should be traced to *Tib* or *tiber*, "a holy place," or "place of sacrifices." In a similarly erroneous manner SWAN VILLAGE might have its name traced to *Sweyn*, the Danish King of England except that we could never find any record of the place being held by that or any other sovereign lord. We do know, however, that the most ancient inn of the parish was situated here, and that it was known as the "Swan Inn" three centuries back.

VII.—RALPH PAGANEL, TENANT-IN-CHIEF OF BROMWICH, FIGHTS THROUGH THE CIVIL WARS OF STEPHEN'S REIGN (1138-1148).

In 1138 civil war broke out in England between King Stephen, who had usurped the throne and Matilda his cousin, the sole heiress of the late king. She laid claim to her father's crown. Her strength lay chiefly in the north and the west, while Stephen's adherents were found mainly in the east of England. When the King set out from Northampton to reduce the borders of Wales, he could not fail to feel an amount of chagrin and annoyance at finding his efforts rendered in a measure futile by the strengthening of Dudley Castle against him. What of wealth and strength there yet remained in the vicinity of Bromwich was now all poured inside the strong walls of Dudley. Outside of such walled protection stalked famine, rapine, and depopulation, Towns were burnt and deserted, Worcester and Nottingham (1140) among the number. Both sides engaged mercenaries, and the people were indiscriminately pillaged all round. Abbeys were desecrated and fortified, Coventry being among the number of those so served. The few wretched hinds, who eked out a living on the wastes of Bromwich, risked the harrying of both the conflicting armies. Being but of the Saxon element they could expect neither the sympathy nor the protection of their proud Norman lord, whose foreign nationality seems intensified by the family use of the baptismal name Fulke, a name which had been borne by no less than five members of the noble Angevin family, whose heir was so soon to become the first Plantagenet King of England. By the way, a short time ago the local newspapers reported that one of the last representatives of this royal house of Plantagenet was recently living in West Bromwich, and finding his name too cumbersome for his humble circumstances, he curtailed it to Plant. If this be true there is an appropriateness about the association of Plantagenet (which in Norman-French signifies the "broom plant") with the town of West Bromwich which also derives its name from the same shrub. Matilda, who had married Geoffrey Plantagenet, a son of Fulke, and a grandson of another Fulke (the Gruff), laid claim to her father's throne immediately upon the death of Henry I., in 1135. Stephen, however, obtained it, and then retained his possession by currying favour with the barons. This he did by restoring lands which his predecessors had afforested, and granting permission to the barons to hunt in the Royal domains; and he further allowed them to fortify their castles as far as necessary for their own security. These concessions affected Bromwich but little. The Saxon hinds were not included, or even remotely considered, in any offer of King Stephen. A great conspiracy was discovered, by the clergy it is said, of these dejected, alien-tongued Saxons, to massacre the Normans, and place on the throne—not Matilda, but—the King of Scotland.

Ralph Paganel interpreted the grant of Stephen in his own way. He fortified his castle at Dudley—but on behalf of Matilda, in whose cause he held the castle (1138). Mrs. Willett (A History of West Bromwich, pp. 4 and 5), says it was *Gervase* who "defended the castle of Dudley for the Empress Matilda in 1137, for which offence the castle was ordered to be dismantled." She then adds—"He again offended by joining the rebels in 1173-4." This is scarcely probable, as there is a period of 37 years between these two dates. It was Ralph, the father of Gervase, who sided with the Empress Maud; for in "5 Stephen" (1140) writes Dugdale, he "was by her made Governor of the castle of Nottingham; William Peverell then lord thereof, being taken prisoner at the battle of Lincoln fighting for King Stephen. Whereupon he instigated Robert, Earl of Gloucester, to enter Nottingham, the inhabitants being destitute of any defensive arms; which he accordingly did; so that the town was miserably plundered, and then burnt by the soldiers." Truly if the serfs of Bromwich Heath were for once safer than those who dwelt in walled cities, it was merely because the scene of action had changed, and that they had less to lose. Only two years previously—that is in the August of 1138—the enraged Stephen had marched against Dudley Castle, set fire to it, and had ruthlessly ravaged Bromwich and Handsworth and the whole district lying round that stronghold. The massacre and sacking of Nottingham may, therefore, be looked upon as a reprisal for what had taken place in this neighbourhood. Ralph Paganel was not the man to hesitate in a case of this kind. Yet the grim baron purposed afterwards, for the good of his soul, to found a monastery at Dudley. He did not live long enough to make this expiation. This pious intention was carried out about 1160 by his only surviving son, Gervase, who succeeded him in the barony

To interpret these incidents aright we must try to realise the horrors of a civil war in those rude times. The land was left untilled, and famine was added to bloodshed. Dudley Castle, in common with all those newly erected or freshly strengthened fortresses, had become little better than a robber's den, from which its owner might sally forth to extort plunder even by torture. As stated in the last chapter, the identity of the actual occupier of the Manor of Bromwich at this time cannot with any certainty be given. But that his life, whoever he may have been, was a busy and an active one, even in time of peace, cannot be doubted; for there was not only actual military service to be performed for his estate, but in that unruly age there were often tedious private jealousies to be settled either by fierce quarrels or by costly lawsuits. We may picture him during the time of this civil war attending on his overlord, either in garrison at Dudley Castle or lying in wait on his own estates, with his handful of followers, to entrap neighbouring squires who were for King Stephen, or more actively harrying their manors, driving off their cattle, and sometimes going so far as to hang their retainers. Maybe there was sometimes a sudden summons from the Baron of Dudley, a hasty ride across the bleak heath and through the hamlet of Tipton, and up the steep and wooded hill to the Castle courtyard: then perhaps a speedy return to muster men-at-arms in a hasty levy of the Baron's tenantry and retainers, it might chance, to fight a sharp skirmish with the Earl Ferrers and his Tutbury men, or possibly to attack the stronghold of some other adherent of Stephen.

VIII.—GERVASE PAGANEL, HIS FIGHTS AND FINES, EXTRAVAGANCE, AND USURY (1161—1194)

William Fitzansculph was the son of the Sheriff of Surrey. He, no doubt, came over with the Conqueror, although his name is not to be found in the Roll of Battle Abbey.

We have seen that among the vast estates with which he was rewarded for his fidelity to the Conqueror, he held *in capite* (that is, directly from the King, as his tenant-in-chief) Bromwich and many of the surrounding manors, including Handsworth, Barr, Aldridge, Rushall, and perhaps Bushbury and Penn; while his chief seat was Dudley Castle, which had previously belonged to the Saxon Earl Edwin, and of which Ansculph was created first baron.

Even the historian Dugdale does not know what became of this great and powerful lord, but it is generally assumed that he had a daughter Beatrice, who married Fulke Paganel, whose issue was Ralph Paganel, as stated in chapters V. and VII. And now Ralph, who had six sons, is succeeded by the eldest, Gervase.

In 1166 a return in the Black Book of the Exchequer enumerates Bromwich amongst the Knights' fees of Gervase Paganel, baron of Dudley. A Knight's fee was a holding, varying in size, for which a Knight rendered the King military service. In Staffordshire a fee averaged 3,000 acres, but this was inclusive of wood and waste. The return of 1166 was made in connection with Scutage ("shield money") which the King (Henry II.) was to receive in lieu of personal service in the field. Sandwell, Wombourne and part of Handsworth were also named as fees in the same barony; and this was the first occasion on which returns were made for such a fiscal purpose. It was Henry II. who invented Scutage, but succeeding monarchs often found this substitution of a levy of money more convenient than personal service in war-time. Towards the close of his reign Henry II. was troubled by the rebellions of his own sons instigated thereto by the jealous King of France. In 1173-4 Gervase Paganel took the part of Prince Henry in his revolt against his father. It was for this offence that his castle of Dudley was demolished (*Note 1*) and in 1176 he was further fined 500 marks for the transgression. This was a large sum in those days even for a great noble. By Michaelmas 1177 baron Gervase had paid 350 marks on account, and it was 1179 before he managed to discharge the balance, "*et quietus est.*" In the following year he landed himself in another money difficulty. He had stood security for some Jew debt of his brother-in-law and late ally in the rebellion, the Earl of Leicester; and now (26 Henry II.) he gives the King "100 marks to be quit of the obligation." Mr. Eyton observes on this extraordinary method of paying old debts in such an entirely new way—"So much money, therefore, went to the Crown, and Aaron, the renowned Jew of Lincoln, held a security that was worthless." As this debt was not fully paid off for many years afterwards, it is easy to understand that money difficulties were not unknown in those days. It may also be inferred that neither the King nor his nobles bore any love towards the Jew usurers: and in the name of holy Mother Church both were ready at any moment to plunder their Israelitish oppressors. No doubt some such moody and revengeful thoughts filled the mind of the troubled baron as he set off from his feudal Castle of Dudley, and crossed Bromwich Heath one summer day in 1189, on his way to Westminster to attend the grand ceremony of Richard I.'s coronation. As the pomp, pageantry and display on this occasion (September 3rd) were so gorgeous, the cost of it all must have added materially to the debts of many who were there flaunting it so royally. As the money for these extravagances came chiefly from the money-lenders can it be wondered at that the proceedings of the coronation were most disgracefully terminated by a massacre of the Jews? Another way to pay old debts.

After a life passed amidst the storms of war with its sieges, battles, revolts, and bloody massacres; to say nothing of the petty worries of financial difficulties; Gervase Paganel, baron of Dudley, and lord of the manor of Bromwich, and of 90 other good English manors besides (*Note 2*) died early in the year 1194, full of years and of troubles, if not of knightly honour and military renown.

* * * * * * *

Two Explanatory Notes on the foregoing will be necessary to its better understanding—

(1). The first is with regard to the dismantling of Dudley Castle after the war of 1174: it is found that in 1273, although the King's licence to rebuild had been obtained nine years, the castle was yet in an unfinished state.—"Salt Collections," vol. ix., p 42."

(2). Among the ninety English manors of Gervase Paganel was included Newport Pagnel in Bucks. The name Paganel is sometimes written Paynel, we modern English, like the later Normans after their period of settlement in France, could never pronounce the guttural sounds of the Danes and the Saxons, and so we have eliminated them from our language; thus "pagan" becomes *paynim* and "Paganel" becomes *Paynel*.

A field name at Walsall (on the Birmingham road) is "The Pannels;" and this is derived from the name of the Paynell family—about the year 1300 Margery Rufus, of Walsall Manor, married a John Paynel, or Paganel.

IX—The Offney Family, resident Lords of the Manor (1155—1180).

We have now to turn back in our history for a few years. So far we have brought the records of the "lord superior" of Bromwich, the great baron of Dudley, up to the year 1194, when Gervase Paganel died.

For nearly three-quarters of a century we have not been able to identify by name the sub-tenant of Bromwich. In 1086 it was Radulphus. In 1166, according to the Scutage returns (Chapter viii.) Bromwich was underheld by William the son of Guy Offney, whose three knights' fees were Ellesborough in Bucks, Sandwell, Bromwich, a part of Handsworth, and Wombourne in Staffordshire; all in the barony of Dudley.

The father, Guy Offney, was also evidently in possession of the same lands as early as 1155 as he then conferred the living and church of Wombourne upon the projected priory of Dudley which Ralph Paganel purposed to found, and which Gervase did establish five or six years later. By 1166 the fierce lord Ralph and his trusty tenant Guy, companions in arms in many a bloody fray, had both passed away, but not before both had shown symptoms of remorse for the much blood shedding of their past lives, and an anxiety to atone for it by deeds of piety.

As noted in Chapter viii. Ralph Paganel left his good intentions to be carried out by Gervase his son. But about 1155 the grant of Womborne to the monks of St. James's of Dudley was formally made by Guy and Christiana his wife, with the consent of his dutiful son and heir William; and further countenanced by the gracious consent of "Walter the Bishop." To this grant, his lord superior who was the prime mover in bringing the Benedictine monks to his new priory at Dudley, naturally gave a ready, if not indeed an eager, confirmation. This ratification was required by feudal law, as these Wombourne lands were then said to be "aliented" to religious purposes, by reason of which their fighting strength would be for ever lost in time of war.

This is the first evidence of a direct personal interest in his holdings, and in the welfare of the locality, taken by the sub-tenant and occupier of the lands. The second instance affects Bromwich much more closely. But before proceeding to record it, a conjectural insight into the cause of this particular tenant's presence in the Manor may be gleaned. The sub- infeudation of vast estates like that of Paganel's barony of Dudley was an absolute necessity; but the introduction of such a tenant as Offney upon lands so close to the seat of the baron is striking. As a rule, lands so close to the castle and home of the baron were held "in' demesne," which signifies that the lord did not grant away the land to be held of him by knight service, but kept it in his own hands, cultivating it either by his servants or by means of farmers. The probabilities are that Bromwich had been so held by Brictruin, as a "socman" under Earl Edwin, while his successor, Radolphus held the manor not quite in the same servile tenure as a husbandman, but as a higher domestic official of Ansculph's household, who needed to be in residence near to Dudley. But Offney was a tenant of a different stamp. He was not an Englishman. His surname was derived from his territorial connection with Offignies in Picardy; and as his family had wealth enough and to spare, some of it to bestow upon religious foundations; the selection of such a tenant seems to have been not exactly fortuitous, but may not unreasonably be attributed in some degree to the straitness of the Paganels' means. For in those days when lands were so easily obtained, current coin was just as difficult to get hold of. The distinctions between real and personal property were even more marked in feudal times than at the present day. Any way it would seem that the appearance of an occupier and resident lord of the status of Offney was a most welcome acquisition to a poor neighbourhood like Bromwich: by present day comparisons we may say that previous tenants of Bromwich Manor had been at the highest, but of the yeoman type, while the Offneys would belong to the class now usually designated as gentry.

The benefits which accrued to the Manor of Bromwich from the presence of the Offneys is at once apparent. To the Paganels at Dudley they are more than vassals— they are neighbours and friends intimate in times of peace, and brothers in arms during the frequent wars of that period. To the Manor they are not merely lords, but they take a deep and personal interest in its religious and social development. After assisting their overlord in his establishment of a Priory at Dudley, they look about for a site themselves upon which to erect a similar foundation on their own Manor, and at their own entire cost. Where in Bromwich was there a spot quiet, retired, secluded. and unreclaimed from its natural wildness, where the presence of good monks would be not only beneficial in a moral sense but a blessing also in a material sense? How the site was sought and found and the monastery established is a tale, the telling of which demands a chapter to itself.

X.—The Founding of Sandwell Priory and the Dawn of Education in Bromwich (1180)

From the time of the Norman invasion (1066) to the period of civil war in Stephen's reign (1148) we have seen the disturbing influences of strife and bloodshed, of fire and famine, all at work in Bromwich for nearly a century. And if they strike the modern inhabitant of the place with horror, may we not ask—What was the effect of the continued prevalence of these bloody wars and civil commotions upon the quiet and contemplative mind in those times?—for mankind is much the same in all ages. Would not retirement from the world he welcome to the meditative mind, facilitating the attainment of a virtuous life, and adding strength to a strong character, by enabling it to follow great ideas without these interruptions of the world's fierce turmoils?

Anyway it is evident that some such thoughts had animated the mind of one man who had taken up his abode in Bromwich, selecting the place primarily because it was far removed from the haunts of men, and, secondly, because it was peculiarly suited to the purposes of a recluse; it was in the depth of a wilderness, it probably possessed a pit or cavern in the sandstone rock, and was certainly provided with a well or spring.

This well lent its name to the locality, in plain Anglo-Saxon it was called Sand Well (but then pronounced, as it still is in the pure unadulterated vernacular of the natives, Sond Well) because it was sunk in the sandstone rock. The hermitage near this well was as ancient, that it dated presumably from before the Norman period, when it offered a place of repose to some more ancient hermit seeking quiet from the troublesome raids of the Danish invaders.

The holy reputation of the ancient hermitage further enhanced by that of its holy well, was sufficient to induce the selection of this site for the new priory. It is worthy of notice that two other religious houses seem to have been erected in this county because of the continuity of famous wells namely at Can-well and at Fare-well.

At no period of its existence was the priory of Sandwell in a flourishing institution. Within two centuries of its foundation, namely in the year 1361 it was at so low an ebb that only one monk remained and he asking the bishop to choose a prior over the empty cells, was himself appointed.

Mr. G. T. Lawley, in an article on "Well Dressing and Well Worship," suggests that the monks eked out their income by traffickings in philters and other miraculous attributes of the waters of the well. It is a fact that the simple English name *Sand Well* was changed by the pedantic monks into the Latin *Sancta Fons*, as if to impress the public mind with Romish credentials for their "holy well." And says Mr. Lawley——" it was the custom every year to adorn the well with garlands to the accompaniment of music and dancing in honour of its patron Saint Augustine who

As early bards do telle.

Gave to Bromwych this holy welle.

The well derived its saintly character no doubt from the policy or cunning of the monks of Sandwell, who would obtain considerable revenue from its real or pretended medicinal virtues."

After settling the site, the next matter for consideration was—In what religious order was the new foundation to be vested? Here again we see the influence of the friendly intercourse between the Offneys and the Paganels. As in 1155, Guy Offney had not only acquiesced in, but kind materially aided, the Paganels in bringing the Benedictines to Dudley Priory, so now in 1180 his son William shows a further appreciation of the same order by introducing them into his own manor at Sandwell. This latter large hearted donor gave also additional lands at Woodford, near

Wombourne to the Dudley Priory, with the amiable assent and goodwill of Juliana, his wife, and of Richard, his heir, conveying the churches of Handsworth and of Ellesborough (Bucks) to the Sandwell Priory at the same time.

The order of monks then introduced into this neighbourhood was that professing the stricter rules of monastic life instituted by St. Benedict, and first brought into England by St. Dunstan about the year 970. The good monks of this order were admirably suited to an area of "waste," and a place so wild and neglected as Bromwich; for by their system of treatment a veritable desert might even he made to smile as a garden, while bogs and undrained lands such as then existed on the boundaries of the parish were in due time converted into cornfields, orchards and rich pastures. The industry of Benedictine monks was a feature in strong contrast to the conduct of the secular canons who officiated at ordinary services as clergy. The laxity of these seculars was directly opposed to the strictness of the regulars; and yet into all St. Benedict had inculcated that strict obedience to a perfect law coincides with perfect liberty. And so the Benedictines of Sandwell, while performing their vows to God, neglected not their duty to men, they worked at many and various occupations, not only reclaiming the barren land and pestilential swamp for pleasant and productive cornlands, vineyards, and pastures; but as a labour of love they also instructed the young, multiplied books and manuscripts, and cultivated all the useful arts and industries of the time. Such institutions were the seats of civilisation in those semi-barbarious times; and in this light we must view the benign influences at work in the Priory of St. Mary Magdalen at Sandwell.

The presence of this newly founded religious house in the manor of Bromwich would necessarily mean a very great social advance for the place. Although but a small priory, it would combine in itself much of the philanthropy which in the present day is to be found represented by the larger and more costly institutions of modern times—the workhouse, the hospital, and the public schools. Before the days of hotels and hostelries, it was also a kind of free inn for all passing wayfarers. But it is as a seminary we may afford it the highest mark of our thoughtful appreciation; for it would meet with little or no welcome when it first lit up the sacred lamp of learning in "darkest Bromwich"; though as years rolled on its rays of light would eventually penetrate the density of the prevailing boorish ignorance, whereby many of the brightest sons of the Bromwich cottars would freely obtain an education that would fit them for admission to the service of mother Church.

Of Dudley Priory the same may also be said; here the monks were of the Clugniac branch of the order, from the Abbey of Much Wenlock, and their garb or habit consisted of cowl and a black loose gown. This branch of Benedictines proceeded from the convent of Clugny in Burgundy, founded in the year 910, and it was distinguished for severer regulations concerning the hours of worship, obedience, and discipline. There were in existence several other branches (for the Benedictine monasteries never constituted one single society) such as the Carthusians, Cistercians, Bernardines, Trappists, etc.

Of the power and influence of the Benedictines in this county of Stafford we may better form an opinion by enumerating their establishments within its boundaries.

At Burton-on-Trent was the Benedictine Abbey founded by Wulfric in the reign of Ethelred, whose charter of confirmation is dated 1004. At Farewell, near Lichfield, was a Benedictine Nunnery. The little Benedictine Priory at Lapley was a cell attached to the great Abbey at Rheims; Algar, Earl of Chester having given Lapley Manor to that French abbey in the reign of Edward the Confessor. And Canwell (near Tamworth) and Sandwell in Bromwich were also both Benedictine.

The Benedictine monasteries are classified as abbeys and priories, the former being of higher rank possessing more extensive domains, and ruled over by an abbot. Priories were smaller, presided over by priors, and in earlier times were nearly always subject to abbeys; thus, St. James's Priory at Dudley was said to be a cell of, or subject to, Wenlock Abbey in Shropshire.

*   *   *   *   *   *   *

Dr. Willmore, in his History of Walsall, says that at Friar Park there "stood a small monastic building of begging friars. They were connected with the Priory of Sandwell. The house stood in what is now called Moat Meadow, near the present Crankhall Farm." Reeves says there was a chapel approached by a drawbridge, some foundations of which were dug up at the beginning of this century. "Near here is a place called Dead Woman's Buryall; thought to have been the cemetery of the monks; and many years ago some human bones were ploughed up, confirming the name which the field still bears."

This is difficult to understand. The name " Fryer's Park" occurs as early as the 17th century, Dugdale enumerating it in his *Monasticon* among the possessions in 1614. But Benedictines were *monks* and not *friars*, and as monks they lived in seclusion, and did not go forth into the world to beg as friars did. The moat and the drawbridge are also inexplicable, unless they were premeditated contrivances to ensure unbroken and absolute seclusion; and looked at in this light the situation in the midst of a burial ground might also be accepted as carrying out the austerities of monkish discipline to a further degree of severity. Taken in this aspect the matter is quite susceptible of explanation.

Sometimes a monastery or priory would select a brother who was thought to be more exemplary than the rest of the monks, and devote him to entire seclusion as an honour. In *Fosbrook's Monachism* is detailed the ceremony by which an anachoret was consecrated to such seclusion. The cells in which the anchorite lived were of stone, and of not more than 12 square feet in area. There were three very small windows and a door, which latter was sometimes walled up, and food was then passed through a window. Or another severe exercise was the singing of psalms, standing in the water of a stream on a cold night—in this case it may have been in the water of the moat. In any case it is certain the "building" in this "park" was not occupied by "friars"; the begging and preaching friars had not come into existence until the 13th century, therefore, the solution of the problem as to the place-name *Friar's Park*, is probably to be found in the confusion which, in course of time, arose in the popular mind, and inability in times after the Reformation to distinguish between a "monk" and a "friar."

XI.—Descent of the Manor of Bromwich from the Offneys to the Marnhams. (1155-1292).

Gervase Paganel had married a widow, Isabel Countess of Northampton, a daughter of Robert de Bellamont, or Beaumont (also called Bossu), Earl of Leicester. By her he had issue only one child, Robert, and as this heir pre-deceased him without issue, the estates passed to his only sister, Hawise. Then the marriage of this heiress of the house of Paganel carried the barony of Dudley to the family of her husband John de Somery.

Our history will now however, have little connection with that of the barony; our attention being directed more particularly to the tenant occupier, or lord of the manor of Bromwich.

Now to trace the family descent of the Offneys, lords of Bromwich, for 137 years (1155–1292):—

(1). Guy Offney married Christiana; he helped to endow Dudley Priory, 1155.

(2). William Offney, their son, married Juliana; he founded Sandwell Priory, 1180.

(3). Richard, surnamed Basset, married Geva, and held the manor. He had a brother, James.

(4). William, their son, died without surviving issue; their two daughters, Margaret and Sara, inherited the manor of Bromwich, divided between them. It is difficult to discover which was the elder sister, Margaret or Sara, but the former married Richard de Marnham, and Sara married Walter Devereux.

Walter Devereux died in 1291 and was succeeded by his son Walter, who in the following year (1292) claimed extensive manorial franchises in Bromwich. Edward I. was a strict ruler, and in the 21st year of of his reign summoned all land holders to show on oath how they held their lands, and "by what right" they did such and such things in their manors. To this *Quo Warranto*, Walter Devereux replied that he held the manor of Bromwich conjointly with Margaret, wife of Richard de Marnham that it was inherited from Richard fitz William (i.e. son of William); and that his franchises, appurtenant to the manor from time out of memory, were the following rights, and prerogatives of his lordship:—

(1) VIEW OF FRANK-PLEDGE, a right to hold periodical courts, with "view" or jurisdiction over tenants, retainers, and servants, for trial of offences committed within the manor, the lord being responsible to the Crown for the prevention and punishment of crime, the "frank-pledge" was a *free* peace *pledge*, or surety for the good behaviour and right government of the district. *Every landless man was bound to have a lord to answer for him in the Courts*. A masterless man was regarded as a vagrant up to two centuries ago.

(2) INFANGTHEF (*in*, preposition: *fagen* or *fongen* "to take": *thef*, "a thief") was, as its Anglo-Saxon terminology implies, a right of the lord of a manor to judge any thief among his dependants taken within his manor or knight's fee.

(3) GALLOWS, the right of erecting this fatal tree for the punishment, by hanging, of certain malefactors; peers, clergy, and often women, being exempt from this form of death—and the two first-named from the manorial jurisdiction altogether. The possession of this right of gallows indicates that the family were of some considerable importance, as such franchise was usually associated only with baronial jurisdiction, and it was not infrequently disputed by the Crown in the case even of some of the barons.

(4) WAYF, a right by which all stolen goods unclaimed became the property of the lord of the manor. Goods *waived* would be such as a thief having feloniously stolen, threw away in his escape from the *hue and cry*. The King's officer—or the bailiff of the manor, if this franchise is held—might then seize the goods, except when the real owner sued for and obtained them within a year and a day. The same law applied to the goods of a felon who fled; but not till a Coroner or other Court of Record had found that he did fly for felony. Similarly things lost or strayed had to be cried and published at a market or a church, or else the year and a day did not run to the prejudice of the loser. From these ancient customs we get the phrase of "waifs and strays. "

How far these four claims were substantiated will be recorded later.

With regard to the division of the Offney estates it must be noted that where land descends to daughters (the holder having no son to succeed him), these are then designated *parceners*, and are but as one heir. The same law applies if the owner had no issue and his sisters became his heirs. In a deed of this period (the originals of which are said to be in the possession of the Rev. Thomas Jesson) it is William Marnham who is styled Lord of West Bromwich, and under feudal law, when a manor was divided between two sisters, it is the issue of the elder who succeeds to the titular lordship, and it would thus appear that Margaret de Marnham was the elder sister. In a Subsidy Roll of the year 1333 detailing the payments towards the expenses of a war, William de Marnham is assessed at 6s., the highest rate of all the tenants in Bromwich. Roger Basset comes next with an assessment of 4s. 6d. The name Devereux does not appear at all, and the inference is that the family had parted with all their interest in the Manor of Bromwich, leaving the Marnhams as sole lords.

But greatness does not always bring happiness, and this was equally true in those times. At the Assizes in 1292 (21 Ed. I.) one son of this knightly family was tried for the murder of another, and though acquitted as having killed his brother in self-defence, the details will not make the circumstances less distressing.

Extracts from the records of a Gaol Delivery of the County of Stafford put us in possession of the whole facts of this domestic tragedy in olden Bromwich.

It appeared that Bertram, son of Richard de Marnham, lord of half the Manor of West Bromwich and resident therein, was in prison under arrest for the death of Nicholas (presumably his elder brother) "son of Richard de Marnham." Bertram being put on his trial pleaded that he was a *Clericus*, and upon this, Walter de Elmdon, rector of the church of Weston, on the part of the Bishop of Lichfield and Coventry, came and claimed him as a clerk [in holy orders], and in order that his status might be known in which he should be delivered up [whether innocent or guilty, for as he was an ecclesiastic he was exempt from the jurisdiction of the civil judges of assize and would be tried in the Bishop's Court] the truth was to be determined by the country: a jury of the Hundred of Offlow and the contiguous parishes stated:—

That Nicolas and Bertram, sons of Richard de Marnham, were sitting and drinking together with others at the house of Agnes the weaver (*textrix*) of Bromwych, in Bromwych, in the dusk of the evening, and contumelious words were used between them and the said Bertram, who was the younger and humble (*junior et humilis*) out of respect for the said Nicholas, got up and left the house of Agnes in order to avoid the malice of the said Nicholas, who was *valde maliciosus*; and Nicholas being irritated at this got up and followed him with a long knife drawn in his hand, and Bertram ran away between two high hedges as far as the door of the said Richard de Marnham in that vill (parish); and the door was closed so that he could not enter the house, nor could he climb over the hedges because of their height, and he could not evade Nicholas except by defending himself. In self-defence he struck Nicholas with his sword on the head and in the breast.

The jury determine that the prisoner is to be given up to the Bishop as not guilty.

"The King afterwards sent for the record."

The leniency may, or may not, have been well deserved in this distressing case of fratricide. But it must be borne in mind that the jurors at these assizes were, with one or two exceptions, knights or heads of knightly families.

XII.—Bromwich under Forest Law.

In a previous chapter (viii.) we have seen that Gervase Paganel was fined in the year 1176 for participating in a rebellion. King Henry II. was at this time traversing the realm to hold Forest Courts. These were oppressive to all classes. The royal forests, of which Cannock Chase was one—and its boundaries approached West Bromwich as near as the banks of the Tame, stretching from Finchpath Bridge at Wednesbury, and

Fullbrook at the Delves—had their own officers and magistrates, their own peculiar code and courts of law, for the protection of Vert and Venison. It would appear that the King took advantage of this same perambulation of the Kingdom to deal with other offences than those against the Forest Laws; for not only was the tenant-in-chief Paganel punished for his disaffection to the throne, but the treasonable practices of certain four of Paganel's sub-tenants, among them William fitz Guy de Offney, lord of Bromwich, were also visited by fines.

During the recent Civil Wars the barons had habitually and defiantly taken advantage of the disturbed state of the country to encroach on the royal forests, the condition of which in time became very unsatisfactory; and very heavy fines and penalties became necessary. The King's officers constantly came into collision with offenders of the very highest rank, who had transgressed against the severe Forest Laws which were then in force. From the Staffordshire Pipe Rolls (the ancient "rolls" or records of the Court of Exchequer, dealing with the Crown revenues) of 1174—1175 we find that three knights and a man-at-arms were summarily executed for the murder of one Gilbert Butler. a king's forester. A few years before this Staffordshire had been severely visited (1166) by Alan de Nevil, the Justice of the Forests, and among the delinquents punished for offending the Forest Laws was Ralph Botterell, lord of Wednesbury. While inside the limits of the carefully guarded royal forests all "vert and venison" (that is, *wood* and *game*) were thus specially protected by elaborate legal machinery: contiguous manors lying immediately outside the forest boundaries were also jealously watched, and it needed a special grant from the King to confer upon Peter de Birmingham the right of "free warren" over Birmingham and Handsworth, permitting this high steward of the Paganels to chase with dogs the hares and rabbits, and to fly his hawks at the pheasants, partridges, and other small game. At the larger game he dared scarcely to look; certainly he would he punished if he made a deer but to pant. Only to the great barons was granted the right of hunting deer and large game; the barons of Dudley having their own "chase," which is the highest form of forest franchise, extending from their castle away to Penn and to Pensnett. "Free warren" was the lowest form of forest franchise, and every lord of a manor seems to have possessed it by the 13th century, if not the next franchise above it namely, that of a "Park" or enclosed preserve. Thus in the reign of Edward III. we find Roger Hillary, of Bescot, possessing the right of free warren in Wednesbury. (see *History of Darlaston*, pp 27 and 28). In Bromwich Manor, however, we find the right of free warren exercised by its lord as early as 1293, and, indeed, then claimed as a grant of the previous reign, namely, that of Henry III. That is to say, the lord of Bromwich Manor might preserve and kill all beasts and birds of warren which by law consisted of hare, coney, roe, partridge, quail, rail, pheasant, woodcock, mallard, heron, and a few others.

But, above all, the grants of (1) *free warren*, (2) of a *park*, and (3) of the *chase* to a subject (like "Sutton Chase," the property of the Earls of Warwick, whose 3,500 acres were afterwards given by Bishop Vesey to the inhabitants of the town in Edward VI.'s reign) was (4) the *Royal Forest*. The royal forest of Cannook was probably part of that ancient Arden, which once had covered the whole Midland Counties; it was hunted by royal owners down to the fifteenth century, as witness the ballad of "The Tanner of Tamworth," relating an adventure of Edward IV. while hunting near Drayton Basset.

With two exceptions, the origin of Royal Forests in England is lost in antiquity, but they certainly existed before the Norman Conquest. The two exceptions are the New Forest, created by William the Conqueror, and Hampton Court, by Henry VIII. There are said to have been no fewer than 68 forests in the possession of the Crown at one time, and 13 chases or forests in private hands, but most of them have long since been disafforested. The district out of which the New Forest was formed was probably very wild and almost wholly uncultivated, but the extension of the forest over private lands and the enforcement of cruel game laws must have caused great indignation in the district, and probably gave rise to the exaggeration with which the story of the making of the forest was told by the monkish historian. Now the New Forest consists of 65,000 acres of which only 2,000 are the demesne lands of the Crown, and are enclosed and cultivated.

Forest Law differed from Common Law, offences being punished not only very severely, but before the reign of King John almost at pleasure. According to Forest Law in 1255 (39 and 40 Henry III.) we find Bromwich given as being in the lordship of Walter de Everoos (Devereux) and two co parceners, in the great barony of Dudley. (It was this charter of Henry III., which was afterwards produced as proof of claim in 1293). Enumerated in the same barony at the same time are given Perry and Hamstead (held by Henry de Pirie), Handsworth (by William de Parles), Little Barr (by Richard de Barre, holding through William de Birmingham), Rushall, Drayton Basset, Enville, Himley, Amblecote, Wombourne, Trysull, Bushhury, Pendeford, Penn, Pattingham and many others. Wednesbury was then in the lordship of Simon de Heronville in the great barony of the heirs of D'Oilli, whose heirs also held Shenstone through Robert de Grendon. (See *Salt Collections*, vol. v., part 1).

XIII.—Law Suits of the Basset, Marnham, and Devereux Families, 1225—1294. Their Manorial Rights in West Bromwich.

Notwithstanding the statement made in chapter xi., that William, the son of Richard and Geva Basset, died without surviving issue, it would appear on closer investigation that William did leave an infant son Richard in the guardianship of one William of Bromwich, probably a large freeholder in the parish. For Geva, the widow, after no doubt enjoying her dower of "one third portion for fire" during the lifetime of her son William, had to sue her infant grandson Richard for a continuation of her enjoyment of the same. This we gather from the Court records of the Staffordshire Pleas of the reign of Henry III (Easter term of the year 1225), the case in question disclosing that Geva Basset sued "Richard, son of William," for her dower, which was stated as a third (always the widow's dower portion) of 4 shillings rent, 6 acres of land and of 5 vivaries, and a messuage in "Bromwic." A Vivary may have been a park, a warren, a fishery, or any other place of preserved animal life. The defendant Richard did not appear, although the summons was duly proved. The dower claimed was therefore taken into the King's hands—that is, the sheriff was, perhaps, put in possession, as Richard was an infant—and the defendant was ordered to be summoned again for the Michaelmas term. William de Bromwic, the guardian of Richard, held none of the lands, except for and on behalf of Richard, and the suit was ordered to proceed against Richard alone. (*Salt Coll.* vi., 33.)

Between the year 1225 and the death in 1291 of the first Walter Devereux, who having married Sarah Basset, the sister of Richard, "the infant" heir, there is a lapse of 66 years, certainly a long period to be covered by one life (supposing Sarah lived as long as her husband, Walter Devereux), but not an impossible hiatus. As recorded in chapter xi., the second Walter Devereux succeeded to his moiety of the Manor in 1291, and in the following year set up his claim to the four manorial franchises (1) View of frankpledge, (2) Infangthef (3) Gallows, and (4) Wayf. Then came the summons of *Quo*

Warranto (*i.e.*, "by what right?',) of that stern monarch, Edward I., issued not only in the case of Bromwich, but of nearly every manor in the country, where the lords thereof were supposed to be presuming too much in their local administration by encroaching on the authority and jurisdiction of the crown itself. From the pleadings in answer to these summonses a vast amount of manorial history of that period may be learnt. The citing of a few cases in the Hundred of Offlow, and of those manors contiguous to Bromwich, will serve to illustrate this. From the Plea Rolls, or court records, of the Epiphany term (7th January) 1293, the following facts are gathered: Walter Devereux was lord of one half of the manor of West Bromwich, and Richard de Marnham was lord of the other half. Walter Devereux was summoned to show his title to hold pleas of the crown, and to have free warren, fair, market, gallows, and wayf in the manor of Bromwich. Walter pleaded that he could not answer to the writ without Margaret, the wife of Richard de Marnham (his co-parcener in the inheritance of Richard fitz William); and Richard and Margaret appeared and disclaimed a fair and market, but stated that they claimed view of frankpledge, infongenthef, gallows, and wayf, in the said manor, by prescription. The King's Attorney disputed their right, but a jury found in their favour. As regarded free warren Walter Devereux stated that Henry III., the preceeding King, had granted to Walter Devereux, his father, and to his heirs, free warren in all the demesne lands in Bromwich, and he produced the King's charter. The question of wayf was adjourned to be heard *coram rege* ("before the King") that is, in the court that followed the king's person, instead of in this itinerant court of the king's justices.

Some of the terms in the foregoing record have already been fully explained. But some of the other technicalities will need elucidation in order to interest the popular reader:

(1) PLEAS OF THE CROWN; were not "*common* pleas," but designated all those suits in the *King's* name, in cases of offences committed against his crown, dignity, and peace. (As Treasons, Felonies, etc).

(2) MARKET AND FAIR. A right by grant or by prescription and usage to buy and sell in the open street or highway, and to take toll for same under certain conditions. A Market was a lesser franchise than a Fair, although it might have been held more frequently. Both were instituted for the promotion of trade and the convenience of commerce. The grant of this privilege was jealously guarded by the King, and it is therefore not surprising to find the claim abandoned in the case of Bromwich, which never has been a "market town."

Proceeding with these local cases through the various stages of summons, pleadings, and judgments some other terms needing glossarial explanations are:—

(3) PILLORY, a right of lords of manors to set up this engine of punishment, for the public exposure of the culprit with his head fastened in a "door."

(4) TUMBRELL or cucking-stool, an engine of punishment for scolds and unquiet women, by ducking them in water. Also used sometimes for brewers and bakers for transgressing the laws in their respective food supplies—these culprits were generally immersed over head and ears in stinking water.

(5) ASSIZE OF BREAD AND BEER, the right of adjusting the weights and measures used in supplying these foodstuffs, and often of fixing their standard of quality.

In these pleas of the Crown (1293) held before John de Berewyk and his fellow Justices Itinerant in County Stafford, we find that the Hundred of Offlow appeared by 12 jurymen, who, among other things presented that the said Hundred "is the King's, and is worth 16 marks yearly"—a mark was 13s. 4d., but the sum mentioned represented a considerable amount in those days. After dealing with the Hundred as a whole—Their finding with regard to pretensions to Manorial Franchises enumerates amongst others (1) that Walter Devereux and Richard de Marnham claim gallows, pillory, tumbrells and assize of bread and beer in the manor of Bromwich, (2) that Agnes de Somery, formerly wife of Roger (tenant-in-chief) claims the same rights in Handsworth Manor, (3) that John de Heronville claimed to have assize of bread and beer in the manor of Wednesbury; (4) that Roger de Mortayn, John Paynel, and Margaret, his wife, all aforementioned privileges in the manor of Walsall; and many other lordships besides. The Sheriff was therefore ordered to summon them, and writs of *Quo Warranto* to be issued.

With regard to Walsall it was found to be held of the King *in capite* at a fee farm rent of £4 annually, by grant of Henry II., whose charter was produced. It substantiated their claims fully: they were to enjoy in peace all their franchises, including two free courts yearly to hear the same pleas that the Sheriff heard in his tourns (*i.e*, the Sheriff's view of frankpledge at the court of the county), to hold fair and market, and all their former privileges.

With regard to Wednesbury the jury of an Inquisition had presented elsewhere that John de Heronville held the manor of " Wodnesburi," which is of ancient demesne of the Crown, and which was worth £4 annually, and it was not known by what warrant. John de Heronville appeared, and stated that he held the said manor in exchange for the manor of "Stontesfeld," in the county of Oxford, which exchange was made between his ancestors and the ancestors of the King, Edward I. (namely, Henry II.); and because the manor of Stuntsfield was of less value than the manor of Wednesbury by 20 shillings a year he rendered to the Exchequer of the King annually 20 shillings. And to ratify this he produced an enrolment of the Exchequer. This showed that originally William de Heronville held Wednesbury by right of his wife: the Sheriff further testified that there were no arrears on account of the difference in value paid yearly into the Exchequer: John de Heronville therefore proved good his title to the lordship of Wednesbury and its extensive franchise as an ancient crown manor.

With regard to Bromwich the law proceedings continue for two years longer.

The Plea Rolls of Easter (Coram Rege, 22 Edward I.) in 1294, supply further records in the suit of *Quo Warranto* against Walter Devereux, and Richard de Marnham and Margaret his wife, his co-parceners respecting the Franchises claimed by them in Bromwych.

Richard and Margaret appeared and stated that they claimed no Pleas of the Crown excepting View of Frankpledge, Infangenthef, Gallows, and Wayf; and that their ancestors had held them from time out of memory; and they appealed to a jury which found in their favour.

The King's Attorney stated that Wayf was a *grossum* (?absolute right) annexed to the Crown, and could not be separated from it without special warrant, and he prayed for judgment on that point. The Sheriff was ordered to summon a jury of 24 for the "octaves of" St John the Baptist—that is "the eighth day after June 24th," or a week later.

Richard and Margaret de Marnham renounced any claim to Free Warren. This right seems to have gone to the Devereux branch of the family.

———————

XIV.—THE STATUTE OF MERTON (1235) AND ITS EFFECT ON BROMWICH LANDS, 1272—1293.

When Fitzansculph obtained his barony of Dudley he was one of 700 chief-tenants, who held the gross total of 60,215 knights fees in England, of which Bromwich was but one. But the Bromwich of 1086 was only a small area of cultivated land, with a few pastures, while the greater portion of what now comprises the parish was wood and waste—waste simply signifying unoccupied land. In due course this waste was gradually brought into cultivation, as in process of time we find other large landowners in Bromwich, besides the lord of the manor. Large open and unenclosed tracts, which lay outside the lands held by the lord of the manor, would have been granted by the sovereign to certain individuals. Such land would certainly be the cultivated land—not "waste" in any shape. By the Statute of Merton passed in 1235, a right was given to the lord of the manor to enclose all common land not absolutely required by the freeholders. It was not customary then to enclose any lands, except those required for the growth of corn and other crops. All the remainder was left open to the cattle of all: and all members of the community, to the very humblest, were permitted to cut turf for fuel, heather for thatching, and bracken for litter. The enclosed part was generally divided into three great fields for a three-course system of husbandry, in which one field in turn was left fallow.

In earlier times the ownership of these enclosed lands had been a collective one, each field being divided into a certain number of equal parts, which were distributed annually by lot among the heads of families in the village community. The rights of common which still survive are but remains of this collective system of ownership—common over wastes being enjoyed by freehold and copyhold tenants of manors for centuries. So late as the Tudor period the cultivation of common fields was practised; the enclosures complained of at that time were enclosure not of waste lands, but of the three great fields of the village.

Each feudal chief became lord of his manor or district, subject to the admitted rights of the larger landowners and free tenants. Presently other claims were put forth by the lord; namely (a) to treat the common lands as his own property, subject only to the admitted rights of free tenants, villeins and serfs, and (b) to enclose portions of waste to his own use, or for the creation of small holdings to be farmed by villeins. This was resisted by the freeholders, but the Statute of Merton in 1235 authorised the lords of manors to enclose parts of the waste, so long as enough land was left to satisfy the wants of free tenants. This was the first Inclosure Act. The last so far as West Bromwich is concerned, was the private Act of 1802.

With this preliminary explanation we proceed to quote certain law cases found in the Plea Rolls of Edward I. concerning either land in Bromwich, or lands held by the lord of Bromwich Manor—all the disputes seeming to be connected, more or less, with the Statute of Merton (1235) :—

I.—At the Michaelmas term of 1272, while the new King, Edward I., was yet abroad, Thomas de Brumwye (that is, Thomas of Bromwich), John de Heronville, of Wednesbury, Henry of Erdington and several others are found *in misericordiâ*, or punished by an arbitrary amerciament for trespass. Thomas of Bromwich was fined 20 shillings, Henry the same amount, and Heronville 1 mark. An *amerciament* was an assessed penalty for an offence, according to its degree, and for which the offender puts himself at the *mercy* of his lord; this is signified by the term "in misericordia;" a *fine*, on the other hand, was a punishment certain and fixed, growing out of some statute. The phrase "de" Bromwich, may possibly be here a territorial title of the said Thomas;

but more probably it simply indicates that he had certain large holdings of land in this parish.

II.—At an Assize held at Lichfield in 1275, a case was tried to find if Ralph de Bushbury and nineteen others had unjustly ousted Richard de Marneham of "Bramwys," and Margaret, his wife, of common of pasture at Bushbury, appurtenant to a free tenement of theirs at Oxley, and consisting of 64 acres of pasture, where they used to common with all cattle during the whole year. The jury found that Richard and Margaret had no right of common in Bushbury. A "free tenement" would be one held without the conditions generally imposed of rendering some feudal service in return for it.

III.—The Assize Roll of 29th January, 1276, of the pleas heard at Kinver before Henry de Montfort contains a case tried to find if Richard de Marnham, William de "Bromwyz," and two others had ousted William de Parles from four acres of land in Handsworth. Richard appeared for all the defendants, and stated that the land in dispute was in "Bromwych" and not in Handsworth, and that it formerly belonged to one Richard, the father of his wife. Margaret, who had died possessed of it. The verdict was given for Richard. This case would seem to indicate that some uncertainty existed as to the exact boundary line between Bromwich and Handsworth in 1276.

IV.—At Assizes held at Handsworth, before the two judges, Reginald de Leye and Hugh de Cave, in 1286, a case was tried if Richard le Sergant of Bromewyz, together with William, son of Simon Atteton, and Walter de Cokesey, had unjustly dispossessed William, son of William Atteton, of certain lands, etc., in "Bromewyz," namely, a messuage, 10 acres of land, and 6 acres of meadow and marsh. All three defendants appeared, but Cokesey stated that he held nothing, nor did he claim anything in the said tenements, except the lordship. William, son of Simon, said he was the tenant, because as his father had died seised of the tenement, he had entered as his father's heir. The other William (son of William), admitted that Simon had died seized of the tenement, but stated that William (Simon's son), had after Simon's death, enfeoffed him (*i.e.* granted him legal possession), William, son of William, in the said lands. The jury found otherwise, namely, a verdict for William, son of Simon. In this case it is interesting to note that Handsworth was the *locale* of the trial, and with regard to "Richard, the serjeant of Bromwich," it may be explained that the phrase indicates that Richard held his lands by some *nominal tenure* of rendering a specified service for them—a *sergeant* literally means a "servant." Feudal *serjeanty* will be dealt with later.

V.—The Staffordshire Assize Roll of pleas before Justices Itinerant, in County Stafford, heard the 7th January, 1293, records that Roger, the Prior, of Sandwell, sued Richard de Marnham and Margaret, his wife, for 7 acres of land in West Bromwich, of which they had unjustly disseised his predecessor in office, the Prior, Richard. The defendants, Richard and Margaret, took exception to the writ, because the prior was named Thomas and not Roger. It may have been that Thomas had changed his name to Roger when he relinquished the world and entered the monastery; any way, there was a legal error, and as power to amend in those days was very limited, the suit had to be dismissed. This and the remaining cases must be looked upon with an amount of suspicion, as they deal with lands claimed or disputed by ecclesiastics. Of some of these church lands a subsequent chapter will treat more fully.

VI.—At the same Assizes of Epiphany, 1293, Richard de Marnham and Margaret, his wife, sued Walter de Cokesey, Thomas the Prior of Sandwell, and five others for unjustly seizing three acres of "waste" (unoccupied land) in West Bromwych. The defendants, with the exception of the Prior, disclaimed all rights; and the Prior stated that the manor of Bromwych formerly belonged to one Richard Basset, and was divided between Sara and the said Margaret, his daughters and heirs, and that the land in question was the purparty of Sara, and Sara had issue Walter Devereaux, by whose concession he, the Prior, holds it. The jury found that the land in dispute was part of the purparty of Margaret, and, therefore, Richard and Margaret are to "recover seisin," that is, regain possession. It would seem that although Walter Devereux had given the concession to the Prior, it was not his to give, being part of the other daughter's portion of the estate—It was in his aunt Margaret's inheritance, and not part of that of his mother Sara. By the term *purparty* is meant that portion of the estate which was first held in common by the two *parceners* when it was divided between them.

VII.—A counter case at the same assizes was to try if Richard de Marnham, Margaret, his wife, and William, their son had illegally disseised the Prior of Sandwell of common of pasture in 40 acres of land in Bromewych, viz. every two years in the open season, and every third year for the whole year, with all kind of cattle. The Prior won this case, possibly because the land in dispute was portion of Sara's inheritance, over which he had acquired rights.

VIII.—From the Prior of Sandwell we come now to another Churchman and his lawsuits about land, namely, the Abbot of Hales Owen. At the same Epiphany Assizes of 1293 a suit was tried to find if Richard de Marnham and Walter Devereux had unjustly dispossessed the Abbot of Hales Owen of common of pasture in 70 acres of "arable land after the corn was carried," "in Bromwych, near Wallshall." Richard pleaded that he held only in right of his wife Margaret, and she was not named in the writ: and both Richard and Walter stated that they did not hold the whole of the land in question, inasmuch as various other persons held portions of it; thus 30 acres were held by William, son of Richard le Serjant, of Bromwych 5 acres by Philip de Lynden, 6 acres by Richard de Rushaker (? Ridgacre), 10 acres by Richard Basset, 10 acres by Richard Hude, 6 acres by William Mustrell, 6 acres by Ralph Swetecok, and 3 acres by Walter Bond. As the Abbot could not contradict the suit was dismissed. In fact, the Abbot seems to have failed to secure the common of pasture, because the rights were actually owned by other persons than those whom he sued.

IX.—Further, to try if Walter Devereux, Richard de Marnham, and Margaret, his wife, had unjustly disseised the Abbot of Hales Owen of common of pasture in West Bromwych, viz., in 310 acres of land in the open season with 600 sheep. The defendants admitted that the Abbot had right of common in the waste of West Bromwych; but stated that the manor of West Bromwych formerly belonged to Richard, the father of Margaret, and of Sarra, the mother of Walter Devereux, and that this Richard had held the manor in severally all his life, and after his death the defendants held it in the same way; and they appealed to a jury. The jury found that the Abbot was seised of common of pasture in the said vill (that is, manor or village of West Bromwich) as appurtenant to his free tenement.

*   *   *   *   *   *   *

Hales Owen Abbey had been founded in the year 1215 and completed in 1218, when Monks from the Abbey of Welbeck in Nottinghamshire had inhabited it. Its Abbots had jurisdiction over Titchfield Priory (Hants) and over Dotfield Priory near Bromsgrove. Henry III. in 1248 gave this Abbey the patronage of the Church of Walsall, with its Chapel, together with all the small tithes arising within the Chapelry of Wednesbury and of Rushall. At these same Assizes of 1293 two decisions of importance to Wednesbury were given: (1) That Wednesbiri was of the *ancient demesne* of the Crown, and therefore its tenants possessed many immunities and privileges; and (2) That Wodensbury was a mother church, and not a chapel appurtenant to the Church of Walsall.

XV.—Side Lights from Bromwich Cases upon English History and Ancient Law Practices.

Keeping still within the thirteenth century or nearly so, and continuing to quote from the records of legal proceedings, much light may yet be shed upon the condition of Bromwich at that period. Unfortunately most of the cases are civil suits, and those relate chiefly to funds (and from the multiplicity of such trials it will be observed that the disputed possession of lands has always been equally fruitful of such legal crops); but in this chapter it is proposed to include a few criminal causes that will enlighten the ordinary reader as to the social condition of the locality in those times, somewhat apart from, but not altogether irrespective of the landed interests. The two things, society and land cannot be entirely divorced, for it was a time of lordship and serfdom—on one side, power and position; on the other, the most abject dependence.

(1).—Manorial Franchises: "the forbidden distress" (1225—1291).

The greatest of the county historians of Staffordshire is the Rev. Stebbing Shaw, whose work in two volumes is most exhaustive. In volume II., published in 1801, will be found the history of West Bromwich, from which extracts will be taken from time to time. Shaw commences this history in the time of Henry III. when, he says: Walter de Everous (Devereux) and his two coparceners held the town of Bromwich of Roger de Somery, and he held plea of all things except the forbidden distress ... the view of frankpledge; and pays the Sheriff for the same, 5s. (this was the contribution of Bromwich to the National Exchequer at that time) and owes suit to the two great Hundred Courts yearly.

Shaw had not seen all those national documents which have since been published, some of which bear upon the courts and jurisdictions of the lords of Bromwich.

The FORBIDDEN DISTRESS is technically called the *plea de vetito namis*. It is where a Bailiff distrains for anything, and is forbidden by his lord to deliver the chattels up if the Sheriff comes to replevy them. The person distrained on then brings a writ "de vetito names," and it would be obviously unjust (says Mr. W. H. Duignen, whose popular interpretation of this legal technicality it is) that such a suit should be tried in the lord's own court, before his own men. Therefore such a suit should go to the courts at Westminster; but, unless expressly excluded would, in truth, be triable in the lord's court.

(2).—How Estates Were Transferred: Bromwich Cases, 1222—1310.

For the sake of security, which in those unlettered days seemed only obtainable through the precise records of a court of law, fictitious actions were commenced for the possession of lands and tenements. All the stages of the suit tended to secure the most public acknowledgments of the feoffment. The records of this method of conveying and assuring lands are met with chiefly under two heads—the *license* of the crown giving the parties liberty to accord; and the *fine* or final accord itself. This "foot" of the fine which *ended* the whole, was the official summary cut in an indented line (hence the word *indenture*), one part delivered to the suitor who could prove authenticity by the exact tally his parchment made by fitting into that part retained by the court.

In this legal sense the word fine is nothing whatever in the shape of a money-fine, but signifies merely the final agreements about lands or rents. Thus certain legal processes are gone through in due form and regular order, one after the other, for recovering possession of the lands or hereditaments. First there is commenced a sort of friendly-suit, secondly follows a *license of concord*, or leave to agree the suit, thirdly comes the concord or agreement itself, usually an acknowledgment from the *deforciants* (those who keep the other out of possession) that the lands in question are the right of the complainant, then there is a *note of the fine* or abstract naming the parties, the parcels of land and the agreement, and lastly there is the *foot of the fine.* These last named always expressed in the Latin phrase, *Pedes Finium.* were the "final," agreements from which there was no departure. In this way a fine was completely levied at common law.

With this explanation we may now enumerate the the following FINAL CONCORDS or PEDES FINIUM (in the reign of Henry III.) of suits connected with Bromwich—in a brief form of abstract, setting forth in order (1) time, (2) place, (3) parties, (4) possessions in dispute, and (5) final agreement made in respect thereof:—

I.—January 14th, 1222, Warwick.

William de Parles—Richard Fitz William (called to warranty by Prior of Sandwell).

Ten acres of land in Sandwell. William remits all claim, for which Richard gives him 100s.

II.—January 20th, 1230, Westminster.

John de Parles—William, Prior of Sandwell.

Advowson of the Church of Handsworth. The Prior remits all claim, for which John gave to the Prior and Church of Sandwell, a messuage in Birmingham.

III.—February 3rd, 1248. Lichfield.

Roger de Bosco and Juliana his wife, and John de Erdington and Alditha his wife— John de Wrosne.

Three and a half acres in Bromwich. Roger, Juliana, John, and Alditha remit their claim, for which John de Wrosne gave them $3\frac{1}{2}$ marks of silver.

IV.—Same time and place.

William le Kittere and Quenilda his wife, and Margery, sister of Quenilda—Walter de la Haye.

Eleven acres in Bromwich. William, Quenilda and Margery remit their claim, for which Walter gave 6 marks. (Endorsed:—Sarra and Helis, daughters of Richard de Bromwyz, put in their claims).

From the Westminster rolls of a later reign we glean the following two causes as they appear in their second stage of procedure, thus:—

The Michaelmas term 3 Edward II. (1310) records that William of Erdington and Petronilla, his wife, paid half a mark for *license of concord* (permission to agree) with "Thomas de Erdyngton" respecting certain tenements in West Bromwich.

From the *Pedes Finium* we afterwards learn more fully that by this *Fine* (*i.e.*, final agreement) a messuage, 10 acres of land, 2 acres of meadow, and one of moor, was settled on William and Petronilla and their issue, and if William should die without issue by Petronilla, it all reverted to Thomas and his heirs.

In 1312 a *license of concord* between Roger Basset of Bromwich, and Richard Paynel and Alice, his wife, is recorded. It was in a plea of warranty of charter respecting tenements in Wednesbury.

By the final agreement the Paynels acknowledged 4 acres of meadow in Wednesbury to be the right of Roger Basset, for which Roger gave them £10.

(3).—LANDS ALIENATED IN MORTMAIN (1294—1302.)

In the previous chapter grave suspicion was thrown upon those legal proceedings in which the clergy were concerned; for there was often collusion between the parties when a cleric was found suing for the possession of lands. At this period the rapidly growing wealth of the church was sapping the very strength and vitality of the nation. Lands going into the possession of monasteries and chapters were said to *alienated in Mortmain*, because the profits on them were lost to the lord, while at the same time the national strength was weakened because they produced no military tenants. In 1278 was passed the *Statute de Religiosus,* prohibiting all such alienations of land. Then the clergy evaded its provisions by setting up fictitious titles to certain lands, with the secret consent of the donor, who connived at the judgment given against him.

Then the *Second Statute of Mortmain* had to be passed (1284), enacting that such cases should be sent to a jury, and if fraud was discovered the lands should be forfeited.

No doubt religious bodies were always popular landlords; they were lax and sympathetic. Still in an age of militarism the lands could not safely be permitted to fall into "dead hands."

From records of Westminster trials (Banco Rolls) 1294, we learn that a jury returned a verdict that certain messuage with $7\frac{1}{2}$ acres of land in Wednesbury were the free alms of the Church of Wednesbury of which Nicholas de Burton was the parson; and that the property in question was not the lay fee of Philip Bonde, of "Bromewych," who held the said tenement; and that it had been *alienated* by Nicholas, the Abbot of Hales Owen.

Possession was therefore recovered by Nicholas, the "parson" of Wednesbury. The next case has been previously given in *The History of Tipton*, chapter viii.

From the Trinity term Banco Rolls, same year, we find that Thomas, the Prior of Sandwell, sued Nicholas Comitassone, of Grete (? Greet's Green) for a mill and half-an-acre of land in West Bromwich and Tipton (probably located on both sides the mill-stream which divides the parishes) as the right of his church. As Nicholas did not put in an appearance, we learn from a postscript to the entry that at the Trinity Term two years later (1296), a jury came to the conclusion (a verdict having apparently been delivered in the meantime in favour of the Prior) that:

(*a*) There was no collusion between the said Nicholas and the Prior. [For, as has just been explained, it was one of the great abuses of the Church which, a few years previously Edward I. had attempted to remedy by legislation. The Church was growing inordinately rich at the expense of the state and to the alarming detriment of its feudal strength; for as a corporate body, which never dies, the church could permanently hold its ever-increasing possessions, which thus became free from fines and other payments on the succession of heirs, and which were totally free from all other feudal burdens, especially the maintenance of armed soldiers. The Crown, therefore, in defence of its own rights passed the *Statute of Mortmain* (*i.e.*, "dead hands," because such holdings were practically dead to the King's revenue and military strength) which forbad this alienation of lands to the church. With legal subtlety it was soon sought to over-ride the Act by setting up a false title to any land, the owner of which was willing to give it to the church for the "good of his soul." This Bromwich case was suspiciously like a fraudulent transfer, hence the finding of the jury on this first point.]

(*b*) That as regards the Mill, a certain William, son of Guy, the lord of Bromwich, and founder of the Priory, gave it, "at a time out of memory"—for the legal memory never extends further back than the reign of Richard I.—to the predecessor of the prior and that one Geoffrey Fitz Warren, lord of Tipton manor in the reign of Henry III., gave the half-acre in question to Richard de la Barre, prior of Sandwell, and that the said Richard was seized of it (that is, was legally in possession) of the right of his church (the priory) before the Statute of Mortmain was passed in the year 1285. The prior consequently "recovered seisin" or got possession. It is evident that between 1294 and 1296 a verdict had already been given in the prior's favour, and that the later proceedings grew out of the Statute of Mortmain.

In 1302 the Prior of Sandwell had a suit against William de Elmhurst and Christiana his wife respecting a messuage in Dudley. This case has also been given in *The History of Tipton*.

(4) PRESENTMENT OF ENGLISHERY, 1293.

We now come to a criminal case, and as near as we can possibly get to secure a glimpse of the social life of the people. Side allusions only have as yet been made to the mutual distrust and jealousy with which the Norman and the Saxon regarded each other in these early centuries after the Conquest. Now to take three direct instances in this immediate neighbourhood. Till the year 1341 the feudal law was administered so much to the prejudice of the Saxon, that if a man was found murdered, he was considered in the eye of the law to be a Norman, unless by particular witnesses he could be proved to be a Saxon. In the former case the whole of the Hundred was heavily fined—the Norman rulers thus demanding vengeance in another form of penalty, as well as by shedding more blood in return for that of the murdered Norman. Hence at these cases of murder, which were rather frequent in those barbarous times the men of a Hundred were always eager to escape fine and punishment, which they did, when witnesses succeeded in proving the victim to be an Englishman and not a Norman, and which was called in the law courts *Presentment of Englishery*. The three cases in this Hundred of Offlow, in the year 1293, are as follows:—

(*a*) "Richard the Clerk," son of the Rector of Barr, was killed in the fields at Barr, by John Mist who was hanged, and other robbers unknown. As the first finder of the body was dead and no Englishery was presented, therefore *murdrum* (the fine for murder) was put upon the Hundred.

(*b*) Brother Robert de Parko, a probationary monk (*conversus*), of Hales Owen Abbey, while at work, evidently, as a tanner or maker of parchment dipping a skin in the ditch at Bromwich, fell into the water and was drowned. The first finder did not appear, and is not suspected, nor any one else. The value of the skin, which was assumed to be the "cause of death," was 2s. In all cases of violent death, accidental or otherwise, the cause of death (*causa mortis* was the instrument, as a cart, mill wheel, sword, or a horse) was valued, and the value so appraised was paid by the owner as a *deodand* to the king. A *deodand* was a "gift to God" to appease his wrath, as it were.

(*c*) John de Brotherfeld killed himself in his own house in the vill (parish) of Handsworth, and the verdict returned was *felonia de se*. His chattels were valued at 2s. 11d., for which the sheriff answers; for by law the goods of a suicide, lawfully found as such by a coroner's jury, were forfeited. This case also produced two other penalties. Both the jury and the vill of Handsworth were fined for falsely valuing the chattels; and the vills of Bromwich and Rushall were fined because they did not fully appear at the inquest before the coroner, as by law they should have done.

5.—THE STATUTE OF WINCHESTER (1285) AND A BROMWICH "HIGHWAY" IN 1307

At a Gaol Delivery 35 Edward I. (1307) at Stafford, the following constituted the jury for the Hundred of Offlow:—

Thomas de Hampstede	William de Sparham
John de Heronville (*Wednesbury*)	William de Stretton
Robert Touke	Gilbert le Hunt
William de Bowles	Osbert de Thamworth (*Bromwich*)
Thomas de Derlaston	William Morel
William Alrewych	William de Jarkeville

Respecting parks, they said—That the Abbot of Hales Owen has a park at Bromwych, through the middle of which runs the high road between Burmyngham and the vill of Stafford, and it has not been cleared according to statute. The Abbot was therefore summoned before the justices, and there denied that any high road ran through the park. He appealed to the jury above. Their decision was that the only right of way was by permission of the Abbot.

It was perhaps because West Bromwich and Wednesbury were not on any ancient highway, that *was* really a main or trunk thoroughfare, that they attained no eminence in mediœval times. Which is the road here brought into question—the present High Street, or the older Walsall Street? Probably the latter.

The interesting fact here disclosed seems to be the actual existence at that time of some useful road from Birmingham, through West Bromwich, to the "vill" or town of Stafford. In the year 1307 it was but ill-defined; and perhaps little better than a bridle-path and as the jury decided, it was not the King's highway, but a private road. The Statute quoted in this case was that of Winchester (1285) which required that all highways should be cleared of woods, bushes or dykes for 200 feet on each side of the road, in order to prevent malefactors from lurking there; ash, oak, and large trees, however, were always exempt and not to be felled to make a clearance. If a park was made at the side of the highway, it was to be at this distance of 200 feet, or such a wall or fence was to be erected as would prevent malefactors coming out to commit offences and escaping back. This law is the cause and origin of those very broad green margins which may sometimes be seen still along many country highways.

(6).—NOVEL DESSEISIN. LAWLESSNESS IN BROMWICH.

In the last case occurred the name of a Bromwich man of whom we are to hear again. He was one Osbert, of Tamworth, a name which would perhaps indicate that he was of Danish extraction. He was evidently a man of position—in other words a considerable landowner. From serving on the jury, we next find him a party in a suit of *novel desseisin*. This assize of *novel desseisin* was where one had unlawfully (and within a limit of time) been dispossessed of his rights, the demandant recited his complaint whereupon the Sheriff (who always represented the crown in the local matters of his county) was commanded to reseise the lands and chattels thereon, and to keep same in his custody till the arrival of the Justices of Assize. After trial, a judgment in favour would recover seisin (lawful possession) and also damages for the injury committed.

At the Stafford Assizes, which commenced the Friday after Trinity, 1300:—Henry le Parker, and Margaret his wife, and Lawrence de Erbury (? Devereux) and Felicia his wife, not appearing to prosecute their writ of *novel disseisin* versus Osbert de Tamworth and Margaret his wife, respecting tenements in West Bromwich, the suit was dismissed, and they and their sureties, viz., Adam de Morf, of Barr and Nicholas, son of Thomas de Barr are *in misericordia*—at the mercy of the King, who might impose a fine.

The Coram Rege Roll of Michaelmas of the following year (1301), records that Osbert de Tamworth of Westbromwich, and Margaret, his wife, Richard le Parker, Richard de Wygemere (? Wigmore), Ralph Swyft, Henry Dun, and William del Hull were all attached at the suit of Walter Devereux (or de Ebroicis) for cutting down trees at Westbromwich *vi et armis*.

The defendants denied the trespass and appealed to a jury, which was summoned for the morrow of the Purification.

At the following Hilary sittings Walter Devereux not prosecuting his writ of novel disseisin against Osbert de Tamworth and Margaret, his wife, respecting the tenements in Westbromwich, is *in misericordia*, but his fine was remitted at the instance of Edmund de Mortimer.

At the Westminster Court, in 1311, the same Osbert, of Tamworth, sued William Attewode, William Robert, of Eselbergh, Thomas Godhope, and three others, for beating, wounding, and ill-treating him at Bromwich two years previously, so severely that his life was despaired of. The defendants claimed and had trial by jury, and it was not till Trinity term 1313 that their verdict was given. The jury found that the chief delinquent, William Attewode, had an ancient feud against Osbert, and had procured the villanous assistance of the other defendants to assault him in a manner so violent as to endanger his life. For this breach of the King's peace and the damage to Osbert, all the accused were committed to prison, and the principal defendant was ordered to pay the sum of £100 (an enormous fine in those days) to the said Osbert.

These cases of forcible ousting, accompanied by such violence, seem to point to great lawlessness amongst the local landed gentry. To go about with gangs of men, and to gain one's end by armed force indicates a somewhat primitive state of society.

XVI.—More Territorial History of Bromwich, from Pleadings in the Law Courts (1223—1296).

It is easy to see that for many purposes, monetary and judicial, national and local, it became necessary from time to time to ascertain the exact position of vassals and sub-vassals. For this purpose Inquisitions were held up and down the country at various times before sworn local juries. Of the returns then made are comprised our earliest national records. Regarding Bromwich we have already taken extracts from the Black Book of the Exchequer *temp.* Henry II. (chapter viii), and from the Scutage Rolls (chapters viii. and ix.), and from the Pipe Rolls. Under the general head of Rolls (*rotuli*), we have still preserved to us many valuable repositories of national and local history. From the Plea Rolls of Henry III.'s reign much of the territorial history of Bromwich is thus gleaned. Not only have we records of cases tried on the spot by Justices Itinerant but of local eases heard *coram rege* ("in the presence of the King"— or his justiciary—wherever he might be), or else *de banco* by the Chief Justices "of the bench" at Westminster. Although we may have to hark back with our 13th century history, we will take a few gleanings.

(A.D. 1223). Geva Bassett sued for her dower against the Abbot of Bordesley, namely, for part of lands and a mill in Bromwich; and other defendants for other parcels of land, some situated in Hamton (Wolverhampton). She recovered dower lands the same year from Ralph Cocus, by default. They are described as—"one-third of one-fourth of a virgate in Bromwich," a *virgate* being a "yardland" of 24 acres.

(1224). From a record of Great Assize between William de Parles (plaintiff) and William Offney "son of William," tenant, of the advowson of Sandwell Priory, we find that the case had to remain over because this "William, son of William" was dead. He had succeeded his brother Richard (son of William) and appears to have died shortly afterwards.

At the same time Geva Bassett is suing for dower the Prior of Sandwell for lands and "one-third of a mill" in Bromwich; various other defendants for property in Hintun, in Wick, in Hamton, in Powick and in Iseburgh (Ellesborough). From the first-named we gather that "Richard, the son and heir of William, son of William," is an infant, and ward to William de Bromle. Richard, son of William, being dead, had been succeeded by another Richard, son of William, his nephew. The small value placed on surnames at that time may be noted by these personal descriptions.

(1225). Geva Basset's pleas of dower still proceeding—in one she is suing Amice Basset for lands in Hamton (? Wolverhampton), and the latter calls Maurice, the parson of Hamton, to warranty on her behalf. In another case she is suing Simon de Merton for lands in Powick. Simon appeared in court and said Geva had no claim to dower in that land because Richard, her husband, neither on the day he married her, nor ever afterwards, held the land in question; that three years before he married her he had given the land to John Blund, his *serviens*, and John held it for a long time, and afterwards John took religious vows (became a monk, and therefore civilly dead in the eye of the law), and wished to sell the land, and he (Simon de Merton) was told he ought to buy the land. And upon this Richard, husband of Geva ordered Simon to come to him, and it was arranged between Simon and John that certain land in Sandwell should be given as security for the money to be received from Simon, and in this way the land remained to Simon; and Geva now claims dower from that land given at Sandwell. As she would not appeal to a jury, and has no evidence to the contrary, she is in *misericordia*.

At the same Westminster pleadings, Margaret, widow of William of Bromwich, sues for dower, the son and heir being also designated "William de Bromwic."

(1227). At Staffordshire Assizes, Thomas the Smith (*faber*) of Bromwich resisted an enclosure in Bromwich which the Abbot of Hales Owen had made by setting up a fence. At the same time Adam the Smith is sued by Geva Basset. Here are two freemen working as smiths in Bromwich at this early period of industrial progress.

In 1230 an assize of Last Presentation disclosed that half of the advowson of Handsworth Church was held by the Prior of Lenton, who sent a Monk with a document (*a chirograph*) to prove the same. With regard to the other half an agreement was come to between John de Parles and the prior of Sandwell, to the effect that John should possess the right on payment of an annual rent of one mark in Birmingham.

In 1247 a similar assize was held and another agreement arrived at.

(1230). William de Bromley (guardian of the "infant" Richard), is charged with causing waste and damage in the woods at Bromwich, Northcote, and Ofelegh (Offley?), and brings a counter-charge of the same kind against Geva Basset, Henry Prestwood and his wife Margaret, for destroying 70 oak trees, damage laid at 100s. The Sheriff is thereupon ordered to take a jury of 12 descreet men of the vicinage, knights and freemen, and proceed to the woods to hold an inquiry into the allegations in the presence of the three last-named complainants.

Three years later Geva denied similar waste and destruction of woods, stating that she had taken nothing but *housbote* (sometimes called *Estover*, and which signifies the ordinary allowance of timber out of the lord's woods for repair of tenements), and *heybote* (the allowance for repair of fences, posts, &c.), and had moreover built a chamber by which the tenement had been improved. A jury were to inspect the wood and park.

(1242). At Westminster Margary the widow of Robert the miller of Bromwich sued the Abbot of Hales Owen for her dower, one-third of the mill, &c. The defence was that her late husband the miller was not a freeman. but a villain, and therefore not entitled to hold lands, and consequently the mill was not his with which to endow his wife. The Sheriff, the Coroner (who always held these powers and jurisdiction in those days) and a local jury on inquiry found that Robert had been a freeman, had been a freeholder, and therefore Margary recovered her dower. (A villain was attached to the soil like a serf—he might be bought and sold with the land, but he could never own it).

In 1260 the Prior of Sandwell charged William de Parles (of Handsworth) Adam de

Pyrie (of Perry Barr) and ten others with coming upon his land at "Brompwich," insulting him, beating and ill-treating his men, and chasing the said Prior with arms in their hands into his house at Brompwich, so that he barely escaped them. But again at a later date even than this we shall come across a more violent assault upon a clerical dignitary—another prior of Sandwell—from which it would seem that the "cloth" was no protection in those turbulent days.

In 1296 (Michaelmas) Margaret Marnham, widow of Richard, sued William, son of Richard, the Clerk of Corfton, for certain meadow and pasture lands in Bromwich. The defendant, William, "prayed a view" of land (*visum terræ*) which could be done when both parties appeared in court. Accordingly the Sheriff by writ sent "free and lawful men" of the vicinage to view the land in dispute—no special number constituted such jury of inspection as this— but four of them would duly report or certify the view to the court. To allow time for this, the suit was adjourned till the 3rd of February, or, as it was then styled, " the morrow of the Purification." She also, sued Margaret, widow of the same Richard, who did not appear; and consequently the Sheriff who always acted on behalf of the Crown, took the lands into his hands, and summoned her again, also for the date of the adjournment.

At the same time she recovered lands in Bromwich from John de Salileye, other parcels of land from John de Linden, from the sons of John Fyne, and from the other Margaret aforesaid, all by default of the defendants. The defendants having been formally summoned to appear on this appointed day, and neither putting in an appearance, or essoining themselves (that is, excusing themselves by the oaths of certain witnesses who testified their inability to attend through some valid cause or other) they were said to be in default, no doubt because their case was too bad to be substantiated at law.

At the Trinity term of the following year, 1297, we find the same suits proceeding. Suits were often delayed purposely when the case was bad; as often as either party appeared in Court, and performed what he had been commanded to do up to that date, he might essoin (excuse by oath) himself three times; and this would take place at every stage of the proceedings. Now as Margaret Marnham recovered certain lands in Bromwich this year (1297) from Richard le Clerk, of Corfton, who was dead, it is because the action for these particular lands had evidently outlasted the lifetime of the defendant. But with reference to the other lands, "the meadow and the pasture," she has now to "call to warranty." Richard her son, the rightful heir of her deceased husband, who only was in a position to "vouch to warranty" as to which were her dower lands. So the younger Richard Marnham was summoned to appear in court on the 18th of November, "the octave of St. Martin," and the summons was to be made both in the counties of Leicester and of Nottingham where no doubt he also held estates. In 1337 William Marnham was certainly concerned in a suit about lands in County Nottingham—North Marnham, South Marnham, etc. Ultimately, the widow obtained possession of these lands—their area is not always described exactly the same on each record, but clerical errors and errors of description were common—at Easter, 1298, by default of her opponents. At the previous Michaelmas (1297) she had also recovered from Walter de Orpede, from Felicia, widow of Philip de la Haye, and from Simon of Oscott several parcels of land in Bromwich, all of them by default.

XVII.—How Bromwich Manor, as part of the Barony of Dudley, went from the Somery Family to the Botetorts (1291—1321).

After the Conquest of England, William I. rewarded his Norman barons for braving the dangers and the undoubted hardships of the invasion by dividing large proportions of the conquered lands amongst them. With consummate tact he gave the more powerful barons their larger estates in separate grants scattered in different parts of the country; and this to prevent the concentration of the forces of any unruly baron against the Crown. By feudal customs each vassal had in return for the grant of land to supply a number of knights fully equipped for war. The number of knights to be furnished was duly specified in the infeoffment or grant. These knights in their turn held lands under the crown-tenants, to whom they owed homage, fealty, and a great variety of services, according to the terms of the tenure, as well as direct payments of money. Some other tenures were merely nominal, as a red rose, a pair of white gloves, holding the lord's stirrup, keeping a pack of hounds, etc. When one held his lands of the King by such a service; as performing some function at the coronation, acting as the King's carver, or his butler, this kind of tenure was known as Serjeanty. In Chapter xiv. allusion was made to Richard the Serjeant who held lands by some such service tenure in Bromwich; but the exact nature of the services this man rendered to the King are not now known. Such service could be rendered to no lord but the King; and was either grand serjeanty or petit serjeanty—the latter generally consisting of supplying annually something towards the King's wars, and in effect payable as rent. Serjeanties could not, as a rule, be alienated to religious bodies.

In 1166 William Offney held 3 knights' fees in the barony of Dudley, viz.:

West Bromwich	...	...	...	...	...	1 f.m.
Wombourne	...	...	...	...	...	1 f.m.
Orton, Oxley, Bradley, and half of Seisdo...		...	...	1 f.m.

He also held in Bucks the Manor of Ellesborough but this was not registered as a knight's fee because he held it by the tenure of "Castle Guard." Evidently this *garrison duty* exempted from foreign service: for that seems to be the interpretation of the omission of the knight's fee of Ellesborough from the *Scuttage Roll*.

In passing, it may be noted that by 1300 (28 Ed. I.) Oxley appears to have passed into the hands of the Marnham branch of the family, whose land-hunger seems to have been very keen around Bushbury. The Devereux branch at a rather later period seems to have been found at the other Bromwich—viz, Castle Bromwich.

Reverting to the knights themselves, the parcelled lands held by them were called "fees," "fiefs," or "feuds ;" and a number of them composed the barony of a crown vassal. Thus Bromwich manor was one knight's fee in the barony of Dudley. A knight's fee was supposed to be so much land as would suffice to maintain him, and enable him to present himself and his retainers fully equipped for the field of battle. Hence a knight's fee represents no definite quantity, but is a variable amount of land, ranging from anything up to 500 acres of cultivated land—in Staffordshire a fee actually averaged 3,000 acres, but this was inclusive of wood and waste. Allusion will presently be made to "Wood Bromwich"—wherever that may have been—and to Wolverhampton Wood; there was unquestionably a large amount of woodland in this locality at that time. It will be noticed, too, that the "fees" became divided up into fractional parts as time went on, no doubt as divided inheritances.

INHERITING LANDS.

Under the feudal system the great allotments of lands originally parcelled out to each great military chief or baron, were at first to be held only for life. But gradually these barons acquired the right of inheritance for their eldest sons or their heirs.

On the death of every chief tenant (*tenant-in-capite*) there was an *Inquisitio post mortem*, or inquiry held on oath by a local jury summoned by writ of the County Escheator (that is, the Sheriff) to find (1) of what lands the person died seized; 2) by what rents or services he held them, and (3) who was the next heir and of what age. If the tenant was attainted of treason, or an alien, his lands were "escheated" or reverted to the crown. The Sheriff, who represented the crown in each county, was known as the *Escheator*. The doubtful dealings of the Sheriffs with the lands of dead men gave us the word *cheat*, signifying "fraud." The Sheriff of Staffordshire about 1272 was Hugh de Heronville, lord of Wednesbury.

In chapter xi. the barony of Dudley was shown to come to the family of De Somery.

In the year 1291 died Roger de Somery, and on December 21st an Inquisition was held, at which Bromwich Manor was shown to be one knight's fee, divided equally between Richard de Marnharm and Walter Devereux, while half a fee each was held by Thomas de Bromwich, and Anselm de Bromwich, who not improbably took their name from the locality of their territorial possessions. William de Castel held half a fee in the same barony—of what castle cannot be now stated: query, Castle Bromwich? The value of each moiety of the Manor is set down as £10; the one-sixth of a fee held by Anselm in Wode Bromwich is also set down as worth £10; the thirty-second of a fee held by Thomas de Bromwich, in Bromwich, is valued at 20s.; this is also the value of one-thirtieth of a fee held by Henry de Cassello in Bromwich.

The widow of Roger was Agnes, and amongst the manors which went to provide her dower, were those of Rowley and Handsworth. (In 1304 Walter Devereux entered a suit against Agnes Somery respecting certain tenements in Bromwich, but afterwards withdrew). The successor in the barony of Dudley was their son John de Somery. To estimate the high position held in the kingdom by this family, it may be noted that in 1308 Agnes was formally and ceremoniously summoned to the coronation of Edward II.; she died soon after this event.

John de Somery, baron of Dudley, received the honour of knighthood in 1306, "by bathing with Prince Edward," on which solemn occasion he received suitable apparel from the royal wardrobe. He was then ordered with others similarly honoured to meet the King at Carlisle, to march against Scotland, and was probably at the disastrous battle of Bannockburn, 1314. He died December 29th, 1321 leaving no heirs. As his younger brother Roger had been murdered in Wolverhampton Wood by a gentleman named Wynterton (who was first outlawed and afterwards pardoned the offence), the barony devolved upon his two sisters. These two parceners were Margaret, the elder, married to John de Sutton, to whom was conveyed the title (as explained in chapter xi.) and Joan, the younger, married to Thomas de Botetort. In the division, Bromwich manor went to the Botetorts (each half fee, held respectively by Richard Marnham and Stephen Devereux, being now valued at 20s. per annum) as did also lands in Saltley, Netheles (Nechells) Bromwich, "Castel" Bromwich, Erdington, Witton, Aston, and many other places, together with the advowson of Handsworth Church—"every other" presentation only.

This Joan, who thus took the superior lordship of West Bromwich to Thomas de Botetort, of Weoley Castle, Northfield, Worcestershire, died in 1388.

XVIII.—How the men of Bromwich were called out to War (1230-1369).

From various rolls of the 13th and 14th centuries we are enabled to gather how frequently Englishmen were called out to fight the battles of their warlike kings and feudal barons; or, as it was termed, to render military service. The summons to war was usually sent direct to the tenant-in-chief of the Crown, who, as a rule, passed on the command to his sub-vassals, whom he gathered under his banner. For instance, Bromwich was underheld by its lord from the Baron of Dudley; therefore, whenever the Baron of Dudley was summoned to war by his King we may fairly assume that the men in the manor of Bromwich stood a fair chance of contributing their quota to the muster who were led out under his flag.

Henry III., in the fourteenth year of his reign went over to France with a large army, but his invasion accomplished little or nothing beyond securing the homage of the Gascon nobility. From the Patent Roll we gather that Roger de Somery Baron of Dudley, accompanied this expedition of the year 1230, inasmuch as it records that he had a *writ of protection*, a document usually issued during times of war, securing the holder against all personal actions and against pleas in the superior law courts during absence. In fact it was a complete protection of property from all legal process while the holder was away fighting for his king and country, and it held good against all pleas except two—pleas of *dower* and of *last presentation*.

In August, 1253, some Bromwich men, under the same feudal chief, no doubt accompanied Henry III. when he crossed the seas to suppress an insurrection in Gascony. Four years later the King's writ, dated from Coventry (24th July, 1257), directed Roger de Somery to proceed to Glamorgan with all his retainers to aid in putting down the invasion of Llewellyn, Prince of Wales, while his *letter of protection* was dated from Woodstock on the 1st of October following.

Coming to the Great Barons' War when the nobles under Simon de Montfort revolted against Henry III., we find that confusion which is incidental to civil war, and it is impossible to say on which side Bromwich men found themselves ranged. It was testified that the whole county of Stafford was against the King, but three of the crown tenants at least stood firm to him, and one was Roger de Somery. This fact, however, does not necessarily imply that the lord of Bromwich, his vassal, sided with him; because another vassal, William de Bermingham, fell at Evesham, slain fighting against the King. This shows how completely the feudal tie was dissolved at this trying period, for Roger de Somery was one of the staunchest supporters of the King. Among other lesser tenants also opposing the royalist forces on this occasion were Geoffrey de Aston and Giles de Erdington. The lands of the misguided William de Bermingham were given to Roger de Clifford, but the superior lord of them, Roger de Somery, redeemed them under the provision of the *Dictum of Kenilworth*, by which submission was so easily purchased after all these civil broils.

With the reign of Edward I. the military records are preserved on separate rolls, and are no longer among the *Patents*. At the Conquest of Wales, Bigod, Earl of Norfolk, was the Marshall, and from the *Marshall's Roll* of 1277 we find the Bishop of Coventry and Lichfield serving (for the demesne of his barony, as a *lord* spiritual) but not the baron of Dudley, nor his vassal, the lord of Bromwich. Some of his neighbours, however, are found rendering knight's service; among them, Henry de Erdington and William de Parles, of Handsworth. On the 25th of March, 1282 however Roger de Somery was ordered to take the field against the Welsh with all his forces when no doubt his Bromwich retainers marched with him towards Harwardyn and Flint. In this campaign the counties of Stafford and Salop were to provide 15 carpenters (*carpentarios*) and 40 sappers (*fossatores*) whose wages were to be paid by the Sheriffs; while proclamation was made that no markets were to be held in the border counties of Gloster, Hereford, and Salop, except at Oswestry nor for the counties of Stafford, Derby, and Lancaster, except at Chester, or wherever the King's *capitaneus* might be. By this master-stroke the King got full control of all his own supplies, and at the same time cut off the extraneous supplies of the Welsh.

As to Roger de Somery he might indeed almost be reckoned among the defenders of the Welsh "marches" or borders. His castle at Dudley is now accounted as being in Staffordshire, but in earlier times (1085) it had certainly been part of Worcestershire (as the town of Dudley has ever been) and as such was undoubtedly part of the border defences. By 1263 Roger de Somery had rebuilt Dudley Castle, and had also fortified Weoley Castle, Northfield, which on the death of his son John de Somery went to the Botetort family, as did also the Manor of Bromwich 1321.

To the Welsh War of 1287 Roger de Somery and all Staffordshire tenants were again summoned. Coming to foreign service on the continent, the *Almain Roll* of 1297 is very interesting. Edward I allied with the Flemings and the German Emperor against the French, crossed to Flanders, but he summoned not only the tenants in chief, but all lords who held lands to the amount of £20 annually. The King's Hereditary Marshall and Constable (the Earls of Norfolk and of Hereford) would not recognise the legality of the summons, and actually withdrew from the army taking with them 30 Bannerets (those who displayed their own banners and had a retinue of knights and squires on the field) and 1500 knights and men-at-arms. The summons (issued as writs to the sheriffs, with a schedule of all those holding lands valued at £20 per annum; certainly reached Bromwich and Wednesbury; for although the baron of Dudley does not appear on the lists, we find Walter Devereux of Bromwich fighting his men under the schedule for Herefordshire, while John de Heronville of Wednesbury is found in the Oxfordshire schedule, a county in which he held Hooknorton manor. Knights and Esquires, and all men-at-arms of lower rank than Bannerets were summoned through the sheriffs, and not directly and personally by writ of summons from the king.

The old belief that William the Conqueror divided the country into 30,000 knights' fees is not borne out by the number of lances which the King was able to bring into the field by his writ of summons. The highest number of lances at any time so available was much nearer 3,000. The lesser tenants of land at £40 or £20 were consequently brought into service. For the Scotch war in 1301 there were 17 tenants in Staffordshire of £40 each thus called up, the whole of the counties of England producing only 835 of them. For the same war John de Somery took out *letters of protection* in 1304, while for the previous year the collectors of *Scutage* had exempted him from the "shield tax," he having rendered his full service actively in the field. Then, as was recorded in the last chapter, he was among the 267 knights (as were also Henry de Erdington and William de Bermingham) who were all made at one time to add splendour and solemnity to the knighting of Edward, Prince of Wales, the eldest son of the king just as he was about to be ceremoniously despatched to the wars in Scotland. By proclamation all the candidates on this occasion were assembled in London at "Pentecost" to receive the King's gift of fitting apparel for the ceremonial: while all tournaments were stopped, so that men and horses could promptly rendezvous at Carlisle. John Devereux is named in the retinue of Roger Mortimer (the Queen's paramour) who was arrested the following year for leaving the army in Scotland without the King's permission; but who was soon after pardoned at the intercession of the Queen. John de Somery was this time in the retinue of the Earl of Arundel. In 1307 Edward I. died, and the Scotch wars continued till 1320, though unsuccessfully, and the baron of Dudley seems to have fought right through the whole campaign; and amongst those of his retinue—were certainly (July 20th, 1319), William Devereux, John de Sutton, William de Bermingham, Henry de Bushbury, Richard Paynel, William de Wrottesley, Richard de Edgbaston, and some other local knights and gentlemen.

When civil war broke out (1322-3) between Edward II. and his outraged barons, who were justifiably jealous of the Royal favourites, the two Despencers, the Baron of Dudley seems to have led out his men—those of Bromwich, no doubt, included—once more in the Royal cause, for we find him afterwards rewarded with the manor of Amblecote of which the rebel James de Stafford had been stripped by the angered king.

In later years, when the Scotch wars were renewed under Edward III., we find a James de Bromwyche fighting in the retinue of Ralph de Stafford (1336), for Staffordshire had on this occasion to array 2,000 men properly equipped, according to the following scale:—

Possessed of £40 or £20 land or rent—arms and horses as customarily required.

Possessed of £15 land, or chattels valued 40 marks —a horse, and to be armed with hauberk, steel cap, sword, and dagger.

Possessed of £10 land, or chattels valued 20 marks—armed as above, but no horse.

Possessed of 40s. land, up to 100s.—sword, bow, arrow, dagger (according to *Statute of Winchester*). The next trace of the men of Bromwich manor being called out appears in 1345, when John Botetort leads them in the retinue of the Earl of Huntington in the renewed French wars of Edward III. where they must have seen both hard fighting and heavy campaigning before Crecy was fought (1346) and Calais besieged. An extract from the *Norman Roll* and dated from "near Calais," September 4th, 1346 names two Wednesbury men, who for their good service in the war were pardoned for all homicides, felonies, etc., a reward (and perhaps a questionable testimony to personal character, if we do not make due allowances for ruder times and rougher manners) which was sometimes granted on the recommendation of the baron or banneret in whose retinue the receiver of the pardon had served. The two men were William Golde and Richard Dillon, "of Wednesbury," who had served under and given satisfaction to John de Grey, of Rotherfeld. It is not unlikely that other men from this Black Country district had also rendered good service as smiths, artificers, armourers, and sappers, for Edward III. as a good general was always most particular in the supervision of his army as an effective working military machine.

In 1361 a John de Bromwyche is named as a Staffordshire knight fighting under Lionel, the King's son, putting down a rebellion in Ireland. In 1369 Walter Devereux was in the retinue of Bohun, Earl of Hereford, in the French wars, and in 1380-1 in that of Buckingham, uncle to the new king, Richard II. And with this a termination is reached of the many and frequent military exploits, in all or most of which Bromwich men played their proper part during the Edwardian period—the most warlike in the whole of English history. These operations took lord and vassal from their native heath to fight in distant parts of England, in Wales, in Scotland, and beyond the seas in Ireland and in France.

*   *   *

*Notes.—(1) *Bishop of Coventry and Lichfield*—this title of the fighting feudal bishop of the diocese is not the one now in use. Soon after the Mercian Kingdom was divided into five bishopries, the see of Lichfield was so far extended as to comprehend the chief part of the former possession of the Cornavii. Peter, elected Bishop of Lichfield in 1075, moved the see to Chester, and Robert de Limesie, in 1102, removed it again to Coventry, tempted probably by the riches and reputation of the monastery founded by Earl Leofric. The five succeeding bishops likewise sat at Coventry; styling themselves *Coventriœ Episcopi* only. Hugh Novant, consecrated in 1188, restored the see to Lichfield, though with much opposition from the Benedictine monks of Coventry. In consequence of disputes between the Chapter of Coventry and that of Lichfield, both parties agreed in the reign of Henry III. that the bishop should be elected both from Coventry and Lichfield; that the *precedence* in the episcopal title should be given *to the former city* (as it occurs in this passage); that the two Chapters should alternately choose their bishop, and that they should form one body, in which the Prior of Coventry should be the principal. From this time the prelate was styled the *Bishop of Coventry and Lichfield*. In the 33rd of Henry VIII. (1542) an Act was passed that the Dean and Chapter of Lichfield should be for ever the entire and sole Chapter of the bishopric of Coventry and Lichfield; "whereof the Prior and Convent of the dissolved priory of Coventry were heretofore the moiety or half-part." From the Reformation to the first half of the present century the double title prevailed; since the time of the reforming Bishop Ryder, however, the simpler designation has been that of *Bishop of Lichfield*.

(2). *Land Values.*—It is difficult to compare ancient land values with those now prevailing The "forty shilling freeholder," mentioned in this chapter, ultimately became the county elector. Money was little used. The Saxons had only silver coins, and gold coins were not introduced till the Conquest. The "pound " was not a coin but 5,400 grains (troy) in silver by weight. This would make the *penny* equal to 3d. and the *shilling* to 2s. 10., if the standard of comparison were permissible. The coinage was often debased even by being clipped in the Royal Mint, while in Stephen's reign every baron had his own mint. Henry II. and John rehabilitated the currency as far as they were able.

XIX.—War Taxes collected in West Bromwich (1291—1333)

Of all human businesses the kingly game of war is the costliest. The last chapter revealed to us the almost chronic state of war in which this country then existed. Having sampled the military services rendered by the men of Bromwich, the next thing will be to see how all these wars were paid for. The lord could command the services of his vassal for 40 days; but campaigns more frequently than not lasted a much longer period, and had therefore to be paid for. To meet these expenses many feudal fines and burdens were invented; as for instance Scutage or "shield tax" in lieu of personal service, described in chapter viii. For special wars of a serious nature, which were popular as well as national special efforts were sometimes put forth. Some of these shall be described.

During the Middle Ages the Papal Exchequer received regular contributions from the English Church in the shape of *first-fruits*—" the first year's income from ecclesiastical benefices or church livings"; and again in the shape of *tenths*. Now in 1288 the spirited policy of the Pope Nicholas IV. induced him to grant the tenths to Edward I. for a period of six years towards defraying the expenses of a Crusade in the Holy Land. In order that these might be collected at their full value, the king caused a Roll to be prepared, which took three years to complete. Drawn up under the direction of the bishops of Lincoln and Winchester, this Roll was finished in 1291, and is known as *Taxatio Ecclesiastica P. Nicholai IV*. An excellent copy is preserved in the Chapter House at Lichfield. So excellently was the work done, the Roll was afterwards repeatedly used as a basis for very many taxings after 1291. The *Valor Ecclesiasticus* held good for all taxes due from benefices, both to our own kings and to popes; and it regulated all such payments till the Reformation (1536). Then the *first fruits* and the *tenths* ceased to be forwarded to Rome, and were transferred to the crown instead; and in 1703 the receipts were appropriated to the augmentation of poor livings, and formed the fund now known as *Queen Anne's Bounty,* a more righteous diversion of public moneys than often takes place.

Bromwich paid its exact tithe or tenth (*decima*), as will be seen in the following extract from the *Taxation of Pope Nicholas IV.* in 1291—for 8 shillings is exactly one-tenth of 6 marks, as is also the 11s. 4d. paid by Wednesbury on an assessment of $8\frac{1}{2}$ marks:—

Bromwych appr[opriated to the]   *Decim.*
   Pr[ior &] Conv[ent] de

Sandwell	...	vi. *marc*	viii. *s.*		
Hunnesworth	...	xxi. *marc*	ii. *m.*	xvi. *d.*	
Wednesbur	...	viii. & *dim.*	xi. *s.*	iiii. *d.*	

Reckoning 13s. 4d. to the mark, the above will be readily understood with the contracted words of the original thus expanded again, and interpreted in English. Without again printing the contracted Latin entry relating to Sandwell Priory (given by Mrs. Willett on p. 149 of her *History*), its purport may be said to be to the following effect:—

Assessment of the Temporal goods of the Prior of Sandwell: The Prior of Sandwell has at Sandwell in the Deanery of Tamworth, 3 carucates of land, and the carucate is worth yearly ten shillings. [The carucate was a variable quantity of land, as much as one plough could "carve" in a year]. And he has in the same place from the profits of the crops yearly, with the pasture, ten shillings. And he has in the same place from pasture land and meadow yearly half a mark. And he has in the same place from two mills yearly ten shillings. And from the returns of the Assize yearly forty shillings. Total £4 16s. 8d., the tithe of which is 9s. 8d.

Thus was Bromwich taxed for a Crusade in which no active work was undertaken; but passing from a religious war to a war of conquest, something may now be learnt of the way Bromwich supplied money as well as men—the last chapter dealt with the levying of forces—when stimulated by the fire of patriotism.

In 1327 the youthful King Edward III. ascended the throne, immediately upon which the Scots determined to take advantage of his minority, and invaded England. The English Parliament met the danger by promptly granting a subsidy to carry on the war of defence against Scotland; namely a tax of one-twentieth part of all movable goods. In county Stafford the collectors were Richard de Hampton and John de Aston, who summoned all the true and loyal men in each vill or parish from whom 4 or 6 assessors were elected. These after being duly sworn, inquired into and made a true return upon the value of the goods possessed by every man of the vill (the boroughs, cities, and walled towns were too few to render aid adequate to the national requirements), both in the house, and out of the house, and to tax the same to their full value. Exemptions from the taxation were made in favor of (1) *Armour* (2) *Mounture* (cavalry horses), (3) the *Robes and Jewels* of knights, gentlemen, and their wives (4) their silver and plate (6) "*des viens de meseaux*"—probably the tools and implements for trade and agriculture (6) the goods of those whose total moveable *property did not reach the value of 10s.* Although the last exemption shows a tenderness for the poor, the villain tenants of each manor were taxed equally with the freemen, which indicates the gradually growing emancipation of the serf (Compare this statement with the ownership of property by the Miller of Bromwich in 1242—see Chapter xvi). Their growing independence is manifested a few years afterwards by revolts and popular uprisings. With regard to the exemption of such luxuries as jewels and plate, it must be borne in mind that wealth and position had their full responsibilities in those days — nothing less than providing the whole military strength of the nation; for there was no standing army then to be supported by taxation. This is naturally the reason why armour and cavalry horses were free from the impost.

The particulars of this taxation are preserved in the Subsidy Roll of 1327, in it the Hundreds are taken separately, but the vills are grouped almost haphazard without any regard to manorial or ecclesiastical administrations. Thus West Bromwich is returned with Darlaston:—

Bromwich..

		s.	d.	
De Joh'e de Marham	...	vj.		
Rog'o Basset	... ...	iij.	j.	ob.
Rog'o de Ruggiacre	... ...	ij.	vj.	qu.
Nich'o de Littlehay	...	ij.	j.	qu.
Joh'e de Salleye...	... ...	iiij.	j.	ob.
Joh'e fabro	... ...		xij.	ob.
Ph'o Godknave...	... ...	ij.		qu.
Will'o Mustrel	... ...	iiij.		ob. qu.
Nich'o Golde	... ...		xviij.	
Will'mo de Bromwych...	...	iij.	iij.	
Rog'o Golde	... ...		xij.	
Will'o Bracun	... ...		xij.	

Derlaston.

De Will'o de Derlaston	...	iiij.		ob. qu.
Agnete de Derlaston	... ...		xxiij.	ob.
Joh'e de Pipe	... ...		xxij.	ob.
Henr' de Wytton...	... ...	ij.		ob.
Nich'o le Bonde...	...		xviij.	qu.
Thoma Lovot	... ...	ij.		
Ric'o filio Roberti	... ...		vij.	

Summa   xlv *s*. ix *d*.   ob.   Pb.

If cast up, the *summa* or total for these two vills amounts to 45 shillings and ninepence half-penny, as here shown—the abbreviation "ob." (*obolus*) signifying "halfpenny," as "qu." stands for quarter of a penny, or a farthing; the silver pennies of the period were actually cut into halves and quarters for circulation. The abbreviation at the end "pb." stands for *probata*, that is "proven" or "checked." It may be calculated that while Bromwich yielded 31s. 9½d., Darlaston produced only 14s. 0½d. towards the total; and the largest taxpayer in Bromwich is John de Marnham lord of the manor, the next being William Mustrel (4s. 0¾d.), the third William of Bromwich (3s. 3d.), and the fourth Roger Bassett (3s. 1½d.) Other explanations to make this list of taxpayers more easily understandable of the ordinary reader may usefully be added: *De* at the commencement of the list evidently means "from," and is supposed to be repeated before every name down the list; while *de* as part of a name signifies "of," as in "Roger of Ridgcare" and "Nicholas of Littlehay." The added description *fabro* means the "smith" who was probably an armourer as well. Nicholas and William Golde no doubt belonged to that family who lent their name to the locality now known as Gold's Hill and Gold's Green.

Another extant Subsidy Roll is a record of yet another taxation for the continued Scotch wars of the same king, Edward III., six or seven years later 1332-3. As before assessors were appointed and sworn on the Holy Evangelists to render a full and true account of each man's goods, and to fairly tax them, saving the things excepted. That the subtaxer of the vill of Bromwich did so righteously apportion each man's contribution to these war charges may be assumed from the checking of the total (*summa*) by the audited mark of the chief-taxers, who went from hundred to hundred throughout the county—the "pb." for *probata* or "re-cast" at the end. The goods of all the Commonalty were to be presented, saving armour, mounture (saddle horses), jewels and robes of knights and gentlemen and their wives, and vessels of gold and brass: in cities and boroughs (as Lichfield and Tamworth) one robe for each man and woman was to be excepted, also a bed for each, an *anel* or buckle of gold or silver and the silk sash (*ceynte de seye*) they used every day, and likewise the hanaper of silver or the mazre of grained wood, from which they drank; and all the goods of lepers (*bien des meseux*) in cases where they dwelt together in a community governed by a Master Leper (*sovereign meseal*), although otherwise they were to be taxed like other people's goods. In cities, boroughs, and ancient demesnes of the crown, if a man's goods exceeded 6s. in value, the tax was one-tenth. Wednesbury was of ancient demesne of the crown. In vills or parishes of the county outside these limits, goods and chattels valued over 10s. were to pay one fifteenth. Walsall and Wednesbury are put together and yield 114s. 1½d. but paying on the other assessment Great Barr, Aldridge, Bromwich and Tipton are grouped together and produce a *summa* of £7 7s. 10d. (See History of Tipton, chapter x.) Towards this total is the contribution of 32s. 10d. forthcoming from

BROMWYCH.

			s.	d.	
De Will'o de Marnham	...	...	vij.		
Rog'o Bassett	...	...	iiij.	vj.	
Rog'o de Rugaker	...	...	iij.	iiij.	
Joh'ne de Salley...	...	...	iiij.		
Will'o de Bromwych ...		...	ij.	x.	
Will'o Golde	...	...	ij.	j.	ob.
Ph'o Godknave...	...	...	iiij.	ij.	ob.
Steph'o del Heeth	...	...	ij.	j.	ob.
Will'o Mostrel	...	...		xvj.	
Will'o Braken	...	...		xij.	
Rog'o Golde	...	...		xvj.	ob.

Philip Goodknave is unquestionably a descriptive personal name. Stephano del Heath, or Stephen of the Heath, pointedly locates the part of Bromwych held by him. The name Braken or Bracun may be derived from the bracken which grew on the heath but as to Salley or Saliley it is hazardous to guess, although as it is certainly a place-name it may be Saltley. At this taxation William de Marnham also pays 6s. for his possessions in Wombourne and Oxley.

Lastly it may be noted that the name of Bassett appears second on these two lists, that of Marnham coming first. Yet Shaw, quoting from the earlier historian of the county, Erdeswick, says:—"Tame being past Tipton, leaveth Bilston two miles west, and two miles from Tame, east is West Bromwich whereof, as I take it, was lord 21 Edward I., one Richard Bassett; and now (1538) one of the Stanleys hath his seat there."

Wyrley, the amanuensis and pupil of Erdeswick, says:—"West Bromwich is so called for that it standeth west of Castle Bromwich. ... It is highseated upon a sandy hill, as it were, a promontory between two rivulets, the one running to the west, and the other, which is the Tame stream, to the east."

Among documents preserved at Southampton is an Indenture dated 13 July, 13

Edward III. (1340) of an Agreement between the Black Prince and Thomas Beauchamp, Earl of Warwick. To this is attached a roll, *Nomina Armigerorum,* that is, of "Names of Esquires" serving under the Earl, among such names being those of

Radulphus Basset (? of Drayton).

Hugo de Bromwyche.

Nicholaus de Egebaston.

&c., &c.

Two problems here offer themselves for solution. First, were the Bassets lords of the Manor of Bromwich later than 1224? And second, may not the full name of the place be given as West Bromwich after the thirteenth century, seeing that frequent reference is made to Castle Bromwich at this period (1291), in the phrases "William de Castel," "Henry de Cassello in Bromwich," and "Castel Bromwich" (see chapter xvii.)?

XX.—The Manor of Bromwich, and its Descent from the Marnhams to the Freebody Family (1292—1500).

Let us look at West Bromwich in the 14th century. Outside the cities, boroughs, and walled towns, such as Newcastle, Stafford, Lichfield, and Tamworth, all the rural parts of the county were organised as manors. This system of dividing the land was to meet a twofold purpose—(1) for the cultivation of the soil, a part of which was retained in the hands of the lord of the manor as his *demesne* or home-farm; while the rest of the estate was divided among tenants who were bound to render certain services to the lord, and (2) for the preservation of internal order, by means of *frankpledge* and the jurisdiction of the manorial courts.

West Bromwich Manor House stood to the north-ward of the church, in that part of the parish now known as Hall Green, and which evidently took its name from the Manorial Hall there situated. This Hall or Manor House was the centre of the whole village life of the place. The manor court was held within its walls, where the lord, or the steward in his absence (for the owner had other lordships to govern at different times, as at Oxley Wombourne, Marnham in Co. Notts &c.; received the homage of retainers, enrolled them in their respective tithing, recovered fines, administered the oath for the peace-pledge, and dispensed justice to all the villagers. Outside his gates, probably on the triangular piece of "green" still marked out by the roadway, stood his gallows. The demesne or home-farm lay largely between the church and the Wednesbury boundary from Friar Park to Finchpath. The villains (literally, "men of the vill" or farm) sunk from pure freedom as they had enjoyed it originally among their Saxon forefathers, now rendered a labour-rent for their holdings, filling the great barn of their lord with sheaves; shearing his sheep at the brook (which we are reminded by its place-name was most conveniently performed at Sheepwash Lane), malting his grain, and hewing his wood for the hall fires. They were certainly *free* as against all men but their lord whose protection they were under, for they sent representatives to the Hundred Meeting (*moot*) and to the Shire Moot; and there was a lower class of *cottar,* and *bordar,* of *labourers* bound to give time throughout the whole year to the work of the demesne farm, while the service of the villain was only compulsory at the time of harvest, and at the autumn and Lent ploughings. Nor were they without many other privileges: they each possessed a little homestead, and cultivated the strip of land around it, with the right of turning out their cattle to graze on the waste of the manor, and as to their labor-rent or *services,* these were strictly limited by *custom,* which was at first mere oral tradition, but which came to be gradually entered on the court-roll of the manor, a *copy* of which at length became equivalent to the villain's title-deed, and hence he was in due time known as a *copy-holder*. When the labor-rent became too difficult to enforce it was commuted for money payments known as malt-silver, wood-silver, larder-silver, etc. With the rise of the free labourer came also into existence the farmer; this was when the lord of the manor no longer cultivated his own demesne lands through the management of a bailiff, but found it more convenient to lease the lands to a tenant for a given rent payable either in money, or in kind, or both. To this leasing, or to the term for the rent it entailed ("feorm" from the Latin *firma*) we owe the derivation of the word "farm."

West Bromwich Old Hall is a building of much later date than of the period with which we are now dealing, although it no doubt stands on the site of the original Manor House.

Continuing from chapter xi. the descent of the moiety of the manor, some few more of the feudal occupants of the ancient Hall may be passed in review:—

(3) RICHARD BASSET married GEVA, and died before 1224: his Manor of Bromwich was divided between Margaret and Sara, his two daughters. (See chapter xiii.).

(4) MARGARET or MARGERY married RICHARD DE MARNHAM to whom she carried a moiety of the manor. She was a widow in 1296. (See chapters xiv. and xvi.).

(5) RICHARD DE MARNHAM, their son, was living in 1322; on the Subsidy Roll of 1327 the name of "John" appears, but in 1330 Richard had certainly been succeeded by his son William; his widow was named CLEMENCE.

(6) WILLIAM DE MARNHAM married ALIANORA, by whom he had two sons, John and William, but died while they were still young.

An agreement made October 13th, 1330, settled the Manor of Oxley (except 100 acres of waste, evidently reserved in accordance with the *Statute of Merton*), and the moiety of the Manor of West Bromwich (with a similar amount of waste land reserved) upon William de Marnham and Alianora, his wife, and the right heirs of William. One-third of the moiety was then held by Clemence, wife of William Blanchard, as her dower portion, but was to revert on her death, to William who was the son of Richard de Marnham. This agreement was finally come to at York Assizes seven years later.

In the same year, 1330, his brother Thomas son of Richard de Marnham, was suing upon a bond; another-suit, which lasted till 1337. In 1337 also William Marnham is connected with the Nottinghamshire Manors of North Marnham and South Marnham.

In 1340 William de Marnham is said to be of full age when he is found suing Nicholas, son of Roger Basset, for certain tenements in West Bromwich which he had demised to him while under age. Nicholas Basset was under the guardianship of Roger de Wirley. In 1345 his brother, Thomas de Marnham, sued Henry Mustral for forcibly breaking into his close at Bromwich and cutting down his trees.

William de Marnham died, leaving a son and heir John under age, whereupon it would appear that his widow Alianora married again, her second husband being John de Alrewas. These two arranged with John de Botetort, the lord paramount of Bromwich—of whom the late William de Marnham as lord paravail had held "a messuage and a caracute of land, by homage, fealty, and a payment of 6d. for Scutage [the service was originally for half a knight's fee, but appears to have been commuted—from 40 days' service in the field of one knight, or of two sergeants as heavily accoutred, but not bringing in so many followers as the knight] when the King's Scutage of 40s. fell due, and by the service of 1d. annually at Christmas—that the young heir and his estate should remain in their custody. The terms of this commutation from feudal service to a money payment are interesting; but more so the reference to the various *feudal incidents* or obligations, as they prevailed in

Bromwich:—(1) The rendering of *homage* to the superior, and (2) the swearing of *fealty* to him; (3) and the payment of scutage or shield money on a regular assessed scale. But the incidence of two other feudal customs is the cause of these facts becoming known— these were (4) *wardship* and (5) *marriage*. Alianora and her new husband having secured from Botetort, as the head of the barony, the custody of the heir of Bromwich, for which they unquestionably would offer some payment or specified consideration, were entitled to *wardship*, a feudal custom whereby the rents and profits of the estate during the heir's minority went to the superior lord, the revenues in this case being farmed by Alianora, according to the arrangement made, and not only was there a great likelihood that this diversion of revenues would be unlawfully and vexatiously prolonged after the heir had attained his majority, but Alianora and the step-father had further secured the right of *marriage* of the heir, another feudal custom by which the guardians could compel the heir to marry whom they thought proper—in the case of an heiress it was generally the highest bidder—and if the ward refused the marriage then they would be entitled to receive as a forfeit as much as the proposed marriage would have brought in. In this Bromwich case a great family quarrel arose.

The young heir, about the year 1348 (on Monday after the Feast of St. Peter in Cathedra, 21 Edward III.), was living on the other Marnham manor, at Oxley near Wolverhampton. The larger the land-owner the larger was his household retinue, and, therefore, the greater necessity to move from one manor to another, no means then existing of moving produce from one part of the country to another, it had to be consumed on the spot where it grew; hence the lord of Bromwich Manor after consuming the produce at Hall Green, would move with his household to Oxley, leaving the Steward or Provost behind as his representative; from Oxley the family would pass on to Wombourne manor house; and so on, according to the size and importance of the family and the number of manors held in demesne. While the youthful John de Marnham was at Oxley on the day named, perhaps with his connivance, and possibly during the absence of Alianora at her husband's manor of Alrewas, a party of horsemen rode up and abducted the lad. The party consisted of Simon Thorley, the knighty Thomas Curzon, the boy's uncle, Thomas de Marnham, and John de Eton, all neighbours and interested persons inasmuch as three years afterwards in the lawsuit which arose out of the abduction of the heir to Bromwich, they distinctly laid claim to the right of his marriage. On the other side the deed of John Botetort was produced, and a claim to £100 damages was laid, and so the case dragged on a weary length from year to year.

(7) By 1362 JOHN DE MARNHAM appears to have succeeded to the estate, as he is then found suing a William Curson. Again in 1384 (7 Richard II.) John has a suit against Henry Costnought for forcibly treading down and consuming his growing corn and grass at West Bromwich with his cattle; as the defendant had not put in an appearance by the following year, the Sheriff was ordered to summon him to the next four consecutive Courts of the Shire, and on non-appearance to outlaw him, as he had no property to attach.

(8). JOHN and WILLIAM DE MARNHAM, sons of William and Alianora, were living in 1388.

(9). A daughter of one, probably the elder, married a WILLIAM FREEBODY, to whom she carried the moiety of the manor of West Bromwich. He is also said to have inherited the manor by will.

(10). ALICE, their daughter and heiress, married WILLIAM FREEBODY, of Dudley, in the reign of Henry VI.

As the widow of William Freebody, she granted a charter, 12th November, 1428, to John Leventhorpe, probably a younger brother of the lord of Wednesbury manor. In the year before this, her husband had certainly been living, as he had then just recovered possession of lands in Sedgeley, Coseley, and Brereley, from one Thomas Newport and Elizabeth, his wife.

(11). WILLIAM FREEBODY, their son, succeeded to the manor of Bromwich. It is recorded as being in his possession in 1436, and again in 1447 (15 and 26 Henry VI.), he holding also the advowsen of Sandwell Priory. At the later of these dates the manor is accounted as part of, or "a member of," Weoley Castle; while at the earlier one it was said to be "held of the king." This same William Freebody also held the manor of Thorp Mandeville, in Northamptonshire, and he was a warden of Dover Castle.

(12). WILLIAM FREEBODY succeeded his father in 1447, and came of age in the following year.

In 1457 this William Freebody, described as "Armiger" or gentleman entitled to bear arms secures for himself and his heirs, in consideration of a sum of 200 marks of silver, large tracts of land (pasture, meadow, and wood) situated in "Great Barre, Little Barre, West-bromwyche and Woddesbury. "

Evidently a family of some importance in these later times, the question is, "Who were these Freebodies"? The name of Frebody occurs locally as early as 1342. A Thomas Frebody together with Richard Dillon and Philip, son of Hugh Aleyn (of Wodnesbury) *chaplain*, were all charged in this year by the parson of Aldridge, with forcibly taking his horse from Handsworth and other goods and chattels value at 100s,, and with beating and wounding the parson's servant so that he lost his services for a long time. None of these defendants, however, seem to have been men of substance. While the Freebodies are comparatively newcomers upon the scene the more ancient family of Devereux seem to have taken themselves entirely away to the Warwickshire Bromwich. John Devereux, knight, is found in 1493 concerned with suits relating to Castle Bromwich, Whitacre, Barr (and the advowsons of the last two) Chartley, and other manors in the vicinity and Bulbroke Manor in Northamptonshire. In 1519 Walter Devereux is concerned in the same and many other estates, including Tamworth, Heywood, and others in the counties of Lincoln, Leicester, &c., &c.

(13). CECILY, daughter and heir of William Freebody, married JOHN STANLEY. This lord of West Bromwich died in 1535.

XXI.—CHANGES TERRITORIAL, SOCIAL, AND INDUSTRIAL IN THE 14TH, 15TH AND 16TH CENTURIES.

Society was slowly changing in West Bromwich as in course of time the lord alienated small parcels of his manor and reduced the extent of it by sub-infeudations, sales, or demises for valuable rent. This process would diminish the means of employment for his villains, who became emancipated as free and voluntary labourers for others, though he still retained his original rights over them. It would also create a new class of landed proprietors whose newer tenures and titles gave rise to innumerable lawsuits, from the proceedings in which much valuable local history of the period may be gathered.

Besides the lord of the manor then, we have these other large landowners growing up in the place. As we saw in Chapter xviii., landowners of £20 and £40 a year in value were called up in the 14th century to render military service and to take their part in common with the holders of the original knights' fees in furnishing the national forces. In the year 1363 a trial took place respecting the estate in "the fee of Bromwich" of the

Golde family. William Golde who was twice married and had one son only, but daughters by both his wives, had possessed tenements valued at 100s. rent, which he granted to his only son, Thomas Golde by deed. Thomas, however died in his fathers life time. On the death of William Golde, his daughter by the first wife, and full-sister to Thomas, who had actually been in possession of the estate by the deed of gift, seems to have succeeded to it as her brother Thomas's sole heir; as he had left no issue. The daughters by the second wife, however, and who were only half-blood of Thomas, had already made a partition of the estate, claiming equal portions of it. The full sister was named Christiana, and had married John Bonde, of Wednesbury, and they produced the deed in question, which was dated from Fynspathe (between Bromwich and Wednesbury) on Friday after the Feast of St. Hillary 5 Edward III. It seems to have been altogether a big family quarrel, and the other parties to the suit who had dispossessed Christiana and her husband were John de Alrewas and Alianora his wife; William de Heronville and Joan his wife; Alice widow of John Tymmesone, and Christiana their daughter; John in the Lee and Alice his wife; and several other members of the Golde and the Bonde families. It is by no means improbable that a piece of land, afterwards known as "Bondthing," was not some of that here in dispute; the place-name being made up of the family-name of *Bonde*, with the terminal *thing*, which signifies "that settled by law, bargain, or by contract." It is interesting, too, to contrast the two old Bromwich surnames, "Bonde" and "Freebody," which unmistakably indicate that one originated from a founder in "bond," or bound as a serf; while the other family founder was a "freeman" or as he called himself a Freebody. Of Fremons there are many, the family being common to Harborne, Barr, and many other places in the locality. There is a Richard Frebody in Rowley, and a man of some importance, in 1332.

In the names of the parties to many other of these mediæval law-suits something interesting may from time to time be observed.

William Bracon, a local name found in the list of taxpayers, had a suit against Roger of Ridgacre in 1341. Curious names are those of Ralph and Eustachia Pauncefot, who contested the ownership of Bromwich lands with the Hillary family in 1339. The old name of Hawkins (Nicholas Haukyns) occurs in West Bromwich as early as 1371, when the bearer had lands from Richard Hervill and Juliana his wife. The name of another old Bromwich yeoman family that of Simcox (John Symcokes), is found in 1449, in an agreement made with John Whatcroft, *armiger* and Joan his wife. Other names are those of Thomas Hynde, John Bromsgrove (1478), John Haddon (1519), against whom appeared Anthony Fitzherbert, the King's sergeant-at-law, the familiar John Smythe (1533), Francis Staresmore, who disputes the rights to many acres of furze and heath in Rowley with William Whorwood; the not uncommon John Taylor and the less common Edward Gamon (1541); and lastly, in 1545, the family name of Orme.

Of Christian names two uncommon examples have occurred in these records: "Geva," as a feminine appellation, is repeated in the person of a Geva Aubrey, from whom the second Richard Marnham demanded (by attorney, in the pleas of Leicestershire 1317), that he should be permitted to pull down a certain house she had erected to his injury in Reresby; and "Clemence," the name of the widow of this same Richard, is often met with in her suits for dower-lands in Bromwich—in 1334 she appears against John Aylwyne, *chaplain*, Roger Golde, and John de Saltley, the name of which last place has been previously found spelt in a variety of unrecognisable ways.

The name of the Hillary family, of Bescot, is of constant occurrence. In 1320 certain lands in Bromwich and Shelfield, namely 2 messuages, 2 carucates of lard (about 200 acres at this period), 30 acres of meadow, 10 acres of wood, 10 acres of pasture and 20d. of rent were settled on Roger Hillary and Katherine his wife, and their heirs male, with remainder to the right heirs of Roger. The other party was Robert Hillary, parson of the church of Sutton. This Sir Roger Hillary was a Chief Justice of the Common Pleas in the reign of Edward III., and died 1356. At Shelfield (near Walsall) his brother William resided; and another brother Thomas Hillary, was Chief Bailiff of the Hundred of Offlow, and held the mill of Finchpath, at Wednesbury (1348). His son the next Sir Roger was pardoned by the king in 1365 for the death of William Woolrich, of Wednesbury. The exercise of the royal clemency towards Richard Dillon and William Golde in 1346 and recorded in chapter xviii., may have been for the offences recorded at the end of the last chapter, and which had been committed some four years previously.

The name Alianora is apparently a variant of Eleanor or Helena. This name appears again (1368) as that of the wife of William Page of Walsall, suing for money lent at Handsworth, and at Bromwych, to Roger Wyrley (formerly the guardian of Nicholas Basset) by the hands of Roger Basset. Before her marriage her name had been Alianora Culy. The Bassets of West Bromwich were connected with the great family of that name at Drayton Basset, and the baptismal name of Roger is of common occurrence in combination with it. Of the Botetort family much has already been said, it may further be noted that at the taxing of 1332 the largest taxpayer in Handsworth and also at "Mere et Forton" was a John Botetort. From the case to be now quoted the intimate connection of the Botetorts with the Manor of Handsworth will be at once apparent.

To the students of Staffordshire history generally it may be interesting to know that another Chief Justice during the middle part of the reign of Edward III was also of this county—Sir William de Shareshill (Shareshill near Wolverhampton). He held estates in Oxfordshire. He was deprived of his judgeship for malversation of office, when he retired to a monastery, and died shortly afterwards. All the judges of this period appear to have been corrupt and to have amassed fortunes by the abuse of their powers. A writ addressed to this judge in 1367 directed him to return the records of a case of trespass between John Botetort,. *chivaler* (or knight), and Henry de Morwode, *clericus*, the parson of the church of Handsworth. Sir John as lord of the manor of Handsworth claimed to exercise the manorial franchises of *free warren* and of *waifs and strays* both of which the parson had violated. For several years he had, by force, entered the park at Handsworth accompanied by the "Personesman;" on one occasion taking six hares and twenty rabbits, and on another two bucks and four does, the damages for the latter trespass being assessed at 10 marks. With regard to the other matter a mare belonging to Morwode had been stolen and left within the demesne of Sir John Botetort who claimed it as a *waif*. The parson re-captured his stolen horse and took it home, as he thought he might lawfully do when he found it wandering loose. The lawsuit was complicated further because Horwode denied the claim to *free warren*; and he also objected to the jury panel summoned to try the case by the Sheriff, Philip de Luttleye, who had married a kinswoman of Sir John's, within the degrees of marriage. The insinuation is significant. The family connections of both these Staffordshire judges seem to have been altogether doubtful characters, and not beyond suspicion by any means.

Many families assumed as their patronymic the name of the place of their origin; this rule will be observed to be very general with the priors of Sandwell. The earliest Norman surnames were territorial titles pure and simple. In these records the most interesting example is naturally that of the native of this parish who called himself Bromwich, or de Bromwich. Attention has been called to this fact previously, a later example is found in a John Bromwich, also a clerk (in holy orders) who in 1565 has a lawsuit over lands in this parish, in Barr, Handsworth, and Aldridge, the names the opposite parties being Pyne and Savage. He also has a case against a very old Bromwich family, the complainants being William Sheldon, *armiger*, and Ralph

Sheldon, gentleman, but the lands in dispute this time are situated near Lichfield. Another family identified with the nomenclature of the locality is that of Sponne, who borrowed their name from the place; and did not as Reeves states, lend their personal names to the locality. For instance, in 1345, John de Alrewas and Alianora, his wife, sue for certain dower-lands, one William atte Sponne. The dwelling place of this William was therefore a well-known spot and presumably called Spon, because a reputed splinter of the true cross was preserved there, perhaps enshrined by some devotee or palmer returned from a pilgrimage to the Holy Land (see chapter vi.)

The particle *atte* or "at," signifying the place at which the person resided, was often used as a means of distinguishing personalities, as were also the particles *de* or "of." In most cases of the use of the latter, however, the proper name of the place is given; as "William de Bromwich" and "John of Tamworth." But in 1304 we get an instance of the use of the common noun in one "Gilbert of the Tune" (tun or town) who is concerned about certain lands in West Bromwich. But surnames now were not as at first, a distinction in more senses than one.

Lands in Westbromwyche, Co. Stafford, and in Oldebury, Co. Salop, form the cause of an action in 1546 between Richard Cartwright, and Richard Hoo and Catherine, his wife, who were probably of Moxley. In 1557 appears a suit of John Clemson against William Wilkes and Joan his wife, among the Bromwich lands in dispute being enumerated two messuages (houses and their adjacent lands), 6 gardens, 30 tofts (a toft was a piece of ground where a house formerly stood), 200 acres of land, 10 acres of meadow, 200 acres of pasture, 10 acres of wood, 100 acres of furze and heath, and 20 acres of moor. In the year following occur the names of Anthony Colle against John Nall and Eleanor his wife. But reverting to the previous case or Clemson v. Wilkes it is suggestive that there were 30 "tofts" in West Bromwich at this time. Does it point to a depopulation to the extent of 30 families? And if so what has caused the decay of the vill or parish?

A variety of causes at once suggest themselves. Was the desolation the result of the disastrous Wars of the Roses? These had terminated more than 70 years, and therefore as a cause may possibly have been too remote. The materials have yet to be collected before any history of West Bromwich at this critical period can be written with authority. The war certainly approached this locality during some part of its 30 years' continuance, as we know that on one occasion Barr Hill was held by a force of Yorkists. Was the decay of the place owing to plague and pestilence? Allusion was made to the prevalence of these scourges of the middles ages in chapter vi. In the year 1517 Oxford had been depopulated by the sweating sickness, which had recurred again in 1528, and may have visited West Bromwich on either occasion. Or was the decrease of population caused by some industrial convulsion?

Workmen combined together in the towns, and serfs fled from the rural districts; agriculture was depressed owing to the growth of sheep farming, and the consequent shrinkage of husbandry. Bromwich offered every facility for sheep rearing on its wide heaths and moorlands, although no record remains of land-inclosure for this purpose, such as had taken place at Rushall (1517), and in other parts of Staffordshire. Anyway, West Bromwich presents an aspect of neglect at this period, for in addition to the several causes of depopulation suggested, there had been the suppression and final closing of the Priory at Sandwell.

Thus the aspect of Bromwich, both social and industrial, was undergoing a marked change. At Finchpath was living a gentleman certainly of equal importance with the lord of the manor; the social position of Thomas Hillary was such as to command for him the dignified office of *Counter* or Constable of the Hundred. Many villains had been manumitted in order to supply Edward III. with armies; for no one but a freeman could serve as a soldier, and even criminals (as in the case of Dillon and Golde) were pardoned for serving on the field of battle with distinction. The empty cottages, to which allusion has been made, were the rude cotts of the *borders* and the *cottars* of the manor—the former occupying their huts and patches of ground on condition they supplied the lord's larder with poultry, eggs, etc, and the latter being similarly sheltered because they were the lord's mechanics and craftsmen, instructed at his charge for his own service. And although this attempt to collate old Bromwich family names has not been very successful, there is one family still largely represented in the parish which originated at this period, and took as a proper name that which as a common noun denoted the office held—the Reeves family are the stock of an important manorial official. There was not only a steward or provost to represent the lord on every manor, but the copyholders and others owing suit and service had a similar headman to represent them; they elected a *reeve*, whose duty it was to check the accounts against the steward, to maintain their rights and privileges, and to speak generally on their behalf in all matters pertaining to manorial service; and to good government as locally administered.

XXII.—The Priors of Sandwell: Their Property and Possessions.

A complete list of the Priors of Sandwell it is not possible to furnish. As a rule a Prior was chosen by the monks themselves, though exceptions to the rule will be noted occasionally in this particular instance.

A Prior was generally esteemed among his fellows for the possession of certain spiritual qualifications; in addition to which he was expected to have a knowledge of glossing, writing, illuminating, and chanting. Holiness of life, with a prudent and thoughtful disposition, would generally point out a fitting brother for the post of Prior. When elected he was entrusted with almost despotic powers: he could punish at will, either by confinement, corporal punishment (flagellation) or by expulsion. Under him were numerous officers, from cellarer and steward down to porter. In the larger abbeys, to every ten monks there was a dean.

Now to enumerate some of the names preserved to us as having held office as

Priors of Sandwell

(1) *William the Prior* is the earliest whose name is recorded, he remitted the advowson of Handsworth Church in 1230 (chapter xv.). He, or an earlier prior of Sandwell un-named, presented Thomas de Bardony to the Rectory of Ellesborough (Bucks) in 1223.

(2) Next there was a *Prior Richard*, succeeded in the office by one

(3) "*Roger the Prior*," whose name was Thomas, and who is named in the Marnham suits in 1293 (see chapter xiv., cases v. and vi.) The name, however, is again given as Thomas in 1294 (chapter xv.)

(4) *John*, prior of Sandwell, witnessed a deed of Ralph Basset in the reign of Edward I., between the years 1272 and 1307.

(5) The next prior (*unnamed*) or his successor William, complained to the Bishop of Lichfield of many trespasses upon the conventual rights and of damage to the priory property.

(6) *William de la Lee*, according to Mrs. Willett, was instituted by the bishop in 1329, and died in 1361. The Bishop of Lichfield apparently exercised a large controlling power over this priory, as many existing records prove. In the complaint previously

mentioned the bishop was petitioned to instruct all the incumbents in the neighbourhood of Sandwell to threaten with excommunication all those who committed offences against the rights and liberties of the Sandwell conventual community. But these two dates are evidently wrong, as in an intervening year (1342) another name than William occurs as head of the priory.

(7). *Richard* the prior of Sandwell in 1342, with Simon, son of William de Burmingham and other defendants, were all sued by the king, that whereas the advowson of the Prebend of Codshall was annexed to the Deanery of the King's Free Chapel of St. Michael's, Tettenhall, and the Dean, William de Sheynton had conferred the prebend then vacant upon Louis de Chertelon, the Prior and the other defendants had presumed to impugn the rights of the king, and to enervate his right of patronage.

It is suggested that the aforementioned William de la Lee had resigned office before his death in 1361, and that Richard was actually in office as prior in 1342. But there is another difficulty. This Richard, whose other name seems to have been derived from the place of his origin, as he is called *"de Tudenham,"* would appear to be in office again (or in conflict) in 1373, if the evidence given in a law case may be relied upon, and also supposing him to be the same Richard living over this extended period of 30 years (1342~1372).

(8). Brother *Henry de Kidderminster*, sole surviving monk in 1361, had in himself the sole right of electing the prior. This he humbly resigned into the hands of the bishop, who thereupon appointed him Prior over the empty cells of the Priory, as is duly set forth in the diocesan register at Lichfield.

(9). Before the certainty of *John de Kyngeston's* date can be settled, the case of Richard de Tudenham, already alluded to, must be again set forth more fully:

A suit tried in 1373 again throws some doubt on the precise individuality of the Prior of Sandwell. John de Witton, William de Marnham, and others were prosecuted by John de Kyngeston, the Prior, for that they came on Thursday "before the Feast of the Apostles Peter and Paul, 44 Edward III." (1371), and with malice aforethought had shot him in the arm with an arrow. John de Witton denied the felony, and further took exception to the writ because *John de Kyngeston* in it was stated to be Prior of Sandwell, whereas one *Richard de Tudenham* was Prior of the said church. He further objected that John de Kyngeston was a monk subject to the Abbot of Cluny in Burgundy, and that neither the Abbot nor Richard de Tudenham were named in the writ. John de Witton was put on his good behaviour while the case stood over, but he was evidently a sturdy Englishman and an awkward opponent to take up this position against the Clugniac fraternity on the ground of its allegiance to an alien head.

Attention may here be directed to a seeming lack of respect for the sanctity of the clerical calling. For here we have a prior, and according to the common acceptation of things, a man of peace, and one whose life should have made him no enemies actually assaulted and shamefully illtreated in a most outrageous manner. A similar violent assault on a prior of Sandwell in 1260 was recorded in chapter xvi. Were these indicative of the ordinary attitude of the lay mind towards the clergy? Or were they but isolated outbreaks in a time when rougher manners and ruder sentiments prevailed? Passing from these representatives of the *regular* or monastic clergy to one of the *secular* or parochial clergy, we had an instance of a somewhat lawless parson (in chapter xxi), who regularly and systematically trespassed on the preserves of the Lord of the Manor of Handsworth, taking hares, rabbits, and deer with the right goodwill of a hardened poacher. Surely he was one of the clergy sung by Chaucer—

> A pricker of a palfrey from Manor to Manor
> An heap of hounds at his back as he a lord were.

It was, however, a Monk of the regulars, of whom this poet further said that he "loved venerie" (hunting), and kept "ful many a deinte hors . . . in stable," and "griehoundes . . . as swift as foul of flight," while

> or pricking and of hunting for the hare
> Was all his lust, for no cost would he spare.

The examples found in West Bromwich of these mediæval clerics would, therefore, be quite typical of the times and manners.

John de Kyngeston resigned the Priorship in 1379 he and William de Dunstable being the sole survivors of the Sandwell brotherhood. They once more dutifully placed in the hands of the bishop the right of election, who appointed

(10) *Richard de Westbury*, a priest and a monk of the order (Benedictine), who was expected to work most strenuously for the revival of the convent's prosperity. It is not improbable that "de Westbury" may mean "of Wednesbury." There was a John Weddesbury, who was prior of Worcester from 1507 to 1518, whose name is generally rendered as Roger Wednesbury.

(11) *John of Tamworth* quickly succeeded, for he had resigned by the year 1400. A pension of 11 marks was allowed him upon his retirement.

(12) *John de Acton* was appointed Prior early in the same year (namely, January 3rd, 1400) by the Archbishop of Canterbury. The patronage of the primate was a new departure in these appointments.

(13) *William Prayne* had resigned by 1436, when his successor was elected "per viam Spiritus Sancti."

(14) This was *John Atton*, who was presented for confirmation in office to the Abbot of St. Peter's Shrewsbury, 4 April, 1436—another new departure in patronage.

(15) *John Bayley* was the last of the Priors, being turned out at the suppression of this Priory in 1526 perhaps one more exemplification of evil-doing begotten of poverty. On the other hand, a pension would have been granted him if he had indeed been a worthy man.

All the mitred and parliamentary abbots (for Abbots as well as Bishops sat in parliament in those times) were of the Benedictine order, to which belonged 113 monasteries in England, Sandwell one of them; and of the lesser class of its houses known as priories, Sandwell was but a small establishment at any period of its existence. Nor does it ever seem to have been unduly rich, or even fairly flourishing. Its endowments and worldly possessions were at no time very vast in extent.

The advowson of Handsworth Church was bartered away at one time (1230) to the Parles family, while a few years previously (1222) some of the priory lands were also parted with for a money payment. The Church of Ellesborough, in Buckinghamshire, was another possession. To West Bromwich Church the priory of Sandwell appointed a *vicar* to do the work for them, the convent having appropriated all the tithes and dues of the parish. A vicar (*vicarius*) was one deputed by a body or corporation to perform divine service, and whose stipend was entirely at the discretion of the community who had annexed the tithes.

Among the most valuable possessions of the Priory were two water-mills, for the return of their value, as given in Chapter xix, is no more reliable than the valuation of a modern executor for probate duty. These mills would prove a steady source of growing income, as the number of landowners gradually increased, and there was more grist to require milling. Tenants of the Manor used their lord's mill, which was probably at Bustleholme. The two mills belonging to the Priory seemed to have been as widely separated as the parish boundaries would permit, one being in Forge Lane, Sandwell Park, and the other away beyond the Heath, on the Tipton boundaries. (See *History of*

Tipton, chapter viii). This latter mill seems to have been parted with by some needy prior before the final crash came in 1526.

The reader may find other particulars of this Priory in Dugdale's *Monasticon*, Vol. IV, or in Shaw's *Staffordshire*, Vol II. That it was never a wealthy community must now be evident, but it is probable on the other hand that the income was at various times fluctuating in amount and precarious in collection. Like all other conventual communities there was always a hankering for patronage, and an anxiety to secure the advowsons of parish churches at which to appoint some unfortunate secular brother to perform the parochial duties for a bare pittance. From the distant living of Ellesborough the Priory was in receipt of "two portions" at the Taxation of Pope Nicholas (1291); one of £1 13s. 4d. per annum, and the other of £6 13s. 4d. These "portions" were no doubt the allotted *proportions* of tithes, etc., as allotted when the incomes of all ecclesiastical foundations were divided and apportioned in earlier times to various specified purposes; as, for the maintenance of the fabric, the relief of the poor, the stipend of the priest, etc. Another statement of the Priory's income was made on the eve of the "Suppression" (1526) when the endowments were said to be £12 a year from *Spiritualities* (presumably income derived from the performance of various spiritual offices), and £26 8s. 7d from *Temporalities*, that is from lands, tenements; and other lay sources of revenue. As a rule *Spiritualities* is a term denoting the profits from livings; as revenues from visitation fees at the ordaining and institution of priests. There was a close connection between this Priory and the patron bishops of Lichfield; and it was by no means so free and independent nor yet so powerful and rich as its neighbour the Abbey at Hales Owen. The possessions enumerated in that same statement were: The holding in their desmesne and in fee, with all tithes, oblations, and profits, of one large messuage with garden, orchard, and other appurtenances in Sandwell; 20 messuages, 1,000 acres of land, 100 acres of meadow, 200 acres of pasture, 300 acres of moor, 100 acres of wood, and 40 shillings in rent in Sandwell West Bromwich, Tipton, Wednesbury, Great Barr, Little Barr, Handsworth, Tofton, Wombourne, Fecham, &c, in County Stafford; valued at £30 per annum clear. The "large messuage" was the Priory itself, a description of which will be given in the next chapter.

At its suppression all its property was at first given by the King to Cardinal Wolsey (1526), but afterwards at the general suppression of all these monastic establishments, it is said to have passed into the hands of Sir Thomas Cromwell. Reeves. in his History of West Bromwich (P. 26), throws some doubt on the first part of this statement, as Wolsey was dead in 1531, and as yet the general suppression had not taken place. But this great confiscation of church property was not the work of a day nor of a year. Sir Thomas Cromwell, afterwards Earl of Essex, rose to high favour with Henry VIII. for his zeal in Church reform. Although not appointed vicar-general till after the downfall of Wolsey, steps had been taken some time, and in fact the work had long been in active progress for the suppression of all the smaller monasteries like Sandwell, whose income was under £200 a year. It is evident a visitation of Sandwell had been made in 1524 or 1526 by some commission empowered to investigate alleged misrule and immorality in religious houses: for there is extant a document of 1527 which is practically the inventory just quoted, and shows how Wolsey employed this particular gift to endow the now Christ Church College he had founded at Oxford.

It is an agreement made in 1527, whereby Edward Sutton Knt. lord of Dudley and Cecilia his wife, remitted to the Dean and Canons of the College of Thomas Wolsey, Cardinal of York, in the Alma Academia or University of Oxford, all rights in a garden, an orchard, a watermill, 20 messuages, 1000 acres of land, 100 acres of meadow, 200 acres of pasture, 100 acres of wood, 300 acres of moor, and 40 shillings rent in

Sandwell, Westbromewich, Tybinton, Great Barre, Little Barre, Horbron, Vernell, Cofton, Woddesbury, Houndesworth, and Fletcheam.

It would thus appear that Sandwell Priory was one of the earliest sacrifices to the cause of church reform. Its seizure by Wolsey, too, and his dedication of its property to the cause of learning, would indicate that this was one of the steps he took in his futile endeavours to stave off the Reformation.

A similar document to the one just quoted is dated the same year, 18, Henry VIII. on the Quindene of St. John the Baptist, afterwards recorded on the Octaves of St. Michael; it is between the same Dean and Canons of the College of Thomas Wolsey, Cardinal of York, in the Alma Academia, or University of Oxford, and the same Thomas, Archbishop of York, and Primate of England, and Legate of the Apostolic See, Bishop of Durham, and commendator of the Monastery of St. Alban's, etc—[here follows a long array of manors and advowsons in sixteen counties, and among them the previously enumerated possessions of Sandwell Priory]—in Sandwell, Dudley, Westbromwyche, Tybynton, Great Barr, Little Barr, Horbronne, Vernell, Coston, Wombourne, Woddesburye, Hondesworth, and Fleatcham, and the advowson of the church of Westbromwyche, in the said county of Stafford. The Cardinal Archbishop acknowledged all these manors, advowsons etc., to be the right of the said Dean and Canons and College, and warranted the same to them against all men, and for this acknowledgment the Dean and Canons received the Archbishop into the prayers which they would say within their College for ever, etc.

*   *   *

The general suppression of all the lesser monasteries certainly did not occur till ten years later (1536), and the greater ones were put down in the year following that—1537. Eventually the Sandwell estates passed into the hands of the Whorwood family from whom they passed to the Legge family by purchase about the year 1700. Among the local incidents of the inspection by the Monastic Commissioners it is recorded (under date 8 August, 1538) by the Bishop of Dover (reporting to Sir Thomas Cromwell) that the Warden of the Friars at Lichfield was "sore diseased in the face, whether of a canker or a pocke I know not." A similar authority tells of the dispersion of church property at Bordesley, where the sale took place on the 23 September, 1538; and that the items specified went to purchasers who were in a good social position, and who yet seem to have had no compunction in securing bargains at the expense of the church— the purchasers were Ralph Sheldon, Mr. Markeham, Fulke Greville, a servant of the Bishop of Worcester, Mr. Morgan, and Thomas Norton. This Bordesley monastery had possessed a water-mill at Wednesbury.

XXIII.—THE LAST OF SANDWELL: THE MONASTERY BUILDINGS AND THE LIFE LED WITHIN ITS WALLS—(1526).

Hints at immorality and misrule among local conventual communities have been given in the previous chapter. These charges, in fact, were naturally brought against them to justify their suppression. There can be no doubt that life in these religious houses was sorely monotonous and wearisomely dull, especially in small ones such as Sandwell, for the larger the company in any human society the more the opportunity for change and variety of experience in life. At 2 a.m. the matin bell rang, when the Monks rose and dressed, and were supposed to be occupied in meditation upon their misdeeds during the time. At another signal they trooped into chapel, stopping upon the threshold to pray for the excommunicated, their heads bowed to the ground. To ensure that everyone was wakeful and attentive to the service, the Prior went round with a dark lantern to see if any were asleep. The monotony of the service was sometimes broken by a brother acknowledging aloud some evil thought and asking for forgiveness of the same, or by a novice advancing to lay on the altar a petition for his admission to the order. If the petitioner were very young, his parents would be present to wrap their hands in the altar pall, while they promised to leave him nothing, lest he should be tempted to leave the Cloister. The service continued till the hour of prime—six o'clock—when at a signal from the superior every monk marched out of chapel and went to labour till ten o'clock. Some went to the mill to grind corn, some to the oven to bake bread, some to the garden and orchard some to the workshop; and those of sufficient ability to the scriptorium to copy old manuscripts or illuminate a book; these last named brothers would have their dinners carried to them, but at ten o'clock all who had been engaged in manual work left off, and went to the library for a book to read during the next two hours. At twelve noon came dinner, the first meal since they had risen. It consisted of fish, vegetables and fruit, and each monk had one pound of bread; and three-quarters-of-a-pint of wine, to last for both dinner and supper. The meal, taken in the refectory, was eaten in silence, whatever was wanted being asked for by signs; for during the repast it was the duty of one brother, each in turn for a week at a time, to read aloud a passage from the Bible or from one of the Early Fathers. From 1 to 3 o'clock was for sleep or reading, at each one's discretion. Then came another spell of work, after which was supper, for which each brother had served out another pound of bread with which to finish the remainder of the wine left over from dinner. After this came Vespers, and after the service bed time, each monk sleeping in habit and girdle. Such was the strict rule of life laid down by St. Benet, and which was led at Sandwell—in theory. That theory did not always coincide with practice is tolerably evident, as this monastery was amongst the earliest of those to be suppressed, and its revenues to be confiscated by the King or his powerful minister Wolsey.

All monastic establishments were modelled more or less upon the same general plan, and many shapeless piles of ruined masonry still remain to mark their sites. But of Sandwell Priory few or no traces now remain, because it was not an erection of stone or of brick, but was chiefly of timber. It was in the mediæval style common to domestic architecture that this ecclesiastical edifice seems to have been erected. Massive oak timbers formed its framing and bracing, and the filling up was not of brick (as we may still see in many old specimens of half-timbered houses) simply because it had been erected before the lost art of brick-making had been recovered in this country. The "filling" was of wattle and daub, with exterior perhaps of rusticated rough-cast, and sometimes a partial inner lining of wood or of plaster, or both.

A survey taken at the time enables us to conjure up a mental picture of the monastic buildings as they appeared at the suppression in 1526.

The survey in question enumerates the following buildings, evidently standing in quadrangular form, the church forming the south side and the dining hall the north side of the "square"; the eastern wing being the house and dormitories, while the western block was another house containing the kitchen, domestic offices and upper chambers. The cloisters, of course were inside the quadrangle.

I. *The South side of quadrangle.*

(1) A CHURCH 57 feet long and 18 feet in breadth, with an aisle on its south side, running its entire length but of just half its width, namely 9 feet. The whole was covered with a roof of tiles, partly in decay, although the timber remained fairly good. The fenestration comprised 5 iron-framed glazed windows, 15 of the panes containing

"imagerie work" of painted glass. Of carved images of the virgins and saints there were a total of five in the body of the church.

(2) A CHANCEL of the same width as the nave, namely 18 feet, and in length 41 feet, stood at the eastern extremity of the church. This was roofed with shingles, but had an inner ceiling. The ceiling was a necessity to protect the ecclesiastical drapery, the holy vessels, and the burning candles from the searching draughts of wind and the insidious leakages of rain, which were always inseparable from a building of wooden construction, the jointing and shrinkage of which could scarcely be expected to stand the wear and weather of time when reckoned by centuries. The shingles on the chancel roof are reported as "in decay." The lights consisted of three "glassed" windows, 10 panes of which were stained designs of "imagery work," contained in a frame of good wrought ironwork. The floor was paved with "brick," and there was the usual sedilia or seat for the priest. There were two carved images in the chancel, one fully gilded and the other only painted, one on each side of the high altar. The length of the chancel was 41 feet, which would appear to have been somewhat extreme, considering that between it and the nave of the church there was, in further extension of the length.

(3) A "BELL-FRAME" or "bell tower of their common width of 18 feet, and 14 feet in depth. This contained a little sanctus bell, and was covered with both tiles and wooden shingles. The bell was scarcely a sanctus or sacring bell, as it was, perhaps at too great a distance from the high alter, it was a bell to ring and give notice when the priest left the Sacristy for the purpose of saying mass. A similar bell still hangs on the eastern gable of the nave of Long Compton Church in Warwickshire, but which was no doubt rung from the interior at the elevation of the Host.

(4) Running out transept-wise from the north side of this belfrey was a CHAPEL, of the usual 18 feet in width, and in length 27 feet. This had a ceiling inside an outer-roof of tiles, and was lighted by three windows, glazed in a frame-work of wrought iron, and which two panes [of painted glass]. Four "old" images composed the saintly statuary of this chapel; which is stated to have adjoined the "house." There can be little doubt that the other chapel was on the south side, because it had a "little window," as had also the chancel, and these two little windows would look out on the outer side of the church and not on the inner or cloister side. They were "lowside" or leper windows for "communicating" these afflicted persons, and were near the ground line, as may be seen in Sheldon Church, Yardley. One of the Commissioners reported to Henry VIII. that where these had possessed little doors for confessing the lepers, they would be "best walled up for ever."

(5) A CHAPEL on the north (? south) of the belframe 18 feet broad as before, with a ceiling (in bad repair) and a tiled roof. This chapel was well lighted by three glazed windows of designed imagery work, another little window of coloured glass on one side, and three windows of nine panes on the other side all in well made frames of ironwork. The floor was paved with brick, and the furniture comprised an altar-table with all the requisite altar cloths, and a small bell for customary use in the services.

II. *The Eastern side.*

(6) THE HOUSE adjoined the north chapel, and therefore "right necessary to stand paved," the monks apparently using this as an entrance to the church on their way to and from the domestic buildings in procession. The breadth of this eastern wing was 20 feet, its total length was 80 feet, divided into three compartments, to make three upper chambers end three lower parlours, with one chimney to serve the whole of them. The chamber floors are described as very "cors," the whole as partly ruinous for lack of fresh painting, and the tiled roof being particularly in need of repairs. These coarse rooms were the "cells." Chimneys were as yet by no means common, even if they had been allowed to the cells, which they were not.

III. *The North side.*

(7) THE HALL or REFECTORY was 57 feet in length, exactly corresponding with the length of the church on the opposite side of the square. The breadth was 21 feet, and the roof was tiled. Either the weight of the roof, or the exposure to the weather on the outside of the block, or both combined, had made the outer or north wall of the hall to be "greatly ruinous, which, if it be not newly made, will shortly be the destruction of the Hall." The flooring too, which was a boarded one, is reported to be in a state so bad as to be described only as 'very evil.'

IV. *The Western side.*

(8) Another HOUSE 60 feet in length and 21 feet broad, having a small well-built kitchen at the end adjoining the dining hall; it is described as "well built," because it was entirely of stone, with cellars, larder, buttery, and other store-rooms cut in the cool sandstone rock, all placed for the convenient and easy service of meals in the Refectory. Under "one roof," but at the other end of this wing, were divers low houses adjoining, with two upper chambers covered with tiles. These houses and chambers are reported as decayed, and it was further stated, "they may well be spared, save only the kitchen."

In the quadrangle, on its northern side, adjacent to the Refectory, and therefore open on the sunny south side for catching the greatest amount of light and warmth, were the CLOISTERS. Like the entire block of buildings these would have round the base a plinth of stone work, but in this case the masonry would rise a foot or two more from the ground-line. The cloisters were built "chamber-wise," the open timbers which carried the heavy tiled roof being sound and massive. Here the good monks sitting within the enclosed area of the quadrangle, held most of their communications with the outer world shut in on all four sides, and yet open to the free air of heaven. In the church, the chapel, and the cell they performed their devotion to their God; in the seclusion of the cloisters they performed their duties to mankind. It was here they wrought with their hands—the scribe at his writing, the steward keeping his accompts, and the illuminator painting the pages of some choice missal or other holy book. It was here the deft-handed brother carved in wood or wrought in some other light material, as his artistic taste and artificer's cunning impelled him to industry and usefulness. It was here the young were instructed, and the mature and the needy were advised, relieved, and ministered to by the brother leech.

In addition to these principal buildings there were standing apart from the quadrangular group, the usual outhouses and farm buildings.

These erections are enumerated as follows:—

(1) A KILN HOUSE [for malting] 21 feet by 13 feet, walls mortared "very evil," but timbers sound and with a good tiled roof.

(2) A STABLE [for cattle] 58 feet by 28 feet at the west end of the church, with a chamber and a gatehouse [for a herdsman or a porter] in decay for lack of tiling. The Bishop, as visitor to the Brethren had bade them on one occasion appoint an efficient porter.

(3) A BARN, adjacent thereto, 72 feet by 24 feet with good timbers and covered with tiles, the ground-silling below, and the daub walls above, are both reported to be in ruinous condition, while the barn doors are said to be very coarse.

(4) A HAYHOUSE, adjoining the barn, was of the goodly dimensions of 64 feet by 21 feet—these large buildings had to store not only the produce of the monastery farm, but sometimes the produce paid as tithes as well. This is reported to be in a state of decay, as regards timbers, walls, and tiles—"howbeit it may well be spared."

(5) A WATER MILL on the stream side, built with good substantial timber, 20 feet by 15 feet, "which was wont to go by the water of the pool, which be now decayed, and with a little cost would be made to go again, for it hath sufficient water belonging to it if the heads of the pool were mended."

"Three pools decayed, with a fair spring running through them." With regard to the demesne-lands or home-farm the monastery was "compassed about with enclosures," which are stated to have produced all "manner of profit," by lettings at rental, by a seignorial right of *wayfs and strays* which the prior seems to have possessed, together with other *liberties* or jurisdictions, independent of the manorial government prevailing in the other parts of Bromwich, the area of this ecclesiastical jurisdiction being clearly marked out between two boundaries, one called *Hores*ton (that is, "the boundary stone," and probably neae *Har*-gate Lane), and the other known as Brend Okr—that is, the Burnt or Blasted Oak. This latter boundary was probably over on the Handsworth sider so that the domain and liberties of the monastery would correspond with that part of the modern borough comprising the Sandwell Ward and the greater part of the area (but not the more populous part) of Lyndon Ward.

Two good reasons exist why so few vestiges of the Priory buildings now remain. First, the materials of which their bulk was composed were not of a durable nature; and, secondly, the existing Hall, in which a few remnants may yet be seen, has been erected on a site some yards removed from the original one. The lower portions of the buildings being of native stone have endured where they have been re-used, as may be noticed round a small yard at the rear of the Hall. Mrs. Willett, or Miss L. J. Selwyn (*Chronicles of Sandwell*, 1875), has professed to be able to identify portions of the cloisters. The "Sancta Fons" still trickles in front of the Hall, and till recent years ran into an ancient stone coffin. As this contained a good lead lining, it is not surprising to learn that it disappeared during structural alterations a few years ago, much to the chagrin of the late Lord Dartmouth, who took some pains, but without result, to trace and recover it—gossip says he had a wish to be buried in this old monkish relic. The cemetery of the monks had been situated next to a shrubbery, in which there was a stewpond and a dovecot, the whole overlooked by the dormitories.

Shaw, in noticing Sandwell, says there were many instruments extant relating to the resignation of the Prior, William Prayne, and the election of John Acton in 1436. This was the one elected by choice "of the Holy Ghost," and the documents were presumably those preserved at Lichfield.

With regard to the possessions of the Priory, the same writer describes the living of West Bromwich as a "rectory"; and, at the close of its career, he says of the Priory lands, 'it was not known who was the patron or of whom, or by what services the lands were held." Feudal tenures were rapidly coming to an end at this period. Much waste of substance had taken place by improvident management of various priors, by neglect, sale, and long leasing of unprofitable character.

The warranty of these lands to Christ Church, Oxford, by Cardinal Wolsey, in 1527, has been already given. The vicissitudes of the estates, and the various hands through which they passed, cannot be with any further certainty stated. In 1558 (12 May, 1 Elizabeth) one Luna Clifford is found to have died seized of Sandwell.

The "*site* of the dissolved Priory"—not the estate, nor yet the buildings which were probably demolished—was granted later to the Whorwood family, of Compton and Stourton Castle.

XXIV.—Halesowen – its Abbey and its Church at the Reformation.

One long, last, regretful glance at monastic Sandwell, and then our eyes must be turned in other directions to view the rest of our historic panorama of the local past. There stood the quaint old priory in the dip of the landscape, its black-and-white half hidden by wild roses and climbing honeysuckle in the bright days of summer-tide. Wandering in meditative mood is a solitary sombre-garbed monk with his face turned towards the old priory mill; and as his eye wanders over the peaceful scene it takes in the wide sweep of meadow-land flecked with sheep, while beyond them the lowing kine stand here and there on the greensward, repairing anon to stand knee-deep in the cooling stream still further in the distance. Slowly the monk meanders along the winding banks of the limpid Tame till he espies the brother of whom he is in search under the grateful shade of a spreading oak, occupied in the gentle craft of the experienced angler. Tomorrow will be Friday and it is therefore with set purpose that the new comer joins his brother in throwing out the fly, and doubling the ripples on the shining surface of the water. Sounds as well as sights harmonise with the peacefulness of the scene. Suited to the dreamy pursuits of the patient anglers is the drowsy hum of the mill's steady whirling grindstones. The old mill itself is white with flour dust, as if hoary with age; while the stilly mill-pond shines through the gently waving foliage like a sheet of glass in the glorious sunlight. A cluster of elms, lofty and leafy, spread their long arms over the ancient mill as if in benign protection of its venerable walls; while nearer yet in the foreground the willows lean over from the banks, with their drooping tresses falling gracefully into the water, as if they were elfin bathers seeking to cool themselves by constant dipping. Still nearer, the reedy sedge sends up a gentle rustle from the flowing waters, which seem to speak to the tranquil minds of the holy fathers in a language of murmuring whispers. And as the shadows slowly lengthen upon meadow and stream, a colony of cawing rooks come noisily homeward to the shelter of the elms. Then the air becomes heavy with delicious odours, perfumes that fall upon the imagination with the same restful effect as have the soothing sights and sounds of this happy dream of Sandwell's bygone and long vanished retreat—all passed away, never to return.

*   *   *   *   *   *

A digression, by moving the scene of action from West Bromwich to an adjacent parish some five miles to the south west, may be pardoned at this juncture; for the period of the Dissolution of the Monasteries, and of the Reformation which quickly followed on, is one of events so momentous, and of the highest social, political, and religious importance, that no detail should be spared which will enlarge our views of the local history, portrayal of which is here attempted. For a brief space, then, the scene is shifted to Hales Owen, where there was an Abbey whose wide-spread influence in the district could not be without some effect upon the affairs of West Bromwich; and whose associations were particularly close with Wednesbury and Walsall beyond. And as a means of comparison and contrast with Sandwell Priory some sketch of this neighbouring Abbey will be valuable to the reader who is intimate with both localities.

Presuming that Monastic rule were in every case carried out strictly according to the letter, and that the accusations of misrule and immorality brought against these establishments were not well founded, then the rule of life at Hales Owen Abbey was by no means so austere as at Sandwell Priory. The discipline which prevailed at the latter, under the rule of St. Benedict, has already been described: but Halesowen Abbey belonged to an entirely different fraternity, namely, a branch of the Austin Canons, as those were called who followed the rule of St. Augustine. This particular branch was known as the Præmonstratensian Order, but more commonly called the White Canons, on account of their dress or distinguishing habit. These Monks went out into the world, conversed at tables, and were by no means so strict, even theoretically, as the Benedictines.

Hales Owen was formerly in Salop but since 1844 has been included in the county of Worcester. But the inception of Hales Owen Abbey seems to have had its origin in Hampshire, for it was founded (with the favour and goodwill of King John) by Peter de Rupibus, Bishop of Winchester, in 1215. It had jurisdiction, too, over the Hampshire Priory of Titchfield, as well as of Dotfield Priory, Bromsgrove.

Among its possessions at one time were the advowsons of Wednesbury and Walsall. King John in 1210 had appointed his own chaplain, "Magister William," to Wednesbury Church, and "Magister Serlo de Sunning" to Walsall Church; but when Hales Abbey was completed in 1218 he granted the two livings to the new foundation. The Abbot's tenure of these two churches however, seems to have been very uncertain. In 1245 the monastery secured a confirmation of the grant of Walsall and its two chapels-of-ease at Bloxwich and at Rushall respectivly, and also of the chapelry of Wednesbury, by a charter from Henry III. All the great tithes of Walsall were promptly transferred to the Abbey, and the rectory thus transformed into a vicarage, had only the small tithes left (about one- sixteenth of the former value of the benefice) for the stipend of the vicarius (1248). But in 1293 a *Quo Warranto* was issued for the recovery by the Crown of the advowsons of Walsall and Wednesbury, and Edward I. at the same time appointed Nicholas de Burton to the living of Wednesbury. At the Assize it was proved that at the time of King Henry's grant, the Church of Wednesbury was not a Chapel of Walsall but had previously been a mother church in no way connected with it. The verdict was therefore for the King, and the advowson of Wednesbury reverted to the Crown. In 1301, the Abbot, Thomas de Hales, exercised the right of presentation to Wednesbury, but only on payment of a fine to the King, and he made himself Vicar of Wednesbury—probably because the small tithes still produced something considerable. In 1305, this right was further secured to the Abbey. See also allusions to these matters in Chapters xiv. and xv.

From its connection with Wednesbury Church we now pass to its patronage of the Church within its own parish. A settlement between the Abbey and the Parish Church of Halesowen had been made in 1270 by Godfrey, Bishop of Worcester, whereby the perpetual Vicar of the Church should have and receive from the Abbot ten marks yearly, a house, with outhouses, orchard, garden, &c., and that the Canons should give him the assistance of another priest, and bear all other extra charges. This was not a bad living, as benefices ranked in those days. But clerical ingenuity has ever been inventive in the augmentation of ecclesiastical revenues.

Among the old customs kept up by the clergy was one known as "Church ales;" and this flourished in a marked degree at Hales Owen. It was a plan for raising money characteristic of that period of voluntary effort, before the local rate-collector was called into existence. Allusion has been made to the apportionment of tithes to a three-fold purpose under the "Law of Ethelred"; but that portion intended for the relief of the poor eventually became absorbed in the general funds of the Church. Not that the poor were neglected. As a matter of fact the poor were too well looked after, even to the extent of pauperising them, and of creating a class of sturdy vagrants. The almoner of a monastery each morning distributed relief in the shape of food, and sometimes of money, to the needy and the sick. As there were no poor laws, and therefore no poor rates, a voluntary fund was created in the 14th Century, and was called the "Church Store" church-wardens actually loaned money at interest, or begged young cattle to rear and sell for the benefit of this fund. But a very common method of raising money, and one that was largely practised at Hales Abbey was the begging of malt and the brewing of ales, which was sold on specially appointed festive days, generally in the churchyard, for the sustenance of the Church Store. For the maintenance of the church fabric and the relief of the poor of the parish it was expected that people would get very drunk. Shakspere confesses with regret, or at least with the after-pangs begotten of strong drink, his attendance at these holiday orgies in the neighbouring villages of Stratford-on-Avon, namely,

Piping Pebworth, dancing Marston,
Haunted Hillbro, hungry Grafton,
Dudging Exhall, papist Wixford,
Beggarly Broom, and drunken Bidford.

At Hales Owen Church these "Ales" were so much in vogue that they were held not only at Whitsun—most "Church Ales" were also called Whitsun Ales" because it was most frequently they were held at this summer festival—but at Easter as well. In 1497 the goodly profit of £2 6s. 8d. was yielded by the Easter Ale. The church too, possessed its own stock of pots, spittoons, and other vessels and utensils for carrying out the custom in a most business-like way. In the year mentioned 8d. was charged in the church accounts for a pewter dish lost during the "Ales" in the town, and a second one is stated to have been lost at Cradley.

At Hales the festivals of St. Stephen and St. Katherine were also kept with great solemnity, and until very recent years the High Bailiff of the Manor is said to have held his annual feast on St. Stephen's Day. In 1497 the sum of 6d. was paid to a reverend member of the Chance family, or as he is styled in the record, "Sir Robert Chance," for singing St. Katherine's Mass; and as it was apparently high festival 3d. was paid for "ringing to the same." The scouring of St Katherine's lamp was carried out at a cost of 2d. on the same occasion. In 1529 the image of St. Katherine, which was carried in procession needed repairs to the face at an expenditure of 4d. The wax tapers burnt at these celebrations were very considerable.

Many other items in the church accounts are equally interesting. The organ-maker at Bromwycham was paid 10s. in 1497 for "repayling the organs"; and at the suppression of the Abbey (1539) the organ of the establishment was transferred to the parish church for which the lord Abbot was paid 4 marks, while the mending and its re-setting up cost 40 shillings. Church music was highly appreciated even here where seasonal depravity was a recognised institution.

And so we come to this stirring period when change and innovation were in the air. The Abbey had escaped suppression when the first general order was issued in 1537, because its income exceeded £200 per annum. But at the general suppression of the larger religious houses ordered two years afterwards, it was overtaken by the same fate that had befallen Sandwell1. According to Dugdale's *Monasticon* the gross revenues of Hales Owen Abbey at the dissolution in 1539 were estimated at £337 10s. 6d., and the net value of them was £280 13s. 2d.

When the closing of the Abbey was found irrevocable, much of its furniture found its way to the Parish Church, including timber, windows, lead, and other stuff worth removing. Three other carriage loads of "stuff" were charged for in addition. To the bishop certain relics were forwarded either as a present or for safe custody. The legend book was mended at considerable cost. A tablet or panel picture of St. Kenelm was removed from the Abbey to the church, and many other tablets and images were likewise transferred at such a cost as indicates the great value placed upon them. The rood, or great crucifix, was not only reverentially removed, but was brought in procession and set up in great pomp, and a "church ale" was held withal to grace the occasion—and to make a profit of £4. All this was done in 1539 or two years after the first order for dissolving these monasteries. As yet there was no fear of the Reformation, but the shadow that foretold its approach was visibly overspreading the land.

In the following year (1540) a box that had contained relics was sold, together with a rood. Seven years later the work of Reformation is in active progress, and all chantries were to be closed. Items in the church accounts are now suggestive of the spirit of reform which was then abroad. There is a payment for drink for those engaged in taking down the images, the removal of which had been ordered as well as the destruction of all altars. The removal of the stones at Jesus' altar is set down at 8d. in 1548, while the pulling down of the high altar and of St. Mary's altar (1549) was accomplished at an outlay of 1s. 2d. In 1552 even the churchyard cross had to go: but in the following year Mary ascended the throne, and it is not surprising therefore to find set down in 1556 a sum of money for mending the cross again, But Mary died in 1558, and the altars and rood-loft were again and for ever destroyed in Hales Owen Parish Church. The surrender of the monastery to the King is dated the Quindene of Easter, 30 Henry VIII. It is—Between the Lord the King, and William Taylour Abbot of the Monastery of the Blessed Virgin and St. John the Evangelist, of Halesowen: of the Manors of Hales, Halesbury, Halesowen, and Hellegraunge, and of 1,000 messages, 1,000 tofts, 1000 cottages, 3,000 gardens, 4 dovecots, 3 water-mills 3 wind-mills, 16,000 acres of land, 6,000 acres of meadow, 12,000 acres of pasture, 1,000 acres of wood, 2,000 acres of furze and heath, 2,000 acres of marsh, 1,000 acres of alders. 1,000 acres of fishery, £100 rent, and a rent of 100 quarters of wheat, 100 quarters of barley, 100 quarters of beans, 20 quarters of oats, 20 quarters of peas, 4 quarters of salt, 6lbs of pepper, 4lbs of cumin; all in Hales, Halesburg Halesowen, and Hellegraunge, and of the rectories of Warley, Hales, etc., in Salop, and of the Manors of Horneburne, Smythwyke, Wornesburn, Swyndon, Rowley, Weddesbury, Westbromwiche, Walsall, Pelsalle, and Lychfylde, &c., &c ... and of the advowsons of the Churches of Clent, Woddesbury, Rowley, and Walsall ... and the Manors of Warley Chirchelenche, Cradley, Dodford, and of the Priory of Dodford, &c. The Abbot acknowledged the right of the King, for which the King gave him £4,000—but this amount is pure fiction, in accordance with the common practice in such cases. A small pension for each monk was all that passed into the hands of the dispossessed ecclesiastics. Some of this property found its way into the hands of Sir John Dudley, Knight, namely, the rectories of Clent, Wednesbury and Walsall.

Surely after the object-lesson afforded by the passing of these events before the mind's eye of the reader, no apology is needed for thus straying into this by-path of our history. A clearer insight has been gained into the events that occurred in this immediate vicinity at that critical period of the nation's history. And the chief impression left upon the mind is the low estate into which the Romish Church had fallen, with the surmise that had she been true to herself, no "Reformation" would perhaps have been needed.

Of the abbey buildings but very few fragmentary ruins now remain, for the fabric seems to have been purposely demolished. The canons who had formed its community numbered thirty in all, and they were patrons not only of Hales Owen, Walsall, and Wednesbury, but also of Harborne and Rushall, and of the two priories previously mentioned, namely, Tichfield and Dotfield. Their sphere of influence was by no means a small one, and further details of the intimate relationships which existed between the abbey and the churches of Walsall and Wednesbury may be found in Dr. Willmore's *History of Walsall*, pp. 110-118.

XXV.—The Manor in the hands of the Stanley Family (1500—1626).

Chapter xx concluded by tracing the descent of the manor from the last of the Freebody family to the first of the Stanleys, thus

(13). Cecily Freebody married John Stanley.

By this marriage West Bromwich was carried into the possession of a new family of manorial lords; and in resuming its descent we will restate the fact by putting it inversely, thus

(13). John Stanley married Cecily Freebody. This John Stanley. Esq., according to Reeves, died in 1533; and p. 39 the same writer quaintly says, "I have read of Thomas Stanley (second son of Sir John Stanley), who died in 1435; also George Stanley, his son, these were the predecessors of the lords of the Manor of Westbromwich, and probably some of them were lords of the manor. John Stanley married Cecily, daughter and heiress of William Freebody, former lord of the manor. I am informed that this Cecily was a co-heiress with another sister as ladies of the manor, and that she succeeded her husband in the manor." This is incorrect in several details.

The founder of the Stanley family was one Henry Stanleigh de Stoneley, who flourished as a Saxon landowner, before the Conquest, when he was possessed of the manor and bailiwick of Wyrall Forest and, says one incautious writer, "thereupon assumed the armorial bearings since used by his descendants viz.: three stag's heads on a bend." The pedigree of the family as given by Mrs. Willett, varies from that printed by Shaw. The latter tree commences with Thomas Stanley, of Elford, a second son of Sir John Stanley, and who died in 1435. Then follows his son George Stanley, who married Eleanor, daughter of John, Lord Dudley, and relict of Henry Beaumont, of Wednesbury. It was their son John Stanley, who married into the Freebody family and so became connected with West Bromwich, and with whom Mrs. Willett commences her pedigree.

John Stanley died about 1534, and at the Inquisition taken at his death it was shown that he held the manor of West Bromwich from Cicely, his wife, by military service and other rents, among the holdings being "17 messuages called Bondsthing," a name which has already been explained in chapter xxi. "Crompes Grownde" is the name of another Bromwich place, on the conveyance of which (1531), appears the names of John Stanley, Thomas Schawe and William Nalle as witnesses. The widow, Cecily or Cecilia Stanley, died in 1552, when half the manor (comprising some 100 acres of land with other messuages and their appurtenances), was said to be held by military service, and half a knight's-fee of Richard Jervis, of Weoley Castle, knight and lord superior. In a deed of the year 1542 she is described as a 'gentlewoman."

John and Cecilia Stanley had three sons and one daughter.

At the Inquisition taken 26 Henry VIII (1534), it appeared that the above John died 7 October in that year, and that Francis was his son and heir, seized of divers messuages in West Bromwich, held of Cecily Stanley, as her manor of West Bromwich, by knight's service, and 22d. rent; by which it is manifest that the Freebodies were formerly Lords of the Manor, and that she carried it in marriage to him. The widow Cecily died on the 6th of May, 6 Edward VI. (1552), her son and heir Francis being then 46 years old, and seized of a moiety of the manor. It is by no means clear how the manor went on the death of John Stanley, whether to his widow Cecily or to his heir Francis. Reeves says "Francis Stanley seized upon certain property during her (Cecily's) lifetime.

(14). Francis Stanley, who seems to have succeeded his father at the age of 30, in the year 1534, was the eldest son. He married Winifred, daughter of Thomas Middlemore, Lord of the Manor of Edgbaston.

"Franciscu Stanley" is the signature appended to a deed dated 1556, conveying to Richard Hodgetts certain lands described as "at Greate, within the demesne of West Bromwich, lying between the land called Crompes Ground and the water of the Tame, in width; and between the King's highway from Greate Green to the town of Duddle, and lands late of a certain Chantry of Tonge in length."

A "Francis Stanley, jun., Esq.," is given by Reeves as the next holder of the manor, and according to the same authority he died in 1658 a year after the other Francis. It is not clear who this second Francis was. There was a daughter of the first named Fraunces. Some fifty-seven years later there was a great-grandson of the first Francis baptised by that name in Bromwich Church, 20 February, 1615. Also in 1617 a "John Lynton and Ffrancis Stanley were married by license of Wolverhampton att Bylston." Like many other families the Stanleys evidently had a favourite baptismal name.

(15). WALTER (or GEORGE) STANLEY was but 11 years of age at the death of his father in 1557 and was proved to hold the Manor of West Bromwich of Thomas Jervis, Esquire, of Weoley Castle, by *fealty*. He married Gertrude Hollys, daughter of Sir William Hollys, of Houghton, co. Notts.: but during his minority his mother (Winifred) acted as Lady of the Manor.

Four interesting documents bear her name, under dates given:—

(A.D. 1571). An indenture of the lease of a cottage made between William Hunt and Edward Davies, the situation of which is described as being between the lands of William Orme, gentleman, the lands of Winifred Stanley, widow, and the Queen's highway leading from Wednesbury to Birmingham.

(A.D. 1574). This is a deed executed under the seal of Winifred Stanley, widow of Francis Stanley, lady of the Manor of West Bromwich. It relates to two cottages of the name William Hunt, the gift and grant of Richard Littlely and John his son, and in which Winifrid, of whom they were held by rents and services, grants release to Hunt, except "suit unto the Great Leet or view of Frankpledge within the said manor." But the place names are interesting, especially those indicating the locality of Finchpath. For instance one cottage is said to be situated "in the Nether Finchpath, within the fee of West Bromwich, called Blake Lake," and in breadth "between the lands of Thomas Ford, gentleman, and Winifred Stanley, and the highway leading from Wednesbury towards Birmingham.

The other cottage was in the way leading from the Church of West Bromwich towards Wednesbury.

(A.D. 1577). A deed of sale by John Partridge of lands in West Bromwich. Again the place-names are interesting. The location is given as "between the land of Winifred Stanley, gentlewoman, called Wall Way; the land of Henry Blakeweye, nigh the highway leading from Blake Lake towards Bromwich Church, the highway leading from the said church towards Hateley Heath; and the land of the said Winifred Stanley, called Wall Moor Furlong; and that croft and close of land called Gold Croft, in West Bromwich now in the occupation of John Partridge; and between the highway leading from Hateley Heath towards Bromwich Church aforesaid, the field there called Knapeney Hill Field, the lane leading from Hateley Heath toward Jone Bridge [Newton] ... and arable land lying in West Bromwich in the fields there called Wigmore Field, between the head land there and the land of Robert Whorwood," &c.

(A.D. 1577). A lease from John Hateley, of West Bromwich, and Thomas, his son, of land lying in, Fynchespath, in the lordship of West Bromwich, to Thomas Parkes, of Wednesbury, also mentions land belonging to Wynyfred Stanley.

By the date 1577 Walter Stanley would have long attained his majority, having been born in 1546 he should be 31. The foregoing documents may perhaps allude to her dower lands and not to the manorial estate of her son. In 1613 Walter Stanley, with rare munificence, founded the "Stanley Trust," in the Parish Church to which allusion will be made later.

Walter Stanley died in 1615, and was buried at West Bromwich. By will he provided for the advancement of Richard Shilton, who was the son of his sister Barbara, who had married John Shilton, a mercer of Birmingham. He favorably mentions another nephew, Robert Shilton; and his two sisters, Francis the wife of John Wolverston, and Jane the wife of a small land owner named Okell (for "Okell's Farm" see *History of Tipton*, Chapter xi) or those bearing his own name, his will recognises Charles, son of Robert Stanley, of Harborne, and Thomas Stanley, of Bromsgrove. Among the bequests to his successor William, he enumerates armour and weapons as a true knight; and certain furniture including a double-gilt standing cup, as a careful householder. The companion cup he leaves to the wife of his heir, Mary Stanley. But his character as a man of shrewd foresight and commendable public spirit is best exemplified in the fact that he left a sum of money for the improvement of the means of communication with his estate; namely money towards the completion of the Bilston causeway, and the highway between Bilston and Tipton. This was just when vehicular traffic was first growing into favor, and the art of road making in England had not as yet been recovered.

(16). WILLIAM STANLEY succeeded to the lordship in 1614, at the age of 29; and presumably did not die that year, as one writer states. According to Mrs. Willett he mortgaged the estates heavily, after barring the entail; in part to his wealthy cousin, Sir Richard Shilton, who became eventually, in 1626, the possessor of the whole, upon paying off the second mortgage held by Sir William Hewitt. "What became of William," says the same writer, " we cannot ascertain, but he must have been much reduced in circumstances, as Sir Richard Shilton made an agreement to pay him £100 a year out of the estates."

William Stanley married Mary Grey, of Enville, by whom he had several children; there were two daughters, one son who died in infancy, and another son, the Francis already mentioned as baptised in 1615, But according to other writers there was a

(17) "SIR EDWARD STANLEY," who succeeded him, and who is said to have been the one who sold the Manor of West Bromwich to his cousin, Sir Richard Shilton.

The element of doubt as to the actual successor of Walter Stanley is not removed by referring to the histories of Shaw and of Reeves. It may not be out of place to suggest that if William did not predecease his father, that his father had some doubt either as to his survival for any length of time—he might have been fatally sick—or as to his moral strength of character in upholding the family name and state. Or why did he so thoughtfully provide for the future of that rising scion of the collateral branch of his family, young Shilton? Events seem to justify some such conclusion; for whereas young Shilton rose steadily in the world, and actually became head of the family and upholder of its dignity, William Stanley, if he survived his father (as some writers seem to doubt) became at first improvident and ultimately a ruined man, as set forth by Mrs. Willett.

XXVI.—The manor held by the Shiltons (1626–1716): Dwelling
Houses of the Olden Times, and their Surroundings.

The Manor of West Bromwich passed in 1626, as described in the previous chapter, from the Stanley family to the representative of a related family, one (18) SIR RICHARD SHILTON, knight, son of a Birmingham mercer. Wyrley's *Church Notes*, written in 1597, says of this Manor—"it is the habitation of Walter Stanley, Esq., my very good friend and kinsman." A note then ads "that his son, William Stanley, sold the manor to his cousin, Sir Richard Shelton, knt."; but Sir Simon Degge tells us "it was sold by Sir Edward Stanley to Sir Richard Shelton of the inner Temple, some time Solicitor General to King Charles, but being found not fit for that employment, was displaced and made of the King's Council Extraordinary; whose son now enjoys it"—the manor. Shaw says further: "This family of Shelton was likewise possessed of the manor of Wednesbury, where [under that heading] we have given their arms."

Although some doubt exists as to the actual vendor, there is no question whatever as to the purchaser of West Bromwich manor; the new comer being yet another illustration of the commercial spirit which animates most Englishmen—an instinct that has converted into landowners and territorial magnates many who were but tradesmen of humble origin.

A Birmingham writer recently gave an interesting account of this class of mediæval trader. About the time of Edward II. Moore Street, in that city, was known as Moul Street, so called in the Anglo-Norman tongue because there was a mill in the neighbourhood, or because it was connected with a family named Moul, who possessed a mill. There lived a John le Moul about the year 1330, and previously a member of the same family was named Alam le Molendin. Many substantial tradesmen and well-to-do burghers had their dwellings in this locality, scattered about the outskirts of the little "Burgh ville." Among these old burgages was, about the time of Richard III., one recently acquired from the Wastlewood family by a prosperous Birmingham trader named Shylton, the founder of the family who afterwards became lords of the manor of West Bromwich. When fortunes were made in trade at this early period these residences of the rich burghers were not stuffy and cramped buildings in a densely populated neighbourhood; these ancient burgages were quaint and interesting old edifices, each with a piece of land called a croft or grange, whereby may be understood a piece of land for either croft or farm purposes, for all these tradesmen were more or less little farmers, and to each of them a barn was an essential possession. It was among such surroundings, and yet close withal to the Market Place, that a fortune was built up in mediæval Birmingham wherewith to purchase the manor and lordship of West Bromwich.

And what did West Bromwich itself look like? In describing the priory buildings at Sandwell (chapter xxiii) a glance was given at the domestic architecture of the period. Of houses there were but few, and these were clustered (if it could be said there were enough to form a cluster) round the church. The cottages were built of oak, the timbers selected and not wrought into shape; the natural fibre of wood when merely cleft by the axe seeming to make it far more durable, and, therefore, more suited for the permanency required of architecture. The use of bricks was as yet but rare. The timber frame-work was filled in with plaster held together either by wicker-work, or with clay in which chopped straw had been kneaded. The roofs were of thatch, and the floors of bare earth trodden hard. Chimneys were rare, except in castles and manor houses: and where they did exist they seem to have been additions, built "outside," as they may still be seen in Lichfield and other quaint old towns at the present day. Where there were upper rooms under the thatch, they were lighted by very small windows set dormer-wise, and were approached by ladders, or by staircases of the very rudest construction. A wood fire blazed on the bare hearthstone, and the long nights of winter were dimly lighted by the blazing of the faggots; for fat, or oil, was too dear for cottager to indulge in. The *bordars*, who held their cottages for a rental of food supply to the lord of the manor, kept large flocks of fowls for this purpose: each *cottar* probably possessed a pig, as swine were very plentiful. Oxen were used chiefly as beasts of burden, beef being eaten only in the homes of the rich. Sheep were kept very largely, but chiefly for the wool. As sure as November came round, every Martinmas saw a great slaughtering of beasts, and a busy salting of beef and mutton, as well as of bacon; for as there were as yet no root-crops known in England, the farmer had to kill off nearly all his stock, keeping through the winter only sufficient animals for breeding purposes. These few were fed on coarse hay and straw and pea and vetch haulm. It was the eating of so much salted meat that made scurvy so prevalent. Another old time disease in England was no doubt traceable to mediæval diet, as suggested by the leper windows at Sandwell (chapter xxiii). Leprosy was then common and is said to have been caused by the eating of rotten fish; for in those times the carriage of fish while was still fresh was impossible owing to bad roads and lack of internal communication—hence the monks of Sandwell kept their own stew-ponds, and jealously guarded their fishing rights in the Tame; while well-to-do landowners prized a vivary or other fish preserve with which they could hold themselves comfortably prepared for the recurring fasting days of the pre-reformation year. In those times a coney-gre or rabbit warren was a somewhat valuable possession among the gentry, for strange to say rabbits were rather rare before the thirteenth century. The Stocks stood near the Church, as does that other manorial institution, the Pinfold, to this day. Drunkards and night-walkers were put in the stocks and all others whose offences were of a trivial nature. The Tumbril (see chapter viii) was chiefly reserved for the punishment of defaulting brewers and bakers, and for common scolds; one of these female offenders in a neighbouring parish has been wonderfully described in the legal jargon of the period as "a common *rixatrix* and *disturbatrix* of the peace." The Tumbril is sometimes known as a *Gome-stool* or Ducking-stool, it would be fixed in that village pond which happened to be most centrally situated for the church and the manor-house.

And what was the manor house like? Let us try to conjure up a picture of life in the old hall. The lord of the manor of West Bromwich at one time had held other estates as well, as at Oxley, Womborne, &c. (chapter xx); and the Sheldons, the lords of West Bromwich at this later period, were also lords of Wednesbury manor. At each manor-house there would be a farm; stables for horses, kennels for dogs, and mews for hawks. Kitchens, cellars, and spiceries were all large and well filled. Spices and perfumes were very largely used before soap was invented; for where uncleanliness was at a discount a pleasant smell was a desideratum. The lord kept his own baker, or at least a bakster (*feminine*); and brewsters, or female brewers, were very general in such households. The candles burnt upon his tables were home-made, the product of the fat of his own sheep or deer. That a rude plenty did make those "tables to groan," when guests and family sat down to partake of meals from wooden trenchers and leathern jacks, would scarcely be an exaggeration of speech. No foreign or fancy dishes garnished the board; but substantial joints of roast beef, baked meats, game pies, and stewed fish; hunks of bread, but of vegetables a scarcity; the whole washed down with copious draughts of ale and wine. We have already noted the store set by domestic utensils, such as *mazeres* or tankards of wood (chap. xix), and gilt drinking cups (xxv); such articles, together with brass pots and crockery, were constantly taken about in the migrations from one residence to another. And on arrival each house was expected to have provisions stored in great abundance; although on departure granaries and store rooms would be bare enough to rouse the steward to renewed exertions. The woodlands would again have to supply fuel for the hearths; pigeon houses or dovecots had a perennial usefulness, the warrens always were ready with food and fur, as the ponds were with fish, The storage of corn was only practised by these large landowners, while the wastefulness and want of forethought by the farmers was the cause of frequent famines. After a bounteous harvest-home no beggar would eat bread that had beans in it, but demanded "cohet and clermatyne" (better breadstuffs), or else bread of clean wheat; he would refuse halfpenny ale, and unblushingly ask for the brownest. After Martinmas the larder was filled with beeves, sheep, swine, and even deer, all salted and cured. Winter provender for cattle was unknown. Breeds could not be improved. People lived from hand to mouth.

Deeds printed by Mrs. Willett (pp 218-9), and bearing the name of Sir Richard Shilton, are under dates as follows:—

A.D. 1637. A conveyance of land by John Stone, of Willenhall, to Henry Ffoorde, of West Bromwich mylner, mentions lands called Barker's Field, &c. lying between the lane leading from Bromwich Heath towards Wednesbury, the land of Sir Rychard Shilton, and the land of Mr. Walsteede. (The lane here mentioned is evidently the one which formerly ran from the Heath towards the Swan Inn at Swan Village, then parallel with the line of the present Great Western Railway, and came out near Wednesbury Bridge, into that known as Mollaston Lane, or Molly Aston's Lane. The family of Walsteede or Walsted belonged to Wednesbury, and were of some importance as their pedigree was recorded at the Visitation of London, 1633-4.)

A.D. 1638-9. An indenture between Thomas Oakley, of West Bromwich, nailor, and Henry Ffoord, of the same, milner; wherein Oakley sells a croft in West Bromwich over against the dwelling house of John Newey (? Oakwood), between the land now or late of Sir Richard Shilton, the land now or late of John Sparrye, gentleman, the King's Majesty's highway, leading from Bromwich Heath towards Wednesberie, and a little lane (? Church Lane) leading from the said highway towards Bromwich Church, &c. Witnesses, Symon Rider, Robert Rider, Humfrey Lowc, George Biker. (It is worthy of note that the "highway" is unmistakably the existing main road over Hill Top and down Holloway Bank; and yet it is *not* designated "Finchpath," as according to some local writers it ought to be called from the vicinity of Black Lake; lower down towards Wednesbury it *is* sometimes known as the "Portway").

Sir Richard Shilton died in 1647, and was buried in the Parish Church, having survived his wife about five years. According to Mrs. Willett (p. 14), Sir Richard devised the manor to

(19) ALICE LOWE, his sister, for her life only; and afterwards to

(20) JOHN SHILTON, his nephew, and son of his brother, Robert Shilton. He is known sometimes as Shilton and sometimes as Shelton. In 1655 he sold Rea Hall in Great Barr, to Henry Stone, the Parliamentarian leader, of Walsall. The document, dated 20th July, is witnessed by one Robert Shilton.

(21) JOHN SHILTON, the younger, succeeded his father in 1665. As he was born on 22nd July, 1659, he was but about six years of age when his father died. When he grew up John Shelton seems to have been either wasteful or improvident.

In 1709 he sold to John Lowe, of Lyndon, Bustleholme Mill, a most valuable property because it was not only a cornmill, but also a "slitting mill, joining together." During the Civil Wars it had been used as a blade mill, and at this time it was productive in the manufacture of slit-rods for the staple industry of nail making. In the same year, and with the consent of his wife and his heir apparent, Joseph, he parted with lands known respectively as Smithy More, Wheatcroft, Little Meadow, and Dam Banks, to the same John Lowe. To another purchaser, John Piddock, *gent.*, he sold "the Hermitage, between the lane called Hermitage Lane, the lane leading from Sandwell Green towards West Bromwich Forge, and other land of the said John Shelton," at the close of the same year. Soon after went Spann Coppice, and then other parts of the estate piece-meal. (Mrs. Willett's *History* pp. 201–204). In 1716 the churchwardens entered in their books the sum of £3 16s. 9d. as "ungatherable" from Mr. Sheldon's estate, and in April of that year they formally seek (by public resolution) to take the advice of "Sergeant Hooe or some other Counsell" . . . "one guiney allowed from the parish as a ffee," as to how the collectors of land tax and the overseers of the poor are to obtain the levies due from "Bromwich Hall and the demean lands thereto belonging." Evidently the Sheltons (or Sheldons, as they were sometimes called) were reduced to very straitened circumstances. Eventually the heavily mortgaged estates were sold under an Order of Chancery to Sir Samuel Clarke, knight, about the 1720. In the meantime John Shelton had died, leaving one son,

(22) Joseph Shelton, who may (1714) have enjoyed for a brief time what remnant there remained of the manorial income . The ruined family of Shelton have disappeared from the parish, unless they are represented by the Sheldons of West Bromwich and Wednesbury, For they had held both these manors, the first John Shelton having purchased Wednesbury in 1663.

Writing in 1798 Shaw says—"about the time the Manor of Wednesbury was disposed of to Sergeant Hoo, West Bromwich Manor was disposed of to the ancestor of the present possessor, Jervoise Clarke Jervoise, Esq., M.P. for Yarmouth in Hants, whose principal residence is Bellmont in that county."

XXVII.—The Last Lords of the Manor, Clarke and Jervoise-Clarke (1716-1819): Horticultural Extraordinary in West Bromwich.

The break-up of the manorial estates under the improvident. Sheltons is the beginning of the end. This dissipation of territorial wealth synchronises with the decay of manorial privileges, and foretells the gradual abolition of feudal forms of government. What

(23) Sir Samuel Clarke, knight, purchased about 1716, was not the whole of the ancient feudal estate of the lords of Bromwich, but only a portion of it. Other considerable parcels of the old manor lands were bought by wealthy men of the neighbourhood, amongst whose names are Josiah Turton, John Piddock, William Silvester, John May Smith, Joseph Worsley, John Mayoe, John Lowe, and Thomas Dudley. Notwithstanding this partition, Sir Samuel seems to have beautified his residence, and to have kept up considerable state there.

West Bromwich Hall possessed a famous garden, In fancy we will stroll round it to observe in what an old-world garden differed from our modern gardens. But first of all, a retrospect of the whole science of gardening will be necessary.

With the Saxons horticultural knowledge was somewhat limited, but we know they had their herb gardens, whence our word "orchard," (*wortyard*). In Domesday Book the existence of *horti* and *hortuli* (gardens and little gardens), is frequently alluded to. The monastic orders encouraged the science of gardening, and brought many rare fruits from the continent, just as they imported many rarities in art, but claustral ingenuity could do little to acclimatise the pomegranate or the citron. Almonds and figs were introduced more for ornament than utility. We are said to owe our peaches, chestnuts, and apples to the good monks; while cherries are said to have been brought to this country by them as late as the 15th century. Birmingham till recent times possessed a noted cherry orchard near the site of Cherry Street. But the Romans are also credited with introducing many of these fruits, perhaps there was a temporary loss of them between the two periods, The monks of Wardon, in Bedfordshire, were famous for a cooking pear, which they cultivated to great perfection, and Wardon pies became a favourite item in mediæval banquets. While the quince and medlar were very well known, apricots and nectarines came only as early as the 16th century. The vine was largely grown; Wednesbury Hall had a famous vineyard which gave its name to a well in Manor House Road. Nearly as much verjuice as wine was the product of English vines; verjuice was so much used in sauces and other culinary preparations that it was obtained not only from the grape, but from vine leaves and from sorrel. Vinegar was also as largely prepared and extensively used. Large nuts are frequently mentioned; they were probably walnuts, as the wood of this tree was known as *masere*, whence the name of the wooden bowls and cups so much in use and so highly valued. Chestnuts and hazel nuts were very common. The earliest notice of the gooseberry or gorse-berry is in an account of the royal gardens at Westminster 1276. Strawberries and raspberries are never mentioned in these old accounts, because they were not cultivated; wild ones only were then known.

Of vegetables the pea and the bean were largely grown; the chief esculent root was the beet, while it is doubtful whether the cabbage was appreciated, if it was known so very generally. Spinach was perhaps more popular. The only alliaceous plants in use before 1400 were onions, garlic, and leek. Of salads, lettuce, mustard, watercress, and hop were most in use. (Reeves mentions a hop-yard at Bromwich Hall in 1836). Pot herbs and sweet herbs were largely used; an old-world kitchen garden would invariably contain shallots, parsnip, carrot, celery, parsley, coriander, dill, savory, poppy, kidney-bean, onions, radish, savoy, cummin, fennel, tansy, sage, rue, lavender. *pulegium* or pennyroyal (with which our not too cleanly ancestors fought the ubiquitous flea) *menta* or peppermint, and rosemary. Monks sometimes kept a special "physic garden" in which to grow most of these, together with their balms and balsams. In all monasteries, manor houses, and castles, there was a still-room for the distillation, concoction, expression, or other preparation of strong waters, oils, essences, syrups, cordials, salves, ointments, broths, washes, and numerous other curatives and concoctions, compounded from roots, berries, herbs, and simples.

Of flowers the most common were roses (red, damask, velvet double, musk, single-white, and Provence double), lilies, sunflowers, violets, poppies, and perhaps narcissus. Margaret of Anjou is said to have introduced the Provence rose. The commonest of all garden flowers were the gilly and the clove pink. There were carnations and the pervinke or periwinkle. Every garden had a pond or well for watering—the formal fountain come in later times with the stiff and stately bedding of Flemish, and the geometrical designs of Dutch gardening. In the wild disordered profusion of an old-fashioned garden a piece of greensward was much appreciated, even more than the lawns and pleasaunces of the later period; bowling-alleys and shooting butts were frequent adjuncts before the 16th century when Flemish influence introduced mounds for overlooking the country, like the *speculatorium* inside the bailey of a Norman fortress. An apiary and a sun-dial were frequent accessories to an old-time garden.

* * *

Descending from the general to the particular, the most amazing fact is the character of the gardening practised at West Bromwich at the beginning of the last century. Involuntarily we are almost made to exclaim—Has the English climate deteriorated since then? Or what great physical change has taken place?

Horticulture was making very great strides in the 17th and 18th centuries, especially with the Dutch gardeners. About the time of the bulb mania in England, Sir Samuel Clarke was evidently bestowing much attention upon his garden at Hall Green. Catalogues of plants consigned to him are preserved in the vestry, and have been printed by Mrs. Willett at some length (pp. 248-258). From Layton Stone, Essex, there were forwarded on 15th December, 1720, a large quantity, each sort and variety properly labelled, for Sir Samuel's two gardens, the parlour garden and the kitchen garden.

For the south-east aspect, "or against the house in the broad gravel walke," there were of vines—

> White muscadine grape.
> Royal ditto.
> Red July ditto.

Vines to grow between the dwarfs or the wall trees undermentioned.

> Newington Nectarine.
>   ,,   Peach.
>   ,,   ,,   Scarlet.
>   ,,   ,,   Early.

With others "to goe between the above."

For the "south-west aspect, or the left-hand side coming from the house, being that side of the wall unto which the end of the barn reacheth":—

Pears,—	Gorls Bury.	Plumbs.—	Mapell.
,,	Diana or Doyne.	,,	Jonhatine.
,,	Done.	,,	Green gage.
,,	Dwarf.	Apricots.—	Turkey.
	etc.	,,	Roman. etc.

"For the north-west aspect or upper end of the Parlour Garden, which reacheth to the summer-house from the eastward":—

Cherrys.—	Bleeding Heart.	Peare.—	Swann's egg.
,,	May Duke.	,,	Summer Bon Creton.
,,	Dwarf.	,,	Bury de Roy.
,,	Lewkeward.		etc.

"For the north-east aspect, or for the wall from the Pump Court Door to the Summer House in the Parlour Garden":—

Plumb.—	S. Katherine.	Cherry.—	Morella.
,,	White Holland.	,,	Black Heart.
,,	Orleance.	Peare.—	Orange Burgamott.
,,	Imperial.	,,	Rosia.

To be planted in the kitchen garden, namely, for the south-eastern aspect of it, were

Apricots.—Mascaline and Royall Orange varieties.

Nectarines.—Red Roman and Newington   ,,

Peaches.—Arlbemarle, Vanguard, Minion, and Bell Chevereuse.

"For the south-west aspect or the right-hand wall from the house," against which wall a house reached to the kitchen Garden, were more peach, apricots, and "plumbs."

"For the north-east aspect, or wall on left-hand from the house, being that wall over against ye Slaughter-house," were more "plumbs" of the Early Amber and Pomegranette varieties.

"Ffor the north-west aspect, or against the house in the kitchen garden" were "peares" of the Jargonell and Amarell kinds, with peaches, nectarines, and vines to go between.

Of standards, for which the gardener had proper directions, there were more pears, apricots, and cherries. Then there were three strong mulbery trees, twenty strong codlins; then

> 100 ffine white rasberrys,
> 100 ffine sorts of goose berrys,
> 100 phi berds,

100 red and white Dutch currants,

2 ffigs

The currants "are for the dwarf wall or the brest wall in the best garden, commonly called the parlour garden." The consignment ends with a memorandum of six quinces to "goe along with" the standards in the orchards and the dwarfs for the parlour garden, all tallied and numbered on lead labels which are to be "nayled on the walls, with nails made through the holes in them; it's thought four-penny nails will be big enough."

A month later another consignment includes fifty-four standard apple trees— French peppins, golden peppins, jennetings, russets, rennets, summer paremaines, winter paremaines, non par elles, bearnards for baking, etc., etc.; black damozeens, white demozeens, and other plums; Windsor and other pears; dwarf plums and cherries for the parlour garden borders, etc., all stated to be vigorous "thriving trees and good bearers, the very best sorts of the said several kinds;" despatched from London on January 21st, 1720-1, by the Wagon of Thomas Shears, who was to deliver them "in good condition and undamaged at West Bromwich Hall, on fryday next."

In the February of the following year, by the same conveyance is sent another lot, mainly apple and pear trees, to take the place of some that died; and with them 100 artichoke plants of the best, strongest, and largest sorts. In the following January (of 1722) another lot was sent by Samuel Gutteridge's wagon, "to be delivered on Satterday next, either at West Bromwich Hall, or else at the houses of Mr John Jesson, or Mr. Richard Jesson, whose houses lie on the road to Tipton." Allusion is again made to some of the previous trees having died, and to "the old great cherry tree which was taken down, and did groe on the south-east wall of the kitchen garden." There was in this lot a box containing Marrowfatt Pease, Admirall Pease, Spanish Pease, Portugall Onyon seed, Melon seed, White Turkey Cowcumber seed "and Cabbage seed" received from Russia in the year 1722," that is, new seed.

The same method of conveyance is used again in November, 1723, to send down many more fruit trees, including these Vines:—

Norbury Portugall Vine layer

Hambro Grape Vine cutting

Le Mune   do.

Black Raisin   do.

Black Muscadine   do.

In less than a month afterwards a bundle of trees —plums, nectarines, and peaches—is sent for delivery "at the Cross Guns" by Gutteridge's servant. Again, "ye 24th November, 1724," the trees include similar lots, with apricot and mulberry in addition, which are to be "planted against the back of the parlour-garden wall in the new piece of ground taken out of the leasow called the Little Stockings, and leading from the back part of the Summer House to the gate between ye new barn and ye Pump Court." These plantings and replantings evidently necessitated a considerable enlargement of the gardens and orchard.

There is a list dated 27th January, 1728-9 of trees that had "miscarried in ye gardens and orchards at West Bromwich Hall, Staffordshire," and which are to be replaced. Then follow numerous similar catalogues of plantings in many following years, the last one being dated 1760, and not the least astonishing item is the "Indian Figg."

It is a big demand on the imagination to call up a mental picture of the local landscape in those days, before the acid fumes of chemical works poisoned the atmosphere and blighted the prospect.

Writing at the very close of last century, the Rev. Stebbing Shaw says:—"The old manor house stands one mile northward from the church, in a flat situation, but well wooded. Like many other ancient family seats still remaining in this country it consists of a large pile of irregular half-timbered building, black and white, and surrounded by numerous outhouses and lofty walls. It is at present the property of the lord of the manor, but under the care of his steward, Mr. Wall, who resides in a modern brick house adjoining." This modern house may be taken to be the present residence of Mr. William Henry Lloyd, J.P.. Mayor of Wednesbury (1892-4), situated at the junction of Crankhall Lane and Hall Green.

Continuing, Shaw says in further description of the neighbourhood at the close of the eighteenth century: —"In the road from hence to Barr, on the verge of the hill called Charley Mount, is a lofty neat looking house of brick, faced with stone, with iron palisade in front, and lately left by two maiden ladies, Miss Loyds, in a singular manner to the Rev. John Hallam, D.D., dean of Bristol." This name should be Lowe, and they were cousins to Dean Hallam (father of the great historian), after whom no doubt Hallam Street was named. Continuing Shaw's extract, it runs:—"The opening valley (of the Tame) is rich and pleasant, and the surrounding country very picturesquely broken, being enriched by the beautiful seats of George Birch, Esq., at Hamstead; Joseph Scott, Esq., at Barr; and the Earl of Dartmouth at Sandwell." The glorious prospect over which Shaw has gazed, and which was the scene of Sir Samuel's daily life is now on the fringe of the murky Black Country divested of nearly all its early beauty.

Reverting once more to the manorial residence of Sir Samuel Clarke with its beautiful surroundings of orchard, garden, and pleasaunce all nestling in the shelter of a well-wooded situation; the Lordship of West Bromwich (of which this domicile and domain were the outward symbols) passed to

(24) Samual Clarke, his son. He married Mary Elizabeth Jervoise, daughter of Thomas Jervoise, Esq., of Herriard in Hampshire, who was descended from William Jervoise, a mercer of London in 1551, and whose descendents enjoyed Weoley Castle in Northfield 274 years. As reference to chapter xxv. will show, this family of Jervis, or Jervoise, had also been lords paramount of West Bromwich.

In 1746 there was a parochial dispute about the Stanley Trust at the church in which Mr. Samuel Clarke took a very prominent part.

(25). Jervoise Clarke, son of the foregoing, succeeded to the estate and changed his name in accordance with the terms of a will of his maternal grandfather, becoming known as Jervoise Clarke-Jervoise, Esq. He was a man of commanding presence and some celebrity, and as previously recorded, became a Member of Parliament. Of him Mrs. Willett writes:—"He was buried in January, 1808 in the family vault within the Parish Church (probably in what was originally the Stanley vault) at the North-East end. When the Church was taken down in 1871, it was necessary to ascertain the position of all the vaults that were in it. The Clarke vault was opened in the execution of this purpose, and the coffin of Jervoise Clarke-Jervoise, M.P. was a very conspicuous object in it. To judge from the coffin, which measured 6ft.6in. in length and 2ft. 6in. across, its occupant must in life have been a very fine man."

(26), Thomas Clarke-Jervoise succeeded his father, but becoming deranged the estates and the Manor House were sold under an order of the Court of Chancery about 1819. At that time there was plenty of fine oak timber growing on the estate, which with what manorial rights were then left, passed by purchase to Lord Dartmouth, after being held for a brief time by its former steward, Mr. Joseph Holford. At the re-opened sale, the purchase money amounted only to some £700. At that time the Pound, the Stocks, and the Whipping Post stood opposite the church, at the corner of Hollyhedge Road and Cemetery Lane, where a cluster of trees has since been planted, presumably to mark the site. All were removed to the present site of the Pinfold at the corner in front of the Ring o' Bells Inn, but the Stocks and Post disappeared about 1849, when the police force were first established in Seagar Street. In olden times Sandwell was an independent "liberty" with its own franchises, as explained in chapter xxiii, But at the present day no vestige seems to remain of the ancient manorial form of government, unless, indeed it be the Pound. Newer forms of government, and more modern institutions pervade the whole of the West Bromwich of to-day.

XXVIII.—West Bromwich a Parish: The Advowson: The Dedication of the Church.

West Bromwich, as a Manor, has received due consideration: now to view it as a Parish. For it is certain that the place, as a separate and distinct entity, existed first as a Saxon Manor. It is not so certain that it was a Parish before the Norman Conquest. While of the first fact we possess historical evidence, of the latter we possess only evidence presumptive.

Arguments have been adduced to prove that a church was first erected in West Bromwich as early as the Saxon period. Briefly recapitulated these are: (1) The commanding site occupied by the church which overlooks the wide stretch of the Tame Valley, and is such as was always chosen by these early church founders, who made their sacred buildings landmarks, as well as rallying places in times of panic and attack by the pagan Danes. The enormous strength still so common to church towers may be traced to this original use of them as watch towers and towers of refuge. The Danes are known to have come up the Tame on many marauding expeditions, and not a few Midland churches are still said to have remnants of human skin nailed on their ancient doors; for it became a practice of the revengeful Christian(!) Saxons when they did gain the victory over the raiders to flay the Danish leaders, and affix their unfortunate hides on the doors of the church, as a warning to other pagan rovers—just as gamekeepers still nail owls on barn-doors; (2) Its situation on an ancient road. It is the one from the great Watling Street, via Queslett, Great Barr, Bromwich (Stone Cross and Hall Green), Wednesbury (Hyde's Road, Walsall Street, High Bullen, and Dangerfield Lane), Darlaston (Catherine's Cross) to Wolverhampton. At West Bromwich a branch runs out below the church, and round the back of Sandwell towards Handsworth and Birmingham. Another branch from the church corner runs to Oldbury, Hales Owen, and the salt district of Worcestershire. Although all these are ancient roads they were at first mere trackways, and then bridle-paths and ultimately became designated highways, although they were never literally "high ways" lifted above the general level for the crossing of swamp, fen, and undrained country, as the Romans practised the art of road-making, unless, indeed, the first-named one from Queslett is the Blake Street of the Romans, as has also been suggested.

Thus much for its surmised foundation in the Saxon era. Of its existence during the later Norman period undoubted internal evidence still exists. But leaving the fabric for later consideration, other matters ecclesiastical may for the nonce claim our attention.

Had the close juxta position of the priory at Sandwell any great influence upon the parochial church? Incidentally many such influences and direct bearings have already been suggested. At Dudley priory the monks were of the Clugniac branch of the Benedictines (chapter x), but unlike the majority of the Clogniac houses in England it was not colonised from Burgundy or France; yet a prior of Sandwell in 1373 was stigmatised by a local litigant as "a monk subject to" the alien Abbot of Cluny (chapter xxii). Was there then, owing to the presence of the priory, any foreign influence brought to bear directly upon the Monastery, and indirectly upon the parish of West Bromwich in general? Although no answer can be definitively given to such a question it certainly offers food for reflection.

The large controlling powers of the Bishop of Lichfield over the affairs of Sandwell Priory, have frequently been noted—(see also Chapter xxii). Perhaps the earliest authentic record of this diocesan authority is the confirmation of the gift of the advowson to Sandwell from Worcester monastery, by the Dean and Chapter of Lichfield in 1255. In this fact of direct episcopal supervision there is again something worthy of cogitation for the mind ecclesiological.

Much has already been said in passing relative to the advowson, or right of presentation to the living of West Bromwich. The earliest record appears as a grant of the Monastery at Worcester to the Priory at Sandwell, between the years 1224 and 1238. The appointment of a "vicar" was noted in chapter xxii; the monastic owners of the great tithes performing parochial duty through one of their own "regular" clergy was a practice somewhat rare, and indicative of a desire to retain as much as possible for themselves. This "appropriation" of Church funds by a religious community is perhaps justifiable; but the "impropriation" by a layman is little less than a sacrilegious robbery. And yet how few of the lay aristocracy hesitated to accept Church property from Henry VIII at the Reformation (chapter xix). The great tithes of West Bromwich and the patronage of the church passed, with the despoiled lands of Sandwell Priory, first to Luna Clifford (1558), then to the Whorwood family (1609), and finally to the Dartmouth family. To learn that in 1843 the Earl of Dartmouth gave £7,481 to the Governors of Queen Anne's Bounty for the augmentation of the living of West Bromwich, is indeed refreshing reading, savouring as it does of a just act of conscientious restitution.

The holder of the benefice, acting vicariously for the priory which held the great tithes, was known as *Vicar*. There was, after the Reformation, a *lay rector*, who held these, in succession, In later years the holder of the benefice retaining none of the tithes was designated a *perpetual curate*, a name which a quarter of a century ago was abolished by Act of Parliament, whereby the holder of the benefice is now properly designated Vicar of West Bromwich.

The County historian Shaw says of the living that it was—

"A *rectory* before the Dissolution in the patronage of Sandwell Priory, but since then the rectorial tithes having been granted to the owner's estate, it has been only reckoned a *donative* in their gift."

By letters patent, 1587, Queen Elizabeth granted the rectory of West Bromwich to Edward Holte for 21 years, at the conclusion of this term, namely, in 1608, by freshletters patent, James I. granted to Francis Gofton, John Osborne, and Sir Henry Fenshaw, Knt., the rectory of West Bromwich. In the following year they sold the living to Sir William Whorwood. In 1701 Thomas B. Whorwood sold the advowson to William, Lord Dartmouth.

*   *   *   *   *   *   *

As late as 1801, according to Shaw, this church was dedicated to St. Clement, while it is now designated All Saints' Church. The possible explanation of this given by Mrs. Willett (p. 33) is scarcely satisfactory. First of all it is evident that the change of dedication was not made (as seems there suggested) at the Reformation; for the church was still known as St Clement's at the end of the last century. Secondly, West Bromwich *wake*, even in the most flourishing days of those annual carnivals, was never of such local importance as those in most of the neighbouring parishes, perhaps because the population was so widely scattered when West Bromwich was but a village community: as it indeed remained up to the beginning of this century. The incidence of the annual wake is always good evidence of the dedication day. When West Bromwich Church was dedicated to St. Clement, the Fair, Wake, or other annual celebration, would undoubtedly fall on or near the day of that patron saint, whose name appears in the Calendar on November 23rd. But the weather at this period of the year, to say nothing of the overshadowing influences of the rapidly approaching Christmastide would militate against any extensive celebration of what was practically an out-door festival. Even at the present day, when the *Wake* celebration has been put forward three weeks, (All Saints' Day is November 1st) the early closing-in of the damp and chilly days forbids would-be revellers to indulge in much open air sportiveness. Therefore there would be little cause for interfering with the holding of Bromwich Wake. But why was the change made? Perhaps it was accomplished at some ultra-Protestant period, when exception was taken to the celebration of other than biblical saints, and when special objection was laid to the Romish practice of promiscuously canonising bishops and other fathers of the church. (St. Clement was bishop of Rome, A.D. 67, and is mentioned by St. Paul in his Epistle to the Philippians. As however a large number of popes had adopted the name of Clement, this may have made it objectionable to some people). Many Wakes were held a fortnight later after the change in the Calendar (1752) from the "old style" to the "new style" of reckoning, although only 11 days were omitted by Act of Parliament that year, namely from September 3rd to September 14th. So that the change from the Julian to the Gregorian calendar while it affected Wednesbury Wake, Darlaston Wake, and other surrounding dedication festivals by putting them a fortnight later in the year, would seem to have put West Bromwich Wake three weeks earlier, which is highly improbable. And, as has been argued, its want of popularity would make the annual holding of the Wake a matter of much indifference to the common people of West Bromwich. Therefore, for this change of canonical patronage from Clement to All Saints, a more subtle reason must be sought—perhaps it was brought about by an excess of religious zeal, or it may have been by the very opposite.

XXIX.—The Fabric of the Church: Five Successive Edifices

I.—That West Bromwich existed as a Saxon *manor* is a fact which has been satisfactorily established, but whether in that same era it attained sufficient importance (by the aggregation of population, or otherwise) to have the services of a priest allotted to it—in other words, to have become a *parish*—is extremely problematical. The existence of a Saxon Church has not been clearly proved.

II.—Of the existence of a Norman Church there exist a few fragmentary pieces of evidence to this day. These are a small shaft and two capitals of Norman design which were accidentally discovered at a recent restoration, with a praiseworthy spirit of veneration they have been inserted for preservation inside the bell tower, probably not far from their original location.

The Norman Church, to which these undoubtedly belonged, dated from about the time of Henry I. As an ecclesiastical structure it would reflect the military spirit of the age by being heavy and massive, and, therefore, as dark and gloomy as its size was diminutive in serving the small requirements of those times. There would probably be the tower then a nave, and thirdly a chancel to terminate the line. This church may have been erected by the piously inclined Offney family mentioned in chapters viii and ix.

III.—The structure of longest duration, however, was probably the FOURTEENTH or FIFTEENTH CENTURY CHURCH, which replaced the previous one. It would be not only lighter and more graceful in every feature, but it would most probably be of considerably larger dimensions than the Norman Church. The architecture of this period would produce a building at once beautiful and ornate, for the art of embellishment was about then at its highest; the enlargement would probably consist of the addition of an aisle. To this decorated edifice further additions are known to have been made at two different times. The first was the Stanley Chapel, erected some time just previous to the year 1575.

The Stanley Chapel is thought to have been at the eastern extremity of the north aisle, as a door step was discovered there in 1871 leading to another floor level. The ancient glass of the Stanley Chapel is said to have been removed to Sandwell Hall in 1854. The faint traces of a fresco and text, believed to have been in this chapel were also found on the old remnant of the original north east wall of the church in 1871.

A further enlargement took place in 1619 by the building of the Whorwood Chapel on the south side. From this period steady decay in the fabric, met always by a debased style of architecture at each attempted renovation, would unfortunately but inevitably set in. Not enriched embellishment, not even restoration as dictated by a reverent spirit or guided by a cultured taste, but mere patching up would prevail at every successive undertaking in the way of reparation. Of the old structure but three vestiges remain to this day. There is the Font, dating, perhaps from a transitional period between the Norman and the Early English; there is the Tower a portion only of whose ancient masonry is now visible to the eye; and the Whorwood Chapel, now used as a Choir Vestry, but whose ancient stones are hidden inside an outer casing put round them at the very last of the numerous restorations. Renewals and repairs of one sort or other have naturally been going on at all periods.

Repairs seem to have been undertaken in 1619, at the time the Whorwood Chapel was erected. The discovery of a beam in which was cut the inscription, "H.T.H.D. 1677," would seem to point to some renewals that year. Another inscription carved in the south porch set forth that this portion of the edifice was repaired in 1706. Perhaps other alterations were made when the existing sun-dial, which bears the names of the churchwardens, Thomas Jesson and T. H. Beeson, was inserted in the south side of the Tower.

IV.—We come now to the EIGHTEENTH CENTURY CHURCH—the "Old" Church of the present generation.

In 1786-8 was carried out, under the name of renovation, what was, perhaps, the greatest act of vandalism to which any church has ever been subjected. The eighteenth century was dull in architecture, if not almost dead in the ecclesiastical branch of the art. Even Shaw placidly writes of these extensive alterations when the greater part of the ancient fabric was taken down and rebuilt, that,

> "The body was much renovated and enlarged, the side aisles being raised, and the whole converted into one large space (!), handsomely pewed, with new galleries round, new pulpit," etc.

Mercifully the tower was spared, as was also the Whorwood Chapel, which afterwards came to be used as the family pew of the Dartmouths.

This restored edifice of 1787 was essentially typical of eighteenth century work. It was as plain as the interior of a barn, and had the usual disfiguring galleries round three sides, the organ being perched up in the middle of the west gallery, and as far as possible from the three decker pulpit which it faced. In later years the galleries were extended along the north and south walls right to their eastern extremities, along which they at first reached but half way. They were so rude in construction that when they were finally taken out they were used as a grandstand on a common recreation ground. The chancel was merely marked off by a strip of moulding along the whitewashed ceiling; in fact, two chancels, if they may be so-called, were thus modestly indicated. Dr. Wilkes, of Willenhall, a learned writer, who lived from 1690 to 1760, had previously made mention of three chancels, east, north, and south. In all probability the north one would be identical with the Stanley Chapel, while the south one may have been the Whorwood Chapel; this latter supposition may at first appear somewhat far fetched till it is remembered that the Stanley Chapel is actually designated a "chancel" in an old manuscript.

In the ancient chapel there were formerly seven marble effigies; of these two only are still preserved. They are at the east end, in the first arch between the chancel, and what is now called the Sandwell Chapel on the south side of it.

Shaw describes all the various monuments, and then says "When the church was repaired most of the above-described monuments were destroyed." The families represented were those of Whorwood, Stanley, Sheldon, Page, Turton, and Addenbrook. More inscriptions are then quoted for the purpose of perpetuating them, and the names on these are Sheldon, Stillingfleet, and Jesson.

The two effigies still preserved are alabaster figures of two members of the Whorwood family, and date from the earlier half of the seventeenth century. They were relegated to the coal-hole in 1787, and are consequently much mutilated. The other five were actually burnt to provide lime for the devout builders of 1787.

What vicissitudes befel this ugly edifice it matters little now. In 1794 a clock was placed in the tower from the manufactory of Thwaite, of London. The single dial now set on a lozenge-shaped tablet on the west front seems to be above the place originally occupied by a circular dial. In 1823, when the project for building a new church—the present Christ Church—was being actively pushed forward, some very extensive alterations were seriously contemplated by a vestry meeting. A recent newspaper writer describing the church, says:—"The upper part of the *steeple* was re-built in 1824." This statement is manifestly wrong in its descriptive language. West Bromwich Church has always been, as Shaw in 1801 describes it, "an old *tower* structure." Most probably the embattled parapet and the crocketed pinnacles at each corner of the tower were renewed at that time. Only the middle parts of the tower therefore, remain of the ancient fifteenth century church. The lower stage of the tower has been re-cased, but as the new masonry was not bonded in with the old stone work it was not considered safe to carry the casing higher. It was rightly felt in 1888 that the tower would stand in its present condition for another century or so. So that the exigencies of architectural construction here harmonised with the right feeling of antiquarian sentiment, and the upper stages of the tower have considerably been left to the view of the parishioners in the same state as that in which the eyes of their forefathers have gazed upon them for some four centuries past at least. The louvre windows are in an earlier Perpendicular style, although the general style of the present building has been kept in that of the Decorated period, which just preceded it.

During the period that the Dartmouth family used Sandwell Hall as a residence they naturally took very great interest in West Bromwich Church of which the earls are "lay rectors." In 1847 they presented an organ valued at 300 guineas. When in 1854 Lord Dartmouth relinquished the use of the Whorwood Chapel as a family pew, it was converted into a Vestry, while the site of the former Vestry was utilised for the extension of the chancel, the enlargement and beautifying of which were also carried out at his lordship's sole cost.

This "old church," as it is still fondly called by aged parishioners, was swept away in 1871, when a rebuilding and remodelling was undertaken on more artistic lines.

V.—THE PRESENT CHURCH is, therefore, a very good specimen of careful "restoration" work. It resembles the 15th century church in its general features, but not exactly in the original arrangement. The nave is now on the north and its single aisle is now a south aisle. The tower originally flanked the nave on its western side, but at the re-building of 1871-2 the tower was considered too narrow to regulate the width of the new nave, and it was, therefore, determined to effect a transposition of nave and aisle. The tower, therefore, now flanks the subsidiary aisle and not the larger nave as formerly, (that is, in the "third" church, not in the "fourth" which was a four sided structure, whose "aisles" consisted merely of passages between the rows of pews) and the tower arch is left open, except for a slight glazed screen, to disclose the ringers.

The clergy vestry is now at the extreme east of the south aisle and beyond the "Sandwell Chapel." The choir vestry, as already mentioned, is the old Whorwood Chapel.

But the great restoration and re-building of 1871 has been more than sufficiently described by Mrs. Willett. It remains now to record the renovations that have been made since that year.

To celebrate the Jubilee year of Queen Victoria, who is the titular head of the Church of England, the parishioners of West Bromwich deemed the repair and enrichment of their parish church a most appropriate commemorative work to undertake at such a time. A sum of nearly £2,000 was expended and the church was re-opened September 9th, 1888.

All the roofs have been entirely renewed with new felt linings. The flooring is now of wood blocks, with marble mosaics down the aisle, and right through both the nave and the chancel. The new oak seats or rather open benches, are as convenient as they are sound in design.

The two front benches are marked with heraldic shields: that on the north with the borough arms showing that it is reserved on state occasions for members of the Town Council; the end seat also having the brass bracket used as a Mace-rest in front of the Mayor: that in the centre of the nave with the family arms of the Dartmouths, presumably indicating the modern substitute for the old-fashioned square family pew which has passed away.

*　　*　　*　　*　　*　　*　　*

By way of recapitulating the various transformations the fabric of the church has undergone nothing can be more to the point than a description of the Mosaics on the chancel floor. As already stated these formed part of the latest renovations undertaken at the Jubilee of 1887. They were designed by the architects (Messrs Wood and Kendrick), and executed by Burke and Co., of London. The description now quoted may be found on a framed drawing of the Mosaics which hangs inside the church:—

EXPLANATION OF THE MOSAICS.

"The object of the five central designs in the chancel is of a two-fold character. First of all they are intended to commemorate the *five churches* which have stood upon the existing site since Saxon times. Accordingly the canopies surrounding the central figures have been designed either in the known style of the church it is intended to commemorate, or, where this is unknown, in the particular *style of architecture* prevalent at the period during which the church was erected; and where the exact date of the building of the church is known it has also been introduced. The *first* church was erected in Saxon times, no remnants of it, however, have come down to modern times.

The *second* was built in Norman times, and it is supposed that the remnants of Norman work now incorporated in the belfry wall, were part of this structure. This latter church was succeeded by a building erected in the *fourteenth century* and re-modelled in the *fifteenth*. Of this building the tower is the only part now standing. Then followed the structure now spoken of as the "*Old Church*," erected 1786 and finally the *present building* in 1872. The first medallion therefore on entering the chancel commemorates the Saxon Church, and the canopies surrounding the central figure represent the Saxon style of architecture in which the church was most probably built. The second medallion commemorates the Norman Church, the third the 14th and 15th century Church, and so on.

In the next place, the figures introduced into these medallions are intended to illustrate the dedication of the church to "All Saints." The figures therefore do not represent any particular person or persons, but the various historical manifestations assumed by the saintly life in the history of the church from the beginning, and as the saintly life was not, and is not, the monopoly of one sex, two of the subjects, the Sister of Mercy and the Martyr are represented by female figures.

In the first medallion is the figure of an Apostle, representing the perfect life.

In the second is the figure of a Sister of Mercy representing the monastic or the devotional life.

In the third is the figure of a Doctor, representing the teaching life.

In the fourth is the figure of a Martyr, representing the suffering life.

In the fifth is the figure of a Confessor, representing the militant life of the Church.

Thus are represented in one way or another each of those particular aspects which the saintly life has assumed from time to time in its conflict with the world, and the symbols with which each figure is surrounded are full of suggestive teaching. The top symbol throughout has reference to God, and the bottom symbol to the world, while those on the right and left hand describe the general character of the saints in the world to come, and are therefore common to each figure. 'They that be wise shall shine as the brightness of the firmament; and they that turn many to righteousness as the stars for ever and ever'—Dan. XII., 3."

Then follow explanations of the various symbols which are added to the central figures of each panel. Thus:—

Figure 1.—An Apostle. Upper Symbol, *a throne* typifying the reward of the perfect man. Lower symbol, *feet treading on a serpent*—triumph of a perfect life over the Enemy.

Figure 2.—Sister of Mercy. Upper symbol, a *descending dove*; lower symbol, *an ascending eagle*, the two signifying the devotional life.

Figure 3.—The Doctor. Upper symbol, *a fisherman's rod and line*, typifying the drawing of men out of the world; lower symbol, a rising sun, which symbolises the ultimate triumph of truth over error.

Figure 4.—A Martyr. Upper symbol is a *crown*, typical of the reward of those who endure to the end, and the lower one is a *palm of victory* to accompany it.

Figure 5.—A Confessor. Upper symbol is a *wrestler's crown of laurel* for those who wrestle with difficulties, and the lower one is the Christian's armour.

All this work of adornment has been one untiring labour of love on the part of the Vicar, the Rev. M. M. Connor, M.A., to whom the executants of the work are indebted for all the ideas and suggestions they have so artistically carried into effect.

XXX.—SYMBOLISM IN THE FABRIC OF THE MODERN CHURCH, AND HOW THE REFORMATION CAME TO WEST BROMWICH (1553).

So long as symbolism is legitimately employed—as it was in the Mosaics described in the previous chapter, and as it is in the oak carving now to be noticed—as a mere expression of fanciful ideas in an adornment of some fabric, no possible objection can be taken to it. But when symbolism has been used to enforce some doctrinal teaching, as in the ceremonial of a religious service, it has often aroused fierce controversy and a bitter hostility which has manifested itself in all too active animosity. Religious wars and persecutions too often have thus arisen. How much bloodshed has the Christian symbol of the cross alone been responsible for?

The use of screens in churches is older than the word "chancel," for the word "chancel" is derived from, the Latin *cancelli*, signifying "lattices," "rails," or "cross-bars," a contrivance with which the clergy and choir were screened off from the congregation. Above the screen which was temporarily placed in West Bromwich church after the restoration of 1871, there was afterwards put up a large carved cross of a richly decorated character. That temporary screen has now given place to a newer and more elaborate one.

The new chancel screen has been erected to the memory of Samuel Lees, who died December 13th, 1890, during his term of office as Mayor of the borough; and also of his parents; and was dedicated on All Saints' Day, 1891. It is of oak, in the style of perpendicular Gothic, and accords with the general architecture of the church. It is divided into five bays by moulded uprights, the upper portions of each bay being filled in with finely carved tracery and cusping; an elaborate, but not too heavy cornice, surmounts the whole. Above the centre stands the Rood or Cross, the remnant of the old temporary screen. On each side of the central bay the dado is filled in with pierced tracery and cusping, with moulded rail and carved bosses, the central opening itself giving admission through handsome gates of wrought ironwork. But among the most distinguishing features of this Screen are the four detached pedestals which stand well out to the front, carrying angels or cherubim; two of which guard the entrance, and two command the extremities.

Here once again comes in the symbolical significance of nearly all outward matters ecclesiastical. As the screen divides the two main parts of the church—the nave from the chancel—so does death, which it represents, divide the Church militant on earth from the Church invisible resting beyond. Above the gate of death stands the cross, by which to Christians the sting of death is removed. On either side is set a guard—as at the entrance to Eden cherubim guarded the "tree of life." Again, at the extremities ministering angels are represented as standing ready to bear the souls of the just to Abraham's bosom.

The full span of the chancel arch is filled in by the screen, which measures 26ft. 3in, across, and rises to a height of 15ft.

The donor of this screen was Mr. Charles Lees brother of the deceased Mayor. The whole is of local production entirely, the design being from the office of Messrs. Wood and Kendrick, of West Bromwich. The carving was executed by Mr. Bridgeman, of Lichfield, and the wrought iron gates were the work of Messrs. Hart, Son, Peard, and Co., of Birmingham.

Shortly after the presentation of this one a similar screen was placed in front of the Sandwell Chapel, at the east end of the South aisle. This is divided into three bays: the central bay has two folding gates with pierced tracery and cusping, harmonising with similar work in the two side bays. The rails are moulded, as are also the uprights, which have miniature buttresses and crocketted terminals. In the tracery will be found two shields bearing the monograms of the departed who are intended to be commemorated; while the bosses carved in the tracery of the gates are elegant floral designs to specially represent the flowers in which they in life were particularly attached—primroses, snowdrops, and Correa Speciosa. This idea for commemorative design is certainly worthy of imitation. The cornice of the screen is finished with finely carved oak brandishing, and in the centre is fixed (on a carved base) the oak cross which formerly stood in the centre of a former screen.

At the foot is carved the inscription—"To the Glory of God, and in loving memory of our parents Job and Mary Haines, and Others of the Family, May, 1893."

This screen also is from the designs of Messrs. Wood and Bendrick, and was executed by the same carver, Mr, Bridgeman, of Lichfield.

Leaving the harmless symbolism of decorative design, let us go back in the history of the church to the time when religious controversy raged around these materialistic representations of great spiritual truths. Three centuries ago it was almost too difficult for the human mind to grasp the idea that the Divine Being was a spiritual essence. So it hankered after outward imagery—and, said the reformers, made too much of this.

In the neighbouring town of Kidderminster may be seen a statue of the great divine, Richard Baxter. What says he of symbolism and ceremony? In his *Church History* we may read—"Multiplied and highly adorned vestments, lights burning on altars, acolytes, etc., are adaptations of heathen rites, introduced at a period during which Christianity and Paganism were struggling for ascendancy as the religion of the State, and ending in a virtual compromise, whereby the ritual of the latter was applied to illustrate the creed of the former."

Before the Reformation such outward forms and visible signs may have been absolutely necessary when the use of a liturgy in Latin made the service unintelligible to the bulk of the congregation. But when an English service was compiled for the use of an English speaking congregation, the reformers claimed that such necessity no longer existed.

* * * * * * *

The dawn of the Reformation, as it broke over West Bromwich, we have already seen (chaps. xxii.—xxiv.) in the suppression of the religions houses between 1526 and 1539. Then in 1547 came the suppression of the Chantries. And now in 1552 the work of "reformation" is found going on in full swing.

In this year a commission was appointed (6 Edward VI.) to go round the country, examine the church property, confiscate all that was considered useless for the reformed services, and to leave behind only such as commended itself to the Protestant mind as absolutely necessary for conducting the services of the church according to the new ideas of the reformed faith. The Commissioners for Staffordshire were all men of high position in the county; and religiously sound they must necessarily have been to become the instruments of the ministers of Edward VI. Their names included those so well known locally to this very day as Giffard, Lyttleton and Wrottesley. On the one hand they had to put a stop to the embezzlement, concealment, and appropriation by private persons of much church property; and on the other to recover and retrieve as much as possible for the King's Exchequer, especially in the shape of church plate convertible into specie, and in money fines imposed on detected offenders. For under the pretence of a great burning Protestant zeal, a concerted system of sacrilegious spoliation had recently been going on, whereby marble coffins were found in stable yards as horse troughs, manor house walls were hung with rich altar cloths for tapestry, costly copes were made into bed coverlets, and ecclesiastical plate was in common use on the dinner tables of the gentry.

By the Spring of the following year the investigation at West Bromwich Church had resulted in a return, which shall now be given—first as it was originally set down in an English partly archaic, and then followed (item by item) with a glossarial explanation in modern English—

WESTE BROMWYCH.

Fyrste,
One challes of sylver parcel gylte with a paten.

> (*One chalice of silver, partly gilt, with a paten* to match. The "chalice" was the wine cup, and the "paten" was the plate for eucharistic bread, used at the Sacrament of the Lord's Supper).

ij   Copes one of blew velvet and the other of cremesyn crule.

> (*Two copes, one of blue velvet, and the other of crimson crewel.* A "cope" was the outer cloak of the priest's vestments used in the processional office; crewel was a cloth of fine worsted).

ij   Vestements one of blew velvet and the other off green crule.

> (*Two vestments, one of blue velvet, and the other of green crewel*).

iij   Candlestyks of brasse, one pyxe bownde abowte with silver, one crosse of latten.

> (*Three candlesticks of brass, one pyx bound about with silver, one cross of latten.* The "cross" and the three "candlesticks" were for the altar; "latten" was an alloy of metals, much resembling brass, but harder, and sometimes grained; it was often used in those times when silver was so dear; A "pyx" was a small box to contain the consecrated water—irreverently scoffed at by the followers of the new faith as "Jack-in-the-box.")

iiij   Alter clothes.

> (*Four altar cloths*, probably richly embroidered).

iiij   towells, one crosse clothe off grene sylke.

> (*Four towels, and one cross cloth of green silk.* The "towels" sometimes called "houseling napkins," were used at celebration of the Communion; all textile fabric were much more costly in those days. The "cross cloth" would be an altar cloth with a cross embroidered upon it.)

iiij   grete bells.

> (*Four large bells.* In these disturbed times even the church bells had often been stolen)

M.D. that there was ij Alter Clothes stolne out of the Churche, by whome the kno not; and also ther was solde by the consent of the whole parish iij candelstyks for the mayntenans of a bryge nyghe ye said towne.

> (This *Memorandum*, while it requires no explanation of its literal and verbal construction, is pregnant with significance. First, there is placed on formal record the fact that property had been *stolen out of the church, but by whom no one would divulge*. This perhaps points to the attitude of the public mind in West Bromwich—the place had very practically "protested" against Romish doctrines. The second point is an important one which cannot be dealt with in this chapter; it is the maintenance of public bridges—a subject which demands a separate chapter to itself, and which must be devoted to it later on.)

There is a second Memorandum to the effect that the Commissioners for Church goods duly delivered into the hands of the two Churchwardens, namely to Edward Hering, and John Hateley,—

On chales of Silver with a Patent.

(*One Chalice of Silver with a Paten.*)

ij Linen clothes for the Holli Communion Table.

(The careful reader will note here the substitution not only of the simple clean linen cover for the more elaborate drapery; but what is far more significant is the disappearance of the word "altar," and the use of "holy communion table" in its place.)

A surples for the Curat to minestre with.

(*A surplice for the Curate to minister with* was probably a plain alb, or linen vestment reaching to the feet. The minister is purposely designated "Curate" in preference to the word "Priest." The richer vestments, as well as the fine altar cloths, were no doubt sold by the Commissioners for the benefit of the Exchequer—in accordance with the terms of their instructions

iiij bells in the Stepull.

(All these "great" bells were left intact, although the small sacring bell, or handbell used inside, and the sawnce or sancte bell rung outside to signal the most solemn parts in the performance of the Mass, seem to have disappeared before the inventory could be taken—bell-metal was deemed precious in those days, and quite worth the stealing. At the present time there are eight bells in the belfry tower, but none of these date earlier than 1711. It is worthy of note that the word "steeple" is again used; but it may be with the same inaccuracy of descriptive language as was noted in chap. xxix.).

The document, indorsed "Westebromewiche," then closes in language which clearly reflects the unsettled opinions of the times, and most unmistakably points out a period of transition in matters of religious opinion and practice. At the end of this brief catalogue of church goods left in the custody of the wardens (and which were deemed quite sufficient for all the purposes of a reformed faith and practice) it says all "safelie to be kepte untill the Kinges Majesties pleasure thereto be furder knowen."

"In witenes whereof as well we the sayd Commissionars as the sayd Churchwardens to thes presents interchaungeabli have putto our hands the xiiijth of May, Anno Regni Regis. Edwardi Sexti, Septimo."

Thus it was that at the Reformation a great attempt was made to abolish from public worship in England so much of that symbolism in church ceremonial which hitherto had been used to "move" the ignorant to an understanding of deep "mysteries."

XXXI.—The Stanley Lectureship: How and Why it was Founded (1613): How it was Worked: and ultimately Transformed (1819).

For fifty years after the "Reformation," notwithstanding that this period synchronises with the "spacious times of Great Elizabeth," the confusion in matters ecclesiastical amounted to little less than anarchy. There were three parties, all of them contending with that bitterness and depth of hatred which always characterises religious feuds. There were first the old Catholics, and then there were the new Protestants divided into two irreconcilable camps, who, perhaps, detested each other more cordially than they did their common enemy the Romanists. Of these two the

State party seemed willing to come to some sort of a compromise with Romanistic practices (of course with the Queen as Supreme Head of their English Church) while the Puritans, who had practically been in existence from the days of Wycliffe, were then known as Separatists; and since then as Dissenters.

The bishops as a class aided and abetted their royal mistress, and upheld the arbitrary principles of Church and State. In the meanwhile the ministry sank lower and lower into disrepute many being so illiterate, that although they had cure of souls, they were quite incapable of preaching—the law only required, so far as public worship was concerned, that they should read the service and administer the sacrament in person once in half a year, or forfeit £5 to the poor.

Now the Puritan party always attached the greatest importance both to preaching and to the moral character of the clergy. They, therefore, began to band themselves together into *local societies* for introducing *further reformation to the Church, without separation,* Queen Elizabeth tried to suppress these associations, believing that *that three or four preachers in each county* would be amply sufficient. In this diocese the Bishop of Lichfield and Coventry showed some independence, boldly writing to his archdeacon (Neal's History of Puritans) to use "the heavenly and most comfortable gift of preaching."

Notwithstanding, all the associations for "exercises" or "prophesyings," as they were called, were suppressed for a time. The Queen imperiously declared that all reforms in religion should "arise from none but herself." Renewed persecution of the Purish clergy led to the founding of the sect of *Independents* by a clergyman in the diocese of Norwich, named Robert Brown. In 1583 the Court of High Commission became a veritable Inquisition in examining suspected persons. The ferment increased till the House of Commons summoned up sufficient courage to brave the royal anger and passed a bill for qualifying ministers. It annulled all Popish ordinations, and *disqualified such as were not capable of preaching,* or were guilty of immorality; and it insisted on a careful trial and examination of candidates by the Bishop, assisted by twelve laymen. The enraged Queen immediately reprimanded the Commons for their audacity, and forbade the Speaker to allow any bills which encroached in this way upon her supremacy.

To the Parliament which met on October 29th, 1586, the Puritan Ministers presented a Petition, accompanied by a "Survey" of several counties— Staffordshire amongst them. This document set forth "that the Bishops had made priest of the basest of the people, not only for their occupations and trades, whence they had taken them; as shoemakers, barbers, tailors, water bearers, shepherds, and horse-keepers, but also for their want of good learning and honesty." Even after this the Commons dared not reform the abuses—several members were sent to the Tower for even proposing to do so.

This *Survey* of 1586 contains the following entry relating to the parish of West Bromwich:—"West-Bromry,—Parsonage; impropriate to Mr. Whorlwood, worth £60. Many Popish. Curate's pension, £6; a layman; no preacher."

It is not to be wondered at that a little later in history we shall find the Whorwood family fighting staunchly for king and church; they seemed to have had a very considerable interest in what had formerly been church property. At this period they were generally residing at Stourton Castle on the confines of the county, but in 1609 they came to live altogether at Sandwell, on an estate which (till 1526) had been for centuries ecclesiastical property. At this period (1586) their possession of the impropriated revenues of West Bromwich Church was so absolute that Shaw designates it a "donative." When it is stated that the living of West Bromwich was a *donative* it implies that the patron could give the preferment as a free gift without making any presentation to the bishop, and without induction by mandate from the bishop or any other. No license would be necessary to perfect the donee's title to possession of the *donative*, for it received its full effect from the authority of the donor alone. Generally, it might he said to be exempt from all episcopal jurisdiction. In the case of West Bromwich this absolute power is all the more remarkable, seeing how much the original holders of the advowson, the Priors of Sandwell, had been under the control of the bishops of the diocese.

According to the *Survey* of 1586, the same Mr. Whorwood was also patron of the parsonage of "Enfield" (Enville) worth the then goodly sum of £100 a year; and held by Mr. Columbyne, a "non-resident and pluralitant," but acknowledged as "a preacher." The impropriated living of "Kinvar" was also leased from the Crown by this Mr. Whorwood; and although producing him £50 a year, the duties were performed by a "stipendiary" for £10; and as he was also set down as "a preacher" he must have been cheap at the price.

But returning to the entry relating to West Bromwich we note that the church was served by a "layman," who was "no preacher." for the small sum of £6 a year, while the revenues yielded as much as £60; and although, as recorded in the previous chapter, the Protestant zeal of the parishioners had led them to steal Romish vestments from the church and to sell other church property for the purposes of public expenditure, yet there still remained numerous parishioners who clung to the old faith—as it says, there were "many Popish."

But West Bromwich, when compared with other places at this time, may actually be said to be a fortunate place. The curates of Bilston, whose names are given as Mounsell and Cooper, are returned as "notorious drunkards and dissolute men." From Cornwall it was reported that the churches there were supplied by "men guilty of the grossest sins; some fornicators, some adulterers, some felons, bearing the marks in their hands for the said offence; some drunkards, gamesters on the Sabbath Day," etc, etc.

The *Survey of 1586* in summing up the whole matter, and attested by Justices of the Peace and other responsible persons, makes the following revelations:

"That after 28 years' establishment of the Church of England there were only 2,000 preachers to serve near 10,000 parish churches, so that there were almost 8,000 parishes without preaching ministers." And all these things were so in the vaunted days of Queen Elizabeth? Yes, but life was unceasingly active then, and events moved very quickly. Perhaps there was not sufficient time for quiet contemplation and the maturing of men's minds upon what were purely matters of opinion. In this same year, 1586, everywhere men were busy preparing a fitting reception of the projected Spanish Armada; which, however, did not come till 1588. In Wednesbury and West Bromwich tongues were busy in the ale-houses gossiping of Jesuits and seminary priests who had not departed the realm as they were expected to do and at whom the finger of suspicion was consequently pointed, as friends at least, if not actually emissaries of the Spanish Inquisition. Some had actually returned from beyond the seas, and were indeed wandering up and down the country disquieting men's minds at fairs, wakes, and markets. Other unpatriotic individuals—perhaps from "religious" motives, such as were held by the more bigoted Puritans—fanned the flame of discontent by stirring to incipient mutiny against a pretended famine. At Sedgley and at Barr the beacons had to be closely watched for fear these "lewd persons" should wantonly fire the beacon light, as had indeed been done at many beacon-hills in the country. In the straightest and largest range to be found under the shadow of the parish church, both at Wednesbury and at West Bromwich, as at all other places in the county, men were to be found on "every Holy-day until Hallow-tide next," after evening prayer practising their archery under the training of a specially appointed corporal in bands of "20 or 30 of the shotte." Under the supervision of the Earl of Shrewsbury, who was lord-lieutenant of the county, the *posse comitatus* or county militia were organised for active service. All the "men of ability resident" in each parish equipped themselves "with least expense to the shire," and were reduced into bands and companies "under ensigns and captains well affected to Her Majesty and the State, the eldest sons of the chief gentlemen, or others of like station." This was in accordance with instructions from the Lords of the Council, dated from Richmond Palace, August 2nd 1586. We know that all these orders were carried out in this locality, because it was reported through the Lord Lieutenant on the 19th of October following that the "footmen" had been organised as directed, that Sir William Aston and Richard Bagott had "viewed" them, and that one of the captains over them was "Thomas Whorwood, Esq." Amidst the commotion of all this marching and counter-marching, and the military activity in every parish of all these drilling bands, what time was there for the calm consideration of matters of mere opinion? At West Bromwich and Wednesbury men had to be up and doing, each parish band under the leadership of their respective local magnates—a Whorwood, of Stourton, or a Comberford, of Tamworth.

And so matters spiritual gave way to the urgency of affairs temporal, and for 27 years things ecclesiastical in West Bromwich dragged on in the condition we have so feebly and inadequately attempted to describe.

It was under such circumstances as these, when the church had sunk into so truly lamentable a condition, that the *Stanley Trust* was founded in West Bromwich. Of all the local efforts or local societies this was one of the best plans for coping with the national evil; and this was a layman's attempt to revivify a moribund church. The action of the Stanley family here contrasts very strongly with the attitude of the Whorwoods. The latter as farmers of lay impropriations made a profit out of the benefice, while the Stanleys found funds for a preacher or lecturer, who was to be distinct from and supplementary to the parson of West Bromwich.

Twenty-seven years after the *Survey*, and in the year 1613, Walter Stanley, lord of the Manor of West Bromwich, gave certain lands of very considerable value in Erdington, Aston, and Sutton, the revenue from which was to support a lecturer or preacher in the Parish Church of West Bromwich. Or, as the deed itself puts it, "towards the maintenance and finding of one honest, virtuous, and learned preacher ... according to the doctrine and religion now established in the Church of England," to preach "every Sabbath-day in the forenoon, and once every principal Feast-day, as on the Feast of the Nativity, Circumcision, Epiphany, Passion, and Ascension of Christ; ... to visit and exhort all sick persons within the parish; ... such preacher shall be a graduate of one of the Universities of Oxford or Cambridge, and a single man unmarried ... chosen by the feoffees and churchwardens; ... if any preacher chosen according to the purport or true meaning of these presents, shall be or shall become a drunkard or haunter of the ale-house, whore-master, or fighter or known to have or use any such notorious crime or fault ... he shall be displaced; and so from year to year on his good behaviour ... He shall be a Peacemaker ... He shall not marry nor take upon him any other cure or benefice during his abode there. He shall not at all meddle with serving the cure of West Bromwich which belongeth to the farmer or proprietor of the parsonage (unless it be upon very urgent necessity, and that very seldom)."

Such were, as briefly as they can be condensed, the chief terms of the Stanley Trust for providing a Preacher or Lecturer when the art of pulpit eloquence was at its lowest ebb in this country; as witness the fact that stereotyped sets of Homilies were prepared at the Reformation for ministers (who were not expected to preach) who should diligently read them to their congregations. (See "Article of Religion, xxxv," in *The Book of Common Prayer*).

Such were the stormy times which followed immediately for a century or so after the founding of the trust, that it was to all intents and purposes a dead letter. A pamphlet, published in 1815, gives an "Account of the Lectureship in the Parish of West Bromwich;" but the earliest authenticated working of the Trust shows that in 1745 the Rev. John Rann was holding the appointment, he was a clergyman and a graduate of Oxford, who held the incumbency of the parish for many years, and who thus violated one of the terms of the Trust by the filling of both these offices. In the meantime mismanagement and peculation seem to have been rife. A house belonging to the Trust disappeared, no doubt quietly appropriated by someone in a position of trust. About the year 1662, when the local iron trade was rapidly reviving upon the Restoration of Charles II., a large quantity of timber had been felled on the Stanley estate, near Sutton, for iron smelting; and with the money realised a house and land in Wednesbury had been purchased. Yet instead of an augmentation of the funds, the only benefit derivable seems to have found its way into the pockets of private individuals, long leases being granted to private friends of the trustees; no doubt "for a consideration." The Wednesbury estate strangely enough proved just as valuable an acquisition, for it was rich in mines which (as was almost essential in those early mining days of the last century) were very readily to be gotten. But again the smiles which fortune seemed to lavish upon the Trust were turned to frowns by—a law suit (1746-52). Eventually the trustees recovered the land, the lease of which had been the cause of the dispute, and also damages to the extent of £91. (In 1849 this land was sold for the making of the South Staffordshire Railway). The fact seems to be that in those days the practice was to treat the Trust property as if it were an absolute private possession. The Rev. J. Rann, for instance, pretended to give possession of the Wednesbury estate to his son-in-law, the Rev. Peter Jones; and the latter it was who had opened the coal-pits upon it which led to the aforementioned law suit. When the trustees tried to remove him from the lectureship, which he had also acquired, he refused to his newly-appointed successor in the Lectureship, the Rev. William Jabet, permission to enter the church; while as to the official residence of the Lecturer, the house claimed was declared to be the property of Lord Dartmouth, the original residence belonging to the Trust having mysteriously disappeared, as already mentioned. The Rev. W. Jabet, though elected in 1746, seems to have been kept out of office till the death of his rival, Mr. P. Jones, in 1752; but for a year after this event he held both the Curacy of the Church and the Lectureship as well. Then the offices were very properly divided, and the Rev H. Saunders became Curate, although the living was at this time under sequestration, owing to the heavy costs of the lawsuit. Mr Jabet held the Lectureship by yearly re-appointments till 1758 when the Rev. Edward Stillingfleet became Curate, and in the following year Lecturer as well. The poverty of the Incumbency seems to have been all-sufficient for repeatedly over-riding the terms of the bequest for both offices continued to be filled by one man till 1815; namely, in 1782, by the Rev. Abraham Elton, and in 1790 by the Rev. William Jesse.

It was on the death of the latter in 1815 that the parish was thrown into a fierce turmoil by a proposal to appoint, as usual to the dual offices, the Rev. C. Townsend. Opponents to the election, who objected that the candidate for the Lectureship was not a celibate, broke out into violent pamphleteering: nevertheless the Trustees made the election by six votes to four. The minority, confirmed in their attitude by an appeal to counsel, would have commenced a lawsuit so high did party feeling run, had not an opportunity for the final settlement of the question presented itself. An Act of Parliament was sought, and finally obtained (July 6th, 1819), for regulating the revenues of the Trust, half of which were to be henceforth devoted to the new church (Christ Church), the founding of which was then being actively and vigorously pushed forward. The other moiety was to remain with the Incumbent of the old church, who was to be permitted to take upon himself the duties of "Lecturer." This was a sensible compromise, because it legally allowed what had hitherto been almost the invariable rule; namely, the appointment of a married man, and the holding of both the Curacy and the Lectureship by one and the same individual. Moreover, thereafter there would always be what the Stanley Trust undoubtedly purposed to have from the very first— two clergymen officiating in the parish. The population was about 9,000 at this time and rapidly increasing. In 1840 a second Act was obtained which permitted the trustees to grant long leases of 99 years on their building estate. When these leases fall in the two ecclesiastical parishes concerned will no doubt be greatly benefited.

*   *   *   *   *   *   *

Although the Stanley family thus appear as thoughtful benefactors, the erection of the "Stanley Chapel" already recorded was not carried out at the sole expense of the Stanleys. The "new" chapel of 1575 "was made at the cost and charges of the whole parish" . . . "Malster Stanley made no more than glazed the windows in the east end of the chancel, and his portion as other men did." This statement (Ryder's MSS) is contemporary evidence, but may be prejudiced nevertheless: there is almost a tinge of jealousy to be detected on the face of it. Any way the new addition to the church was always designated the "Stanley Chapel." Walter Stanley could not found a chantry— chantries had been suppressed. He could not endow a chantry priest, so he founded a Preachership, which was the new equivalent.

XXXII.—HOLDERS OF THE BENEFICE FROM THE "REFORMATION" TO "BLACK BARTHOLOMEW" (1662).

It has been recorded how in pre-Reformation times the great tithes (of wheat, grains, &c.) of the parish were "appropriated" by the religious fraternity of Sandwell; and how in post-Reformation times the same revenues were held by "impropriation" by a layman. So far we can trace the ecclesiastical history of West Bromwich, naming the holders of the advowson right down to the present time. But it will be remembered that the priors of Sandwell also held the living of Ellesborough. What became of that at the Dissolution? The history of that distant Buckinghamshire parish would seem to have still been involved with that of this locality for a century or so afterwards. For among the Braye MSS., preserved at Stanford Hall, Rugby, are several bundles of ancient deeds relating to properties in various parts, and including some belonging to Ellesborough, alias Eselborough, Rowley, and Tybynton or Tipton. (These MSS. are not quoted, but merely referred to by the Historical Manuscripts Commission. The same published volume of the Commission, by the way, mentions that the Excise, which was then let out at rents to farmers of the revenue, produced for the year commencing September 29th, 1665, £312,180. Or this amount Staffordshire brought in the sum of £2,900.)

But to return to West Bromwich. The church as served in olden times by one of the "regulars" from the Priory, but how the services were conducted after the disturbed times of the Dissolution, and then of the Reformation, it would be difficult to say. It was a period of neglect as well as of reform and innovation. It would be interesting to discover who was the last priest of Bromwich of Romish ordination, and who first of the English ordination. The earliest of whom we have record was (1608) the Rev.

Thomas Johnson, in whose time the Parish Registers began and the Stanley Lectureship was founded. His seems to have been a strange experience. He was married one year (to Maudlin Sibbes, 2 November 1635), died the next (November, 1636) his posthumous child was baptised some three months later, and his widow was remarried, all within a year or two (28 April, 1638).

Then comes next (1645?) the Rev. Edward Lane, whose daughter's baptism is recorded 27th April, 1646, and who seems to have made way for a successor of more pronounced Puritanical views when Cromwell came into power in 1648. This was the Rev. Richard Hilton.

This brings us to the most interesting epoch in the history of the English Church. Mr. Hilton was one of those ministers who conscientiously declined to *conform* to those practices of the "reformed" Church of England which were deemed too closely allied with those of the Roman Catholic Church, and because of which, as "Protestants," they had seceded from the older hierarchy. In the previous chapter fuller allusion was made to these controversial details. Suffice it to say here that in all the parish churches of England the clergy had practically conducted the services according to the dictates of their own consciences, for there was no uniformity of worship throughout the length and breadth of the land. During the Commonwealth the authorities naturally levied towards the side of Presbyterianism. But the Restoration of Charles II.(in 1660) soon made its influence felt. The Presbyterians were persecuted, and the episcopal form of Church government took a new lease of life. In 1662 the *Act of Uniformity* was passed, compelling the service in every church, chapel, or other place of public worship, to include the book of Common Prayer, and the minister to declare his "unfeigned assent and consent to all and everything contained therein," and forbidding any person to preach or lecture in any part of England, unless with the permission of the Archbishop of the province, before whom he must assent to the "thirty-nine articles." When the Act came into force on St. Bartholomew's Day (August 24), more than two thousand ministers, holding Presbyterian opinions, formally left the church rather than comply with the obnoxious Act, among them Richard Hilton, of West Bromwich, that renowned champion of religious liberty, Richard Baxter, and many more learned and devout men, who preferred ruin and poverty to compliance with this rigorous law. The Rev. William Fincher, vicar of Wednesbury, resigned his living—very fittingly, on St. Bartholomew's Day, since his church was dedicated to that Saint—and left the parish, which a cruel law made it impossible for him to longer remain in.

Wednesbury sustained a great loss indeed by the harsh Uniformity Act of 1662. In order still further to harass and persecute the Nonconformists the *Conventicle Act* was passed, which provided that if more than five persons besides the family attended for public worship in any house or place, they should be fined £5, or undergo three months' imprisonment, for the first offence; £10 or six months for the second offence; and for a third offence £100 or transportation for seven years. Many preachers persevered and were imprisoned; and the Quakers especially dared to hold public meetings, and were imprisoned in large numbers; while ordinary religious people were afraid to pray in their own houses if five strangers were present as guests. This terrible persecution, however, did not suffice; and in 1665 the *Five Mile Act* was passed, which forbad any of the Nonconformist and ejected ministers to come within five miles of any town sending members to Parliament, or of any village in which they had previously ministered, under penalty of £40, and a further penalty of six months' imprisonment if they refused to take the oath of non-resistance. Still further, the ejected ministers were forbidden to keep any school. The great Richard Baxter had been a schoolmaster at Dudley Free School. Under such restrictions it became hopeless to continue public worship; but the very severity of these enactments, aided by the *Revocation of the Edict of Nantes*, scattered good seed abroad, and finally led to the triumph of that wide civil and religious liberty which had been so ruthlessly assailed.

Birmingham, as a non-corporate town, and not being honoured by sending a member to Parliament, soon became a true city of refuge for the persecuted and oppressed. Dissent from the Church rapidly increased, even in spite of a second *Conventicle Act* in 1670, which reduced the penalty on hearers, but enforced fines on preachers and those who lent their houses for religious meeting. Even after the death of Charles II. the persecutions were continued, the "meeting-houses" of Protestant Dissenters were closed, ministers were dragged from their pulpits, houses were visited and ransacked, and even the rooms of the aged and sick were invaded. Spies and informers abounded, and ministers had even to travel in disguise. The venerable and honest Richard Baxter was tried before the infamous Judge Jeffries, who denounced him as a "snivelling, canting Presbyterian," fined him five hundred marks, and sentenced him to be kept in prison till he paid the fine, and to be further bound "to be of good behaviour" for seven years. In houses where meetings were held, holes were made in the walls, so that the preacher's voice could be heard by more than one household, and in some cases trap-doors and passages were provided, so that he could escape arrest. The unconcealed Romanist views and practices of James II., however, alarmed the Episcopalians, and some proposals to pacify the Nonconformists were made through the "dispensing power" of the King. A license office was opened, and an indulgence granted (on the payment of fifty shillings) for permission of householders and their families to worship in their own way. A license dated April 29th, 1679, was granted by the Lords in Council "to Mrs Elizabeth Legge, a papist, to stay in town, she being very weak and sickly. She and her servant lodge in Berey Street, next door to the sign of The Dolphin, in St. James' Fields." This old lady was the widow of William Legge, and the mother of the first Lord Dartmouth. In Birmingham thirteen houses were licensed for worship to Samuel Willis, John Wall, Joseph Robinson, Samuel Taylor, Samuel Dooley, John Hunt, William Fincher, Richard Yarnold, Thomas Gibson, William Yarrington, William Webley, John Pemberton and Richard Careless, the fathers and founders of Nonconformity in Birmingham. Soon after a second declaration of "liberty of conscience," the first regular society of Nonconformists in Birmingham was founded, and the names of the ministers (November, 1684) were Brian, Evans, Fincher, Baldwin, and Spilsbury. There is a curious letter of that date, which describes these five as "now resident"; and then it adds, "we had some others and one Dr. Long, but he's now away. We have others which come to our town often, at one Sweetman, that lives 2 miles off at Mosely, and one Turton, a very dangerous Nonconformist, and it is said will suddenly be resident in Birmingham. As for Mr. Oasland, I am informed that he comes often in these parts. I know not the man, I am told he lives in Worcestershire, hard by Bewdley."

The "indulgencies" and "licenses" of James II. were followed by legal and not "dispensing" powers. When William and Mary came to the throne, and a farther but still a small instalment of religious liberty was conceded in 1689 by the *Act of Toleration*, which exempted "their Majesties' Protestant subjects dissenting from the Church of England from the penalties of certain laws therein mentioned," but did not include the *Test and Corporation Acts*, or those referring to all who denied the doctrine of the Trinity—Acts which remained in the Statute Book till almost our own days. Among the biographical sketches of Calamy are the following local names of the ejected ministers of neighbouring churches, the story of whose lives is full of interest:—Samuel Willis, rector of St. Martin's, Birmingham; Thomas Bladon, vicar of Alrewas; Thomas Wilsby, rector of Wombourn (Staffs.), ("who had some trouble for preaching in those parts especially from Sir Richard Holt, of Aston Hall"); Samnel Bryan, vicar of Allesley, "six months in gaol with great patience and cheerfulness"; Thomas Baldwin, jun., vicar of Clent; William Fincher, "ejected from Wednesbury, an heavenly good man and of a most sweet temper"; William Brookes, from Hintes (Staffs.); —Bell vicar of Polesworth(?) Josiah Bassett, of Cradley; George Long, M.D., ejected from Newcastle-under-Lyme, who after his ejection studied medicine at Leyden, settled at Birmingham, was persecuted there, fled to Ireland, returned to Newcastle, and died in Bristol, aged 84, in 1712, Samuel Fisher, of Thornton-in-the-Moor, Cheshire, who lived many years in Birmingham, preached in a licensed place of worship in 1673, and wrote a pamphlet "On Honouring the King," from his "Study in Birmingham, March 10th, 1673"; and William Turton M.A., the first minister of the Old Meeting House, Birmingham. This last named was no doubt connected collaterally with the West Bromwich family of Turtons.

For many of these particulars we are indebted to Calamy's *Nonconformists' Memorials*; and it may not be out of place to put on record here the characters of these good men in the immediate vicinity of West Bromwich, who two and a half centuries ago were content to give up all that makes life happy for conscience' sake, and to go forth into the world bereft of everything but their own self-respect.

The biographical extracts from Calamy must needs begin with West Bromwich; they need little or no explanation, except perhaps of the abbreviations descriptive of the benefices abandoned by these self-sacrificing men, as V for Vicarage, R for Rectory, C for Curacy, D for Donative, Chap. for Chaplaincy, and Col. Ch. for Collegiate Church. Calamy says:—

"BROMWICH (WEST). Mr. Richard Hilton, born near Oxford, and brought up in that University. He conscientiously discharged the duties of the ministry at this place till 1662, when he parted from a people who had a great respect for him. He afterwards spent some time at Philip Foley's, Esq., as chaplain, and then removed to Walsall, where he lived many years, and died about 1706, aged 82. He was a good scholar, a judicious divine, and all his days a hard student, a man of great simplicity and plain-heartedness, and a very substantial and useful preacher. His general talk was regular and exemplary. He was frequent and fervent in prayer, careful in the spending of his time, and exact in all proceedings. He had drawn up a covenant with God, which it was his custom to read over every Lord's Day morning to quicken him in his work. He was generally respected even by the worst of men; being quiet and charitable, and inoffensive in his whole deportment. In the close of his days, being asked about his Nonconformity, he professed an entire satisfaction in it, and hoped God would enable him, if there were the same occasion, to do the same again. He lived in self-denial among a poor people, doing good both to their souls and bodies; and when dying showed his great concern for their future provision and spiritual welfare.

WEDNESBURY (commonly called *Wedgebury*). Mr. William Fincher, younger brother to Mr. R. Fincher, ejected at Worcester; born at *Shell*, near that city; both of them had a liberal education. There was a third brother who was a Non-conforming minister. Mr. W. Fincher, after his ejectment, preached frequently at *Guarnal*, in Sedgley parish, and other places. At length he retired towards the place of his nativity, and often preached in the troublesome times at old Mr. Mence's, near Worcester, who had married his sister. He was a good and heavenly man, of a most sweet temper; very humble, and never seen in a passion. He was also a solid, close, awakening preacher. He died at Birmingham.

BLOCKWICH (chap.). Mr. Toogood.

LITCHFIELD. *St. Chad's* (£80). Mr. Thomas-Miles.

        St. Mary's. John Butler, M.A.

PELSHALL (chap.). Mr. Wilson.

ROWLEY. William Turton, M.A. (of the Brades, afterwards minister at Oldbury and at Birmingham).

RUSHALL (v.). Mr. Robert York, a religious, active man, and a lively preacher. He died young, of consumption, in 1667.

SEDGELEY (v.) Mr. Joseph Eccleshall. He left the university about 1654. On preaching a lecture at Dudley, some of the people at Sedgeley heard him and prevailed with their vicar, Mr. Parkes, who was old and infirm, to invite him to be his assistant. In a few years he succeeded to the living. He preached his farewell sermon on August 17, 1662, to a large congregation, all in tears. On August 24, no one coming to officiate, he went into a pew, prayed, read the Scripture, expounded and preached. Afterward, although he lived a mile from the church, he ordinarily attended public worship there and gave his hearers what personal help he could in private. The succeeding vicar, for some years, was violent. . . . The Oxford Act forced him [Mr E.] to Kinver, where he preached in private, and went afterwards with his hearers to church to hear Mr. Jonathan Newey, a worthy man who succeeded Mr. Morton. He then came secretly by night to his own people (not daring to be seen by day) to do what service he could, and returned by night till the rigour of the times abated. He then appeared in public and continued his ministerial work among his old people, with little allowance from them, living chiefly upon a small estate of his own. There were two meetings kept up in the parish because of its largeness, two or three miles distant [? one at Willingsworth], and Mr. Eccleshall administered the sacrament in both. Here he continued his service several years till he was silenced by death. His funeral sermon was preached by Mr. Oasland.

TATENHALL [R.] Mr. Thomas Buxton.

TIPTON [C or D] Mr. Richard Hinks. Before the Restoration he offended the neighbouring minister and other good people by his rigorous notions, and by assisting in raising soldiers for Lambert against Monk. (For further particulars of this *Independent*, and also of Rev. J. Eccleshall, see HISTORY OF TIPTON, Chap. XXII.). His successor, Mr. John Taylor, suffered him to live in the parsonage house upon easy terms. He was afterwards imprisoned for preaching.

WALSALL. Thomas Byrdal, M.A. He died a very little before the Act of Uniformity took place, but he had so far declared his mind that he may properly be numbered with the silenced ministers. (Here follows a list of this minister's works, all posthumous).

WILLENHALL, [Chap.] Mr. Thomas Baldwin, junior. He was probably the son of Mr. Thomas Baldwin, ejected from Chaddesley in Worcestershire. Though he might have been expelled from Willenhall Chapel at the Restoration, the proper place of his ejectment seems to have have been Clent.

WOLVERHAMPTON [Col. Ch.] John Reynolds M.D. He was ejected from hence In 1661," etc., etc.

This Rev. John Reynolds, who was ejected from Wolverhampton, is connected with West Bromwich also. A letter written the following year by Sir Bryan Boughton, says of him:—"Reynolds has been preaching at a conventicle, as he always does when plots are in agitation." His son also of the same name was a remarkable man. In 1721, he gave up a living in London and settled in Walsall, assisting the Rev. Mr. Godley as pastor of a congregation of Dissenters. This Rev. John Reynolds was a friend of the Rev. Matthew Henry, and the author of several well known religious works. His "Discourse of Reconciliation," was strongly recommended by Dr. Watts. While preaching at West Bromwich, in 1727, he was suddenly taken ill in the pulpit, and died at Walsall a few days later. This eminent divine and theological student was buried at West Bromwich, and in her Diary under date of March, 1738, Mrs. Sarah Savage says:—"Looking out of my window I see Bromwich Church where that excellent man, Mr. Reynolds was buried. I have desired that my bones may be laid by his especially that I may stand with him at Christ's right hand in that day." A *Life of Reynolds* gives full details of a good and useful career.

So much for these staunch upholders of religious freedom who flourished in this immediate locality. If any reader desires to have a clearer conception of what took place in 1662, the opening chapter of Mr. Walter Besant's novel *For Faith and Freedom* will give it. There may be read an account of the scene which must have been repeated at hundreds of parish churches on "Farewell Sunday," or "Exile Sunday" (as August the 23rd was called in that year), on the day previous to the "Black Bartholomew of England."

Complications in the ownership of advowsons and in presentations to livings naturally arose with the requirements of the new Act of Uniformity. The case of Sutton Coldfield rectory is one in point. This advowson had been purchased in 1586 by John Shelton, the Birmingham mercer, who was a trustee of Birmingham Grammar School. His grandson, John Shilton, who had bought the manor of Wednesbury, and was sheriff of the county in 1660, had presented to the said rectory in 1662, the year of the passing of the Act. But, being a Nonconformist, he found it an awkward position when family interest demanded that he should present his own son-in-law to the benefice, his daughter Katherine (sister to the second John Shelton who sold the two manors of West Bromwich and Wednesbury about 1710) having married one John Riland, "clerk." To simplify the situation, the Rev. John Riland "purchased" the living from his nonconforming father-in-law in 1689. The conflict between self-interest and the dictates of conscience was thus most ingeniously overcome.

XXXIII.—The Living of West Bromwich, and its Holders from 1662 to the Present Time

Taking up the thread of local Nonconformist history again, for a few more brief allusions, it may be useful to put on record again the fact that Birmingham Old Meeting was formed by three of the previously mentioned clergymen of the Established Church, who were ejected from their livings in 1662 by the Act of Uniformity. Many other Nonconforming divines were also brought into Birmingham, as recorded in the previous chapter. The three were Thomas Baldwin, jun. of Clent, whose name was recorded on a brass in the Old Meeting House, William Fincher, of Wednesbury, ejected from the vicarage of that town and whose virtues were also written in brass; and the Rev. William Turton, M.A., the first minister at the Old Meeting, who "was the happy instrument of forming a body of Presbyterian nonconformists into a regular society" in the year 1686. (A descendant of this last named is Sir Thomas Turton, Bart., of Starborough Castle, Surrey.) Mrs. Catherine Hutton Beale, in a work of historical reminiscences (published by Cornish Brothers) surmises that the religious opinions of these founders were at first Trinitarian, but being free and unfettered they soon afterwards became Unitarians. The chapel was erected on joint stock principles being built by eleven proprietors or shareholders The shares were £20 each, or £220 in total value. Under the chapel vaults formerly lay the remains of the Colmores, the Russells, the Bedfords, the Lawrences, and many other old dissenting families of the city. The building has been entirely swept away to make room for the enlargements of New Street Station.

To fill the place in West Bromwich vacated by the worthy Richard Hilton in 1662, came the more complacent SAMUEL ADDENBROOK, who held both the Incumbency and the Lectureship. During his term of office the Churchwardens' Books were commenced (1678); since when are to be found in them many useful records of Vestry Meetings for conducting parish business. A copy of the Terrier is in existence from this time, and is dated 1693. The fabric of the church as it existed from this time to the great alterations of 1785 has been fully described by Dr. Wilkes of Willenhall; there was a tomb to Matilda Addenbrook, wife of the Incumbent, dated 1709. He himself died, 1710.

His successor was the REV. JOHN RANN, in whose time the living was bringing in £20 per annum. This stipend allowed little enough for requisites of any kind: in 1723 this minister's "Master of Arts hood" had to be purchased for him by the Churchwardens.

During this Incumbent's tenure occurred the Sacheverell Riots (1715) when both the Meeting Houses in Birmingham were partially destroyed; and when the Tory "Jacks" came from Wednesbury yelling seditious songs in praise of the Pretender, and attacked West Bromwich Meeting House. Two of these rioters were shot. Thus much for "Church and State."

In 1743 Mr. Rann resigned West Bromwich for the better living of Rushall, where he died in 1771 at the age of 84. Of him Saunders' *History of Shenstone* says: "Damaris Dolphin, third daughter of John Dolphin, of The Moss, was wife of Mr. Rann of Caldmore, Walsall, late of the Delves, and minister of Wednesbury (?) yet Vicar of Rushall in 1769." Their daughter Damaris married the REV. PETER JONES, the next minister of West Bromwich and a Prebendary of Wolverhampton, whose transactions with the Stanley Trustees have already been alluded to.

The poverty of the living has already been disclosed in dealing with the maladministration of the Stanley Trust. To eke out the income no doubt no opportunity was missed for demanding fees at every performance of a religious rite. Reverting to the Terrier of the fees allowed to the minister of West Bromwich Church, of the data 1693, we learn that he was allowed all the accustomed "surplice fees," for every burial in the church 1s., for every burial in the churchyard 4d., and mortuaries according to the statute in that case made and provided. Respecting the latter the Rev. J. Rann thus certifies in the parish register:—"I do here certify that while I was minister of West Bromwich, I always received mortuaries from housekeepers worth forty-seven pounds and upwards in moveable goods, according to the custom of my predecessors. July 13, 1762."

The same registers record the following entries;—"1692: For breaking up the church 5 times, 16s. 8d. 1704: Received for breaking up the church for Hobbeage's grave, 3s. 4d. 1740: For breaking the church, 3s. 4d. 1744: For breaking the church, 6s. 8d." The breaking of the church means taking up part of the floor for the purpose of making a grave.

The incumbency of the Rev. Peter Jones probably terminated by financial difficulties resulting from the prolonged lawsuit between him and the Stanley Trustees, mental worry, brought on by the expense and uncertainty of the law, has killed many men. He died January 17th, 1752. Before his death he signed a Terrier (July 22nd, 1751) of lands and profits belonging to the Church: these included a house, two bays of buildings, a garden, and one-quarter of an acre of land; also the lands of Walter Stanley's Trust, together with the Wednesbury estate, producing £2 13s. 4d. per annum, which had been bought with the money realised by selling the timber on the said Trust lands, £20 a year paid to the Curate by the Impropriator, Lord Dartmouth; all the Burying Fees, viz., 6d. for burying in the Churchyard, 1s. in the Church, and 2s. in the Chancel, with a registration fee of 6d.; Wedding Fees—by banns 2s., and by license 5s.; and Mortuaries according to the Statute.

The repetition of this term "mortuary" brings us to an interesting antiquarian subject. The certificate given by the Rev. J. Rann is dated 1762, nearly twenty years after his resignation of the living; from which it is evident he had been appealed to in order to discover what the living could really be expected to reach. In explanation, the term *mortuary* signifies a sort of ecclesiastical heriot, being a "customary" gift claimed by and due to the minister of the parish on the death of a parishioner. It was, perhaps, a kind of expiation and amends to the clergy for the personal tithes and other ecclesiastical duties which the laity in their lifetime might have forgotten or neglected to pay—in fact, it was funeral conscience money. The "custom" evidently prevailed in West Bromwich to a considerable extent, and the way it was carried out was this:—

The "mortuary" was carried into the church along with the corpse when it was brought to be buried, and as it was a voluntary donation it was often designated a *corse present*. The custom varied in different parts. When a clergyman died the bishop sometimes claimed his best horse, spurs, bridle, and saddle, his cloak, hat, gown, and tippet, and also his best signet ring. When a prelate died the King could once upon a time claim the dead bishop's best palfrey with its furniture, his cloak, gown, and tippet, his best cup and cover, basin and ewer, his gold ring, and his mew or kennel of hounds.

The Rev. William Jabet succeeded Mr. Peter Jones, but as the living had been sequestrated owing to the excessive law expenses incurred by the previous holder, he held office as curate-in-charge for one year only. His only source of income was probably the Stanley Lectureship, and this office he retained for several years, from 1746 to 1758 in fact.

The Rev. Henry Saunders followed, but he is better known locally as the author of the *History of Shenstone* (of which parish he was afterwards curate), than as minister of West Bromwich. He never held the Lectureship, and as the living was sequestrated his connection with West Bromwich must have been an unremunerative one.

The Rev. Edward Stillingfleet became Incumbent in January 1757, when the living was released from sequestration; and he also in the following year succeeded Mr. Jabet in the Lectureship. He seems to have held both offices till 1782.

The Rev. Abraham Elton succeeded to the dual offices in 1782, and resigned in 1790 on succeeding to the family baronetcy, when he took up his residence as Sir Abraham Elton, at the family seat Cleeve Court, Somersetshire. During his incumbency it was that the great re-building of the Church took place in 1786.

This brings us to the consideration of another source of ecclesiastical income—*pew rents*. The second Churchwardens' Book commences with the year 1787, and the first entry relates to the redistribution of the pews and seats in the rebuilt edifice. Allusion has already been made (chap. xxix) to the fact that the Dartmouths claimed the old Whorwood Chapel as their family pew. The following is an extract from the first of the Churchwardens' Books—"March 9th, 1701,—We, the inhabitants of West Bromwich whose names are subscribed, doe hereby unanimously agree, consent, own and acknowledge that the Little Chancell that is on the South side of West Bromwich Church aforesaid, and all the propriety right, title, interest, claime, and demand whatsoever thereto belongeth to the Right Honourable The Lord Dartmouth, and soe to remain and continue to him and his heirs for ever, without any lett, trouble, denyale, interruption, molestation, or disturbance of us or any of us. Witness our names—Bayley Brett, John Lowe, Richard Sterry, George Simcox, Job Simcox, Richard Brooks, John Jesson," &c., &c.

This was the year (1701) when Lord Dartmouth had just bought the Sandwell Estate and the advowson of the church; the parishioners of West Bromwich were evidently anxious to propitiate the newly arrived magnate.

Some years later occurs the following entry:—"18th March, 1738—It is agreed at a Vestry Meeting that ye churchwardens shall assert and maintain ye Parishes right to the seat in the church now claim'd by Mr. Thomas Jesson and Mr. Jesson Lowe in case Mr. The. Powell's right to it be disalowed, at ye cost and expence of ye Parish."

In those times (and there are yet some few survivals of the same old custom) the right to sit in a particular pew in a church arose from either (1) *prescription as appurtenant to a messuage,* or (2) from a *faculty* or grant from the ordinary, the bishop having the disposing of all pews not claimed by prescription —that is, as the Dartmouths claimed theirs as being appurtenant or attached to Sandwell. When so appurtenant to a property, pews might descend by immemorial custom, without any ecclesiastical concurrence, from ancestor to heir.

Coming to still later times, a Vestry Meeting held in the "Workhouse"—perhaps because the Vestry itself was too small—resolved on April 3rd, 1775, "That the parish's right to all the sittings in the gallery shall be maintained at the expense of the parish, and the Churchwardens are hereby desired to support and maintain that right. And whereas certain persons have, without *proper leave and license from the parish,* taken away one of the seats in the upper part of the said gallery, containing nine sittings or more; and also made other alterations, the Churchwardens are hereby desired to take care that the said seat be *again put up,* and that everything be restored to the same state as it was in before such alterations. And whereas certain persons *calling themselves singers,* and others, have hindered and molested some of the parishioners in coming into the seats; and made other disturbances in the Church; it is hereby agreed that if any person or persons shall hereafter offend in like manner they shall be prosecuted at the expense of the parish, and the Churchwardens for the time being are desired to carry on a prosecution against them.—Edward Stillingfleet, Minister." Evidently this parson was at loggerheads with his choir over their sittings.

The entry of 1787 alluded to, was a notice of meeting for Monday, November 26th, to make allotments and appropriate the newly-erected seats, pews and sitting places; and to which were particularly invited all the subscribers to the re building fund. This notice was formally and carefully read out on the Sunday preceding the meeting. At the meeting it was resolved to appropriate and allot the pews among the subscribers in proportion to the sums they had respectively subscribed and paid. The Minutes most precisely set forth the details of the allocation then made—No. 1 pew "adjoining the Clarkes Reading Desk and opening into the south aisle, to the Rev. Abraham Elton, clerk, the present minister or curate of West Bromwich aforesaid, and to his successors, curates of the said parish for the time being." This was the vicarage pew. Then No. 2 went to the Whyley family of Oak House, No. 3 to John Wright; No. 4 to Richard Jesson, No. 5 to William Bullock the elder; No. 6 to Joseph Jesson; No. 7 to William Bullock the younger and James Bullock; No. 8 to Edward Elwell—this opened into the north aisle, and was adjacent to the seat of Jervoise Clarke Jervoise, Esq., Lord of the Manor; continuing on the north aisle, No. 9 went to Isaac Hadley Reddell; No. 10 to Elizabeth Lowe for the use of the aforesaid Whyley, Wright, Jesson, Bullock, Jesson, Bullock, Bullock, Elwell, Riddall, and Lowe, and their respective families residing and dwelling in the parish—a sort of common possession for these high and mighty families of West Bromwich. Then certain seats in the North Gallery, Nos. 11—17, were allotted to the lord of the manor for the use of himself, his tenants, and occupiers of his houses in the Manor. Several seats in the South Gallery, Nos. 23—27, went to Lord Dartmouth for his tenants on the Sandwell estate. Other appropriations have set against them the names, Thomas Penn, Joseph Barts, Charles Jevons, John Blake, and Daniel Whitehouse.

For similar proceedings see the *History of Tipton,* Chapter xxvi. In modern times, and chiefly through the efforts of a most admirable incorporated society, sittings have been almost universally freed. West Bromwich Church having received a grant in aid of its building fund from this society, is now under an obligation to throw open a certain number of its seats—as is duly set forth on a notice-board fixed at the entrance to the church in the south porch.

And now to resume the succession of Vicars:—

To the Rev. Sir Abraham Elton succeeded—in both Incumbency and Lectureship—the Rev. Wm. Jesse, who held the two offices till 1815, a period of 25 years. His son acted as his Curate during several years.

On the death of the Rev. W. Jesse, his son in-law the Rev. C. Townsend, succeeded to the living, and afterwards to the lectureship. The Act to amend the Stanley Trust and the building of Christ Church were incidents of Mr. Townsend's incumbency. He was unmistakably a pluralist, for besides these two appointments in West Bromwich he also held the Rectory of Calstone in Wiltshire.

His West Bromwich curate, the Rev. James Spry succeeded him on his resignation of that living in 1836. Mr. Spry died in 1865, and was buried out-side the east end of the chancel. His successor was the Rev. F. Willett, whose wife (a daughter of Mr. J. N. Bagnall, who wrote the *History of Wednesbury*), wrote the last *History of West Bromwich*. In 1881 Mr. Willett was succeeded by the Rev. Muirhead Mitchell Connor, M.A., of Corpus Christi College, Cambridge. As mentioned in Chapter xxviii., the Earl of Dartmouth in 1843 gave £7,481 in augmentation of the living, now producing £270 per annum. Nominally, it is a Vicarage, net yearly value £431, in the gift of the Earls of Dartmouth. See also the close of Chapter xxxi. for the division of the Stanley Trust Funds between the old Parish Church and Christ Church.

XXXIV.—Catholicism since the Reformation: "Auscott" (1694) and Oscott (1794) Sedgley Park School (1763); Father Ignatius and West Bromwich (1832).

One great blunder was committed by the Romanists at the Reformation. To combat the efforts of the Reformers they introduced into England the new order of Jesuits. Had they been content to leave the fight in the hands of the older hands, whose work for all the centuries they had been domiciled in England had been of a most beneficent nature, there had been more hope of success. With what regret we took leave of the history of Sandwell Priory in chapters xxiii. and xxiv. But the Jesuits were not only aliens, they were everywhere received as enemies to good order. Englishmen decline to welcome any stranger whose policy, whether military or religious, is avowedly aggressive. So the name of Jesuit became a by-word in England. It took at least two centuries to remove the national distrust of everything Catholic. From the reign of Mary to that of James II. English Catholicism meant daily self-sacrifice, and the life practised by its followers was one of devoted resignation and stern self-repression.

Between 1535 and 1583 there were no less than fifty-four put to death under Henry VIII. and Elizabeth, who are now designated English Martyrs, and whose festival is kept by English Catholics every 4th of May. In addition, there are 261 "Venerable Servants of God who suffered death in England for the Faith, from 1535 to 1681." It was a brief respite the Romanists enjoyed under the Catholic James II. They snatched "a fearful joy." But all this time, although the nobility who clung to the ancient faith might from time to time become a little too conspicuous to the public gaze, it is difficult to portray the retired and fearsome lives led by the humbler Catholics. And yet, as we read in chapter xxxi., there were "many Popish" in West Bromwich in the year 1586.

Before James II. could come to the Throne, however such was the public terror with which the reign of a Catholic monarch was contemplated by the average Englishman, that the whole of society throughout the land became honeycombed with plots and counterplots. Let us see how these intrigues affected society in this immediate locality whose history we are attempting to trace.

The most infamous of all these plots was known as the "Popish Plot." The central figure of the so-called "Popish Plot" was our local magnate, Lord Stafford, the victim of that notorious arch-liar Titus Oates. As affecting our local gentry it is on record that the unfortunate Viscount Stafford, lying in the Tower made an urgent petition to Parliament on 10th May, 1679, that Mr. Henry Vernon and Mr. Thomas Lane, of Bentley, two material witnesses at his forthcoming trial, and both magistrates of Staffordshire, should have express summons to be present on his behalf. It availed him little. After two years imprisonment he was arraigned (30th November, 1680), found guilty, and brought to the scaffold. Five years later the attainder was reversed, the Lords then declaring he had "died innocent."

The local gentry were naturally affected by these turmoils, more or less, in every neighbourhood. Just previous to the incident above recorded, an Indictment of Grand Jury before the Justices of Middlesex on 3rd December, 1678, found Henry, Lord Arundel of Wardour; guilty of high treason. This indictment, affecting a peer, was made returnable to Parliament on 12th April, 1679. Among the justices named in the record of indictment was Humphrey Wirley Esq. The Wirley family were connected with Tipton and Handsworth parishes.

The license to the "papist," Mrs. Legge (1679) was mentioned in chapter xxxii.

The absurd fear of a Catholic heir to the throne found a vent by the overhauling of the commissions of the peace, for fear that the magistracy should use their influence, which was then very considerable, against Protestant supremacy. The names of families involved in the history of West Bromwich came into prominence. For instance, Worthly Whorwood was placed in the commission of County Kent 9 March 1680; while Brome Whorwood had been removed from the Oxfordshire bench 21 February 1680. On 10 April of the same year (1680) Thomas Jervoise was removed from the Southampton commission of the peace. All these names were closely connected, either then or at other periods, with the history of West Bromwich.

And what of religious reprisals in foreign Catholic countries? In the reign of Charles I. (1628) England had actively interfered on behalf of the Hugenots and now in the reign of James II. when Louis XIV. was increasing the persecution of the French Protestants, a general feeling pervaded England, and manifested itself in parliament, in favour of the oppressed Hugenots. Before the revocation of the Edict of Nantes (1685) appeals were made throughout England, and on May 14th 1682 a collection made in West Bromwich Parish Church realised "the sume of £1 4s. 3d. for ye relief of distressed protestants driven out of ffrance." This record in the Church Books is "subscribed Samuel Addenbrooke Minister, Job Simcox, John Carles, Churchwardens."

But reverting to the "Popish Plot" there is a local connection with this historical episode which is even more intimate. In the hamlet of "Auscot" (this is the spelling of Oscott in Camden's *Britannia*, 1610), and in a house on the site of the present Maryvale Orphanage at Queslett there lived a priest whose name—singularly enough for our history—was Andrew Brommich (or Bromwich) who ministered to the wants of the Catholics of this neighbourhood. In 1679, owing to the excitement caused by the Titus Oates' Plot, he was seized and imprisoned at Stafford, tried before Lord Chief Justice Scroggs, and *sentenced to death for ministering as a Catholic priest*, For some reason not known, he was reprieved and finally released, he returned to his little mission which he served till his death, 15 October, 1702. An old chair, which belonged to this worthy priest, is still reverentially preserved in the College Museum at Oscott.

In 1685 James II. ascended the throne of England. The Catholics were not slow to take advantage of the fact, as may be gathered from many incidents in the history of this immediate neighbourhood.

In Birmingham, Masshouse Lane takes its name from the Roman Catholic Church (or Mass House, as such edifices were then called) erected in 1687, and dedicated to St. Mary Magdalen and St. Francis. The foundation stone was laid March 23rd, and the opening was performed by Bishop Giffard, of Madura, September 4th of the following year, and on 16th August, 1688, the first stone of a Franciscan convent was also laid adjoining to the Church, which latter was consecrated September 4th. The church was 95ft long by 33 feet wide, and towards the building of it and of the convent, James II. gave 125 "tuns of timber," which were sold for £180; Sir John Gage gave timber valued at £140; the Dowager Queen Catherine gave £10 15s.; and a Mrs. Anne Gregg £250. This would appear to have been the first place of worship put up here by the Romanists after the time of Henry VIII.; and even then it was not allowed to stand long; for the Church and what part of the Convent was built (in the words of the Franciscan priest who laid the first stone) "was first defaced and most of it burrent within to near ye vallue of 400lb., by ye Lord Dellamer's order upon ye 26 of November, 1688, and ye day sevennight following ye rabble of Birmingham begon to pul ye Church and Convent down, and saesed not until they had pulled up ye fundations. They sold ye materials, of which many houses and parts of houses are built in ye town of Birmingham, ye townsmen of ye better sort not resisting ye rabble, but quietly permitting, if not prompting, them to doe itt." The poor priests found shelter at Harborne, where there is another Masshouse Lane, their "Masshouse" there being a little further on in Pritchett's Lane, where for nearly a century the double work of conducting a school and ministering to their scattered Catholic flock was carried on. It is believed that St. Bartholomew's Church covers the site of the short-lived Birmingham "Mass House." So that from the days of Queen Mary this church was the first regular meeting place of the Catholics of Birmingham. It was indeed short lived. James II. abdicated 11 December, 1688, William of Orange having landed November 5th of this year of tumult and revolution.

Skipping the reigns of William and Mary, and of Anne, before anything else closely affecting the history of local Catholicism can be unearthed, we come to the Hanoverisn succession. There is a "List of Roman Catholick Non-jurors who refused to take the Oath to George I. in 1715," and which was printed in 1745.

Among the local names and forfeits are found the following staunch Jacobites:—

	£	s.	d.
William Davies, of Handsworth, yeoman	10	0	0
Robert Kildeck, of West Bromwich, bridle buckle maker	3	0	0
Thomas Parry, of Bilston, locksmith	3	13	0
William Smith, of Sedgley, naylor	–	–	–.

It was a century after the destruction of the Masshouse before the next Catholic Church was erected in Birmingham. This was St. Peter's Chapel, off Broad Street, erected about 1786, and whose windows were at first hidden away from the street frontage. This second edifice has proved a more permanent one.

In Wolverhampton, a chapel attached to the private residence of the Giffard family (who retained their old faith) was used even when public worship according to the Romish practice was proscribed by law. This church, SS. Peter and Paul's, in North Street, is still in use; adopted in 1725 and rebuilt in 1743, it is said to possess a singular feature common to many Catholic churches of that period—the secret passage so useful when "priest-hunting" was a recognised demonstration on the part of "good Protestants." For twenty two years this building, which can be described not only as "unpretentious," but as necessarily "retiring" for obvious reasons served as a cathedral to the Midland district, comprising parts of the Catholic dioceses of Birmingham, Nottingham, Shrewsbury, and Northampton. In 1804 Bishop Milner came to reside here, and is now buried in the vaults beneath the church.

Going back to the scene of the worthy Andrew Bromwich's labours, other priests succeeded him and the place at Queslett, near Oscott, evidently grew in importance; for in 1752 the Catholic bishop Hornyold (co-adjutor to Bishop Stonor, Vicar-Apostolic of the Midland District) had the mission house pulled down, and a larger one was built by subscription on the same site, so as to make a home if necessary, for the Midland Bishops of the Catholic Church. The Rev. Pierce Parry, who was priest of the Mission from 1782 to 1785, built a new chapel in 1778, which is practically the one still in use at Maryvale. His successor, the Rev. Joseph Berington, improved the building and laid out the grounds (1785–1793). The next priest, the Rev. Anthony Clough, died after a few months' residence, and then, till the founding of Oscott College, this mission was served by the Rev. John Kirk, then President of Sedgley Park School. It was with this good priest the idea originated of making Oscott an Educational Establishment.

From the Reformation to the French Revolution English Catholics had mostly to be educated abroad (at Douai, St. Omer, and Liege chiefly), but the latter event swept away these useful seminaries. By this time tolerant England had grace enough to permit the establishment of Catholic Colleges such as Stonyhurst and Oscott. It was exactly a century ago namely in 1794 that the Oscott Ecclesiastical College was founded, for the accommodation of six students by the Midland Bishops, Drs. Talbot and C. Berington This—"the old College," in the valley near Queslett, and now "Maryvale Convent and Orphanage"—was used from its foundation in 1794 till 1838, when the new Oscott College on the hill was erected to take its place. Its first president was the Rev. Dr. Bew who had fled at the Revolution, from the care of a Paris college and who held office here till 1808. Almost from the first it was decided to admit laymen as well as clerical students; and many Catholic gentlemen interested themselves in the management of the College; its popularity may be gauged by the fact that as early as 1800 the building had to be enlarged to accommodate 60 students instead of the 8 as originally intended—when projected merely as an Ecclesiastical College: this number grew to 72 in 1804.

Among the early students trained at Oscott may be mentioned, among many others of note, the name of the Hon. Charles Langdale (Charles Stourton), afterwards a leader of English Catholics; and Henry Howard, grandfather of the present Duke of Norfolk. A new student in 1804 transferred from Sedgley Park School was Henry Weedall, destined to be three times President of the College, and associated with it after history, welfare, and prosperous development.

In 1805 Francis Martyn, the *first Catholic Priest who had been entirely educated in England* since the Reformation, was ordained and sent forth from Oscott. He was sent to Bloxwich, and from there started missions at Walsall, West Bromwich, Stourbridge, Bilston, and Dudley.

Identified with the history of this locality is yet one more important Catholic institution—Sedgley Park School. After the "subversion" of their religion, Catholics could neither learn nor teach without exposure to heavy Penalties; parents were liable to £10 a month, and the Catholic schoolmaster to £2 a day. Education was therefore sought abroad at Douay, St. Omer, etc. Catholic schools were practically unknown in England from the reign of Elizabeth till the establishment of Sedgley Park School. No doubt there were many short-lived academies, as under a Rev. Mr. Palin at Rowney Wood, near Beoley in 1740, and one at Edgbaston about the same time. In 1762 the Rev. W. Errington opened a school at Betley, near Newcastle-under-Lyme on Lady Day of the following year (1763) the whole establishment comprising twelve scholars, was bodily removed in a covered wagon to Sedgley Park. This place, generally known locally as Park Hall, was a mansion of the "noble family of Dudley and Ward," and the removal of the family about the time Lord Ward was created Viscount Dudley and Ward afforded an opportunity for securing it at an easy rental. Thomas Giffard, of Chillington, became guarantor for the rent. In 1754 John Milner arrived as a scholar— he who became Bishop Milner in due time. John Bew, afterwards a Doctor of Sorbonne and President of Oscott College, was another famous scholar. A list of the notable men educated at Sedgley Park would be too long to print here. Associated with this school will be found such names as Walsh, Weedall, Francis Martyn (1790), and many who became either bishops or attained to other high positions in the Catholic hierarchy. A history of the school, written by one "parker" Dr. Husenbeth, and dedicated to another, the first Bishop of Beverley, was published in 1856 by Richardson and Son, London. It is illustrated by views of the school at various periods; and at the end is a most interesting glossary of words used at the school—quite worthy the attention of Dialect societies. Sedgley Park School was thus one of the first as it was one of the most famous of Catholic seminaries permitted in England after the Reformation. It has been closed some years.

With the more tolerant attitude of succeeding generations, and with the establishment of educational facilities, the re-planting of a Catholic hierarchy became possible about 1840. In 1838 St. Chad's Cathedral was erected in Birmingham from the designs of Pugin at a cost of £60,000. Even in 1848 there were but seven priests in the whole of Birmingham; there are now ten or twelve different Catholic churches. The cathedral, of course, was to become the seat of a bishopric. The present bishop is the Rt. Rev. Edward Ilsley, born at Stafford 1838, educated at Sedgley Park School and Oscott College; he succeeded Bishop Ullathorne in 1888.

The first Catholic Bishop of Birmingham, however was Dr. Milner, appointed Bishop Apostolic in the Midland District, with the title of "Bishop of Castaballa," and who died in 1826. It was owing to the prejudice in the minds of English Protestants against Catholic prelates being allowed to assume the actual titles of the diocese they governed that Bishops Milner and Walsh were designated by foreign titles, and were generally known as Vicars Apostolic. But in 1850 Cardinal Wiseman boldly took the step of changing this state of things, and on October 27th Dr. Ullathorne, previously known as "Vicar Apostolic of the Midland District," was enthroned as first "Bishop of Birmingham." This diocese includes Warwickshire, Staffordshire, Worcestershire, and Oxfordshire.

Although St. Chad's Chapel had been opened in 1813 by Bishop Milner, it is Bishop Walsh who must be considered the founder of St. Chad's Cathedral. It was in 1834 he presided at the preliminary meeting to consider the practicability of such a scheme. For 22 years he presided over this Midland District as Vicar Apostolic, and he died Vicar Apostolic of the London District 1849.

*   *   *   *   *   *   *

With West Bromwich there was connected, and that somewhat intimately, one of the most conspicuous figures in English Catholicism, which the nineteenth century has produced. This was Father Ignatius, otherwise the Hon. and Rev. George Spencer. This famous priest was a scion of one of England's noblest families, being the son of the Earl Spencer, K.G., who at that time (1799) was First Lord of the Admiralty. He was born at the Admiralty, London, December 21st of that year, but in 1800 was taken down to Althorp; he was educated at Eton and Cambridge, and in his twenty-second year took orders in the Church of England.

With the disappearance of the many legal disabilities in 1829, Catholics in England were enabled once more to lift their heads more freely. It was about 1830 that George Spencer left the Church of England to join the Church of Rome. After being received and duly ordained he was appointed by Dr. Walsh to begin a mission in West Bromwich. He "set about it immediately and got an altar for it from Lord Dormer in Walsall." His church in West Bromwich was opened on the 21st November, 1832, and he was settled down as a Catholic pastor near where he had hunted as a Protestant layman, and preached heresy as a Protestant minister." (The quotations are from *The Life of Father Ignatious, of St. Paul, Passionist* by Father Pius, published in Dublin, 1866). Father Spencer had applied to the Bishop for the poorest and worst mission in his diocese; it was because priests with private incomes could better subsist in poor missions that Bishop Walsh placed him at West Bromwich. From there he often visited his sister, Lady Lyttelton, at Hagley, but was only received on condition that he would not speak of religion. Going through Dudley on these occasions determined him to beg among his aristocratic friends in London for a new church he purposed building in Dudley; and for this purpose he actually went to the Duchess of Kent, whom he found with the Princess Victoria beside her. He seems, however to have returned to his West Bromwich Mission without having accomplished much, for he purposed shortly afterwards to start on a tour in Ireland "collecting alms for Dudley." But in 1835 he began to spit blood, and was fetched by his family to be nursed at Hagley, "allowing him to be set down at Stourbridge to say mass." His daily private life at West Bromwich is recorded in detail, and is described as self-denying and laborious. When he opened his Dudley mission he slept on the bare floor of what served as the sacristy, wrapped in a large cloak; he did this rather than sleep at an inn. A quoted letter dated 1837 says—"Mr. Mackey was engaged painting a picture for Father Ignatius for his chapel at West Bromwich, and we saw a great deal of him. He was devotedly attached to his sister." His "director" was the Rev. Mr. Martyn, under whom he served his novitiate to the work in Walsall, three months before he came to West Bromwich. Father Martyn seems to have taken the Dudley Mission as soon as Father Spencer had built the church there. A day-book of accounts for 1838 is printed, in which are many quaint entries, among them 9d. paid to the watchman, 6d. for sealing wax, turnpike 8d., and for a horse at Dudley 6s.—all reminders of other times and other ways in West Bromwich life. As a Passionist he preached, and as a good Catholic he continually prayed for the conversion of England. Of the treatment he sometimes had to put up with, it is recorded that some fellow spat in his face one day when he was "going to say mass in one of the little places he had opened near Bromwich"; an episode which disturbed the equanimity of the good man himself much less than that of his housekeeper. His private income was not large, yet he managed to found the Bromwich and Dudley Missions, and to give a large part of the land on which Oscott College is built, and to which he was removed from West Bromwich in 1839, and where it was felt his influence over the students (in the specially created office of Spiritual Dean), would be exceptionally valuable. In 1848, he undertook a peculiar mission—a begging tour through Birmingham, Wolverhampton, Derby, Nottingham, and Leamington, to obtain funds for a church of the Passionist Fathers (whose order he had joined in 1847) at Aston Hall in North Staffordshire. In his life and travels Father Ignatius was cosmopolitan. Keeping here only to his local influence, we again find him in the neighbourhood "giving a retreat" at Sedgley Park in 1850, and again in 1852. It is difficult in these days of religious freedom and universal tolerance to realise that it was only in 1852 that Lord Derby's proclamation was published against priests appearing abroad in the streets wearing religious habits. In 1853 Father Ignatius gave a retreat to his old parishioners of West Bromwich and to the nuns in Wolverhampton, having been in Dudley the previous year. As a sample of devoted industry we may read that, in mission work, "he preached morning and evening, heard confessions daily pledged 200 young teetotallers, and received £14 in voluntary offerings." And "this mission was his 242nd of the kind, and the number of his teetotallers, since he himself took the pledge from Father Mathew in 1842, was 60,000." After the strain of such a life as this, it is not surprising to learn that he fell down dead October 1st, 1864, while entering a friend's house in Scotland. His obsequies at Oscott were imposing, as befitted the termination of a career so extraordinary, of one born to luxury, but who had abandoned all and had become qualified for enrolment "in the catalogue of saints, as the first English Confessor since the Reformation."

The following is a contemporary account of the opening of Rev. Father Spencer's church in West Bromwich and it indicates the hopes and aspirations with which the undertaking was regarded by the Catholics:—

"On Wednesday, the 21st of November, 1832, a new church, dedicated to God, under the patronage of St. Michael and the Holy Angels, was opened for the celebration of Catholic worship, at West Bromwich. The Right Rev. Dr. Walsh celebrated High Mass on this occasion. There were present nearly 30 of the clergy, and after the Gospel, a Sermon was preached to an exceedingly crowded congregation by Dr. Weedall, president of Oscott College, and Grand Vicar of the Midland District, in which, with admirable power of reasoning and elegance of language he set forth the necessity of a Divine and infallible guide, like the Catholic Church, to lead men to a settled and reasonable belief of the mysteries of revelation. Oscott being but five miles from West Bromwich, a choir was furnished from among the students, who, under the direction of Mr. Sharman, performed the music of the High Mass with most excellent taste and perfect execution, and of course added exceedingly to the impressive effect of the solemnity. There were evening prayers at three, which were followed by a sermon from the Right Rev. Dr. Walsh, Bishop of the Midland District, who, in a feeling and paternal strain, exhorted the Catholics to adorn their profession with holy and exemplary conduct, and thus to overcome the prejudices which exist against their religion among their Protestant brethren, while he entreated the rest of his hearers to attend no longer to partial, and unjust representations of our religion from the mouth of its adversaries, and explained to them in particular the true principles of Catholics on several points upon which these mis-statements have been spread abroad. We are happy to say that satisfactory proofs have already appeared of the favourable impression made by these two sermons on this Protestant part of the congregation, who till then had perhaps few of them witnessed Catholic ceremonies, or heard the principles of religion fairly set forth. After this short account of the opening of the West Bromwich church, our readers will no doubt be pleased to learn some of the circumstances under which this establishment has been formed. We trust that the mention of them may be animating to the hopes of those whose hearts delight in watching the steps by which religion is recovering her ancient footing in England, and may encourage the zealous exertions of those whose life is devoted to this sacred cause. It is not many years since the strongest prejudices prevailed against our religion in this very neighbourhood, and the existence of a Catholic was hardly known in the place. What a change do we already see! Yet we trust it is but the beginning of a far greater work. We now see in one of the most conspicuous situations in this parish a beautiful Gothic church, capable of holding conveniently 300 persons, measuring in the clear within the walls 80 feet by 30, which at every service since the opening has been filled with a respectful and attentive congregation. The Catholic Church of West Bromwich may be called a daughter of that of Walsall; for the Rev. F. Martyn, of Walsall, was the person through whom were made the first converts to faith in this place, and the seeds were thus sown, from which we hope an abundant harvest may in due time be reaped. About four or five years ago the, Catholics here, who had no nearer place to attend their duties than Walsall, amounted to such a number as to justify the attempt to form a new congregation. The first plan was to purchase and convert into a chapel a small Dissenting meeting. But as a good title to this building could not be made and the prospects of success at that time, became so much more promising, this scheme was relinquished and the present handsome Church was begun under the direction of Mr. Ireland, the architect, and we rejoice to say that the confidence in Divine providence which encouraged the undertaking of this expensive work for the glory of God has not been disappointed, for unlooked for resources have been found by which pecuniary embarrassments, which it might naturally be expected would attend it, are in a fair way of being soon removed.

The Hon. and Rev. Mr. Spencer has been appointed to the care of this Mission, The indefatigable zeal, the unostentatious simplicity and humility, and the unaffected charity of this gentleman induce us confidently to hope that under the divine blessing Religion is about to make great progress in the new mission. Will not the faithful reader offer a fervent prayer to the Giver to all good gifts in furtherance of this desirable object?"

This edifice, which was a substantial structure of a Gothic character, very well served its purpose from 1832 to 1877, and would perhaps have been still a welcome memorial of the life and labours of Father Ignatius to many of his old West Bromwich parishioners. But the Rev. J. J. Daly thought the site at the corner of St. Michael's Street worthy of a more ambitions building. His enterprise, notwithstanding the doubts of many of the older and more discreet members of his congregation, brought about the erection of the present building, which was opened on March 19th, 1877, by Cardinal Vaughan, then Bishop of Salford. Its architecture may be thus described:—The plan of the church consists of nave, with north and south aisles and sanctuary with side chapels and a sacristy. The church has a central west doorway, with baptistery on the south; and the north aisle has a porch containing the staircase to western gallery, and a proposed future tower. (There is no attempt at orientation, by the way.) Internally the nave arcade has three arches on either side, with clerestory windows over. These arches are in richly molded bricks with stone labels, supported on massive stone piers, with well proportioned molded caps. The sanctuary has a rose window with the reredos under, and is divided from the nave by a rood beam, with the crucifix in centre, and the usual supporters, viz., the Blessed Virgin and St. John. There is a western gallery in which is the organ. The whole of the interior is lined with buff brickwork, and the aisles are stone flagged, and the church has open benches to seat 300 worshippers. The centre roof has massive timbers, and is of the waggon-head type of construction with lean-to roofs over the aisles. The fenestration is in the east, west, and northern walls, the southern not being available for light because of the adjoining priest's residence. Throughout, the whole edifce has been consistently designed and possesses the spirit of the middle French period of Gothic architecture. In the western front is a central arched doorway, and over it are three long pointed windows connected by lancet arches, surmounted by a rose recess, and the gable terminating in a richly floreated cross finial. On either side of the main gable treatment are massive buttresses, the one on the north being octagonal and containing the tower staircase. The north elevation is quietly treated, and has pointed windows with labels over. The whole presents a simple yet dignified effect, which, when the tower and spire shall have been built, will add to the architecture of the improving, if not already imposing, High Street of West Bromwich.

Since its establishment the parish priests in charge have been the Hon. and Rev. George Spencer, appointed 1832; Rev. George Bent, 1839; Rev. Thomas Revill, 1853; Rev. John Wyse, 1861, Rev. Louis Groom, 1863; Rev. J. J. Daly, 1872; Rev. E. A. Platsier, 1880; and the Rev. J. Fox, 1891.

*   *   *   *   *   *   *

Thus the history of Catholicism in this Midland district has been roughly outlined up to date, and West Bromwich has played no unimportant part in that history. It is happily a story of progress; from bigotry and prejudice to religious toleration, and from passive toleration almost to religions equality. *That*, too, will ultimately be reached if— no one church is allowed to acquire domination and unfair preference over the other in any direction whatever; not even in the matter of religious teaching in the public elementary schools, for instance. There can be no real liberty of conscience in the absence of absolute religious equality all round.

XXXV.—The River Tame in Local History: The "Tame Bridge Case," from 1606 to 1894.

So far we have treated of the human history of West Bromwich without particular reference to its natural features.

When a place possesses any striking and prominent physical feature—as a harbour for shipping, a rock for defence, or a hill to dominate the neighbourhood—it is easy to observe how readily that feature enters into the whole life history of the place.

The only physical feature of West Bromwich which attracts the least notice is a stream of very meagre dimensions, which almost encircles the parish till it makes of the place a kind of peninsula.

Streams have three chief uses, viz., for navigation, for irrigation, and for drainage. With regard to the first, a glance may be sufficient to discover that for navigable purposes this stream, the Tame, is altogether too small. It has been said that the Danes used the Tame water for their invading boats (see chaps. ii and iv), but it must have been then "overflowing," as its British name signifies, and not improbably it was then more frequently in this condition in some of its adjacent reaches; for instance, the Tame Valley would be flooded after every heavy rain fall. In the name "Bustleholme," the syllable *holm* is a Danish word signifying "an island in a river or lake," which would seem to point to both of these conjectures having a substantial basis—to a Danish occupation, and also to a flooded river sufficiently large for internal navigation. For irrigation and domestic water supply the Tame, like most streamlets, was once amply sufficient. For drainage, too, it once served every reasonable purpose required of it; but that was before the accession of a dense population to its banks, with manufacturing processes to pollute its waters and even to poison its banks. Of its present condition little need be said here except that it is now more like a dirty ditch, and, notwithstanding the efforts of local governing authorities and protecting Acts of Parliament, its cleansing capacity seems altogether too small for the density of population on its banks. Sewage farms and Drainage Boards have as yet done little to remove the cause of the threatened litigation—from riparian landowners and neighbouring corporations—which has been in the air ever since Lord Norton and the Birmingham Town Council suspended hostilities seventeen years ago. (It was in 1877 that a United Drainage Board was formed for Aston, Balsall Heath, Birmingham. Handsworth, Harborne, Kings Norton, Northfield, Perry Barr, Saltley, and Smethwick).

As a parish boundary the Tame serves as a clear line of demarcation to West Bromwich on every side except the south-east; dividing it from Oldbury, Rowley, Tipton, Wednesbury, Walsall, Great Barr and Perry Barr.

Natural water-courses were nearly always adopted in ancient times as boundaries between areas of different jurisdictions; it is important to remember that the Tame was so used as part of the ancient "metes and bounds" of Cannock Forest, whose government was described in chapter xii. In the early Plantagenet period the bounds of the Chase were thus legally fixed: They began at the Bridge of Finchespathe, descending by the Thame River to Holebrok, and thence by the brook of Holbrok to the vill of Waleshale, and thence as far as le Bolestile, and thence to the water called La Bourne, and descending La Bourne to the high road near the Park of Drayton, and from that road near Watlingstreete as far as the Thame River . . to the Trent . . the bridge of Coven . . by road to Pendeford, Fossemoore, Oxley . . Wolverhampton, and by the high road to the bridge of Finchepathe.

The River Tame rises in two main heads: one, the northern, on the borders of Cannock Chase, with several subsidiary feeders from Essington, Wednesfield, and the outskirts of Wolverhampton, joining it near Bentley; and the other in the south, on the borders of Worcestershire, near Warley, Rowley, Dudley and Tipton, both joining together at Bescot. The former coming into Wednesbury through Darlaston is sometimes known as the Willenhall Brook, and is met at Bescot by the Walsall Brook. The latter, coming into Wednesbury at The Bridge is joined there by the Lea Brook, now a foul ditch from the adjacent Chemical and Iron Works. This head (also joining the first at Bescot) flowing northwards from the Dudley and Tipton side of West Bromwich, makes a bend after confluence at Bescot, and flows back again in a southward direction towards Barr and Handsworth, passing Hamstead Hall on the right and Perry Barr Hall on the left bank. Joined by the Rea near Saltley, it passes on through Fazeley towards Tamworth. Its pollution after passing through all this populous manufacturing district of the Black Country is the subject of a complex problem, which the various local governing authorities have been for a long time engaged in trying to solve. With the enormous access of population during the last century the stream cannot of itself, and unaided by some artificial means, be the natural scavenger to the district it was in ancient times, and at the same time retain its purity. No fishing can be expected from its filthy malodorous waters now-a-days. Waterpower is superseded by steam-power, and its mill dams have disappeared. In place of them may be found sewers and drains emptying their sewage and trade refuse into the stream. For a full and scientific account of the river in its present condition there may be consulted THE POLLUTION OF THE TAME with map (Steen and Co., Wolverhampton, 1891) by Mr. Herbert Manley, the medical officer of health for West Bromwich.

As the Tame once passed through a thickly wooded district it was very favourably situated for working mills without the expense of storing large bodies of water in pools or dams; at a very early period this natural feature was taken advantage of as is manifest from the large number of ancient mills formerly situated along the Tame banks.

Our history in this connection will almost exclusively arrange itself round the two institutions connected with water-courses—namely, Mills and Bridges. In the latter connection we shall see the course of traffic and communication, first of a military character and afterwards of a commercial nature. With the former will be associated the progress of industry; from peaceful agriculture to military manufactures, and finally tending towards those general hardware products for which the district is so famous. The growth of mills along the streams of all the district around this side of Birmingham, and now known as the Black Country, is the best evidence of their original importance. It would seem that the most petty stream capable of storing sufficient water to fill a mill dam was called into requisition at an early period of the manufacturing era. When feudalism had died away, and men had time to devote themselves to the arts of peace this was the case nearly everywhere. For instance, the Edgbaston "bourn" and the Rea at Edgbaston Lane had each its mill; then there were

Speedwell, and Pebble Mills and Ladywell Spring, and a cutting or channel from the Rea turned two more mills near Birmingham old manor house, the water returned to do duty again at Deritend, at Saltley, and at Nechells.

But the most valuable mineral resources were found on this side of Birmingham; hence the heavy trades remained here even when mill-power was no longer a necessity. Still it is interesting to remember that the little brook from Handsworth was diverted to supply and work Aston furnaces (a remarkable instance of economy and adaptability) and lower down this water supplied a corn mill at the Birmingham boundary, and again a thimble mill at Nechells and at least one more before it reached the Tame. The water of the Tame itself was greater, and all the mills from Bustleholme to Kingsbury have an older and a more lasting look about them. All these survivals of the mills themselves or their names, serve to remind us of the time when a mill was one of the proudest distinctions of a lordship, and as worthy of notification by the king's surveyor as a church.

With regard to the history of iron smelting before the era of Dud Dudley, and his exertion about the middle of the seventeenth century to introduce the use of pit coal, all furnaces were fed with charcoal, that is, with charred or chark'd wood from the forests. As the woods of the Black Country rapidly disappeared under this system, new furnaces had to be erected – further and further away from our mines of ore, where the woods were yet unburnt, as at Erdington near Bromford Forge, at Aston near Aston Furnaces, and at Witton and Perry near Holford Forge. And so the centre of the iron trade was moving away from Wednesbury and West Bromwich till the use of our mineral fuel brought it back again.

Then not only the increase of mill power, but the conversion of many of the greatest power mills from corn to blade mills, affords an insight into another advance in trade, and also the treatment of iron ore for the making of iron "piggs." Even Dud Dudley had gone as far as Little Aston to do his smelting, while the Jennens family of Birmingham in addition to working Aston Furnaces, were using their great wealth to establish iron works even further away from the coal pits of Wednesbury and Tipton. In the reign of Elizabeth (1599) a lease of a Hammer Mill and "Chafery" (an iron-forge) at Little Aston upon Coldfield was granted to Thomas Parkes of Wednesbury. To this work there was a "Finary" (or second forge for "refining") and subsequently it was carried on by Philip Foley (1681). The families of Parkes and Foley may be claimed amongst the earliest of English ironmasters. They were the originators of the practice, when the woods and forests here were first exhausted, of taking the iron stone to the woods elsewhere.

*   *   *   *   *   *   *

Incidental to the Reformation in West Bromwich it was recorded (chap. xxx) that in 1552 "there was sold by the consent of the whole parish three candlesticks (part of the ancient church furniture) for the maintenance of a bridge nigh the said town." This indicates in a most unmistakable manner the importance attached to bridges in olden times. The art of road making may have been lost; but where a bridge had once been built it was never allowed to disappear altogether—hence the extraordinary and unusual effort to raise funds for the repair of this bridge "nigh" West Bromwich. Three observations may be made on this transaction: (1) the value of the candlesticks would be considerable because all wrought metal was highly prized in those days; (2) although bridges were never allowed to pass away entirely, they were often in a state of great dilapidation where (as was evidently the case in West Bromwich) no regular income was provided for maintenance and repair; and (3) it is difficult to suggest what bridge it was which was here the common care of the "whole parish."

Tame Bridge, near the Delves, is a county bridge dividing the parishes of Wednesbury and West Bromwich. The repairing of this bridge was formerly a condition attached to the possession of two closes of land, situated on the left-hand side of the road, just over the bridge towards West Bromwich. To this condition there was also added an obligation to repair the road skirting the said land.

This land, and the obligation attaching to the possession of it, belonged for a long time to the Corporation of Walsall. Very recently, however, the land is said to have been freed from this ancient obligation and has become enfranchised by the payment of a lump sum to the County Council of Staffordshire, who undertake all future responsibilities in respect of the repairs to the said bridge and of the adjacent length of road way. The removal of ancient landmarks has made it difficult to determine how far that length of roadway, the repair of which was thus provided for, extended beyond the bridge. The first clue would be the extent of the "two closes" originally charged with the cost, the distance of the second close from the bridge being clearly the limit of the obligation. Originally the necessity of maintaining Tame Bridge in sound condition, as set forth in the trust, imposed a liability to keep in good repair "a wooden bridge, and way adjoining as far as a place called *Fryars Park Corner* at a certain tree standing in a lane called *The Dead Woman's Buryall.*" If these place-names appear on the West Bromwich Tithe Map, or on the Estate Plan in the office of Lord Dartmouth's steward ("Fryers Park" being part of his lordship's estate) then all doubt and uncertainty as to their exact location will be set at rest at once and for ever. If, however, these two place-names are lost, we must proceed to the identification of their probable location by inference. By the construction first of the Canal, and afterwards of the Railway, it is apparent to the most casual observer that the road from the bridge into West Bromwich parish has been considerably diverted. The carrying of the road over the railway was evidently accompanied by a considerable shortening of it. The direction in which Tame Bridge itself "sets" will indicate that the ancient road wound round towards Friar Park and then came back again into the present road near the old cottages at the foot of the incline to the railway bridge. It is this diversion of the ancient roadway by the railway engineers that has probably caused the loss of the old landmarks—for "Fryers Park Corner" is undoubtedly in the direction of the Park, towards which the old Tame Bridge still sets.

Besides mentioning a "lane," the old records distinctly call the place a "corner." This would seem to indicate that from the ancient *road* over the bridge there also set off a *lane* from a certain *corner*; in other words we had here a junction of two roads, or two lanes, for the "road" in question was never a turnpiked highway. This junction was the nearest approach the locality afforded to a "cross roads," and it was in this spot that some "dead woman" had been afforded a hasty and an unceremonious buryall." It may have been that the "dead woman" had been found drowned in the stream; that there was the usual parochial dispose as to which of the three neighbouring parishes was liable for the interment of the unknown unfortunate, and as an easy way out of the financial difficulty the uncharitable but very common verdict of *felo de se* was returned, so that the body might be buried readily and cheaply in the public highway, a custom abolished only in 1823.

For nearly three centuries disputes have arisen as to the liability for these repairs.

In 1606 an Inquisition was held at Wolverhampton before William, Lord Pagett. Robert Stanford, knight, and others, when evidence of the liability of certain feoffees of Walsall, seized of a close in West Bromwich and near Tame Bridge, "to keep in repair a bridge called *Tame Bridge*, and a wooden bridge, and a way adjoining as far as a place called *Fryers Park Corner* at a certain tree standing in a lane called *The Dead Woman's, Buryall*," was given on oath by Roger Fowke, of Aston, gent., Thomas Coxe, of Coxe Green, gent., and others. These feoffees were the Corporation of Walsall, and they duly acknowledged their liability, and repaired the bridge. A copy of the proceedings of this Inquisition is preserved in the Town Chest of Walsall, and the ruling of the Commissioners will be found explicit. (Calendar of Walsall Deeds, 159).

In 1782 the Walsall Corporation accounts showed that the borough paid a certain sum to Mr. Elwell for the work of repairing the Tame Bridge.

In 1837 Reeves writes:—Tame Bridge Meadow belongs to the town of Walsall, and the rent of £5 per annum is applied for the repairing of the bridge over the river there, and of the road leading to and from it. In 1855 another inquiry also decided that the Corporation of Walsall were legally liable for the repairs to Tame Bridge. The last time the question was raised in a court of law was a few years back, at Staffordshire Quarter Sessions, and it was then stated that the Corporation admitted their liability, and were actually then doing the work.

In a similar manner Fullbrook Bridge divides the parishes of Wednesbury and Walsall, and in this instance the liability for maintenance is said to have been borne out of the Moseley Dole, belonging to the latter borough.

With the introduction of newer forms of government it was only to be expected that modern ideas would end this old-world arrangement—for it was indeed a very common idea in olden days to charge certain lands and properties with the repair and maintenance of roads and bridges, and this was because local government was then scarcely organised up to the point of looking after lonely places distant from the centres of population. The County Council for Staffordshire have therefore wisely made it their duty to terminate the old-fashioned and unsatisfactory state of things which has prevailed so long. At the present time Mr. Franks holds the two fields near to the bridge, and under the conveyances of such lands was liable to maintain the bridge. To terminate a tenure so antiquated, and to get rid of the ridiculous responsibility whereby the care of a public bridge was in the hands of a private individual, he entered into negotiations with the County Council and agreed to pay them £100 on condition that they adopted the bridge and that portion of the road approaching thereto which he was liable to repair. This may or may not have been an equitable arrangement, but it certainly possessed the merit of being a definite settlement of a very long standing difficulty. The county at once proceeded to spend at one outlay more money than they had received. The road which Mr. Franks, under his covenants, was liable to repair, was the road over the bridge, and between the bridge and the place known as Dead Woman's Burial. This was accepted to be a place situated some 160 yards from the bridge at the West Bromwich end, and at the foot of the slope now leading to the railway bridge. The length of the road, therefore, which the county will in future maintain under this agreement will be from the bridge parapets at the Walsall end to the foot of the inclined approach to the railway bridge at the West Bromwich end. Happily, therefore, there is now no longer a "Tame Bridge Case" to dispute about.

XXXVI.—Bustleholme Mill: Old Forge Mill: Finchpath Mill and Bridge

A little lower down the stream from Tame Bridge and towards Newton is Bustleholme Mill, which after centuries of work, remains a going concern to this day. And Bustleholme, with its mill and waterwheel, is still a picturesque spot. In 1594 it was in the lordship of Wednesbury when the Comberfords held that manor. They that year parted with it to the Stanleys, of West Bromwich manor, together with all their "right, claim, and demand in all those fludgates upon the water of Tame near Bustleholme in West Bromwich and of the soyle whereof the said fludgates stand, and all that parcel of ground stank or dam in length 30 yards and in breadth 15 yards" the rights not only including the water, but the right of fishing (no doubt valuable enough in those days) between Tame Bridge and the said fludgates. As late as 1709 liberty was reserved (on lands purchased by John Lowe) for the Sheltons as lords of the manor to come at pleasure to *fish with nets* or otherwise in the said millpool or river from Tame Bridge to the Mills.

The mill, or at least the adjoining lands, seemed next to have passed into the hands of an old local family named Simcox. In the marriage settlements of Francis Symcox and Alice, daughter of John Hayteley, deceased—and this is another old yeoman family of that side of West Bromwich parish—mention is made of (1) a "mansion house where Johan Symcox, my Mother, dwelleth", (2) a croft near Stone Cross, in the lane leading from West Bromwich church towards Walsall, (3) three "closses" adjoining the Stanley lands and the Longe Crofte; and (4) Little Croft near the "layne" leading down to Bustleholme Mill.

In 1663 the mill was occupied by John Simcox, the elder, who is styled ironmonger, and which signified either a maker of iron or of iron goods—in other words that he was equivalent to an ironmaster of the present day. Besides the Bustleholme lands he occupied 80 acres in a "leet or common field" there, known as Linedone Field. Evidently this was a family of good position as they married into the family of the Sheltons, lords of the manor.

Other lands in the vicinity, known respectively as Smithy More, Wheatcroft, Little Meadow, and Dam Banks—the first two names point to the nature of the occupation, and the second two names suggest the location—were sold in 1709 (as previously recorded in chap. xxvi.), to John Lowe, also an "ironmonger." At this period the mill was a corn mill and a slitting mill combined, its ancient work of grinding grain being now supplemented by the newer services to which water-power had been applied, namely, the nail-making industry. (See WEDNESBURY WORKSHOPS, pp. 20–24). This very combination of agricultural with manufacturing industry is characteristic of the early days and primitive ways of the great local iron trade.

Mention is made of 49 yards of "cinder bank" "alongside of the mills (and mill buildings) as the water runs," and a long stone wall for supporting the carrying troughs; all of which points to the existence of a very extensive industry there, to say nothing of further mention of the fishing rights between the mill and the Tame Bridge, which apparently, could not have been unimportant. With regard to the busy road traffic to and from these mills, which must have been considerable, there was called into existence a way or road for "all sorts of carriages from the mills" through the aforementioned Smithmore Meadow; and another "passable" way through the Lower Stone Pitt Leasow, which was held by one John Culwick.

And then follows descriptive language which helps again to identify the locality of "Dead Woman's Burial." Speaking of another private road leading from these mills to the main road between West Bromwich and Tame Bridge, it says that the private road from the mill ran into the public road at "Dead Woman's Burial Gate."

In 1732 Bustleholme Mills were being worked as a "Rod Mill and Oil Mill," by Jesson Lowe, in succession to his father, John Lowe, of Lyndon. In 1743, the mill, under the same management, was supplying Thomas Jesson, of the Forge, with bars.

Sixty or seventy years later Bustleholme was worked by a man named Morris whose father had been with John Wilkinson, the celebrated ironmaster, of Bradley. After lying idle some years it was worked by G. B. Thorneycroft. It was indeed but by the merest accident that this rural spot was not selected by the Bagnalls, when they first started in the iron trade, and erected the earliest blast furnaces in West Bromwich—but they were put up at Gold's Green instead.

*   *   *   *   *   *   *

Another ancient Bromwich mill is that known as the Old Forge, which was placed on the point of that Tame which approaches nearest to Sandwell and which was probably the priory mill in olden times. After the suppression of the Monastery it seems to have been adapted to the iron industry, and was used as a hammer mill. The meadows near it were open fields, formerly known as Hammer Mill Meadows, in which various people (according to Mr Stone) possessed doles. The particular form of the iron trade followed in Bromwich and in Handsworth was the same as at Wednesbury in those early times—nail making. Mention is made in a deed of 1657, between the Wyrley and Smallwood families, of certain lands in Handsworth Park, lately in the occupation of one Thomas Dutton "naylor." By the terms of this lease Sir John Wyrley reserved to himself as Lord of the Manor, the right of cutting timber on the said lands, while Smallwood was to grind all the corn and malt used in his house at the Manor mills of the lordship at "Hampsteed" within the parish of "Hansworth," "being there well used and to pay all levies, lones, and taxes assessed and charged by vertue of any lawe or authoritie whatsoever." This William Smallwood seems to have been a hatter—an industry not then located in any particular centre for hat-making was practised in Bilston by an isolated craftsman as late as 1816—and it is curious to note that the rent he was called upon to pay was at that somewhat late period in kind as well as in coin. He had to pay £7 10s. per annum in money "at the dwelling-house of Sir John Wyrley, called Hampsteed Hall," and there also "two fat capons" on the first of November every year. These two facts carry back the imagination to the time when rent-day at a hall was a periodical institution in every manor, and to a still earlier period when money was so scarce a commodity that payments were oftener made in kind or in service than in coins of the realm.

*   *   *   *   *   *   *

The identity of "Finchpath" must undoubtedly be connected with *both a mill and a bridge;* because this ancient place-name is invariably associated with one or the other if not with both. Both being adjuncts to a stream, reference to the records of that lordship which had most control over the water-rights of the said stream may throw some light on the subject.

That lordship was Hamstead, held for a very long period by the Wyrley family. (See HISTORY OF TIPTON, pp. 7—10). The researches of Mr. J. H. Stone, of Handsworth, enable us to give the history of this lordship in considerable detail.

Thomas Wyrley was succeeded by his son, John Wyrley, and in 1590 Humfrey, the son of John, was married to Katherine, daughter of Edward Holte, of Duddeston (both being then under age), by whom he had several children. His wife dying, he married (about 1606) Knightly Wyrley, by whom he had five children. In January, 1626, Humfrey Wyrley and Knightly, his wife, levied a fine in favour of John Wyrley, Esq., and John Parkhouse, gentleman, of the manors of Purye Barre *alias* Perrye Barre and Tybbington *alias* Tipton, and of 31 messuages, 20 cottages, 10 tufts, *10 water mills*, 1 columbar (that is, a pigeon-house), 31 gardens, 30 orchards, 300 acres of land, 200 acres of meadow, 150 acres of pasture, 200 acres of wood, 600 acres of furze and heath, 100 acres of moor, 31 acres of marsh, 31 acres of land covered with water (which indicates that the science of land drainage was almost unknown in those days), with free rents, view of frankpledge, free warren, etc., in Tibbington, Pury Barre, Great Barre, Handsworth, Holford, and Hamstead. Also free fishery in the waters of Tame and Barbrooke. The fine was enrolled Easter Term, 3 Ch. I. (1628).

At this time the Wyrleys were working their Corn Mill at Hamstead, and a most valuable possession it was. Perhaps more so even than that at Bustleholme or the Old Forge Mill near Sandwell. Alter leaving Hamstead the Tame flows through Perry Barr, where considerable water was stored. The Perry Corn Mill was then the property of the Wyrleys, as previously it had been of the earlier owners of the Manor, the ancient family of Pyrie. The division of the Perry lordship is peculiar; it is not improbable that at an earlier period there had been two distinct lordships—Pyrie and Little Barr. One of these passed to the Stamford family. The divided manors became designated Hamstead, Perry Barr *alias* Little Barr, and Oscott.

There is in existence a lease of this Perry Mill made in 1632, between Humphrey Wyrley and John Curtler, of Walsall. The "moitie or one-halfe parte" of the mill, with water courses, half the "mylle house," mill pool, "fleames, dammes, stancks, easements, liberties, &c., were let for 11 years at £6 yearly; Curtler to "sufficientlie upholde repaire, and Wyrley to provide sufficiente tymber." "Proviso that Curtler shall not keepe any loade horse to the said mylle, nor fetche nor carry any corne or grayne to or from the said mylle, unless it be from Walsall, aforesaid, or from the *Mylles at Wednesbury*, which the said Curtler now holdeth."

At one time there were three water mills in Wednesbury, though the water power there was not so reliable as lower down the stream. The proviso seems intended to suppress competition with nearer mills, and it is clear the business at Perry Grist Mill was much the more profitable if Curtler could convey his grain from Walsall or Wednesbury to relieve the strain on these other mills of his in those places.

(To increase the value of all the neighbouring mill-power, Birmingham trades and other local industries were at this time, remarks Mr. J. H. Stone beginning to make demands on such water power for the purposes of Blade Mills, Slitting Mills, Polishing Mills, and Fulling Mills; and in somewhat more recent times, Paper Mills.)

The exact locality of these several Wednesbury mills cannot now be specified. Elwell's Forge is no doubt on the site of one. Another in later times was perhaps that one known as Heller's Mill at Hateley Heath; one may possibly have been at Sparrow's Forge on the Willenhall Brook, and the corn mill, now unused, at Wednesbury Bridge was no doubt erected on the site of a former and more ancient mill.

Finchpath Mill may have been the one at Hateley Heath, or it was at least nearer to that locality than Wednesbury Bridge—say in Hyde's Road.

Mills change in feature, as from grist mills to iron mills. and they even pass away altogether, leaving little or no trace behind them to mark their sites. Bridges on the other hand are more enduring. Very few bridges indeed, erected in ancient times, have been allowed to pass away entirely, leaving behind no modern structure as a substitute. This being so it is instructive to observe that before Telford's bridge over the Tame, known as Wednesbury Bridge (1820), there would appear to have been no earlier structure spanning the steam at that spot.

The rows of cottages dating from the last century which line both sides of the main road approaching this bridge from the West Bromwich side are at a low level, corresponding with the ford which formerly used to mark the road through the bed of the stream.

To contend that an ancient bridge once stood there but fell into decay and passed away would be idle. There were in mediæval times many trusts and religious bodies charged with the maintenance and repair of such useful structures. For instance, there were the Pontife Brethren, a religious fraternity instituted for the special business of bridge building and repairing. Amongst mediæval institutions there were such things as *pontage, pontagium,* or *brudthol,* the right to take toll on bridges, the tax of course going to the support and repair of the bridges. Another ancient term, *trinoda necessitas* signified a "triple obligation," which was a certain charge on the ownership of lands (such as existed at Tame Bridge) for maintaining neighbouring roads and bridges.

Another illustration of these fixed charges or burdens on land may be found at Handsworth. There the "Bridge Trust" was so called because it was originally established for the repair of eight bridges within that parish, five being for carriages, and three being only footbridges. This Trust was so well endowed that its surplus moneys have been utilised to endow the Bridge Trust Grammar School. This work of transferring the application of public funds to more modern uses and better purposes was initiated about 1813 by Mr. George Birch. Some reformer might follow his example in Wednesbury with the overgrown funds at the disposal of the Hopkins' Charity in that parish.

Similarly the obligation of repairing Fullbrook Bridge between Wednesbury and Walsall was imposed on certain lands of the Moseley Dole—some 200 acres at Bascote in Warwickshire.

XXXVII.—Is Hill Top the Ancient Finchpath?

The present writer has always been of opinion that the ancient Finchpath was the Hydes Road—that is, the *ancient highway* between Wednesbury and West Bromwich, which passed through Oakeswell End, Hydes Road, Hall Green, and Stone Cross. This was undoubtedly the *King's highway* between the two parishes in olden times, passing those important buildings, Oakeswell Hall and West Bromwich Manor House, in its numerous windings between the two ancient parish churches. Hill Top and Holloway Bank are newer names for a comparatively new road, which would appear to have been a mere *bridle path* over Bromwich Heath until the beginning of the Eighteenth Century, when its "holloway" was dug out for the track of the long lines of pack-horses plying regularly between the mines of Wednesbury Old Field and the Aston Furnaces. At Wednesbury Bridge no trace of a more ancient bridge can be found, so that this cannot have been the site of Finchpath Bridge. It is not improbable, however, that the ancient trackway called Portway Road, went *through* the Tame here, and continued its line along Mollaston Lane towards the Worcestershire salt district—a relic of the ancient Britons, and a road probably adopted by the Romans when they came.

The Rev. Samuel Lees, of Hill Top, has gathered such a mass of valuable information to prove the identity of Hill Top with the ancient Finchpath that it cannot be ignored. He says: Hill Top bore the name of Finchpath for five hundred years, from the time when the justiciaries set out the result of their enquiry as to the ancient boundaries of Cannock Chase in 1286—as mentioned in the previous chapter. The "bridge of Finchpath" alluded to is undoubtedly Wednesbury Bridge, the bridge leading from Wednesbury to Finchpath or Hill Top. The name is variously spelt. A selection of examples from old deeds may be interesting, the dates are those of the documents. In very old deeds, without date, of early Plantagenet times, and possibly earlier, it is spelt as Finchespath, Phinchespad, and Ffynchespath. We then have later:—

1338—Finchespade.	1460—fynchspathe.
1385—fynchespathe.	1479—Findespath.
1399—fynchpade.	1577—Fynchespath.
1399—fynspath.	1696—Finch Path.
1422—fynspathe.	1700—Finspott Hill.
1428—ffynchespath.	1727—Finch Path.
1446—Vinspath.	1759—Finchpath Hill.
1457—fynchespathe.	1785—Finch Path Hill.

Hill Top was Finchpath Hill; Black Lake, called "Blake Lake" in 1399, was in Nether Finchpath; land near "The, Swanne," the inn which gave the name to Swan Village, had cottages near to "Finchpath End"; and there was an "Over finchpade" named in 1385 which cannot be located.

The earliest dated deed I have seen was shown to me by H. O. Crompton, Esq., of Birmingham. It is dated at the feast of S. John the Baptist in the 12th year of Edward III., that is the 24th of June, 1338. An extract will have a special interest for readers in Wednesbury:—"I, John, son of Nicolas Golde of Fynchespade grant and concede and by this present Charter confirm to Richard, son of Thomas atte Gate of Wednesburie a certain piece of land lying in Wawecroft; in length between my lands and the highway which leads from fynchespade towards Wolvernhampton." Amongst the witnesses are "John Dymmoc, John Henris, John of Grete, Henry atte Gate, Henry of Derlaston," and others. Grete is an old family or place name preserved in Greets Green; and in Great Bridge, which is really Grete or Greet Bridge.

Wolvern hampton is interesting. It was not till a long time after Wulfrun had, by charter of 996, given lands to the monastery in "Hamtun" that it became known as Wulfrun's or Wolvern Hampton. But what was the gate at Wednesbury? It must have been well known? Turnpikes were centuries later. Was there any defensive enclosure at Wednesbury? If so, where! [Was there a gate at the entrance to the Portway?]

The earliest mention I have found of the newer name, "Hill Top" is in a deed kindly shown to me by George Whitehouse. Esq., of Harville's Hawthorne House. It is dated 1747, and is a conveyance of land from "Mr. Joseph Woreley, yeoman, of Lindon, to Mr. Thomas Dudley, of Tipton, otherwise Tibbington." The land is "situated at or near to a place called Hill Top, in the aforesaid parish of West Bromwich," and one of its boundaries is "the road leading from Hill Top aforesaid to Wedneshury." The land is part of that on which the house stands in which Dr. Trimble now resides.

But after 1747 the name of Finchpath still lingered in documents as it probably did in common speech. Hill Top is called Finch Path Hill in 1785. A parallel case of change may be found at West Bromwich. Where the centre of the town now stands there was a common at the commencement of this century. The parish name was given to the town when built. But older people never went to West Bromwich; they went to shops "on the common" or "on the heath," or to "Brammich Heath." This old mode of speech is now dying out.

Black Lake, however, keeps an unchanged name. In 1399 land is described "as lying in length between Whytelake and Blakelake." Where was Whytelake? Blacklake has been a continuous name for 500 years. It is probable the Swan is as old. Can anyone inform me as to the locality of "Coven Moore and Birchie Croft"? They were properties attached to the "Swanne" in 1613. In a lease of 1655 of a house "called or known by the signe of the Swanne." "Coven Moore," "Birch leasow," and lands known as the "Shepheards" are included.

The name of Finchpath in some of its forms appears in the deeds for Meyrick House, of properties which were in the possession of my own family, and many other properties at Hill Top. The name of an old house, which occupied the space of the Poplars (Mr. Mitchell's) and the Woodlands (Mr John Field, J.P.) was Finchpath Hall. The name crops up at intervals in places on the high road from Wednesbury Bridge to Black Lake. I believe it is never found beyond these limits north or south. Eastward it is not applied beyond Hateley Heath and Ridgacre, or of a line thence to the Tame. Its western limits seem to have been an ancient bridle path, to which I will refer presently.

So much for the main road, the axis or centre of Finchpath. To ascertain its limits let us approach it by some ancient road. Dial Lane will serve as one, This lane was known as Brickhouse Lane about 1600. In 1800 it was called Woodwards Lane, from an ancient family resident in a house, part of which, with half timbered gable, still stands. After the erection of the Dial Works, at the angle, it was called Dial Lane. Deeds of various properties in this lane refer also to Finchpath.

A conveyance from James Smith to Thomas Dudley, in 1727, describes the land as in "the lane leading from Great Bridge to Finchpath." Another property is described in the same year as "near a place in West Bromwich, called Finchpath." In 1759 (June 13) a property was conveyed from Thomas Dudley to Thomas Bratt in "the lane leading to Finchpath Hill" and in 1785 "John Sargent and Trustee" conveyed to "John Wilkes and Trustee" another property in the "lane leading from Great Bridge to Finchpath Hill."

There was a way (probably a *Bridle-path*) from the old Swan Inn, at Swan Village, which formerly went across to beyond the Fountain Inn at Wednesbury Bridge. It began at the Swan, crossed part of the present Gasworks; the road between the Gasworks and the Swan Village Timber Yard was diverted by the extension of the former; and went near to Black Lake Colliery, from this point there was a connecting line with the main road by Jones' Smithy, opposite Jacques' School, and another branch went into Dial Lane. From Blacklake Colliery it then proceeded, leaving the Bye Pit on the left, and Maskells on the right entering New Street (formerly Brick-kiln Lane) by Peggy Taylor's Hut. This road was kept open by my uncle, the late Mr. John Lees, who proved it to be an old road when an attempt was made to close it 50 years ago. It then crossed the triangular piece of vacant ground between the junction of Hawkes Lane and New Street, known at the time of the enclosure in 1802 as "War Hall Green," one of the very numerous heaths, greens and commons in this parish. It proceeded along Tunnel Road over the Hollow Meadow, passing Bilperts Row destroyed for the Canal, and entering the high road by the turning north of the Fountain Inn. So that before it entered the high road it passed the cottage of Mr. Clifton, better known by his nickname of "Honest Munchin," the deliverer of John Wesley in the Wednesbury riots of 1743.

On the earlier line of this road we find a certain place called Finch path End (*25 Charles II.*) Then on the right, the land as seen by the following grant: "9 Richard II (1385). Grant by Richard son and heir of Thomas Gold of Over-finch-pade to Robert son of Philip Janneys of the same in the fee of Weste bro'wych, between the land of Wm. Tymmesone and the highway from fynches pade towards Burmicha'm. Given at West Bromwich, Sunday after Feast of the Purification of the Blessed Mary: *Witnesses*, Richd. on le Heathe; Thomas Godknave; John Symkoc; Willm. in le Wode." On the right of this line, near to, we have another grant. (Dec 8, 1399.) "Grant by Robert Janyes, of West Bromwych to Robert Asseheley, of one croft of land in the fee of West Bromwych, and lying in length between Whytelake and Blacklake, and in breadth between land sometime of William Tymmesone and the highway from fyndepade towards Byrnech'm. Given at West Bromwych. Conception of Mary. *Witnesses*, Nicholas Hawkys; William Lyttal Hay; Robert Tolle; Henry Ryder; Phylyppe Goodknave."

In these documents the road at Blacklake appears as the highway from "fynches pade" (or Hill Top) to Birmingham. The names of Gold or Golde, of Hawkys or Hawkes recur and are family names which reappear in Golds Hill, Golds Green and Hawkes Lane. (See also chaps. xix and xxi. for these old personal names.) Proceeding further along the road described we get beyond the junction of Tunnel Road with Castle Street. Here in the marriage settlement of Phebe Turton in 1696 we come to land "known by the name of the Square Leasow, now into two parts divided, seytuate and lying in Finch path in the parish of West Bromwich."

Again, that the road from Wednesbury through Hill Top, across Bromwich Heath to Birmingham was an ancient highway from Wolverhampton, Willenhall, Darlaston, and Wednesbury to Birmingham, may be next shown by documents and other facts.

A road is called the King's Highway as far as the "bridge of Finches path" (or Wednesbury Bridge) in 1286. It is described as "the high way which lead from fynches-pade towards Wolvern-hampton" in the deed of 1338 quoted. In deeds recited above, it is called at the Blacklake end of the road in 1338 " the highway from finch pace towards Byrnechm," and in 1384 "the highway from fynches pade towards Burmicham." In the following grants (1460) we have another form. "Grant of William Colyns and Agatha, his wife, to William Wingeley Chaplain," of a messuage "and curtilage adjacent in West Bromwich, between the highway leading from Wednesburie towards Burmyngham," &c. "Given at fynspath. Sunday after St. Matthew the Evangelist. *Witnesses*: John Symcoks, John Say, John Swettcock." Mrs. Willett's book gives other forms as to the same length of road from Wednesbury Bridge to Carter's Green, which vary from the King's Majesty's Higheway leading from Bromwich Heath towards Wednesbury" to, in Commonwealth times, for the same property, "*a* roadway "leading, etc. This reference is to property near Wednesbury Bridge. In the other direction we find that the road in front of Oakwood House (Councillor Cheshire's residence), now Old Meeting Street, is described in 1638 as "the King's Majesty's highway leading from Bromwich Heath towards Wednesburie." Oakwood House is built on Oakley's Croft (see Willett, page 219). The road on the far south end of Bromwich Heath near the Beeches is called "the Kings Majesty's Highway leading from Birmingham towards Wolverhampton" in 1670.

*   *   *   *   *   *   *

In addition to all this evidence of the Rev. Samuel Lees, there is also testimony of Mr. W. H. DUIGNAN to the same effect. The latter authority also says:—

"Finchpath" means *Finch's Road*—probably the way to Finch's house. "Finch" is an Anglo-Saxon personal name. There is a "Finchfield" two miles beyond Wolverhampton.; "Finchale" in Durham; "Fincham" in Norfolk; "Finchdean" in Hants; "Finchingfield" in Essex; "Finchley" near London, &c. The majority of place names have their origin in Anglo-Saxon personal names: "Wodnesbury" is Woden's Bury—*Woden's fortified place or dwelling*. Woden is a personal name. It has been said that Wednesbury is named after the Saxon god; but that is very unlikely, for if Wednesbury was founded by the Saxons when still pagans, the early missionaries would very promptly have changed its name."

Very few authorities would agree with Mr. Duignan in this last conclusion. As to his first statement, it has been suggested by some one that "Finchpath" simply means *a fishing* path by the stream side!

XXXVIII.—ABOUT BARR: BARR BEACON, PERRY BARR AND PERRY BRIDGE, AND GREAT BARR.

The name BARR is one which is applied to a very extensive range of the countryside lying to the E., or rather N.E., of West Bromwich; and with which its relations are so intimate, that some small space must here be devoted to its history and description. It may be said that there are three Barrs, the nearest to West Bromwich is Great Barr or Barr Magna; then there is Barr Beacon, a height attaining some 653 feet above the sea-level, about two miles further away; and Perry Barr, which is included within the Poor Law Union of West Bromwich.

While most of the neighbouring manors and parishes have become populous urban districts, Barr still retains nearly all its rural characteristics, except Perry Barr, which is becoming a mere suburb of the great city of Birmingham. Up to the close of last century there was a quaint old custom still lingering at Great Barr. There it was the practice of the clergyman of the parish, every Christmas day, to give to each person, gentle or simple, resident within his parish, and who chose to go to his house for same as much bread, beef, mustard, and vinegar as the recipient could eat. Later this was changed into a money gift to the inhabitants of Great Barr and Aldridge, a total sum of £26 13s. 4d., providing a portion equivalent to 1s. 6d. each.

As an eminence dominating the whole country round, BARR BEACON must have been repeatedly occupied or used in the war-like times of old. Britons, Romans, and Saxons, Danes, and English have all in succession utilised its commanding position. Its occupation during the Wars of the Roses was alluded to in chap. xxi. Perhaps the last military display on that height was that of September 23rd, 1799, when amid great popular enthusiasm colours were presented to the Volunteer Association under Captain Joseph Scott (of Barr, and afterwards Sir Joseph) during the Napoleonic scare.

*　　*　　*　　*　　*　　*　　*

Evidence has already been offered in favour of the theory that Barr Beacon and Aldridge were important centres even before the Romans came. British and Druidical occupations of these spots were noted in chap. ii. This being so it is not difficult to believe that one of the most ancient Trackways in Central Britain crossed the Tame near PERRY BARR, and which led through Wednesbury and Oldbury to the salt springs of Droitwich. This was entirely independent of the Roman road which was made later. Perry Bridge would, of course, date from the making of the later and more artificial road. Some writers claim that the Romans had a camp on the hill to the south of this bridge, the formation of the ground there favouring the theory. The bridge they built would be some two hundred yards to the east of the site of the one now existing, where the line of Icknield Street may yet be traced. The Saxons were neither bridge builders nor yet masons. They let the Roman Bridge fall into hopeless dilapidation, and probably resumed the use of the old natural trackway in the line of which the present Perry Bridge was erected early in the Middle Ages.

Hol Ford, the junction of Hol Brook with the Tame has left no trace of a ford alongside the bridge, yet as the name implies a ford did exist there, but probably in front of a house close there, called Perry Pont, in the village of Perry. The Hol Brook itself was always forded; the road by the bridge was called Hol Ford Brugge as early as 1309.

The date of Perry Bridge is very early. Perry lay outside both the royal Forest of Cannock and the noble Chase of Sutton; the brook as a boundary would be regarded in the eye of the law as included within the jurisdiction of the Forest Laws: and in all cases of forest trespass the Law viewed the demarcation of the Tame water as arbitrarily as if it were an unscalable wall reaching up to the very heavens. Sutton Chase (see chap. ii) has part of its bounds defined as extending as far as the Hole brok and as far as the Thame, and as far as the Hol Ford Brugge (1309).

The road from Lichfield through Aldridge led over this bridge, and was much used in the mediæval feuds of neighbouring lords, for instance in the marches of the hired forces of Freebooters and Welshmen engaged by either Bassett of Drayton, or Somory of Dudley, when these fierce nobles fled out at each other in their perpetual baronial jealousies. In 1271 it must have been the scene of fierce bustle and turmoil when used on one occasion by the forces of certain other feudal magnates, more closely attached to the locality, if lesser in degree. This was a night attack on the Park of Handsworth by Adam of Perry, Sir William de Parles, lord of Handsworth, and his son; who having lost their lordship to one Sampson, a Lichfield money-lending Jew, broke into the Park by night and took away 60 head of cattle by force. Sir William paid dearly for his lawlessness—he was beheaded five years later for felony.

Over this bridge has been carted many a fat buck, poached either from Cannock Forest or else from Sutton Chase, for the road led to the eastern boundary of the former, and the western bounds of the latter. Stolen venison is said to have found notorious receivers in the monks of Sandwell, deer stealers have been traced over this bridge as far as Solihull in the opposite direction, too. During the Civil Wars a noteworthy incident took place close here. In October 1642 and again in the following April Charles I. held a kind of Court at the King's Standing on Perry Common, when all the royalist gentry of the neighbourhood (including Hopkins of Wednesbury, and Whorwood of Sandwell) sent him what help they could in his cause against the Parliament. While his main supporter here would be Sir Thomas Holte of Aston, the lord of Perry Barr, Edward Stamford of Perry Hall, was active as a colonel in the King's army, and recruited from the whole neighbourhood around.

Later on in the struggle, when Prince Rupert skirmished round Birmingham, he pursued Captain Turton and his troops as far as Smethwick on their way to Turton's residence in West Bromwich—The Oak. And we can in imagination picture the dashing but wary Rupert relinquishing the aggressive in so doubtful a locality, and pushing on next day to the trusty city of Lichfield, marching his flushed forces over this Perry Bridge before entering on the wide expanse of Perry Barr Common, or the more deserted solitudes of Sutton Chase.

Perry Barr is believed to obtain its distinguishing appellation from *Per* and *Perain*, "pear trees" (British). In Domesday Book it is called Pirio, when given as the possession of Drogo. In later times William Wirley gave his son Philip certain lands and tenements in both Pirie and Parva Barra, from which it is apparent that Perry and Little Barr are two distinct places. In the time of Edward I. John, lord of Little Barr, obtained a license from the Earl of Warwick to enclose his wood, which being within the metes and bounds of Sutton Chase, could only be secured by a payment—the price in this case being six barbed arrows, to be delivered annually at Sutton Manor House. In the reign of Edward III. the village of Perry was held by John de Perry under William de Birmingham by service of a knight's fee, £10.

In 1518 Eustace FitzHerbert died lord of Perry and Sutton Coldfield. By the marriage of one of his daughters it was carried to Thomas Smith, whose father had been a Baron of the Exchequer. In 1546 Perry Hall and estate were sold to Sir William Stamford, attorney-general. During the Civil Wars Edward Stamford was dispossessed by the Parliament for taking up arms on behalf of the king, as just recorded, although his wife was permitted to rent the hall as her residence. In 1646 he compounded for his delinquencies, and one of his sons sold Perry Hall in 1669 to Sir Henry Gough, knight.

The Goughs are an old family. Matthew Gough distinguished himself in the Welsh Wars between 1424 and 1450. He was killed in the last named year while defending London Bridge against Jack Cade. Henry Gough entertained Charles I. at Wolverhampton at the outbreak of the Civil Wars, and gave a large sum to the royal war chest. He declined a knighthood, but this honour was conferred on his grandson Henry, of Perry Hall, by Charles II. His descendant, Henry Gough, born 1749, was created Baron Calthorpe in 1796.

WITTON.—Domesday Book informs us that in Perry Barr there were 3 hides held by Drogo, and also in Witton was 1 hide valued at 20s. Witton is beyond the boundaries of Staffordshire, being a part of Warwickshire. In Domesday Book the name is written Witone, and afterwards the place seems to have been connected with the lordship of Aston, Erdington, etc. When its boundaries were in dispute in the reign of Henry III. it was set down as *Wicton*, from the bend of the river there. The various holders of the lands have been John Dyxele (1291), William de la Hay, Thomas East descending to Henry East of Hay Hall, Yardley; sold to John Bond, a Coventry draper; sold again in 1573 to Edward Kynardsley, whose son alienated the manor to John Booth, barrister.

*   *   *   *   *   *   *

GREAT BARR is by some authorities said to derive its name from the Hebrew *barrah*, "to eat sacrifices" because it was anciently the spot where the Druids performed their sacrificial ceremonies. It is mentioned in the Domesday Book (1086) as being held by one Drogo, under the great baron Fitzansculph. By the time of King John we find it divided into two separate and distinct manors, Magna Barr and Parva Barr, one Guido (? Wyrley) holding the former. In the reign of Edward II. it passed from John Somery to Sir Robert de Stapleton, who had lands in Aldridge also, and who settled the estate on his wife's relations, the Birminghams. By descent Great Barr (or a moiety of the manor) was conveyed in 1573 to William Barroll. In 1618 William Scott is in possession of Great Barr. Frances Lady Scott brought it to her husband John Hoo, a nephew of John Hoo, barrister who had bought the manor of Wednesbury in 1710. Their son Thomas Hoo died intestate in 1791, when Barr passed to Joseph Scott, created a baronet in 1806. Sir Joseph built a new mansion, replacing the old manor house. a quaint half-timbered edifice, in which had resided the last of the Hoo family; who as a country gentleman (and a sheriff in due course) had lived in great affluence in the old fox-hunting style. An old account book of the estate gives the prices current in the year 1667—for a strike of barley as 1s. 6d., and for a strike of wheat 2s. 8d.: the following year barley was 1s. 4d. and wheat 3s 6d.

In the year 1800 Barr Beacon was occupied for a month by a detachment of Engineers, taking the bearings of the different stations, as seen from the Beacon summit, for the Government Ordnance Survey. The stations are Lickey Hills, Walton Hill, Clay Hill, Wrekin, Castle Ring, near Beaudesert, Weaver Hill, Oxpit (Derbyshire), Sutton (Notts) Holly Hill, Bardon (Leicestershire), Corley, Asbury Hill (Northants), Epwell (Oxon), and Camden (Gloucestershire).

Illustrations of Barr will be found in Shaw's County History. Here are given three capital engravings: one is a view of "The old house at Barr," inscribed to Joseph Scott, Esq., another is a "N.E. view of Barr Chapel" and the third, a "S.E. view of Great Barr Hall." In the letterpress will be found a full account of all the feudal possessors of the manor, and a history of the place down to the close of the last century.

XXXIX.—Fragment of a West Bromwich Rent Roll of the time of Elizabeth.—Circa, 1590-1603.

Mr. W. B. Bickley communicated to the "Midland Antiquary" (vol. iii.. pp. 72-73) a mutilated fragment of the rent-roll of West Bromwich chief rents, *temp* Elizabeth. "Chief rents" were the rents of the freeholders of the manor and thus often called *reditus capitales*. They are also denominated "quit rents" or *quieti reditus*, because on payment of them the tenant goes quiet and free of all other services. They were but small amounts, and payable by the tenants of a manor in token of subjection. Sometimes they were called "white rents," because paid in silver money, and so distinguished from "corn rents," etc.

. . . . . .
. . . . . .

(Commencement torn away.)

Edward Pershowse of sedgley his Land ...	...	...	...	ijd.
Edward Groves for Ward's Land of Birmicham ...	...	...	iijs.	iijd.
& for Bustellhome Late Wards ...	...	...	...	vjd.
Homfray Gybbins of Ascote for his Land...	...	...	...	xxjd.
John Dutton a'ls tumlinson for George P'trig	...	...	...	• • •
Land in Wigmore Late Stamfords ...	...	...	...	vjd.
& for Bustellhome late Osbornes	...	...	...	iijd. q.
Will'm Lane for his p'te of Bustellhome ...	...	...	...	vjd.
Will'm Orme for his p'te of Bustellhome ...	...	...	...	vjd.
And for tandies Land in greete ...	...	...	...	iijs. iiijd.
and for p'ocks in nechiles Late hinds ...	...	...	...	iiiijd.
& for Squiers Land	...	...	...	iiijd.
Thomas Wood for his pt'e of smithes Land in Wigmore	...			jd. ob.
Thomas Cotten of Cotten Bridge for his p'te of smithes Land...				xjd.
Will'm Orme of Tomworth for his p'te therorf ...	...	...		jd.
Homfray Jones for Bellfelds w'ch he holdeth of Sr. William				
Whorwood	...	...	...	xviijd.
Rechard more for Wilks Sponeheath...	...	...	...	vjd.
Thomas Birche for a Cottage w'ch Gdman. Darbie holdeth	...			vjd.
& for Will'm P'tridge howse in hawle end		...	...	jd.
John P'tg of Hawle end for Will'm Huntes Land...	...	...	xiiijd.
John Osborne for his howse...	...	...	...	jd.

. . . . . .
. . . . . .

(Part torn away).

John Trulove for a Cottage Late Joan Yates	...	...		vjd.
Mr. Walter Lytteltons Chefe Rent ...	...	...	vs.	jd.
Theares of Thomas Birche of Holt Hill	...	...		xxiijd.
Mr. P'sehowse of Renols Hawle- for Chantrie	...	...		
Land in grete Called newhawle and small heathe	...	...		xvjd ob.
Thomas p'trige for a Cottage and Land in greete...	...	...		iiijd.
Willm Orme of Rowley for his Land Called Lady Rudding	...		vjd.
& for a meadow in the occupation of george Write ...	...		ijd.
Willm Hunte for Cophawle and Land Thereto belonging	...	iijs.	vd.

Symon Ryder for his Land	...	...	...	...	...	...		xiijd.
Edward Dudley of typton for his land			...	...	...	...		xijd.
Thomas Dudley for his Land in greete			...	...	...	...	ijs.	vijd.
John sabin for his house and Land...	...	...	...	...	...			vd.
John Woodward for his Land...	...	...	...	...	...	...	ijs.	xjd ob.
Thomas Sheldon for Hawks Land ...	...	...	...	...	...			xvd.
& for his Land at Blake Lake bought of Mr. Stamford				...	...			ixd.
Gregorie Shepord for his p'te of Hawks Land	...	...	...	...			iijd.
Willm Turton junior for Hadley's Land at Oldberie Mill				...	...			xxd.
John Turton for his Land late Willm...	...	...	...	...			
Taylors old time gamons	...	...	...	...	...	...		iiijs.
Willm Jesson for Willm Hunts Land...	...	...	...	...	...			jd ob.
Edward Davies for his p'te of Hunts Land...	...	...	...	...			ijd.

• • • • • •
• • • • • •

(Part torn away).

& for golde Crofte	...	...	...	...	...	...	...	jd.
Willm Hobbens for all his Land		...	...	...	...	...	iijd ob.
Raffe Tunkes Junior for all his land...	...	...	...	...	...		vd.

(struck out)

cheffe rent

S. mariday	vli.	xs.	vid.
micaellmas	5li.	10s.	6d.

Some little explanation of the foregoing may be necessary to its understanding by the ordinary render unacquainted with the peculiarities of old documents. At this period there was no settled orthography; everyone spelt according to individual taste. Even the use of capital letters will be found somewhat erratic, proper names as often as not commence with small initial letters, although it is significant of this era of landlordism and territorial supremacy, that the word land is invariably spelt in this document with a capital L. The mention of Sir William Whorwood's name would fix the date as some year between 1590 and 1603. Walter Stanley would be Lord of the Manor at that time.

Of abbreviations the form *p'te* signifies "part," while even the proper personal name of "Partridge" (an old West Bromwich family of many branches) is invariably cut down to *P'trig. Gdman* is equivalent to "Goodman," a generic name then used for all householders, and here it is in happy combination with "Darbie"—Darbie and Joan are accepted types of happy goodman and goodwife. For *p'ocks* it is presumable we may read "paddocks"; for *a'ls*, "alias." People very often had two surnames in those early times, when surnames were little more than nicknames; and *w'ch* is the legal penman's shortening of "which."

It is interesting to note that lands are often identified by the name of their previous holders, as "late osbornes"; while some holdings are broken up into "parts" for newer tenants.

Important local family names are those of Persehouse—one branch of Sedgley and another of Reynold's Hall, Walsall, Stamford, of Perry Hall; the family of Birche, identified with the spot now called Birchfield: Ryder. a family who left records of parish events between 1558 and 1638, Dudley, a family of innumerable branches in the locality; Hawks, who lent their cognomen to Hawke Lane; Turton of the Oak, a family generally found on the popular, Puritanical, and Parliamentary side, and Jesson, one of the modern families longest planted in this parish. It was possibly the freeholder Shepord, who lent his name to the "Shepherd's" mentioned in chap. xxxvii., just as the

Freebody family (chap. xx.), have a place in Dudley named after them, "The Freebodies." The name While is evidently but another form of Whyley.

Of the places mentioned *nechiles* is evidently Nechells; *spone heath* was doubtless near Spon Lane; *hawle end* points towards Hall Green; but where were *newhale* and *smale heathe* in the neighbourhood of Greets Green or Great Bridge ?

In the money column *ob.* signifies obolus or halfpenny as q. stands for a quarter of a penny, or farthing, and *li* for "libra" the pound. The two half-yearly totals at the end are strangely enough given in different characters; the first for *S. Mariday* ("St Mary's Day" or Lady Day) is after the Monkish Latin fashion expressed in the Roman numerals for £5 10s. 6d., while the second rent day of *Micaellmas* ("Michaelmas"), has the total of the rent roll recorded in the more modern method of Arabic figures.

XL—A RENT ROLL OF 1649, IN WHICH ARE TRACES OF MUCH OLDER LAND SYSTEMS.

Another rent roll of West Bromwich Manor is still extant; and although it is half a century later than the last the study of it will prove both interesting and instructive. The great fact it bears home upon the reader's mind is the antiquity of West Bromwich; for, if rightly interpreted, we may trace a Saxon origin of the parish, first, in the survival of certain purely English name words, and secondly in the preservation of place-names, which reveal the former presence of an old Teutonic system of communal government.

First the Rent Roll shall be given as it stands:

Rents payable unto JOHN SHELTON, ESQ., *at the feast of St. Mich. Tharchangell only as followeth:*

Anoq. d'ni 1649.

	£	s	d.
Wm. Ward for his house and groundes...	3	6	8
John Turton a mess. and grounds...	5	0	0
Wm. Preston for his Tenem't	1	7	0
Edw. Dixon, a cot and close	0	15	0
John Ensworth a mess. and groundes ...	1	2	11
George Kendricke a mess. and lands ...	3	6	8
John Bird a cot and close	1	5	0
Wid Reignolds	0	10	0
John Bennet a mess. and lands ...	1	0	0
Waltr. Stevens ju. a mess. and lands	5	0	0
James Evans a cot and 2 closes...	0	12	0
Walter Vale a cot and lands	2	5	0
Wm. Hadley and Mr. Wilmot rigdacres grounds	3	10	0
Wid. Bridgen a mess. and lands...	1	6	8
Wid. Bridgen for dam Hay	2	0	0
Tho. Bassett a pasture and a mede	1	13	4
Tho. Gretton a mess. and lands...	5	0	0
Wm. and Walter Wyley a mess. and lands	2	0	4
Mich. Poultne a mess. and lands...	2	6	0
Gregorie Haddocke a mess, and lands...	1	6	0

	£	s.	d.
Tho. Nurthall a mes. and one p'cell	0	13	0
Rich. Partridge for Whorhall. *pd.* 3 *li.* 18.	11	0	8
Edw. White a mes. and crofte	0	1	8
Tho. Reeves 2 closes w'ch White held	1	5	8
Mr. Fowke and Mr. Foley for a mede w'ch White held	2	0	0
Wid. Orrie a cot and lands	2	0	0
Robt. Willmott a mes. and lands...	14	0	0
Tho. Nurthall for broad fields	1	15	0
Walter Stevens sen. a cot and lands	2	6	0
Mr. Fowke and Mr. Foley for ye rod mill	10	10	0
Francis Penn a mes. and lands	2	0	0
Henry Hunt a mes. and lands	3	6	8
George Syncox a mes. and lands...	8	0	0
Mr. Foley for the fordge	7	10	0
Edward Dudley a mes and lands...	4	3	4
Wid. Rawley a mes. and lands	6	15	10
	£121	**3**	**9**
George Syncox for 3 closes w'ch Partridge held	2	10	0
Edward Bybie a cott.	0	10	0
Wid. Poole for Broomy close	0	15	0
Wm. Osborne a medowe and grounds	5	5	0
Rich. Parkes a cot. and 3 closes...	2	10	0
Robte. Flynt for the farme at Church	10	0	0
Mr. Fowke and Mr. Foley for Tame bridge grounds	2	0	0
Tho. Hurley for a pingle	0	2	0
Wm. Stanley for a croft	0	12	6
John Yardley for a cot	0	1	8
Thomas Reede a little close	0	3	4
Henry Wasse a cot	0	6	8
Wid. Kerbie a cot and hemlecke...	0	5	0
Ralphe Bott a cot and crofte	0	1	8
Edward Bylie for mill meadows...	0	10	0
John Caste a cot and garden	0	5	0
Edw. Tranter a cot	0	10	0
Roger Osborne for Whiles ten'te	4	0	0
	28	**7**	**10**

RENTS OF DEMESNE LANDS.

	£	s.	d.
Wm. Ward for dych land	5	0	0
Ralphe Marshe for Biddles crofte	1	10	0
Wm. Preston for gorstie crofte	1	5	0
Jo. Deeley and Wm. Allen for pescroft...	0	13	4
John Deeley for the Whittington mede...	2	15	0
Tho. Reeves for Broad feild	1	5	0
John Deeley for Cronell	2	0	0
Robte Flynt for hey p'ke	5	0	0
Mr. Wm. Foord for rod mill moore	4	0	0

	£	s.	d.
Tho. Reeves for Crumtree	1	13	4
Tho. Reeves for p'ke meadowe	5	0	0
John Deeley for a little patch and for the paddocks...	0	13	4
	30	15	0

FEILD LANDS SETT.

	£	s.	d.
Wm. Preston 6d. worke in marshe flatt...	0	12	0
Jo. Deeley for 4d. worke in marshe flatt	0	8	0
Thom. Reeves 3d. worke in gorstie corn...	0	6	0
Tho. Gretton 4d. worke	0	8	0
Ed. Curtler 1d. worke in gorstie corn'...	0	2	0
Ed. Bybie 2 little pikes	0	1	6
Wm. Reeves, 4d. worke in gorstie corn'...	0	8	0
Wm. Penny 1 odd selion	0	0	2
Robte Flynt 2d. worke at Lydiyate	0	5	0
Robte Flynte for 1d. worke of feild land	0	2	0
The halfe years chiefe rents	5	5	11

RENTS OF LANDS LATE MR. FOLLYOTTS.

	£	s.	d.
Tho. Edwards for his house and grounds	2	11	2
Wid. Rider for a little meadowe...	1	0	0
Jo. Stamps for a house and grounds	4	10	0
Jo. Stamps for land w'ch Edwards and Granger did hold	3	2	6
Jo. Wyley for a house and garden...	0	6	8
Tho. Hadley for Wid. Bulls house and grounds	2	0	0
Gregory Woodwards for house and grounds	1	13	4
Wm. Jesson for a little barne	0	0	6
Mr. Rotton for his farme at Harborne	20	0	0
Henry Osborne, of Handsworth...	15	0	0
	35	0	0

MONEY PAYABLE BY JOHN SHELTON, ESQ.., AT TH' ANNU'C, 1649.

	£	s.	d.
To Tho. Sheldon of Crankell for p'te of ye lands w'ch Jo. Coley held ...	0	0	4
To the bayliffs of the hundred for frith silver...	0	4	4
To Mr. Jo. Syncox for a passage over the lane to Bustleholme	0	0	6
	0	5	2

(*undorsed*) Westbromwich
rent rolle at
Th' archangell only 1649,
JOH. HOPKINS.

£	s.	d.
121	3	9
28	7	10
30	15	0
2	10	8
15	4	8
198	1	11

It will be observed that the outgoing amount of 5s. 2d. is payable not at Michaelmas, but at the opposite half year, viz., "The Annunciation," or March 25th. The endorsement, too, seems to be inaccurate in the last two totals, which cast up to £2 12s. 8d. and £15 4s. 2d. respectively; but these may be mere clerical errors in transcription. The contribution of "frithsilver" or *peace money* paid to the Bailiff of the Hundred illustrates the subordination of Manors to Hundreds, and of the Hundreds to the County. The name "Crankell" evidently stands for *Crankhall*. John Hopkins was the Steward of the Manor, or the Seneschal. But to go back to the beginning of the document:—

(1) In the first list of lands and rents (amounting to the then goodly sum of £121 3s. 9d.) we note that Bustleholme Rod Mill was let at a rental of ten guineas a year, while the rent of the Forge of Mr. Foley was only £7 10s. 0d.; against the Whornall lands it is noted that only £3 18s. 0d. had been paid some time previously, perhaps because it was then newly enclosed from the common lands. Several widows seem to be in possession of lands which had no doubt been formerly occupied by their husbands. Of abbreviations we have "mes." for *messuage*, a dwelling-house with the land adjacent assigned to its use; "tenem't" (or "ten'te" in another list) for *tenement*, which was larger in signification than *messuage*, as it comprehended not only the house but all corporeal inheritances exercisable with the same, "mede" means *meadow*; "p'cell" stands for *parcel* or piece of land: and it may be added here that a croft was generally a small close of land adjoining a dwelling house. Every house then (except in cities) had its croft or paddock attached.

(2) In the second roll (which totals to £28 7s. 10d.) attention may be directed to several of the items. Again we find the name of the two iron-masters. Fowke and Foley, as occupiers of the Tame Bridge Grounds, near their Rod Mill and Forge at Bustleholme. As already noticed in Chaps. xxxv. and xxxvi. the value of water-power was just then attracting to the stream sides all manufacturing concerns when the processes needed "power." These waterside works, too, were getting nearer the wooded country of Sutton and Cannock, for the woods of South Staffordshire had for centuries been gradually disappearing through the devouring and insatiable furnace-mouths, the woodlands ever receding as the ironstone pits steadily advanced. As it was found impracticable, or at least unprofitable, to cart the wood from a distance, the other alternative was to take the ironstone to the woods. Hence sweet-smelling corn mills were converted to noisy hammer mills or dirty blade mills. Among the first to undertake these newer commercial and manufacturing enterprises in this district were those families so quaintly described under the old-style designation of "ironmongers"—Foley, Parkes Jennings, etc. The Oldford, or Hol-ford Mill, at Perry Barr, was another mill similarly worked by the Foley family at an iron-forge. The next item of interest is the place-name "Broomy Close," which seems to distinctly re-assert the presence here of the plant *broom* from which the parish originally derived its name of "Broomwich." Then in the use of the common noun "pingle" we have another confirmation of the fact that the purest Chancerian English was spoken in this locality. "Pingle" is another form of "pike" or *picle* (in some parts called also *pightel*) and is a good English word for a little close of land surrounded by a hedge. The form "pike" will be found mentioned in the fourth list. Some philologists connect the word with the Italian *picciola*. "Hemplecke" would probably designate an enclosure from the *waste* planted with *hemp*, the cultivation of which in olden times was somewhat strangely regulated by law, for by *33 Hen, VIII. c. 17*, a crop of hemp (or of flax) might not be watered by any running stream or common pond under pain of 40s.: while about a century later by *15 Car. II. c 15*, if even a foreigner exercised the trade of dressing hemp (or flax) to make tapestry, twine, cordage, etc, after three years he would acquire the

privilege of naturalisation, the industry being then thus encouraged somewhat artificially by legislation. In the very earliest Workhouses which were erected, "idle" paupers were nearly always set to work to beat hemp.

(3) In the third list by "Demesne Lands" we are to understand the Home Farms, which in earlier times had been cultivated by labour-rent or services of the tenants occupying the tenemental portions of the Manor, according to ancient custom; as has been previously explained in chapters ix. and xx. demesne lands were generally measured by plough-teams (*carucæ*).

In the supervision of the cultivation of these demesne lands it was the duty of the Steward or Seneschal when he first came to the manor (on his round from one manor to another) to see how many acres ought to be reaped "by boon or custom," and how many for money. But how scarce money was even at this comparatively late period, may be gauged by scrutinising the monetary totals of this Rent-Roll. It does not aid us much if we place the value of money at twelve times its present value; even at twenty times current values our minds will fail to grasp the vast discrepancy.

"Gorstie Croft" was named after the prevailing *gorse-bushes*, from which also that well-known spot Gosta Green derived its appellation. "Pes Croft" was no doubt so-called because of the crops of *peas* it produced.

(4). The fourth roll is a list of "Field Lands" now "set" to tenants. These tenants had in the earlier feudal period been known as *villains* or *natives*. They were the tillers, not only of their own small holdings, but of the lord's lands as well, for besides sometimes now paying him a small ground rent they had always been required to perform certain stipulated services for their lord, such as ploughing his demesne lands so many days in the year with their own teams (*carucæ*); carrying his corn so many days at harvest-time; and so on. These "days' work" to be thus rendered as rents were gradually commuted to money payments, as the system of villainage steadily decayed, and men became free. It will be seen that in West Bromwich the average rate of commutation seems to be 2s. for each "day's work." As to the nature of the "feild lands" "set" to these freed men, they were undoubtedly survivals in *name only* of that system of collective ownership by the inhabitants of the whole parish as a village community; a system which characterised the origins of all Saxon settlements such as these which here sprang up under the shadow of Woden's Hill. By this system, only that portion of the land which was suitable and necessary for the production of corn and other crops was enclosed and cultivated, the remainder being left open to the cattle of all (as set forth in chap. xiv.), and where every member of the community was entitled to cut turf and bracken for fuel and litter. The enclosed part was generally divided into three great *fields*—hence the name here surviving—for a three-course system of husbandry, of which one field in turn was left in fallow. Each of these fields was divided into a certain number of equal parts which were distributed annually by lot among the heads of families constituting the village community. Such was the system of Communism which anciently prevailed in West Bromwich, Wednesbury, and all the more ancient Saxon settlements, and of which the only remnant in 1649 was this lingering place- name. Modern Socialists in West Bromwich will not fail to observe that these common lands had been absorbed into the estate of the lord of the manor, who was then deriving £2 12s. 8d. a year from them, to say nothing of twice that amount set down as a half-year's chief rents. One other point only needs elucidation: a "selion" of land was a ridge of ground rising between two furrows, but whose exact dimensions were variable and uncertain.

(5). The last roll is rent of lands apparently acquired from the Follyot family. These lands would probably be in Warwickshire, although the two largest parcels are only on the Staffordshire borders, namely, in Harborne and Handsworth respectively.

XLI.—The Whorwood Family (1577–1701): The Period of the Civil War.

After the dissolution of Sandwell Priory in 1526 the monastic estates passed through the hands of various favored individuals, who however held them but for comparatively short periods owing perhaps to the unsettled state of things during the Reformation decades. After Wolsey's original seizure (1526), "the site of the dissolved priory," was held till 1558 by the Cliffords. The first holders to remain on the estate for a prolonged period were the Whorwoods to whom it was next *granted* and who came to West Bromwich towards the end of Elizabeth's reign.

The Whorwood family are traced back by Shaw's pedigree to one John Whorwood, of Compton, whom we may consider the founder of this notable family. He had issue amongst other children (1) John who died 1528; and (2) Richard, the other of William, founder of the Tipton branch of this family. (See History of Tipton, chap. XVII) .This John, the eldest, had issue (1) John, who married Joyce daughter of Sir Ed. Grey, of Enville, one of the noble houses of England remaining to this day; and (2) William, an attorney-general to Henry VIII, and whose eminence in the legal world enabled him to secure for a wife, Mary, daughter of Brooke Corbyn (of Corbyn's Hall), a baron of the Exchequer, when she became a widow she entered the family of the Sheldons, of Beoley, by a second marriage. This William is mentioned as possessing lands in Rowley with "rights of heath and furze" (1533), in chapter XXI.

The third John, and grandson of the first John, Whorwood, had amongst other issue, two sons of whom our local history must take cognisance. The first and eldest, was Edward, who is described as "of Compton," and who no doubt passed into possession of the ancestral mansion at Compton, to him and his branch we shall refer later on. The other was Robert, who is more intimately connected with West Bromwich and its history.

(1) Robert Whorwood, of Sandwell, is the first of this family who can be found in actual residence at Sandwell. although even of him Reeves says:—"His residence was Stourton Castle, near Kinver." The earliest date at which the name can be found recorded in connection with West Bromwich is June 12th, 1577. In a sale of lands in this parish the deed of this date mentions Wall Way, the older name of Wall Face, where the Hill Top Branch Library now stands; and it proceeds to mention land at Wigmore, near to some in the possession of "Robert Whorwood, Esq." The next mention is in Ryder's Memoranda—

"1587.—Paid to Mr. Whorwood for my tithes the 1st of May, 5d."

Three years later when Robert died 13th October 1590, he was found to be seized of the *manor* of Sandwell; also a mill and divers lands in West Bromwich, Barr, Handsworth, and Tipton (with its rectory—see *History of Tipton*, chap. xxi.) held in capite by Knight's service, and the hundredth part of a Knight's fee.

As noted in chap. xxviii. the rectorial tithes having been granted to the holder of the old monastic estate—which, by the way, is here distinctly designated a "manor"—the "rectory" of West Bromwich became a "donative." But the earliest record of the Whorwoods being in actual receipt of the tithes is that of the *Survey* of 1586, mentioned in chapter xxxi)., when they were bringing in £60 a year to the Impropriator "Mr. Whorwood," who was paying a Curate a stipend of £20 out of this revenue.

(2) Sir William Whorwood, his son, succeeded in 1590. In an indenture of the year 1594, he is described as "William Whorwood, Esq., possessing certain lands near Barditch, near to the ancient way from Wolverhampton to Birmingham. And to the ancient way from West Bromwich to Smethwick. His wife was Anne heiress of Henry Field, she

died in 1599. He was a Justice of the Peace, and in 1604 was also Sheriff of the County. He is described as a knight. and of both "Sandwell and Stourton Castle." In 1609, by an Indenture dated 17th February (chap. xxviii.) he formally acquired the advowson of West Bromwich. In the enumeration of his possessions at the time of his death they are set down practically as those mentioned in the possession of his father, with the additional item of 400 acres in Fryer's Park. It was while attending in London on business that Sir William died suddenly at his town house in Basingshaw, at 6 o'clock in the morning of July 1st, 1614. His body was brought to West Bromwich for interment, and in the old parish church pulled down in 1786, were the tombs of himself and his wife. They were of alabaster, standing close together in the "south chancel," within iron rails, "on the southmost a man on his back with a book in his left hand." By his wife Anne he had issue thirteen children, five sons and eight daughters. In his will he provided for the erection of a chapel on the south side of the church, and which was "to resemble that of Mr. Stanley on the north side"—(see chapter xxix.). The Whorwood Chapel was completed in 1619.

In addition to the Whorwood tombs just mentioned there also formerly stood another monument in the northern side of the chancel to Field Whorwood, fourth son of Sir William and his wife Anne (neé Field). who died July 1658 at the age of 66.

Sir William Whorwood, in the year 1614, gave, by will, £6 12s. to be paid equally to thirty three poor inhabitants of West Bromwich and such poor of Handsworth as dwell along the highway near Sandwell, viz., to every one a like portion as near as they can divide it, payable at West Bromwich Church on Christmas Eve and Good Friday, for ten years after his decease; and after ten years then £10 yearly for ever one of the tythes of West Bromwich. Lord Dartmouth now pays this, which is known as the Tithes Dole. Till 1816 it was distributed annually at the Hall.

One of the Whorwood's left a piece of land known as Monk's Meadow, and situated somewhere near the Smethwick boundary of the parish, for the support of a school in the parish. All trace of this charity would seem to be entirely lost.

Sir William was 51 years of age at the time of his death.

(3) THOMAS WHORWOOD, OF SANDWELL, KNIGHT, succeeded to the family honours in 1614, and although his wife Ursula, daughter and heiress of George Brome, had on his marriage ten years previously brought him very extensive estates in Oxfordshire, he does not seem to have upheld the family dignity as might have been expected. He was a man of headstrong will and hasty temper, and given to miserable fretfulness after each ebullition. He made himself very ridiculous for his many base acts and degrading penury. Having brought upon himself much mental anxiety by giving way to his passion on one occasion, and commanding his Bailiff to kill a man at Kings Norton, he died a short time before he was to have been censured in the Court of Star Chamber in 1635 at London. He was only in his 47th year, had attained the honour of knighthood, and served as Sheriff in 1632. He founded a benefaction in the parish now known as the *Brick-kiln Dole*. It was in 1635 Sir Thomas Whorwood, Knight, purchased land galled the "Brick-kiln Land," out of the arrears of rent devised to the poor of West Bromwich by the will of Sir William Whorwood, deceased, and gave it to trustees for the poor for ever. The first trustees were Edward Grove, Thomas Grove, John Turton the younger, etc. Trustees in 1691—John Turton, of The Oak, Thomas Jesson, John Lowe, Henry Hunt, John Turton, of Hately Heath. In 1722 John Turton, Josiah Turton, etc. etc. This Dole was always given away in single shillings on St. Thomas' Day. In 1870 the vicar, churchwardens, and trustees met together and came finally to the conclusion to spend the money arising from the Dole in blankets, to be divided among the ecclesiastical parishes. Instead of a shilling, spent and gone in a few hours. many a family is now yearly thankful for the comfort of a warm blanket. With regard to this

Dole, among the church papers is a notice, dated 1862, which says—The land is situate at the back of the lodge grounds. The mines under this property have been sold to William Izon, Esq., and £619 1s. 4d. paid to the Official Trustee of the Charity Commissioners at the Bank of England, for investment in Government Securities.

(4).—Brome Whorwood bore the name of both father and mother, and his career was somewhat of a romantic character. He was married (1634) about a day before his father's sudden death, to Jane, daughter of William Rider, who had been harbinger (or courier) to James I. The first documentary reference to him is an Indenture of 1637, which mentions "Brome Whorewood, Esq.," as possessing land in the parish near the "Monnynges." But to pass on to the more stirring times of "The Great Rebellion." With the approach of the first distant rumblings of the political thunder of that commotion and unwanted violence occurring in Parliament, differences of opinion begin imperceptibly to manifest themselves between neighbours who had been hitherto close and friendly, and even among members of the same family. The best known families of West Bromwich were no exception to this rule. The Whorwoods became divided among themselves, while the estrangement between the Whorwoods and the Turtons, who had often worshipped together in the same parish church soon developed from mere distrust into open hostility. To be fair to both sides, it may be conceded that those who became known as Cavaliers sided with the king from high chivalric motives; while those stern grave warriors who were derisively called Roundheads were actuated by an intelligence equally high, and which enabled them to look far ahead into the future for the logical outcome of all the King's acts of misrule in the past.

Gradually, but orderly, just like chessmen arrayed on the board for the pending struggle, every man of note fell into his right position, as his character and his circumstances dictated. Stourton Castle, the ancestral home of the Whorwoods, was rapidly fortified on behalf of the King, but within two years had fallen into the hands of the Parliamentarians. Yet the owner, John Whorwood, is found on the Cromwellian side fourteen years later. Brome Whorwood, of Sandwell, remained a consistent and uncompromising Royalist to the end. On the other side, when (March 9th, 1642) Charles refused to give up the command of the Militia, and Parliament issued their own independent commissions, Captain Turton, of The Oak, became one of their first russet-coated officers in these parts. Edward Dudley, of The Green House, Tipton, who had married a daughter of Richard Sheldon of Wednesbury Hall, was another unyielding Royalist. His father-in-law was a Wednesbury yeoman (Salt. Coll. X. pt. II. p. 64), and apparently not of the same family as the Sheldons who then held West Bromwich Manor. Yet Sir Richard Shelton lord of the manor, although unfitted to take active part in the strife, was at heart a Royalist, having been some time a Solicitor-General to Charles I. Soon after 1647 his nephew and successor, John Sheldon, purchased the manor of Wednesbury, and as he was Sheriff in 1660 seems also to have steered tolerably clear of partisanship, notwithstanding that he was an avowed Nonconformist (chap. xxxii.).

This Edward Dudley was a man of means and of considerable social importance. He was fined £14 for not taking the order of knighthood at the coronation of Charles I. From State Papers, namely, the "Calendar of Committee for Advance of Money," we gather that when the Commonwealth came into undisputed power in 1649, that there was a petition to the Committee in the October that "delinquent" Dudley should be sequestered, his estate being set down at £200 a year and more. From the same papers, an entry of January 14th, 1650, states that "Magdalene Lewne lived with her brother (Colonel) Leveson in Dudley Castle all the late war. John Perry of Sardon and Rich. Perry of Wednesbury, owe her £450." Reverting to Edward Dudley's case, the evidence against him seems quite clear and circumstantial, Richard Caddick of Sedgley lodging the petition against him. In the following month, namely on November 16th, John Caddick laid information that Dudley had assisted the late King; and in the following January renewed information alleged that he had sent men and arms into the King's garrison—presumably Dudley Castle. Yet in 1659 another "Edward Dudley of Tipton" received a Captain's commission to raise a troop for the Commonwealth. Evidently he was a nephew of the first Edward, and regained the confidence of Cromwell and Fleetwood by lending large sums to the Parliamentary treasury. They were awkward times to live in. It was sometimes expedient for families to change sides. Among other local notabilities who took part in the great struggle were the Parliamentarians, Captain Henry Stone and Colonel "Tinker" Fox, both of Walsall; that world renowned loyal gentleman, Colonel Lane of Bentley, George Haw of Caldmore, and William Hopkins of Oakeswell Hall, Wednesbury, both staunch Royalists also. On the same side, Sir Thomas Holte had to withstand an attack on his mansion, Aston Hall, while Sir Edward Leigh turned his residence, Rushall Hall, into a real garrison, around which considerable fighting raged, and where William Hopkins and Colonel Lane were taken prisoners by the Earl of Denbigh, May 22nd, 1644. Rushall was then placed in the hands of Captain Tuthill. War contributions were levied on the unfortunate population by both contending factions. The Earl of Denbigh advanced in June and encamped on Bromwich Heath preparatory to making the attack on Dudley Castle with a larger force. The governor of the castle at this time was Lieutenant-Colonel Beaumont. Advancing from Bromwich Heath, the formation for attack was performed on Tipton Green. The Royalists, who had been reinforced by a brigade of horse and 1,000 foot soldiers, sent by the king from Shrewsbury, ambuscaded all the hedgerows and approaches to the castle. The sturdy Roundheads, however, charged every line, and drove the enemy steadily before them, but leaving some 60 of their number dead upon the field. Beyond this the besiegers gained no advantage, and both sides claimed a victory. In 1646 the castle was quietly surrendered to the Parliament.

Another Royalist was Colonel Edward Stamford, of Perry Hall. On that October day in 1642, when King Charles held his muster of the local Royalist gentlemen on Perry Common, Edward Stamford, Sir Thomas Holte, and Brome Whorwood acting almost in the capacity of hosts (from the close contiguity of their three several mansions), gave welcome to their king and comrades, eager to speed the great enterprise on which they were about to embark. On the 23rd day of that month the first battle of the Civil War was fought on the opposite boundary of Warwickshire, only some thirty miles or so away, at Edgehill.

Of the actual movements and activities of Brome Whorwood in all the changing episodes of the Civil War, research has yet failed to disclose the details. As the King was generally destitute of money and of arms, and as Brome Whorwood had considerable wealth, it may be imagined that the Royal coffers were generously supplied from time to time from the resources of the owner of Sandwell. The fortification of Oxford and of Lichfield on the King's behalf would busily employ the Whorwood retainers; hard riding between these points of communication by swift and secret messengers was best undertaken by men well acquainted with the dangers as well as the intricacies of the road. Brome Whorwood held the extensive Oxfordshire estate brought into the family by his mother, as well as Sandwell. It is probable that when Charles fell so fiercely on Waller at Cropredy Bridge on the last day of June, 1646, that many of the loyal gentlemen of Warwickshire and Staffordshire were also in the thick of that local fight.

In three years the cause of Charles was lost, but that there had been no lack of loyal support on the part of Brome Whorwood may be inferred from the severity of the penalty meted out to him. When the committee sat in London to consider each royalist's delinquency, and to award the penalties in proportion either to the offender's activity in the campaign, or else to his means—and in raising money for the Parliamentary cause the latter consideration was by no means an unimportant one—we find the "composition" apportioned to some of the Staffordshire "malignants" set at the following amounts:—

Sir Simon Degge, of Callowhill, was let off on payment of £7.

Richard Shelton, of Tettenhall, paid only £40 3s. 4d.

William Hopkins, of Oakeswall Hall, Wednesbury who was taken prisoner in actual combat at the siege of Rushall Hall, £195.

Colonel Thomas Lane, of Bentley Hall, a man of larger means and greater influence, captured at the same time, £225.

"Bromley" Whorwood, of Sandwell Hall, was fined the excessively large sum of £872. When the Earl Denbigh lay encamped on Bromwich Heath he would appear to have given a very high estimate of the importance of the lord of Sandwell.

Whether the heaviness of this forfeiture was due to Brome Whorewood's wealth, or to his prowess, it would be impossible to say. It would seem from some authorities that this disastrous termination of his brief military career weighed upon him so heavily that he died very shortly after the year 1654, and was succeeded by his son, Thomas Brome Whorwood.

(5) THOMAS BROME WHORWOOD has been confused by some writers with Brome Whorwood his father whom he succeeded some time shortly after 1654. He became the last of the family to live at Sandwell and as he did not leave the parish till 1701, he was master of Sandwell for the long period of half-a-century.

A deed dated 24 March 1670 of the sale of the Barditch property mentions adjoining land there as "the land now *or late* of Broom Whorwood Esq." and more lands of his near a "a certain common field" called "Wiggmorefield." An endorsement contains a memorandum of agreement between the two parties to this sale "that the money formerly paid to the Abbot of Sandwell, and now to Broome Whorwood Esq. and his heirs shall be effectually excepted by this" &c.

In 1680 T. Brome Whorwood was removed from the Commission of the Peace for the county of Oxford, not being able to inspire confidence in the Ultra-Protestant Ministry at that period of unrest and suspicion.

A Terrier of 1693 setting forth the profits accruing to the curate holding the living of the parish of West Bromwich, "Thomas Broom Whorwood Esq. being Impropriator, alloweth to him that supplieth his cure there, in money a salary of £20 per annum, and a house to live in, with the garden and backside adjoining," and all the customary fees &c.

After being connected with this parish for a century and a quarter the Whorwoods give place in 1701 to the newer family of the Dartmouths. By a document dated April the 3rd in the first year of the eighteenth century, Thomas Brome Whorwood, granted and conveyed to the Rt. Hon. William Lord Dartmouth, his heirs and assigns for ever, the rectory. premises, &c. of West Bromwich." Thus terminated their connection with West Bromwich, and their further history must be looked for in Oxfordshire and elsewhere.

*   *   *   *   *   *   *

Going back in Shaw's pedigree to the third John Whorwood, of Compton, it was mentioned that his eldest son who succeeded to the patrimonial acres was named Edward—brother of the Robert Whorwood who first took up his residence at Sandwell. Edward was succeeded by Thomas of Stourton and Compton, who in 1572 was Member of Parliament for Staffordshire, with John Fleetwood as his colleague in the representation of this county. He was also Sheriff of the county more than once, certainly in 1573 and 1596; he died about 1617. Then Shaw's pedigree becomes obscure. Issue of the foregoing Thomas is given as Gerrard, who died about 1583, or some 60 or 70 years before his own son John, who is said to have sold Compton about 1650 to John Foley Esq. Probably it was John's son who transacted this sale. As to "Gerrard," that will be found a favourite baptismal name of the Tipton branch, as the registers of that parish will reveal nearly a century later (1667).

This John Whorwood of Stourton Castle, Compton, and Dunsley, was a man of sound character and great ability. He became an active Parliamentarian, exercising considerable influence on this side. He lived at Dunsley, near to Kinver. As a magistrate exercising official functions during the time of the Commonwealth. When marriages were performed as a civil ceremony in the presence of a justice of the peace, we have the following preserved on record:— "The purpose of marriage between Thomas Heming of Old Swinford, the sonne of Francis Heming, of Rouse Lench, in the county of Worcester, and Elizabeth, ye daughter of William Rushton, of Wolverhampton, was published there several Lord's Dayes in the parish church of Wolverhampton, March 2, 9, and 16, 1655, and they were afterwards married at Dunsley Hall, before Mr. John Whorwood, March 22nd, 1655."

The pedigree then gives a (second) Sir William, but of Stourton Castle instead of Sandwell Hall, as the issue of this John. The next in descent is given as Wortley Whorwood, who sold the chief of the family seats, namely, Stourton Castle, and this again to the newly rich family of the Foleys. The enterprise and commercial spirit of the Foley family, then engaged in the iron-rod and nail-making trades, have been already commented upon. Here they become possessed of a magnificent family residence, historically famous as the birth-place of Reginald, Cardinal Pole, and which the Foley family have continued to possess up to the present day. Wortley Whorwood purchased Denton Court, near Canterbury, and leaving the Midlands altogether, took up his residence in Kent, where his sound Protestant opinions placed him on the Commission of the Peace for that county where all England was disturbed by those supposed Popish Plots of 1680. Here again was diversity of opinion among the different branches of this family. Wortley was made a magistrate while Thomas Brome was removed from the bench. Men's minds were then often distraught, and factions opinion ran so high in the seventeenth century that the sequence of events ran farther than from thoughts to words—for words begat blows, and hence all this civil strife and political commotion.

XLII.—The Dartmouth Family come to Sandwell (1701): their Antecedents from 1326: Lord Dartmouth the Suspected Traitor (1691).

The welcome accorded to Lord Dartmouth and his family by the parishioners of West Bromwich has already been noted. It was done by a formal resolution of the Vestry meeting on March 9th, 1701, acknowledging his lordship's proprietary right in the "Little Chancel" (afterwards known as the Dartmouth Pew) or Whorwood Chapel. The legal conveyance of the estate from the Whorwoods to the Lord Dartmouth is dated April 3rd following.

This William, baron of Dartmouth, who now took up his residence at Sandwell, was the second to bear that title. He was the only son of his father the first baron, and was born 14th October, 1672. He took his seat in the House of Peers, 22nd November, 1695, at the age of 23, and came to West Bromwich at the age of 29, very soon after his marriage. Enjoying the confidence of Queen Anne he was sworn in 1710 one of her principal Secretaries of State, and in the following year, September 25th, was advanced to the dignities of Viscount Lewisham, in Kent, and Earl of Dartmouth. In 1713 he was appointed Lord Keeper of the Privy Seal. His lordship had married, July, 1700, Lady Anne Finch, third daughter of Heneage, Earl of Aylesford and by her (who died November 30, 1751) had issue six sons and but two daughters, viz., (1) the Lady Barbara, married, July 27, 1724, to Sir Walter Bagot, of Blithfield, in this county, bart.; and (2) Lady Anne, married, in October, 1739 to Sir Lister Holt, of Aston, in the neighbouring county of Warwick, bart.

On the death of Queen Anne the Earl of Dartmouth was made one of the Lords Justices of Great Britain, being at the same time High Steward of Dartmouth.

Now as to the antecedents and family history of this new comer at Sandwell:

*   *   *   *   *   *   *

"This antient and respectable family, it is said, came out of Italy into this kingdom, though the exact period when is not ascertained, Hugh de la Lega, and Richard, son of Osbert, were Sheriffs of Bedfordshire and Bucks from the 10th to the 16th of Henry II. and William de la Lega (as the name is written in antient records) was Sheriff of Herefordshire 17 Henry II. Those of Herefordshire have always been esteemed the elder branch, but those of Legg's-place, near Tunbridge, in Kent, were resident there for many generations before Thomas Legge, whose name generally heads the family pedigree." The acknowledged founder of this noble family, Thomas Legge, in the year 1326, was Alderman of the Company of Skinners, and served the office of Sheriff of the City of London in 1343 and was Lord Mayor in 1346 and again in 1356, the years of Cressy and Poitiers respectively. In 1338, this opulent citizen had lent Edward III., towards carrying on the war with France, £300, which was a very considerable sum in those days, and was far more than any other citizen had advanced, except the Lord Mayor, and Simon de Francis, who lent each £800 in the ensuing year. Alderman Legge, a merchant prince, married Elizabeth, daughter of the noble house of Thomas Beauchamp, Earl of Warwick. He was succeeded by his eldest son, Simon. Simon Legge married Margaret, daughter of Sir John Blount; and his eldest surviving son was William Legge, who going into Ireland, settled at Cassilis, when he married Ann, only daughter of John, son of Miles, Lord Bermingham. He died at the advanced age of ninety and was succeeded by his son.

Edward Legge became vice-president of Munster, in Ireland, during the lieutenancy of his kinsman. Sir Charles Blount, and Lord Mountjoy. This gentleman married Mary, daughter of Percy Walsh, Esq of Moy Vallie, and had six sons and seven daughters.

The eldest son, William Legge, was brought out of Ireland by his godfather. Henry Danvers, Earl of Danby, and sent by him as a volunteer under Gustavus Adolphus, of Sweden; and he served afterwards under Prince Maurice, of Orange, in the Low Countries. On his return to England, he was first constituted Keeper of the King's Wardrobe during life; and was made soon after Groom of the Bedchamber. Colonel Legge, during the Civil Wars became eminently distinguished by his faithful attachment to King Charles I., and for his persevering exertions in the royal cause, before and after the execution of the king. At the battle of Worcester, he was wounded and taken prisoner, and would have been executed, if his wife had not have contrived his escape from Coventry gaol, disguised in her own clothes. He was high in favour after the restoration, and enjoyed several lucrative and honourable offices. Colonel Legge married Elizabeth, eldest daughter of Sir William Washington, of Packington, in the county of Leicester and granddaughter, maternally of Sir George Villers, of Brooksley, in the same county. He died in 1672.

We now come to the greatest of the Legge family; or at least to the one who looms largest amongst all those past shadows who have flitted across the pages of the nation's history.

* * * * * * *

Colonel Legge was succeeded by his eldest son, George Legge, Esq. Sent to sea at the age of seventeen and who became a naval and military officer of eminence. From 1667 to 1672 he commanded a line-of-battle ship, and was wounded in the taking and destroying of the Dutch fleet. He was appointed in the latter year Lieutenant Governor of Portsmouth; in 1673 advanced to the Governorship; and soon after was further appointed Master of the Horse, and Gentleman of the Bedchamber to James, Duke of York, afterwards James II. and to whom he became closely attached. In 1677 Governor Legge was Constituted Colonel of a regiment of foot, and nominated Lieutenant General of the Ordnance, of which he was soon afterwards (1682) made Master with a commission for viewing all the forts and garrisons of England. He was subsequently sworn of the Privy Council. Charles II. also granted him a charter to hold a Fair twice a year, and a Market twice a week upon Blackheath in the parish of Lewisham, Kent from which parish the second title of the ennobled family is now taken. The same monarch elevated this favourite courtier to the Peerage, 2 December, 1682, as Baron of Dartmouth, in the county of Devon, with remainder after his own male heirs, to his brother William and his heirs male. His lordship was soon afterwards sent as Admiral of the whole English fleet to demolish Tangier, with a commission as Governor of that city and Captain-General of all his Majesty's forces in Africa. Upon his return he obtained a grant of £10,000, in reward for his services in that quarter of the world. During the succeeding reign of King James II. Lord Dartmouth enjoyed the confidence of that most Catholic monarch, and filled some of the most important offices. In 1685, after the rebellion of the unfortunate Monmouth had been quelled at the battle of Sedgemoor the last ever fought on English soil, the Duke, as a prisoner of war, was received at Vauxhall, London, into the custody of George Legge, Lord Dartmouth, and conveyed in a state barge down the Thames to Whitehall Stairs. After the rebel's affecting interview with James II. he was conveyed to the Tower. On his way he implored the intercession of Dartmouth. "I know, my Lord, that you loved my father [Charles II.] For his sake, for God's sake, try if there be any room for mercy." Dartmouth replied that the King (James II.) had spoken the truth (in the recent interview), and that a subject who assumed the regal title excluded himself from pardon.

In 1687 Dartmouth was appointed Admiral of the Fleet, which indicates the unbounded confidence James II. placed in him. Peculation and corruption at the Admiralty had been rife, but the King had just accomplished reforms in that department, and placed under Dartmouth a fleet of thirty ships of the line, all third rates and fourth rates, lying in the Thames. "The loyalty of Dartmouth was not suspected, and he was thought to have as much professional skill as any of the patrician sailors who, in that age, rose to the highest naval commands without a regular naval training, and who were at once flag officers on the sea, and colonels of infantry on shore."

When William of Orange set sail the second time to invade England in 1688, the same breeze which favoured his voyage from Holland prevented Dartmouth (who is said to have then commanded 38 ships of the line and 23 frigates) from coming out of the Thames. His ships were forced to strike yards and topmasts. Two of his frigates, which had gained the open sea were shattered by the violence of the weather. At length Dartmouth was able to proceed, and came in sight of the Dutch topmasts in Torbay. Just at this moment he was encountered by the tempest and compelled to take shelter in Portsmouth Harbour." At that time James II., who was not incompetent to form a judgment on a question of seamanship, declared himself satisfied that his Admiral had done all that man could do, and had yielded only to the irrepressible hostility of the wind and waves. At a later period the unfortunate prince began, with little reason, to suspect Dartmouth of treachery, or at least of slackness."

When the cause of James II. was hopelessly lost, preparations were made for flight. Dartmouth, lying at Portsmouth, refused to transport the young Prince of Wales to France. He was still zealous for the crown, and had done all he could with a disaffected fleet. He was also equally zealous for the Established Church. Then news came that a free Parliament had been convoked, and Commissioners named to treat with the Prince of Orange. Joy ran clamorously throughout the fleet, and an Address warmly thanking the King for making gracious concessions to public feeling was drawn up on the flag ship signed by the Admiral first, followed by the names of 38 captains. Dartmouth soon found that all these promised concessions were parts of a great fraud on the nation. Although Dartmouth was grieved and angered at this, after James and his family had fled to the Continent, and William assumed the reins of government in England, the Admiral was removed from his command, and the sailors were conciliated by assurances of speedily receiving their overdue pay. As to Dartmouth himself, Macaulay says he "had as little scruple about taking the oath of allegiance as he afterwards had about breaking it."

Dartmouth, though he had sworn allegiance to the new sovereigns, William and Mary, "was one of their most active enemies," continues Macaulay, "and undertook what may be called the maritime department of the plot to restore James II. His mind was constantly occupied by schemes, disgraceful to an English seaman, for the destruction of the English fleets and arsenals." And who so capable a traitor in this respect as one who had held command of both fleets and forts? But to continue our extract from Macaulay: "He was in close communication with some naval officers, who, though they served the new Government, served it sullenly and with half a heart, and he flattered himself that by promising these men ample rewards, and by artfully inflaming the jealous animosity with which they regarded the Dutch flag, he would prevail on them to desert and to carry their ships into some French or Irish port"— Ireland being a Jacobite stronghold at that time (1690). After the defeat of James II. at the Battle of the Boyne, however (July 1st), the Jacobites were crushed. For this plot only one traitor was sacrificed to the executioner, of course one of humble origin, an innkeeper of Rye who had conveyed information to the French Fleet, about the time they had defeated the combined English and Dutch fleets off Beachy Head. The danger subsiding, the arch-traitors like Dartmouth and Clarendon became busy again. "and drew from their pockets libels on the Court of Kensington, and letters in milk and lemon juice from the Court of St. Germains." It was then determined that the head of the conspiracy, Viscount Preston, should carry to St. Germains various resolutions and suggestions of the conspirators; and in the important packet of secret missives one was a list of the English fleet, furnished by Dartmouth. At dead of night, the last night of the old year of 1690, Preston and his gentlemanly accomplices in treason embarked on a smack from near the Tower. Not being challenged by sentinel or by guard frigate their spirits rose. Getting out a hamper of beef, mince pies, wine, and other Christmas cheer, they had scarcely sat down to enjoy themselves when a swift vessel came flying after them. On being boarded, they were promptly arrested; and in his agitation Preston dropped the fatal packet. Preston was afterwards convicted and sentenced to death, but ultimately pardoned. In confessing, he named Clarendon, Dartmouth, and other accomplices. "The treason of Dartmouth was of no common dye. He was an English seaman; and he had a plan for betraying Portsmouth to the French, and had offered to take the command of a French squadron against his country. It was a serious aggravation of his guilt that he had been one of the very first persons who took the oaths to William and Mary. He was arrested and brought to the Council Chamber. In a narrative written by himself he admits that he was treated with great courtesy and delicacy. He vehemently asserted his innocence. He declared that he had never corresponded with St. Germains, that he was no favourite there, and that Mary of Modena (the ex queen) owed him a grudge. "My lords," he said, "I am an Englishman. I always when the interest of the House of Bourbon was strongest here, shunned the French, both men and women. I would lose the last drop of my blood rather than see Portsmouth in the power of foreigners. I am not such a fool as to think that King Louis will conquer us merely for the benefit of King James. I am certain that nothing can be imputed to me beyond some foolish talk over a bottle." His protestations seem to have produced some effect; for he was at first permitted to remain in the gentle custody of the Black Rod. On further inquiry, however, it was determined to send him to the Tower. After a confinement of a few weeks he died of apoplexy, but he lived long enough to complete his disgrace by offering his sword to the new government, and by expressing in fervent language his hope that he might by the goodness of God and of Their Majesties, have an opportunity of showing how much he hated the French." Such is Lord Macaulay's estimate of this man's character. He died October 25th, 1691, after an adventurous career, terminated by a three months' imprisonment in the Tower, and at the comparatively early age of 44. Although a prisoner of State, all proper respect was paid to his funeral, the Tower guns being fired when he was carried out to be interred near his father in the Minories, where a monument of white marble is erected to his memory by Barbara, his lady, who died January 28, 1717-18. aet. 68, and was buried in the same vault with him. She was daughter and co-heir of Sir Henry Archbold, of Abbots Bromley in this county.

XLIII.—The Lords of Dartmouth (1691–1894).

Of George Legge, Baron Dartmouth Admiral of the Fleet, there is a medallion portrait in *Old Yorkshire* (Longmans, London, 1889), a copy of which was presented to Alderman Farley by the late Lord Dartmouth. Regarding the aspersion of this great man's character by Macaulay, it may be noted that a *Vindication* was published in 1856 by F. Devon, Assistant Keeper of the Records. "It was there shown that the great historian founded his accusations on untrustworthy testimonies, and many important documents were brought to light clearly proving Lord Dartmouth's loyalty."

William, First Earl of Dartmouth was but Baron Dartmouth when he came to reside at Sandwell in 1701. He had been educated under the celebrated Dr. Busby at Westminster School, and then went to King's College, Cambridge, where Dr. George Stanhope, afterwards Vicar of Lewisham and Dean of Canterbury was his tutor. He was but 19 when he succeeded to his father's title in 1691. As we have seen, by his steady adhesion to the principles of the "Protestant Succession," he not only redeemed the family position as Court favourites which was no doubt in considerable peril when his father died in the Tower, but was clever enough to get his father's barony made into an earldom. At the Court of Queen Anne we may picture him a stately and gracious courtier exercising his influence to secure for his neighbour John Hoo, Sergeant at law, of Bradley, and Lord of Wednesbury Manor, the much coveted privilege of a charter for holding Fairs and Markets in Wednesbury (1709), similar to that which Charles II. had granted to his lordship's father for Lewisham markets.

There is extant a letter dated February 15th of the same year, 1709 (and published in *Dartmouth MSS*.) from Sir Cleobury Holte to Lord Digby at Mr Nicholas's house in Old Spring Gardens, London, desiring him to use his influence with Lord Dartmouth to obtain for Mr. Ranshe, the son of a neighbour, the Cursey of West Bromwich; Mr Adenbroke, the minister there being on the point of death! The old minister, however, did not die for some little time afterwards (1710), and then was succeeded by the Rev. John Rann—probably the same candidate, whose name had been mis-spelt.

It was on the accession of Queen Anne (1702) that he was sworn of the Privy Council. The following anecdote is also taken from the *Dartmouth MSS*:—

"Queen Anne a little before she died told the Earl of Dartmouth that she never had bought a jewel for her own use in her whole life, and of all the vanities in the world looked upon them as the greatest, but thought they were proper for presents because a great value in a small compass, The Earl of Oxford brought Mr Pitt's great diamond to Queen Anne and told her several gentlemen of the House of Commons said it was a pity it should go out of the kingdom, and had a mind to move in their House to have it presented to Her Majesty. She desired he would stop the motion, for she should be very sorry to see the people's money thrown away upon such a bauble for her, and told the Earl of Dartmouth she thought it was a much greater pity that Greenwich Hospital was not finished."

While this favoured courtier and friend of princes was deeply engaged in the higher affairs of state in London, his own private West Bromwich business was managed for him by his steward resident there. Glimpses of his connection with this parish may be gained by reference to the following pages of Mrs Willett's History:—pp. 203-4, conveyances of land in 1709, p. 228, allusion to a similar transaction in 1748, p. 96, the name of his agent, Mr. Thomas Scott, appears attached to a parish notice of 1716 agreeing to take legal advice of Sergeant John Hoo of Bradley; on p. 101, his lordship heads a subscription list of money collected in the church under authority of a *brief* for the relief of distress caused by a fire at Willinbrow, September, 1738, and on p. 89 it is recorded that in 1747 the Vicarage House in Church Lane was claimed as part of his lordship's property, which claim the Stanley Trustees were unable to withstand.

The Earl had six sons and two daughters. Of these it will be here necessary to mention but three, viz.:—

(1) George, Viscount Lewisham, eldest son of the above William, first Earl of Dartmouth, married Elizabeth, sole daughter and heir of Sir Arthur Kaye, of Woodsome, in Yorkshire, bart. and died of the small-pox at his house in Holles Street, Cavendish Square, August 29, 1732. By his said lady (who afterwards married Francis North, Earl of Guildford) he had issue (besides a son and daughter, who died young), William, Lord Viscount Lewisham, who became the second earl of Dartmouth and two-daughters, Anne and Elizabeth.

(2) Heneage Legge, second son of the first earl, born 1703-4, admitted a student of the Inner Temple at the age of nineteen, was December 12, 1734, chosen High-Steward of the city of Lichfield. In February 1739, he was sworn one of the King's Council; and in 1749, constituted one of the barons of the Exchequer. In June, 1740, he married Catherine, daughter and one of the co-heirs of Jonathan Fogge, Esq., of London, and died August 29, 1759, leaving issue one son and two daughters.

(3) Robert is mentioned simply because his brief record of life appears in the West Bromwich Registers; he was baptised 21st July, 1716, and buried 19th December, the same year.

The two first mentioned, when they grew up, had in the natural course of events to be educated.

In the *Dartmouth MSS*. preserved at Patshull, there is a document dating from about the beginning of the last century, headed "An Account of the Charges of the Journey from Sandwell to Oxford, and of my Lord Lewisham's and Mr Legge's settling in the University." It runs:—

	£	s.	d.
Coach hire from Warwick to Oxon...	4	18	0
To Sir Charles Holt's coachman, postillon and groom	1	0	6
At the George-on-the-Tree	0	6	0
„ Warwick	3	6	0
„ Kenton	0	5	6
„ Banbury	1	7	0
„ Middleton Stoney	0	6	0
To the Manciple and servants belonging to Magdalen College ...	4	15	0
„ „ President's man	2	2	0
Matriculation	8	11	0
To the Vice-Chancellor's man...	1	1	0
Caution Money	40	0	0
Instead of a treat in the Hall...	10	0	0
To the University bell ringers and waits.	0	10	0
Given at the library, museum etc.	0	15	6
Admittance in the comon Room	7	3	0
A dozen of wine, the first time the gentlemen dined in the Hall ...	1	0	0
To the waiters at the high table	0	10	0
To the sextons and beadle of St. Mary's, to Mr Holt's man	0	10	6
„ „ Porter of the College...	0	2	6
For two night gowns	7	12	6
„ „ every day gowns	18	0	0
Brocade and silk for lining	51	13	0
Making the best gowns, buckram, silk, &c....	3	5	6
Nine dozen of gold loops, £3 10 0 per dozen	31	10	0
Upholsterer's bill	14	4	10
For two Capps	2	0	0
„ a bob wigg	1	1	0
„ two dozen of bands	1	10	0
A journey to Blenheim...	1	2	6
Expenses at the Angel Inn	6	10	7
For my lodgings	0	15	0

etc., etc.

The total amount is £241 16s. 0d. At the end is written—"The tutor is to have 20 guineas a year for each of the gentlemen. The necessary woman four pounds a year for each. The lodgings £20 a year."

Their father, the Earl, must have been a truly remarkable man, in as much as he not only regained the family prestige when it was in a critical position, but actually brought to it an accession of new honours and fresh dignities. Of him, Shaw says—"The above noblman, William, first Earl of Dartmouth, who had behaved with the strictest honour and integrity throughout his life, deceased at his house in Blackheath, in Kent, on December 15th, 1750 aet 79, and was succeeded in his virtues as well as honours and estates, by William, his grandson and heir, second Earl of Dartmouth, Viscount Lewisham, and Baron Dartmouth."

WILLIAM, SECOND EARL OF DARTMOUTH, was born in 1721; and, for his more polite education travelled through France, Italy and Germany, and on his return to England took his seat in the House of Peers, May 13, 1754. In 1775, January 11, he married Frances Catherine, sole daughter and heir of Sir Charles Gunter Nicoll, K.B., by whom he had several children.

Like his grandfather he held various high positions of state namely—First Commissioner of Trade and Plantations, to which he was appointed 20 July, 1765; afterwards he became (1772) Secretary of State for the Colonies.

His connection with West Bromwich seems to have been slight, so far as it is on record, in 1751 we find him paying the Curate's stipend of £20 per annum; and in 1787 claiming his pew at the allotment after the re-building of the church.

Of his children—

(1.) George, Viscount Lewisham, the eldest, was born 3 Oct., 1755.

(2.) Henry became a barrister.

(3.) Arthur Kaye (Sir) K.C.B., joined the navy and became an Admiral of the Blue. He was the sixth son, born in 1766.

(4.) Edward died Lord Bishop of Oxford, 1827; born 1767.

(5.) Angustus George, the eighth son, born 1773, was also in holy orders, and held a family living as rector of Lewisham.

The second earl was a man of great piety and earnestness, the friend of Cowper, the Rev. John Newton, Vicar of Olney, the Countess of Huntingdon and others connected with the religious revival of the last century. He is alluded to by Cowper as "one who wears a coronet and prays," a somewhat rare combination in those days. He is also believed to be the nobleman addressed by Newton in the book called "Cardiphonia." The earl died in 1801, and it is remarkable that the first two holders of the title enjoyed it no less than 90 years, namely, from 1711 to 1801. Or if the barony of Dartmouth only be considered, these same two—a grandfather succeeded by his grandson—bore the title Lord Dartmouth, from 1691 to 1801—the marvellously long period of 110 years.

GEORGE, THIRD EARL OF DARTMOUTH, K.G. (of whom there is also a portrait in *Old Yorkshire*), born 1755, succeeded his father in 1801. In 1774, while but nineteen years of age he was returned M.P. for Plymouth, and in 1780 for Staffordshire. Two years after this—the same in which he married Frances, daughter of the Earl of Aylesford— he was appointed one of the Lords of the Bedchamber to the Prince of Wales. In 1789 he was made Lord Warden of the Stannaries. The exceptional honour of being called to the House of Lords during his father's lifetime befell this heir to a peerage, for in June, 1801, he was summoned to the Lords in his father's barony, but his father, the Earl, died almost immediately afterwards—in July, the following month. He was appointed President of the Board of Control the same year. In 1802 he was made Lord Steward of His Majesty's Household, and in 1804 Lord Chamberlain.

The third Earl had twelve children, Henry the fifth (who afterwards took holy orders) was baptised at West Bromwich 29th October, 1803.

In the summer of 1807, his lordship resigned the Coloneley of the Birmingham Loyal Volunteers, on the plea of ill-health. He died in November, 1810. He was a man of the mildest and most amiable manners and Reeves quotes the following lines which were made upon him at Eton School by his schoolfellow the Earl of Carlisle—

Mild as the dew that whitens yonder plain,
Legge shines serenest midst your youthful train,
He whom the search of fame with rapture moves
Disdains the pedant, though the Muse he loves;
By nature formed with modesty to please
And joins with wisdom unaffected ease.

He was much beloved, and inherited all the amiable qualities of his family—for indeed the serious minded Charles I had dubbed the one of his time, "honest Will Legge."

WILLIAM, FOURTH EARL OF DARTMOUTH, born 1784, was married twice (1) in 1821, to Frances Charlotte, daughter of the Earl Talbot, she died in 1823; and (2) to Frances, daughter of Viscount Barrington; she died 1849.

He succeeded to the Earldom in 1810, and died in 1853, having had issue by both his wives—by the second wife the large family of six sons and nine daughters. The baptisms of four children are recorded in West Bromwich registers, namely—Frances Elizabeth, October 16th, 1829, Louisa Jane Cecil, January 21st., 1831; George Barrington. February 28th, 1832; and Beatrix Maria, May 12th, 1833. He was a D.C.L. and F.R.S., and altogether a man of refinement and culture. It was this Earl who bought Patshull, when the rural aspect of Sandwell was first threatened by the advance of local manufacturing concerns.

All his life at Sandwell he manifested a retiring disposition. At Jaques' School, which was first established in New Street, but was afterwards better known at Hill Top, he maintained a number of poor boys, who were generally known as "My Lord's Scholars." He paid for their education and clothing, the dress consisting of corduroy knee breeches and green coats. At one time his lordship was Chairman of the Board of Guardians. He it was who began the earliest mining in West Bromwich upon any large scale, opening up those three collieries, now near the very centre of the town, near to Pitt Street, the Cronehills, and the Terrace; this commercial spirit he manifested some twenty years or so before his death. But into all, his character was that which distinguished most of his family—he was before all things a faithful son of the Church. When Alderman Farley, as a young man of 17, first essayed to do something for the town, he applied to Lord Dartmouth for assistance to establish a Mechanics' Institute. His lordship's characteristic reply was to the effect that, although the proposal was a good one, he thought religion must always precede education, and the practical outcome was the ultimate building of St. Peter's Church at Greets Green, the locality originally suggested for the Mechanics' Institute.

His close connection with West Bromwich is but thus casually alluded to by Mrs Willett:—(p. 91), his large control over the Stanley Trust in 1815: (pp. 92, 113, and 115) his generous support of the new Christ Church in 1818–19: (p 93) his selection of the clergy for this new church, which power (p. 132) was exercised in 1829 according to the Act of Parliament: (pp.123,133) his influence and intervention being solicited in 1835, to stop Sunday tippling in the parish, and (pp. 58, 115) his munificent gifts for augmenting the living of West Bromwich, alluded to in chap. xxxiii. Much of this lord's time was spent at Woodsome Hall, in Yorkshire, where the family has also large estates,

WILLIAM WALTER, FIFTH EARL OF DARTMOUTH, born 1823, succeeded his father in 1853 and died in 1891, the year that his brother, the Rev. Hon. Angustus, became Bishop of Lichfield. The late Earl was educated at Eton and Christ Church, Oxford, taking his B.A. in 1844 and his M.A. in 1847. He sat in the House of Commons (as a Conservative) for South Staffordshire from 1849 to his elevation to the Peers in 1853. He was a magistrate for Staffordshire and Shropshire, and a Deputy-Lieutenant for this county till he succeeded Lord Wrottesley as Lord Lieutenant. He was a Captain of the Staffordshire Militia from 1843 to 1854, and became one of the first Captains of the 27th Staffordshire Volunteers in 1860.

In 1846 he had married Lady Augusta Finch, daughter of the Earl of Aylesford, and a year or two afterwards was the first of the family to go into residence at Patshull. His earliest act of benevolence in West Bromwich after succeeding his father in 1853, was to give up his right to the Whorwood Chapel or Pew in 1854, and to add "a small sanctuary" to the church, which in 1871 he permitted to be removed at the general rebuilding of the fabric, the stained glass in the windows, which were a family memorial, being preserved and re-used. At the re-opening services, one of the special preachers was very fittingly the Earl's brother, now Lord Bishop of the diocese. When land has been required for the enlargement of the churchyard it has twice been freely given by the Earl; in 1859 he gave an acre on the south side, and in 1875 he gave upwards of an acre at the east end. (His predecessor had carefully bargained for £80 as the price of an acre on the eastern side in 1823).

His relationships with West Bromwich were close and cordial, and perhaps he showed more public spirit in the real sense of that term than any other member of his family. For instance, it is to him West Bromwich is really indebted for Dartmouth Public Park; he took a deep interest in the establishment of the West Bromwich District Hospital, of which the Countess laid the foundation stone, to the Institute he was a generous donor (giving altogether £1,500) and became its first president, he presented to the town the mayoral chain, and in return, in recognition of all these tokens of kindly interest in the welfare of West Bromwich, a portrait of the Earl in his peer's robes was presented to the Countess, a replica of the picture being also hung in the Municipal Council Chamber.

He leased the Sandwell Park property for that great commercial enterprise in local coal mining. But the relinquishing of Sandwell Hall as a residential seat had long been acted upon; for like his father the Earl was an enthusiast in forestry and floriculture, the pursuit of which had long been impossible at Sandwell, owing to the ever crowing murkiness of the surrounding skies. In the adjacent Black Country. The late Earl, however, was always proud to boast himself a West Bromwich man, although he never resided at Sandwell after his succession to the title; as a staunch Churchman, a sound Conservative, and a generous patron, his memory will long be cherished in West Bromwich.

WILLIAM HENEAGE, THE SIXTH AND PRESENT EARL OF DARTMOUTH, was born May 6th, 1851, and succeeded his father at the age of 40. He was educated, as his father had been, at Eton and Christ Church. He is a magistrate for Kent, Salop and the West Riding of Yorkshire; and Lord Lieutenant and a County Alderman for Staffordshire. He is also Honorary Colonel of 1st Volunteer Battalion S. Staff. Regt. He sat in the Commons when Viscount Lewisham as Conservative representative of West Kent 1878-85, and from 1885 for same constituency under the name of Lewisham till his elevation to the Upper House in 1891. With his party's triumph he secured the office of Vice-Chamberlain of Her Majesty's Household in 1885-6, and like all previous holders of this title, has been *persona grata* at Court.

Lord Dartmouth is patron of nine livings:—In Staffordshire—(1) Pattingham Vicarage (2) Patshull V. (alternately), (3) Christ Church V. (West Bromwich), (4) West Bromwich Vicarage. In Kent—(5) Lewisham V., (6) Forest Hill V., (7) Sydenham. In Yorkshire—(8) Farnley Tyas Perpetnal Curacy. In Bucks—(9) Olney Vicarage.

His seats are Patshull House, Wolverhampton; Woodsome Hall, Huddersfield; and Sandwell, now deserted.

His eldest son is William, Viscount Lewisham born 22nd February, 1881. There are two other sons and two daughters.

The Earl's arms "Azure, a buck's head cabossed argent," and his crest of 5 ostrich plumes, have with other "differences "been adapted in the construction of the West Bromwich Borough armorial bearings. His motto is *Gaudet tentamine virtus*, "Virtue rejoices in trial."

XLIV.—THE SEATS OF THE LEGGE FAMILY; SANDWELL, WOODSOME, AND PATSHULL.

During the Civil Wars the career of Colonel William Legge was romantic and adventurous. He had gained his first military experience in the Low Countries under Prince Maurice of Saxony. On his return to England he was made Groom of the Bed Chamber to Charles I., and afterwards as Lieutenant General of Ordnance under Lord Newport he gained more experience in the first expedition against the Scots (1639). When the Civil War broke out he served under Prince Rupert at the Battle of Newark and was taken prisoner at Dunsmore Heath and again at Lichfield. In 1644 he was governor of Chester and of Oxford: at the latter city he no doubt came into frequent contact with the Whorwoods. He was one of the three companions of Charles I. in his flight from Hampton Court, and according to Lord Clarendon he possessed "better judgment and understanding" than the other two, Ashburnham and Berkeley. After the execution of the King, Col. Legge was imprisoned successively at Plymouth, Bristol, and Arundel, and then obtained permission to go abroad. He returned in 1650 with Prince Charles, accompanied him to Scotland, and shared his defeat at Worcester. His escape from Coventry Gaol has already been alluded to. During the Commonwealth he was ever busy with Royalist plots, and on the Restoration of Charles II. reaped his rich rewards. Readily he secured his old appointments in the Bed Chamber and the Ordnance. Then followed command of a Company of Foot in the Tower, with the King's House in The Minories, the lieutenancy of the Alice Holt, the Woolmer Forests, in Hampshire, and lastly, a pension of £500 for his own and his wife's lives. He died in 1670 (not 1672 as stated on his monumental tablet in The Minories), at the age of 80, and was succeeded by his renowned son, first Baron of Dartmouth and Admiral of the Fleet.

This "KING'S HOUSE" in The Minories is the first residence of the family to which attention may be called.

In the preceding chapter passing allusion was made to the family residence at Black Heath in Kent and to Lord Lewisham's town house in Holles Street.

*   *   *   *   *   *   *

The acquisition of Sandwell Hall in 1701, as a real country seat—the first by this branch of the Legge family—has already been described. The second seat, Woodsome, in Yorkshire, came a few years later by marriage. WOODSOME HALL is an Elizabethan stone building about the year 1600. It will be remembered that George, Viscount Lewisham, eldest son of the first Earl of Dartmouth, married the daughter and heiress of Sir Arthur Kaye, baronet, of Woodsome, Yorkshire, and by that alliance brought these Yorkshire estates into the Dartmouth family. When Lord Lewisham died in 1727 these estates passed to his son William, who became the second earl. The hall is a quaint old place full of ancient furniture, and many portraits of the Kaye family. It is surrounded by pleasant woods, from which it derived its proper name of Wood's-ham. An engraving of the hall, a fine portrait of the late earl, taken in 1889 etc., illustrate the volume *Old Yorkshire*, mentioned in the previous chapter.

*   *   *   *   *   *   *

To West Bromwich readers a description of SANDWELL HALL, as it was in the zenith of its prosperity as the chief seat of a titled family, should be not unwelcome. The following was written by Shaw (who gives a fine engraving of the place) about the year 1798:—

"DESCRIPTION OF SANDWELL HALL

This mansion, which has been some time the principal seat of the family, is situated on the site of the priory, some of the foundation, &c., of which is still traceable in the back part and offices, where may be seen a stone coffin that was dug up there.

And on the lawn in front is still remaining the well, before mentioned, now guarded by iron rails, as seen in the engraving. The size and architecture of the house (which is of brick neatly stuccoed white) and its external appearance and situation, may be seen from the view [given by Shaw] better than expressed by any verbal description.

Besides the rooms mentioned with the following pictures, there is a handsome library and a large, neat chapel.

CATALOGUE OF THE PICTURES.—THE HALL.

Four large landscapes of Tangiers, in Africa, and the neighbouring country, taken upon the spot, when the first Lord Dartmouth was sent to demolish that fortress. Over the chimney is a large picture of the Battle of Rocroy.

THE LITTLE PARLOUR.

Beginning over the door leading to Lord Dartmouth's apartment:—

(1) A head of the Hon. Heneage Legge, afterwards Baron Legge; by Sir Godfrey Kneller.

(2) A half-length of old Colonel William Legge, father to George, Lord Dartmouth; painted by Houseman.

(3) A half-length of Mrs Legge, wife of Colonel Legge, daughter of Sir William Washington; by Gascar.

(4) George, Lord Dartmouth; by Vivian.

(5) Barbara, Lady Dartmouth, daughter of Sir Henry Archbold; by Houseman.

(6) William, first Earl of Dartmouth; by Sir Godfrey Kneller.

(7) Head of Lady Anne Holte, daughter of William, Earl of Dartmouth; by Highmore.

(8) Lady Anne Finch, Countess of Dartmouth; by Sir Godfrey Kneller.

(9) George, Lord Lewisham, father to William second Earl of Dartmouth; by Highmore.

(10) Elizabeth Kaye, Viscountess Lewisham, with her son William, second Earl; by Highmore.

(11) A head of Hon. Henry Bilson Legge, afterwards Chancellor of the Exchequer; by Sir Godfrey Kneller.

LORD DARTMOUTH'S SITTING ROOM.

A half-length of Frances Katherine Gunter Nicoll, Countess of Dartmouth; by Sir Joshua Reynolds.

MY LORD'S DRESSING ROOM.

A whole length of Charles Blount, Earl of Devonshire, which was engraved by the Antiquarian Society.

EATING ROOM.

Opposite the chimney—

(1) A whole-length of George Villiers, Duke of Buckingham; by Cornelius Janson

(2) A whole-length of John Digby, Earl of Bristol.

(3) Over the chimney, a whole-length of the Hon. Commodore Edward Legge, when a child; by Richardson.

WITHDRAWING ROOM.

(1) Over the eating room door, a head of William Chittins, groom of the Bed Chamber to King Charles II.; Ryley.

(2) Over the library door, a head of Sir Henry Archbold, father to Barbara, Lady Dartmouth; by Johnstone.

(3) A half-length of Lady Mary Villiers, Duchess of Richmond; by Vandyke.

(4) A half-length of Catherine Villiers, Countess of Pembroke; by Sir Peter Lely.

Two large pictures of ducks, etc.; by Honderkoster.

Two landscapes, opposite the chimney; by Lucatelli.

Opposite the windows—Two large pieces; by Nicola Poussin.

Two landscapes under them; by Mola.

Two small ones, by Gasper Del Oechiale; and a Dutch piece.

On the side with the chimney—Holy Family, said to be painted by Guido.

Landscape by Vernet.

GREEN BED–CHAMBER.

(1) Over the door leading to the library, a head of George, Lord Lewisham, by Sir Godfrey Kneller.

(2) Opposite the window—A head of the Hon. Baron Legge, by Zeaman.

(3) Barbara, Lady Dartmouth, half length.

(4) Hon. Mrs. Legge, wife to Baron Legge, by Zeaman.

GREEN DRESSING ROOM.

Over the door leading to the Green bed chamber.

(1) Anne, Lady Brudenell, daughter to George. Viscount Lewisham, by Hudson.

(2) John Lord Viscount Mordaunt.

(3) Elizabeth Cary, Viscountess Mordaunt; painted by Louisa Princess Palatine, daughter to the Queen of Bohemia.

(4) Sir Edward Legge.

(5) Under Lord Mordaunt, old Sir Christopher Musgrave; by Ryley.

(6) Mary Villiers, Countess of Fevorsham; by Sir Pater Lely.

(7) Prince Rupert, by Dobson.

(8) Mrs Sneyd, daughter of Sir Walter Bagot; by Hudson.

(9) Over the chimney, George, Lord Lewisham, and his sister, Lady Barbara Bagot; by Richardson.

(10) Robert Harley, Earl of Oxford, Lord Treasurer; by Sir Godfrey Kneller.

(11) Queen Anne, by Sir Godfrey Kneller.

(12) Young Sir Christopher Musgrave, in red; by Sir Godfrey Kneller.

(13) Mrs Musgrave, afterwards Mrs Crauford, sister to the first Earl of Dartmouth; by Sadler.

(14) Heneage, Earl of Aylesford, father to Anne, Countess of Dartmouth; by Sir Godfrey Kneller.

(15) Under the picture of Lord Aylesford, Mrs. Elizabeth Legge; by Ryley.

(16) In the centre at the bottom, Mr Thare.

(17) Mrs Graham, sister to Mrs Elizabeth Legge; a copy by Ryley.

BLUE BED–CHAMBER UP ONE PAIR OF STAIRS.

(1) Over the stair-case door, a head of Prince Maurice; by Dobson.

(2) Over the chimney, a half-length of Elizabeth Banks, Countess of Aylesford; by Richardson.

(3) Lady Clothea Rich.

(4) William, first Earl of Dartmouth.

(5) Lady Elizabeth Finch, Lady Bingley; by Sir Godfrey Kneller.

(6) Over the dressing-room door, a head of old Col. William Legge; by Dobson.

(7) Mrs Legge, his wife.

(8) A half-length, of Lady Goodrick; by W. Wright.

(9) A head of George, Lord Dartmouth.

LADIES' BLUE DRESSING ROOM.

Over the chimney, a whole-length of Esme Stuart, Duke of Richmond when a child, by Vandyke. Over the doors three pictures of dead game.

Near the bedroom door, a head of Lady Barbara Bagot; by De Gaze.

A head of Mrs Graham, by Sir Peter Lely.

Under the heads, two flower pieces, by Carlo.

Between these four small views of Rome and in the centre, a landscape with ruins.

Opposite to these, a beggar boy and Sigismunda, both by Morland.

Between them a landscape by Wyke, and a drawing of our Saviour, brought from Italy by the second Earl of Dartmouth.

Under the beggar boy a small whole length of Anne Butler, Countess of Newport, by Dobson.

Under Sigismunda a small whole length of Montjoy Blount, Earl of Newport, by Dobson.

GENTLEMAN'S BLUE DRESSING ROOM.

Over the doors two pictures of dead game.

Opposite the dressing room door, a half-length of Lady Anne Porter, by Sir Peter Lely.

In the centre, Lady Washington, sister to George, Duke of Buckingham, and mother to Mrs. Legge.

A half-length of Sir Walter Bagot, by Richardson; under, Lady Washington's picture.

A Madonna and two landscapes.

Opposite to the windows—Lady Mary Finch, Marchioness of Halifax and Duchess of Roxborough, by Sir Godfrey Kneller.

Left hand of the door—Viscount Townshend, by Doll.

By the chimney—Sir John Goodricke, by Gascar.

Over the chimney—a half-length of the Duchess of Richmond, Duke Esme, and Lady Mary Stuart, afterwards Countess of Arran, by Wright.

YELLOW DRESSING ROOM.

Various drawings by the family and their relations.

YELLOW BED CHAMBER.

Over the chimney a half-length of Anne, Countess of Dartmouth; by Sir Godfrey Kneller.

ALCOVE BED CHAMBER.

Over the chimney, head of Admiral Dean.

LADY CHARLOTTE LEGGE'S ROOM.

(1) Over the door next the chimney, Lady Buller and her daughter.

(2) Over the closet door, Sir Henry Washington.

(3) Over the chimney, battle-piece, by Wike.

LORD AND LADY DARTMOUTH'S BED CHAMBER.

Over the chimney, a head of the second Earl of Dartmouth; by Kettle.

LADY'S DRESSING ROOM.

Half-length of the second Earl of Dartmouth; by Gainsborough.

LADY'S INNER ROOM.

Contains heads of the second Earl of Dartmouth's eight sons.

(1) Lord Lewisham, in red; by Sir Joshua Reynolds.
(2) Hon. William Legge, deceased; by Sir Joshua Reynolds.
(3) Lieutenant colonel Charles Gounter Legge, deceased.
(4) Heneage Legge, deceased.
(5) Henry Legge, deceased.
(6) Captain Arthur Kaye Legge, in the sea-service.
(7) Edward Legge.
(8) Augustus Legge.
With several drawings. etc.

Having now done with the house, we shall conclude with a few observations upon the park and pleasure grounds, which, though situated near a manufacturing country, and about four miles from Birmingham, and close to the turnpike road thence to Wolverhampton, Dudley. etc., yet being shut out from all those inconveniences by a lofty park wall, and rich phalanx of plantations on rising ground to the south, and encompassed on the north-west by the fine barrier of hills, on which is seen the neat residence of the present minister and parish church, with Wednesbury spire peeping behind, while, from the well-wooded valley towards the north (from whose boisterous attacks the back part of this mansion is sufficiently protected), gradually arise to the horizon the picturesque hill and spire church of Walsall, with Barr Beacon and Mr Scott's beautiful woods, &c., on the right. The whole of this fine scene is beheld to the greatest advantage on the side of the hill in the park, in the direction in which the view [in Shaw] was drawn, or still higher up from a seat in the plantation, along which are beautiful shady walks, that lead to a pleasant vale across the park, south-west. The park and whole estate is well stocked with all kinds of timber, particularly oak. On the west side are large suitable buildings for his lordship's farm; and towards the north good pools of water."

Reeves says (1837) "the mansion is of brick, stuccoed white, and forms a square and was very much improved about 1805." Other items of interest added by him are:—Its exclusion from the busy world by high walls and a thick plantation (the handsome entrance gates, still an ornament to the road, are a special copy of a classic specimen on the continent); its handsome library and neat chapel; and the cost of a painting there, "The Temptation of St. Anthony," by Carracci, brought by Lord Dartmouth in 1826, as being noteworthy at £787 10s. He then refers to the encroachments of the local ironworks on the pleasant landscape, and quotes:—

    "Yet want there not e'en here some lucid spots
    The smoky scene to cheer, and by contrast
    More fair, such Dartmouth's cultivated lawns!
    Himself, distinguished more with ornament
    Of cultured manners and supernal grace."

The late earl, after the death of his father (1853) eventually placed the hall, when abandoned as a family residence, at the disposal of various charitable institutions connected with the Church of England. It was used for the education of poor children; then as a ladies' school; and afterwards, under the management of Miss Selwyn, sister of the late Bishop of Lichfield, for the reception of ladies in reduced circumstances. It is now void, although the Park is regularly used for a Volunteer's rifle range, and occasionally as a camping ground for them.

*   *   *   *   *   *

Patshull House and estate, near Wolverhampton, were purchased by the Earl of Dartmouth in 1848, and Lord and Lady Lewisham took up their residence there in the autumn of that year. In 1852 the Earl left Sandwell, and himself settled at Patshull. In the November of the following year (1853) he died, and was buried in a vault, now closed, in Patshull Church, delightfully situated within the park and close to the hall.

This mansion, on the immediate border line of Salop and Staffordshire, is a handsome stone building in the Italian style, with terraces, velvety lawns, gardens, vineries and pleasure grounds. The park contains two lakes, one of 64 acres and the other 21 acres, arranged to resemble a river, with a cascade of 30 feet in length. The ancient manor of Patteshull was held in Edward I.'s time by the Bagots, and in Edward III.'s reign belonged to the Sir William Shareshill mentioned in chapter xxi. It then passed to the Astley family, who sold it, with Pattingham, to Lord Pigot for £100,000 and a celebrated diamond, about 1801. The Astleys were great cock fighters, and the carving of the gamecock will be found extensively repeated about the building. The Pigots improved the grounds and lakes very much. During the Civil Wars Patshull House was garrisoned by a "Popish troop," and besieged by Captain Stone under the orders of Sir William Brereton. Though strongly fortified it was taken owing to the drawbridge being left down, when the sentinels were surprised, the garrison put to the sword, Mr. Astley (then the governor), several noblemen, and two Jesuits being taken prisoners.

XLV.—The Turton Family of "The Mill."

Another important local family is that of the Turton's. Their origin seems to have been somewhat humble. They were at first yeomen, who, combined with farming on a small scale, the pursuit of the iron industry, then chiefly concerned with nail making. In this respect the foundation of their fortunes was exactly similar to those of the Foley family, of the Parkes family, now represented by Earl Dudley, and of the Paget family, of which the Marquis of Anglesey is now the head—all sprung from local nail-makers. The Turtons of West Bromwich clung to the Oldbury and Rowley Regis side, from which they probably came, and where they perhaps acquired the first instalment of a freehold estate which ultimately grew to considerable proportions. Their first landed possessions in West Bromwich seem to have been all in the vicinity of Bromford Lane.

A copy which was made of a deed in 1629 by William Turton seems to disclose that the family had been interested a century previously (namely, in 1531) in certain West Bromwich lands. Some of this land was known as Tonky's land or "Luttleys" some was near "the oake called Harvyl's Oke," and another piece was "six days earth of land in the common field called Stycroft." In their possession also is another deed between two members of another yeoman family of West Bromwich, the Ormes, dated 1615. It conveyed land which seems to be identical with the first-named as it is thus described—"that meadow called Sharpeling's Land (sometimes Lytley's)": it also conveyed a "meadow called Over Huckleys, alias Braynford Bridge, now in the tenure of Francis Symcoxe"; and a meadow called "Whyte's Croft, alias Gorstie Croft."

In a third deed, dated 1617, a sale is made by "William Orme of Longdon gent." to John Turton, a yeoman of West Bromwich (who some seventeen years later acquired The Oak) of two pieces of land, the second one of which seems again identical with the one already noted: they were (1) land called Slowe's Land, lying between lands of William Stanley, of Thomas Turton (from whom John afterwards purchased The Oak) late of Richard Smalbrooke, and Oxley's Lane and the Common Heath of West Bromwich): (2) a pasture called Over Lutleys alias Bromford Bridge Leasow between the land of the said Thomas Turton, of William Turton the elder (their father), Tinker's Lane, and the lane from West Bromwich Heath towards Oldbury. It is thus evident that this energetic yeoman family of the Turtons were rapidly acquiring lands on the Oldbury side of the parish; and in course of time they came to own a very considerable estate.

By 1663 a grant of Arms to the Turtons is officially recorded at the Herald's Visitation in that year; and as in those days very particular inquiry was made into the claims of those who wished to bear these heraldic symbols which were supposed to distinguish nobles and gentry from common people, it may be inferred that the family could trace descent from those really entitled to the distinction, or had accumulated sufficient money to buy the coveted honour. At least this may have been the case with that branch who resided at The Oak; the senior branch remained in trade till the eighteenth century and the term "gentleman" is not so frequently applied to the members of this line. Before, however, the family greatness ripened to this extent a more humble frame of mind possessed some of its earlier founders. For when Charles I. came to the throne in 1624 it was sought to thrust the honour of Knighthood upon the family, whose growing wealth was common knowledge and whose importance was duly noted by the Sheriff responsible for the King's taxes; but the honour was modestly refused by the thrifty Turton selected by the King.

It was sometimes usual for the Stuart Kings to create knights wholesale, and to make a commercial profit of the transaction by demanding fees, or imposing a fine on refusal. The answer of William Turton, of Westbromwich, was put in "in writing in these words. vizt., that he at the time of His Ma'ties coronation was possessed of no lands at all in fee simple, fee tayle, or for terms of life, nor sithence to this present day hath had any above the value of twenty pounds p' ann'; that his father is living and that estate he hath is in rev'con after his father; and that he is mistaken in the sheriff's returns.

But he further saith that at the time of His Ma'ties Coronation there was one William Turton thelder who dyed some three years sithence and was seized of some forty pounds p' ann; and standeth still in the Sheriffe's Books and returned by the names of William Turton thelder of Westbromwich, and his heire doth live at Birmingham, in Warwickshire, and is returned upon this commission for Shropshire," etc., etc.

The county of Salop was no doubt the shire accountable for recording the family possessions, because Oldbury, like Hales Owen, was then in Shropshire. The heir residing in Birmingham would be one Ann Turton, a widow, of whom mention will be made in due course.

The more convenient way of dealing with the history of this West Bromwich family will be to divide it into two branches, one dwelling at The Mill and the other at The Oak.

The Pedigree of the Turton family is headed by the statement that they are descended from the Turtons of Turton Tower, County Lancaster. This hardly squares with the boast of a modern representative of the family that they "had resided at The Oak for more than seven hundred years" (Reeves p. 43).

The West Bromwich branch of the family is therein said to have come from Dudley, and their genealogical tree is headed by one

(1) NICHOLAS TURTON OF DUDLEY, who lived (according to a pedigree in the British Museum) about 1470. His son was

(2) WILLIAM TURTON OF DUDLEY, who was succeeded by his son,

(3) JOHN TURTON, "of West Bromwich, naylor." This member of a very extensive and prolific family seems to have been the first to settle in the parish; and like the Pagets of Wednesbury, who were also nailers, they managed to develope into landowners. There was a lease of lands called the Turhills in Rowley Regis, made to this John Turton in 1595. He was married twice: by his first marriage he had a son Adam, from whom was descended the William Turton living in West Bromwich in 1818, but his better-known son, by the second alliance, was

(4) WILLIAM TURTON THE ELDER (generally so designated because his son William was his contemporary for a number of years) who in 1592 purchased two Mills from one Thomas Cowper, or Piddocke. These Mills were "The Mill" (as that is called, where the Messrs Izon's Works now stand) and Bromford Mill, the latter being probably a Blade Mill. Both the pools belonging to these Mills are to be seen still; Bromford Pool is near the Bromford Iron Works.

The allusive extracts from Rider's *Hypomnema:—*

"1592.—Thomas Cowper, alias Piddocke, of Kings Bromley, conveyed to William Turton, the elder of West Bromwich, two mills and one meadow, called the Floodgate Meadow."

Other extracts from Rider allude evidently to the same William:—

"1599.—Paid to William Turton for rent, land in new leasowe.

1601.—Paid to William Turton his whole year's rent.

1602.—Paid to William Turton the elder.

1602.—Paid to William Turton the *younger.*

1602.—Copy of a Writ of Procedendum brought to the Court of West Bromwich, in which the name of William Turton appears.

1603.—Thomas Hadley sealed and delivered a deed to William Turton, giving possession of the Croft near his house.

1621.—Paid William Turton senior his rent due for an acre of land in the new leasowe."

The second entry dated 1602 is an exception, self-manifest; while in the third entry of that year, the Court alluded to is the Manorial Court, from which some action had been removed to a higher Court, and was sent down again to be proceeded with, it not appearing to the higher Court that the suggestion had been sufficiently proved.

In 1613, when the Stanley Trust was first founded, William Turton the Elder and his three sons William, John, and Thomas, were all thought fit to serve on the new Trust, and in the deed are all described as yeomen.

These three sons were also left as Trustees to their father's "Pudding Land Dole," a benefaction derived from lands variously in Lyndon near "Hargett Lane"; in Church Field; and in the "Pudding Land" lying in West Bromwich between "land of William Stanley (in the occupation of George Kenrick) between the King's highway leading from Birmingham towards Wolverhampton, and the lane leading from Greete Bridge towards Harvell's Oak, which premises the said William Turton purchased of one Wm. Colmore, of Birmingham, gent."

"The Mill" seems to have been a family residence, and also a nail-making establishment (worked by water power) out of which the family wealth was all amassed, It being the patrimonial property, descended in the eldest line of the family, William the Elder died in 1628, and it passed to either

(5) (*a*) ANN TURTON, widow of the first-born son, "William the Younger," dead some years. She by deed dated 31 October, 1635—quoted by Mrs Willett, p 167—bought of one "William Cartwright, of Oldburye, within the parish of Halesowen, County Salopp, Brandford Leasow in West Bromwich, between the river or water of Tame," etc.

But in this deed she is described as "of Birmingham," probably because she had returned to her paternal home there on the death of her husband, "William Turton the younger," in 1621, She was a daughter of "Thomas Smalbroke of Birmingham," Subsequent extracts from Simon Rider's MS. would seem to allude to this Anne as in receipt of moneys previously paid to her deceased husband:—"Paid to Anne Turton, widow, my rent for tiath hay at Oldbury, for Sir Thomas Littleton, the 19th October, 1621." From this we gather that her husband William was dead: that she was in receipt of tythes; and that the family interests lay on the Oldbury side of West Bromwich. There is a second record—"Paid to Anne Turton, widow, the halfe-year's rent due for the meadow before my door at the Annunciation last past, the 10th day of April, 1623. 15s."

Her son William, born 1607, she had carefully educated at Oxford where he matriculated at Queen's College in 1624. In 1626 he entered as a student at Middle Temple, as if destined for the Law, instead of Trade.

(5)(*b*) It was this WILLIAM TURTON, a grandson of William Turton the Elder," most probably succeeded to The Mill in 1628. He was eldest of the eight children of William Turton the younger, by his wife Anne. From an extract taken from Rider's MS. (Willet p. 239) it would appear that the Turtons were also in the chain trade as well at this time. This William died in 1663, and was succeeded by another,

(6) WILLIAM TURTON (mentioned in the earliest entry of the Churchwardens' Books), who seems to have died unmarried in 1681, when The Mill passed to his next brother

(7) RICHARD TURTON, of "Mill House" (as it was now called), who, if not actually working the nail-rod mill, was certainly a man of considerable means, as in 1682 we find him (with one George Devenish, of West Bromwich) letting the other branch of the family residing at The Oak, and of whom some account will be given in the next chapter, have large sums of money for Kings Norton corn mills and other properties in that parish and in West Bromwich. This arrangement kept the estate in the Turton family—for having acquired territorial greatness few families care to part with it again—and enabled the owner of The Oak (another William Turton) with the acquiescence of his son and heir John Turton, also described as a "gentleman," to make "effectual provision for the payment of his debts, and raising portions for his younger children."

Richard died in 1685, and we have on record the following heads of the will of Richard Turton, of West Bromwich, gent., proved 17th July, 1685:—To his sister, Eleanor, his messuage called the Mill, in West Bromwich, and all his lands in the Parish of Oldbury; to his kinsman, Joseph Turton, a rent: charge of £40 upon his lands in West Bromwich; to his cousin Mary Brown, £20 for a ring; to his cousin, William Turton, of Orgreave, £20; to his cousin, John Turton, and Ann his wife, £20 each; to his cousin, Phillip Turton, and Mary his wife, £20 each; to his cousin, Mary Yates, £20; to his cousin, Elleanor Fflynt, £20; to his sister, Mary Freeth, £10; to the children of Mary Freeth, Joseph and Phœbe, a legacy. The residue to his sister, Eleanor whom he left sole executrix. A codicil mentions among others, his cousin Joseph Simcox and his sister Elizabeth, 10s. each.

(8) JOSIAH TURTON, son of another brother (Joseph, who married a Freeman of Barr) is next found in possession of The Mill. In an Indenture of 1708 he is designated an "ironmonger" as if he were still in the iron, blade, and nail trade, and mention is also made of his *corn* mill towards Greet Bridge: at the same time his dwelling is called The

Mill, and he purchases the Mill Closes, or enclosed lands adjacent thereto from John Shelton.

In 1701 his aunt Elinor Turton of The Mill had died and bequeathed £5 per annum "chargeable on an Estate at The Mill aforesaid now in the possession of Josiah Turton viz £2. 10 to the Poor Inhabitants of West Bromwich, and £2. 10 to the Poor of Oldbury in the County of Salop, to be disposed of at the discretion of the Minister and Churchwardens, on Good Friday, for ever." She was sister and heir to Richard. After the death of Josiah in 1735 "The Mill" and Bromford Mill came to a family of the name of Abney, but by what means has not been ascertained. The Dole was afterwards called "Abney's Dole", the money is now paid by the Izon family whose iron-works occupy the site of "The Mill."

The acquisition of the property by the Abneys was provocative of much litigation which ensued. A Miss Abney married one Roger Holmes, and they left two daughters, who both died insane at Lichfield, and therefore intestate. In the course of time three separate claimants appeared to this property. After a lengthy suit in Chancery, these claimants at last submitted their claims to a solicitor for arbitration. The claimant, who was apparently the nearest of kin, was one Edward Holmes, a labourer in Plymouth Dockyard, and on him the property devolved, but with mortgages upon it for the benefit of the other two parties. As, however, the mines, which were thought to be very valuable, have proved not to be so, the ownership of it cannot be very profitable.

Josiah Turton seems to have been the last of his name to reside at The Mill, his son William having pre-deceased him in 1728. Of this William little can be gathered, except that he was one among the Stanley Trustees newly appointed in 1722.

*   *   *   *   *   *

Notes on Hales Owen.—How came Hales Owen to be accounted part of Salop? It was in this wise: In Saxon times the name of the place was Hala, and William the Conqueror gave it to his kinsman Roger, Earl of Shrewsbury, who naturally included it within his own county as part of Shropshire, although geographically it lay in Worcestershire, quite twelve miles away from the Salopian borders. Thus the *manor* remained a detached portion of Shropshire till a rectification took place in the present century, although the parish has always included parts of Worcestershire. How was the second portion of the name "Hales Owen" acquired? It was in this way: In 1102 the Earl of Shrewsbury's estate was confiscated and among them Hales which in 1177 was given by Henry II. to his brother-in-law, David ap Owen, Prince of Wales. As Hales was not an uncommon place name, when his son Owen succeeded to the estates in 1204, it was distinguished by the addition of his personal name, and ever afterwards bore the semi-Welsh title of "Hales Owen."

XLVI.—The Oak House and its Owners: The Turton (1634) and the Whyley Families (1768)

William Turton, the Elder had, besides his first born William, in whose line descended The Mill property, four other children. His youngest was Richard, "of Hartlebury," educated at Oxford. Next came a daughter Elizabeth, married into the Simcox family. Then came

(1) Thomas Turton, of The Oak, the first of the family, who can be so designated. Either he or the next tenant very probably altered and enlarged this residence till it

attained the dignity of a family mansion house. There are to be traced in the building existing evidences of two styles of architecture, which perhaps admit of this conjecture.

In 1629 his son and heir William married Judith a daughter of Symon Perkyns, a wealthy tanner of Lichfield. In the marriage settlements the jointure included lands in this parish known as Over Leaw, Tonke's Leasowe's, Wall Meadow, Grove, Tinker's Lane Meadow, Rick Meadow, Glover's Grove, and Clay Hay; all of which had been of the inheritance of William Turton the Elder, and several of which have already been mentioned by name in the preceding chapter. This "son and heir," William Turton, is described as of Hateley Heath, a part of the parish in which his line apparently settled. The paternal residence, The Oak, seems to have been on the estate known as the Litley's (1625) or as Over Lutleys (1650). In 1634 Thomas Turton was resident in this "mansion house, with its appointments" when (with the consent of his wife Alice and of his "son and heir apparent" William and his wife Judith) he sold it for £350 to his brother "John Turton the elder." Both these brothers are then described as *yeomen*, and not yet as *gentlemen*.

Apparently John Turton the elder did not enter into residence at The Oak after he had purchased it. But in the following year (1635) "for the sum of £620 by John Turton the younger, his second son, paid" he leaves in trust the said mansion house (which his brother Thomas still inhabited) with all its lands, meadows, etc., for the use of his said son "John Turton the younger," and then for William; (his grandchild) and his heirs for ever. Here then The Oak estate is settled in the line of John Turton and the difference in the consideration money in so short a space of time would lead one to suppose that great improvements and alterations had been specially effected for this purpose.

The "Building News" in 1877, a technical paper of high standard, supports the view that the house was probably altered about this time, when it was a century old or so. Accompanied by most interesting drawings to illustrate its article, the paper in question says:—

"This old mansion is a good specimen of the half-timbered work of the 16th century, though now sadly out of repair for want of attention. The brick part seems to have been added subsequently, as the brickwork is built on the face of framing. The plan is simple, consisting of porch, hall, three sitting rooms, and kitchen, etc., with bed rooms over. The lantern tower, which gives the house its picturesqueness, is approached by a steep staircase from landing. The interior is but slightly altered from its original state, most of the rooms still retaining their ancient panelling and quaintly-moulded chimneypieces."

The place took its name from an ancient oak tree which stood on the green in front of the house. This old landmark became hollow with age, and was at last destroyed by fire at the very beginning of this century. And this monarch of the forest did not stand alone; in the year 1768 many of these 'kings of the forest' were felled to make lock gates for the navigation, then being first made through this parish. There have been several falls of timber on the estate since and some of the trees were of great magnitude.

No doubt it is difficult for the modern inhabitants of West Bromwich to conjure up a picture of this locality when the crystal waters of the stream ran pleasantly between two banks of velvety green, and when all the landscape around was thickly clothed with the wide-spreading foliage of magnificent oaks. And yet this in truth was the aspect presented by the neighbourhood of Bromford Lane and The Oak right into the last century.

Having thoroughly examined the Oak House very recently (1894) partial dissent must be offered to the opinions of a writer in a Birmingham newspaper, which a few years ago published a view of this "manor house" (sic), with the accompanying remarks:—"The present occupant cares little or nothing for its interior beauty, and has desecrated its beautiful old wainscoting, or allowed it to be so disfigured, with a coat of green paint. Other carved woodwork, of exceeding richness and beauty, has been whitewashed over. The individual with a romantic turn of mind, fond of spending breath in sighs of vain regret over departed glory, need only pay a visit to the Oak Road, West Bromwich."

The edifice is no doubt at the present time much dilapidated, but at the time it became the residence of a seventeenth century family of wealth it was as imposing as it is still picturesque, and its surroundings were as desirable in 1635 as the most beautifully situated mansion can possibly be at the present day.

[The first son of John Turton the Elder was William Turton "of Alrewas." His son, Sir John Turton Knt., born at Alrewas in 1637, became a Baron of the Exchequer in 1689, and a Justice of King's Bench in 1696: he bought the manor of Alrewas, and was buried there in 1707. Sir John's son was another William Turton, born 1663, who went to Oxford very young in 1678, and became a Barrister of the Middle Temple in 1685.]

(2) JOHN TURTON OF THE OAK had married in 1624 Elizabeth, daughter of George Hawe of Caldmore, and Sister of the staunch Royalist George Hawe, with whom Queen Henrietta Maria stayed for one night in 1643, and who was fined £212 in 1646 by the Parliamentary Committee. John certainly resided at The Oak, and no doubt he entered into occupation at once, and did not wait till the death of his uncle Thomas in 1646. His marriage had brought him land and property in King's Norton, which his successor had to raise money upon in 1682. But what was it which brought about this change in the family fortunes of this branch of the Turtons? Was it this owner of The Oak who became Captain Turton of the Parliamentary forces, when the great Civil War broke out? And did he suffer for his participation in that great struggle, after the Restoration of Charles II. in 1660? We have learnt (chaps. xxxii. and xxxiii.) that the Rowley branch of the Turtons suffered in the religions persecutions of the Clarendon Code—it was a Rev. William Turton of The Brades (educated at Brasenose, 1653) who was ejected in 1662. It therefore, comes well within the range of probability to permit the imagination to play about The Oak House—with its quaint old timbered walls, and its mysterious lantern chamber having a convenient approach to the roof-leads for overlooking a wide stretch of country—as a centre of romantic incident during those stirring times of the Cromwellian Wars. Little has as yet been written of the many probable romantic episodes of the Civil Wars connected by various associations with the history of West Bromwich parish.

Roundhead soldiers are known to have thrown up an earthwork on Bromwich Heath which was afterwards called Camp Bank, and further to have marked their occupation of the place by hanging a local Royalist in chains there.

There is yet another West Bromwich association of which much might be made. Jane, the wife of Brome Whorwood, it was, who (according to Anthony Wood, the quaint Oxonian writer) conveyed to Charles I when he was a prisoner in Carisbrook Castle, the special saw made to cut the iron bars, and some aqua fortis to assist it. The king in a small time did the work. The bars gave him liberty to go out with his body till he came to his breasts; but then his heart failing he proceeded no further, so afterwards he was kept closer." The same writer gives an artless account of Mistress Jane Whorwood's interview with Lilly the Astrologer when she sought to learn the most auspicious time for attempting the king's escape. The Whorwoods at that time were residing at their Halton seat in Oxfordshire, and not at Sandwell—see chap. xii;

(3) WILLIAM TURTON DE LA OAK next resided in the mansion in succession to his father, who lived to a ripe old age. William was married twice, (1) to Sarah Smalbroke, by whom he had four children, who all died young, (2) to Eleanor Page, a daughter of Robert and Elizabeth Page, of Leighton, Huntingdonshire, the tombs of all three of whom formerly stood in the "east chancel" of West Bromwich Church. By this second

marriage he had issue five children. Of the three sons John was the eldest and succeeded to the Oak. William the next son, was born in 1663; from him descended Sir Thomas Turton, of Starborough Castle, Surrey, created a baronet in 1796.

Of the impoverishment of William Turton of the Oak and of his son John, both now described as "gentlemen," and of the monetary assistance they received from Richard Turton of the Mill House in 1682, cognisance was duly taken in the last chapter.

(4) JOHN TURTON DE LA OAK succeeded his father in the estate, now encumbered or considerably reduced, at the age of 22. His father's will (dated 1682, the same year as the transfer of the Kings Norton and West Bromwich lands to his cousins Devenish and the Turtons, of The Mill) mentions (1) one Nathaniel Wiley, a tenant: (2) his heir, the aforesaid John, (3) his son William, who became ancestor to the baronet, and (4) his son Robert who was to be a clerk or apprentice, To Eleanor his dear wife, he bequeathed "the bedd, bedstead curtains, valances, chair, stools, and furniture of all sorts which is now in the parlour where my cozen Devenish lodgeth, with sheets and other linen necessary for the furnishing of the room; and I also give unto her a bed and furniture convenient for the lodging of a maidservant; and I also appoint that my said wife shall have the use of six silver spoons, two silver porringers, and one little silver cup during her life." To his daughters Elizabeth and Sarah Turton he bequeaths "all the linen of all sorts that were their grandmother Turton's."

Of the Wiley family, whose name is just introduced, much more has yet to be learnt. In 1688 "Isaac Wiley, of West Bromwich, naylor," purchased meadow lands at Wigmore, bounded by Penny Lane on the north, Bellfields, the land of Brome Whorwood on the west, and Ditchland, belonging to John Shilton on the south and east: and also "two day's work of land" in Churchfield, near to Penny Stile. The Wileys were evidently of some position in the parish, as several members of the family filled the then honourable position of churchwarden, namely John Whyley in 1681, John Wiley in 1683, Nathaniel Wiley in 1695, William Wiley in 1705, Isaac Wyley in 1715, William Wyley in 1720 and 1725, and Nathaniel Whiley in 1732, 1733, 1740, 1741 and 1742.

A flat stone in the "middle aile" of the old church thus recorded the deaths of John Turton and his father:—

Here lieth William Turton de la Oak, Gent,, who departed this life the 27th July, 1682, in hopes of a joyful resurrection. In memoria æterna justus erit.

———————

Also in this grave lieth the body of John Turton de la Oak, Gent. eldest son of Mr. William Turton above named, who died 6th December, 1705, æt. 45. Saneti cum Deo vivunt.

———————

On the Terrier of 1693, John Turton is also set down as "gentleman"—the only one of the feoffees therein so described.

When John Turton died in 1705, his son and heir John was a minor, 13 years of age. His widow Dorothy is therefore found transacting the business of the estate; and there is in existence a lease granted by her (as guardian to the heir) of lands etc., to William Ward, Esq., of Willingsworth near Wednesbury. The heir came of age in 1713 and Dorothy died in 1726.

(5) JOHN TURTON, ESQ., OF OAK HOUSE, attained his majority in 1713, and was master of The Oak for the long period of 55 years. When he died in 1768 he was the last of his name to reside at The Oak, and the occupation of the mansion by the whole line of Turtons only just exceeds 130 years; by no means a lengthy tenure for a family to occupy a residential seat.

John Turton took considerable interest in all parish matters. His name appears in the Churchwardens' books under the following dates:—

1718.—Riding with other freeholders through the encroachments of the lord of the manor's wastes.

1719.—Agreeing to indite cottagers at next Quarterly Assession for erecting cottages and encroaching on wastes.

1725.—At a public meeting to suppress sparrows in the parish as destructive vermin.

1731.—Agreeing to go "prossessioning" round the parish with the minister.

1735.—Opposing a workhouse for the parish.

1765.—Electing a workhouse governor.

The will of John Turton is dated 1749, but he did not die till nineteen years later, at the age of seventy-six. He appears never to have been married, but at the age of 43 had a natural son by "Mrs Ann Whyley, of Charlemont." The will bequeaths the Oak estate to this illegitimate son, known as William Whyley, and in default of issue to the said William Whyley, the property was to go to that branch of the Turton family (non-resident in West Bromwich), in which the baronetcy afterwards existed, and of whom Reeves gives an account on p. 45. Had William Whyley needed a guardian by the earlier decease of his father, Nathaniel Whyley, of Wigmore, was nominated in the will for that responsible duty.

(1) Mr. WILLIAM WHYLEY OF THE OAK, born 1735, succeeded to the property in 1768, when the oak-felling alluded to was undertaken, on the advice of the recently-deceased owner. William Whyley married Jane Edwards, who lived till 1837, and was 82 years of age at the time of her death. He at once assumed a high position in the parish, had his family pew at the re-allotment in 1787, and some of his dealings with the lord of the manor are set forth in the following document:—

14th November, 1777.—Indenture of this date between Jervoise Clark Jervoise, Esq., Lord of the Manor of West Bromwich, of the one part, and William Whyley, of the Oak, in the Parish of West Bromwich, of the other part. Whereas, William is seized in fee of three closes or parcels of land called the Calves' Croft, Tillatts Close, and Tinker's Meadow which said lands formerly belonged to John Turton, gent., deceased, who was heretofore the owner of a certain mill standing near to the same, formerly called Turton's, but now called Abney's Mill, and of other lands there lying between the said mill and other lands of W. Whyley; and whereas a private road, called Tinker's Lane, was formerly made use of to and for the said Mill through said closes, which said road has been disused for upwards of 50 years; and whereas said Jervoise apprehended the said road to have been formerly a common and public road or way, and as such the ground and soil belong to him as Lord, and did some time since lay claim to the ground and soil as a part of the waste of said Manor, but is now satisfied of the contrary. Whereas William Whyley hath some time since, with permission of said Jervoise Clark Jervoise. inclosed and fenced a certain piece of ground, part of the waste land of the said Manor, called Bromwich Heath, lying near to the dwelling house of William Whyles, called the Oak, or Oak House; and hath also obtained permission to inclose another piece of the said waste land . . . which two pieces so adjoining together are bounded on the south by the land of the said William Whyley, lying before his house, used as a court, containing about seven yards in depth from the said house, other land of William Whyley, called the Orchard, and by the cowhouse, &c., fronting the Oak Green. The said William Whyley hath also inclosed another small piece of ground, part of a certain common or waste within the said Manor, commonly called Greet's Green.

William Whyley died in his 65th year in 1800.

(2) WILLIAM WHYLEY, JUNIOR, was but fifteen at the time of his father's death in 1800; he lived only to attain the age of twenty-one, dying in the year 1806.

* * * * * * *

The Oak is still a picturesque building although its environments are of so sordid a character. In a dirty closely built neighbourhood it yet entrances the eye and stimulates the imagination. And while one deplores the loss of its past glories a hope arises that the public spirit of West Bromwich will rise to the occasion, and gratefully seize the proffered opportunity of preserving this relic of the past for the enjoyment of future generations of Bromwich men, justly proud of their native place, and of the part it has played in history. It would be the height of public ingratitude to churlishly refuse the offer of this interesting old building, which the Mayor (Alderman Reuben Farley, J.P.) has recently purchased, and proposes to present to the borough for the purpose of an Art Gallery and Museum, until such time as West Bromwich is in possession of a building specially designed for the reception of pictures, curios, and other objects of interest. No reasonable expenditure of the public moneys in putting the fine old house into a state of proper repair could possibly be objected to by right-thinking ratepayers. A West Bromwich newspaper in publishing (28th September, 1894), a capital view of The Oak, from a drawing by Mr Thomas Keys, of Thynne Street, very rightly says: — "There can be no doubt that the Mayor rightly interpreted the feeling of the town when, hearing that the building was for sale some short time ago, he concluded that the inhabitants would like to have it preserved to them, and to cherish it as one of the old land marks. By his prompt action in purchasing it, in order that he might present it to the town, he has intensified the obligations under which he has already placed his birthplace. To what purpose the old building will be devoted is, we suppose, a matter yet to be decided, but the suggestion of the donor that it might for the present, at any rate, be used as a museum and for the storing of pictures, seems to us a very excellent one, and will no doubt receive at the hands of the Corporation the respectful attention it deserves."

A good engraving of The Oak, as it was 60 years ago is to be found in *Reeves' History*. And in any picture the building must necessarily be interesting. But a rumour than Mr Henry Irving sent his scenic artist to sketch the interior of the house, for the purpose of utilising the sketches in his recent production of "Becket" is scarcely to be credited: the fact that there is a gap of nearly five centuries between the period of Becket and that of The Oak, makes the idea somewhat preposterous, However the house is one of which West Bromwich may justly be proud, and its preservation is urgently called for. Careful restoration at the hands of an architect imbued with the spirit of his art will imply the expenditure of money: but whatever the sum, it may be looked upon by all right thinking inhabitants as a sound investment for the benefit of an appreciative posterity.

XLVII.—OAKWOOD AND THE JESSON FAMILY.

Oakwood is a residence of a later type than The Oak. It is situated on the main road between Black Lake and Carters Green, The name is sometimes supposed to be derived from the site being known in olden times as Oakley's Croft, (in 1638 there was a West Bromwich nailor, named Thomas Oakley, who is then found buying several crofts.) This land was purchased in 1679 by Thomas Jesson, who built the house upon it. Or as the internal timbering, panelling, and in fact the whole of the woodwork is of oak, this alternative derivation of the name Oakwood is sometimes suggested therefrom.

The earliest recorded connection of this family with the parish is in a 99 years' lease, dated 20th April, 1560 (3rd year of Elizabeth's reign) whereby one HENRY JESSON let a croft in this same locality of Black Lake to a tenant named John Davys, who built a cottage thereon. Another indenture of the following year (1561) sells this property, which brought in the then considerable sum of 20s. yearly; and also another property consisting of a cottage, with garden croft, and meadow, all situated in the adjacent vicinity called Haytley Field, and in the occupation of one FRANCIS JESSON; the consideration money being £50, and the purchaser William Hunt, of West Bromwich.

An indenture of 14 June, 1605 (3rd year of James I's reign) was made between one party of the same name (William Hunt) but now described as "of Smethwick," and another party, granting a lease of a cottage with its croft, together with a croft called the Moore in Hateley field, between the land of the said Hunt in the occupation of WILLIAM JESSON, and the highway leading from Lydeatt towards the common called Hateley Heath.

The next member of this family discovered in West Bromwich, and the one who heads that part of their pedigree given by Mrs Willett, is NICHOLAS JESSON, buried at the parish church 20 January, 1626. His son, JOHN JESSON, married Amy Darby, of Rowley, and died the year before his father, namely, in 1625. His widow married again (1631) her second husband being Thomas Grove, also of West Bromwich, belonging to another family of whom something must be said in due course.

John Jesson the younger is named among the original Stanley Trustees of 1613, and is classed with them as a yeoman.

A surviving son of John was GEORGE JESSON, born 1619, who became executor to his step-father, Thomas Grove. Both George Jesson and Thomas Grove are found in 1643 as witnesses to a lease at peppercorn rental, of two cottages, etc., in Finchpath, on the King's highway from Bromwich Heath towards Wednesbury. In 1658 George, acquired for his son, Thomas, a minor, the remainder of a lease of a property called the Bridge End Croft, held by the nominal fancy tenure of "one rose flower" yearly. Interest is at once aroused by this place-name. The question naturally arises, Where was this Bridge End Croft? Did the "bridge" span the brook at Hydes Road? or at Wednesbury Bridge! If at the latter spot, the problem then is: How did this seventeenth century bridge fall out of existence, and become lost to all knowledge in the eighteenth century? The name "Wednesbure Bridge" is found in use in 1620 (*Willett*, p. 222); and allusion to the aforementioned properties of William Hunt describes their location (1661) as being near the "Great Portway leading from Wolverhampton towards Birmingham,", and another cottage as being on the "said Portway leading from Wednesbury towards Birmingham." This evidence seems unmistakeably to point to Wednesbury Bridge; because this structure is still approached to this day from the Wednesbury side by a Portway Road; and the old cottages clustering around it were known till very recent years as Bridge End. The use of "End" in the nomenclature of street localities has already been explained, and till the first decades of the present century the term was used in Wednesbury at the three most ancient centres of its population; namely, in the Bridge End just mentioned, and for the groups of dwellings lying around its two most important residential seats, Oakeswell Hall and the Manor House; and designated respectively "Oakeswell End" and "Hall End."

When the 1658 lease is made over, of this "Bridge End Croft," at "the yearly rent of one roase flower upon the Feast of St. John Baptist, if it be lawfully demanded," George Jesson is therein described as a "yeoman." Another property acquired by him (in 1666) was the remainder of a lease from Brome Whorwood of lands called Bald Hills, it was for some 20 acres abutting on the Hayes Meadows, "the mines of stone or cole" and all quarries being reserved. This land is now known as Balls Hill, although the original name would seem to indicate that it was once an elevated knoll *bald* of trees and of all foliage, while the surrounding landscape was well wooded; and that most probably with oaks, as the name Oakwood would imply. The property called Barditch, or Barr Ditch, on that side of the parish called Smethwick Lane, was purchased by George Jesson in 1670. He died in 1678 and was buried at the old church on 28 November.

THOMAS JESSON, his eldest son, was born 1645. He it was who built Oakwood, as already mentioned. He is described as of Sutton Coldfield in the conveyance of a certain Barker's Field, near the Portway from Wednesbury towards Bromwich Heath; and again in the deeds of the previously described pastures called Oakley's Croft adjoining the said Portway and a lane leading from the Portway towards West Bromwich Church (this lane was either Church Lane or Witton Lane). Thomas Jesson became a trustee of the Brick Kiln Dole in 1691, in the January of which year he took part in the overthrowing of boundaries illegally erected around some of the waste-lands of the manor. This was the year, too, in which he became churchwarden. Thomas Jesson had several brothers, but their connection with the parish seems to have been of the very slightest. One of them JOHN JESSON, of "Bilston and of Graisley," was present at a vestry meeting of West Bromwich parishioners in 1701, and took part in the proceedings as one entitled to do so. As the family of Thomas, "of Sutton," died out, the Oakwood property is found in the possession of the descendants of John, who died in 1712.

THOMAS JESSON, son of John, was born 1697, and was one of a family of six children, his eldest brother being the Rev. Cornelius Jesson, Vicar of Wombourne and Trysull, buried at the latter place in 1756. Thomas was churchwarden of West Bromwich in 1734, and in a conveyance of lands situated near the church, dated 1728, he is described as an "ironmonger" or iron merchant. He was a trustee of the Pudding Land Dole in 1722, and was nominated to the Stanley Trust in 1746.

Thomas Jesson died at the age of 70 in 1766. Of his large family of twelve children but two of the sons survived him. Richard, of the Leveretts, became High Sheriff in 1804, and his son Thomas, born in 1779, lived for some time at Charlemont Hall, which he sold in 1825. But another son of Thomas, and an elder brother of Richard, was JOSEPH JESSON, born 1736. He was churchwarden for three years following his father's death, namely 1766 to 1768, and at the rebuilding of the church in 1787 claimed his pew at the general allotment. The next year, 1788, he was again a churchwarden, when money was borrowed on the "security of the parish" to pay £180 due on the alterations.

Joseph Jesson died in 1816, and was succeeded by his son, THOMAS JESSON, "of Severn Hall," who, in 1818, is the largest subscriber next to Lord Dartmouth to the fund for building Christ Church, he also served on the Committee of Management for carrying out the scheme. He died 1837.

His son, THOMAS JESSON, of "Oakwood," was born in 1801.

The late Thomas Jesson, like all his ancestors, took an intense interest in all parochial and ecclesiastical matters. For 25 years after the death of his father he served the office of churchwarden, and on his retirement a Vestry meeting in 1862, expressed their deep debt of gratitude to him for the very faithful and conscientious manner in which he had invariably discharged the duties of his office for the whole period of that 25 years. In the civil government of the parish he was also equally zealous, he had been a prime mover at a Vestry meeting in 1853 for the taking of the necessary steps in obtaining a local Act for the improved government of West Bromwich. At the last restoration of the Parish Church in 1871, he naturally took a most prominent part.

For his second wife he married Mary Charlotte Izon, of the Lodge, West Bromwich, but by his first wife, Susanna, daughter of Joseph Smith, Esq., of Summerfield, West Bromwich, he had a family of two sons and two daughters. Both the sons have gone into the Church. The Rev. Henry jesson, born 1842, was formerly "assistant priest" St. Andrew's Church, and is still located in his native parish, holding the benefice of St. Peter's, Greets Green. His brother, the Rev. Thomas Jesson, born 1843, was also at one time in the parish, acting as a curate at the Old Church; he is now at Bath. He resided but a few months at Oakwood after the death of his father.

So far only that part of the family has been dealt with which brings the line down from the beginning of the seventeenth century to that member still resident in the parish at the present day, and which for about two centuries has been connected with Oakwood. But there have been other branches of this somewhat extensive family, who have exerted considerable influence over the past history of this vicinity. In earlier times the name was spelt Gesson. The Walsall branch have lent their name to Jesson's Lane in that ancient borough. But in West Bromwich itself there was a Richard Jesson, who was a Justice of the Peace from about 1765, a period when the office would mark him as a personage of importance not only in the parish, but in the county as well. He, and several other members of the family who have not been mentioned, also held the office of churchwarden many times during the eighteenth century.

Going back still further at the Herald's Visitation of 1664, the Thomas Jesson who afterwards built Oakwood in 1691, but who is then described as "of West Bromwich and Sandwell," was disclaimed. That is, he claimed the right to bear arms, a distinction then reserved for "gentlemen," but his pretensions could not be made good, to the satisfaction of the authorities.

From George Jesson, who flourished in the 17th century, most of the family have been iron merchants, their grant of arms is dated 1854, and is to the descendants of Thomas Jesson, who married Mary Chambers in the middle of the 18th century. The pedigree, certified at Herald's College, has several of the collateral branches shown.

XLVIII.—Dagger Hall and the Grove Family: the Household Stuff of a Seventeenth Century Yeoman.

The late Mr Thomas Jesson, who died at Oakwood in 1873, was a magistrate for the county of Stafford. And now to revert to the Jessons' connections, by the marriage of 1631, with the Groves:—

The earliest mention of the Grove family in West Bromwich is the appearance of the name of Edward Grove as a witness to lease of land in Fynchespath, dated 20 April, 27 Elizabeth (1584). But on the other side of the parish, Henry Grove of Hondesworthe was a yeoman, whose will is said to have been proved 11 September, 1589, in which he mentions his sons Edward and Thomas Grove, his wife Elene, bequeathing her "my best feather bedd with bolsters and pillowes and all things belonging to the same;" his wife's son, William Cookes; Henry Grove, his son Edward's son and "to cozen Robert Grove, one weyning calf" is left.

Search for this will has failed to find it at Lichfield, although one of Richard Gesson *alias* Jesson was found to have been proved in 1592.

Some confusion may now possibly arise in the identification of the two specified sons, Edward Grove and Thomas Grove, inasmuch as two other members of the family, named also Edward and Thomas respectively, were buried some 80 years afterwards. These latter would in all probability be grandsons at least of the Henry Grove of Handsworth.

To Thomas Grove a payment, in 1602, of 2s. (? rent) is recorded by Symon Ryder. Edward Grove was one of the original Stanley Trustees in 1613: and in 1635 both Edward and Thomas were equally honoured by being made Trustees of Whorwood's Brick Kiln Dole. In 1638 Thomas (with one Edmund Darby) took a lease of pastures and closes called Turhills. When Thomas Grove's name occurs as a witness to the lease of the Bridge End Croft in 1643, it is worthy of note that the occupier, one "Walter Vale (or Ffale), is described as a "husbandman," a class living also on the soil, but of distinctly lower rank than "yeomen."

On February 12th, 1631, Thomas Grove had married Amy Jesson, widow of John Jesson, whose stepson (George Jesson) became his executor, and by 1637 we have a second Edward Grove, probably a son of the former Edward.

EDWARD GROVE THE YOUNGER, of West Bromwich, yeoman, purchased (1637) from another yeoman family of Oskote (Oscott) named Gibbons, a cottage (?Dagger Hall) with garden and hemplecke in Lyndon; together with four crofts of pasture, a "one-acre or dayes earthe of errable land", the said cottage was near the highway called Hargate Lane, and two of the crofts were near the land of Edward Grove the elder, "and to the way there, leading from the dwelling-house of the said Edward Grove the elder towards Birmingham." Now this locates the residence of the elder Grove with a tolerable amount of exactness; presuming we can decide which *was* "the way towards Birmingham" in those days—the older way by Forge Lane, or the present main-road.

From a conveyance by this same Edward Grove, of Lyndon, yeoman (dated 1667), it becomes evident that either this house, or one erected on land bought from the same Gibbons, was "known by the name of Dagger Hall," because the land conveyed abutted on the south side thereof, and on the west end thereof, upon "the lane leading from the said house towards the church . . . which said piece of ground is now marked and paled out from the greate gatepost of the said Edward Grove." The purchaser, William Turton, made a draw-well on the north end of the house, eastward to the corner of the garden. This well was intended for a pump, and its importance in those days may be gauged by the fact that there is added to the document a second and supplementary agreement by which Turton formally let and set to Grove the use of the well and pump for watering "the cattle of the said Ed. G. that depastured there."

There are extant receipts for rents paid by Edward Grove to one Matthew Ruston "for all his lands in West Bromwich" in 1661, at both half-yearly rent. days, "Saint Mary day" and "St. Michall the Archangel." Also similar receipts for 1662, 1668 and 1677.

This second Edward Grove would appear to have buried his first wife Mary, October 1657, and to have contracted a second marriage with Mary Persall on October 20th, 1664. Their first child was buried on July 24th, 1665; but a second was baptised by the name of Mary on June 22nd, 1666. Mary Grove became by marriage one Mary Billingsley, of whom more anon.

A "Mr Edward Grove" died at the beginning of the year 1669 and was buried on January 5th. His brother, Thomas Grove, was executor to his will, but as he died in the August following, the executor of Thomas, namely, the aforementioned George Jesson seems to have carried out the provisions of both wills.

This step-son, George Jesson, has left behind him most interesting records of his administration of the estates: interesting because they throw a flood of light upon the daily life and habits of the yeoman class in this locality. The first document is:—

A Bill of the funeral expenses of Edward Grove, whoe departed this life the 2nd day of January, 1668-9, as folleth:—

	£	s.	d.
Payd to Edward Jesson for bread and cake...	5	5	0
Payd to Sarah Thorne for ale...	0	12	0
Payd for wine	0	6	0
Payd for suger...	0	5	0
One quire of riting piper	0	0	5
Fine incke	0	0	3
For ginger	0	0	6
A peare of hose for the child...	0	0	6
For gloves and mase	0	0	9
For one quarter of veale	0	2	2
For fore capuns...	0	4	0
For one grouse	0	1	6
For a peace of befe	0	1	0
For towe rabets...	0	1	0
Payd to the Clarke	0	4	0
Payd to Ann Blumer	0	2	0
Payd to Thomas Briscoe	0	2	10
Payd to Robert Grice...	0	1	6
Payd to Samewell Westwood...	0	0	6
Payd for laying him out and windden him...	0	1	6
Payd for tobackoe	0	2	0
Payd for tobackoe pipes	0	0	4
Payd to Edward Grove, Henry Grove, John Grove, and Thomas Grove for carring him to church, and layinge him in his grave, twelvepence apeace...	0	4	0
Payd to my cusen John Grove, for taking the Inventory and ingrossing it	0	5	0
Payd to George Jesson for copinge out the will	0	2	0
Payd for provinge the will and the commission for taking my oathes	0	15	0
Payd to Mr White for his funerall sermon and a mortorie, and for giving me my oathes	0	16	8
Payd to Thomas Belaingam for keeping the plompe which was due at Christmas last	0	1	0
Payd to James Cope for the starlings, the moles, and towards the making of the hedges	0	2	6
	£10	0	11

Apart from the unconventional orthography—and the spelling of the numerals and quantities *two, four, pair* and *piece* are indeed deliciously free from all grammatical constraint—the funeral accounts here rendered are most instructive, Here may be observed the large amount spent in those days on the pomp and ceremonial of a funeral. Considering the relative value of money, the funeral baked meats are set down here at a very considerable sum. It was the custom to have grand funerals, followed by great feasting, at which the smoking of tobacco was apparently no small part of the entertainment.

Charges are made for writing notices and legal documents, and even for the material with which they were written. The funeral cake was evidently a costly one. Perhaps the spices were used on the corpse; there is an item for winding the body in its cerements. Even the bearers were paid. The mortuaries and other ecclesiastical fees were fully explained in chapter xxxiii. The receipt for the breaking up of the floor of the church, to make the grave or vault, is also preserved.

But why the charges for destroying vermin should be included in funeral expenses it is difficult to suggest. Nor can the preceding item referring to "the plompe" be readily explained. The receipt alluded to, however runs:—

"October 13th, 1669.—Received then of George Jesson for taking upp the seates when Mr Edward Grove was buryed, and setting them down again the some of two shillings and four pence."

The next document is a brief rent-roll, drawn up by the administrator in which the allusion to a bolster is obscure, although "line" evidently signifies Lyne or Lyndon:—

My cosens tennants as followeth:

	£	s.	d.
John Osborne for his howse	0	16	8
And for the towe craufts	1	0	0
Robert Grice for his howse and land...	1	5	6
Robert Grice for the barne	0	2	6
James Cox	2	0	0
My Ante Grove...	0	5	0

Rent due at Allhallowtide.

	£	s.	d.
Rafe Cullwicke—rent due at Chrismas	5	10	0
Widdowe Baker...	0	19	0
The howse in line	1	10	0
My ffather Grove received of his maid for a bolster	0	4	0
of Edward Dudley for Line Barne	0	12	0

The next two accounts appear to refer to the commercial relations and transactions between the two deceased brothers. Here we obtain an insight into the prices current for farm produce at that time, and of the value of furniture and household utensils which it was then common to bequeath by will.

A bill of what money my ffather Grove hath received of my
Uncle Edward Grove.

	£	s.	d.
Three tun of hay	3	0	0
For boards which came from line	1	0	0
For one cow	2	10	0
Received of Elizabeth Dawes for one coverlet and one box	0	11	0
Received of Henry Lowe for pewter...	0	13	0
Received of John Deeley for one flichen of bacon...	0	15	0
Received of James Bun for the cubert	0	11	0
Received of William White for one cofer and two blankets	0	7	6
Received Goody Large for one chaf bed and two blankets	0	6	4
For one coffer and one chaire...	0	4	4
For one spade	0	0	4
Received of Thomas Simes for a peare of bedsteads	0	9	6

A few notes on the foregoing may serve to add interest to its perusal. A cupboard was the most useful article of furniture in a yeoman's kitchen; on this "cubert" or dresser the wealth of the family pewter would be displayed, and a service of pewter was a sign of comparative wealth when silver-plate was at so high a value. The coffer, too, was essential to a man of substance when bankers and banking were unknown, and money was always stored up in the safest part of the house. And with regard to the "chaff bed" sold to "Goody"—or the old Goodwife Large—be it remembered that while feather beds were heirable property, common people knew not flock or cotton wool beds, but were content to sleep upon beds stuffed with chaff, or sometimes with herbs.

A note of my unkle Grove's debts, and whic money father Grove
paid for my uncle Ed. Grove.

	£	s.	d.
Mr Thomas Groves acquitance	2	0	0
George Jesson's ,, ...	2	0	0
To father Grove...	5	0	0
Unkle Grove's funeral expenses	10	0	11
Paid to Mary Grove for keeping the child...	1	10	0
Paid to the churchwardens	0	1	6
Paid to John Stamps for the poore...	0	1	6

One quarter's rent was due to my mother Grove for her dowry
    out of my father Grove's land at Oldbury.

The next document shows that the mother had died also, and accounts for the household expenditure during her last illness. Then appear the small family legacies, and not the end the household furniture with its valuation which came to the executor as residuary legatee:—

Money to be allowed me upon act.

	£	s.	d.
Paid for my father Groves funeral expenses	11	12	1
The charge of housekeeping between my father Grove's death and my mother's	10	19	8
Mother Grove's funeral expenses	8	19	2

Legacies.

	£	s.	d.
To his sister Coper	0	10	0
To Thomas Coper	0	10	0
To Mr Thos. Grove	2	0	0
To Cozen John Grove...	2	0	0
Imp: The cast mettle plate belonging to the hall fire	0	11	0
The great brasse pann...	0	19	0
One spitt	0	1	0
The truckle bed...	0	3	4
One forme	0	1	0
The axe	0	1	0
	01	16	10

"Received these goods above written in part of a Legasie given by Thomas Grove, lately deceased, by mee George Jesson."

In the following settlement and destination of the goods, chattels, and household stuff one is struck with the pettiness of the accounts. But that those times cannot fairly be placed in comparison with the present will be made obvious by directing attention to two items. First, the value placed on a joint stool should serve to remind us that the humblest article of furniture was enhanced in value if its joints were framed together and not the product of the rough hedge-carpentry which finished its work only with axe and adze. The second allusion which emphasises the difference in the periods is that of a loom as part of the household equipment. But as late as 1712 and 1720 the Wednesbury registers mention weavers and tow-dressers among the ordinary avocations of the locality.

I sold to my Ant Grove these things under written:—

	£	s.	d.
One great kettle...	0	10	0
A nurse chair, one fflichen of bacon...	0	10	0
And the store pig	0	7	0
One joyned stule	0	1	10
One warming pan	0	2	0
Two little joyned stules	0	1	0
All the flax, and the woole, and the litle wheele...	0	4	0
One chest, one coffer	0	6	6
Two smuthinge irons...	0	0	10
One ffallinge table		1	0

One feather beed at seaven peenee the poound cometh to one poound eight shillings and six pence and for kiping the cowe the some is besides, ...

	£	s.	d.
Sold one kettle, 15 pounds weight at 10 pence the pound, comes to	0	12	6
Sold three pewter dishes att 6 pounds and one quarter att	0	6	0
Sold one brasse chafinge dish att	0	1	4
Sold one table with two tressells in the buletinge house, att		2	0
Sold one coppinge knife, att...			6
Sold the little table in the hall	0	4	0
Sold one chafe bed, att...	0	2	10
Sold one chaire in the hall chamber, att	0	2	0
Sold one coffer in the kitchen chamber to Will White, which he hath not paid for	0	3	0
Sold two peare of ould blankets to Will White, which he hath not paid for, att	0	4	0
The great chest, att	0	11	0
Sold one wine sheet, one bag, and one axe...	0	5	0
One lume, not paid for, att	—		
Sold one hurdle to Thos. Briskoe, not paid for	0	0	4

Delivered to my Ant Grove—one great kettle, one dabnet, one brasse mortar and pestle, one brasse limer, one brasse candlestick, one little kettle, two barrels, one burning lume, one skelle, one kimnell, one brasse pott, one churne, fiare shovle and toungs, two joyned chaires, one deske stule, a nurse chaire, one flicken of baken, and the store pig.

Left with Mistress Selly—7 fowles, and fore guislings, and one patted woden bole.

	£	s.	d.
To Thomas Simcox one bedsteds	0	9	6
One cofer	0	2	2
To Humphrey Rowe the great brasse poote at 9 the pound	1	16	0
One table boord...	0	4	0
One corne showlle	0	1	8
One barill	0	3	6
To Thomas Simcox a peare of coberts	0	2	6
To William White a sacor	0	0	4

In the butrey, tenn shillves in the darke rume; seven shillves below the entrey; towe benches in the halle.

Goods received at time unsold—One table and forme in the halle, one londwin (?) and bare of iorne, the screne, towe candlesticks, towe peare of beeadstides, six silver spownes, one jacke and wates, one coffer, one old bible, and a peare of gold waits, one little book, one cofer and linings, one smothing irone, one dripin ponn and broache. [spit], *one fether beead and beead trillinge, Imwaeitnoel*

What shillves and benches are lafte in Mrs Selly's rumes, as folleth: towe joyned beeds and cords, and mats, in the hall, one longe table, one joyne forme, towe joyne benches, one other bench, in the butrey, tenn shillves, in the dark rume seaven, belowe the entry towe, one lous irn, one iorne bare, and geeale.

∗ ∗ ∗ ∗ ∗ ∗ ∗

Edward Grove had an only daughter, Mary, who married James Billingsley. Their only daughter, Mary Billingsley, married Charles Magenis.

Sarah Magenis survived her husband, and then by will devised all her lands in West Bromwich and Wednesbury to her second son, Constantine Magenis. The will of this Sarah Magenis, widow, of Alcester charges him on arriving at 21 years of age to pay £125 to each of her four daughters. But as Constantine died before attaining his majority, the estate passed to his brother Charles Magenis. The release to Charles, from the four husbands of these sisters (Catherine, who had married William Mantell; Frances, who had married Edward Watton; Ann, who had married Richard Hawkesford, and Sarah, who had married Henry Baddily) is dated 17th October, 1734.

The will of Charles Magenis, dated 3rd April. 1745, gives power to his trustees, Robert Aglionby Slaney and Richard Rann, to sell the estates if necessary.

The indenture of Sale, dated 22 September, 1748, is made between the said trustees, R. A. Slaney (of Walford, Salop), and R. Rann (of Birmingham), and Rebecca Magenis, widow of the said Charles (who had been a Birmingham merchant) of the one part; and Thomas Jesson, ironmonger of West Bromwich, of the other part, and by the terms of it, the latter party purchases (1) two closes of pasture in West Bromwich, in the tenure of John Worsley, near Dagger Hall, (2) a parcel of land in Churchfield in the same occupation, and near lands held by Nathaniel Whiley, under Lord Dartmouth; and (3) the use of the well or pump standing near Dagger Hall, yielding and paying therefor one peppercorn upon the feast of St. Michael, if lawfully demanded.

———

XLIX.—The Lowes of Lyndon; Charlemont Hall.

Another connection of the Jesson family was that of the Lowes of Lyndon. The earliest mention of the Lowes is perhaps that in the Ryder MSS., of a John Lowe, living and owning land in West Bromwich about 1632; and apparently the next is of one Humfrey Lowe, who witnessed the sale of Oakwood (or Oakleys Crofts), in the year 1638, and who was mentioned in chapter xxvi.

Then there was an Alexander Lowe who heads the pedigree given by Mrs Willett and whose son, John Lowe, is unquestionably the one who first interests us most by his frequent appearance in local history. Other sons of the same "Alexander Loe" were:— Alexander, born May, 1632; Henry, 1636; and Paul, born 1639.

There was an Alice Lowe, a sister to whom Sir Richard Shilton left his Manor of West Bromwich, in 1647, but whether she was wife or widow of any member of this family of Lowes is not known.

John Lowe, the eldest of the sons just enumerated was born in 1628, and is registered as the son of one "Sawnders Loe," on October 26th; from which it may be surmised that at the time of his birth, the father had not as yet acquired sufficient of wealth or of dignity to entitle him to the enjoyment of his own full baptismal name—perhaps he was at that time but a workman, whose development and evolution into a capitalist and an employer of labour was then in the womb of the future.

John Lowe married Priscilla Robins, of Bilston, on July 9th, 1655, and by the time his firstborn (John) was born in November, 1658, we find him described as an ironmonger or ironmaster. His name occurs in the Parish Books in 1691, and again in 1698, in connection with the protest against illegal enclosures of the waste-lands. In 1691 he became a trustee of the Brick Kiln Dole. He died in 1702, leaving a family, which included John, Benjamin, etc.

John Lowe, junior, in 1689 married Elizabeth Jesson, and his alliance with this family is a sufficient indication of his worldly prosperity, and of the social position he occupied in the parish. From the Churchwardens' Books the following Statement has been abstracted, and from it we gather that as an ironmaster he was engaged in the local staple of nail making, and that he had large transactions with the Parish Overseers who seem to have then employed the able bodied paupers in the same branch of trade. The extract whose accountancy certainly needed emendation, reads as follows:—

The accompts of Mr John Lowe, junr., concerning the buying of nayles delivered to ye Parish Nayler in July, 1697.

	£	s.	d.
which come to	105	16	06
due to him for Nayle bags	000	12	08
due to him for Iron delivered to Nayler	000	04	07
due to him for Interest ye 26 July next	004	12	00
	119	05	09½

According to other Vestry records John Lowe, junior, is found taking part in parish business in 1690 and 1698: and again in 1701, as mentioned in chapter xxxiii. After his father's death the family prosperity seems to have continued unabated, the nail rod manufacture being still carried on with vigour and enterprise, In 1709 John Lowe of Lyndon purchased Bustleholme Mill which he used for corn grinding, for nail rod splitting, and for oil expressing, as mentioned in chaps xxvi. and xxxvi. But as he is generally styled "ironmonger" we may conclude that his business chiefly lay in the nail and nail rod trades. When the manorial estate was being broken up in 1720 John Lowe is found among the purchasers of the ancient manor lands.

About this time his brother Benjamin and his son Samuel are also found taking active parts in parochial affairs. In 1698 Benjamin Lowe was churchwarden, but the name of Samuel does not appear till 1704, and then he would be but a boy. Benjamin was again warden in 1711 and 1712. There is also mention of a Josiah Lowe in 1716 and 1718, and in fact the family name is of frequent recurrence; but after 1725 the name of John Lowe begins to disappear. He died in 1729.

John Lowe, by his wife Elizabeth Jesson, had five sons and four daughters, and is supposed to have built Charlemont Hall as a residence for his growing family. Of these it is necessary to mention John (born 1689), Samuel (born 1691), Jesson (born 1698), Benjamin (born 1708), Elizabeth (born 1701), Mary (born 1702), and Sarah (born 1711). As the two first-named daughters were living at the original family house in Lyne as the tenants of Samuel Lowe in 1748; and as Jesson Lowe probably lived with his other sister Sarah, near Bustleholme, where he was working the mills, it has been thought that Samuel must have been residing at Charlemont in succession to his father, if even he was not the one who actually built the hall. Charlemont was at first called Crump Hall, and as we do not find any records of the eldest son, John Lowe, being engaged in any local trade or other business affairs, it has been surmised that he entered the army and was the Cornet Lowe, whose political escapades made this place somewhat notorious. At this time he would therefore probably be living under his father's roof at Charlemont or Crump Hall.

But why was the name changed? Had the re-naming of the Hall anything to do with incidents in the military career of John Lowe? Had Cornet Lowe followed the fortunes of Marlborough along the iron frontier of France?

Charlemont the original, is one of the strongest of French fortresses, situated on the left bank of the Meuse. It no doubt obtained its name from the feet that the small town and castle there were erected on a steep mount by the river, and which commanded every direction, by Charles V. in 1555. Charlemont is so impregnable that practically it has never been attacked, although it will garrison from 11,000 to 25,000 men, and yet may be defended by 3,000. But there was another Charlemont in Ireland, and as this place came into notoriety about this time, perhaps it may be accepted as a piece of Whiggery—or shall we say, of political waggery?—that Crump Hall had its name altered by a Whig owner to Charlemont Hall. The Irish Charlemont was the last important fastness which the Irish occupied in Ulster, and it was taken by Schomberg in 1690, when fighting for the Protestant cause of William III.

George I. came to the throne in 1714, and the accession of the House of Hanover was naturally unwelcome to the adherents of the House of Stuart. No matter how wise or circumspect was the conduct of the new king and his Whig ministers, it was quite sufficient to drive the Jacobites to extremities, and with the accompanying irritation of the high Tories, an appeal to arms was only to be expected. After some months serious riots broke out, and in this Midland district they assumed the form of an attack upon the Dissenters, which became so alarming that the Riot Act was passed, which is still in force. These civil tumults culminated in the Pretender's Rebellion of 1715.

Dissenters hitherto had not only lain under every disability, but had been the object of an active tyrannical oppression of every kind, civil as well as religious. Staffordshire was described as being in 1714 a "most Tory county" and in the excesses perpetrated here neither Whig nor Dissenter escaped insult or injury. It may fairly be assumed that if Cornet Lowe were not acting impartially in an official capacity that he was a Whig in sympathy. Anyway in the local riots of 1715 (which will be found more fully described in the History of Tipton, chap. xxxi.), two of the mob who were unroofing the West Bromwich Presbyterian Meeting House were shot by him in his defence of the building on July 14th. These two men, Francis Gibbons of Sedgley, and Thomas Royston of Wolverhampton, were buried at Wednesbury on the 17th following. And as indicative of the persistency of the mob's violent attitude it may be added that their purpose was afterwards effected, and the meeting house was burnt to ashes. Refer back also to chap. xxxiii.

Premonitory symptoms of a second great Jacobite rising now approaching, namely that of the Young Pretender in 1745, were further local riotings. There can be no doubt that there were many Jacobites in Wednesbury, Walsall, and the immediate vicinity of West Bromwich. But, as before, there was a strange admixture of political frenzy with religious intolerance in this renewed outbreak, a description of which may be found in The Wednesbury Papers pp. 36-39. What was the exact part played by Cornet Lowe in the Shrove Tuesday Riots at Wednesbury in 1744, it would be impossible to say. But a Tory writer has described him as a "ringleader" on that occasion.

JESSON LOWE, even if he did not reside at Charlemont may be taken as the representative *head of the family in trade* in succession to his father "John. Lowe, junior," whose death occurred in 1729. In 1722 both Jesson and his brother Samuel were trustees of the Pudding Land Dole, in 1738 Jesson and John (? his eldest brother, the Cornet) are both contributors to a church collection, and in 1746 Jesson was one of the surviving Stanley Trustees. John and Jesson Lowe are both found in 1734 agreeing formally to the provision of a Parish Poor-house. That Jesson Lowe was as active in his own private business, as in the public affairs of the parish, may be taken for granted; in chap. xxxvi he was mentioned as having parted with various tenements near Bustleholme Nail-rod and Oil-pressing Mill, together with the "close of land wherein the said mills and premises stand"; in the deed mention is also made of all the stables, outhouses, warehouses, and manufacturing premises which he had purchased from his late father "John Lowe, of Lyndon, alias Lyne, gentleman." This may possibly have meant a complete or a partial retirement from commercial pursuits, as there is a suggestion of other ideals of life in the assumption of the descriptive affix "gentleman." If any branch of his business were relinquished, it may have been the oil department, as it was certainly not the iron making, for we find in 1743, and even later, that Mr Thomas Jesson, of The Forge, was being supplied with bars by Jesson Lowe, who was evidently a large iron-maker.

That Jesson Lowe also filled a position of some social importance, even to taking upon himself high county rank, is apparent from the fact that he held office as High Sheriff in 1752. His death took place in June 1758, after a very long and painful illness.

If John Lowe, the eldest, were identical with Cornet Lowe, the record of his death may have to be sought very far afield from West Bromwich. Any way it cannot be traced in the parish registers, nor yet that of the second son, Samuel, although the name of Samuel Lowe transpires at the Vestry Meeting in 1765. From Samuel, Charlemont seems to have passed to his maiden sisters.

Surviving the brothers were the three sisters, none of whom seem to have married. Sarah, the youngest died in 1774. In 1786 Miss Lowe is named as part "owner" of the Singing Gallery which then stood at the west end of the Old Church, and at the reallotment of the pews in the re-built church, Elizabeth Lowe claimed a family pew in the year following (1787). The second sister Mary, died in 1792, at the age of 90; but the eldest, generally known as Madam Betty, survived till 1793, dying at the advanced age of 92. Portraits of Cornet Lowe and of Madam Betty, were formerly to be found hanging in Charlemont, and are still extant.

Here we bring to an end the stock of the family founded by "Sandy Loe." in disposing of the members of the last generation we have had to assume that the eldest, John, became a soldier who spent most of his life away from West Bromwich; that Samuel became resident head of the family, and that Jesson Lowe became head of the manufacturing concern, and did not live at Charlemont, although Reeves' *History* makes him set fire to the house.

Reeves writing in 1836, also says: Sixty years ago there was a Hop Yard near the Hall, in which was a Well, the water of which was considered medicinal, and was regularly drunk during the summer season by the three maiden ladies then living at Charlemont Hall. Elizabeth, Mary, and Sarah Lowe.

The description of "Charley Mount" given by Shaw (who miscalls the three ladies by the name of "Loyd") was quoted in chap. xxvii. On the death of Elizabeth Lowe, the Hall passed by will to her cousin Dean Hallam of Bristol, who in turn devised it to Henry Hallam, the great historian. In 1807 the property formed part of the marriage settlement upon his wife, Julia Maria Elton, the daughter of a former incumbent of West Bromwich, whom singularly enough for the ownership of this little estate he married. When however, another estate was settled upon Mrs Hallam by way of substitution, in 1812, Charlemont was purchased by Mr Thomas Jesson, in the following year, for his own occupation.

Since Shaw wrote his description of Charlemont Hall about 1790, the house has been enlarged, and the road thrown further from it. In fact one of the walks in the grounds was formerly the public road, probably diverted at the time when the Enclosure Act came into force in 1803. The old road passes round to the back of the house which originally was its front. The hall is a well-built residence, with staircases, flooring, panelling, etc. all of oak. The east wing is a new addition of the year 1855. By Reeves the house is described as a "fine mansion." This was when the Halford's were tenants. Mr Halford had been steward to Lord Dartmouth.

From Mr Jesson, who planted trees and otherwise improved the property, it passed in 1825 to Mr Samuel Dawes of The Leveretts, Handsworth, from whom it was acquired in 1854 by Mr J. N. Bagnall.

Of its occupants several startling incidents are related. Twice has the Hall been threatened with destruction by fire; the first time, according to Reeves it was Jesson Lowe, who, retiring to bed one night about 1750, left the candle burning on a table covered with papers, which caused a conflagration. Or, according to Mrs Willett, it was Mr Thomas Jesson, who sometime in the present century, committed this indiscretion. A second fire took place in 1879, during the present occupancy.

As tenants to Mr Jesson, a family named Price resided at Charlemont about 1822. The ridiculous tale related of them, and quoted in The History of Tipton, p. 37, is one of sacrilege (!) by using the discarded roof of Tipton parish church, for which "no good ever came to them afterwards", it tells of the consequent death of the children at an early age and of the disreputable drunkenness and retributive death of the one grown-up son; and as a fitting climax to all this, is added the discovery of the head of the family with his throat cut in his bedroom, an affair we are asked to believe, which was all hushed up, and not even the formality of an inquest held upon it!

A succeeding tenant was Mr Joseph Halford, of whose connection with the place Reeves relates the following incident, which is not only of a much more pleasing character, but which seems to carry us back through such a long vista of time to find Wednesbury and West Bromwich indulging in the pleasures of the chase. He says:— "There is an excellent pack of Harriers belonging to Mr Halford, of Charlemont. I believe the Gentlemen dine at the Turk's Head Hotel Wednesbury [at that time kept by Mr. John Russell, who had a training ground and paddock for his hunters at the back of the Hotel, where Russell Street now is], at the close of each season. The following occurrence I have extracted from a newspaper of Saturday, Feb. 15th, 1834:—"As Mr Halford's Harriers were hunting on Tuesday week, within a few miles of the kennel at Charlemont, they rousted an outlying deer, which they immediately pursued; after a severe run, which continued without a check for over 40 minutes over a course of country which, at a moderate calculation, could not he much less than 12 miles, the hounds had actually killed him when the horsemen came up, there being only seven of the hounds up at the time, a few of which were found worrying him, while one or two others were observed lying in an almost exhausted state near him. One hound in particular, which was noticed to press him very hard at the last, was picked up in an apparently lifeless state, but being bled and rubbed in a few minutes came to himself. This run, we think, stands unparalleled in sporting history, when we consider the small size of the hounds, and the gallant style in which he was killed.'"

Since 1871 Charlemont has been occupied by Mr John Hunt Thursfield, a Wednesbury solicitor, who for twenty years previously had lived in the High Street of that town. His father before him was a solicitor who had been articled to the

Wednesbury firm of Messrs Crowthers, and who was a contemporary of two other well-known local lawyers, Mr Elisha Caddick of West Bromwich, and Mr Charles Adams, of Darlaston. His mother too, came of a legal family, for she was the daughter of another solicitor, Mr James Hunt, who in his youth migrated from Walsall to the Metropolis where he became the London agent of Messrs Crowther. Mr Thursfield's father dying young, his brother-in-law, Mr Charles Hunt took his practice, to which Mr Thursfield ultimately succeeded.

Mr J. H. Thursfield for forty-four years filled the post of clerk to the Wednesbury division of the County Magistrates, from which position he has just retired. In 1890 and again in 1891 Mr Thursfield was chosen Mayor of Wednesbury, in the public life of which place he has taken a fairly good part, but always in a quiet and unobtrusive manner.

L.—The Family of Rider (or Ryder): The Rider ms. "Hypomnema": A Yeoman's Revolt against Villein Services.

In the last year of the reign and intolerant times of Queen Mary, was born in West Bromwich, one Simon Rider. Evidently he was of good parentage belonging to the yeoman or small land-owning class; and a man of some education he must have been, as he graces his book of local "memoranda," which he kept from year to year, with the Greek name, *Hypomnema*. From this source of parochial information—and West Bromwich may be congratulated on the possession of so unique and ancient a record—much may be gathered of the Rider or Ryder family, and of other local families besides.

From this interesting old MS. (a small quarto of 146 closely written pages, preserved but uncatalogued in the Salt Library), we learn that the writer Simon Rider was born April 8th, 1558, and baptised a week later. His father was a certain Robert Ryder who is mentioned in a deed of 1527 (19 Henry VIII) whereby one William Hogetts, a baker of Dudley, grants a piece of land to Harrye Carus, a priest and the Vicar of Dudley; this land being therein described as situated between a close belonging to a Chantry in Walsall Church, and the highway leading from Robert Ryder's to the town of Dudley, and both places continuous to the water called Tame. This location, a part of the parish lying towards Dudley and near the Tame brook, we may possibly recognise further on as the seat of the Ryders' residence.

The father of Simon died 24 May, 1579. Some six months previously, Simon Rider had married at Halesowen (25 November), where he apparently settled down to live. Or if not at Halesowen, perhaps he resided at Oldbury; or it may have been that he possessed residences in both those parishes, as he formally records that he came to live in West Bromwich on 4 June, 1580, and then some following entries chronicle the birth of his children in all three parishes. Thus we read:—

(1) "My son Nicholas, born at Oldbury 31st May, baptized at Halesowen 2 June, 1579."

(2) "My daughter, Joanna, born at Oldbury, 15th March, baptized at Halesowen, 18th March, 1580."

(3) "My son, Robert, born at Oldbury, 23rd December baptized at Rowley, 1582."

(4) "My daughter, Margerie, born at West Bromwich, Friday, the 9th July, baptized at West Bromwich, 11th July, 1585."

(5) "My daughter, Anna, born at Oldbury Saturday, 2nd December, 1587, baptized at Rowley, 3rd day of December."

(6) "My daughter, Amy (?), born at West Bromwich, 30th April, baptized at West Bromwich, 2nd May, 1589."

(7) "My son, Simon born at West Bromwich, 4th day of October, baptized 8th October, 1591 "

(8) "My son, Francis, born at Oldbury, 24th January, baptized 25th January, 1593."

(9) "My daughter, Margaret, born at West Bromwich, 31st July, 1595."

(10) "My daughter, Maria, born at West Bromwich, 15th September baptized at West Bromwich 27th December, 1597."

(11) "My son, John, born at West Bromwich, 24th April, baptized 2nd May, 1600."

Along with this register of numerous births, is also one of a death in the memorable year of the Spanish Armada; it runs:

"My mother, died 31st December, 1588, buried at West Bromwich, 1st January." Of more distant members of his family we have a record:

"Robert Rider, son of Robert Rider, son of Nicholas Rider, born at West Bromwich, 30th March, 1636, and baptized 1st day of April."

A Death Register of his family did the careful Simon also keep with equal precision, a self imposed duty which is highly commendable, considering that Church Registers were then not too firmly established for the preservation of family and parochial records:

"My daughter, Margeria, died 17th July, 1622; Buried at Rowley, 18th July.

"My daughter, Anna, died 7th October, 1622; Buried at Madeley, *in ecclia* 8th October." [Burial inside the church denoted the social rank of the deceased, only wealthy families secured intramural interments].

"My son, Nicholas, died 10th August, 1623; Buried at West Bromwich, 12th August. [This was the eldest, but he left a son Robert to become Simons heir].

"My wife died 21st December, 1629. Buried at West Bromwich 22nd December, aged 70, etc."

"My daughter, Amy, died 5th March, 1632; Buried at Cannock [perhaps married and settled there] 7th March."

"My son, Francis, died 12th December, 1633; Buried the same day at Rowley Regis."

It will be observed how brief was the interval between the occurrence of death and burial of the body in those times.

Beyond noting the vital statistics relating to the members of his own family, Simon Ryder preserves for us similar figures respecting other important local families As thus—

"1601.—Mr John Shilton, of Birmingham deceased 8th March.

"1603.—The tenth daie of October Mr Symon Stanley was buried.

"1603.—The second daie of November Sir William Walker Clerke was buried att hondesworth.

"1613.—Richard Sheldon, of Wednesbury, died the ninth day of September.

"1615.—Walter Stanley, Esquire, died the 8th Aprile Anno Domini 1615, and was buried the tenth day of Aprile following.

"1615.—Thomas Russell, co-heir of William Orme, died the 22nd day of November and was buried the 23th day of November, att Rowley Regis.

"1616.—William Orme, of Rowley, deceased 7th March. Buried the 8th March at Rowley.

"1636.—The fourth daie of September—John Furnetbie, prebend and official at Lichfield and parson of Handsworth and Aldrich, was buried at Handsworth."

Entries respecting the deaths of the Whorwoods and his transactions with them, have already been quoted in the Chapter xli.: and in Chapter xvii of THE HISTORY OF TIPTON, the writer also mentions under date December 20th, 12 Hen. VIII, Richard

Jennyn, Clarke, who was Vicar of Wednesbury at that time (1521) and who in 1553 received a pension of £2 14s. 4d. for a suppressed chantry.

But Simon Rider's Diary is something more than a Family Register—these births and deaths are simply grouped together here to throw some light on the writer's family history, as to who he was and the manner of man he was. His careful and methodical records throw many valuable side-lights on the local history of that time.

But it will be more orderly, perhaps, to take next his recorded business transactions with various members of his somewhat extensive family circle.

1589.—"Itm. paid to my Aunt Rider her rent the 27 day of Marche, the which I paid to
William Knowles his boy in presence of John Baker.
Paid to my Aunt Rider her annuity 21 April.
Paid to Agnes Rider her annuity the 20th October—6s. 8d."

1601.—March 14th. "A note of my son Nicholas his marriadge money.—A note how I
bestowed the said marriadge money."—20s. went to Thomas Grove for rent of
"Newe leasow" on 19th April, 1602, and £5 to Walter Stanley. lord of the manor,
the "28th day of Maie."

The same year, 1601, another marriage portion is thus mentioned:—
"20th September. My daughter Joanne, her marriadge goods.
Itm. paid for her gowne cloath, 31s.
Itm. for baies to line yt [baize to line it] 7s. 6d.
Itm. for triming of it, 16s.
Itm. her hat, 8s. 6d.

1615.—"My daughter Amye had a brasse pott weighing twelve pounds 22th of Maie."
[This she received as part of the paternal household stuff due to her].

The next entry illustrates how the head of a family was expected sometimes to make provision for even a generation beyond his own issue:—

1636.—"I accounted with my sonne John Ryder the eleventh day of february, and he
was then in my debt five pounds for which he ys to find my grandchild's apparell
of all sorts three years—daughter of my son Symon,"

*   *   *   *   *   *   *

We may now leave the domestic for the social side of the family's history.

The MS. gravely informs us that Simon Rider was elected Ale Taster at the Court Leet held October 19th, 1583, and that his associate in the office was one Thomas Parsons. Although these quaint manorial officers are still annually elected in Wednesbury and other ancient manors, the duties of this office no longer call for actual performance, as they formerly did when the lord of the manor was responsible for the quality and measure of all Ale sold within his manorial jurisdiction. But the relationship existing between the Rider family and the Stanleys, who were then the lords of West Bromwich manor does not seem to have been of a very cordial nature. One sign of friction has already been noted at the close of chap xxxi. The Rider MS. distinctly declares— although the record seems to be subsequent to the fact by several years—that the honour of erecting the "new chancel or chapelle" did not belong to the Stanleys notwithstanding that it was known as the Stanley Chapel but that Henry Tey, a wheelwright of West Bromwich "did say unto me, Robert Rider," (who evidently set his son Simon the praiseworthy example of keeping records) that the chapel was built at the cost and charges of the whole parish, "John Wilkes and William Emsworth (churchwardens) being the greatest doers in it." "And he said . . . some of the stone was got from Highfield and some from Hamstead, and he said that the master's (? master mason's) name was Harwell, and they that made the roof were called Warnoll and

Hollies." There are given the names of the wardens for the three succeeding years, namely, Robert Bate and Robert Hadley; Humphrey Walker and Henry Farre; Robert Rider and Thomas Partridge. "The next year it was finished . . . And I, the aforesaid Robert Rider asked him the question for this cause: Henry Partridge asked me at the church the same day whether I did remember that my father and his grandfather were churchwardens when the new chancel was in building. . . . Henry Tey spoke these words aforesaid (29 January 1575) in the presence of me the said Robert Ryder, Joanne Ryder my wife, Henry Corns Simon Ryder, William Ombersley and Agnes Hickmans." There is surely evidence here of some suspicion of a secret jealousy treasured against the Stanleys. And apparently it is handed down from father to son for a few years later Simon disputes the right of the Stanleys to make him, as a tenant of the manor, pay a *Heriot*. This "heriot" was sometimes the best live beast or *averium* which the tenant died possessed of: and sometimes the best inanimate thing, as jewel or plate; but always it was a personal chattel, and was no charge upon the lands. In some manors a composition in money, as ten or twenty shillings was paid; and sometimes a double rent was paid on the death of a tenant, and nearly always on the part of those holding by copyhold tenure. Now Robert Rider had died in May, 1579, and here we have his son, Simon, at the next manorial court defying the lord of the manor's claim to a *relief*, or payment on entrance to the enjoyment of his holding, into which this Danish custom had been transmuted by feudalism. Here is Simon's record of the matter (Walter Stanley, lord of the manor, was a minor, represented by his mother, Winifred):—

"In the first day of October, anno 1579, Mistress Wynifrede Standley, the late wife of ffranncis Standley, Esquire, deceased, did keep a *leete* or great courte by her steward, William Booth, of Birmingham, the elder, gent., at which court I, Symon Ryder, was, and the steward demanded of me whether my land was harriotable and ought to pay *harriott* to the lady of the manor. I sayd it ought not, etc. . . . and to confirm my saying I did shewe unto Maister Walter Standley there presently two deeds . . . the other containing only Huckwalls—my *chief rent* for sich field is yearly 4d."

In 1630 this land, "huckwalls," is mentioned again as being rented by his daughter-in-law Mary, who is apparently the wife of his youngest son, John Rider.

Continuing the extract from Rider's MS. we have the gist of the two deeds to which he refers, and which go back to the period when the lands in question were held by villein tenants, as recorded in chapter xx.:—

"It doth appear that one Margery Marnham in her widowhoode did grant unto Walter, the son of Nicholas Erdynton . . . and the other deed doth come of the grante of Richard Marneham, being chiefe lord of West Bromwich, unto William, the son of John Erdinton, containing Huckwalls; and Maister Walter Standley demanded to have a coppy of the same deede, and the steward, at his desire, did copy them out."

By the next year's court, the heriot remaining still unpaid, there appears some threat of levying a distress for it. By common law distresses were incident to every kind of *rent-service*. But Simon Rider, among his other accomplishments, was well versed in law; and he proceeds to argue the legal distinction between *heriot-service* and *heriot-custom*; the first being: due upon special reservation in the grant of the lands, amounting to little more than a mere rent; and the latter depending merely upon immemorial custom. He implies that no heriot can be claimed by usage or custom, and that the only service to be rendered originally was that of *homage*, and even that was not made hereditary by deed, in fact there was no reservation whatever. He writes:—

"Item the 25th day of October, Anno. Dom, 1580.—Mystrys Winifred Standley kept a leete at West Bromwich, when I, Symon Ryder, was to agree with her for my knight's fee, and my land being equally and undifferently .... was esteemed to be the tenth part of a knight's fee, for which I payd unto her per yd. And whereas one of those deeds was granted by Margery Marnham to Walter, son of Nicholas Erdinton, for his homage and service, with distress at her charges as in the same it doth and may appear, wherefore the steward doth say that I ought to do homage unto my chief lady, which I think I ought not to do, by cause it was granted to him only for his homage and service, and doth not say of his heirs. . . ."

Then the writer sets forth the feudal ceremony of doing *homage* to a lord, or "becoming his man" [derived from *homo*], and of the supplementary rite of swearing *fealty*. He does not contend that in this case the lord is "bound to warranty", therefore the inference is that no *homage ancestral* ever existed. For a mutual trust always subsisted between lords and vassals, whereby the lord was bound to protect his tenant vassal in the enjoyment of the lands granted to him. In his own language he says the first service he declined to perform was thus rendered .—

"When a free man shall do *homage* to his lord of whom he holdeth in fee, he shall hold his hands together between the hands of his lord, and shall say thus:—I become your man from this time forwarde for life for membre and for wordly honor, and I shall owe you my faithe for the lands that I holde of you, saving the faithe that I do owe to our Sovraigne Lady Queen and to my other lords.—*17 Edward II.*"

And the supplementary *service* he thus describes:—

"When a free man shall doe *fealtie* to his lord he shall hold his right hand upon a book and shall say thus:—Heare you my lord R. that I, P......... shal be to you both faithful and true, and shall owe my fidelytie unto you for the lande that I holde of you, and lawfully shall doe such customes and services as my duty ys to you, at the termes assigned, so helpe me God.—*17 Edward II.*— Robert Rider, arbitrator, 1571."

LI.—The Rider Family and "Dunkirk."

The Ryder family, who lent their name to Ryders Green, although they do not appear to have lived in this parish for more than a century and a quarter— from the days of Queen Elizabeth (1580), to those of Queen Anne (1703)—seem to have had many associations with West Bromwich, both prior to and after this space of time.

ROBERT RIDER probably flourished in this neighbourhood from the days of Bluff King Hal, but whether resident in West Bromwich or not cannot be determined. Probably his residence was at Rowley although we find him coming to West Bromwich for the transaction of business, as the following document testifies:—

"Item the 29th day of September, ann. 1572.—Payd unto Richard Jennens, of Wednesbury, yeoman, five pounds of currant english money to and for the use of Robert Byrom, late of London, bricklayer, in the presents of Syr Henry Blakemore.—Rychard Barker, John Hawks, Roger Walton, Richard Bennet, Robart Wright, John Watt, alias Comson, Jhon Hopkis, junior, &c."—[*Marginal Note*: "Paid in Bromwich Church Porch. by Robart Rider, my father—*die et anno infra scripto*.]

This side annotation discloses a West Bromwich example of that ancient custom of paying debts in the church porch, where the sacredness of the edifice was supposed to lend a more solemn ratification to the transaction—it was a sort of religious receipt-stamp.

The next document has also very interesting references to ancient practices: these as to very remote forms of *land tenure*. The one reference is to the ancient strips of cultivable land allotted to members of the village community of, perhaps, pre-historic times; and the other is to the quaint legal practice of *livery of seisin*, to which allusion will be made presently.

"Item the 23rd day of October, 1573.—I, Robert Rider, was at the sealing and delivering of a deede from Richard Jennens, of Wednesbury, to Jhon Jesson, of West Bromwhich—the which deed contained three [ancient communal allotment] lands of arable land lying in Monney field—also I was at the sealing and delivering of another deed granted by the aforesaid Jhon Jesson to Richard Jennens—conteayning one [ancient Wednesbury allotment] land of arable land lying in the Church-feild of Wednesbury—and I sawe livereye [delivery] and season [seisin] to these deeds the daye and yeare above mentioned."

Robert Rider was not only a man well-known but he seems also to have been a man of considerable leisure. He is recorded as taking part in several legal formalities connected with the transfer of lands in some of which he is not at all directly interested, beyond witnessing the fact to vouch for its proper legal performance. The custom (already referred to) was that known as *livery of seisin*, or giving feudal possession of lands by the symbolical delivery of a twig or a turf cut therefrom, and presented by the vendor or feoffor to the feoffee.

With his son Simon he was present in 1575 when "lyvery and season" were done by "Jhon Parkshouse, of Hurst Hill," of lands called Winses Ground, to the mortgagor Gregorie Woodwarde; when the latter renewed the mortgage immediately and for the re-conveying ceremony Robert Rider "digged the turfe with his bill, and Gregorye gott a twigge of an oke, the which grew over the water of tame."

In 1576 he records that he "made an entry"— part of the same formality of taking possession of lands—of lands called "Saulley's Moore" and of part of another piece called "bircholt," which was "before Whersted", here he "cut a bough of an oke and digged a turf and stucke the boughe in the turf" "to beare witness" that he "entered" in his "owne right." This formality he repeated on the first-named "moor" land where he "hanged that bough and turfe upon an oke which grewe in the sayd more." This conveyance seems to have been necessary through the default of one "Jhon Bissell," through whom also Hugh Shelley had similarly to establish his claims and to bring his mother to see him perform the ceremony with all its due legalities. The memorandum runs:—

"Item the 18th day of October, anno domini 1677.—Hew Shelley, sonn and heire of Thomas Shelley deceased did make an entry in the meadowe at my father's house in his owne right in the name of all the lands which his father sold (?) to Jhon Bissell: and a gorse at Birmicham: and there came with him his mother and two young men, and she sayd that the last yeare before he made his entrye in the afforesaid manner."

Robert died the 24th of May 1579, and it was perhaps due to his influence or his example that his son Simon followed out the practice of systematically preserving these records of local personages and noteworthy incidents in the social life of the place. Simon records a similar transaction at which he himself was present, but not his father, as early as 1575. This was the *livery of seisin* of a croft of land near Rowley Church, done by William Orme "to obtain feoffys" (or grant the lands) to some 21 trustees represented by two only who were then present.

Simon Rider, who has left us all this wealth of useful and interesting local memoranda, married his wife, Joane, at Halesowen, in 1578. (She died in West Bromwich at the age of 70, where she was buried 22nd December, 1629.) About a year after the death of his father, and of the birth of his eldest son, Nicholas (1579), he took up his residence at West Bromwich, at the Greets Green Mill. As a miller he worked this one of the three contiguous mills then marking the course of the Tame stream in that immediate vicinity.

In the last chapter the personal records of his own family were given in some detail. Here are just a few more entries of a semi private nature:—

(1) "Paid to John Osborne, 28th January, 1599, for three years' clerk's wages (videlicet for 1596, 1597, 1598), 6d. a year—in the whole 1s.6d.

(2) "Vicessimo secundo die Januarii, anno 1600, et anno Elizabetha 43, Paid to John Osborne for clerk's wages for the years 1599, 1600, 12 pence, before John Partridge the younger, then Churchwarden.

(3) "Paid to Simon Ward, 17th April, 1621, for my Easter reckoning and my household, 3s.; for my mill 2s.: for amercements 16 pence: for my chief rent 8 pence: in toto 5s."

NICHOLAS RIDER, the eldest son of Simon, was born 1579, married 1601, and died in 1623. Apparently he pre-deceased his father. His son bore the name of ROBERT RIDER, and became Simon's heir. He married in 1632, and had a son whose name was also Robert, born, as recorded in the previous chapter, in 1636. But the heir, if not the oldest surviving son, was named Nicholas as we shall find when we come to deal with his successor. But in the meantime we have an important and highly interesting document in the *Marriage Settlement, dated 30th March, 1632,* of this Robert Rider, yeoman, grandson and heir of Symon Rider, with Joan Sydenhall, conveying to Trustees, namely Charles Waringe, gentleman, Thomas Waringe his son, both of Solyhull (the Wearing family. Originally of Warwickshire, are long since settled in West Bromwich), and Francis Rider, of West Bromwich, yeoman; the said lands being thus described:—

"All that part of their messuage, dwelling house, or tenement, now or late called or known by the name of the Parler, with the eight chambers over the same, the closet or study thereto adjoining, and the large buttery near unto the same, with all appurtenances, and the back side thereto adjoining, and the garden called the (?) garden, and two bays of the west end of the barne and the cowe house, or close to the west bay of the sd. barn adjoining, with all appurtenances unto the sd. Simon Rider and Robert Rider, and the heirs and assigns of the sd. Robert, the usual gates and ways to and from the orchard and garden, &c. . . . with free ingress, egress, and regress to and from the same. And also all that close pasture, or parcel of ground called Newlands, and all that close. . . . called Blakehay, and all that close called *Huckwalls,* and all that meadow called *Huckwalls' Meadow,* situated between the land of John Woodward, the land of Edward Duddeley, the land of John Lowe, the land of John Foxall, the land of Richard Stone, and the lane leading from the King's Majesty's highway, called the *Portway,* towards the nether end of Greet's Green."

The explicit naming and locating of a lane from Portway towards Greet's Green lends confirmation to the suggestion advanced, in the opening paragraph of chapter xxxvii., that the Wednesbury Portway Road once continued the line of its ancient trackway towards the salt mines of Worcestershire.

NICHOLAS RIDER, who succeeded to the family honours, made a marriage with a lady named Palin, which was destined to have an important bearing on the family fortunes in the near future. The marriage settlement made on this occasion, under date 9th September, 1663, can also be quoted.

"Indenture made between Nicholas Rider, of Greet, in West Bromwich, son and heir of Robert Rider, of Greet, deceased, of the one part and Charles Waring, of Berry Hall, in the Parish of Solyhull, Esq., Thomas Palin, of Deamesdale, Co. Staff., gent., and Ann Palin, one of the daughters of Richard Palin, late of Deamesdale, deceased, of the other part. It is witnessed that in consideration of a marriage then intended to be had and solemnized between the said Nicholas Rider and the said Ann Palin . . . the said Nicholas Rider did grant, etc., to Charles Waring and Thomas Palin and their heirs . . . all that messuage or tenement, situated and being in Greet, wherein the sd. N. Rider and Joane Rider, mother of the said N. Rider, did lately inhabit and dwell, and also all the barns, gardens, outhouses, hemplecks, fold, yards, etc., and also all that water corn mill, commonly called Rider's Mill, and all the ponds, pools, fleams, streams, etc. . . . Also all the crofts, pastures, etc., called the Great Barn Field, the Little Barn Field, the Long Croft the Peas Croft, the Great Stockwell Field, the Birch Hall, the Gorsty Bank, the Broad Meadow, the Oat Leasow, the Cony Leasow alias Conbury Field, the Moor and the Mill Meadow, and all that close called the Little Stockwell Field, also all those closes called the Newlands, and those closes called the Blackheys, and that close called Luckwall's Leasow; also the Huckwall's Meadow, alias the Long Meadow.

Covenant by said Nicholas Rider that he was lawfully seized and had good right to convey, free from incumbrances, except the estate for life of the said Joan Rider in some part of the said messuage, and in certain meadows."

From this it would appear—(1) that Nicholas had "lately" been living with his widowed mother in the family residence near the water-mill, (2) but that they no longer lived there; and (3) that the widow Joan retained a life interest in the property. Now it is not unlikely that this was the period when the family residence may have been thought too humble in its pretensions for the bringing home of a bride won from the Palin family, who indeed appear to have been people of some substance in the county. It is therefore suggested that this was the time when the old family half-timbered homestead was enlarged and almost rebuilt as a more ambitions residence aspiring almost to the dignity of a mansion house; and which is now known as "Dunkirk." It was merely a "let-off" *part* of that tenement which in these *abstracts* is designated "The Parlour", and the payment of the then considerable sum of £5 to the London bricklayer, just recorded as having been made in 1572, may have been for the first enlargement from a humble cottage to a yeoman's more commodious homestead.

DUNKIRK, even at the present time, is divided into two tenements; the occupants of which are fittingly engaged in the old time callings of dairying, and of smithing and inn-keeping respectively; and indeed where they still cultivate the time honoured custom of extending a homely hospitality to the unexpected guest.

The first view of Dunkirk strikes the beholder with the dignity of its simplicity. The plan is oblong terminated at each end by a well pitched gable, while the front also consists of three three-storied gables, the centre one projecting well in front of the two flanking gables. The windows are nearly all of three lights with bold stone mullions, and a hood mould proclaiming the period of architecture as one intermediate between the Tudor and the Annean. The middle portion formerly contained the hall and staircase, while the two wings were occupied as living rooms.

A closer inspection reveals the fact that behind this building are the remnants of a sixteenth century half timbered house, connected with the main building by a lean-to roof. This is built on a plinth of peldonstone quarried from the adjacent collieries. Its characteristically low ceilings, compared with the loftier rooms of the front part of the house, seem to disclose the fact that about 1660 an accession of wealth or at any rate a desire for more domestic conveniences dictated to its owner the desirability of rebuilding on a more ambitious scale. And yet the newer work is most severe in its plainness, with the almost absolute absence of decoration. The only difference observable in the external work is, that while brick work has succeeded timber framing (in its natural order) the old English bonding of the bricks in the earlier portion is also succeeded by the Flemish bond in the newer part; itself also marking, or rather confirming the hypothetical date of the latter. Perhaps the poverty of ornamentation which prevails everywhere enhances the artistic value of the flowing, curves of the saddleback coping bricks, which top the remnants of the ancient garden walls. Inside everything is equally plain and substantial; and at one time it may have been the difference in the levels of the two floors—between the old and the newer buildings—which provided hiding places in a mezzanine of which local legends speak, but of which no traces now remain.

But why was the "hall" named "Dunkirk"? Dunkirk would appear to have borrowed its name from the French seaport which is so called. The almost self-evident meaning of the name is "the church on the downs:" but whether by stretching the legendary use of this house as a Catholic church, a local applicability of the designation can be claimed for it, is not so very certain. Or that the original Dunkirk was a nest of freebooters, whose hands were turned against everybody, and especially against English and Dutch Protestants, can have lent any deep meaning or covert suggestiveness to the borrowed use of this name for a Romanist rallying place, is equally a matter for inconclusive surmise. Any way it was a well-known fact throughout the nation, at the time when Dunkirk Hall was in its zenith of prosperity, that the port of Dunkirk had been captured from the Spanish by Cromwell in 1658, that Charles II. sold it back to the French for £400,000, and that by 1713 the English had insisted in the demolition of its fortifications. These political facts may have had some local bearing and significance, as suggested for the naming of "Charlemont" in this parish. Dunkirk the sea-port occupied a large share of public attention at that time (1700) as one political pamphleteer gives his tract the startling title "Dover or Dunkirk?"

On the death of Nicholas Rider, in 1703, his will (dated 21 September, 1702), appointed as executors Thomas Whitgreave, Gilbert Merry, Thomas Palin and John Pidgeon, who were directed to sell him real estate for the payment of his just debts, the surplus then to be divided among his surviving children Simon, Elizabeth, John, and Catherine Rider Thomas, the eldest, having died in 1702. Against these executors and also against Isabella, widow of the testator, and against others concerned, the creditors of the deceased Nicholas filed a bill in Chancery, Easter, 1708, praying that the trustees and executors might come to a settlement by selling the real estate, and paying the plaintiffs what was due to them. Isabella then filed a cross petition against both creditors and executors to establish her jointure or dower. Both causes were heard together before the Master of the Rolls; but this Chancery suit, like many others, lingered in the law courts for a wearisome century, and it was not till 1812 that the Rider estates were put up for auction at the Swan Inn in a tardy attempt at settlement. But, again, Fate was adverse. The buyer, one Alexander Stansbie, paid only one-third of the purchase money, the remainder being paid in equal amounts by Edward Blount of Bellamour, and Thomas H. F. Whitgreave. When in 1816 Stansbie became bankrupt his share of the Dunkirk estate was ultimately acquired by Thomas Price, of Bescot, and Henry Price, of Charlemont, ironmasters of Tipton, allusion to which family was made in chap. xlix. When Henry Price died his share became vested in his brother Thomas.

The intervention of the Whitgreave family into this winding-up of the Rider affairs was due to the fact that they represented the interests of the Palin family, whose intermarrying with the Riders in 1663 has just been noted in the marriage settlement of that date. The Thomas Whitgreave of 1702 lived at Moseley, none of the family ever lived at Dunkirk (and therefore could never have been murdered there), and the modern representative of the Whitgreaves resides at Burton Manor, near Stafford. The account of Dunkirk given by Reeves is very confusing, as there is no doubt some substratum of truth underlying its various details, although the dates are obscure and the personal names more than doubtful in their accuracy. The name "Isaac Hadley" he gives on p. 149 as that of an Overseer of tho Poor in 1799; and in his Directory for 1837 printed at end of the book the same name occurs as that of a "black miller, Spon Lane." But here is Reeves' marvellous chronicle verbatim:—

"Dunkirk is situated on the west side of the parish, joining to Tipton: it was originally the abode of Roman Catholics before and after the Reformation. The Romans [Catholics] had a Chapel here and the place being retired they continued to hold their religious meeting for several generations. I am informed the Chapel was a large upper room in the back part of the hall; there is also a secret hole from the upper floor to the lower part of the house. Tradition informs us that the last Roman Catholic proprietor was murdered in the garden, at the old house at Rider's Green, formerly occupied by Mr Isaac Hadley, and that the Catholics were driven out by the Protestants. After the Romans [Catholics] left the place the estate fell into the hands of government about the year 1803, when the waste lands were enclosed, a person whose name was Dodd, said he was agent for government, and thought to claim the allotment; he actually made money of it, and defrauded government of the rents of the estate. The family of Gutteridge lived upon the estate for upwards of 100 years. The Rider's family are said to be right heirs to Dunkirk estate, and they originally enjoyed the same. The front part of the house was rebuilt about 150 years ago."

An Edward Rider is found enrolled amongst the inhabitants of West Bromwich as late as 1735 in the Churchwardens' Books. But the direct line of Riders failed by 1800, and the Whitgreaves were no doubt induced to come forward and vindicate their rights on account of the estate, though small, proving a valuable mining property. Mortgages and incumbrances had gradually overwhelmed its productiveness for the last dozen years of the life of Nicholas Rider after whom (1703) none of the name ever occupied Dunkirk. Did the rebuilding, and the consequent attempt to live in a grander style than the estate could possibly warrant, have anything to do with the collapse of the family fortunes? In 1691 Nicholas and his son and heir Thomas Rider, mortgaged Huckwall Closes, previously known as Newlands, and the Black Hayes, to Joseph Moore, in 1693 the Great Barn Field, the Little Barn Field, the Peas Croft, and the Long Croft, were similarly pawned; in 1694, the Answorth Leasow or Windmill Field, with the windmill thereon, were also mortgaged to the same Joseph Moore, to whom they further gave a bond for a penal sum of £60 in the following year. Indebtedness by bonds to Thomas Bracegirdle, William Stanlay, Ann Cherrington, and others on the part of Nicholas, was discovered on his death in 1703. So that the estate had been heavily involved for some time before his decease. Still some remnant of the Rider estate was apparently worth the effort of an attempt at recovery by the Whitgreaves.

Mr Thomas H. F. Whitgreave died in 1816 leaving George T. Whitgreave, his eldest son heir-at-law. Between him, Edward Blount and the Price family, a Deed of Partition was executed in 1829. The trustees of the Price family, of whom John Walker Turton was one, eventually sold their third part of the estate, including the old mill and water course, to the Birmingham Canal Company, who are the present owners. Dunkirk which was about a quarter of a mile from the mill, is now the property of Alderman Reuben Farley, J.P.

The name of Gutteridge's Pool and Mill has been retained almost to the present time, and up to a quarter of a century ago, with its ancient water-wheel, it was a place sufficiently attractive as a pleasure resort for boating. Near by was the ancient Sheepwash of Sandwell Monastery. The Mines Drainage has now taken the water away.

LII.—The Hateley Family of Hateley Heath: The Rise and Decline of English Yeomen.

Whether HATELEY HEATH gave its name to, or derived its name from, some personal appellation, is uncertain. The place was originally called *Longmor*. A variant of the name is *Hak-le-heath*, and the cognomen of the associated family is sometimes spelt *Haickley*: this suggests that the place-name was derived from a personal name, perhaps that of a Norse chief Haco (the possessive form of which is Hac or Hack) and from which the family name of Hackwood is also derived.

In this chapter it is proposed to treat of the English yeomen in general, with West Bromwich examples of the class, and a special reference to the Hateley family.

As early as 1428 a Roger Hateley de Lyndon (with Margerie, his wife) rented lands in Finchpath from one Christina Wylkys, widow, and to the deed of agreement a Nicholas Hayteley was one of the witnesses. Roger Hayteley was himself a witness to another deed in 1446, whereby Henry Gesson acquired lands (held of the chief lord in fee) in the same locality of "Vinspath," one piece being called *Longmore*, and near the lands of one William Stony, who perhaps lent his name to Stony Lane. By the time of the Reformation this family of Hayteley had made itself a firm social standing, inasmuch as in 1552 John Hayteley was Churchwarden, as recorded in chap. xxx. Now a yeoman was one of a large class of small agricultural freeholders who down to the end of the 17th century formed a most substantial and important part of the population, and who, in spite of their often defective means of farm cultivation, throve and formed—it is not too much to say—the very backbone of the country. In speaking of the rise of the yeoman class in the period between 1401 and 1582, Professor Rogers says: "It cannot be doubted that the yeoman and the husbandman at a fixed rent were the persons who suffered least from a rise in prices. Labour to them was relatively cheaper, and what they had to sell was relatively dearer." As a consequence of this the yeomanry of England were an increasing and flourishing set of men, for they bought land, and it is beyond doubt that they were comparatively rich. In 1584, for instance, we have Thomas Hayteley granting a lease of lands in Finchpath, to some one under him.

But besides the Hateley family, there may be discovered in West Bromwich numerous other families owning lands, and otherwise largely interested in landed estates during Elizabeth's reign, the close of the period indicated by Mr Thorold Rogers. To enumerate a few recorded in *Salt Coll.* Vol xiv.:—

(1) ORME FAMILY. A Rowley family, mentioned among many other farmers and landowners in Chap. xxxix., who sold land to the Turtons in 1615, and had transactions with the Riders in 1615 and in 1579, all of which has been already recorded: according to this *Salt Vol.* p.170 they became interested in "50 acres of land, 15 acres of meadows, 40 acres of pasture and 12 acres of wood in Westbromwyche," which were to revert to William Orme, son of Joyce, after the joint and separate lives of Thomas Meyre and his wife, the said Joyce (1574). William Orme three years later (1577) acquired all the "tithes of . . . and grain in the parish of Wednesbury, otherwise Weddesburye" (p 195). Two years later William and his wife Alice parted with "5 acres of moor in Westbromwyche" (p. 207), but the year before had acquired many acres in Rowley Somery (not Rowley Regis, or part of Rowley Crown lands, but a part of that parish once attached to Somery's barony of Dudley).

(2) TONKS FAMILY. In 1531 part of the Turton estate had been "Tonkys land." In 1574 Nicholas Tunckes acquired from William Cumberford over 100 acres of useful

lands in wood and pasture, besides 200 acres of furze and heath, in Westbromwiche and Wednesbury (p. 168). About the same time Henry Tunckes acquired a small holding in "Westbromwyche and Greete" (p. 171).

(3) BIRCH FAMILY. George Byrche obtained (1574) an annual rental of £38 10s. issuing from Westbromwyche lands (p. 167), and two years later Thomas Byrche bought a small estate for £40 (p. 187).

(4) BISSELL FAMILY. This name has already occurred in dealing with the Riders' possessions. In 1577 this family parted with a considerable estate to Richard Smalbroke (p. 195).

(5) PARTRIDGE FAMILY. This family name has occurred many times in previous chapters. In 1577 John Parteryche, his wife Eleanor, John his son, and his wife Katherine, parted with eight acres to Robert Whorwood *armiger* (p. 190). Two years later they sold to one William Mucklowe a larger and more valuable holding (p. 202).

Passing on from the Reformation period, we come to another epoch-marking period in the evolution of English yeomen. In the time of Cromwell they were used to excellent advantage in connection with the Civil War; they were always ready to fight if occasion demanded it, and they fought with an almost irresistible determination. Our West Bromwich example is found in Captain Turton (mentioned in chaps. xxxviii, xli. and xlvi.), who no doubt upheld the character of this class of England's famous sons.

Another writer (Whitelock) says of the yeomen: "The able and substantial freeholders" were "well armed within with the satisfaction of their own good consciences, and without by iron arms, they stood firmly in battle, and charged desperately." It was this class of men who in the Civil War cared for neither kind nor lord, and yet who within a hundred years of that time were absolutely of no power in the country.

Intermarriage within their own class no doubt built up the fortunes of many of these yeomen families, till they gradually assumed very respectable dimensions. We have seen how the West Bromwich family of Turton, after the turmoil of the Civil Wars had passed away, produced a Baron of the Exchequer in one of its branches, and a Baronet in another. As an example of this knitting together of small landed possessions we may quote the settlement made by John Haitley on his daughter in 1620. According to the Parish Registers "Walter Vale and Elnor Haickley" were married November 23rd of that year, and the *Settlement* is dated November 6th, and runs:—

"To all Christian people. John Haitley, of West Bromwich, sendeth greeting in our Lorde God everlasting. Know ye as well for and in consideration of a marreage shortly, by God's permission to be had and solemenized between Walter Vale, son of Symon Vale, of West Bromwich, husbandman, and Elianor, my daughter, do for other good causes and considerations, me the said John Haitley, moving, I the said J.H. have given, granted, enfeofed, and confirmed . . . unto Symon Warde, of West Bromwich, yeoman and Nicholes Rider, of the same parishe . . . yeoman . . . all that messuage, cottage, dwelling house, or tenement . . . wherein I the said John Haitley doe now dwelle, in finchepath, neare unto Wodnesbure Bridge, and also all that cottage . . . adjoining to the aforesaid dwelling house, wherein one Elizabeth Parkes widow, nowe dwelleth and also all and every the houses, barnes, stables buildings, out-houses, foulde, gardanies, orchards . . . and parcels of ground . . . situate . . . between the land nowe or late of Willm. Stanley, esquire, the land of Ralphe Tomkys, deceased . . . to the use and behoof of me the said John Haitley, for and during the terme of my naturale lief . . . and after the decease of me . . . then to the use and behoof of the said Walter Vale and Elianor my daughter . . . Indented in the presence of . . . Walter Stevens, Francis Brookes, Symon Rider, Nicholas Rider, and others."

Reference to chap. xxxvi will recall a similar marriage between Francis Symcox and Alice, daughter of John Hateley deceased (1626). These Simcoxes are another old landed family in West Bromwich; As early as 1403 three members of it witnessed a conveyance of lands, of William Hayteley de West Bromwych (Willett pp. 186, 208, and 211).

About the period of the Civil Wars there were in England some 160,000 to 180,000 of these small freeholders, which was an exceedingly large number, but a hundred years later they were being recognised as a class of the past. Chamberlagne in his "State of Great Britain"—a work published at the end of the 17th century—said of the freeholders of England, "they are more in extent and richer than in any other country in Europe." He added that a rent of "£40 or £50 a year is very ordinary," and that "£100 or £200 in some counties is not rare."

In this vicinity, now commonly designated the Black Country, some of the yeomen endowed with a business capacity above the average of their fellows, developed into our earliest ironmasters. Examples of these in West Bromwich have already been named—for instance, the Turtons, Lowes, Simcoxes, and Jessons have all produced "iron-mongers" or else "nailers," not to mention the families of Jennings, Foley, and Parkes beyond the confines of this parish. In other localities less favourably situated these freeholders unfortunately became the ready prey of the landlord influence in the Houses of Parliament, which influence was most undoubtedly exerted to their great detriment. The average yeoman was fond of his farm life: he was free and contented, and that perhaps, was enough. Even in the height of his prosperity he was somewhat ignorant of the science or art of his calling; but as he managed, we are told, to grow some twenty five bushels of wheat to the acre it may reasonably be supposed he was prosperous. It was about 1760 when the process of extinction of the yeomen class became rapid. How few yeomen are there in West Bromwich to-day?

Another writer (Arthur Young), in 1786, "regretted the loss of that set of men whom we call yeomen . . . who really made up the independence of the nation." He added that he was "loth to see their lands in the hands of the monopolising lords."

In looking over and examining a number of published particulars of various parishes for 1780 we find the following facts concerning an agricultural parish in Staffordshire. The total number of houses is given as 332, being made up thus: Gentlemen's or farm houses with land from 400 acres in extent down to 100 acres, 30; houses with land from 100 to 50 acres, 8, ditto from 50 to 20 acres, 9 ditto from 20 acres downwards, 41; houses with only gardens, 204; cottages, 40; total, 332. Many small lots of land which had no houses thereon were farmed by people living near to them, and about one sixth of the land of the parish was occupied by the owners of it. Included in these figures were five "gentlemen's seats," ten public (or ale) houses, and two turnpike gate houses, and there were also in the parish seven mills, five of which were driven by water-power and two by wind.

The survival of the Hateley family in West Bromwich, therefore, from 1403 to the present century, is almost exceptional in the history of the yeoman type. Joseph Hateley was a churchwarden in 1807, and that his family retained its social position is evident from the fact that in 1818 he subscribed £100 to the New Church Fund (of which he acted as Secretary), while James Hateley, junior gave £5. When the new Christ Church was opened in 1829. Mr Joseph Hateley became the first Minister's warden (a) there. Two years later Mr Hateley served on another important Parish Committee to deal with

---

a At first designated "Chapel wardens," as there was some hesitancy to use the word "Churchwarden" for an officer of a mere *ecclesiastical district*, which was not a legal *civil parish*. The administrative duties of churchwardens of *parishes* were then very considerable.

the question of the Magistracy in West Bromwich. With the disappearance of the Hateley's the last link between modern manufacturing Bromwich and the Bromwich of the old agricultural era may be considered finally and irrevocably severed.

LIII.—Two 17th Century Wonders—A Giant and an Earthquake.

In olden times the people were extremely fond of the marvellous, and all that was in anyway out of the common was always sure of an eager and credulous reception. Therefore it is not surprising to learn that in the seventeenth century, a village as insignificant as West Bromwich then was, actually produced two wonders—a giant, and an earthquake. The records preserved of these are more interesting than the phenomena themselves, for while much exaggeration has no doubt gathered round the story of the giant, the description of the earthquake makes it out to be but a very mild occurrence indeed. We will take these two notable "wonders" in turn.

The Giant was one Walter Parsons, a blacksmith, whose birth-place has been located near West Bromwich old church. The family of Parsons was represented by William Parsons and Agnes his wife living in the reign of Mary. In the succeeding reign of Elizabeth there was a Thomas Parsons who was elected ale taster along with Simon Rider in 1583.

Dr. Plot, in his Natural History of Staffordshire, published in 1686, gives the following:—

Not at all inferior to any of these in matters of strength was one Walter Parsons of West Bromwich, in this County, though he was not so much admired as theirs, who were men but of a middling ordinary size, whereas Parsons had a stature proportional to his strength; being so very tall when he was a young apprentice, that they were forced to digg a hole in the ground for him to stand up to his knees, when he struck at the anvil (for he was first a black smith) or sawed wood with another, that he might be at a level with his fellow workman. At length he became Porter to King James the First, where he behaved himself so generously, that though he had valour equal to strength yet he scorned to take advantage to injure any person by it; upon which account we have but few experiments left us of his great strength, but such as were sportive: as that being affronted by a man of ordinary stature as he walks London streets, he only took him up by the waistband of his breeches, and hung him upon one of the hooks in the shambles, to be ridiculed by the people, and so went his way, and that sometimes by way of merryment, he would take two of the tallest Yeomen of the Guard (like the Gizard and Liver) under his arms, and carry them as he pleased (in spight of all resistance) about the Guard Chamber; where (if I am not misinformed) that is his picture which hangs at the end next to the stairs, leading down into the court toward White Hall Gates. There is another picture of him, as I have been told also by some, in the great room at Popes Head Tavern in Popes Head Alley, but whether they are the true pictures of him or noe, it being uncertain that they were drawn in the just proportion, I took not the pains to have them measured, choosing rather to collect what his height might be, from a true measure of his hand yet remaining upon a piece of wainscot at Bentley Hall, by which it appears that from the *carpus* to the end of the middle finger, it was eleven inches long, and the palm six inches broad which (abatements being made interchangeably) is much about the size of the hand of Edmund Malloon, a youth of 19 years old, born at Port-Leicester in Ireland, for his extraordinary stature shown publickly here in

Oxford 1684, which though from the *carpus* to the end of the middle finger it were twelve inches long, yet the palm was no more than five inches broad, *i.e.*, it fell as much short of Parson's hand in the breath, as it exceeded it in length. Now the proportion of the stature of Edmund Malloon to this hand, being as $7\frac{1}{2}$ to 1, that is being 7 foot 6 inches high, thence we may rationally conclude that Parsons must also be thereabout, both much about the height of John Tates, born at Schoonhaven in Holland, the length of whose cubit (as Mr Ray tells us) was 25 inches and $\frac{1}{2}$ the length of his hand to the wrist 11 inches, and his middle finger 7 inches. All short of the stature of Martin Wierwski, a Polander, who, at the age of 42 years being presented to the Emperor Maximilion the Second as a rarity of nature, was found full eight foot high. And so was one of the Someries, Baron (and founder of the Priory) of Dudley, if we may believe either his stature, or hollow of the stone chest in which his body lay, both which as Mr Erdeswick testifies measured 8 foot, than which had the body been anything shorter, it could not with conveniency have been laid there, considering how they anciently cut their stone coffins."

This is Plot's account, written within half-a-century of the event. This Bromwich prodigy, whose stature had afforded so much gratification to that "wisest fool in Christendom," James I., died in the succeeding reign of Charles I., and was succeeded in the office of Royal Porter by William Evans, a Monmouthshire giant, 7 feet 6 inches high, or two inches taller than Parsons. An account of both these giants is said to have been contained in an old book published in 1678. An epitaph for Parsons has been concocted, thus

"Beneath this mossy surface lies
A Philistine of wondrous size;
At Bromwich born, he won renown
For *greatness* up in London town.
A *porter* at King James's call,
He was a man both *stout* and tall;
Parsons by name, he ere was seen
A head and shoulders o'er the dean,
And e'en the bishop with his see
Was not so *great* a man as he."

*   *   *   *   *   *   *

The Earthquake is chronicled in a Tract, here reprinted in full. A copy from the Library of James Comerford, Esq., was sold in London some years ago. The specimen in the British Museum is a very tattered copy, but a transcription was made in 1851 by the late C. H. Bayley, Esq., and reprinted by him in West Bromwich. He says he found it bound up with seventeen other Earthquake Tracts, in a quarto volume numbered $\frac{444 \text{ b } 21}{8}$. Although Dr. Plot makes no allusion to this natural phenomenon, notwithstanding that he was collecting the materials for his History shortly after the event yet a record of the Earthquake will be found in Alrewas Church registers, under date 1675, January 4. It is also on record in Northamptonshire, but if it did no more harm than shake down the pewter plates from the kitchen dresser, then indeed no harm was done. The Tract is entitled

A True
Relation of the Terrible
E A R T H Q U A K E
AT
West Brummidge
In Staffordshire, and the places adjacent,
&c., &c.

With Permission. ROGER L'ESTRANGE.

London: Printed for D.M. in the year 1676.

Then the pamphlet runs:—

"We cannot certainly forget the very blustering tempestuous weather which happened here at London on the third and fourth days of this Instant January the winds blowing with that impetuous fierceness and violence, as if all *Æolus* his two and thirty sons had been in an uproar; and though the damages thereby susteyned at Sea in several parts were very great, yet we shall pass them by with silent pity, and onley mention a very rare and wonderful Accident which happened at the same time at land, which was thus.

At a place called West Brummidge in Staffordshire within four miles of Brummingham (that famous town for ironware, scituate on the edge of Warwickshire), on the said Tuesday, the fourth of January instant, in the afternoon, the wind thereabouts for several days before having been very calm, and more still than is usual for the season. On a sudden a strange rushing noise was heard in the Air, and so continued for some time, to the great admiration of many people that heard it, which was the more increased for that they could not perceive any very sensible blast or strong gust of wind, which might be the occasion of such an uncouth murmur, but this their wonder was by and by forced up to the highest pitch of amazement and terror, when they began to perceive the Ground to quake and tremble under their feet.

Which it did so evidently, that pewter dishes fell from off the Shelves on which they were placed, in several houses; nay, as it is attested by divers credible Eye witnesses, it made the very Stones in the Streets and lanes to beat and knock against one another.

The Inhabitants, in fear run out of their houses dreading they would be shaken down upon their heads, but blessed be God no harm was done that we hear of.

The Earthquake was not onley in this single Town but in all other villages near, for several miles in Staffordshire, and divers parts of Warwickshire.

This account was sent up to a person of good repute, by Trade an Iromnonger, in Whitechappel, from one of his correspondents, desiring to know if any such thing was observed at London, they in the country apprehending it might be general.

The continuance of the Earthquake was above half an hour, which was followed by mighty violent and tempestuous Winds for two or three days together.

The true copy of a Letter sent to an Eminent Artist in London:—

Sir,—There was here last night viz Jan the 4th about six in the evening a noise as of motion, taken to be an Earthquake, which frighted us as if the Houses would have come on our heads; but 'twas soon over, and was perceived in most parts of this Town, and as I hear, in divers other places. Several Credible persons affirm they saw or felt the Ground rise or move, and the Windows shake strangely; but I do not yet hear of any harm susteyned. If this intelligence may pleasure those profound Speculatures into the mysteries, of nature, which I understand compose a great part of your happy Studies. I am sir, so far

      Yours.

              T. B.

Kidderminster
    Jan 5th 1675-6.

For the assisting weaker understandings, the better to apprehend the cause and reason of these Tremblings of the Earth, they must know, that naturalists define an Earthquake to proceed from Winde or dry Vapours shut up within the Earth; and heated there by the penetrating Influence of the sun, which puts them forward to finde or make their passage out of caverns: and with the violence of their Irruption, the Earth to a vast distance, is moved and shaken. They happen more usually in Spring or Autumn, than Summer or Winter, and especially after great Droughts succeeded by hasty Rains. For the earth being before chapt and cleft, the Wind and Vapours in vast quantities insinuate and get into the same, which by a sudden glut of Wet being stopt and shut up, they are forced to break their way forth in manner aforesaid. The Signs of an approaching Earthquake are either Astronomical or Physical. Of the first sort are bad Aspects of the Planets *Jupiter* and *Mars* in any of the Earthly signs, as *Taurus*, *Virgo*, or *Capricorn*. Of the second, Extreme cold, unusual stillness of the air, clouds drawn out to a great length, Water in Wells troubled and stinking. etc.

Pliny 2 Book chap. 84, and Gellius Lib. 2 Noctium relate: The ancients were so struck with fear when an Earthquake happened, that they always set aside a Thanksgiving Day for their Preservation, but kept silent the name of the God to whom they dedicated such festival, because they were not certain to which of their feigned Dieties they were to attribute that stupendious power of shaking the Earth, and 'tis conceived by many of the Learned, that upon that most prodigious and universal Earthquake which happened at the Crucifixion of our blessed Lord and Saviour the affrighted Athenians might (by reason of such their custom) erect that Altar *Ignote Deo* (to the unknown God), observed afterwards by St. Paul, and mentioned Acts 15. Which terrible Pangs of Nature, when the God of Nature suffer'd, 'tis very probable Pliny means, when he saith: L. 2, chap. 84, in these words: The Greatest Earthquake that has been known in the world since the memory of Man, was in the Reign of Tyberius Cæsar, whereby in one Night Twelve famous Cities of Asia were thrown down and destroyed.

We shall conclude with one story out of Ecclesiastical History: It is from Nicephorus Lib. 13, cap. 3, who relates, That in the daies of Justinus Cæsar, there was such an Earthquake at Antioch, that it demolisht a great part of the city, and that about thirty months after, there hapned another greater than that, under Euphemius, then Bishop there; and that at that time it was revealed by Divine Oracle or Inspiration, to a devout and religious man inhabiting there that they should write the name of God over their Doors in this manner.

Christus nobiscum. State

That is in English
Christ is with us. Stand ye:

And that this being done the Earthquake ceased, without doing any damage.

The same Author tells of another earthquake at Constantinople, when Theodosius Junior was Emperour, which continued six moneths together, and at last was driven away by the Peoples singing through the streets this Anthem taught them miraculously by Angels:

> Sanctus Deus Sanctus Fortis,
> Sanctus Immortalis, miserere nobes.
> FINIS."

Thus ends this quaint old pamphlet, the orthography of which is like its Latinity, not altogether unimpeachable.

LIV.—The Independents; West Bromwich "Old Meeting."

Resuming the history of religious life and movement in West Bromwich, we naturally take up the narrative again with the story of the Independents. West Bromwich possesses no less than four chapels belonging to this denomination, namely, Ebenezer Church in Old Meeting Street, Swan Village; Mayer's Green Chapel; High Street Chapel; and the Salem Chapel in Sheepwash Lane, which last named was dealt with in *The History of Tipton* p. 28. Not only are the Independents numerically strong in West Bromwich, but their chief glory lies in the fact of possessing in "The Old Meeting" Chapel, a place of historic interest, dating as it does from the Act of Uniformity, 1662, almost the earliest date possible for the founding of such an institution. No better, or more succinct account of this place of worship can be produced, with all its gradual developments through a long series of interesting associations, than that written by one of its ministers, the Rev W. Kelly, in 1893; in the March of which year a Bazaar was held to raise funds for re building the Schools.

In a pamphlet this writer traces the inception of Independency right from the very Reformation period, claiming John Hooper, Bishop of Gloucester, as the first Nonconformist. Then proceeding reign by reign he comes to the revolt of the Puritans against diocesan episcopacy and episcopal ordination. In the reign of James I. he says the Puritans were tolerated, while the Independents and Baptists were imprisoned or banished, Then Oliver Cromwell comes on the scene as the leader of the Independents, But after the disappearance of that religious champion, the restoration of Charles II. in 1660 made the last state of this people worse than the first. Referring back to chaps. xxxii. and xxxiii. the consequences of the Act of Uniformity in this immediate locality will be found there fully recorded.

The names of Richard Hilton, of West Bromwich, and Thomas Badland ejected from Willenhall, are inseparably connected with West Bromwich Old Meeting. Mr Hilton, always a hard student, husbanded his time with jealous care. His mind was richly stored with knowledge, he spent much time in prayer, and on Sunday his spiritual zeal set fire to the discourses he had prepared. He was very judicious in everything he did; his simplicity of manner and blameless life endeared him to his hearers, his discourses were weighty and profitable, and even the worst of men were constrained to respect him. When he was silenced and ejected from the Parish Church many of his attached hearers came out with him, and these formed the first nucleus of a Nonconformist community in West Bromwich so that The Old Meeting is a direct offshoot from the Old Church.

Rev. Thomas Badland (1663) became the first minister of the "Old Meeting." Mr Badland (aged 28) had been ejected from the Incumbency of Willenhall, Staffordshire, in 1662. Worcester was his native place and he made his way there. Passing through West Bromwich he met with the Rev Richard Hilton, just ejected from the Parish living here at that same time, and Mr Badland acted as minister to the faithful few who were valiant enough to resist the demands of the State and to come out of the parish church with their pastor Mr Hilton. Mr Badland reached Worcester sometime in 1663, and Rev. Mr Hand, who was ejected from Oldbury, probably accompanied him and it is recorded that Mr Hand acted as Mr Badland's assistant when the latter formed the first Nonconformist Church in Worcester in 1663. The first Church Book in connection with this new Church in Worcester is dated 1687, and Mr Badland died in 1698, aged 64 years. (See "Worcester Sects" by Noakes). He was therefore Minister in Worcester for 35 years. The present Congregational Church in Worcester was founded in 1708, and rebuilt in 1858. Close by its pulpit is a marble tablet to the memory of "Rev Thomas Badland, a faithful and profitable preacher of the Gospel in this city for the space of

35 years, He rested from his labours May 5th, A.D. 1698. Aet 64. *Mors mihi vita nova.*"
We are unable to discover any records to show how the Protestant Dissenters of West
Bromwich got along under the intolerance and ill-usage to which they were subjected.
It is not known whether Mr Hilton was minister on the departure of Mr Badland, and
if so, how long his ministry continued before he went to be private chaplain to Mr R.
Foley. The Church held its meetings in a room or private house, probably in the house
of one of Mr Hilton's attached friends. Nor do we know in what year the first Meeting
House was built, but we find that on December 23rd, 1699 John Lowe bequeathed a
perpetual annuity (now known as the Holyoak) of £2 10s. towards the support of the
ministry of the Old Meeting. A deed dated March 30th and 31st, 1714, states the uses
for which the then newly erected chapel was put up. At this period. with the exception
of the Quakers, the "Meeting houses," as they were termed, of the denominations were
guarded by trusts of a general character, which neither specified the sect to which they
belonged, nor the doctrines which were to be preached. They were secured by deeds to
the congregations of "Protestant Dissenters," worshipping in that place, who were
allowed to choose such person as minister as a majority might elect, No creeds,
confessions, or articles of belief were subscribed to by either ministers or churches, but
declarations of their faith, made at general assemblies or conferences, were common to
all Dissenters. The particular deed of the "Old Meeting" states that the building "was
and is intended for a Meeting House for the worship and service of God, and fitted for
that purpose," The trustees were 15 in number—John Lowe, Josiah Turton, Richard
Brett, Richard Witton, Thomas Brett, Samuel Lowe, — Turton, Bailey Brett, John
Mayo, William Silvester, Edminy Weaver, Jonathan Clare, Richard Nock (the elder),
Thomas Nock (the younger) and Richard Nock (the younger). The trustees had power
to expel any of their numbers who became scandalous or offensive, to fill up vacancies
so caused by expulsion, or by death, or removal from the neighbourhood, up to the
number of 15. Elizabeth Jesson appears to have given the land for this purpose, and the
building was raised by subscription. This was the building referred to in Reeves'
History in which we are told that a lawless mob set fire to the Dissenters' Meeting
House in 1715, and that a young man in the act of unroofing it was killed by the slugs
from Cornet Lowe's blunderbuss. For about a year afterwards the building lay in ruins,
but was rebuilt by the Government in 1716. Mr Badland is said to have been connected
with the chapel till 1687.

Rev. R. Witton, M A, (1725), nine years after the re-building, was called to the
pastorate, and for 40 years he was a living protest against the interference of the State
in matters of belief or modes of worship. As years enfeebled his strength he was obliged
to find an assistant, and this he found in the Rev. William Howell, who succeeded him
in the full pastorate at his death in 1765. His ashes lie in the old portion of Ebenezer
Churchyard, close by the scene of his 90 years' faithful work, and his tomb in
inarticulate speech bears tribute to his memory thus:—"Here lie the remains of Richard
Witton, M.A., forty years Pastor of this church. Justly esteemed and beloved for his
cheerful and unaffected piety, his inflexible integrity, his open and benevolent temper,
his faithfulness and zeal in the service of his divine Master. He died December 28th,
1765 aged 82 years." Witton Lane takes its name from this pastor.

Elizabeth Brett, in 1765, presented the Church with two Sacramental Cups of
hammered silver bearing this inscription,—"The gift of Elizabeth Brett for the use of
the Protestant Dissenting Society at West Bromwich, Staffordshire, 1765."

Rev. William Howell (1765) was sole minister from 1765 to 1776 in which year he
passed behind the veil. Desiring to be laid beside Mrs. Savage, he was buried in the All
Saints graveyard. The only note extant respecting him is that on March 15th, 1752, he
preached the funeral sermon of Mrs S. Savage, taking as his text Daniel ii., 13. This Mrs

Savage was sister to the celebrated commentator, Rev. Matthew Henry, and mother-in-law to the Rev. R. Witton, M.A.

Concerning the four ministers of the "Old Meeting" who successively followed little is known beyond their names. They were REVS. JOSEPH ROSS; W. ROBINS; HUMPHRIES; BRAYBROOK. The average length of pastorate of these ministers was two years, and this may account for the fact that little is known of them.

Whether the last of the four, Mr Braybrook, removed or died is not clear, but in 1785 the REV. G. OSBORNE was chosen minister, and it was placed on record that, "having received a learned education with a view to the Christian Ministry, he entered upon the office of Pastor to the Dissenting Church at West Bromwich, in the year 1785 from whence he removed to Worcester, in the year 1792. He was highly esteemed as a preacher; his discourses were truly serious, judicious, and evangelical. As a tutor he was also eminently distinguished, and rendered highly useful to his pupils by his classical attainments and general knowledge." He had the honour to be one of the first promoters of Sunday Schools (founded by R. Raikes in 1780-1), and by the exercise of the most ardent zeal in that good work was the happy means of stimulating those exertions which have raised these institutions to their present high state of excellence and usefulness. His benevolence made him beloved of the poor.

Rev. MR McGEORGE was in 1793 asked from Wolverhampton to take the oversight of the Church. A scrap of paper in the Ebenezer safe, bearing the following memorandum, is the only record of Mr McGeorge left in West Bromwich:—

	£	s.	d.
Journey to Worcester.			
Walked to Birmingham			
Breakfast	0	6	
Hostler	0	3	
Horse hire	12	0	
Dinner	1	0	
Wine	0	$7\frac{1}{2}$	
Horse	0	7	
Hostler	0	1	
Tea	0	8	
Turn pike	0	3	
Horse at Worcester	1	6	
Breakfast	0	8	
Porter	0	$2\frac{1}{2}$	
Turnpike	0	3	
No Dinner	0	0	
Tea	0	6	
Coach	2	0	
Coachman	0	3	

"Mr McGeorge's Expenses to Worcester" £1 1 4

Many dissenting Churches were at this time Presbyterian only in name, and the fact that many of these drifted into pronounced Unitarianism may find its explanation in this: (1) the Churches were bound by no doctrinal trust deed, and (2) the greatest intellectual forces of the time were in sympathy with Unitarian views. Many churches openly declared themselves to be Unitarian. For a long time the "Old Meeting" was Presbyterian, and Nonconformists were then granted what were called "Indulgences"—licences to preach, to hold meetings, &c.

At a Church meeting on Wednesday, March 4th 1794, the REV. JOHN BERRY of Rumsey, "was asked to become Pastor at a salary of £70 a year, which is £10 more than has hitherto been raised for the Minister of this place." Mr Berry accepted the position and laboured here from 1794 till 1797. On January 13th, 1796, John Addington and Bailey Brett made application to the Clerk of Stafford County Court to have licenced "a house in the parish of West Bromwich, on the side of the road leading from West Bromwich Heath to Hill Top, and intended to be used as a place of meeting for Protestant Dissenters from the Church of England."

Mr Berry was succeeded in 1797 by Rev. Joel Maurice, of Stretton-under-Fosse, who was a man of grave and judicial character, an evangelical preacher, and well acquainted with Puritan theology. He died on December 26th, 1807, and a monument in Ebenezer churchyard marks the resting place of his dust, and bears the following inscription:—"Sacred to the memory of the Rev. Joel Maurice, late pastor of this congregation, and also for upwards of 30 years over a numerous congregation at Stretton-under-Fosse, Warwickshire, where his labours will be remembered by many with affection and gratitude. Having borne honourable testimony to his Master's cause for a period of nearly 50 years, he could with truth exclaim in the words of the Apostle II Tim. iv. chap., 7 and 8 verses (being the last from which he preached). He died December 26th, 1807, in his 70th year."

In April 24th, 1807, at the age of 86 there passed away another notable personage, Mrs. Esther Bulkley, who was grand-daughter to the celebrated Commentator, Matthew Henry. Before her death she gave her grandfather's exposition of the Old and New Testament, in five large volumes, to the Church, to be under the care of the Pastor for the time being. Four of these volumes are still in a good state of preservation in the Ebenezer safe.

In 1808 the Rev. James Cooper, born at Walsall, educated at Rotherhan, College, and for a short time minister at Wirksworth in Derbyshire, was chosen to fill the vacancy. Mainly through his exertions the Old Chapel, now too small for the purpose required, and dilapidated by over a century of use and abuse, was superseded by a more capacious and imposing structure—the present Schools. The site of the Chapel was now changed from the position of the caretaker's house, and the cost of erection was £800. Mr Cooper removed in 1829 to another charge after a ministry of 20 years, and died at Norwich, May 27th, 1863. In 1830 his place was filled by Rev. W. Foster, who removed to London in 1834.

Rev. J. C. Gallaway, M.A., a young man, fresh from College, began his ministry in October, 1834, and during his nine years stay prosperity attended the "Old Meeting." A religious awakening took place there in 1840, the church grew, and a larger and more convenient sanctuary (Ebenezer, for now its name was changed), was erected in 1839 by the side of the present schools at a cost of £2,400. A piece of land measuring 33 by 24 yards was bought of Mr Jesson for this purpose and on it the present Chapel, and stabling at the back, were erected. In 1843 Mr Gallaway resigned and became pastor at St. John's, New Brunswick, North America. Returning to England he became the secretary of the Chapel Building Society. His last years were spent on the spot endeared to him by the memories of his early ministry, and on September 16th, 1886, he "fell asleep," and his ashes lie under the shadow of the Sanctuary he built for God. In 1839 Mr Gallaway received into the Church a young man who was destined to take no small share in the work at Ebenezer —Mr John Eld, who is still a deacon, and who became at this time a devoted worker in school and church, elected to the diaconate in 1841. He was for many years superintendent of the Early Morning Adult School.

Rev. W. H. Dyer, who was chosen to succeed Mr Gallaway, began his ministry here in December, 1843. He was a man of grave disposition, of much logical and analytical power. On April 28th, 1853, be relinquished his charge here to fill the place vacated by the death of Rev. William Jay, of Bath. He afterwards became a barrister.

REV. WILLIAM CUTHBERTSON, B A. (1853), became a fit successor to this office. William Cuthertson, B.A. was then a student of Spring Hill College, Birmingham. He commanded good congregations until his departure to Australia in 1856. He subsequently held pastorates at Bishop Stortford, and Markham Square, London, and was chairman of the Congregational Union of England and Wales in 1879. Crossing the Atlantic in 1882 he held pastorates at Chicago, and Woodstock, Canada, and in 1891 returned to West Bromwich, thus completing the circuit, and is now the able and eminent pastor of the High Street Congregational Church. His was the first example for many years of a minister taking office at the "Old Meeting" (Ebenezer) without signing a declaration of faith.

Rev. JOHN WHEWELL, of Belper, was chosen minister, and laboured successfully here from February 1857, till his removal to Coventry in October, 1868. In the year 1864 Mr John Blackham was chosen a deacon, and Mr Isaac Hartill was promoted to the same office in 1868. The other members of the present diaconate with the dates of their appointment are—Mr D. Harford 1883; Mr S. N. Williams 1883; Mr G. E. Vaughan, 1883; Mr J Tickle, 1885; Mr Postlethwaite, 1885. Vignette portraits of these eight deacons accompanied the pamphlet, from which all these copious extracts are now taken.

During Mr Whewell's ministry (1857 to 1868) nearly 126 members were admitted to Church fellowship, on profession of faith, 140 Church meetings were held, all of which the Pastor attended, and in all the Church's proceedings there was not a discordant note. A dispute between the trustees and Messrs Badger over damage done by the latter to the Chapel property was decided on the arbitration of Mr J. L. Hornblower. Messrs Badger, in 1863, paid £729 3s. 1d for damage done to the property, and £229 10s. for encroachments in mining operations. In 1863 the schools were belted with iron rods, and other repairs done to the Chapel and Schools, and in 1864 the recess behind the pulpit was enlarged to make room for the new organ, built by Mr Banfield. The cost of the new organ was £240 and the builder allowed £120 for the old organ. The money subscribed for these repairs, together with the amount received from Messrs Badger, was £1,047 11s. 4d. The repairs were commenced in January 1864, and the Chapel re-opened in April of the same year. On May 29th the Rev. J. C. Gallaway (late pastor, then of London) preached the opening sermons, and on the Monday a public tea was held, and addresses were given by Revs J. C. Gallaway, M.A., W. H. Dyer, W. Cuthbertson, B.A., and J. G. Jukes. A statement on behalf of the trustees was then made by Mr C. Stringer, one of the deacons, and the Church's legal adviser.

REV. H. LUCKETT, of Gainsborough, was the next to be chosen as pastor, and he began his ministry on Sunday, January 24th, 1869, which ministry closed on December 30th, 1877. The Rev. Grattan Guinness held a fortnight's services in May, 1871. On April 17th, 1870 the Early Morning Adult School was commenced, with Mr James Lewis as superintendent. This office was afterwards filled by Mr John Eld from December, 1873, to May, 1884. This school has done good work, and as many as 640 men have met for instruction at 7.30 on the Sunday morning. Since 1884 this school has been under the efficient leadership of Mr S. N. Williams, who had previously been general secretary from 1873. The pew rents were abolished in January, 1880, and the church's finances revived under the weekly envelope system. In 1881 the Witton Lane property was sold for £903 7s. 9d. The chapel was renovated, the aisles raised, the heating pipes covered with gratings, and the property insured for £4,000 in 1885.

The Pleasant Sunday Afternoon movement which has now become a national "institution," commonly recognised by the mystic initials "P.S.A.," originated at this place of worship in 1875, its founder being Mr John Blackham.

REV. J. BAINTON, of Bideford, succeeded Mr Luckett (1878), and on receiving a call to the Congregational Church, at Heywood, Manchester, gave up his charge on September 12th, 1886.

In 1884, Mr George Green (Evangelist), conducted two special missions, with marked results. At the church's annual meeting on January 1st 1885, the pastor reported that 90 members had been added, making the total membership 211.

Mr Timothy Hartland having rendered devoted service for 50 years as choirmaster resigned and a testimonial was presented to him on January 1st, 1886, in recognition of his labours.

REV WILLIAM KELLY, A.T.S., of New College, London, was unanimously invited to the pastorate, and began his ministry on March 6th, 1887. His ordination service was held on March 30th, 1887, at which service the scripture was read by Rev. R. Aylward, West Bromwich; a statement on behalf of the church was made by Mr John Eld, questions to the minister were asked by Mr William O'Neill, London, the ordination prayer was offered by Rev. C. A Berry, Wolverhampton, the charge to the minister was delivered by the Rev. Samuel Newth, M.A., D.D., Principal of New College. Other ministers present were Revs W. Oakley, T. Lord, and F. Docker, of West Bromwich; B. B. Williams, of Dudley, and J. Byers, of Wednesbury.

On September 15th, 1890 the old vestry, 11ft. by 9ft. was taken down, and there were erected on the old site, at a cost of £318, three Vestries of the following dimensions:—13ft. by 11ft. 3in.; 13ft. 6in. by 13ft., both on ground floor and one over these two 25ft. by 17ft. 6in. Rev C. A. Berry, preached at the opening of these vestries on December 3rd, 1890.

The REV. W. KELLY resigned in June 1893, having received a call to Sheffield. A portrait of him accompanied the Bazaar Pamphlet, which he compiled. During the six years of his pastorate over £1,000 was raised for building purposes. After paying the £318 just mentioned, the balance has been retained towards the erection of new Schools for the use of the 500 Sunday Scholars in attendance there.

The REV. OWEN LLOYD MORRIS, of Brecon College, succeeded in September, 1894, his ordination taking place on Friday, October 19th. He is the latest of a long and worthy line of pastors, of whom few chapels can show such an unbroken list.

The "Old Meeting" became known as "Ebenezer" (*Stone of Help*), in 1839; a custom having then grown up of assuming distinctive names for "congregational" chapels. A picture of the building headed the historical sketch to which we are indebted for this chapter. The white stuccoed facade, classical in design, stands back from the main road behind palisades. In the old burial ground will he found the graves of the Kenricks and other local families of note. By the side of the chapel is the School, also faced with white stucco, its door in the centre having over it a quaint sort of triptic light, the central panel being larger than the outer one, and rising above them with a semi-circular head. This schoolroom was once the chapel, has more recently been used as a Board School and will soon give place to a newer and more modern school building when the Bazaar funds, now in hand, have been sufficiently increased.

LV.—NONCONFORMITY MILITANT: MAYERS GREEN INDEPENDENT CHAPEL.

Recalling the historical evolution of Nonconformity, we found the Puritans in course of time became divided into Presbyterians, Independents, and Baptists. The Independents separated from the Presbyterians because the latter sought to establish a "uniformity" according to their own views, they called themselves Independents because they objected to the divine right or control of a Presbytery, or Court of

Delegates. The name "Presbyterian" occurs locally (but perhaps inaccurately applied) in Wednesbury PARISH REGISTERS of the year 1702, an entry therein running thus: "John the son of John and Elizabeth Cashmore was baptized by a Presbyterian minister, at St. Margaret's Chapel *alias* a barn in the parish of West Bromwich." The "Old Meeting" is similarly called "Presbyterian" in the same Registers when alluding to the rioters' attack thereon in 1715: and the places are, therefore, no doubt identical.

This attack has been many times described, but to do full justice to an episode of such historical import it has needed the pen of an eye-witness. There is happily, in the possession of Mr Charles Osborne Ellis (a member of the present Board of Guardians), a private, trustworthy, and original account of this notable incident, in the handwriting of one of his ancestors. This old document adequately meets all the requirements of historic truth, the writer was one Thomas Maullin, born the 29th September, 1684, and his testimony is now forthcoming as that of an eye-witness of the scenes he describes; his MEMORANDUM (which has never been published before) is characteristic in its faithful reflection of the times:—

"*February the 1st*, 1715, there was a very great and high wind that blew down a great deal of Building, and did a great deal of dammage. And on the 22nd day of Aprill following there was a great and total Ecclipse of the Sun, insomuch that Several Stars Appeared, and people could not see to work out of Doors. And on the 20th day of June following there Happened a very great Storm of Hail that broke a great many glass Windows, and quite Spoiled Several fields of Corn and flax. Soon after this arose that great Storm out of the Bottomless Pitt (that is) that most odious and unnatural Rebellion that was raised against his Majesties Person and Government, a Short Account whereof as it was carried on in these Parts is as followeth:—

"*A Short Account of the Proceedings of the Mob at Westbromwich and Severall other Places.*

The first battell that was fought at West Bromwich was on the tuesday, the 12th day of July, Annoq. Dom. 1715, about Six of the Clock at night the Mob Came to the Meeting house, and as it is said they stood about a hour before they began to fight, but the Mob was quickly forced to run, and was very much wounded. "The next battell was wednesday, the 13th day of July, about Six of the Clock at night, and about Six-and-thirty of the Mob were taken Prisoners, and in the same night the Mob came to Mr May's, where the Prisoners were kept, and broke the house, and let out Severall of the Prisoners, but were again beaten and forced to run, and eight more were taken Prisoners.

"And on thursday the 14th of July James Clarck and the Limemen raised the Mob again and Came with more rage and fury than ever they had before with Guns and other desperate weapons and it is said they discharged three Pieces first and killed Mr Abell's horse. In which battell one of the mob of Wolverhampton was wounded and died in the night following and ffrancis Gibbins of Sedgly was wounded and died on the morrow and a great many of the Mob were taken Prisoners. And on friday the 15th of July the Sheriff came to the Meetinghouse and Commanded both Sides to lay down their arms and accordingly our side did and after the Sheriff and the rest of the Company were gone from the Meetinghouse the Mob came again to the Meetinghouse and broke into it and Pulled Down the Pulpit and Some of the Seats and then the Sheriff and his Men with other Assistance Came to the Meetinghouse and met one of the Mob as he was bringing out Some of the Seats and Severall shot at him and killed him and the Mob was again forced to run.

"And on Sunday the 17th of July the Mob came again and fired the Meetinghouse at West Bromwich and the Meetinghouse at Oldbury and the Meetinghouse at Dudley. And on Munday the 18th of July the Mob went to Sturbridge Meetinghouse and there they pulled down the Pulpit and Seats and Carried them out and burnt them.

"And its thought if the Worcestershire Sheriff had not met them and taken Some of them Prisoners they would not easily have been suppressed.

"And likewise it pleased Almighty God to put it into the heart of Mr Bayleys to Ride to London to acquaint the Parliament with their gross proceedings the Design of Which was to bring in a Popish Pretender and depose our Rightfull and Lawfull Sovereigne King George upon whose Head Let the Crown Long flourish."

Nonconformity in those early days of its existence was truly a church militant. Not only did the preceding chapter disclose the noteworthy fact that in West Bromwich many of its oldest and best families stood identified with the cause of dissent and religious freedom, but that the espousal of the cause then meant active participation in a constant fight with the aggressive forces of an intolerant Government supported and abetted by its unscrupulous partisans. In the great cause of religious liberty we have seen Captain Turton don his armour, buckle on his sword, and depart from the Oak House to fight as an Independent on the battlefields of Cromwell, and in this later struggle of 1715, we find Cornet Lowe of Charlemont taking his life in his hand to defend that Meeting-house which he and his father had helped to found, and against which came repeatedly and relentlessly the more formidable forces of a wild. Jacobite, High Tory mob, of infuriated rioters—(Refer also to Chap. XLIX.)

Three-quarters of a century later but little amelioration can be claimed in this direction. From a JOURNAL kept by a young lady during the "Church and King Riots, we learn that on Thursday, July 16th, 1791, a West Bromwich man of eminence—the philosophic and learned James Keir, whose residence was then on the sunny slopes of Hill Top—was dining with a semi-private party at a hotel in Birmingham where as friends of freedom they were quietly celebrating the French Revolution. Again the passions of the rabble were inflamed by the Tories, who posing as a "Church and King Party"—and therefore superior to their dissenting and law-abiding neighbours—objected to such a celebration. Denying liberty to others, they took a license for themselves, and gathered a mob round the hotel. The company of diners, however, broke up peaceably at five; and, says the diarist, "several of the gentlemen drank tea with us, among the rest was one churchman, Mr Keir: They were congratulating themselves on the pleasant and orderly manner in which all had been conducted, talking over their toasts." James Keir was not only a churchman, but was acknowledged on all hands as a loyal gentleman, in presiding at that dinner over an assembly of eighty of the keenest intellects of the day (including Dr. Priestley) his loyalty had in no wise diminished. Yet almost immediately after this tea the fierce Priestley Riots broke out and Birmingham Dissenters suffered shamefully. The Wednesbury colliers marched through Bromwich into Birmingham on this occasion, terrifying the peaceful inhabitants *en route* by their fierce demonstrations.

*   *   *   *   *   *   *

Just previous to this, an offshoot of the Wednesbury Independent Church had taken root in West Bromwich. In 1785 some nine male members of the Wednesbury congregation joined themselves together for Sunday prayer meetings at MAYERS GREEN. It is known that at least three of these families were resident in West Bromwich. Presently they secured the use of a Barn at Virgin's End for the purposes of a meeting house; neighbouring ministers came regularly to conduct the services, particularly the Rev. Mr Bradford, pastor of Lady Huntingdon's Connexion at Birmingham, and whose chapel there was specially spared in the '91 Riots, because this branch of the Independents was acknowledged by the mob to be little more than a Calvinistic branch of the Church of England. Another minister who had rendered kindred service at West

Bromwich, was the Rev. Mr Moody, who was one of the earliest students sent out from the Countess of Huntingdon's newly-established College at Trevecca, in South Wales. His remains were in after years interred in the Chapel graveyard here. From the same college came also the Rev. HUGH WILLIAMS who may be reckoned the first pastor of Mayers Green Chapel. He having preached in the Barn as soon as it was formally licensed as a meeting-House, was invited to stay on permanently. He was publicly ordained in 1787, and in the same year land was purchased in Messenger Lane—the site of the "Old Burial Ground," as it is now called—and the first little chapel, only some 36 feet by 30 feet, was erected thereon at a cost of £285. This modest edifice was opened on Shrove Tuesday, February 5th, 1788. The contract for the building of this place of worship was signed by William Smith, Samuel Winchurst, John Bibb, William Fisher, John Davis, Thomas Horton. Benjamin Timmins, James Cash, and Rev Hugh Williams. It stood then fronting the wide common and was at that time most pleasantly situated. In 1790 it was lengthened and a front gallery was erected at an outlay of £173. In 1799 Mr Willams suddenly left, after an honourable career of some twelve years, to take a pastorate at Stafford. He died at Handsworth in 1823 aged 65 years; and he, too, lies buried in the little graveyard here, in accordance with his own expressed wishes.

The REV. THOMAS MADDIN came as his successor on the special recommendation of Lady Huntingdon's chaplain, in 1799. (The great George Whitfield, by the way, had been adopted as the first chaplain of the Countess). Mr Maddin's stay here, however, was a little under a year.

REV. JOHN HUDSON came by invitation, and commenced his ministry in June 1801. Just previously the worshippers here had formally resolved themselves into a "church," and the first deacons elected were William Smith and Francis Johnson. The young pastor, fresh from Hoxton College, devoted himself assiduously to the work, and more seating accommodation had soon to be added, while an old debt of £250 was also paid off. His public ordination (6 May 1802) excited some considerable stir, the Church of England at that time resenting the idea of these ordination services being held by Dissenters. Growing prosperity next induced the purchase of a larger piece of land on the opposite side of the road—the site of the present Chapel and Schools—from the Waste Lands Enclosure Commissioners, the price being 5d. per yard.

In 1804 Sunday Schools were established in rooms built specially for the purpose by Benjamin Messenger, at the commencement of the lane now bearing his name. Although side galleries had but recently been added to the chapel, it was now resolved to pull it down and build a more commodious one on the new site opposite. The new chapel was accordingly commenced in 1807, and was opened in the following year, on April 13th, but as no artificial lighting had been provided to admit of evening service, one of the officiating ministers (the Rev. Thomas Grove, of Walsall) had to preach a "double sermon" in the morning. Towards the erection Mrs Jane Whyley, of the Oak, contributed the magnificent sum of £1,000. A memorial tablet in the building fittingly records this fact, and describes the donor as the widow of William Whyley, senior, a daughter of the Rev. John Edwards, of Leeds and a member of the church for 50 years.—(See also Chap. xlvi.)

With this substantial aid the total of £1,550 was soon paid off. As the material in the old chapel had been frugally utilised, a malt-house of Mrs Whyley's had been requisitioned as a temporary meeting-house during the building operations. Soon after the opening of the chapel the first benefit club in Bromwich, and probably in this part of the country, was established in connection with this place of worship. The site of the old chapel was walled in and used as a burial ground. At the present time, however, this "garden of sleep" is in a somewhat neglected condition and calls for attention. The Sunday schools built in 1807 were enlarged to double their original size in 1813, under the successful management of Mr John Reeves. To pay off the new liability incurred sermons were preached by the Rev John Greig, M.A to whose character there is in the chapel a tablet dated 1828, bearing very high testimony. The support accorded to these schools in voluntary subscriptions from the year 1805 to 1843, the year Mr Hudson resigned, amounted to £2,711, an average of £74 per annum. The certificate of License for the "Independent Meeting in Mares Green" is dated 1810, and shows that the building was registered by the Bishop of Lichfield and Coventry", as a place of public worship for the use of Protestant Dissenters" in accordance with the provisions of an Act (*I. Will. and Mary, Cap.* 18.) for exempting Protestant Dissenters from penalties, &c. In 1812 the first collection here was made for the London Missionary Society: and during the next thirty-one years there was collected for it the sum of £1,725, which yields an average of £55 13s. 0d., so that beyond being a self-supporting community, considerable sums were contributed to this and many similar extraneous purposes. The Rev. John Hudson died in October 1864, aged 85, and was buried within the precincts of this chapel; a tablet records his faithful pastorate for the long period of 41 years. He was the father of Robert Spear Hudson, founder of the well-known firm of soap manufacturers ("Hudson's Soap") a member of the Congregational body whose donations to the cause amounted to £20,000.

Rev. Basil Henry Cooper, B.A., of London was ordained in April 1844, to succeed the Rev. John Hudson. The old school room was now pulled down, and the present two-storied school was re-erected at a cost of £1,050. Day schools were opened in them, another great advance in the social development of this church. Mr Cooper, who was author of "The Free Church of Ancient Christendom," resigned his charge in 1852. The Chapel was licensed for the performance of marriages in 1845, during his pastorate.

The Rev. W. Creed, son-in-law to Rev. J. Hudson, succeeded, he resigned in 1859 in consequence of ill-health.

Rev. J. G. Jukes next became pastor, and remained till 1873; upon his resignation a good number of the congregation, some of them influential members, seceded with him, and became the nucleus of another congregation in the parish—that now meeting in the High Street Chapel.

Rev. Joseph Hall, who came to Mayer's Green next, left a large congregation at Hounslow to regret his departure. He was a man of good presence, and always well liked by those who came into contact with him. He had a successful ministry, and was succeeded by the Rev. J. H. Snell, after whom came the Rev. T. P. Hookey. The present pastor is the Rev. W. H. Muncaster, M.A., B.D. The congregation is large, influential, prosperous, and thoroughly representative of the town.

Mayer's Green Chapel is a large and substantial brick building, with an imposing central entrance lobby between two fluted columns surmounted by a frieze and cornice. A fine organ, in a recessed chamber behind the pulpit, cost £650. The chapel is very handsomely pewed, and with its large galleries will seat comfortably 650 worshippers. Its school rooms are the centre of much social activity; not only are there schools and classes of various kinds, but a library and a gymnasium provide respectively for the mental and physical recreation of the people, while clubs and societies for a variety of objects supplement these numerous religious and educational agencies.

Mayer's Green is a place-name which has appeared in a variety of different forms, as *Mare's Green, Mayor's Green*, etc. But it is not improbable that the place was so called from an old family named Meyre (chap. lii.) or Mayoe who formerly resided in the parish. Reference to Willett's History will disclose a John Mayoe buying a parcel of manor lands in 1720 (p. 17): & John Mayow, churchwarden in 1708 (p. 130): there is named a Mayoe's Meadow in 1709 (p, 203): and Thomas Meir held lands in West

Bromwich as early as 1584 (p 217).   MAYERS GREEN BIBLE CLASS—About 1855 or forty years ago, Sir James Scattergood commenced his Bible Class for Adults at this Chapel. This class soon became well known in Birmingham and throughout South Staffordshire. It was attended by men from Birmingham on the one side, and Dudley on the other, as well as by others from intermediate places as Oldbury and Great Bridge. None were admitted under 18 years of age, and the members and visitors were of different ranks and all denominations. Independents and Wesleyans of all shades, Churchmen, Roman Catholics, and others sat side by side with men who honestly doubted, and were allowed the rare opportunity of expressing their doubts as freely as they pleased. The subjects taken were some of them simple for beginners, but generally the subjects were special because the times were special, the Bible was attacked by philosophers, sceptics and professed Christians, and the subjects were arranged accordingly. The Bible, as affected by the writings of Lyell, Darwin, and other scientific writers, by the speeches and writings of Bradlaugh, Barker, Watts, Gordon and other sceptical writers, the Bible as affected by the writings of Bishop Colenso, and other professed Christians formed subjects for years and years of inquiry. Bible truth, consistent with itself and with the character of God, formed subjects of another kind and for another class of minds, some subjects occupying twenty and thirty more successive Sundays. The time devoted to the work each Sunday varied from two to four hours, according to the subject and the audience. After about twenty-five years the then existing forms of scepticism gave place to others of less consequence, attacks on the Christian revelation almost ceased, and the class then became an ordinary Adult Bible Class. It passed into the hands of Mr S. Pitt on the failure of Mr Scattergood's health in 1880. On this change women were admitted after a great struggle, and it subsequently so increased as to contain some eight hundred members.

LVI.—THE CONGREGATIONALISTS, BAPTISTS, AND UNITARIANS

Still pursuing the historical development of Puritanism—a movement inaugurated almost from the Reformation—it is proposed in the current chapter to bring this section of our history to a completion. The earlier divisions among the Puritan ranks resulted in the formation of the denominations known as Presbyterians, Independents, and Baptists. Later came the Unitarians."

Our narrative of local incident, reflecting the national movements of all these various sects, is resumed with one more glance at the INDEPENDENTS. At the present time, however, this body is more generally known as CONGREGATIONAL. For while the old Independents objected to any foreign communion controlling their proceedings, the modern Congregationalist goes further, and declares that each member of a Congregation has a personal share in its affairs.

The CONGREGATIONAL CHURCH, in HIGH STREET was shown to be an offshoot from Mayers Green Chapel. Its establishment was supported by men of influence, including Mr R. S. Hudson, a West Bromwich man of some considerable wealth, mentioned in the preceding chapter; and of whom a portrait and a brief memoir appeared in "The Christian Globe" of 21st August 1884. Incidentally it is mentioned in that memorial sketch that the £1,000 which were contributed to the building of Mayers Green Chapel, in 1808, by Mrs Whyley, of The Oak House, were the proceeds of an auction sale of timber growing on her estate; a feet which forcibly thrusts upon the mind a deep sense of the altered conditions of life in West Bromwich at the beginning as compared with the end of the nineteenth century.

In May, 1878, those members of the Mayers Green Congregational Church who had seceded under the Rev. J. G. Jukes, laid the foundation stones of their present chapel in High Street. For the first four years they had met to conduct public worship in a small room in the centre of the town; but for the last year or more the services had been of necessity transferred to the Town Hall. This growth justified their intention to expend £4,000 on a new chapel. The proposed building was designed to seat 1,000 worshippers, being 100ft. by 50ft., with galleries on three sides. It is constructed of pressed bricks, with Bath stone dressings, and makes some pretensions to ecclesiastical style by possessing a clerestory carried on columns. To the right and left are two storeys of vestries and class rooms, with separate entrances. To the front street is presented a handsome gable end flanked by wings containing the gallery staircases, all in a style of highly decorated French Gothic, projecting still further forward is a long vestibule, presenting a row of three gablets.

The contract was £2,700 for the first portion of the work; and on this stone laying day it was announced that £2,220 had already been raised. The stones were laid by Mr R. W Hudson, of Bache Hall, Chester, and Mr Thomas Rollason, of Handsworth to whom silver trowels were presented. The former gentleman was the grandson of the Rev. John Hudson, formerly pastor at Mayers Green, and son of the late Robert Spears Hudson, the benefactor of Congregationalism already alluded to. The chapel was opened in April, 1879; its successive pastors have been the Revs. E. Waldron Skinner, Robert Aylward, E. Watt Smyrk, and W. Cuthbetson.

*   *   *   *   *   *   *

THE BAPTISTS next present themselves for consideration. And at once we are met with the leaven of "Antinomianism" which hereabouts seemed to work through this body. The Antinomians (so called from the Greek *anti-nomos*, "against the law',), were a sect or originating in Germany in 1535, and were said to believe that the moral law was not binding upon Christians, under "the law of grace." Although even the great Baptist divine, Spurgeon, has said "I am rather fond of being called an Antinomian, the term is generally applied to those who hold the truth pretty firm and will not let it go," yet this sect was John Wesley's special abhorrence. Under date March 22nd, 1746, he writes: "I came to Wednesbury. The Antinomian teachers had laboured hard to destroy this poor people." And again in 1776 he says he preached at Dudley in the midst of "Antinomians and backsliders." And now as to the workings of these people in West Bromwich:

A History of The Midland Association of Baptist Churches (published in Birmingham in 1855), gives the following account of West Bromwich "Bethel" Baptist Chapel in Cutler's End, or Dartmouth Street as it is now called:—

"This church originated in a laudable desire on the part of a few earnest Christian brethren to preserve the Gospel pure from the Antinomian leaven which had found encouragement in this locality. A Baptist church existed in this place in 1796, was reconstructed about the year 1810, and became a member of the Association sometime prior to 1818."

The chapel erected in the Sandwell Road in 1812 is still in existence, and till recently bore witness to the distinctive principles of the Baptist denomination. Continuing our extract:—

"For many years it continued sound in the faith and was useful, but it gradually sank into hyper Calvinism, and varied its course only to reach occasionally the lower and darker depth of Antinomianism. It is now (November, 1855) extinct. About 1834, a few who mourned over the scene of disorder and decay decided on an effort to save the Baptist cause from utter disgrace and ruin."

The church which thus became extinct seems to have been known as West Bromwich "Providence" Chapel.

The seceders, for a time, met in the house of Mr Jeremiah Richards. Though few in number, they made up for this deficiency by their devoted earnestness. Money was raised, land was purchased in Dartmouth Street, and in 1835 "Bethel" Chapel was erected. For fifty years this building served as a sanctuary, till it outlived both its popularity and its stability. It was in an out-of-the-way situation, and the progressive spirit of the age began to desire something better. The town had increased in population in an extraordinary manner. When the first Baptist Chapel was erected in 1812 the population was 7,500: in 1835 when the second chapel was put up, the population was 20,000. After 75 years of labour, the population had risen to 60,000, but only one Baptist Church was found in the parish. The first chapel for a great number of years was not used by any community; and in 1884 the second one had to be taken down.

Even as far back as 1867 the need for a new chapel had been felt. Project after project was discussed only to be laid aside as involving a responsibility too great to be then undertaken. It was not until about 1876 (during the ministry of the Rev. W. J. Acomb) that a forward step was decided upon. At that time a fund was started, and after many efforts a fresh piece of land was purchased in High Street, a situation both prominent and central. At this point however, it was found necessary to stop and await a more favourable opportunity for carrying out the larger work. It was not until 1884 that the task of raising a new building was seriously entered upon, and even then it was not undertaken voluntarily, but through force of circumstances.

Subsidences of the earth caused by the mining operations of the district had, during the course of years, seriously damaged the old chapel. Rents and fissures were plainly visible in the brickwork, and often the solemnity of a service was destroyed by the falling of pieces of mortar, or by the still more alarming cracks that were distinctly audible as some fresh part of the building gave way. Under the stress of these circumstances it was not surprising that the congregations should become small by degrees and sorrowfully less. At any time a fresh subsidence of land might have been attended with disastrous consequences, and therefore, acting upon advice, the trustees closed the building.

For a time the congregation met in the adjoining schoolroom, but there again misfortune attended them. While holding the Sunday school treat in the July of 1884, an accident occurred which might have resulted most seriously. At one part of the proceedings, when a large number of teachers and scholars were congregated together in the schoolyard, the arch of a large rain water cistern gave way throwing some thirty or forty children and teachers into the well, a depth of seven or eight feet. In the confusion that followed, mothers saw their little ones vanish from their sight as though the ground had opened and swallowed them up. The cries of the children, mingled with the screams of the parents, created a most painful scene, and though the incident caused more alarm than injury, it sealed the fate of the old place, which was at once abandoned, and eventually taken down. Pending the opening of the new sanctuary the congregation and the school met in Prince's Assembly Rooms.

A Birmingham magazine published an account of this new chapel, accompanied by a small woodcut illustration, in April 1887. The building is of red brick, with white stone dressings in the early decorated style of the Gothic period. The elevation to High Street is irregularly disposed, having a central narthex, and at the eastern angle a square buttressed tower, 70 feet high. This tower has a pointed doorway, the arch of which is filled in by stone tracery; in the stage above is a single-light window; in the next stage some arcading appears; and in the belfrey stage above are coupled windows; the whole topped by an embattled parapet, with pinnacles at each corner, that on the south angle being higher, more massive, and capping a small projecting staircase-turret (tourelle) in the mediæval style. The narthex is entered by a double doorway under a pediment; and above this a large wheel window pierces the main gable of the chapel, which has a stone coping finishing in an elaborate finial at the apex. The side elevations are broken up by two projecting gables at the rear. The dimensions are 65 feet by 41 feet, and accommodation is provided for 500 persons. The pulpit is of polished pitchpine and mahogany, standing on a platform, and having in front an open Baptistry. Including land, the total cost has been about £4,300, to meet which a claim for £350 was made on the colliery proprietors who damaged the older chapel. At the back is a schoolroom (a necessary provision for nearly 300 children attending there) containing four classrooms, connected by a covered passage with the vestries. The architects were Messrs Ingall of Birmingham. The new pastor, the Rev. A. W. Oakley, entered on his work here, August, 1886 and a notice of his career appeared in the Birmingham Magazine, *Thought and Work*, already mentioned. The foundation stones were laid September, 1886, and the opening of the chapel was celebrated in April, 1887. The furnishing and equipment had run the total cost of to £5,100, so enterprising was the management by this time.

The compiler of the aforementioned *History of the Midland Association*, from which extracts have already been taken, was the Rev. W. Stokes, himself at one time a pastor of Bethel Chapel, West Bromwich, He gives the following list of ministers among whom he found himself enrolled:—Mr John Parker, from Bond Street, Birmingham, was the first pastor. He removed to Cosely in 1837, and was succeeded by Mr W. Stokes early in 1838, the members of the church being thirty-one in number. This minister resigned in October, 1843 having accepted the call of the church at Newhall Street, Birmingham. The members were at that period seventy-four in number, and the cause at Smethwick was commenced during this ministry. With occasional intervals the following ministers have been pastors since Mr Stokes:— Messrs W. D. Corken, W. Lloyd, T. E. Wycherley and W. Jones. The church is at present without a pastor; and the members are about 56 in number. But notwithstanding their comparatively destitute condition, the members conduct a useful and extensive tract distribution society, and in proportion to their numbers the largest Sunday school in the association." This, of course, was up to the year 1855.

A minute of the Church Book of the year 1838, and therefore in the earlier days of Mr Stokes' ministry is worth preserving. It runs:—"That the ordinance of Baptism be postponed until the first Sabbath in November, being ill-convenient for want of water. 2nd, That a reservoy be sunk to procure water, and a spout to convey the water into the baptistry." During the ministry of Mr Jones a Sunday school was erected at the back of the chapel. His successor was Mr Sneath, of Cradley, who held office from 1855 to 1860, then came Mr Hanson till 1868. Next Mr Newton held the pastorate till 1873, and in the following year came the Rev. W. J. Acomb, of whom mention has already been made. From 1878 the ministry was held by Mr Clarke, the immediate predecessor of the present energetic Pastor, the Rev. A. W. Oakley, A.T.S., late of Broughty Ferry, and a former student of Rawdon College, Leeds. To his devoted services, backed by the never-failing encouragement of Councillor Garrat and an active congregation full of self-denying labours is largely due the present prosperity of the Baptist Church, and the high efficiency of its numerous religious and social agencies.

The meetings of the "Midland Association" date from 1655, commencing that year at Warwick. After 1659 they had to be held in secrecy till 1690. In 1841 the meeting, was held at West Bromwich "Bethel" Chapel, the Rev. W. Stokes being Moderator. All this is duly set forth in *The History* aforesaid and much more of great local interest including a chronological list of events from which, however, only three items are here selected:—

1830. West Bromwich "Providence" Chapel admitted [to the Association].

1839. Church formed at Wednesbury. Wednesbury Church admitted.

1846. Providence Church, West Bromwich, re-admitted.

The first chapel—that of the year 1812—in Sandwell Road is now being used again as a place of worship by the "Wesleyan Reform Union." Attached to this building is a Burial ground, the land for which was presented in its early years by Mr George Cutler, a supporter of the Baptist denomination. It was a Mrs Benjamin Cutler, too, who paid the mortgage off the chapel.

* * * * * * *

The UNITARIANS first appeared in West Bromwich when the Rev. H. McKean, óf Oldbury, commenced to conduct the services in the Summit Schools, Spon Lane. July, 1859. Sunday schools were at once established, and in 1860 some further organisation was attempted, which was, however, more thoroughly gone into again in 1866. In 1868 a move was made to the Assembly Room, Lombard Street, which had to be relinquished in the following year. At first it was thought the movement would collapse, but in March, 1874, the Midland Christian Union, under whose auspices the higher organisation had previously been attempted, invited the Rev. John Harrison to re-establish the services. Under Mr Harrison public worship was resumed in St. George's Hall, and then a sum of £890 was very soon promised towards the erection of a proper chapel. Lodge Road Chapel was soon afterwards erected at a cost of £1,400, and was opened April, 1875. At the Council meeting of the Midland Christian Union, held at West Bromwich in April 1876, the Committee reported that they did not retain Mr Harrison as a minister attached to the Union any longer, but that as it was most desirable the congregation should be untrammelled in the management of its own domestic affairs, he had been appointed as minister to the Lodge Road Chapel. This pastor is as unconventional, and in outward appearance as unclerical as his flock are unfettered by creed; the trust deed of the chapel contenting itself with saying that the building is provided for the worship of God, no reference being made to any sect whatever. Mr Harrison is a popular platform speaker, and an earnest preacher; his discourses indicating a wide range of reading combined with an intimate knowledge of human nature.

The Chapel is in red brick, with stone dressings, in the Early English style; it will seat about 200 persons. There are now good commodious schools at the rear of the chapel.

LVII.—THE STORMY DAWN OF WESLEYANISM ON THE HORIZONS OF WEST BROMWICH, IN 1743.

Having traced the local history of that line of thought which was evolved from the Puritanism of Elizabeth's reign, the next trend of religious opinion to which attention must now be directed, is that which flowed from the second English Reformation—that of the eighteenth century, when Wesley gave to the world of believers his system of church government and religious practice which became known as Methodism.

The connection between West Bromwich, Wednesbury, and all the surrounding district, and the founder of Wesleyanism, is indeed a close and an intimate one. The history of local Methodism is undeniably of the very greatest interest. Happily there is available a vast amount of trustworthy recorded incident. So rich in record is this locality, that Reeves, the historian of West Bromwich, compiled a "History of the Rise and Progress of the Wesleyan Methodists in Birmingham, Wednesbury, Dudley, West Bromwich, and Its Vicinity, 1742-1842."

This work, which bears the later date (1842), is still in MS., and was purchased in 1860 from the widow of its author by the Rev. Samuel Lees, of Hill Top. It is now the property of that reverend gentleman's nephew, Mr S. Lees Taylor, postmaster of Tipton; and by the special permission of both the contents of this unpublished work have been placed unreservedly at disposal for the purpose of this present history. That portion of it which has long been on record in the printed works of John Wesley and others, will be drawn upon but little, but that part of Reeves' work which is purely local in its references, and which has probably never been in print before, will be eagerly welcomed by the present writer and no doubt by very many of his interested local readers.

The Rev. Charles Wesley was the first to appear on the scene here, in the September of 1742, when he preached to immense crowds in the "Coal-pit Field" at Wednesbury— which was probably Wednesbury Old Field. As some of his hearers became devoted converts, holding their evening meetings quite regularly, the Rev. John Wesley, at the special and earnest request of his brother, was also induced to make a visit to Wednesbury as early as possible. This he did in the January following (1742-3); and like his brother he also selected for his open air preaching the natural amphitheatre of the Holloway. This place, although in West Bromwich parish, furnished then (as part of the Bridge End) a recognised integral portion of Wednesbury's industrial population. This "End" of the town—before the lanes became united into one continuous network of streets, every detached centre of population was designated an "End"—was situated on the right bank of the stream which gave the town its chief water supply: it was on the line of the ancient "Portway;" and its population were just then engaged in developing the newer route to Birmingham, which at that particular period was beginning to be extensively used by regular trains of pack-horses, or rather load-horses, carrying panniers of coal, despatched from the mines of Wednesbury Old Field to the Furnaces at Aston, or the innumerable smiths' hearths in Birmingham. As the name "Holloway" implies, it was a road partly natural, but which by artificial means had been further hollowed out for the purpose of easing the heavy traffic carried on by these tramping trains of sturdy carriers over the crest of Hill Top, at the outset of their journey towards Birmingham. This besetting difficulty once surmounted, there was little or nothing to disturb the further solitudes of a journey, which lay over an expanse of sandy heath stretching almost away to the confines of Warwickshire, except it were the jangling of the horse bells, or the cracking of the driver's whip as he plodded along at the head of the leading horse, in whose wake a long running-chain compelled the others to follow. Such was the system of traffic which the Holloway made possible before the canals had provided a silent highway for the carriage of heavy goods and raw material or the turnpike roads had been made fairly passable for the regular running of wheeled vehicles. At the turnpiking of the road in 1727-44 no doubt the road was somewhat diverted, Reeves says the Holloway was "an amphitheatre of nature" which was "in great part filled up about the year 1821." This was the date of Telford's second making of the great Holyhead Road.

In 1742 West Bromwich contained but two places of worship—the Old Church and the Old Meeting; and it is by no means certain that the Independents of the latter were not as actively hostile to the reforming Methodists as the Churchmen themselves. The whole spiritual life of the locality was then at a very low ebb, the populace being generally given over to amusements of such brutalising influences as bear and bull-baiting, and dog and cock-fighting. As yet legislation had not attempted to regulate the hours of labour, and men therefore worked only and as long as they liked, and idled whenever they chose. The colliers were a steadily increasing body of workmen at Wednesbury; but the pursuit of coal-mining had not as yet crossed its boundaries into West Bromwich, whose chief industries then consisted of gunlock filing and nail-making, principally the latter. Its only large iron work was the Old Forge at Wigmore, whose place was afterwards supplied by Bromford.

On the 8th of January, John Wesley arrived in Wednesbury at 3 in the afternoon, at 7 he preaches in the upper room of the Market Cross, which was filled from end to end. At 5, the next day, Sunday, he preached again in the same "Town Hall," and he records that "at eight we met in the place where my Brother preached, made as it were for a great congregation. It is a large hollow, scarcely a mile from the town, capable of seating four or five thousand people. They stood in a half circle one above another." The Vicar of Wednesbury, Mr Egginton, as yet friendly in his attitude towards the Reformer, preached a plain, useful sermon in the afternoon; but almost all the congregation afterwards went down to the "hollow" where "abundance of people were already waiting for us," so that even the spacious "Holloway" could not contain this vast concourse which had gathered from all the surrounding parts; in eager expectation of a sermon from Wesley. That same night twenty- nine of his converts joined themselves together and became the first Staffordshire "Society" of Methodists, meeting at the house of one John Sheldon in the Holloway. As this spot lies outside the boundaries of Wednesbury, it yields to West Bromwich the honour of forming the first Society of Methodists in this district. By Tuesday following it boasted a hundred members, who all took an affectionate leave of Wesley on the morning of Wednesday, the 12th, when he departed for Evesham. Thus ended John Wesley's first visit to Staffordshire, an eventful epoch for both Wednesbury and the Bridge End of West Bromwich.

In April following (1743) John Wesley rode in two days from Sheffield to Wednesbury. Here he "found things surprisingly altered. The inexcusable folly of Mr W——s had so provoked Mr Egginton (the Vicar) that his former love was turned into bitter hatred." From the Friday of his arrival, to Sunday, which was the 17th of the month, all remained quiet. But on the latter day the Vicar preached such a "wicked" inflammatory sermon against this new "Society" which the earnest and devoted Methodists had formed, and whose numbers in a couple of months had largely increased upon the first hundred, that Wesley took pains to prepare his followers for the threatened persecutions which he could see looming in the immediate future in consequence of this hostile clerical attitude. While he was further exhorting his flock on Tuesday, the 19th, in the open air, a clergyman who was "very drunk" rode up and in sheer wantonness tried to ride down some of Wesley's hearers. Reeves surmises that this abandoned priest of God was the Rev. Mr Rann, curate of West Bromwich.

The next to appear here upon the scene is Mr Charles Wesley, who says that on May 20th he "got once more to our dear colliers at Wednesbury." He found the flock had grown to upwards of 300, and on the following morning he held a conference with those who had responded to his brother's ministry, and inspected a piece of ground given by a Dissenter to build a chapel upon. They all then walked together from Wednesbury to Walsall and as they were singing hymns as they walked along, this aroused such opposition that an assault was made on the preacher three times, the raging rabble losing set on by the "principal men" of the place. Here we have the first overt demonstration of armed opposition. Fearlessly, however, did Charles Wesley stalk through these "Ephesian beasts" of rioters, the next day addressing nearly two thousand hearers in Birmingham, returning to Wednesbury in the evening, and taking his leave of the vicinity on the day following, May 23rd. Till this exhibition of hostility we have so far seen nothing but the sunshine of prosperity, and the most encouraging promise of future fruitfulness. But jealousy seems now to have awakened great fear in the breasts of the local clergy. The success of Methodism meant the decline of Episcopalianism. The larger the new societies, the less satisfying the churches. Therefore, this demonstration against Charles Wesley was but the beginning of tribulation in store for the Wesleyans. Exactly a week after his departure, open rioting began, and a systematised attack was made upon all known followers of the Wesleys.

John Wesley records in his "Journal" that it was Saturday, June 18th, when he received intelligence of the riots in Staffordshire, and that he was not at all surprised, after the recent advice pointedly given to the ignorant populace, not only from the pulpit, but from the Episcopal chair. Setting out on the Monday, and travelling from Wycombe via Oxford and Birmingham, he got to Wednesbury on Wednesday, the 22nd, riding straight to the house of his staunchest adherent there, Francis Ward, who had married a sister of the John Sheldon, just previously mentioned. According to Reeves, the said house was fifty yards from Wednesbury Bridge, and in 1842, he says, was occupied by Mr James Richards, axle-maker. This house of Francis Ward's, which was the centre of the great historic episode now about to be described, is still standing, being numbered 92 in Bridge Street, and is the property of the Holden family, who own The Mounts and much more of the surrounding property. If never purchased for preservation by the Wesleyan body, it surely deserves to have had a tablet or something of the kind inserted in its front chronicling the great part it played in the stirring incidents of the fateful year 1743.

The disturbances had commenced here on May 30th, and had been resumed on June 20th. John Wesley had arrived in Wednesbury to comfort and console his flock on June 22nd, and then had departed to obtain legal advice on the matter at Tamworth. On Sunday, the 26th, many of the poor persecuted people went to Birmingham to meet there Charles Wesley and receive strength and comfort at his hands. Of these riotings, which began at Darlaston and raged so fiercely in Wednesbury, a very full account appeared in print as early as 1744 in the form of a pamphlet published promptly after the events by Wesley himself, and entitled "*Modern Christianity exemplified at Wednesbury.*" It consists chiefly of a number of depositions, some of them on oath, by eye-witnesses of the turbulent and unlawful proceedings. Part of it relates to West Bromwich directly, and the following verbatim extracts must be quoted, as they refer to events during this outbreak of the early summer time.

"*On June 20, John Baker, Thomas Griffiths*, and *Daniel Oniens*, at the head of a large mob, came to my house, *Jonas Turner* by name, of *West Branwick,* near *Wensbury*, and asked, "Whether I would keep from these men and go to the church?" I answered, "I go to the church very often, but I never see any of you there." Presently *Daniel Oniens*, with a great club broke part of my windows with one blow. Others laid hold of me and said, "You shall go along with us." I told them "I would not." They dragged me by force about 60 yards, and then I got loose from them. Afterwards they broke all my windows, and threw into my house three baskets full of stones to break my goods."

"Some Time in *June*, about Four in the afternoon, a mob came to my House in *West Bramwick*; I was within, and my two daughters without. They threw in stones and bricks so fast that I thought I should have been knocked on the head. Whereupon I opened the door and ran out amongst them. One of my daughters cried out, "My mother will be killed," on which they fell to throwing stones at her, She ran into a neighbour's house, but before she could shut the door they broke the bottom off with a brick-end. They followed my other daughter with stones and one with a great stake. She run into another house, much frighted, expecting to be murdered. I asked them "how they could come and abuse us thus ?" upon which one came with a large club, and swore "if I spoke another word he would knock me on the head and bury me in the ditch." Then he went to the window end broke two or three panes of glass, which were all that were left. A woman then came with a club and broke to pieces part of the tiling of the house.

Of this I am ready to make an oath.

Mary Turner."

Besides this evidence of Jonas and of Mary Turner, similar testimony is given by a John Turner also: but he apparently lived on the Wednesbury side of the brook. Another deponent, amongst a dozen or two, who testifies as to events occurring in Wednesbury and Walsall on May 30th and again on June 21st is one James Jones, of whom more anon.

On October 20th following (1713; John Wesley was again in Wednesbury, and preached "at noon in a ground near the middle of the town"—probably on the High Bullen, then an open green known as Hancock's Cross. (John Hancokes of Wednesbury served on a jury *20 Ed. III.* or A.D. 1377. See *Salt. Coll.*, vol. xiv.) In the afternoon while writing in the house of Francis Ward the rabble again collected round the door with the fierce cry, "Bring out the minister!" Then occurred the well-known episode, so often told and re-told, of his seizure and haling to Squire Lane's at Bentley Hall. A picture of this incident, as the fearless and intrepid Wesley walked bareheaded up Bridge Street towards the Red Lion posting house, has been painted by the great artist Marshall Claxton, and was purchased in 1865 by Mr Charles Nixon, of Birmingham for £400.

The ridiculous charge of "singing psalms all day" and "making folks rise at five in the morning" having failed to obtain condign punishment from either Squire Lane at Bentley, or Justice Persehouse at Walsall, John Wesley eventually got back to Wednesbury before ten at night, having providentially sustained little hurt owing partly to the fact that William Sitch, Edward Slater, John Griffiths, and Joan Parkes, when all the rest of the society had fled for their lives, had still staunchly and unflinchingly stood by their great leader for the whole of that terrible journey. Wesley lost only a little skin from his hands, and the flap of one waistcoat-pocket; (Reeves says that in the other pocket was a £20 note); and how miraculous were his several escapes may best be gathered from the Journals of John and of Charles Wesley. A great marvel is that John Wesley was not pitched headlong down a Wednesbury coal-pit on that occasion.

Under date October 25th Mr Charles Wesley writes in his diary that he was much encouraged by the patience of the brethren in Wednesbury, and as agreed upon with his brother, he responded to their pressing invitation to preach to them in the "midst of the town"—otherwise the High Bullen. He accordingly went to Wednesbury, and came "to Francis Ward's, from whence my brother had been carried last Thursday. I found the brethren assembled," he writes, "standing fast in one mind; in nothing terrified by their adversaries. The word given me for them was 'Watch ye, stand fast in the faith, quit yourselves like men, be strong.' Never was I before in so primitive an assembly." The next day he again preached openly and boldly to this intrepid people, and took several new members into the society, among them one—"upon trial" only—a worthy commonly known as Munchin, who had been the captain of the recent mob, but "whose heart the Lord had opened," so that he now fearlessly stood by the "*mon* of God" whom he had helped to rescue from the mob. But this particular incident of the previous Thursday's proceedings demands special attention by itself.

The mob from Wednesbury, Darlaston and Walsall had held John Wesley in their hands for several hours, and although they had fully intended to kill him, a few blows from which in his ecstatic excitement he had felt no pain, were the only hurt he received. The young woman and the three men already named were not quite all who in that yelling crowd had stood by him for protection. At last this man Munchin, the acknowledged captain and leader of the rabble, had turned to Wesley and said, "Sir, I will spend my life for you; follow me and not one soul here shall touch a hair of your head." Accordingly with the help of the other three or four he undertook to convoy Wesley back to the safe asylum of Francis Ward's house, and he directed the return to Wednesbury over the meadows from Walsall, and then through Friar's Park; Munchin carrying on his back across the stream at this spot, first John Wesley and then his well-to-do adherent, James Jones; afterwards proceeding along the brookside, "the backway" to Francis Ward's. An interesting account of all this appeared in *The Home Mission Record* of January 1868, from the pen of a local writer, whose appended initials S.L. practically disclose his identity: and accompanying the article was a wood engraving depicting John Wesley's strange method of re-entering the confines of Wednesbury perched on the back of Honest Munchin, who is seen sturdily wading the roaring torrent, anxiously watched from the banks by the other faithful friends. The real name of this man—for in those days nearly every one in Wednesbury was known by some nickname—was George Clifton. His cottage was situated in the lane which ran at the rear of the Fountain Inn, Holloway Bank towards Golds Hill; Honest Munchin, as he is now generally called, was therefore really a West Bromwich man. (Refer back to chap. xxxvii). This preserver of Wesley from his would-be murderers, died at Birmingham in 1789, and his tombstone in St Paul's Churchyard there gives his age as 85. A son of this man, says Reeves, died in West Bromwich Poorhouse about 1842, very old and quite blind. As to the James Jones whom he also bore across the flooded stream, he was one of Wesley's first itinerant preachers, and a man of some wealth, as he erected in this county at his own expense the first chapel (1755) for the denomination at Tipton, of which parish he was a native, (*History of Tipton* p. 29). Wesley called him to travel as early as 1743—this year we are chronicling—but he desisted in 1749 settling at Handsworth, but afterwards taking up his residence at West Bromwich. Reeves says that he died in 1783 in the "house now in the occupation of Benjamin Haynes"—1842. See also *Methodist Memorials*, p. 225.

The determination on the part of the local clergy to try their utmost to root out Methodism was worthily backed up by the Magistracy refusing the protection of the law to these persecuted people. It was at this juncture (October, 1743) there appeared that famous notice issued by Justices Lane and Persehouse, authorising a search for, and the arrest of, those "disorderly Methodist Preachers" who were "going about raising routs and riots." After this it cannot be a cause for wonderment that the mob violence found its way from the extreme confines of West Bromwich, at Bridge End, to the very heart of the parish near to Lyne and Mayers Green. A chronological table recording the march of events in this eventful year affords much food for thought and speculation; as may be seen below:—

January 8 (1742-3)	— John Wesley arrives in Wednesbury at the express desire of his brother Charles.
April 15 (1743)	— John Wesley at his second visit found the Vicar of Wednesbury turned against him.
May 30 ,,	— Riots break out in Darlaston and Wednesbury.
June 18 ,,	— Wesley receives news of the Riots.
,, 20 ,,	— Riots resumed for about a week.
,, 22 ,,	— John Wesley arrives in Wednesbury to strengthen and comfort his flock.
Oct. 20 ,,	— John Wesley in the hands of the Wednesbury Mob.
,, ,,	— Magisterial Notice issued against the Methodists.
November ,,	— Mob violence spreads from the outskirts to the centre of West Bromwich.

LVIII. — The Great Shrovetide Riots of February, 1743-4.

Except that the Rev. George Whitefield was in the neighbourhood of West Bromwich in the December of 1743, the stirring events of that year have been pretty fully chronicled in the preceding chapter. About the commencement of the following year (1744) a communication as under was made to John Wesley, and incorporated by him in his pamphlet:—

Mine and *Mare's Green* have been long noted for Wickedness of every kind; for cursing and swearing, Sabbath-breaking, idleness, and all manner of Debauchery. Few thereabouts used to go to church or trouble themselves about Religion, till some of them heard Mr *John* and *Charles Wesley*, who then had a Desire to flee from the Wrath to come. In order to this, they set apart one Evening in a Week, to meet and encourage one another, by reading a chapter, singing a Psalm or Hymn, and praying and conversing together.

The Revellers, finding their old Companions had forsaken them, were enraged at them more and more; insomuch that they came one Evening when they were met, in *November*, 1743, and unroofed the shop that was aside the house, and thrust down the Walls.

The next time we met they came in more fury than before, threw great stones, broke the windows and looking-glass, and made the roof of the house to crack and sink, and seem every moment as if it would break in upon us; insomuch that we were obliged to press out in the dark, in the midst of a shower of stones.

We thought it would be best afterwards to meet in the day, and accordingly we did. Immediately they blew a horn, to gather their company together. When they had gathered fifty or sixty they went from one house to another, threatening to kill those who would not go along with them. They went together to a house, where were things of value with a great shout, swearing they would plunder. The woman of the house went out and ask'd What they wanted? They did not make much reply; but part of them immediately went into the garden, and dashed in pieces things which cost several pounds.

We made a complaint hereof to a justice, Mr *W.G.* He took a warrant to fill up, and asked us, "What number there was in all?" We told him "About sixty." He then said, "What, you are *Methodists*! get about your business, you shall have no warrant; I am informed you are the vilest men that live."

> George Hadley,
> Samuel Hadley,
> Jos. Moore.

On the three signatories of this document Reeves makes the following comments.—

"J. Moore (as I have been told) lived near the Old-End (or Moore's End) sold clothes, and preached about the parish.

"Mr J. Moore, it is said, was a man of such talent that Madame Abney of The Mill in this parish, sent him to Oxford College (*sic*) and he became a Minister in the Established Church, at London. I have also been told that Mr Moore married Madame Abney.

"George and Samuel Hadley, were the sons of Mr Humphrey Hadley, Claypit Lane. Samuel died September 5th, 1747, aged 29 years."

The resumption of the previous summer's riots occurred with renewed vigor towards the end of January (1743-4). James Jones forwarded to Wesley a faithful account of what be describes as a kind of "invasion" of Staffordshire—England was at that time expecting another invasion of the Pretender. The tumult seems to have begun at Darlaston on the 13th of January, and by Monday the 23rd a thousand people of that parish were regularly and systematically engaged in almost daily demonstrations of violence against all avowed Methodists, On the 31st, Wednesbury Church Hill became the rendezvous for the mob, drawn from Darlaston, Walsall, West Bromwich, and all the countryside round. On Feb 1st Charles Wesley came from Birmingham, through West Bromwich, to Wednesbury, but met with no interruption.

On Monday, February 6th (so James Jones reported to John Wesley), the Methodists were in possession of information to the effect that their determined adversaries were under a binding oath to plunder them on the next day, Shrove Tuesday. Nevertheless, the society continued in prayer, keeping the day "as a fast." Francis Ward's house (in Bridge Street) being specially marked out for attack it was attempted to remove his goods, but this seems only to have precipitated matters, for a detachment of the mob got wind of the attempt, gutted the building, taking away even his fire-grates, and destroying the whole of his furniture. As Wesley comments on this, "Had the French come in that place would they have done more?" These particular rioters certainly did more; they crossed the brook; "they went to another village called *West Branwick*, and then returned back again to Wednesbury" devastation marking the line of their march only too clearly.

All the night was the mob gathering; having given a taste of their quality at Hobs Hole by despoiling the house and goods of John Griffiths the elder whom they had threatened on the 31st of the previous month), they hung around the Church Hill rather quietly till the signal was given at ten the next morning. Of the whole of the scandalous outrages perpetrated at those infamous Shrove Tuesday Riots (1743—4) it would be impossible to speak here. Those relating to West Bromwich, however, cannot be omitted.

As Reeves claims John Turner to be a West Bromwich man—he lived most probably, however, in the Potter's Lane, Wednesbury—his evidence, as printed in Wesley's tract *Christianity Exemplified at Wednesbury*, shall be given first:—

According to your request, I send you some account of what the Mob did on *Shrove Tuesday*. When I heard they were in Town and broke and stole all before them, I got out our beds and Wearing Apparel, and hid them in the Hedges, and went and stood aside of a Hedge, about 60 yards off my own House.

When the Mob came they began with breaking the windows. They then broke and stole all they could lay Hands on. They search'd and found Beds and Linnen which I had hid, and took all that they thought worth carrying away. I waded through the Brook to try if I could save some of my Goods, which a man was pulling out of the Ditch where I had hid them; his name was *David Garrington*. He told me *It would be the same here, as it was in* Ireland; *for there would be a* Massacre *very quickly, and he wished it was now*. When they were gone, my Wife, and I, and two Children came home. Our House was all laid open for both Doors were gone, and all the Windows, and the Middle Posts were broke out. Being wet and very cold, we gathered up some of the Chips (for our Goods were mostly broke into Chips, and strew'd about the Rooms) and made a Fire; but the Wind blew the Smoak so about, that we could not bear to sit by it. We knew not what to do, till one of our neighbours sent us Word we might come to his House. But one went to *Walsal* the next Day, and told the Landlord, who came and told them that received us, "They must turn out." And we expected there would not be an House to receive a *Methodist* in the whole country.

On *Ash Wednesday* I was helping Mr *Eaton* to remove some Iron, which they had not found the Day before; when Mr *William Horton* came with a Paper in his Hand and 100 Persons with him. He press'd Mr *Eaton* to sign it, who refused. Then they laid hold of me, and swore I should. I told them I would not. They caught hold of

my Collar, shook me, tore my Shirt and Waistcoat, push'd me from one to another, and ask'd again, "Will you sign the paper yet?" I told them No. They then got a cord, put it about my Neck and swore they would hang me out of hand. Others cried out, "Draw him thro' the Brook." But one of them snatch'd away the Cord, and said "If I would not set my Hand, I might go about my Business." They followed me, however with many Stones; but, by the Providence of God, I was not hurt.
March 5, 1743-4.   JOHN TURNER.

Then follow in order the testimonies of William Sitch and Mary Turner; and the very full statement of Thomas Parkes, all three witnesses being of West Bromwich parish:—

Having notice that the Mob was coming, I *William Sitch*, of *West Bromwich*, and my Wife (who had been deliver'd but a Fortnight) thought it best to go out of the House, and leave it to them, My wife, with her young Child, was forced to stay in the fields, none daring to take her into their House. At length one Man did, but he was in a little time persuaded to turn her out again. The Rioters plundered my House three several Times, and did all the Mischief they could; but blessed be God, I could rejoice therein. He has said, *As thy Day, so thy strength shall be.* And never did I find his Promise fulfilled more than at that Time.   WILLIAM SITCH.

On *Shrove-Tuesday*, after two large Mobs were past by, came four or five Men to my next Neighbour, *Jonas Turner's* House. I and another Woman followed them, to see what they would do. They first broke the Windows, then broke down the Door, and went into the House. Soon after they were in, they flung out a Box at the Chamber Window, and swore, if any touched it, they would murder them. Soon after they flung out a Bible, and one of them came out, and in great Rage cut it into Pieces with his Ax.

MARY TURNER, OF WEST BROMWICH.

They first that came to my House (*Thomas Parkes, of West Bramwick*), *on Tuesday, Feb.* 7, were five with great Clubs, whom I met at the Door. They demanded, "Whether I would deny hearing these Parsons?" I told them, "No; for I believed they spoke the Truth, as it is in Jesus, and if I were to deny them, I should deny him that sent them." They told me, "If I would not, they would plunder my House." I replied, "They must answer it at God's Bar, and I would meet them there." I asked, "Whether I had done them any Harm." "They said "No; but they have me keep to the Church." I told them, "Some of you may know that I worship among the Dissenters, but I love a good Man, let him go where he will, For there is but one Church of Christ, and if you do not belong to that Church you had better never have been born." I told them, "God has allowed me Liberty of Conscience and so have the King and Parliament, and I hope my Neighbours will too; but if not, a Day is coming, when the Persecuted and the Persecutor shall stand together: and if you wrong me now, God will right me then." While I was speaking, I caught hold of their Clubs, and the Words seemed to have some Influence on them: But by this Time there was a great Body of them gathered together; so they broke my Windows, and then the Door, and flock'd into my House, and began to break my Goods. But here the Lord suffered them not to go so far as they had done in other places. For they soon fell to plundering and loading themselves with the Things I had for myself, a Wife, and seven Children.

However, in a while I had prevailed with some of them to stop. But then they said, "I must set my Hand to their Paper." I told them, " They were cloak'd over with the name of Protestants, but none but a *Popish* Spirit would tie Men's Consciences." So I commended my Cause to God and withdrew from my House and them. As I went along one who thinks herself a Christian said, "Now I might see

God was against me." I told her "I did now feel that God was for me, and that he loved me never the less for this: For God loved *Job* on the Dunghill with only a Potsheard, as well as he did in all his Plenty." I thought she, in effect, bid me "curse God and die." May the Lord make her a Christian indeed!

When I returned to my House and saw it in Ruins, I found nothing in my Heart towards my Persecutors but Love. Neither could I doubt of God's Love to my Soul. All that is within me bless his holy Name! One day six or eight of the Mob got me among them, and said, "They were going to make Law, and we should all set our Hands to it. "I told them I would submit to the Laws of God and my Prince, but I could not to the Laws of the Devil." One of them swore "He would break my windows again." I ask'd him "if ever he heard of Jesus Christ doing so? And how he durst, when he must answer it at his Bar?" At which he stood silent.

Of the last witness Reeves says, that Mr Parkes died at Hill Top; and that Mr Philemon Parkes, schoolmaster, was his son.

Of the next deponent and his testimony much has to be said. If the initials S.L. stand for Samuel Lowe, then it was not his brother John, who held the military rank of cornet, as was surmised in chap. xlix. In either case the Lowes were "Presbyterians of the Old Meeting." It is interesting to observe the attitude assumed by the Presbyterians and Independents towards the Wesleys. Clearly they were as actively hostile as the Church party. Under date, February 1st, 1744 is recorded by Charles Wesley, that at Dudley the great preacher, "had been cruelly abused by a mob of Papists and Dissenters, the Dissenters being stirred by Mr Whiting, their minister (Presbyterian). It is probable he would have been murdered but for an honest Quaker, who favoured his escape by disguising him in the broad hat and drab coloured coat." Then the Diarist on the 2nd set out for Wednesbury, which he aptly describes as "the field of battle," where he at once with characteristic courtesy paid a visit of condolence to "Mr Egerton's widow," otherwise Mrs Egginton; for the Rev. E. Egginton, Vicar of Wednesbury, died soon after the beginning of the destructive riots of which he had been the chief instigator. [It was his successor the Rev. E. Best, whom John Wesley met by appointment in March, 1752.] In marked and striking contrast with that of all other denominations, is the position taken up by the fearless Quakers. Beside the rescue incident just given, we have another one recorded as happening very soon afterwards. According to his diary Charles Wesley preached on February 3rd, at "Tippen Green," within sight of Dudley, where a friendly Captain Dudley had kept off all persecution. Passing through Birmingham, where they tried to drown the voice of the preacher as he held forth in the Bull Ring by clanging the church bells, he preached again at Wednesbury, and got to Nottingham on February 6th, the day before the Shrove Tuesday. Intelligence of the mischief having reached Charles Wesley through friends at Lichfield he returned on the 9th and, "met our brother Ward who had fled for refuge." Then occurs the passage, "The enemy had gone to the length of his chain," an assertion based on the following episode: A Quaker happening to ride through Wednesbury they swore he was a preacher, pulled him off his horse, dragged him to a coal pit, and were with difficulty prevented from throwing him in. But this worthy member of the Society of Friends, with a courage nothing could daunt, carried the case to a successful prosecution of his assailants at the following Assizes. And from that moment the tumults in Staffordshire subsided. But not till liberty of conscience and freedom of speech had been thus vindicated at the instance of a Quaker.

And now as the chief persons concerned in the next deposition. Reeves says:—"John Sheldon, farmer lived at the Holloway, at the house now (1892) in the occupation of Samuel Harrison. It was in front of this house that Charles Wesley in 1742, and John Wesley in 1743, first preached to thousands of their attentive hearers from Wednesbury,

West Bromwich, Darlaston, Tipton, etc. John Sheldon it is said was the first man to shelter and protect John Wesley. Both he and his wife retained their piety to the end of their days; he died about 1801 at the advanced age of 101, and she two years earlier aged 99 years." Of John Sheldon and his wife during the trying ordeal of the Shrovetide Riots, the original pamphlet of 1744 gives us a most interesting sketch:—

"On SHROVE-TUESDAY, about eleven o'clock SARAH, the wife of JOHN SHELDON of *West Bramwick*, being told the Mob was coming to her House, went and met them at the Gate. Mr S——, Mr J——, and Mr S——L——, Cornet, were at the head of them. She asked John Baker, who was the captain of the Mob, What they were come for? He answered, "If she would have nothing more to do with these people, not a penny-worth of her Goods should be hurt." She made no reply. Then they broke the door open, and began breaking and plundering the Goods. One coming out with a fire-shovel. she begg'd him not to take it away. He swore "if she spoke another word he would beat her Brains out."

After they rifled the House they went to search the Barn. Some Goods were hid there, which she thought would go with the rest; so she went and sat contentedly down in the ruined House. But a Man of their own as bitter as the rest till then, desired they would not pull up the cow's stakes; so they looked no further; but seeing a Calf, they beat and lamed it in such a Manner, that they were obliged to kill it. *John Sheldon* was this while helping *Thomas Parkes* to hide his Goods, tho' he knew by the Noise they were breaking his own in Pieces. Between Two and Three he came to his House with *William Sitch*. William asked Sarah how she did? saying, "For his Part he took joyfully the spoiling of his Goods." She answered, "That seeing so much Wickedness, she could not rejoice but she blessed God she could bear it patiently, and found not the least Anger in her." *John Sheldon* seeing the Spoil they had made smiled and said, "Here is strange Work." His Wife told him, "If she had complied with their terms, not one Pennyworth would have been hurt." He replied, "That if she had complied to deny the truth, and he had found his Goods whole on that Account, he should never have been easy as long as he lived; but he blessed God that she had rather choose to suffer wrong."

Reeves further says:—"It is said the only article saved was the clock, which stood up in a corner, and the last man who left the house saw it, threw a brick-bat but missed it. This clock is still to be seen (1842) at Mr John Sheldon Peters' house, Hill Top."

The following List is printed in Wesley's tract but in copying it into his MS. Reeves has added to several of the names the places in which these ill used and much wronged people dwelt. In reprinting them here the place names are put in brackets for Reeves does not seem very certain as to their accuracy; although the death of John Eaton, August 21st, 1753 aged 60 years, is written down. with a more emphatic hand. Brerely and Bumblehole, it may he noted, are in Sedgley parish.

The Mob continued to rise for six days together. The damage they did in and about *Wednesbury* at the lowest computation, is as follows:—

						£	s.	d.
Benjamin Constable	...	...	(Wednesbury)	...	...	103	0	0
Humphrey Hands	...	...	(do)	...	...	44	6	7
John Eaton	...	...	(do)	...	...	43	11	0
John Bird	...	...	(do)	...	...	43	0	0
Richard Bolton	...	...	(Bumble-hole)	...	...	40	0	0
Francis Ward	...	...	(Wednesbury)	...	...	22	14	6
Godfrey Ward	...	...	(do)	...	...	22	6	4
John Turner	...	...	(West Bromwich)	...	...	20	0	0
William Mason	...	...	...	...	...	19	10	4

Thomas Parkes	...	...	(do)	...	...	14	0	0
John Sheldon	...	...	(do)	...	...	9	6	6
Lydia Partridge	...	...	(Near the Bridge)	...	...	2	0	0
Joseph Perry	...	...	...	...	...	1	10	0
John Darby	...	...	(Brereley)	...	...	8	13	6
Jonas Turner	...	...	(West Bromwich)	...	...	3	12	0
Richard Spittle	...	...	...	...	...	2	17	0
Jos. Spittle	...	...	(Darlaston)	...	...	1	5	0
Edward Holdbury	...	...	(Holloway)	...	...	4	10	0
Humphrey Hadley	...	...	(West Bromwich)	...	...	13	11	0
John Griffiths (sen.)	...	...	(Wednesbury)	...	...	6	6	0
Benjamin Watson	...	...	(do)	...	...	2	11	0
Thomas Smith	...	...	...	...	...	7	15	6
Edward Smith	...	...	(do)	...	...	2	5	0
William Sitch	...	...	(West Bromwich)	...	...	5	6	0
Daniel Constable	...	...	(Wednesbury)	...	...	2	13	5
Henry Addinbrook	...	...	(do)	...	...	15	14	4
Joshua Constable	...	...	(Darlaston)	...	...	14	11	0
Jos. Stubbs and Robert Dakin	...	(do)	...	...	2	0	0
Jonathan Jones	...	...	(do)	...	...	3	0	0
William Small	...	...	(do)	...	...	4	12	7
Thomas, Edwardly	...	...	...	...	...	5	0	0
John Griffiths	...	...	...	...	...	3	15	8
Edward Slater	...	...	(Wednesbury)	...	...	9	12	10

£504   17   10

House property, furniture, wearing apparel, all suffered equally at the hands of the Mob. The detail of the destruction in Wednesbury parish alone, which was the head centre of the whole of the rioting, is too voluminous to include here. Portable property was carried away wholesale to be turned into money at leisure. As to the sufferers, they "gave God glory that Satan was not allowed to touch their lives," ... "they lost all besides" ... and rejoiced with joy unspeakable." ... "In the latter end of March when Mr Charles Wesley was sheltered from the storm in London, he was not unmindful of his persecuted friends in the country, and in a few weeks he raised the sum of £60 in behalf of the Methodist families in Wednesbury, some of whom were deprived by wicked and cruel men of all the property they had in the world. This sum he committed to the care of Mr Butts, and sent him to distribute it among the most destitute."

The "gentlemen" who had set the mob to work had threatened to turn away collier or miner from employment who did not do his fair part. Respite had been offered if the persecuted Methodists would sign a document to the effect that they would never again invite these preachers to address them. Of course this offer had been rejected with scorn. On the Ash Wednesday the organisation of the Mob had aimed at terrorising a much wider area, and dividing into two or three companies, they had spread themselves in various directions, one marching six miles away from Wednesbury to Aldridge, plundering *en route*. These spoils, however, were recovered by the better disposed gentry of Walsall, who stored them first in a public room (?Guildhall) and then restored them to the proper owners. Likewise "Mr Wood, of Wednesbury" (a great inventor and ironmaster—See *Wednesbury Workshops*, p. 116)—told several that they should have back their goods on the aforementioned conditions—"to receive the preachers no more."

With reference to the two local magistrates whose names Wesley merely indicates by the initials J. D. and W. G. it must be borne in mind that in 1743 justices were very few and far between. It has been suggested that J. D. may have been John Dolphin, and W. G. may very probably have been Walter Gough, of Old Fallings, the only foundation for this suggestion being the fact that these two names occur as those of local notables in a Turnpike Act of 1748.

LIX.—THE FOUNDING OF LOCAL WESLEYANISM, 1744-1770.

When the dangers experienced by the Wesleyans from outside persecutors had in course of time gradually disappeared, their continued existence as a separate sect was almost immediately threatened by far more insidious foes from within—for "heresy" and "doubt" began to raise their treacherous heads. So far, Methodism had passed through the fiery ordeal of persecution, and had emerged purified by the process.

Allusion has already been made to John Wesley's encounter with the Wednesbury Antinomians (Chap. lvi) in 1746. Wesley doubts if that pride of heart had not made their leader, Stephen Timmins, almost mad, there was such "an uncommon wildness and fierceness in his air, his words," and behaviour. The same evening (Sunday March 23) "another of their pillars" in Birmingham, named John Ward, alias Mouse-trap Ward, defended the use of their pet phrase of "being perfect in Christ, not in themselves." As Ward contended that he might take any article out of a shop if he stood in need of it, and that he had a right to all the women in the world if they gave their consent, Wesley in his wrath writes "Surely these are the first-born children of Satan!" Not only were these Antinomians found in Wednesbury, Birmingham and Dudley, but Reeves says: "West Bromwich was at that time and for many years after, over-run with Antinomians. The following are the names of some of them—John Ward (?Birmingham) Stephen Timmins (the leader, from Wednesbury) John Sedgley, John Carr, John Price, Thomas Parkes, William Turner, Thomas Hutchinson, John Hall, Thomas Hall, Francis Clemson, etc.

Thirty years later (27 March, 1776) John Wesley makes this record: "I preached at Dudley in the midst of the Antinomians and backsliders." But as it were to soften the pain he adds to this entry, "In the evening I preached to our old flock at Wednesbury, and the old spirit was amongst them."

The year 1751 brought Wesley again into conflict with the Baptists of South Staffordshire. On April 3rd he writes: "I made an end of visiting the classes, miserably shattered by showers of strange doctrines. At one I preached at Tipton Green where the Baptists also have been making havoc of the flock." While preaching at Dudley two days previously, he "had desired John Haime to preach at Wednesbury. But when I came he had just begun the hymn. So I had an opportunity of speaking again to that willing people. What a work would have been in all these parts if it had not been for doubtful disputants! If the Predestinarians had not thrown back those who began to run well, partly into the world, partly to the Baptist, and partly into endless disputes concerning the secret counsels of God. While we carried our lives in our hands, none of them came near; the waves ran too high for them. But when all was calm, they poured in on all sides and bereaved us of our children. Out of these they formed one Society here [Wednesbury] one at Dudley, and another at Birmingham. Many indeed, though torn from us, would not stay with them, but broke out into the wildest enthusiasm. But still they were called Methodists, and so all their drunkenness and blasphemies were imputed to us."

Also on the day previous, namely, the 2nd of April, preaching to the Wednesbury flock in the rain which they patiently endured, he "gave them all an earnest caution not to lean on broken reeds, on opinions of any kind; and even the Predestinarians received it in love, and told me it was highly seasonable."

This Calvinistic doctrine of "particular election" or *predestination* (which even Arminius also defended), seems to have been rampant in this locality. As to the Antinomianism it was also but a local manifestation on the part of an obscure church, and by no means characteristic generally of the Baptist body, than whom no denomination is so strict in all matters relating to doctrine and church discipline.

And with regard to the discipline and early organising of Methodism; we find that several converts, in West Bromwich and elsewhere, threw open their houses for the meetings of the society as soon as formed there. At these meetings the brethren came together for prayer, singing hymns, and reading the scripture. Among those who opened their houses were James Wheatley and Joseph Heywood. Of James Wheatley we learn that he lived in the house opposite Dagger Hall, and was for some time "a preacher, late in connection with Messrs Wesley and the Conference." He was "the first preacher expelled by Mr Wesley in 1751." After this "he preached about the parish, and sometimes on a Sunday evening in his own house." He tried to obtain a following of his own, and to accomplish his purpose he bought a piece of land on the Heath—now Paradise Street—and began to build a room in which his followers could meet, but he did not finish it. Thus early in the history of local Methodism did, schism lift its head!

About 1760, five young men banded themselves together for religious purposes and mutual improvement generally: they were James Mayo, James Bayley, Thomas Russell, Thomas Ault, and Francis Asbury. Of the last named we have yet much more to learn. It was the custom of these young men to walk to Wednesbury every Sunday morning to the 5 o'clock service, and when it was over they returned to West Bromwich and attended church twice, going back again at 8 o'clock to the evening service at Wednesbury. (For many years the societies met at 5 in the morning, but this was ultimately altered to 8 o'clock). The preachers at Wednesbury at this time were Mr Mather and Mr Fugill. These preached at West Bromwich and at Wednesbury in turn; using the dwelling-house of the more loyal Joseph Heywood, already mentioned, in the former parish.

In 1764 the room, which had been partly built by James Wheatley, was bought by James Bayley and Joseph Russell. They finished the building, and it was opened as a Methodist preaching room—the first erected in West Bromwich.

Even with the master mind of John Wesley to guide its affairs and to direct its policy, it took time to organise Methodism into a systematised order of church government. The names of some of these early leaders in West Bromwich will occur again in tracing the history of the establishment of Wesley's new hierarchy. For instance there was Francis Asbury: he was fifteen when he joined the society, and at the age of seventeen he began to preach (1762). The year following he was appointed "Leader of the Society Class at West Bromwich Heath," a position he retained till he entered the ministry in 1767.

Preachers at first being scarce, sermons to the members of these societies were consequently few. And although Wesley, himself, was so many times staying on the confines of West Bromwich parish (at Wednesbury Bridge) and had at first always used the Holloway we do not find many recorded instances of his preaching in the heart of the parish. Here are some set down in his JOURNAL.

"1768. March 20th. About one I preached on West Bromwich Heath; in the evening near the preaching house [? Meeting Street] in Wednesbury. The north wind cut like a razor. &c."

"1770. Sunday, March 18th. At half an hour after one I was to preach at Bromwich Heath, but the house would scarce contain a fourth of the congregation; so I made a virtue of necessity, and preached in a ground where there was room for all that came.

"1774. March 19th. At noon I preached at Bromwich Heath, and the room being far too small stood in Mr. Wiley's court-yard, notwithstanding the keen north east wind." (This is, no doubt, at Mr Whyley's, the Oak House).

"1779. Sunday, March 21st. Just at the time of preaching at Bromwich Heath, began such a storm as that which ushered in the year. Yet as no house could contain the people, I was constrained to stand in the court yard. For a moment I was afraid of the tiles falling on the people; but they regarded nothing but the word. As I concluded we had a furious shower of hail."

The first preachers were frequently removed, sometimes at the end of three months, and often at six months. The first preacher who laboured in the Staffordshire Round was John Houghton, dating from 1744; the next Thomas Williams 1745. These good men were of course in the thick of the riots and persecutions. Then there was John Nelson who records in his diary in 1745 "I found peace at Wednesbury . . several who had been persecutors were converted." Another preacher however, Richard Moss, says "Monday June 17th, 1745. I came to Wednesbury But the brethren would not suffer me to stay, the constables being resolved to press me." This was, no doubt, an activity on the part of the Wednesbury constables, inspired by that precious manifesto of the Magistrates Lane and Persehouse. Near the close of 1796, Joseph Cownley encountered violence from a Darlaston mob, and again in Wednesbury and Walsall. A charge of "superstition" was actually brought against these infant societies.

About 1747, Samuel Taylor, late vicar of Quinton, also laboured in the Staffordshire Round. Once when preaching at Wednesbury he exclaimed aloud, as he noted the threatening aspect of some hostile hearers, "Were I but called to the honour of martyrdom, as my great-great grandfather was, I trust that I should be able to stand in the day of trial, and like him, go through the flames to Glory." His allusion was to Dr. Rowland Taylor, of Hadleigh, in Suffolk, who suffered death during the Marian Persecutions in 1555. But he was not to suffer at the stake in Wednesbury Market Place, in emulation of his historic progenitor; the sullen assembly preserved peace.

Of John Houghton, we learn that he was again in those parts in 1748, when he was taken before Lord Dudley to answer for "preaching." His lordship, on asking what was the offence, met with the reply, "He preaches and he prays without using a prayer book!" His lordship then inquired, "Does he repeat the Lord's Prayer?" "Yes, my lord." "Did he pray for the king?" "Yes, my lord." "Why then," said Lord Dudley; "Mr Houghton, you may go and preach and pray wherever you please."

In 1749 Mr John Madden was another preacher who laboured in this Round. But as there were no "Stations of the Preachers" printed till 1765, it is difficult to discover the names of all the itinerant ministers of the early Wesleyan period.

But during these early days the personal presence of John Wesley on many occasions did much to strengthen the cause. In 1752 he met Mr Best, the Vicar of Wednesbury, by special appointment, and speaks very highly of the Vicar's good intentions. In fact, Wesley records that in his own flock "the genuine Gospel runs and is glorified" in Wednesbury. "On Wednesday, March 23rd," continues Wesley, "I spent an agreeable hour with Mr ——, Curate of W——, an honest upright man." Yet the year before (1751) Charles Wesley, arriving at Tipton, had received from James Jones a melancholy account of the Society at Wednesbury, which from 300 "was reduced to 70 weak, lifeless members." Many of the old converts who had borne the heat and burden of the day had removed from steadfastness; the wranglings and janglings of the Predestinarians had done the mischief.

On July 8th Charles Wesley says "At six I preached on Bromwich Heath to a multitude of the poor, who heard me gladly, and I knew not when to leave off." On the 10th he gave an exhortation to the people of Wednesbury, among whom a revival apparently took place before his brother came some months afterwards. "The curate met me," he writes, "a well-disposed youth, just come from college, where his tutor Mr Bentham, gave him an early prejudice for religion. He invited me to his lodgings, joined with us in serious conversation, and singing, and seeming ready for all good impressions." Thus recognised by the regular clergy there was more hope for the spread of Methodism "The society was all in a flame of love. They made me full amends for my sorrow at Wednesbury." Taking his leave on July 12th, he adds, "Sister Perrin met and found much grace among the women, Half-a-dozen more wandering sheep I gathered in, and restored to their brethren." Thus all was left well for John Wesley's next visit, as we have seen.

As the detailed information respecting these visits of John and Charles Wesley are obtainable so easily from their respective published JOURNALS, so also we have a work of reference which similarly aids us with regard to the earliest Wesleyan preachers into whose labours we are now making investigation. The work in question is a local production entitled METHODIST MEMORIAL, and was compiled by the Rev. Charles Atmore on the same plan as Calamy's "Nonconformists' Memorial." It contains brief notices of most of the early preachers, with a chronological list of all the preachers living at the time of its publication. The preface is dated "Wednesbury, 17 August. 1801," but the book was printed by "Richard Edwards, Broad Street, Bristol," and "sold by G. Whitfield, City Road." Of the writer, BIBLIOTHECA STAFFORDIENSIS contains the following entry:—

"Rev. Charles Atmore, Wesleyan Minister. 'The Grace of God manifested.' In a short Account of the Life and Death of Mrs. R. Emmet of Halifax, and Mrs Slater and William Wright of Wednesbury. Dated Wednesbury, 31 January, 1801." See also *Wesleyan Magazine* (1805), 78-82.

LX.—BISHOP ASBURY OF HANDSWORTH AND OTHER LOCAL NOTABLES OF EARLY WESLEYANISM.

An illustrated volume entitled *Black Country Methodism*, by A. Camden Pratt (*London, C. H. Kelly, 1891*), is a most interesting work, especially to readers in this neighbourhood where so many local associations with the founding of Wesleyanism abound.

That Methodism found a congenial home in the hearts of Black Country men is quite manifest from its present flourishing condition, and from the uninterrupted steadiness with which it has grown ever since its first inception here. Of the early workers in the cause, and their devotion to its highest interests, some brief account will be necessary to the ordinary reader unconnected with the denomination; and no better beginning can be made than with "the five young men" who banded themselves together in West Bromwich in 1760.

FRANCIS ASBURY was the son of Joseph and Elizabeth Asbury, and was born in Handsworth, near the foot of Hamstead bridge August 20th, 1745. While Francis was quite a child, the family removed into Barr parish, and it has been said Francis was born there, but this is not correct. He says in his *Journal*, Vol. II page 133, "My parents had but two children, a daughter called Sarah, and myself. My lovely sister died in infancy; she was a favourite, And my dear mother being very affectionate, sunk into deep distress at the loss of a darling child, from which she was not relieved for many years. It was under this dispensation that God was pleased to open the eyes of her mind, she living in a very dark, dark, dark day and place. She now began to read almost constantly when leisure presented the opportunity. When a child, I thought it strange my mother should stand by a large window poring over a book for hours together. From my childhood I may say I have neither '——dared an oath nor hazarded a lie.' . . . My foible was the ordinary foible of children—fondness for play, but I abhorred mischief and wickedness, although my mates were amongst the vilest of the vile for lying, swearing, fighting, and whatever else boys of their age and evil habits were likely to be guilty of; from such society I very often returned home uneasy and melancholly; and although driven away by my better principles, still I would return, hoping to find happiness, where I never found it. Sometime I was much ridiculed, and called *Methodist parson*, because my mother invited any people who had the appearance of religion to her house. I was sent to school early, and began to read the Bible between six and seven years of age, and greatly delighted in the historical part of it. My schoolmaster [one Arthur Taylor, sen., who kept school at Snarls Green, Great Barr], was a great churl, and used to beat me cruelly; this drove me to prayer, and it appeared to me that God was very near to me. My father having but one son, greatly desired to keep me at school, he cared not how long, but in the design he was disappointed; for my master, by his severity, had filled me with such horrible dread, that with me anything was preferable to going to school. I lived some time in one of the wealthiest and most ungodly families we had in the parish; here I became vain, but not openly wicked. Some months after this I returned home, and made my choice when about thirteen years and a half old to learn a branch of business, at which I wrought about six years and a half, during this time I enjoyed great liberty, and in the family was treated more like a son or an equal than an apprentice.

Soon after I entered on that business God sent a pious man, *not* a Methodist, into our neighbourhood, and my mother invited him to our house, by his conversation and prayers I was awakened before I was fourteen years of age. It was now easy and pleasing to leave my company, and I began to pray morning and evening, being drawn by the cords of love, as with the bands of a man. I soon left our blind priest, and went to West Bromwich Church: here I heard Ryland, Stillingfleet, Talbot, Bagnall, Mansfield, Hawes, and Venn, great names, and esteemed Gospel ministers. I became very serious, reading a great deal—Whitfield and Cennick's sermons, and every good book I could meet with. It was not long before I began to enquire of my mother who, where, what were the Methodists? She gave me a favourable account, and directed me to a person that could take me to Wednesbury to hear them. I soon found this was not the church, but it was better. The people were so devout—men and women kneeling down, saying *Amen*. Now behold! they were singing hymns—sweet sound! Why, strange to tell, the preacher had no prayer-book, and yet he prayed wonderfully. What was yet more extraordinary the man took his text and had no sermon-book: thought I, this is wonderful indeed. . . . On a certain time when we were praying in my father's barn, I believe the Lord pardoned my sins, and justified my soul; but my companions reasoned me out of this belief, saying "Mr Mather said a believer was as happy as if he was in heaven." I thought I was not as happy as I would be there, and gave up my confidence, and that for months; yet I was happy; free from guilt and fear, and had power over sin, and felt great inward joy. After this we met for reading and prayer and had large and good meetings, and were much persecuted, until the persons at whose houses we held them were afraid, and they were discontinued. I then held meetings frequently at my father's house, exhorting the people there, as also at Sutton Coldfield, and several souls professed to find peace through my labour. I met class awhile at Bromwich-Heath, and met in band at Wednesbury. I had preached some months before I publicly appeared in the Methodist meeting houses; when my labour became more public and extensive, some were amazed, not knowing how I had exercised elsewhere. Behold me now a local preacher, the humble and willing servant of any and of every preacher that called on me by night, or by day; being ready with hasty steps to go far and wide to do good; visiting Derbyshire, Staffordshire, Warwickshire, Worcestershire, and indeed almost every place within my reach for the sake of precious souls, preaching, generally, three, four, and five times a week, and at the same time pursuing my calling. I think, when I was between one and twenty-two years of age, I gave myself up to God and his work, after acting as a local preacher near the space of five years."

It was in 1760 that Francis Asbury, then only 15 years old, joined the young men, as recorded in the last chapter. In 1762 he began to preach (locally) and the following year was appointed Leader of the Society Class at West Bromwich Heath, retaining this position until he entered the ministry in 1767—admitted on trial at the Bedfordshire Conference. The Conference of 1771 appointed him for America. He landed at Philadelphia October 27th, and was present at the first Conference held in America, 1773. In 1784 he was ordained Bishop by the unanimous vote of the General Conference. [Wesley claimed that in the Primitive Church bishops and presbyters were the same order. And as the American brethren were totally disentangled from the State and from the English hierarchy, he was at liberty to follow the Scriptures and the Primitive Church, and so appointed Methodist Bishops, or Superintendents, of whom Asbury and Dr. Coke were the first. Asbury was known as Bishop of Baltimore in the Methodist Episcopal Church.†] Bishop Asbury, in the course of his career, preached nearly 18,000 sermons, travelled nearly 150,000 miles, presided at 270 Conferences, and is said to have ordained more ministers (nearly 3,000) than any other man ever did. Extracts from his correspondence inform us that in 1809 he was "sinking under the weight of labour and infirmity; last year I had to travel on crutches several hundred miles, the face of the country is such I cannot use *wheels*"—*(Letter to Dr. Coke)*: That "the annual duty of our Superintendents is great; they have to visit eight conferences, and make arrangements for nearly 620 preachers; they have to ride near 6,000 miles in eight months through wildernesses and devious lonely wilds, sometimes waterbound, but never weatherbound."

It was Francis Asbury who organised the first Sabbath School in America. This school was established for the benefit of the slaves in the Southern States, 1786. Bishop Asbury died near Fredericksburg, Virginia, 31st March, 1816. He was conspicuous for his piety for plainness of dress and simplicity of manner, for zeal, perseverance, and endurance of sufferings. The motto engraved on his seal was "Show thyself approved of God." A minute account of his career may be found in The Pioneer Bishop by W. P. Strickland (*Manchester* 1860). See also Methodist Magazine. Vol. xxxiii, p. 84 and p. 483 (1810).

To perpetuate the memory of this good man there has been erected in his native parish of Handsworth an Asbury Memorial Chapel. In America Cokesbury College took its name from Coke and Asbury.

---

† In a 64 pp. pamphlet, entitled *The Increase, Influence, and Stability of unestablished Religion,* written by one Jacob Stanley, dating from Wednesbury, 25 June, 1813, and printed by Joshua Booth, also of Wednesbury, the writer deals very vigorously with this question, and in the course of his argument says, "You may call men *bishops* or *deacons* but unless they have the qualifications essential to these offices they no more resemble Apostolical bishops and deacons than an idiot resembles a philosopher or a knave an honest man" A copy of this work is preserved in the Wednesbury Free Library.

Methodism was planted in America in 1769. By the Peace of 1783 the independence of the United States was established. Wesley was at first head of this American Methodist movement, but at a general conference held at Baltimore, commencing Christmas Eve 1784, the movement was placed on a new footing. Wesley appointed Dr. Thomas Coke and the Rev. F. Asbury, general superintendents or bishops of the Methodist Episcopal Church in America. From this moment Wesley gave up his personal authority over the American societies to their own Bishops, Presbyters, Deacons, etc. At this conference there were present 60 preachers, 21 others were absent. Richard Whatcoat and Thomas Vasey, itinerant preachers, had also been sent out to America by Wesley; for the assistance of Dr. Coke he had appointed these two elders or presbyters. The recorded numbers of membership with the Methodist Episcopal Church in U.S.A. about that time were—

1787 — 25,347 members.
1791 — 57,621   ,,
1800 — 49,115 whites, 12,236 blacks.

JAMES MAYO, another of the "five young men" was appointed to succeed Francis Asbury as Leader of the West Bromwich Society. He led the class till he removed to Birmingham in 1779. Reeves makes a note—"John Mayo lived next door to the room"— that is, the preaching-room in Paradise Street.

THOMAS AULT, another of the band, was the successor of James Mayo. He conducted the class for more than twenty years, and then he resigned because the members ceased to attend Church, "a step of which he could not approve." Mr Ault was Parish Clerk of West Bromwich for twenty-five years, and in a letter of an autobiographical nature he says—"My father and mother were religious and lived at Aldridge where they suffered the loss of their goods by a lawless mob about 1743, two years before I was born. I was instructed in the principles of religion from a child, and had serious thoughts when I was about seven years of age. When I was sixteen I began to seek the Lord earnestly . . . My father and mother came to live at Barr about the same time, and I became acquainted with Francis Asbury. He and me (*sic*) and three or four more used to go to Wednesbury in the morning of the Lord's Day to the preaching at 8 of the clock, and when that was over, twice to West Bromwich Church, and at 5 in the evening to Wednesbury again. . . . The local preachers [at the preaching house partly built by Wheatley] were James Mayo and James Jones, and others that came sometimes from Birmingham. James Mayo was leader of the class for some years, the number of which seldom was so many as twenty; this continued till 1779, when he went to live at Birmingham, and as they were left without a leader, at the request of Mr Bayley and the people I undertook that task, and was leader for more than twenty years, till they left off going to church, which was a step I did not approve. Since that time I wish them well, and hear them sometimes, but am not joined to them. Thomas Ault. May 14th, 1821." The writer was in his 76th year at this time; he rejoined the society 7th February, 1822, and died 23rd October, 1825, aged 80 years, his funeral sermon being preached by Mr Seth Morris. He had lived with the wife of his youth 56 years, and for 54 years of that period in the house adjoining the Room, namely, from 1769 to 1823. From 1769 to 1799 his house had always been open for the reception of the preachers, both local and travelling. He was the eldest son of one Robert Ault, a local preacher, who lived the later portion of his life in Spon Lane.

JAMES BAYLEY and THOMAS RUSSELL, who make up this notable quintette of primitive Wesleyans, were both personally known and remembered by Reeves. Bayley was a park keeper at Sandwell for forty-seven years, and died 19th December, 1798, aged 71. Russell was a carpenter, who dwelt in Over-end, and died shortly after his colleague, Bayley.

*   *   *   *   *   *   *

Of JAMES WHEATLEY it is furthered noted by Reeves that after his expulsion by Wesley in 1751 he went to reside at Norwich, where he had a Society and a Chapel. his people being called Lambs, and his chapel The Tabernacle. He requested John Wesley to take to his Society, and then left the place. About 1759 he came to live in West Bromwich again, leaving it once more in 1764. Towards his preaching-house he is said to have collected £20, intending it to be much larger than it was.

"JOSEPH HEYWOOD lived near old Stephen Timmins, and the house was taken down about the year 1836"—apparently this was in West Bromwich perhaps near Wednesbury Bridge.

HENRY FOXALL was born in Monmouthshire, 24th May, 1758, and in his youth lived with his parents at The Old Forge, West Bromwich. He was accustomed to hear in his childhood the preaching of the Gospel both by the Methodist preacher, and at the Church, in West Bromwich. He saw true religion daily exemplified in the lives of his mother, of Mrs Asbury, and of many of his neighbours. About 1793, he removed to Ireland, and it was there he was converted under the preaching of an itinerant Methodist. Emigrating to America he settled at George Town, where he acquired much wealth. He erected at his own cost, in the city of Washington, a commodious chapel (opened by the venerable Bishop Asbury) in lieu of a small school-room previously used for meetings. It was called "The Foundry," partly in allusion to Mr Foxall's business. This benefactor for years subscribed £50 to the Wesleyan Missionary Society, and at his death bequeathed 5,000 dollars to the Society, and a like amount to the Methodist Connection in America. He paid a visit to this country in 1816 and preached in this neighbourhood, and during a second visit in 1823 he died at Mr Crockett's, Handsworth, and lies buried in West Bromwich churchyard.

RICHARD COATES was an Itinerant Methodist Preacher of the Staffordshire Circuit. By his hard work in this locality he brought on an early death— Conference had appointed him only in 1764—and he died at Wednesbury at the age of 28 in the year 1765. He was buried in Wednesbury Churchyard, and his funeral sermon was eloquently preached by Mr Mather.

RICHARD WHATCOAT, connected in early life with Darlaston, also became a bishop of the Methodist Episcopal Church of America. See *History of Darlaston*, pp. 130-131.

HARVEY WALKLATE MORTIMER was born at Newcastle, Staffordshire, 1753. While apprenticed at Hill Top, West Bromwich, he became a zealous Wesleyan (1770). He died 1819 in London, treasurer of the City Road Chapel. See *Methodist Magazine*, Vol. xlii., p 384.

LXI.—WESLEYAN PLACES OF WORSHIP.

At first any special place of meeting, devoted exclusively to the use of the very earliest Wesleyan societies was generally designated "The Room,"— at Newcastle-upon-Tyne it was "The Orphan House," and one place mentioned in the last chapter was "The Foundry"—a name that gave way in time to "The Preaching House," and ultimately to the more convenient designation of "Chapel."

It was the custom so long as the ROOM at West Bromwich (1764) was occupied for Preaching, for the men to sit on the right hand side of the preacher and the women on the left. "The Room was about 24 feet square, with a pillar in the centre. There were three pews on the right hand of the Preacher and one on his left hand. These had only been erected a few years."

This Room did not come into very extensive use for some years, Wednesbury continuing to be the centre of Methodism for a considerable period. And not only did such men as Asbury and his colleagues find their way thither, but its influence was sufficient to attract a man moving in the highest spheres of life like the second Earl of Dartmouth. (*Harper's Weekly* once described Asbury as "the greatest hero of their nation next to Washington.")

This Lord Dartmouth was a personal friend of John Wesley, who sometimes waited upon his Lordship at his residence at Black-heath, Kent. In the early days of Methodism, his Lordship would sometimes attend the preaching at Wednesbury, and Reeves was informed by an old Methodist that he was wont to say, "When I am here, I am Brother Dartmouth—but anywhere else I am My Lord Dartmouth." The Rev. Mr Sidney speaking of him says, "Lord Dartmouth was one of those excellent men who in a period of wide spreading error and apathy towards real religion, enjoyed the privilege of a knowledge of divine truth, and manifested a sincere love for the Preachers of the Gospel. He was the friend of several zealous Clergymen, and was glad to welcome to his house a despised follower of a despised Master."

Writing in 1778 (Monday February 2nd) John Wesley says:—"I had the satisfaction of spending an hour with that real patriot Lord D——. What an unheard of thing it is, that even in a court he should retain all his sincerity! He is indeed (what I doubt Secretary Craggs never was)

'Statesman, yet friend to Truth.'

Perhaps no prince in Europe besides King George, is served by two of the honestest and two of the most sensible men in the Kingdom." Bearing so truly noble a character, it is not surprising to learn that Lord Dartmouth should have made periodical pilgrimages from Sandwell Hall to Wednesbury Preaching House (see chap. xliii).

In 1771 Francis Asbury preached for the last time in The Room at West Bromwich, ere he departed for America. About this time the Society here consisted of James Bayley and his wife, Robert Ault and wife, Ann Firm, Sarah Mallin, Ann Cutler, Mrs Taylor, Samuel Clift and wife, Samuel Cutler and wife, Jonathan Turton, Joseph Heywood, and Thomas Ault and wife. Occasionally Mrs Foxall, Mrs Asbury. and the families of Brettell and Mortimer, and others would attend the preachings. Till 1803 the Society rarely reached a maximum of twenty members.

In 1790 John Wesley paid his last visit to Staffordshire. It was Monday, March 22, that he records how he "went to his old friends at Wednesbury, where the work of God greatly revives. Business has exceedingly decreased, and most of them have left the town." Reeves had in his possession a Class List of the West Bromwich Society for this year (1790) which contained the following names—Thomas Ault, Ann Ault, Samuel Bayliss, John Barton, Ann Barton, Ann Tonks, Jona. Turton, Mary Taylor, Elizth. Timmins, Joseph Partridge, Jabez Ault, Willm. Horton, Willm. Bissaker, Francis Moss and Elizth. Ivey—the last marked "gone away to Birmingham."

About the year 1800 James Heaton, a native of West Bromwich, joined the Society, he succeeded Thomas Ault, who with John Barton had latterly kept the little Society together, after its continuous but unobtrusive existence of about forty years. At the Conference of 1802 the Revs. T. Taylor and Peter Haslam were stationed at Birmingham, and these two made a practice of preaching at West Bromwich on alternate Monday evenings, and visiting the friends too, from home to home. William Ault was added to the Society, George Taylor was appointed a Leader, and so was James Heaton who as a local preacher came to reside at Spon Lane for greater convenience. The Sunday preachings about this time were fixed for 11 a.m. instead of 8 a.m. as had previously been the custom. It was in 1803 that the first Prayer Meeting was held at Ireland Green by "six men from Wednesbury," who met regularly "under

Thomas Simcox's tree." It is remarkable how the workings of earlier Wesleyanism always radiated from Wednesbury as its central point. The first Sunday School in West Bromwich had been that at the Old Meeting, opened in 1786. Next the Old Church Sunday School was opened in 1788. The first Wesleyan Sunday School was now opened in 1803, at the Preaching-room, in Paradise Street, William Ault and Joseph Russell actively taking up this department of work. In 1764, when the Room was built, the population of West Bromwich was but about 2,000. The congregation grew very steadily till further accommodation was sorely needed, and consequently, in 1805, it was decided to build a new CHAPEL. A piece of land was bought, situated at the corner of the Common, the site of old St. George's Hall. The first stone was laid by Mr Heaton, in March, 1806, near the north-west corner of the building, which was 30 feet long and 32 feet wide, inside measurement. The New Chapel was opened by Rev. Richard Reece, on Christmas Day 1806, the collections realising about £9. In the same year (1806), was established "The Friendly Society" which soon became a flourishing institution.

The Appendices to Reeves MS. Book are so full of interesting detail and local colouring that it is to be hoped Mr J. Lees Taylor will one day get the whole of it printed. *Appendix I.* gives the sums collected towards "entertaining the Preachers that come to preach the Gospel in Mr Wesley's chapel at West Bromwich." The exact dates and amounts are set down from 1785 to 1788. Then the payments are curious. May 15th, 1785, John Ault was paid 4s.6d. for three times entertaining the preacher. Later, the item "Entertainment" is more frequently set down at 2d., $2\frac{1}{2}$d., or 3d. "Candles" is an item often recurring, so is "Ale" at 2d. or 4d., and sometimes "Rum" at 2d. or 7d. "Cleaning," "besoms," and "brushes" testify to the cleanliness of The Room as does "Horse-corn" to the only means of locomotion then available for the itinerants. *Appendix II.* gives extracts from a Vestry Book ranging from 1805 to 1822, with entries relating to Class Money, Monthly Collections, Tickets, Love Feasts, Sacraments, &c., the members' names appearing in detail.

With the old "Room," old members were also passing away. On December 18th, 1806, died Edward Bagnall, coal-master, of Wednesbury, in his 45th year. He was a good man and a generous supporter of the Wesleyan cause. In April had died in London Mrs Mortimer, aged 48 years who was a daughter of Francis and Jane Whitehead, of Wednesbury. This Jane Whitehead died at Wednesbury September, 1807, in her 81st year; and it is recorded on her gravestone that she was one of the first Methodists to join John and Charles Wesley; she was a daughter of that John Griffiths, of Hobs Hole who had suffered so severely in the Riots. Her husband died 1816. Thus were at this time passing away some of the pioneers of Wesleyanism.

Methodism at The Old Forge, West Bromwich, had also been strong enough to possess its own chapel—about 1790. But when The Forge stopped working, the Superintendent of the Wednesbury Circuit reluctantly gave his consent for the sale of the building to the Independents, but not till about 1821.

In 1811 West Bromwich became the head of a Circuit, the first minister being the Rev. John A. Lomas. This was an epoch in the history of West Bromwich Methodism. In 1813 a large new Sunday School of two rooms was erected for 200 scholars; It was opened on December 26th of that year.

A West Bromwich Circuit Plan of 1821 gives the following places: West Bromwich, Birmingham, Barr, Nineveh, French Walls, White Heath Gate, Glass House, and Greets Green. The most active members of society were now Mr John Bagnall,: founder of the well-known firm of ironmasters, and Mr Job Franks. In 1821 the society, numbering 280, drew some of its members from outlying places such as Nineveh (Handsworth) and French Walls (Smethwick). The Chapel being found now too small, it was elongated some 20 feet at a cost of £350, and re-opened on October 24th of this year (1821), the collections realising £70. It may here be noted that John Bagnall died November 23, 1829, and that the Rev. Jacob Stanley, of Wednesbury preached his funeral sermon (John Wilkinson, of Bradley, the great iron master, had also befriended the Methodists of Moxley and Bilston.) The year 1824 was marked by the establishment of a Methodist Tract Society in West Bromwich.

When in 1831 the Rev. R. Pickering was appointed to the Circuit, the chapel was again too circumscribed in its dimensions for the still growing numbers of its regular attendants. A sum of £586 was expended in adding another thirty feet to the length of the building, and immediately on its re-opening, in 1832, every available seat was "let." The trustees soon afterwards (7th November, 1833) held a vestry meeting, and to put things on an orderly footing appointed Mr John Bagnall as treasurer and Mr James Hartley as secretary. (The Hartley family had then recently come to reside in Spon Lane, and the moral, social, and religious influence exerted by them was highly advantageous to the cause). A leader of the singing was also appointed at a salary of £2 a year, while no less than four beadles at a guinea a year were found requisite for upholding the dignity and maintaining the orderliness of the chapel services and proceedings.

Ideas and numbers still continued to expand, and it was soon afterwards determined to convert the chapel into a schoolroom, and to erect an entirely new place of worship. A Building Committee was appointed including the names of John Silvester, a man who was thorough in everything he undertook; Thomas Bagnall, an ironmaster; and James Hartley, connected with the Crown Glass Works at Spon Lane. An architect—Mr Cutts, of Birmingham— according to instructions prepared plans which he submitted to the committee at Mr Bagnall's, the Oak House, in June, 1834. The estimated cost of the proposed chapel was £3,000, and the designs were approved at that figure. The site in High Street was purchased from Mr Carter at the price of £700. Before active operations could be commenced, the minister (the Rev. R. Pickering) died. With much care, however, the work was carried out, and the chapel was opened 5th June 1835, the total collections at all the services realising upwards of £700, while the gross cost of the undertaking approached nearer to £5,000 than £3,000.

The old Chapel was made into two schoolrooms. In January, 1838, Day Schools, including an Infants' Department were opened there in Paradise Street, Mr Bakewell being appointed master. On every hand there were thus indications of the continued vigorous growth of Wesleyan Methodism in West Bromwich. The High Street Chapel still stands a monument of solidity, characteristic of the men who erected it. Architecturally, its two chief pretensions are those to commodiousness and substantiality. Its seating capacity is 2,000, which as becomes the mother chapel of the parish is no mean figure.

Wednesbury, from its close connection and intimate association with the personality of the founder of the sect, naturally became the first great local centre of Wesleyanism in these parts. When in after years Birmingham outgrew Wednesbury in local influence a division took place, after which West Bromwich was worked from Birmingham, although Harvill's Hawthorn and Swan Village Chapels still remained for years in the Wednesbury district.

Harvill's Hawthorn Chapel, as a matter of fact, was an offshoot of the Wednesbury society. The earliest services were held in Martin's Farm which stood on the site of The Hollies, Councillor Peters' residence at the corner of Coles Lane. When Mr James Botteley came to reside at Hill Top this little society began to grow rapidly. An endeavour had been made about this time by Mr Cooper, Pastor of the "Old Meeting," to establish services in a Barn at Harvill's Hawthorn; but meeting with little success, Mr Horton was induced to let the Barn to the Wesleyan Society, whose numbers had now grown so much as to make their Farm House accommodation quite inadequate. That portion of the Barn at first brought into use was quickly outgrown, and then the threshing floor, and at last the whole of the Barn were brought into occupation. To meet the further requirements of this growing body of worshippers, a gallery was erected at one end, to which an outside brick staircase gave access, chiefly for the use of the pupils of Mr Marshall, who had established a school in Wittons Lane. So this society continued to grow till in 1830 a chapel was built, which is now converted into the residence for the minister. The present chapel was erected in 1850, Mr Simpson, of Leeds being the architect, and Mr John Lees the builder. It cost £7,000, and seats 900 worshippers, being 64ft, by 54ft. Collections at opening services amounted to £620.

Hill Top Wesleyanism is of both ancient and sturdy growth, as the history of Harvill's Hawthorn Society so clearly makes manifest. One of the earliest adherents of John Wesley, as already fully noted, was John Sheldon, who lived at Holloway Bank, and suffered in the Great Riots. His son had eight daughters, every one of whom married a man prominent in the Wesleyan body, and who are represented now by descendants still (or till recent years) well known in local Wesleyan circles, such as those who bear the name of Field, Woodward, Peters, Bayley, and others.

Sheldon lived to a great age; the character of the man may be very fairly gauged by the fact that, as he lay on his bed, when a year or two over a century old, he was able to compose verses of which the following is a sample (dated May, 1802):—

> Then shall I drink full draughts of bliss,
> And see dear Jesus as He is;
> Then shall I sing and praise and bless
> The Lord my Strength and Righteousness.

The very earliest prayer meetings of this congregation are said to have been held in Widow Cox's cottage which also stood near the top of Coles Lane. Till 1864 Harvills Hawthorn Chapel had been in Wednesbury (chief, or Spring Head) Circuit; in this year a sub-division took place, and it was included in the Second Wednesbury Circuit, afterwards known as Wednesbury Wesley Circuit. Ultimately, as Harvills Hawthorn Chapel was the real head of the Circuit, it became also its nominal head, although now generally called Hill Top Chapel, and head of the Hill Top Circuit. This was no means a happy alteration, for there are many places in England known as Hill Top, while the name Harvills Hawthorn is probably unique.

Connected with the later history of Hill Top Chapel was a man, who, had he lived in earlier times would assuredly have been canonised as a saint by a more appreciative church. His life and good works deserve more than the passing notice that can be given to them here. Thomas Halbert had originally been a navvy, but when he came to take up his residence in the Black Country got employment as a chain-tester. Associating himself with Hill Top Wesleyan Chapel he gradually commanded a respect bordering almost on veneration. For years he gave all his spare time to home mission work, and that in his own immediate neighbourhood, among those who could watch his own daily life and religious consistency—surely the greatest test to which erring man can be subjected. His chief labours lay in Bible selling while engaged in public-house mission work on Saturday afternoons; this he carried on so persistently and successfully, but with such self-sacrificing devotion, that his neglected body gave way under the strain, and he died of overwork at the comparatively early age of 55. When he so unexpectedly passed away on January 4th, 1879, it suddenly dawned upon his friends that a saintly career had just terminated. Thomas Halbert was honoured with a semi-public funeral, an illustration of the procession being printed in an eight page memoir which was issued at the time from the Methodist Book-room.

Swan Village Chapel was the third one erected in West Bromwich. It was a small building, opened on January 2nd. 1831, by the Rev. Ed. Oakes. It cost about £250, and is now enclosed within the Swan Foundry of Messrs Roberts. The present chapel on the main road, with its schools and vestries, was erected in 1865, at a cost of £2,600.

Spon Lane Chapel, accommodating 650 worshippers, was opened St. Bartholomew's Day, 1841, when the total collections realised £195. It has cost £3,500, and is in the Smethwick Circuit, as is also Ryders Green Road Chapel.

Beeches Road Chapel, erected in 1873, is the more "fashionable" and suburban of the Wesleyan places of worship. It accomodates only 375, but cost £3,500.

Greets Green Chapel, in a poorer neighbourhood, was built the same year (1873), to seat 450 people for £1,780.

Carters Green Chapel, which stands on the site of the old Junction Inn, a hostelry which formerly marked the bifurcation of a great highway, was put up in 1876 to accomodate 750 worshippers, at a cost of £5,200.

Overend Chapel, is a smaller fane with only 140 seats built in 1878 at an outlay of £740.

Lyng Lane Chapel, erected 1880, is slightly larger (175 sittings), but cost a little less, namely £668.

In Park Street, a rented cottage which will hold 50 worshippers, is used.

Altogether there are in the borough of West Bromwich 18 Wesleyan chapels and schools, of an estimated value of £35,855, with a total accommodation (in the chapels) for 5,600 persons. Of the day schools something will be said in a future chapter. The chapels in High Street, Hill Top, Swan Village, Carters Green, and Beeches Road are all licensed for the performance of marriages.

In 1838 a return gave the Wesleyan body credit for possessing in West Bromwich accommodation for 3,550 worshippers, 10 Sunday Schools with 1,375 scholars, besides 280 scholars in the Day School.

For further details the readers is referred to Methodism in West Bromwich *from 1742 to 1885* by James Hall, an interesting little work of about 40 pages, prepared for a Jubilee meeting, 8 June, 1885.

LXII.—The Primitive Methodists and Other Denominations.

Seeing the great importance which Wesleyan Methodism assumed in the religious life of West Bromwich, it will not be surprising to find that one of the off shoots of Wesleyanism has also taken up a remarkably strong position in this borough.

The second split in Wesleyanism was that which gave birth to Primitive Methodism—its founders (about the year 1811) claiming that their Methodism was that which was more truly analogous to the primitive form of Methodism practised by the immediate followers and early converts of John Wesley.

In Primitive Methodism West Bromwich was originally a part of the Darlaston Circuit, which at first comprised the whole of the Black Country district, extending beyond Wolverhampton on the one side, and Birmingham on the other, and including Lichfield. In 1812 one Sampson Turner joined the Primitive Methodists at Cannock Lane, and then went with others to spread the teaching in Pelsall, Brownhills, and Walsall Wood. These teachers were then heard and believed by a Darlaston man named W. Carter, who with two neighbours named Humpage and Bowen, formed the nucleus of the Darlaston church. This church subsequently missioned the whole of the Black

Country district. So rapidly did the work progress, that by 1819 or 1820 the Darlaston Circuit extended into Shropshire. In the latter year Thomas Brownsword missioned Dudley and formed a church there, embracing Netherton, Old Hill, and Stourbridge.

By 1840 the Darlaston Circuit had 1,070 members which grew in the next two years respectively to 1,120 and 1,150. By 1843 the members reached 1,300 but trade depression immediately after this adversely affected these numbers.

West Bromwich was made an independent circuit in June 1849, the elder Darlaston circuit having by this time reached a numerical strength of 1,900 members in its churches and 4,000 scholars in its Sunday Schools, dimensions altogether too unwieldy for efficient management. West Bromwich at this time setting up a claim for an independent circuit was at first refused by the Darlaston officials but on the appeal being made to Conference the petition was granted.

The West Bromwich new circuit made great advancement, successfully working a locality where hundreds of the congested population were induced to lead better lives by the influence of Primitive Methodism. It early opened ten new places of worship, and called out an extra minister to assist in this work of extension. The numbers reported for the first year of its working were 1,100, being an increase of 257 for the twelve months. Since then the West Bromwich circuit has steadily progressed; out of its area has been carved the Tipton circuit, the life of which, however, has been somewhat chequered, owing to the fluctuations of a diminishing trade, and the closing of many of its ironworks. At present the West Bromwich circuit has 509 members.

The Primitive Methodists have now in the West Bromwich Circuit 15 Chapels besides preaching-rooms, and Sunday Schools, which gives them the religious instruction of nearly 4,000 persons, under a superintendent, an extra minister, and 30 local preachers. For the ministerial office in this denomination a severe course of four years' probation is necessary, and then the salaries are by no means high. Queen Street Chapel is at the head of the Circuit. It was built in 1847 to accommodate 750 worshippers at an outlay of £2,500.

Lyng Chapel was opened in 1851, the building having cost £450. In 1856 a school-room for 300 children was added, which was enlarged to hold a larger number in 1860. In 1872 funds were raised by a special effort to wipe off the debt upon these undertakings, and ground was also secured for the erection of new schools and chapel to cost £1,500. The other chapels are:—

Spon Lane	...	built	1852,	to seat	500,	for	£1,460.
Greets Green	...	,,	1848,	,,	360,	,,	£1,400.
Golds Green	...	,,	1836,	,,	360,	,,	£1,300.
Gun Village	...	,,	1851,	,,	400,	,,	£900.
Witton Lane	...	,,	1862,	,,	400,	,,	£890.
West Smethwick	...	,,	1878,	,,	200,	,,	£700.
Great Bridge Street		,,	1883,	,,	200,	,,	£800.

Cophall Street (a house is used.)

* * * * * * *

The CATHOLIC APOSTOLIC CHURCH in Victoria Street was built in 1870, and is a neat little structure, which cost £700. The denomination to which the worshippers attending it belong, was founded in 1829 by a pious but somewhat eccentric Presbyterian divine named Edward Irving; hence they are sometimes called Irvingites. In this community there is a fourfold ministry of Apostles, Prophets, Evangelists, and Pastors, the chief pastor of a flock being termed an angel. In 1842 a liturgy was published, and certain vestments were adopted. Later, lights on altars and incense burning were added to the ritualistic adjuncts of its public worship. The Irvingites recognise no earthly leader, but their mission is declared to be the re-uniting of the scattered church, and a solemn preparation for Christ's second coming. At this Victoria Street fane may be found an attractive yet Protestant service, performed in a perfectly "free" church.

* * * * * * *

The other centres of religious working within the borough, but which are unattached to any particular sect or denomination, are (1) the Gospel Blue Ribbon Mission in Pitt Street, and (2) the Salvation Army Barracks in Queen Street.

The Evangelical churches of the parish have formed a Sunday School Union to promote friendly intercourse between the teachers and officers of the different schools, and to qualify them for the more efficient discharge of their duties.

Lastly, there is the agency of the Young Men's Christian Association, who in this town boast very good headquarters at a specially erected building in St. Michael Street. Here are to be found the usual lectures, classes, and competitions, all conducted for the special purpose of raising the physical, mental, moral, and spiritual welfare of the youth of the town.

LXIII.—Modern Ecclesiastical Parishes.

For West Bromwich during its long existence as a village one church amply sufficed to supply all the spiritual needs. But for the modern town it has been necessary to split up the ancient civil parish into numerous ecclesiastical districts, and these have been both formed and altered from time to time during the present century. So far as the history of the Established Church in West Bromwich has yet been traced, it has dealt only with the Establishment as represented by the old parish church; that history terminating with chap. xxxiii. In resuming, precedence must be given to that oldest daughter Church, which being situated nearest the centre of the commercial life and activity of this busy modern borough, has to some extent usurped the importance of the old mother Church—Christ Church in the High Street.

Even from the re-building of the parish church in 1783, there had been a feeling that an additional new church was rapidly becoming necessary to meet the growing wants of the parish and some of the largest subscribers took this wider view. At a Vestry Meeting held 29th July 1818 the following gentlemen did "agree to subscribe towards the erection of a New Church, the sums affixed by them to their several names."—

	£	s.	d.
John Salter	100	0	0
Joseph Hateley	100	0	0
William Robbins	100	0	0
W. Bullock	100	0	0
James Bullock	50	0	0
Edward Elwell	30	0	0
Samuel Whitehouse	50	0	0
Rev. Chas. Townsend	100	0	0
	630	0	0

By August 8th, this total had grown to £2,639 including £100 each from Samuel Dawes, William Izon, J. P. Blakemore, Joseph Halford, William Turton, and William James and Co., £500 from Lord Dartmouth, and £150 from Thomas Jesson.

Advantage was next taken of the provisions of an Act lately passed for erecting new churches in populous places, and application was accordingly made to the Commissioners under the Act. Lord Dartmouth caused £7,500 to accumulate for the benefit of the living (*Willett,* p. 115, and pp. 92-93). A committee was appointed October 14th, 1818. to conduct all the business connected with the building of this New Church or Chapel of Ease; and an advertisement in *Aris's Gazette* asked for plans and estimates of a "new stone church in a plain style of Gothic architecture," sufficiently spacious to contain 2,000 persons. The Earl of Dartmouth laid the first stone of the building September 25th, 1821. At a meeting held 22nd February, 1823, allusion was made to the bankruptcy of the contractor, and the edifice was not completed till the close of 1828. Exclusive of £200 for the site, the cost was no less than £18,446 2s. 6d. The consecration took place on January 17th, 1829, and the formal opening on Sunday, April 26th, following.

On the most commanding site to be found in the new High Street was produced an edifice in Tixall stone, which at first no doubt presented a pleasing white, or at any rate a clean, appearance; but as a foundry then closely adjacent belched forth upon it dense volumes of sooty smoke it soon lost its pristine appearance and its cleanliness has since been more and more deeply hidden from view by the accumulations of succeeding years of Black Country "atmosphere." Instead of its native whiteness it now presents the dinginess of a smoke grimed chimney. The designer, Mr Francis Goodwin, of London, achieved as great an architectural success as his times and opportunities would permit. This architect was engaged about the same time in erecting several new churches in the Midland district, St.George's, Birmingham, being one among the number, and while none of them may claim to be architectural triumphs, they are all of them more than passable. considering the times in which they were built. The style adopted here was supposed to be that of the later English or Decorated Gothic; the dominant feature in this particular design being a really good western tower, with pinnacles reaching to a height of 114 feet. This tower, together with those stately ranges of crocketed pinnacles marking the length and breadth of the edifice, combines to produce that beauty of outline which is its finest and most pleasing feature. It contains a peal of twelve bells. Of the interior there is very little which displays the spirit of English Gothic, owing most probably to the exigencies of providing such an undue amount of sitting accommodation within so limited an area. The imaginary aisles, flanking an undefined nave, have their position but vaguely suggested by the shadows of overhanging galleries. Yet the ribbed roof which spans the almost rectangular plan of the whole body of the church is not without its merits. Nor can the novel feature of its cast iron tracery in the windows be allowed to go altogether undefended. Surely if it be permitted in these days of advanced architecture for the craftsmanship of the skilled mason to be dispensed with in favour of traceries moulded in terra cotta the same license may more legitimately be claimed for the use of moulded iron in a district peculiarly famed for its iron working. Anyway, the ironfounders of the Black Country would bear with much equanimity the fine contempt of superior ecclesiologists if more of their wares could he similarly introduced into the decorative portions of local church building.

To inclose the burial ground of the new Church a Palish Vestry Meeting held 3 October, 1828, authorised the Churchwardens to borrow a sum of money on the credit of the Church Rates. At a similar meeting, held earlier in the year (21st April) the minister of the "New Church or Chapel," the Rev. William Gordon had appointed Joseph Hately, the secretary to the Building Committee as his warden, while the people's warden chosen at the same time was Edwin Bullock.

But as yet the "New Church" was scarcely allowed even to use its own distinctive name of Christ Church, and was kept in leading strings with a firm hand. The Parish

Vestry accounts for January 19th, 1829, show the following disbursements made on account of the "New Church":—

		£	s.	d.
To	Cash, four constables, three beadles, and clerk	2	0	0
,,	Singers	4	7	0
,,	Cakes		3	0
,,	Collation at Hardware's and wine at Church	6	1	0
,,	To Cashmore, attending three days...		7	6
,,	Mears for large bell	152	12	0
,,	Frame and fittings	35	4	0
,,	Small bell	51	17	4
,,	Frame and fittings	20	0	0
,,	Communion table and chairs...	16	0	0
,,	Commandments, Prayer and Belief...	36	13	0
,,	Lettering and numbering the seats...	12	15	0
,,	Copper gutters to windows...	9	17	0
,,	Gangways along roof	10	16	0
,,	J. Dickenson, pulpit and vestry furniture...	16	0	6
,,	Borini, looking glass...		6	6
,,	Candlestick, etc, ...		3	9
,,	Bateman, communion plate...	61	12	0
,,	Gas apparatus for lighting, as ordered by the Bishop	110	0	0
,,	Bebb and Mallin, beadles' cloths	10	0	3

Dec 29th.

To Evans and Cashmore, assisting to keep order 1 2 0

April 20th, 1830.

To Mr Bebb, beadles' coats 5 7 0

From 1829 Christ Church may be said to have managed its own affairs without any further interference from outside.

Mr S. B. Reed (who for seventeen years has held office here as churchwarden) possesses a rare little pamphlet which gives the details of the subscriptions amounting to £658, wherewith the fine peal of bells was acquired for the church in 1847.

About 1878 was effected a restoration (chiefly of the interior) costing about £4,000, of which sum over £700 went to the purchase of a new organ. In 1882 the tower pinnacles were restored by Messrs Wood and Kendrick, architects; and the same West Bromwich firm undertook to superintend the erection of the new vicarage near the north east of the churchyard; a substantial official residence which cost about £2,500 some four years ago.

The register dates from 1829; the first minister is commemorated by a carved stone font.

The vicars of Christ Church have been the following:—

1829.—Rev. William Gordon.
1849.—Rev James Bradshaw.
1872.—Rev. R. Hodgson.
1883.—Rev. C. H. Joberns.
1891.—Rev. M. Crofton.
1894.—Rev. C. W. Carrington.

There are three curates-in-charge of the following mission churches, respectively, one to each, namely, (1) *St. Philip's* District Church in *Beeches Road*; 2) *St. Mark's Mission, Duke Street*; and (3) the *Mission Room, Pitt Street*.

The living is a vicarage, net yearly value £290, with residence, in the gift of the Earl of Dartmouth. Notwithstanding the original intentions of the founders, the building now accommodates only 1,200 worshippers; 800 seats are "free."

*   *   *   *   *   *   *

St. James' Church, Hill Top, was built in the year 1841, the foundation stone having been laid by the Countess of Dartmouth. It was originally intended as a chapel of ease to the parish church of West Bromwich, the Rev. J. L. Neville being curate-in-charge. In June 1844 it became the centre of a newly formed parish, a District Chapelry, and the first incumbent was the Rev. Francis P. Sockett. About the same time the National Schools were erected, and a minute of the year 1845 records the appointment of Mr and Mrs Wilkins the first master and mistress. Church and schools have thus gone hand in hand for fifty years.

From time to time noteworthy gifts have been bestowed upon the church. In 1841, Mr James Bagnall. of Meyrick House, gave a valuable organ. In 1845 Lord Dartmouth generously gave about £300 to be invested in the names of trustees, the interest to be perpetually devoted to the insurance and repair of the church. In 1853, Mr James Bagnall presented the stained-glass east-window. Two more windows were presented in 1862, one (on north side) by Mr Benjamin Whitehouse, of Harvill's Hawthorn, and one (south side) by Mr Isaac Horton, of Clapham Rise, London. In 1876 Mrs Sarah Dunn invested £85, the annual interest on which was devoted as a dole to the "godly poor of Golds Hill," a district which then formed a portion of St. James's parish, but which was formed into a separate parish in 1887 under the incumbency of the Rev. R. B. Robson, The edifice, erected by voluntary contributions, together with £300 granted by the Society for Promoting and Building Churches, is built of brick, its west front presenting twin turrets as its most striking feature. The schools adjoin, on the north side; and the whole area is neatly fenced in with good iron palisading.

It was supposed to have 1,009 sittings, of which 590 were "free." But recently the pew rent system has been abolished, and the whole 850 seats were declared free and unappropriated.

The present Vicar, the Rev. J. Watkiss Jones, found on coming to the Vicarage (1889) that there was already in existence a Restoration Committee with £300 in the bank. Under Mr E. Pincher, architect, the fabric of the church was carefully repaired, a tower was built to hold the bell, and the vestry was very considerably enlarged. The work of restoration was then laid aside for two years. In the autumn of 1892 the Church was closed for internal restoration and improvement. The pews were removed, the organ taken away from the West gallery, and re-built in an organ chamber, by Messrs Nicholson and Lord, of Walsall. A Choir Vestry was constructed; together with choir stalls, the whole Church was cleaned, painted, and decorated, and various extensive improvements were carried out by Messrs H. Smith and Son. Several handsome gifts were bestowed, including a pulpit, an oak lectern, and a font. The work of restoration cost about £1,000.

The register dates from 1844; and the vicars of the parish have been so far:—

      1844.—Rev. F. P. Sockett.
      1869.—Rev. F. P. B. Hutton.
      1872.—Rev. R. Wall.
      1889.—Rev. J. Watkiss Jones.

The living is a vicarage, gross yearly value £270, in the gift of the Bishop of Lichfield.

*   *   *   *   *   *   *

The ecclesiastical parish of HOLY TRINITY was formed in 1842: the church situated in TRINITY ROAD, is a building of brick, in the early English style, erected in 1841, at an expense of nearly £3,000, of which £500 was granted by Government; the site of the church, parsonage house, and schools was generously given by Mr Silvester: the church consists of chancel and nave, and a tower with pinnacles containing one bell: the chancel was burnt in 1861 but immediately restored. The register dates from the year 1842.

The living is a vicarage, gross yearly value £398, with house, erected in 1845, at a cost of nearly £1,000, in the gift of trustees, and held since 1874 by the Rev. Arthur Benjamin Irvine, M.A., of Trinity College, Dublin. The first vicar (1842) was the Rev. H. S. Beresford, who was succeeded in 1845 by the Rev. W. Cardall. Then came the Rev. B. Willmore, whose son Mr F. W. Willmore is the author of "A History of Walsall." In 1871 the Rev. W. S. Escott became the immediate predecessor of the present vicar.

A complete list of the wardens was printed in the magazine of this parish for December, 1894.

* * * * * * *

ST. PETER'S is an ecclesiastical parish, formed in 1861: the church, situated in WHITEHALL ROAD, NEW TOWN, was consecrated in July, 1858, and is a building of stone, consisting of chancel, nave, aisles, and a small tower containing the bell. The register dates from the year 1858.

The living is a vicarage, whose net yearly value has been set down as £330, in the gift of the Bishop of the diocese but *pro hac vice* the Crown. It has been held by the Rev. Charles Massey, M.A. (of Trinity College, Dublin), who was succeeded in 1878 by the Rev. Walter Frederick Bradley, of Durham University. The present vicar is the Rev. Henry Jesson, who is a West Bromwich man by birth, and one who belongs to a family of staunch churchmen. (See Chap. xlvii.)

* * * * * * *

ST. ANDREW'S ecclesiastical parish was formed in 1879 from the parishes of All Saints, Christ Church, St. James and St. Peter; the church, in OLD MEETING STREET, was opened in December. 1867, but its register dates only from 1879. It is a cruciform building, consisting of chancel, nave and transepts, and will seat 450 persons, all the sittings being free. Alongside the north of the nave are a side-chapel and a choir-vestry. All the interior fittings are extremely plain. The exterior presents so unimposing a view that an ordinary wayfarer, who was at all pre-occupied, might walk along the high road between Carters Green and Black Lake without ever becoming aware of the vicinity of a church, and when pointed out to him he would then seem to have little more than a great mass of tiled roof to gaze upon. The living is a vicarage, net yearly value from the Ecclesiastical Commissioners £200, in the gift of the Vicar of West Bromwich, and held from 1879 to 1895 by the Rev. James Benjamin Crump, M.A., of Queen's College, Cambridge. The present Vicar is the Rev. W. C. Weston, previously curate at St. John's. In 1894 a commodious and substantial residence for the Vicar was built next to the church, on its south side. It is from the design of Messrs Wood and Kendrick, and the proportions of the house quite overshadow those of the adjacent church. With a boldness of conception only equalled by the daring of its execution, this massive vicarage house has been faced throughout with the ordinary brick of the neighbourhood, best Stourbridge bricks being used for quoins only. The result is satisfactory, and will most probably be more so with the lapse of time, when the murky atmosphere of this Black Country region has given to its colouring the tone which apparently is expected of it.

This church works St. Michael's Mission in Bull Lane.

* * * * * * *

The ecclesiastical parish of St. John the Evangelist, was formed in 1879 from that of Christ Church: the church situated in Sams Lane, and erected in 1878, is a brick building in the Early English style, consisting of chancel, nave, and south aisle, and affords 400 sittings. The register dates from the year 1879.

(Connected with this parish is the Good Shepherd Mission in Hall Street. A Men's Club with a gymnasium has been established at the schools, Newhall Street.

The living is a vicarage, net yearly value from the Ecclesiastical Commissioners £210, in the gift of the Bishops of Lichfield, and held by the Rev. Cyril Tidswell Holmes, M.A., of Clare College, Cambridge previous to the present vicar, the Rev. Newton T. Langley. The first Vicar was the Rev. H. N. Churton.

*   *   *   *   *   *   *

St. Paul's parish, Gold's Hill, already mentioned, has a small mission church. The living is worth only about £30 a year but there is a good residence attached to it. The work, however is considerable, as the population consisting mostly of the poorest class in a typical Black Country district, reaches nearly 4,500. In Brickhouse Lane is St. Mary's Mission.

*   *   *   *   *   *   *

St. Mary Magdalene's is a mission church connected with the old Parish Church. It is situated at the corner of Workhouse Lane.

St. Mary the Virgin's at Hateley Heath was also served by the clergy of All Saints', till demolished five years ago.

LXIV.—Schools, School Boards, and Educational Progress.

It was surmised (ch. x) that the earliest educational establishment within the confines of West Bromwich was the Scriptorium of Sandwell Priory. When the monasteries were abolished, the schools went with them. In some parishes another class of school was instituted, now known as Grammar Schools, which were sometimes endowed by the munificence of wealthy citizens, or as frequently by property transferred from some chantry guild, or other religious establishment suppressed at the Reformation. Unfortunately for West Bromwich nothing of this kind happened here. The nearest approach was the right of West Bromwich to participate in the benefits of the free education provided under the will of Solomon Woodhall in 1796. (See *History of Tipton* pp. 23 and 34). There was once also the endowment of Monk Meadow left by the Whorwoods for the support of a school (ch. vi. and xli.), but now that too has been "lost."

West Bromwich almost as a consequence, and also perhaps because it long preserved its rural aspect between busy Birmingham on the one side, and the smoky Black Country on the other, became the seat of numerous private boarding schools. *Pigot's Directory* for 1835 gives a long list of schools and academies in West Bromwich, most of them private adventure establishments and including among them some whose names are famous even to this day, such as those of Joseph Jaques at Black Lake and John Marshall at Springfield, Witton Lane. The former school was mentioned in ch. xlii., and the latter in ch. lxi. Other well-remembered names are those of James Beddoe, Summerfield Academy; George Borwick, Heath Academy; Edward Gittoes, Great Bridge; John Richardson, Oak Road; Michael Skelly, Field House and several others.

The public schools therein enumerated are but four, namely, the Catholic Charity School in High Street; an Infant School at Lyne; a National School for Boys in New Street and one for Girls in Hall End. It was in 1838 the Wesleyan Day School in Paradise Street was opened (ch. lxi.)

At first public elementary schools were chiefly aided by the two noted School Societies; the Church Schools receiving their support from the National Society, and so getting the name of National Schools; the Nonconformist (or rather undenominational) schools deriving their grants from the British and Foreign School Society, became known as British Schools. It was not till 1839 that grants were made to schools from the public purse, and with public aid naturally went along Government inspection. From the Report of Her Majesty's Inspector for 1844; It would appear that only one school in West Bromwich had placed itself under Government inspection in those very earliest days of State-aided education, and the report, which reads as follows, is very interesting read in the light of our modern experience:—

"Trinity School, West Bromwich:

I.—Numbers.

	Boys.	Girls.	Infts.
Population for whose benefit the School was erected ...			2,711
No. of children for whom school accommodation is provided ...			310
No. of children on books for last six months...			153
No. of children in average daily attendance			98
Fee for each child		2d.	or 3d.
No. attending at time of Examination...	70	43	0
No. of Classes	4	4	0
Average age of Monitors	9 4-5th	10 1-3rd	0
No. of Paid Teachers (exclusive of Monitors or P.T.'s)	0	0	0

II.—Attainments.

	Boys.	Girls.
Reading (a) Simple Narrative	22	24
(b) With ease	0	0
Writing on paper	13	10
Arithmetic (a) First four rules	18	37
,, (b) Compound rules	6	0
,, (c) Proportion and higher rules	4	0

Mental Arithmetic, Geography, Etymology, English History,
Vocal Music 0, English Grammar 13. (no Library.)

III.—Expenditure.

Stipend: Master, £50; Mistress, £35; monitors, 0.
Sundries: Books, stationery, etc., £12 2s. 4d.;
repairs, furniture, etc., £5 17s. 4d.; fuel, £5 8s. 6d.

IV.—Income.

Endowment 0; subscriptions, etc., £15 9s., fees £76,
annual collections, £33 7s. 1d.

V.—Remarks.

Date of inspection, August 15th. "I can record no favourable
impression of this school."

The inspector who made this report of 1844 was the Rev. Henry Moseley, M.A., F.R.S. In the following year (1845) St. James's National School at Hill Top was opened (ch. lxiii) By 1850, to the list of elementary schools already noted must be added (1) British

School at Black Lake, Henry J. Norrish, master; Susanna Sargent, mistress. (2) Wesleyan Day and Infant School at Harvills Hawthorn, Samuel Sadler, master; Ann Austin, mistress. And (3) The Infant School at Lyndon is given as *Ebenezer*, with Ann Bannister as mistress.

By 1855 the list of public elementary schools had been extended a little by the addition of All Saints' Infant School in Churchfield, Kenrick's British School at Spon Lane (George Fillmore, master), Bagnall's Free National School at Gold's Hill (Thomas Crabtree, master), the Independents' British School in Sheepwash Lane, and some others. The academies and boarding schools are found still numerous, and evidently thriving so far. After this no great changes occur until the era of School Boards.

Taking early advantage of the Elementary Education Act a School Board was formed for West Bromwich in 1871. An educational census was at once taken, from which it appeared that there were in the parish 2,825 children between three and five years of age, and 9,337 between five and thirteen making a total of 12,162 children within the district of the Board, for whom school accommodation was required. From this number 421 were deducted for children attending schools where the fee was over 9d. per week, and 2,348 (or 20 per cent.) for absentees, leaving 9,393 as the number who ought to have been present at school at any one time.

The then existing provision to meet the requirements of these children was ascertained to consist of—

    (*a*)   14 schools containing 36 departments in receipt of
            Government aid and having room for...   6414

    (*b*)   6 schools not under Government, containing 7 departments
            and room for   1850

    (*c*)   5 Private adventure schools, accommodating   429
            Making a total of accommodation for   8693
            And leaving a deficiency of...   700
            to be provided for.
            This deficiency was afterwards increased by the closing of
            the schools at Mayer's Green and Greet's Green, to   1544

But, although the deficiency for the whole parish at the time of ascertaining the accommodation was comparatively small, the supply of schools was very unequally distributed, there being sufficient provision in Christ Church and All Saints' districts, a small deficiency in Trinity, and a considerable one in St. Peter's and St. James's.

On these returns H.M Inspector recommended the erection of schools at Greet's Green and at Hill Top. At the latter place, however, a new voluntary school was erected, which met the deficiency of accommodation there. Gun's Village was another locality requiring school places. The Board made temporary provision by renting rooms. These were at (1) Mayer's Green and Queen Street, opened for for Boys, Girls, and Infants, in January 1872: and in March following, schools were commenced in the rooms connected with the Wesleyan and Primitive Methodist Chapels at (2) Greet's Green. In the same month (3) the schools for many years previously supported by Messrs Kenrick and Sons, were transferred to the Board; and in June 1873, the rooms adjoining the Primitive Methodist Chapel (4), Gun's Lane were opened to afford school accommodation for the children in the neighbourhood of Gun's Village and Dartmouth Street. The Board then controlled 4 schools with 11 departments; by 1874 the average attendance at these four Board Schools was 1,149.

To put into force their powers of compulsory attendance at school, an Attendance Officer was appointed in May 1872. Between July 22nd, 1872, and January 31st, 1874, some 500 persons were prosecuted for failing, to cause their children to attend school and the fines imposed amounted to £84. Leniency with the defaulting parents had failed to produce any good result whatever. Some little trouble was next experienced in dealing with half-timers, of whom there were 400 in the parish; many boys under 13 years of age also being found to be employed full-time. Employers of labour, however, soon put themselves right by complying with the law. Another difficulty at the outset of the Board's career was that of Dame Schools, and other schools of private adventure, where few or no registers were kept, and where no efficient education was really being given. The compulsory enforcement of attendance at first filled these schools, to which the children of indifferent parents naturally flocked, in order to escape the rigour of the Act. Several of these schools were condemned by the Magistrates, and closed in consequence. By 1874 there were 130 children of school age returned as being "taught at home." Of the 12,162 children returned in 1871 as being of school. age, 8,366 were under proper instruction, and 3,796 were not. By 1874 it was calculated there were 12,400 of school age, and an increase of 3,263 under efficient instruction, a gain of 39 per cent, as the first fruits of the Board's operations. The details of this increase appear in the following table—assuredly no mean result for the expenditure of only £4,600 of which £3,450 came from the rates, £400 from Government grants, and £758 from children's fees.

School	January, 1871. Average Attendance.	January, 1874. Average Attendance.	Increase. Average Attendance.
I.—BOARD.			
Summit	286	334	48
Greet's Green	——	326	326
Mayer's Green and Queen Street	——	297	297
Gun's Village	——	192	192
II—VOLUNTARY.			
St. James's National	314	367	53
St. Andrew's ,,	96	205	109
Trinity ,,	313	503	190
Christchurch ,, Walsall Street	305	436	131
Christ Church ,, Newhall Street	143	193	50
All Saints' ,,	293	364	61
St Peter's ,,	409	447	38
Messrs Bagnall's, Gold Hill	277	354	77
St. Mary the Virgin	——	100	100
St. Mary Magdalen's	89	112	23
Wesleyan, Great Bridge	318	494	176
,, Hill Top	241	408	167
,, Bratt Street	296	478	182
,, Spon Lane	22	105	83
St. Michael's, R.C.	75	97	22
Ebenezer	127	207	80
Bethel	75	190	115
Ragged School, Moor Street	150	187	37
III.—PRIVATE.			
Dame and Private Schools (7 the first year. 5 afterwards)	463	351	d'creas
IV.—EXTRA-PAROCHIAL.			
Messrs Chance's, Smethwick	80	120	40
Totals	4472	6857	2485

The second School Board was elected in March 1874, and Messrs T. Davis and J. Cooksey were re-appointed to their respective positions of chairman and vice-chairman. At Greets Green new Board Schools were erected, and formally opened in December, 1876. Costing about £4,800 for the accommodation of 700 scholars, the outlay was brought to a very economical average of under £7 per child. Meanwhile a new class-room had been added to Queen Street Board School, and early in 1876 the Board had purchased Moor Street School with all its fittings for £1,200; the Ragged School formerly held here now became known as a Board School. The school-room in Dartmouth Street belonging to the Baptist Bethel Chapel, and previously conducted as a private school, was taken over by the Board in October, 1876, and opened as a Mixed School under a master. Besides acquiring over 3,000 square yards of land at Guns Village for the erection of a new school, this Board proposed just as it was going out of office to open a two department school at the premises attached to Lyng Primitive Methodist Chapel.

When these were in operation, the Board Schools, would then afford accommodation for 3,073 children allowing 8 square feet per child (except at Greet's Green) made up as follows:—

		No. of Departments	
1. Dartmouth Street, Mixed...	... ...	1	250
2. Gun's Village Mixed and Infants ...	... ...	2	212
3. Greet's Green	... ...	3	700
4. Mayer's Green and Queen Street ...	... ...	3	700
5. Moor Street, Mixed... ...	... ...	1	379
6. Lyng, Boys and Infants	... ...	2	312
7. Summit	... ...	3	520
			3073

The other Schools under Government Inspection afforded accommodation for 5,919, as follows:—

		No. of Departments	
St. James's	... ...	3	476
St. Andrew's	... ...	1	176
Trinity	... ...	3	486
Christ Church	... ...	3	622
Christ Church, Newhall Street	... ...	2	268
Wesleyan, Great Bridge	... ...	2	569
Wesleyan, Hill Top ...	... ...	3	692
Wesleyan, Bratt Street ...	... ...	2	718
Wesleyan, Spon Lane ...	... ...	1	271
All Saints'	... ...	3	461
Messrs Bagnall's	... ...	3	434
St. Peter's	... ...	3	415
St. Mary Magdalen's	... ...	1	111
St. Mary, the Virgin	... ...	1	60
St. Michael's	... ...	1	142
			5919

In Private Adventure Schools recognised by the Board as giving fairly efficient Instruction, there was room for 784 children.

The total School accommodation therefore stood thus:—

1. Board Schools 3073
2. Denominational Schools... 5919
3. Private Adventure Schools 784

                                                                9776

All the efforts of this Board resulted only in an increase of 65 in the average attendance, from 1874 to 1877. As an explanation it was stated that the "increased number not under instruction was composed chiefly of children under 5 years of age." The Board, therefore, reduced the fee for these infant children to a penny per week. The expenditure of this Board had risen to over £12,000 for its whole term of office, of which £4,281 was the amount of the loan obtained for the building of Greets Green School.

The Board elected in 1877 was somewhat of a polemical body. It discussed methods for wringing the last penny of the school fees from parents, and gravely decided that the appointment of another Attendance Officer was unnecessary if the Teachers would devote themselves to the systematic performance of the extra-official duties of an Attendance Department. The religious controversy raged for months, as might have been expected of this body till finally an Extraordinary Meeting adopted on November 1st, 1878, the Syllabus of Religious Instruction used by the London School Board. The adoption of this illogical and invertebrate system of "religious" instruction was carried in the face of earnest protests from the Nonconformists of the parish. So highly had the bitterness of debate run, that an ill-advised attempt was now made to secure an injunction restraining the Board from letting their schoolrooms to a very vigorous Liberal Association which existed at that time, and which had made its influence severely felt in the controversy. The Master of the Rolls of course refused the application.

The provision of more school accommodation was forced upon the Board. The Moor Street School recently purchased for £1,200, was improved and greatly enlarged by the addition of a new Infants' Department, which raised the cost to £2,950. The Gun's Village Schools were finished in April, 1879, Their accommodation was for 600 children provided at an outlay of £6,715; and to them were removed the Boys and Girls from the Dartmouth Street School leaving that building for future use as an Infants' Department. In December, 1877, the Ebenezer School was transferred to the Board, giving them the control of 454 more school places; and in March, 1878, the Wesleyan body also transferred their Spon Lane School, with accommodation for 271 scholars to the Board. The school buildings at Golds Hill erected in 1855 by Messrs Bagnall (chiefly for the children of their own workpeople) were at this time to be sold; the Board therefore acquired them, November 1878, at a valuer's price of £2,800. The buildings, accommodating 457 scholars, were repaired and improved at a further outlay of £1,825; this included two dwelling-houses for teachers valued at £800. The Park Village School for 230 younger children was opened in February 1878. The enlargement of the Summit Infant School was compelled by the attitude of the Education Department: and the rebuilding of the Lyng School was undertaken at an estimated cost of £5,446, for three departments to hold 826 children. The great changes therefore which this Board may be said to have effected, were the conversion of three Denominational Schools into Board Schools, namely Ebenezer, Spon Lane, and Golds Hill. In the same period St. Andrew's and St. Mary's Schools ceased to be under Government inspection, while St.

John's Girls' and St. Mary Magdalene's Infant Schools were both closed. The expenditure of the Board naturally went up by leaps and bounds with this rapid accumulation of its responsibilities. For to the seven Board Schools previously enumerated must now be added four more, viz.—

8. Ebenezer, Mixed and Infants (8 sq. ft. each child) for 454.

9. Gold's Hill, Boys', Girls, and Infants (10 sq. ft. each child) for 457.

10. Park Village (8 sq. ft. each child) for 230.

11. Spon Lane, Mixed (8 sq. ft. each child) for 271.

During the three years ending 29 September, 1879 the Board spent £34,863, of which £11,000 was derived from the rates, and nearly £15,000 from loans raised for building purposes, the remainder was chiefly made up of Government grants (£4,724) and the children's fees (£2,816).

Of the fourth Board (1880-1883) there were only two original members who had served on the first elected Board, namely, Mr Alfred Caddick and Mr Scattergood. The former became Chairman, and with the triennial report issued in February, 1883 he gave a concise resumé of the Board's work from the very first, complimenting their Clerk, Mr George Hillmore, on the invaluable assistance he had rendered throughout the Board's trying period of incubation. [It is interesting to note here that Mr Fillmore is still (1895) ably filling the office to which he was appointed in 1871.] The Chairman in his review dealt with the statistics of the Board's operations in a masterly manner, and in connection with the resultant figures of comparative attendance, he testified to the great efficiency of the work performed by their Visiting Officer, Mr Coleman, in placing West Bromwich so high in the scale of the country's tabulated percentages. But the chief feature of the Board's policy as directed by this highly capable chairman was the rescission of the resolutions adopting the London syllabus of religious instruction; and the substitution of the daily reading of the Bible in all Board Schools, by the head teachers, without note or comment. Central classes for pupil teachers and assistant teachers were also established and held every Saturday morning. The Lyng Schools in Sams Lane were formally opened on October 4th, 1880 and in June, 1881, it was proposed to erect new schools at Black Lake, to replace those held in the Ebenezer Rooms. At the same time there was a falling-off in the attendance at Golds Hill Schools where the wage-earning opportunities of the population were diminishing. It is worthy of noting here that just previous to the era of limited companies, it was often a pleasing feature of the relations between capital and labour, for extensive employers of labour to provide elementary schools for educating the children of their workpeople; such schools were those of Messrs Bagnall at Golds Hill, Messrs Chance at Spon Lane, Smethwick; and Messrs Lloyds, Foster and Co., at Wednesbury, &c.

The tables which accompany this fourth triennial report are very elaborate. From them it appears that this Board's total expenditure was £38,827, while *Table II* gives in detail the Board's loan account, showing a repayment of £1,651 and an indebtedness of £22,981.

Before the next Board came into office in March, 1883, the town had been incorporated. Of this new Board, Mr Daniel Howard became chairman, a position he retained on succeeding Boards up to his retirement (1895). The Bible reading resolution was rescinded, and the reading was now to be accompanied "by explanation and instruction"; but this instruction was to be of such a wonderfully colourless description as not to "attach children to any particular denomination," 'In provision of school accommodation the Black Lake Schools for 1068 scholars were completed and fitted at a cost of £10,000; they were opened September 14th, 1885, when the chairman presented an illuminated clock to adorn the turret. A Cookery Department was included in this outlay. Lyng Board School was enlarged and others were improved.

While Trinity schools increased their accommodation by 53 places, St. John's School which had held 216 children was closed.

The financial statement shows an expenditure of £43,442; and a loan account of £35,433, with a repayment of £3,435. A sum of £16,400 was drawn from the rates, at 6d. to 8d. in the pound.

Succeeding Boards have done nothing very heroic; their school buildings, however, have been fairly good ones. To keep pace with the growth of population, an increase of accommodation has been found necessary from time to time. The new Spon Lane Board Schools, to supply the place of the two hired schools (The Summit let by Messrs Kenrick at a nominal rent, and the premises in Spon Lane belonging to the Wesleyan body) were opened in February, 1889. They accommodate 1,406 children, and strangely enough are built in two storeys, an expedient which should never be resorted to unless in some crowded city where sites are expensive. The total cost of these schools was £9,293.

The new schools in Beeches Road were opened in March 1893; they supplied the place of the temporary schools previously held in Mayers Green and Queen Street. With a Cookery School, and all complete, the cost was £11,372. Additional accommodation was provided for 220 children at Greets Green, and an Infants' Department was opened by the Board in Bull Lane. Of the voluntary schools All Saints' accommodation was increased by 88 places, and St. James's School was enlarged. On the other hand Hateley Heath and Hall Green Schools, which for some years were carried on chiefly at the expense of Miss Lloyd, were closed, as was also Trinity Infant department, and later (March 1893) St. Andrew's School, having 176 school places was also discontinued.

The central classes for teachers were discontinued in 1886; and while the teaching of cookery to girls has been extended, the art of swimming among the boys has been directly fostered and encouraged. The substitution of the Government Fee Grant, by the Act of 1891, for the collecting of weekly fees from the children, relieved the West Bromwich Board from what it had always considered one of its primary duties. One of the latest bye-laws has raised the "standard" of total exemption from the obligation to attend school from the "fifth" to the "sixth." West Bromwich School Board in 1890 joined the Boards of Walsall and of Burton-on-Trent in a scheme for jointly erecting a Truant School at Lichfield for 100 boys. The estimate was £8,000, but when the scheme was carried out the cost of the school was found to have reached £13,000, which involves the annual payment by this Board of £231 18s. 8d. for principal and interest.

The financial statement for the three years ended 29 September, 1894, shows among the receipts:—(1) Government Grants earned £17,228; (2) Fee Grants on attendance £8,956; from the Rates, at 9d. in £, £22,650, etc. The Loan Account shows that while £11,918 had been repaid, there was still an indebtedness of £50,211, repayable over periods of 30 or 50 years, £8,861 having been repaid during the triennial period under review

---

LXV.—West Bromwich Institute.

We pass next from the history of Elementary Education to the consideration of the facilities which exist in the modern borough for graded instruction in the higher branches of learning.

West Bromwich Institute began in 1881 as a mere lecture-giving movement, similar to the present Wednesbury Institute. But in 1882 a town's meeting was held, at which it was declared that a scientific and literary institution located in a permanent and special building of its own was highly desirable for the good of the community, to supplement the rudiments of knowledge acquired in the elementary schools. A committee was appointed, They purchased the site in Lodge Road for £1,676, selected the designs of Messrs Wood and Kendrick, and accepted the tender of Mr Thos. Rowbotham, of Birmingham, at £7,975. The building was opened in May, 1886, it is principally of red brick and terra cotta, in the Tudor or late Gothic style. It is elegant, commodious, and replete with every convenience for carrying on the special work for which it was designed. It is conveniently situated near the Town Hall and is one of the chief architectural ornaments of the town. The ultimate finishing cost was about £12,500, from which the generosity and public spirit displayed in the subscription list may be well gauged.

West Bromwich has been most fortunate in possessing from the commencement of its municipal life, a few leading citizens, who, whilst carefully guarding the commercial interests of the borough, have recognised the importance of developing to the fullest extent the educational work begun in the elementary schools. Therefore, after successfully establishing a Free Library—which grows daily in its influence for good upon all members of the community—it was thus eventually resolved to erect an Institute for the teaching of science, literature and industrial art. The generous donations of the late Earl of Dartmouth, the present Mayor (Alderman Farley), Messrs Ryland, Kenrick, Salter, Chance, Heelis. Macaulay, Dr. Underhill, and many others, enabled a building to be erected, which, thanks to the architects, Messrs Wood and Kendrick, is a great credit to the town, the gross outlay upon it exceeding £15,000. It had for its object two distinct features; first that of providing high class lectures, entertainments, etc., and second, the technical education of the rising generation, To promote the first lectures, upon scientific and literary subjects were to be given every week during the winter months, besides an occasional dramatic performance, whilst to develop the second classes in every subject likely to be of use to those wishing to study the principles underlying the many industries of the district, were opened. Both departments were highly successful and happily for West Bromwich are still flourishing. There is a nightly average attendance of 450. Directly the Technical Classes were opened their popularity and usefulness became manifest, and probably in no other borough has there ever been such a rapid development in the highest branches of technical education. Many of the classes have become so large that the present building is already too small and will, at an early date have to he enlarged.

Educational work, to be sound, is extremely expensive; yet for five years the whole cost of maintenance was entirely defrayed by those who had so generously contributed to the erection of the building. Neither time nor money was spared by them to make the work thoroughly effective.

This state of affairs was obviously unjust, inasmuch as a benefit shared by the whole community should not have its expenses borne by a willing few. Therefore when the monies derived from the "Excise and Customs Act, 1890," for the purposes of higher education were available, and when the "Technical Education Act, 1889," had been adopted by which a Local Authority may raise a rate not exceeding a 1d. in the pound, the Committee of Management, then known as the Institute Committee, made overtures to the Town Council for these public monies to be devoted in West Bromwich to those purposes for which they were intended, the Town Council of course taking charge of the schools as representatives of the public. In spite of the usual opposition on the part of the short-sighted few who are always to be found in the most public spirited community, the schools were eventually transferred to the Municipality, and are now known as the Municipal Technical Schools,

Being affiliated to the Science and Art Department, valuable scholarships, medals and prizes are offered yearly in competition, besides Local Scholarships, Free Studentships, and Prizes given by the Borough Member (E. Spencer, Esq.,) the Mayor (Alderman Farley), Messrs Chance, Ryland, Salter, and many others.

To assist the work in the Central School, three Branch Schools are now established in Greets Green, Black Lake, and Spon Lane. An educational ladder is thus formed by ascending which, a youth, let him be ever so poor, may reach to the highest distinction in Technical Science or Art. The Art School is under the direction of Mr Joseph A. Pearce, a highly successful principal, among whose qualifications as a teacher may be mentioned the fact that he took the highest possible award given by the Science and Art Department in 1886, namely, the Gold Medal and Travelling Scholarship. He has published a Report on Continental Art Teaching—*vide* "Blue Book," 1886—and together with his wife, who is also on the staff of the Institute, exhibits regularly at the Society of Artists in Birmingham, Manchester, and other places. The Science Department is under the direction of Mr Lloyd Whiteley, F.I.C., F.C.S., of University College, Nottingham.

LXVI.—Early Administration of the Poor Laws, from 1525 to the Close of the 18th Century.

The first dispensers of relief to the poor of this neighbourhood were no doubt the monks at Sandwell Priory. Perhaps when wealthy enough they kept an *almoner* there. Anyway, vagrants and sturdy beggars were plentiful enough. After the suppression of the monasteries the management of vagrancy and the relief of the deserving poor were problems which provoked all kinds of legislative nostrums. The Poor Laws date from 1535. In 1601 every parish was charged with the support of its own poor, and their relief was entrusted to *Overseers*, superintended by the *Magistrates*. The poor were classified as the "idle," who were to be made to work, and the "impotent," who were to be relieved.

The History of Wednesbury (p. 127) gives the names of the parish officers of West Bromwich in 1646, they were Thomas Jesson, Constable, and John Wawde, and Walter Stevens, Overseers of the Poor.

In 1691 the Overseers were compelled to furnish at Vestry Meeting lists of the poor to be relieved; and the Justices were then to add any names they thought fit.

At one time it was necessary to the exercising of any trade that an apprenticeship should have been served at it. The churchwardens and overseers were consequently engaged extensively in the *apprenticing of pauper children*; and a person merely occupying lands in a parish, although he resided out of it, was actually compellable to receive a parish apprentice. An apprentice, on the death of his master, might be ordered by the justices to serve the residue of his time with the widow, or executor, or other successor under certain conditions. Or he might under other circumstances be free. Illustrative of the exceeding strictness of the law we have in West Bromwich Churchwardens' Books, under date April 6th, 1696, a Certificate signed by the Minister and Wardens that Jonathan Brooks was "free from his master and father" to serve any other person. Perhaps otherwise he might have become chargeable to the parish by the recent death of his "father and master." Anyway it is apparent that the parent was not able to maintain the child.

For the greater ease of parishes in the relief of their poor, the churchwardens and overseers, with the consent of the major part of the parishioners, were to purchase or hire any house or houses and to contract with any person or persons for the keeping and employing of the poor; and there to keep and employ such poor, and to take the benefit of the work and service of the said poor. They might also set up any trade for the setting on work and relief of the poor, and might keep a stock of necessary material to work upon. In West Bromwich was kept a stock of iron (in the form of nail-rods), and the trade set up was that of nail-making. An account of this parochial employment for the year 1697 was given in ch. xlix. But up to this time West Bromwich had shirked its duty of purchasing or hiring any *Poor-House*, or proper Work-house establishment; contenting itself with the provision of employment in private forges in consonance with the theory of "profitable employment" then in vogue.

But the same authority might also build on the waste lands of the parish (of which there were then plenty in West Bromwich) with the consent of the lord of the manor *dwelling-houses* for the use of the impotent poor. At a "publique meeting" held at West Bromwich on October 8th, 1716, the "trustees for the poores land in the occupation of Thomas Jesson doe consent and agree that the parishioners doe erect houses upon partes of the said premises for the use of the poore;" and as all the large land-owners mutually promised to execute the work at once, it is just suggestive that their action has been delayed till the force of circumstances actually drive them to the "perfecting of ye same." (*Willett*, p. 97). The Vestry Books then give us a curious entry two years later. It was required by law that the Wardens and Overseers should meet together at least once every month in the church upon the Sunday in the afternoon after divine service to consider "of some good course to be taken" in the performance of their parochial duties. So at West Bromwich on March 21st, 1718, it was agreed that "only one shilling be allowed to any officer going into monthly meeting, and noe ale to be allowed upon any account whatever."

In 1721 the constable was bidden to give "noe money to any vagrants." No doubt the sturdy pauper was becoming unmanageable in the parish; and the provision of a regular parochial establishment was slowly but surely being forced upon the overseers. By January 24th, 1734-5 it had to be "agreed that there shall be a house fitted and prepared with such necessaries thereunto for the setting of the poor of the Parish of West Bromwich on work, and for the relief of the lame and impotent of the said parish." Perhaps, after all, the cottages promised in 1716 had not yet been provided for the infirm poor. The resolution now passed most carefully proceeds (no doubt under the provisions of the *Permissive Workhouse Act* of 1723) to deal with ways and means thus—"And for the defraying and payment of the charges of the said *Workhouse* it is alsoe agreed that the same shall be paid by the usuall four-penny levey of the Poors Rate, and such leveys to be collected in manner hereafter named—That is, one levey in this present year; and to continue the collection of two leveys yearly afterwards, more than the charges of the maintenance of the poor, untill the expenses above-said be fully satisfied and paid." This heroic resolution is signed by John Lowe, Jesson Lowe, Thomas Jesson, and other parishioners; but three months after another resolution was passed thus—"Whereas an entry was made on the four-and-twentyeth of Jany. last past for erecting a Workhouse in the parish of West Bromwich: Wee, the freeholders and tenants within the said parish whose names are underwritten, do oppose the erecting of such Workhouse as a thing that will be of great damage and pernicious consequences to the said parish of West Bromwich:" signed by John Turton, Ralph Moor, and others. This was passed on April 8th, and as evidence that the opponents of the Workhouse were in earnest, similar resolutions were passed in rapid succession on April 18th, June 13th, July 9th, and August 22nd.

On September 26th the resolution took this form: "Wee, the inhabitants whose names are subscribed, do hereby protest and declare against the erecting of a Workhouse, buying any lands or buildings for that use; or that the poor shall be kept in any workhouse or otherwise than usuall, at the perill of the officers; or that the money which hath been granted be applyed to any other use than the relief of the poor as usuall, and not putting them into a workhouse.—Edward Horn, John Turton, Edward Rider," etc.

Whether a parochial controversy raged round this question cannot now be determined, but it would seem like it from the allusions contained in the following notice given "March ye 19th, 1737," by the Overseers for the Inhabitants "to meet them att ye house of William Morris on Fryday next att four a clock in ye afternoon, to consent upon the agreement that was made at Joseph Gutheridg's; and then to determine whether or not *ye law charges* expended on *each side* shall be raised by leveys and laid upon the inhabitants, and applied to pay *boath parties* in the manner as is particularly sett forth in the said agreement. Agreed at the meeting that no law charges or expenses of either side shall be allowed to the Overseers in their account over and above such as are for the *immediate reliefe* of the poore."

As is always the result in cases of this kind, the constituted authorities in the end had to perform their duty, and provide the Workhouse. The grumbling ratepayer has always to submit to the inevitable, and generally he but makes his burden all the heavier by a policy of futile procrastination. Of the Poor House provided *Reeves* says (p. 125):— "West Bromwich Poor-house was originally a nail warehouse"—very likely the one used in connection with the parochial employment of the able bodied paupers, both male and female, in nail making—"belonging to Mr Turton" [who had opposed the Workhouse scheme]. "Studs are said to have been made here also. The premises were purchased from John Fidoe" [? of the Wednesbury Quaker family] "for £87 18s., expenses in repairing, fitting up, and paying some cottage rent for the poor, £288 2s. 8d. Total £376 2s. 8d. The title deed bears date the 11th day of August, 1735. Family in the House, October 6th, 19 persons: Job Reeves and Jesson Lowe, churchwardens; William Webb and Joseph Wall, overseers of the poor."

Jesson Lowe's name does not appear in the list of churchwardens given by *Willett*, pp 129–131.

"There were six levies in 1735, and which amounted to £181 1s. 8d."

Whether this date, 1735, is the correct one, and Jesson Lowe had his way immediately on the passing of the resolution of January 24th, 1735, it is certain a workhouse had been provided about this period, 1735-1737. By 1754 it was necessary to put the building into a state of repair, and a Vestry Meeting at the house of Richard Reeves gave authority for the same to be done out of the Rates, the order being signed by Ralph Moore and Joseph Stephens, as churchwardens, and further by Jesson Lowe and Samuel Lowe. *Reeves* professes to give (p. 125), a list of the Governors of the Poor House, starting with "Mr Smith," to whose name he adds—"In Mr Smith's days the Poor in the House wore an iron collar round their necks, with their names and parish engraved thereon, it was after a few years discontinued, and again used in 1766 for a short period." The same writer also says (p. 163), "The poor were buried in West Bromwich Church till Mr Rann's days [1745] without coffins." Although *Willett* (p. 104), extracts from the Vestry Book, under date November 29th, 1765, the record of a "Meeting for electing a Governor," when after "taking the votes of those who paid Church and Poor Rates, Joseph Sanders was found to have the majority"—no mention of Sanders is made by *Reeves*, whose list runs—"Mr Clem. Fisher, Mr Green, Mr George Stephens 1772, Mr Goodwin Smith 1775, Mr Thomas Clarke 1775-1789, Mr John Parkes 1789-1803, Mr William Smith 1803-1812, Mr Charles Starkey 1812-1835, Mr Francis Taylor 1835."

In February 1833 a meeting was held for the purpose of determining what stipendiary parochial officers should be in future employed, when it was resolved— "That a House Governor and Matron be appointed, the duties of the Governor to be to ascertain the settlement of all paupers applying for relief and to have general care of the Poor House, his salary to be £70 per annum. A collector also to be appointed to collect Poor, Highway, and Church Rates, his salary to be £60. A general Clerk and Accomptant to be appointed, salary £60." It is evident that not only registration had been lax in former times, but that the law of pauper settlement bad not been very closely regarded; for in 1773, "Amey, an old woman out of the workhouse, known by no other name," had be buried.

LXVII.—WEST BROMWICH POOR LAW UNION.

As to the early statistics of local pauperism with its one-parish-power administration of the Poor Laws, some figures are forthcoming for comparison with the large and populous union of the present day. "A Rate or Assessment," says *Reeves*, p. 148, "made upon the several inhabitants of West Bromwich upon the 15th day of June, 1750, for the relief of the poor, being the second levy of fourpence in the pound"— apparently the standard poundage in those days—"produced a total of £30 14s. 3½d." He also records "a valuation of the lands, buildings, tithes, and premises within the parish of West Bromwich, in the County of Stafford, made and proportioned at a reduced value, for the purpose of an assessment to the relief of the poor in the years 1799 and 1800, by Richard Fowler and Richard Court:—

	AC.	ROOD	PER.		*Annual value*	
Total ...	5,155	1	36	...	£7,520 14	
Rate at 5d. in the £		...	...	£156	13	7½

ISAAC HADLEY
THOMAS WOODHALL } *Overseers of the Poor."*

After the Inclosure Act of 1802 had added considerably to the landed value of the Parish, we have (*Reeves*, p. 163) a fresh "Assessment of the new enclosure of the Parish of West Bromwich, dated 20 August, 1805:—

Quantity.			*Value.*		
AC.	ROODS.	PER.	£	s.	d.
241	1	11	372	12	0

RICHARD JESSON
EDWARD ELWELL } *Churchwardens.*

PAUL SHELDON
JOSEPH LLOYD } *Overseers."*

Agricultural lands, however, can never compare in value with lands used in connection with mining and manufacturing, for mark the rapid rise in value during the next thirty years—the valuation of lands, buildings, tithes, mines, etc., in the parish was by September, 1836, estimated at £75,000 per annum.

The first enlargement of the original workhouse was agreed upon at a Vestry Meeting on 21st March 1774, as the establishment was then found "insufficient to receive the poor applying for relief; and also all necessary workshops should be built." As to the numbers for which provision had to be made some idea may be gathered from figures given by *Reeves* p. 126:—

		Poor in the House		Out-door Paupers
1798, October 1st	...	39	...	243
1802, July 20th	...	37	...	247
1817, June 16th	...	72	...	444

(Increase no doubt owing to Napoleonic wars just closed, 1815).

1831, March 26th	...	53	...	508
1832, March 25th	...	57	...	490

Then as to finances we have—

		Disbursements for the year			Amount of the Poor Rate	
For 1831	...	£3,120	6	6	£635	5	10
1832	...	£3,432	19	5	£626	14	2
1834	...	£3,492	9	$4\frac{3}{4}$			
1835	...	£3,128	7	$4\frac{3}{4}$			
1836	...	£2,397	18	5			

"The average number of persons in the Poor House 43, at a weekly cost of 3s. 6d. each."

In 1809 the financial straits of the country during the weary progress of the wars against Napoleon may be gauged by the fact that Church levies, if not poor rates had to be enforced by legal process in West Bromwich, and even the Canal Company were in arrear. By 1829 the Poors' House had been allowed to fall into "a ruinous state," no doubt for want of capital expenditure upon it during the hard times. The overseers of both the old Parish Church and also of the new Christ Church were instructed to procure plans and estimates for a new building "upon land belonging to the parish." Frequent are the references to this piece of land; it was specially reserved at the time the common lands were enclosed for purely parish purposes, and as it has never yet been properly occupied, its ultimate fate is still enshrouded in doubt to this day. When the old workhouse in Stolley Lane was occupied, this piece of land, which is situated in the Cronehills some 300 or 400 yards away, was once used as a produce garden to supply the paupers with vegetables; but beyond this stage of usefulness it never progressed. As we shall hear yet again in this chapter of the difficulty of dealing with the land in question, the problem to be solved may be stated to shape itself somewhat in this form—The land was legally reserved in 1802 to the parish of West Bromwich for purely parochial purposes; as by 1834 it had been put to no particular use (that is to say it had no buildings erected upon it to raise it from "prairie value") the newly constituted Board of Guardians of that year could not fairly take possession of the property, inasmuch as they represented not West Bromwich alone, but other outside parishes who could not possibly claim any vested rights in the said "reservation." And so the matter stands. Although it would seem to most people that being "parish land" it should now fall under the control of the Town Council, the legitimate successors to the Parish Vestry.

But to proceed with the historical development of Poor Law administration. By the amendment of the Poor Laws in 1834 Boards of Guardians came into operation, the great principle here involved being that the power of relief was transferred from the Overseers of a Parish to more fully constituted Boards of the people's elected representatives. Another feature was the grouping of smaller parishes into a large "union" of parishes for the more economical working of the Act. Yet for the area of each Board's jurisdiction the civil parish was still taken as a unit, and parish boundaries were never intersected, although county boundaries were—as for instance, Oldbury, although part of West Bromwich Union, is not a Staffordshire parish. Why

Tipton could not have taken the place of Oldbury it has always been difficult to discover. Tipton *is* in Staffordshire, but remains in the Worcestershire Union of Dudley to this day.

In our Introductory Chapter I. we glanced at the many and important changes which these new Poor Laws of 1834 wrought in the constitution and government of West Bromwich.

On p. 164 of *Reeves* will be found the valuation of West Bromwich parish in 1836 (£75,000), while on the preceding page are the names of the Board of Guardians of the newly constituted Union—presumably those of the first elected Board, of which the Earl of Dartmouth was chairman. This nobleman took a deep, personal interest in the working of the new Act, and remained in the position of chairman for some years. The Board meetings were held at the Dartmouth Hotel till 1857.

In February, 1849, it was resolved in Vestry—for as yet the Vestry meeting with all its ecclesiastical influences was a dominating power in the Parish— "to pay out of the Poors' Rates the debts incurred for enlarging, improving, and repairing the Workhouse" in Stoney Lane.

We now presently come to the time when it was deemed advisable to close the separate parochial workhouses, and for economy and the concentration of administrative energy to erect one large "Union Workhouse" in West Bromwich; the parish which headed and gave its name to the poor law union, comprising West Bromwich, Wednesbury, Handsworth, and Oldbury, with Warley. And the first difficulty encountered seems to have been the long standing problem of utilising or selling the Cronehills parish land. At a meeting on September 26th, 1856, consent was given to the Guardians of the Poor to sell a "piece of land situate in Sandwell Road and near the Cronehills, alloted for the use of the Poor House by the Commissioners under the *West Bromwich Inclosure Act*, and containing about 4 acres." It had previously (5th January, 1855) been resolved "That this Meeting do consent to the sale to the Guardians of the Poor of the West Bromwich Union of the land alloted for the use of the poor." This land is described farther on as "a piece of land formerly part of a croft in the Parish of West Bromwich, containing a frontage of thirty yards or thereabouts next the road to Lyndon, and the like frontage next Stoney Lane, together with a dwelling-house and buildings erected thereon, used as a poor-house and called the West Bromwich Workhouse."

Whether the first named "parish land" ever came into the absolute legal possession of the Guardians or not, it is certain they have never had the courage to use it. The new Union was erected in Hallam Street, nearer the Parish Church than the old Workhouse had been. This building was opened on September 25th 1857, and by many was thought altogether too large, and by far more commodious than would ever be required for the purposes of the united parishes. The inmates at the opening numbered 216 made up as follows:—

	West Brom-wich Parish.		Wednesbury and rest of Union.
Sick and infirm	44	... ...	84
Able-bodied ...	12	... ...	4
Children	44	...	28
	100		116

Developments, with accompanying extensions and improvements, have followed one upon another, especially since the appointment of the present Master, Mr William James Gilpin, in September 1871, till the institution has more than doubled itself in all its departments. In some instances it has more than trebled itself, taking the numerical strength of the material dealt with, the inmates now number (14th June, 1895), as under:—

Union of West Bromwich

Sick and infirm	...	...	...	...	613
Able-bodied	...	...	...	...	106
Children in House	...	...	...	...	75
Total	...	...	...	...	794
Children at Wigmore		...	...	...	198
Grand total		...	...	...	992

One of the earliest developments after Mr Gilpin's arrival had regard to the treatment of pauper children. Up to the age of four years children may (and do) safely remain in the Workhouse; but after that age it is well to endeavour to remove them as far as possible from all the contaminating influences and taints of concentrated pauperism. Various means are adopted to effect this. West Bromwich Union joined with the Walsall Union in the formation of a School District, their respective contributions to the undertaking being in the proportion of about 2 to 1. The district school was erected at Wigmore, a convenient situation for both the contributing unions, and was opened on May 1st, 1872, when the number of children drafted in was—

From the West Bromwich Union	...	...	157
„ Walsall „	...	...	56
			213

For the two years previous to this the West Bromwich children had found no accommodation in the Workhouse, but had been boarded out at Stoke-on-Trent, where the authorities had possessed an excess of accommodation. At Wigmore the boys are now under the control of a Superintendent, and the girls of a Matron: the former are taught the trades of the tailor, shoemaker, baker, and gardener, while a proportion assist and learn all they can from the engineer; the girls are employed in the laundry and at other useful domestic avocations. The boys get military drill; and, by way of brightening the lives of the whole establishment, a good juvenile brass band is conducted among them. At the age of 14 the boys are apprenticed, and the girls are sent out to domestic service. but for two years after leaving they are visited and supervised by the chaplain.

After the care of the pauper children, the next class of paupers demanding constant and careful attention is the sick and infirm. At the Workhouse the Infirmary is a distinct department, and is even popular with the poorer stratum of society, for in case of illness the poor will willingly go into the Infirmary, whereas they would indignantly refuse to go into the Workhouse itself. By some curious attitude of the popular mind there is no "disgrace" in accepting assistance from the poor rates through the Infirmary. At first this department was intended for 120 inmates; but the tendency of modern pauperism is an increase in the number of the aged, infirm, and sick, requiring shelter, while the other classes shows signs of diminution. Hence the number now accommodated in the Infirmary has grown to 250. It is so constructed as to be separate in its service and management from the other departments of the " house", there is a head trained nurse, who has five under-nurses, and two night-nurses to assist her. The doctor visits daily.

Old married couples are allowed to live together; West Bromwich finds accommodation for six such couples ample provision for this humane regulation.

While pauper lunatics are sent away for proper treatment in the County Asylums at

Burntwood or Stafford, the imbecile, epileptics, and other harmless insane paupers are retained at the workhouse. They are housed in that portion of the building which was once the children's schoolroom ; but a separate ward, properly constructed, will, no doubt, be provided as one of the developments of the immediate future. The imbeciles are under the care of a man and his wife; the men are employed at gardening, and the women in their own laundry.

With regard to the able bodied paupers, there is, happily, a tendency towards the gradual extinction of this class. During trade depression its ranks are spasmodically swelled by the inclusion of the "unemployed", and the same periodical increases mark the occurrence of severe winter seasons. But when the individuals are closely examined there is always found a large proportion of these able-bodied paupers to be really mentally deficient.

Lastly to be considered, and certainly the least satisfactory of the departments, is the Casual Ward. A new ward for these tramps was provided eight years ago. And whereas the average received weekly was over 250, it has now fallen to 80. This gratifying decrease among the professional paupers relieved here may unhesitatingly be ascribed to the improved methods adopted for their treatment. It is now a system of "isolation and detention." The tramps are no longer herded together, for their own further contamination and degradation, and then allowed to depart next morning after the unprofitable task of picking a regulation amount of oakum; but they are now isolated as far as ever is possible in dormitory and in employment—the men breaking stones and the women in laundry work—detained always one clear day and not allowed to depart till the second morning, and never on Sundays at all. If the tramp turns in twice a month, the detention is extended to three days, and for three times a month to five days a system which has shown itself very satisfactory in its working and results. The Workhouse now occupies eight acres of land and has cost nearly £40,000.

For the distribution of out-door relief the parish of West Bromwich is now divided into two districts, designated respectively the North-east and the South-west.

LXVIII.—WEST BROMWICH DISTRICT HOSPITAL.

In considering the eleemosynary institutions of the town it is but a natural step to proceed from the rate-aided Workhouse to a Hospital supported by voluntary effort. The District Hospital, the area of whose beneficent operations includes the districts of Wednesbury, Oldbury, Great Bridge, and West Smethwick was built in 1869, (and originated from a Dispensary formed and carried on by public subscription in High Street, West Bromwich, in 1867,) the foundation stone being laid by Lady Dartmouth on September 21st, 1869. The building, which was designed by Messrs Martin and Chamberlain, of Birmingham, stands in its own grounds covering an area of 6,000 yards on the Lodge Estate. The original cost was £8,000, and the building contained two wards—males' and females'—each ward being provided with eleven beds. In 1881 an addition of two further wards was made, one for children and a second men's ward, at a cost of £2,600, the accommodation now being 55 beds. Further additions were made in 1890, an administrative department and two circular wards being built at a cost of £7,700 and which addition provides for twenty-eight beds, these wards are on the circular plan, which is adopted for the greater access of air and light and for better ventilation by a central shaft, and were designed by Messrs Wood and Kendrick, and were practically the first in these parts.

The Eye Department was instituted in 1893 and six beds are kept specially for eye cases, all of which cases were previously treated at the Wolverhampton Infirmary.

The Hospital is supported by voluntary contributions, and depends entirely upon private subscriptions and donations, and on the Hospital Saturday and Sunday movements for funds to carry on its work.

The following figures will indicate the steady growth of the institution from its foundation:—

The number of subscribers has risen from 57 in 1867 to 473 at the present time, while the amount subscribed by them has similarly increased from £134 to £762 in 1894. The Hospital Sunday collections in 1871 realised only £169, while last year the places of worship collected £231 for the same object. The Hospital Saturday collections in 1873 were only £499, while with a systematised method of collecting in most of works and factories of the district the movement in 1894 resulted in a total of £2,062 finding its way into the hospital exchequer, Of the numbers treated the 439 out-patients who benefited by the Dispensary of 1867 have given place to 8,118 out patients who drew upon the resources of the hospital in 1894; while the in-patients, who numbered only 84 in 1872, when the hospital was opened, are now replaced by about 920—this being the number who occupied beds in 1894.

LXIX.—The Earlier Forms of Local Government in West Bromwich.

Of local government in West Bromwich the earliest historical form was that of the *Manor*. Many allusions have been made in the preceding chapters to the manor, to the lord of the manor, the manorial court, manorial officers, and to the customs of the manor. At its original Saxon settlement, it was the "Wich" or "Wic," or village situated in the "Broom"; or "Brom-wich." As such Teutonic settlement, its government was a pure democracy; its three governing officers being directly elected by the people in *Tun-gemot* or Town-meeting assembled; namely, (1) the *Reeve* or headman,whose modern counterpart may now he found in the Mayor or chief magistrate; (2) the Bydel or *Beadle*, a messenger-officer, now represented by the head constable; and (3) the *Tithing-man* or petty constable. In course of time came a vast change. After the Conquest, if not before, it was the lord of the manor as feudal autocrat who appointed these (or similar officers) at will, and the independence of the ancient village was lost in the newer form of lordship, or manor.

Manor is a word which merely signifies a "dwelling place," namely, that of the noble who was lord of it. When the popular control was lost most ecclesiastical parishes became also feudal manors, but not all. Sandwell has sometimes been called a manor by itself. Parishioners were practically the tenants on the manor, the manorial officers were, in the feudal period, responsible to the lord and not to the people. Once more, however, local independence began to emerge from this state of feudal dependence. The *Vestry Meeting* gradually grew to take upon itself the lost functions of the ancient *Tun-gemot*. With this resumption of English independence officers were once more elected, rates were granted, and *by-laws* (*i.e.* "town laws") were enacted. With the complexities and gradual evolution of a growing development the officers to be appointed naturally became now more numerous. The Vestry Meeting (so called because held in the ante-room of the parish church where the vestments hung) elected (1) the constable; (2) (*a*) the parish clerk for ecclesiastical work, sometimes assisted by (*b*) the vestry clerk for civil affairs, and who corresponds with the town clerk of to-day; (3) the beadle, a messenger or crier who gradually assumed the powers of the tithingman or petty constable; (4) waywardens or surveyors of highways; (5) churchwardens for the care of church property, assessing of rates, and for the calling of the vestry meetings; and (6) in the later centuries, the overseers of the poor—as set forth in the chapter dealing with Poor Law administration.

Into all this, manorial customs prevailed in many places up to the present century, in an attenuated form no doubt: the powers of the vestry being chiefly exercised for church purposes, and for administering the poor-laws. For instance, the manorial courts appointed various other officers for purely civil business, such as the *ale-taster* mentioned and explained in chapter 1. But to recall a few of the recorded references to these ancient offices and their borders in West Bromwich:—

In 1720 we read (*Willett*, p. 100) "that the Headborough be allowed nothing for ale tasting." The *Headborough* in Saxon times was the chief of the ten pledges in swearing the frankpledge by tithings, the other nine being sometimes designated "handboroughs," or inferior pledges. In our chapter on the Poor Laws we noted that the *Constable* was the officer who dealt with vagrants and sturdy beggars; but the official who often undertook the task of flogging them was the *Beadle*. Allusions to the Beadle are frequent in the vestry records. In 1788 Richard Stanley was appointed Beadle for the year, while to another ancient office, that of Parish Clerk, John Perkin was appointed, with a remuneration of one shilling per week for cleaning the church, to which was added in 1796 a guinea a year for winding the clock. In 1831 William Barton was granted £5 per annum in place of the £1 previously paid him as Parish Clerk. See also Thomas Ault's accounts, as Clerk in 1815, on p. 134 of *Willett*. But reverting to the Beadles, the chief glory of this office in the later centuries, was the gorgeous uniform which always accompanied it. This livery of office was of itself almost sufficient to strike terror into the hearts of evil doers. When Christ Church was opened in 1829, "Isaac Richards and John Wilson were appointed Beadles," and "allowed a complete suit of clothes every second year, and a great coat every fourth year." The cost of these two lots of clothes has already been given—it was no less than £10 0s. 3d. and £5 7s.

As to the "local habitation and the home" of this old form of parish government, that is practically disclosed in its familiar designation "The Vestry." In 1786 special instructions were given for erecting a proper vestry at the newly-restored church, this was no doubt for the convenience of conducting all parish meetings in due form. Yet the quaint old custom of conducting business in the church porch—the precincts of the church again denoting the ecclesiasticism of all old parochial forms —has been alluded to in ch. li. and lxvi.

The functions now performed by the modern Highway Committee, through their able and specially trained executive officer, Mr J. T. Eayrs, the Borough Surveyor, were anciently attempted by the elected representatives of Vestry, the Waywardens of the village lanes and by roads.

The Waywardens of West Bromwich were in 1724 known as *Supervisors of the Highways*, and it was then agreed (April 23rd) that they "doe allow to every teame 3d. a day for every day that they come in and noe more; and likewise that every labourer have three halfpence a day for every day and noe more." As required by law, these accounts were allowed by two Justices, John Lane and John Dolphin.

But not only in Highway matters, nor yet merely in Poor Law Administration, as previously described, did the Justices take part in local government. To these two departments, and of course, to the local administration of justice, must be added many other functions which they were by law called upon to exercise in their respective counties. The magistrates were then appointed only from among the local gentry and great landowners, and to them were entrusted very large and extensive powers in their own particular areas of jurisdiction, of an administrative and judicial nature. Till the country was rife for the more democratic forms of government, the Magistracy exercised a large controlling power over all the elected representatives of the people, such as Overseers, Waywardens, etc.

Among the chief of their executive arms was the constable. But as an elective parish officer he was more or less amenable to popular control; yet sometimes this subordinate official preferred to consider himself as answerable only to the Magistracy. As recorded by *Willett* (p. 99) the Constable in 1721 seems to have set his authority against that of the Supervisor or Surveyor of Highways, while in the matter of the administration of justice the Vestry had to restrain his hand in the disbursement of fees by passing a resolution to the effect that the constable "give but 4d. to any *hiew and cry*, and that he set down the day of the month whence the *hiew and cry* came and whither sent." So that apparently the Constable's accountancy was discredited, and that for his work in tracing and capturing felons and other offenders by passing on the hue and cry from parish to parish, he had been charging the rate-payers too much. No doubt as social life advanced, the efficiency of the parish constable was found to be less and less to the satisfaction of the public. The protection afforded was in fact found to be totally inadequate for populous places, if indeed it had not failed in every emergency during the period when Bromwich was but a village community. *Reeves* shows (pp. 84-88) this inadequacy on several memorable occasions, namely, at the Sacheverel Riots in 1715, the Wesley Riots in 1743-4, Bread Riots in 1801, a Colliers' Riot in 1831, and the Election Riot in 1835.

In 1819 also, resort had to be made to the extra assistance of specially sworn constables, a fact which is preserved on record because the payment of these special constables from the parochial funds was evidently challenged by a Meeting of aggrieved Ratepayers. The Churchwarden who had authorised the payment was perhaps surcharged, and then appealed to expert opinion on the matter. Here is that opinion, as set forth in a letter kept in the church safe:—

"Dear Sir,—I have perused the Resolutions of the Inhabitants of West Bromwich assembled in Vestry of the 19th May, 1819, and carefully considered the question; how far you as Churchwardens are justified in paying the salaries of the seven Special Constables appointed by the Vestry Meeting. I do not think the Special Constables can be considered as your assistants for all the purposes mentioned the resolution. For instance, they are "To suppress the disorderly proceedings of any persons publickly assembled together on the Lord's pay without lawful occasion." Now it is no part of your duty to suppress the disorderly proceedings alluded to unless they take place in the church or churchyard. The Constable of the Parish is the proper person to preserve the peace and suppress the disorderly proceedings alluded to.

"By Resolution 2.—'The Assistant Constables are to see that the *public houses* are not kept open during the hours of Divine Service on the Lord's Day, nor after 9 o'clock at night, nor for the purpose of *tippling* during any part of the day.' The Churchwardens as well as the constables are by Statute (4 *James* II. 5, *s.* 7), and their oaths required to prevent tippling as well on Sundays as other days. Whether the Magistrates have ordered all public houses in your parish to be closed at 9 o'clock at night or not, I think it is the Constable's duty and not the Wardens' to see that they are closed at that hour.

"The Third Resolution is 'To see that the butchers, hucksters, and other shop-keepers do not keep open their shops on the Lord's Day after nine o'clock in the forenoon.' "The 4th Section requires 'The Assistant Constables to assist the

Churchwardens in clearing the churchyard and *church-porch* of all idle persons loitering there during the time of Divine Service. CLEMENT INGLEBY."

This Clement Ingleby was an attorney of the highest standing in Birmingham, and a Commissioner in Bankruptcy, etc. There seems no doubt the Churchwardens had, in this particular instance exceeded their duties. But on the other hand, as we have seen, the powers of the Churchwardens were then very considerable. For instance, the churchwardens (1) were to join with the overseers in making rates for the relief of the poor, (2) setting up trades for employing them, (3) placing out poor apprentices, (4) settling poor persons, etc. All these functions were noted under the head of Poor Law Administration. But the further duties of the churchwardens being here noticed related to their connection with the church; they (1) were to see that all the parishioners duly resorted to their parish church during divine service: (2) they were not to permit anyone to stand idle, walk, or make any noise in the church, (3) they were to chastise disorderly boys, (4) they were to search *ale houses on Sundays*, that no persons be found within them during divine service, etc. The performance of this last-named duty had evidently exercised the West Bromwich authorities very considerably for some time. In August, 1807, a Vestry Meeting declared its opinion that already there were more than sufficient public ale-houses in the parish, and requested the justices to grant no more licenses; in 1814 a similar Meeting repeated the declaration, and opined that the facilities for drinking promoted idleness and disorderly and vicious habits—bull-baiting was then rife, and "Saint Monday" was always honoured by idleness and debauchery. With regard to the evil of "tippling," as late as 1835 the churchwardens had specially waited on Lord Dartmouth to consider steps for effectually suppressing "tippling in the public and beer houses on the Sabbath Day." At this period the Acting Magistrates for West Bromwich division were: the Earl of Dartmouth, Sir Edward Dolman Scott, Bart., Edward Grove, Esq., of Shenstone Park, Chandos Leigh, Esq., of Aldridge, and the Rev. E. G. Simcox, of Harborne. Their Clerk was Mr James Male, and two or more of them sat every Saturday, at Scott Arms Hotel, Barr, and the Dartmouth Hotel, West Bromwich, alternately. That both the judicial and executive machinery was at this time very defective is evidenced by a declaration of the Vestry on 21st September, 1831, that there was "a lamentable increase of crime"; that there existed in the parish "a class of persons without visible means of subsistence" who were sources of vice and debauchery strongly calling for a more efficient police, and coming to the point asked openly for a "sufficient resident magistracy" and an effective police to carry out the law, It must be remembered that the days of the parish constable were then approaching an end, and that the public attention was being directed towards the necessity of an organised county constabulary. On the other hand an appeal was made to Quarter Sessions, July 1842, evidently by the "economical" class of ratepayers, "believing that the Constables, Watchmen, and other officers are quite sufficient to keep the peace and protect the parish; and being convinced after a trial of nearly three years that the Police officers stationed in the parish are unnecessary and a vexatious burden upon the poor rate," that the Police force within the parish be discontinued to relieve the "overburdened" ratepayer! So that merely to save the rates, these parishioners would have reverted to the effete Parish Constable and the decrepit Watchman again; even at this most critical time when West Bromwich was fast emerging from its state of village-dom, and becoming a populous place and a busy centre of growing industries.

As evidence, however, of the rural character so long preserved by West Bromwich, may be noted the war waved by its agriculturist up to recent times against "vermin" and what were considered to be destructive birds. In 1746 it was agreed by the Vestry that the churchwardens should pay 2d. per dozen for sparrows' heads. Urchins (or hedge-hogs) were also deemed inimicable to the welfare of the farmer, and 4d. each was the price set upon their lives. On p. 134 of *Willett* will be found an account rendered to the parish by James Smith (? churchwarden) for the destruction of these "vermin." This was at the beginning of the present century, One piece of evidence also remains that there was at least a small amount of public spirit existing in the parish; this was a resolution passed 15th October, 1830, in favour of the Emancipation of Slaves. But if the the leaders of English social life were not yet awake it cannot be wondered at if as yet local government of the parishes retained so many of the antiquated and inefficient forms to this very late period.

The Ale-taster to whose office reference may once more be made by way of illustration, may be considered in some fashion as the manorial prototype of our modern Food and Drug Inspectors, for it was his special function to maintain the standard of quality of all beer brewed within the Manor. But the protection of all public rights and privileges, as secured by the Manorial Courts, supplemented by popular government as then conducted in vestry meetings, was of the very feeblest description. And that one department of local government which we now deem of paramount importance, was till almost recent times all but ignored. That was the care of the public health. It is not therefore surprising to learn that whenever disease broke out in an epidemic form, its ravages nearly always assumed such formidable proportions as to drive the authorities to despair. The visitation of Cholera to this locality in 1832, has already been described by many writers.

Reeves says (p. 124)—"In West Bromwich the first case was on July 15th—a poor man, a boatman, of the name of John Cavan; from this time until October 15th we had 297 cases and 62 deaths. The Ranters' Meeting in Sams Lane was fitted up for a Hospital."

As early as 1828 (16 October) the Vestry had given some casual attention to "nuisances", but now that an epidemic had appeared to stimulate their vigilance it is on record that under date September 14th, 1832, a meeting was "held to receive a statement of the present expenditure of the Board of Health, and to grant a further sum of money to the Board for the purpose of carrying out the Cholera Act and the orders of His Majesty's Most Honourable Privy Council: it was resolved to adjourn to the Schoolroom in Hall End, where it was resolved to place at the disposal of the Board of Health the sum of £250 to be paid out of the Poor Rates."

Perhaps it was part of the same work of putting their house in order which induced the Vestry the same year (10 December, 1832) "to have a Plan of the Highways in the Parish made by Mr William Saller," although there is a suspicion from the terms of the resolution that the Vestry was still more concerned about encroachments on the common lands than they were about the public health. Even the attention which Vestry paid to roads and highways was generally that which had for its purpose an excuse to escape from liability to repair them at the public expense. So late as July, 1842, the repairs of Temple Street, running from the Turnpike Road towards the Windmill in Tantany Lane, were formally repudiated by a Vestry meeting.

LXX.—THE IMPROVEMENT COMMISSIONERS (1854–1882): LOCAL ACTS OF PARLIAMENT AFFECTING WEST BROMWICH.

Up to the year 1854, West Bromwich was governed as we have seen, by the Parish Vestry and (more latterly) the Surveyors of Highways; the latter body was elected in Vestry in the March of each year (qualification being ownership of land valued at £10 annually, or possession of £100 in property), or in default of election, they were appointed by the Justices under the *Highway Act, 1835.*

By this date (1854) there were in existence some churches and chapels; but these were the only class of public building to be found within the confines of the parish. Not only was there an absence of proper public buildings for conducting the municipal and social life of the community, but the streets were ill-lighted and totally unpaved, the roads were atrociously bad, the place was undrained, and its death rate was high. The population had then reached 35,000, and it was therefore felt that the formation of a Local Board under any general and adoptive Act, would not meet the requirements of the case; the parish was in all essentials a "town," and its government needed to be provided with full and adequate powers for dealing with it as such:

In 1853 a vestry meeting was held (on October 14th), when it was moved by George Frederick Muntz, Esq., M.P. (Sandwell), and carried unanimously. "That it would be of great public advantage if the parish of Wrest Bromwich were sufficiently paved, drained, lighted, cleaned and otherwise improved, and a Local Board of Health established therein; and whereas the said purpose cannot be effected without the authority of Parliament, it is therefore the opinion of this meeting that the necessary steps should be immediately taken for obtaining a Local Act for the parish of West Bromwich in the ensuing session of Parliament." A committee was appointed, consisting of above forty of the inhabitants, among them George Frederick Muntz, M.P., Rev. James Spry, Rev. James Bradshaw, Rev Benjamin Willmore, Thomas Jesson, Henry Dawes (Charlemont), Thomas Davies, William Salter, John Chance, Charles Bagnall, etc. The outcome of this was the obtaining of the West Bromwich Improvement Act of 1854, which incorporated the Improvement Commissioners and conferred powers upon them for the better paving, draining, lighting, cleaning, and otherwise improving the parish, and for constructing cemeteries and maintaining and regulating markets. Further powers were conferred by an Amendment Act in 1855, and another Amendment Act again in 1865. Thirteen members were to be elected. and three others to be appointed by the Staffordshire Quarter Sessions in each month of October. The Act provided that the Commissioners should reside within seven miles of Christ Church (which was recognised as the centre of the new urban district, in preference to the old Parish Church); that they should be rated at £25 per year to the poor rate, or seized of £100 per year in leaseholds or freeholds, or be possessed of £2,000 personally. With this local Act was incorporated the Commissioners' Clauses Act of 1847, by which owners and occupiers were given the following votes for electing their Commissioners:—For any property for which an occupier was entered, if it be rated at less than £50, one vote; £50 and under £100, two votes; £100 and under £150, three votes; £150 and under £200 four votes; £200 and under £250, five votes; above 250 six votes. If the person were also owner as well as occupier of the said property, he was entitled to double the number of votes. Such was the effect of a franchise like this, that four partners of one firm have been known to walk into a polling booth and record 48 votes. No individual could have more than twelve votes. Mr Reuben Farley was a Commissioner for about 20 years, and the Chairman from 3rd October. 1874, to the close of the Board's career. He himself was entitled to 12 votes, his partner in the works to 12, and his partner in some leasehold collieries to 6, total 30. The checking of the votes was always a difficult task as there was no voters' list and the rate collector had to calculate each voter's number of votes to be allowed. It was open voting, written out so that every one might know how the votes were given. Thus were the 13 elective members placed in power; as to the three magistrate Commissioners they were not always forthcoming so easily as this, owing to the restrictions of the residential qualification.

No doubt the coming of the Great Western Railway, which placed West Bromwich in more direct communication with the outside world, had a very stimulating effect upon the public life of the place. The opening of the Grand Junction line in 1837 had little or no effect, as it merely skirted the parish at Newton Road, even farther out than the parish church was from the centre of population. The opening of the Stour Valley line ten years later had given the Spon Lane end a fillip, but the Great Western inaugurated quite a new era for West Bromwich when it tapped the centre of its population in 1854.

In 1801 the population of West Bromwich was 5,887, scattered in detached residential quarters, or mere aggregations of houses, over an area of 5,710 acres. Practically it may be said that the place was always a village, remaining comparatively stationary till the enclosure. in 1804, of its extensive wastes; the boundaries of which extended roughly from Overend to Carters Green in one direction, and from Messenger Lane to the Turks Head in the other. Till 1804, the Common stretching from Hill Top to Sandwell Park along both sides the main road to Birmingham afforded shelter for the partridge and the pheasant, and a safe cover for the hare and the rabbit. Near the present railway bridge in Lodge Road was one of the highest points of land, and on it grew till 1764 a clump of trees where six roads converged, and which constituted the travellers' land mark in crossing the heath, To the north-east could be seen the Old Church, Lyne, and Mayer's Green. Scattered between the church and the green were the cottages of the greater part of the inhabitants of the parish. On the other side, toward the south, stood another cluster of cottages, called Old End. This part of the parish had been enclosed about 1690. Near by was the Oak House, not in such an apparent hollow as it now seems to lie in, but almost on a level with the clump of trees and surrounded by stately oaks over the tops of which peered its lantern turret and its gabled roof—the former marking the military look-out of the roof-leads, and the latter affording no clue to the sinister provision of the casernes for the sleeping of a garrison amidst its roof-timbers. As yet the track across the Heath had scarcely felt the importance of its new dignity as a coach-road—for the ancient main road from Wednesbury to Birmingham had wandered from Oakeswell Hall round West Bromwich Old Hall, Stone Cross, Church Vale, and Mayers Green—and the cutting through Holloway Bank was yet regarded as an engineering feat of wondrous magnitude. Still the Hill Top portion of the road was not without its points of interest, there was Oakwood, the family seat of the Jessons, the Old Meeting with its lingering traditions of the fanatic mob's attack upon it, and further off, the "The Woodlands," in its sunny gardens and pleasant slopes, as built by the eminent scientist and philosopher, Dr. James Keir.

From the date of the Enclosure Act, the growth was steady, proceeding at the rate of about 800 per annum increase for at least 50 years. Thus the

Population in	1811	was	7,485
,,	1821	,,	9,905
,,	1831	,,	15,337
,,	1841	,,	26,121
,,	1851	,,	34,591
,,	1861	,,	41,795
,,	1871	,,	47,908
,,	1881	,,	56,295

The increase became much more rapid after mining industries were introduced, which was not till much later than in any of the other Surrounding Black Country parishes. But at the end of this period namely, in 1881, there was still half the area of the parish being used as agricultural land.

The town, in the meantime, had become the recognised seat of the hollow-ware trade (See Wednesbury Workshops, pp 25-29) to which were added other extensive industries in the shape of chemical works, brick works, spring-balance, safe and tube factories and other large iron-works, to say nothing of its coal-mining development at Sandwell and the lesser collieries. Such had been the progress of West Bromwich when were called into existence the Town Improvement Commissioners who governed the parish for the next 28 years, namely, from 1854 to 1882, and under whom the town then made even more rapid progress; as will be clearly seen as we proceed.

This Board of 16 Commissioners was organised for departmental work in seven committees, six meeting in the day time, and one at night. Most of the members served on several committees, and a quorum consisted of two. These committees were respectively designated: (1) The Highway, (2) The Sanitary (3) The Markets and Baths, (4) The Cemetery, (5) The Gas, (6) The Finance, and (7) The General Purposes. To these must be added the Free Library Committee, which according to the permissive Act calling it into existence, consisted partly of commissioners, and partly of other gentlemen who interested themselves in the work of the institution. In tracing the development of the place's local government, it may be convenient to deal with the departmental details under the heads of the various committees. Of these the most ancient and representative in its character is the *Highway Committee.*

At this time (1882) there were sixty miles of roads within the boundaries of West Bromwich which were repairable by the parish. In addition to these maintained by the Commissioners there were five miles declared "main roads" under the Highways and Locomotives Amendment Act, a proportion of the expenditure upon which was paid by the County, Already some seven miles of paving had been laid down, and at this juncture the tramways were being promoted, by which it was proposed to lay down five miles of double lines along the highways.

Next should come in for consideration, as indubitably the highest in importance. the work of the *Sanitary Committee.* But as sanitation in this modern epoch has dominated every other branch of local government, it is somewhat difficult to select the details of special effect in this matter of taking a direct care of the public health. Its highest development was perhaps resolved in 1878, when a public park was provided as the lungs of the town. This pleasantly situated open space, comprising fifty-six acres of undulating land, was lent to the town for a period of ninety-nine years, at a nominal rent, by Lord Dartmouth, in compliment to whom it was named "Dartmouth Park." The Commissioners did not hesitate to spend £8,000 on this desirable acquisition, laying it out in drives, walks, ornamental waters, cricket and recreation grounds, refreshment rooms and shelters, keeper's lodge, and everything complete for the public enjoyment. But the real details of this committee's onerous duties are not such pleasant reading, dealing as they do with nightsoil removal, zymotic disease, and death rates, and the problems of drainage. In the last-named connection the Commissioners commenced the sewerage scheme of deep drainage, and purchased 282 acres at Friar Park for a sewage farm.

The Cemetery Committee had to undertake a branch of work for which the Commissioners were specially empowered. (For the overcrowding of the church burial ground, and its enlargement from time to time in 1773, 1823, and 1859 see *Willett* p. 74). At a cost of £6,400 some 16 acres of land, not far removed from the old parish churchyard, were laid out, with chapels and an entrance lodge, for the purposes of a public cemetery. Generally it required a rate of 1d. in the pound to support the burial department.

The Market and Baths Committee were also specially empowered to act. The provision of baths was but one of those sanitary precautions to which allusion has been made. At an outlay of £6,000 a building was erected which contained commodious swimming baths and private baths for both sexes; which altogether attracted some 27,000 bathers to patronise them in each year. The provision of a market did not result so satisfactorily. When the embodiment of the town's progressive public spirit eventuated in the erection of the block of public buildings which since 1875 have ornamented the High Street, a Market Hall was included along with the Town Hall, Free Library, and those other public offices which go to make up that pile of buildings. But the exemplification of public spirit is one thing, and the overcoming of prejudice and life-long proclivities is another. The Market Hall was never popular and soon became a signal failure. At an expenditure of £5,000 it was made replete with every modern convenience, its well-lighted spacious area, 147 feet by 87 feet, being fitted with 62 stalls, and 12 look-up shops: while at the rear was an open market with pig-pens and sheep-pens all provided. Yet it is now practically deserted; several causes no doubt contributed to this discouraging result. Chiefly, local prejudice is in favour of open markets—a small one has flourished on Saturday nights for years without official recognition on private land between High Street and Paradise Street—and secondly, the market was "up-steps," and was not a thoroughfare between any two centres of traffic—fatal objections which left it stranded far from the bustling tides of the people's lives.

In a thriving community such as this, there could not but be many interests to be safeguarded and served by a *General Purposes Committee*, whose deliberations produced among other things the aforesaid Public Buildings in 1875. This massive group of buildings, designed by Messrs Alexander and Henman, of Stockton-on-Tees, and built by Messrs Trow and Sons, of Wednesbury, include a Town Hall, which was opened on Tuesday, August 10th, 1875, and to which was presented a fine organ by Mr Alexander Brogden, at that time M.P. for the borough of Wednesbury, in which West Bromwich was then comprehended.

The *Free Library Committee* had got to work a little earlier. The Lending Department soon possessed over 10,000 volumes, yielding an average circulation of 62,000 volumes per annum. The Reference Department became possessed of nearly 2,000 volumes, of a character both valuable and useful. For the purchase of books a voluntary fund of £1,500 was raised with but little effort.

One of the latest Committees, but one whose business was perhaps of the most weighty description, was the *Gas Committee*. In 1876 the Corporation of Birmingham bought up the various private undertakings which supplied their town with gas. One of these companies was the Staffordshire Gas Company, whose works had been erected at Swan Village in the parish of West Bromwich. Even REEVES considers the planting of this novel industry in the parish of sufficient historic interest to write upon it (pp. 122-3) as follows:—

"The Birmingham and Staffordshire Gasworks are situated near the Swan Inn, and were erected in the year 1825 (under an Act of Parliament), at the expense of £120,000 raised in £50 shares. If any person had predicted a century ago that a Beacon would be set up in West Bromwich, that would light the streets and shops of Birmingham, he would have been treated as a fanatic or if any one had told us, only a few years since, that we should have lived to hear, that the vast ocean had been crossed in a steam vessel, and to see our streets, houses, and places of worship lighted up by the burning of air, we should have smiled at the idea for a moment, and then have dismissed it as an incredible wonder, the offspring of fancy or folly. We have lived to witness these things. These Gas Works are the largest in the kingdom, and supply part of Birmingham; also, the parishes of West Bromwich, Handsworth, Wednesbury, Darlaston, Bilston, Tipton, and Oldbury; they have upwards of 90 miles of main pipes, 200 retorts, 10 gasometers, each capable of holding 2,500 feet of gas. A committee of proprietors meet once a fortnight at the Birmingham and Staffordshire Gas Company's Office, Old Square, Birmingham.

> J. F. Ledsum, Esq, *Governor.*
> Mr J. Brunton, *Engineer.*
> Mr Joseph Rowlinson, *Clerk."*

All the parishes supplied by the old gas company had the opportunity of purchasing that part of the plant and mains by which their respective areas were fed with the artificial light. Some elected to purchase and some not to do so. Wednesbury among the latter, is still supplied with gas by the Corporation of Birmingham, in succession to the old Staffordshire Company. West Bromwich, on the other hand decided to acquire control of its own gas undertaking. Therefore it was necessary in 1876 to go to Parliament once more, and obtain powers whereby the Commissioners might purchase from the Corporation of Birmingham (who had themselves been recently empowered to acquire the Swan Village Gasworks and all its appurtenances) so much of the gas undertaking as they wished to control, and which was situated within the limits of the parish, and to light the said parish with gas. On the arbitrator's award they paid Birmingham £70,750, which with stamps and extensions came ultimately to £71,650. They then expended over £70,000 on the erection of new works at Albion, the Swan Village Works being retained by Birmingham to supply Wednesbury and other outlying districts.

Lastly, we may here glance at the *Finance Committee* upon whom rested the grave responsibility of providing the ways and means for all the other committees. The total indebtedness of the Commissioners on mortgage in 1882 was £221,500; the chief items of this amount were £27,000 on account of Public Buildings (reduced from £31,000 in 1876): £11,000 for Footpath paving (increased from £4,000 in 1876); £18,600 for sewers, a new item; nearly 8,000 for park; and over £147,000 for gas works which of course produced a revenue for the ratepayers. The ratable value of the parish was about £200,000. The rates were then about 2s. 8d. in the £ altogether (say 1s. 4d. payable each half year) inclusive of the Free Library fixed rate of one penny the Highway Improvement, Sanitary, and Cemetery rates. The rates had been higher, namely 2s. 10d. and 3s, but a diminution had then set in owing to the profits made on the gas-undertaking going to the relief of the rates.

Such was the civic progress and standard of public life to which the town had been brought by its Commissioners in 1882.

LXXI.—The West Bromwich Gas Undertaking.

The manufacture and supply of gas, besides being a revenue producing department of the local authority is also now its largest departmental concern; and therefore deserves here a chapter to itself, coming just between the work of the late Commissioners and that of the new Municipality.

The gas undertaking of the Borough was established on 1st July, 1880, under powers of an Act of Parliament, promoted by the late Board of Improvement Commissioners. The gas supply (as mentioned in the last chapter) was previously in the hands of the

Birmingham and Staffordshire Gas Light Company, until purchased by the Corporation of Birmingham on 1st January, 1875.

The Board of Commissioners opposed the Bill of the Birmingham Corporation for the acquisition of the Birmingham and Staffordshire Gas Light Company's property, and succeeded in obtaining the insertion of a clause empowering the purchase of that portion of the gas undertaking which was contained within the district of any Local or Sanitary Authority or Authorities, by agreement, or failing agreement, by arbitration, provided steps were taken for that purpose within a certain specified time.

The insertion of this clause was a victory for the local authorities concerned, but was not obtained without the usual expenditure of money. Parliamentary oppositions are proverbially expensive luxuries in which to indulge, and West Bromwich came out of the fray with a bill of £1,800. This amount was subsequently made a charge not on the rates of the town as it might well have been, but upon the gas undertaking, so that the ratepayers were not directly charged with the cost even of the initial proceedings.

The West Bromwich Improvement Commissioners under powers contained in the section referred to, had promoted a bill in Parliament in the year 1875 to enable them to purchase the right of supplying gas in West Bromwich, and in the following year (1876) the bill received the Royal assent. The expenses of obtaining the Act, although an unopposed measure, were £1,368.

The local authorities of Smethwick, Tipton and Oldbury also promoted bills in regard to their respective districts, and notice of purchase thereunder was in due course served upon the Corporation of Birmingham, by the four local authorities. The West Bromwich Commissioners failing to come to an agreement with Birmingham as to the terms of purchase, the matter was referred to arbitration. The parties failing also in the selection of a single arbitrator. the West Bromwich Commissioners appointed the late Sir Frederick Joseph Bramwell, Civil Engineer, London and the Corporation of Birmingham appointed the late Mr Thomas Hawksley, Civil Engineer, London, as arbitrators. The arbitrators nominated the late Sir Henry Arthur Hunt, C.B., London, to be umpire, to decide on any matters on which they should differ. The inquiry was characterised by considerable spirit and earnestness on both sides, and it is to be feared, at times with some little display of feeling. A large number of the most experienced gas engineers and accountants of the day were examined as witnesses and it is not a matter of surprise to learn that considerable divergence of opinion existed between the witnesses of each side The inquiry occupied some forty days, but the arbitrators being unable to agree as to the amount of compensation to be paid to Birmingham, the decision lay with the Umpire. The Umpire's award as regards West Bromwich was to the effect that the Improvement Commissioners were to pay the Corporation of Birmingham the sum of £70,750, and in addition the cost of any extensions of mains and meters made in the town between the date of the award and the date upon which the supply was formally taken over, namely 1st July, 1880. The value of the extensions was afterwards arranged as £546, so that the total amount paid to Birmingham was £71,296. The stamp duty on the deed of transfer executed between the two parties was £354.

The sum paid for the acquisition of this portion of the concern may, to many people, appear excessive, but when it is mentioned that most of the witnesses called by Birmingham estimated its value at amounts from £200,000 and upwards, it will be admitted that West Bromwich did not, alter all, make a very bad bargain.

There can be no doubt that the case as regards West Bromwich was laid before the arbitrators with consummate skill and ability, the credit of which is due to Mr Reuben Farley (Chairman of the late Improvement Commissioners, and present Mayor of the Borough), and to the late Mr Charles H. Bayley (Clerk to the Board). It is matter of common knowledge that the former gentleman spent many sleepless nights during the progress of the negotiations.

The Improvement Commissioners were not as yet in a position to supply gas, as no manufacturing plant and processes were included in the award. It was necessary, therefore, to select a site for the erection of works, and it was ultimately decided to purchase a plot of land of about five acres in extent on the Union Estate at Albion, fronting Oldbury Road, and bounded on one side by the London and North-Western Railway Company's Stour Valley line, and on another side by the Birmingham Canal Company's main canal to Wolverhampton. The site is therefore convenient for receiving coal, etc., and for shipment of bye-products; and, lying relatively low, enables the supply of gas to be maintained throughout the town without working an exceptionally high pressure.

Designs for the works were publicly invited, and subsequently the design sent in by the late Mr G. W. Stevenson, Memb. Inst. C.E., London, was accepted and the construction of the various works and plant was carried out under that gentleman's supervision. The execution of the works was not effected without difficulties, but by tact and perseverance these were overcome, and gas was duly forthcoming to supply the town on the evening of 1st July, 1880 as previously arranged. During the forenoon of that day the purchase money payable to Birmingham was handed over to their representatives, and at twelve o'clock noon the chairman of the late Board of Commissioner, (Mr Farley) with some little ceremony turned the gas into the mains of the town. In celebration of the event Mr Farley, with his accustomed generosity, entertained the members of the Board principal officials, the engineer, and others to luncheon in the Town Hall, at which mutual congratulations were exchanged.

The members of the Board of Commissioners who formed the Gas Committee at the time of the transfer were the late Mr Joseph Cooksey (chairman), Mr Reuben Farley, Mr John Field, Mr John B. Lees, Mr Samuel Roberts, and Mr Joseph H. Siddons.

Mr Cooksey occupied the chair until November 1882, when the present Mayor of the Borough (Mr Alderman Farley) was elected, and he has filled the position down to the present time.

The Gas Committee lost no time in arranging for a private siding from the works to the London and North Western Railway, in order to facilitate deliveries of coal and other materials; also for the making of a basin to connect the works with the Birmingham Canal. These matters were carried out and completed shortly after the works were opened, and have proved of considerable advantage, both pecuniarily and otherwise.

The works were designed and constructed for the making of 200,000,000 cubic feet of gas per annum, and the quantity made during the first year of the undertaking was 125,867,000 cubic feet. The production has steadily increased with one or two slight exceptions down to the present time, the quantity made during the year ending 31st March, 1895, being 205,752,100 cubic feet.

No very considerable extensions have as yet been required in the manufacturing plant with the exception of the apparatus for washing and purifying the gas, which was augmented in the year 1891. An additional gasholder was also constructed in the year 1893, thereby materially increasing the storage capacity of the works.

The amount expended on capital account, including land, works, apparatus, mains, also purchase money paid to Birmingham, as well as costs of arbitration proceedings and the expenses incidental to the consolidation of the debt and the issue of Corporation stock in lieu thereof to 31st March, 1895, was £197,563 19s. 11d., of which £17,094 2s 5d. has been extinguished and paid off.

The period originally fixed by Parliament for repayment of the debt was 60 years dating from five years after the commencement of the undertaking. During these five years no provision was required to be made towards redemption of the debt but the Gas Committee, however, very wisely resolved to commence repayment with the first year's working, and continued to do so each year, With the result that at the end of the five years referred to the sum of £5,800 was wiped off.

When the general debt of the borough was consolidated under an Act of Parliament passed in the year 1889, the whole of the existing debt including that of the gas works was made one debt instead of a number of separate debts with varying periods of repayment as previously, and Parliament prescribed that the whole should be redeemed in one equated period of 41 years, dating from July, 1889. The result is that instead of the gas debt being continued until the year 1945 as originally fixed, it will be extinguished in the year 1930, so that in 35 years from the present time the gas debt will he liquidated the ratepayers then obtaining a valuable property, free from encumbrances, and a property which, if the existing conditions continue, will not have cost them one penny.

The powers of borrowing moneys contained in the original Act of Parliament having become exhausted, the Corporation in the year 1885 petitioned the Local Government Board for further borrowing powers, and a provisional order was passed by Parliament in the following year authorising the Corporation to borrow a further sum of £50,000, with the consent of the Local Government Board, for the purposes of extending the works, plant, and mains when found necessary.

The additional powers have been exercised in the construction of a gas-holder, and in the extension of the purifying plant already referred to, and in the extension of mains in various parts of the borough.

At the time the late Board of Commissioners commenced the supply of gas, the prices charged to consumers ranged from 3s. to 2s.4d. per thousand cubic feet, but a reduction was speedily made to 2s. 9d. ranging to 2s 3d. per thousand feet, and a further reduction was made in 1884 when the prices were from 2s. 5d. to 2s. In the year 1886, however, the prices were advanced, and made from 2s. 8d, to 2s. 3d. which have continued to the present time. These prices, having regard to all circumstances compare very favourably with other towns of the same size as West Bromwich.

The gross profits made from the commencement to 31st March, 1895, have been £140,596 14s. 7d., out of which sum £86,385 6s. 6d. has been paid in interest on the debt, and £22,412 19s. 6d. set aside for extinction of the debt. Out of the balance remaining, £4,000 was applied to the formation of a Depreciation Fund, and lastly the sum of £17,500 has been paid over in relief of the General District Rate of the Borough. In the early years of the gas undertaking £3,000 per annum was contributed in aid of rates, but circumstances then were exceptionally favourable for making large profits, the works were new requiring very little expenditure for repairs and maintenance, and coal and labour moreover were very low, whilst the bye-products commanded a high price. For several years past a very different condition of affairs has obtained; coal and labour have greatly appreciated in value, whilst the bye-products have been seriously depreciated, in two cases nearly 150 per cent. The result is that the profits have suffered accordingly and the contributions made in aid of rates have proportionally diminished. In the fifth year of the undertaking the contribution was reduced from £3,000 to £1,500 and during the three following years entirely ceased. The contributions were however resumed in 1888. and continued for four years at the rate of £1,000 per annum. During the last three years no relief to rates has been experienced from the gas works owing to the Gas Committee being engaged in the formation of a working capital by the accumulation of surplus profits. A sum of £10,000 has now been accumulated for this purpose, and it may be that contributions in relief of rates will be resumed.

In the years 1893 and 1894 the Gas Committee made extensive alterations in the retort house, and adopted the regenerator system of firing for heating the retorts, whilst at the same time the productive power of the retorts was augmented to an extent which will meet the requirements of the borough for some few years. The outlay consequent upon these alterations has been largely met out of the depreciation fund already referred to, and the Gas Committee considered themselves justified in this expenditure in view of the advantages over the old system of working, and the economies to be effected thereby.

Nearly 22,000 tons of coal are required annually to produce a proper supply of gas for the borough at the present time, and 43 miles of mains are laid for the distribution of the gas to the 5,200 consumers at present supplied.

The late Board of Commissioners appointed as manager of the works, at their inauguration, Mr William Littlewood, of Manchester, and he continued in the managership until March, 1895 when he resigned. Mr Thomas Glover, assistant at the Carlisle Gas and Water Works was appointed to succeed Mr Littlewood, and he holds the position at the present time. The distribution of gas (or the out-door department) is under the superintendence of Mr W. H. Wayte, formerly with the Birmingham Corporation, and he has had charge of this branch of the undertaking from its commencement in 1880 to the present time. The late Board appointed their clerk (Mr Charles H. Bayley) as secretary, and he occupied the position until his lamented death in the year 1882, when the accountant (Mr Thomas Hudson, who was appointed in 1880) succeeded to the secretaryship also, and still retains the office. As a matter of fact the last named has been the presiding genius throughout the whole of these newer complicated financial arrangements and readjustments; and to him it is very largely due that they have all turned out so advantageously.

LXXII.—Incorporation as a Municipal Borough (1882).— A Parliamentary Borough (1885)—A County Borough (1890).

Public spirit seems to have reached high-water mark in West Bromwich, when in 1882 a petition was presented to the Privy Council for the incorporation of the parish as a municipal borough. No less than 1,053 inhabitant householders signed this petition, and these represented a ratable value of £24,696. There was no disposition whatever to find fault with the government of the Commissioners; but there was an avowed and laudable aspiration for the enjoyment of the very highest form of municipal life possible. By order of the Privy Council an official enquiry was held before the Hon. T. H. W. Pelham, at the Town Hall, on May 25th. The arguments then adduced in support of the petition were:— (1) The enjoyment of a simpler franchise and the right of the ballot, or secret voting; (2) greater facilities for raising loans at easier rates of interest, and the lightening of the ratepayers' burdens in this respect; (3) a rise in the status of the town by the conferring upon it of a higher civic dignity; (4) with the enjoyment of this higher dignity under a Mayor and Corporation (and perhaps a local bench of magistrates) there was a possibility of the larger employers of labour being induced to remain in residence within the confines of the parish in order to take part in its government, and so to assist in elevating and improving the social conditions of the place; (6) an assumption of a stronger position from which West Bromwich could ask for separate and independent Parliamentary representation—for since 1869 it had been only a part of a Parliamentary borough, of which Wednesbury, as an old market town, had been made the head, and (6) the strengthening of a claim for the removal of the County Court from Oldbury to the larger centre of population found in West Bromwich.

There was no opposition offered, and a Charter of Incorporation was granted, bearing the date 1882. The Town Council was constituted of a Mayor, six Aldermen, and 18 Councillors, divided among six electoral divisions or wards.

The newly-constituted borough was divided into six wards, namely (1) Sandwell, (2) Lyndon, (3) Hill Top, (4) Greets Green, (5) Town Hall, (6) Spon Lane; exactly as a map prepared for the official inquiry by the surveyor, Mr J. T. Eayrs, had laid down. All the evidence produced on this occasion has been printed in a pamphlet, and not the least interesting portions of that production are the map aforesaid, and the numerous instructive Tables and tabulated Returns prepared by the various officials. As a record of the condition and status of West Bromwich in 1882 nothing could give a clearer and more concise view; the returns relate to Population, Public Debts, Highway rates, statistics of bathers at Public Baths, and of volumes issued from the Free Library: Plans of new erections sanctioned, Expenditure on Drainage and Highways, Sanitary and Vital statistics, Voters in the proposed wards, an Analysis of the Public Expenditure, and the incidence of the Rates from 1871: the proportion of Agricultural Lands included in the parish acreage, returns from the Board of Guardians and the School Board, a list of Commissioners, and figures testifying to the representative value of the petition itself. No doubt the guiding spirit of the whole movement was the Clerk to the Commissioners, Mr C. H. Bayley, to whom it would doubtless be a labour of love; for few towns ever possessed a more patriotic citizen than Mr Bayley, one of whose chief delights was in original antiquarian and historical research, especially relating to the town and district of West Bromwich. By his lamented death at this juncture Mr Alfred Caddick was called upon to occupy the honourable post of first Town Clerk.

Before proceeding to survey the progress made under the fostering care of its municipal government, it may be recalled, as previously recorded in chapter I, that West Bromwich was taken out of the parliamentary borough of Wednesbury, by the Re-distribution Act of 1885, and erected into a separate *parliamentary borough* by itself. The first Member of Parliament for West Bromwich was Alderman Blades (1885), succeeded in 1886 by Mr Ernest Spencer.

The next advance in the status of the town was in 1890, when it became a county borough, independent of the county authorities altogether, and obtaining full and direct control of those financial "aids" made from the national exchequer towards certain portions of local government which Parliament had from time to time determined to subsidise in order to secure their more effective discharge.

LXXIII.—Municipal Progress—Corporation Stock—Rating.

While it would be a work of supererogation to set forth here all the minor improvements effected by the new form of local government adopted in 1882, being so fresh as they are in the minds of the inhabitants; still it will not be out of place, nor throw our review out of its perspective, if allusion is made to the two most important departmental branches of municipal work—sanitation and finance.

In dealing with the public health (the first and greatest care of every local governing body which acts as a sanitary authority) the new municipality have been consistently successful. An epidemic of small-pox, complicated by the presence of fever, in the first year of the town's incorporation proved somewhat embarrassing. But the outcome was the very prudent provision of a very good permanent *Infectious Hospital* within two years (1884). Many improved regulations were made for the management of the Cemetery, and a mortuary was erected at a cost of £360.

The *Sewering* of the town has been ably carried out at a cost of no less than £150,000, and the method adopted is known as the separate system; that is, the storm water from the streets and the fronts of the houses is kept separate from the sewage and rainwater of the back-yards. The cost of the 284 acres of Friar Park secured originally by the Town Commissioners was £20,000; but portions of this were afterwards sold off, so that the present Sewage Farm covers only 230 acres. About 14 acres were laid out for intermittent filtration purposes in areas of about two-acre plots, the work being done chiefly by the "unemployed." Then a further area of 21 acres was laid out at the east end of the farm, and this whole area thus prepared deals with the sewage of 10,700 houses, representing a population of 53,000 persons, Of these 31,000 are on the "low level," which also receives the drainage of a portion of Smethwick, representing a population of 4,400 there. A steam pump now lifts some of the low-level sewage for treatment on the higher land, which was unavailable by gravitation. At present the land is not drained and the sewage merely flows over the surface. Two small roughing tanks have been constructed of 25,000 gallons capacity each, to intercept sludge and solid matter from the high-level, and after passing these the sewage passes on to the filtration areas. There is much yet being done to clear and prepare the other portions of the Farm: and the difficulties encountered in this work of dealing efficiently with the matter have been almost insuperable at times. The Borough Surveyor, Mr Eayrs, now recommends a system of precipitating tanks for the treatment of the low-level sewage.

Then with regard to *Public Parks*—for the provision of open breathing spaces is but a higher development of sanitary science—

"Dartmouth Park" was extended in 1887, 9 acres being added, of which 6½ acres are occupied by a boating lake, and ½ an acre is used as an open bathing pond. A boat-house and shelter have also been erected. The new Lodge erected at Beeches Road entrance brought the total outlay from the rates to about £4,800. A kiosk near the lake was erected and presented by Alderman Farley.

"Greets Green Recreation Ground," upwards of 5 acres in extent, was presented in 1892 by Alderman Farley. It was laid out, and the Lodge, with branch Library and Reading-room, and a District Fire Station brought the cost to £1,900, chargeable on the rates. A band-stand was given by subscription.

"Kenrick Park", comprising nearly 20 acres, near Union Street, Spon Lane was given in 1895, by Messrs Kenrick Bros., and is now about being laid out at an estimated cost of £3,000.

*   *   *   *   *   *   *

And now for matters financial and the public rating—by which indeed all public affairs are more or less affected. When the Borough was incorporated in the year 1882 the public debt was as follows:—

Public buildings	...	...	...	...	...	...	...	26,869	17 7
Dartmouth Park	...	...	...	...	...	...	...	7,678	17 6
Fire Brigade	...	...	...	...	...	...	...	1,550	0 0
Street Improvement	...	...	...	...	...	...	...	2,246	9 7
Footpath Paving	...	...	...	...	...	...	...	11,501	5 10
Stables	...	...	...	...	...	...	...	1,250	0 0
Cemetery	...	...	...	...	...	...	...	2,600	0 0
Free Library	...	...	...	...	...	...	...	1,854	4 4
Works of Sewerage	...	...	...	...	...	...	...	18,626	0 0
								74,176	14 10
Gas Works	...	...	...	...	...	...	...	145,387	5 11
						Total	...	£221,564	0 9

According to the population, the general debt shows an average of £1 6s. 4d. per head, whilst the total debt shows an average of £3 18s. 8d.

A considerable expenditure of money upon public works has taken place in the Borough since 1882 more particularly on Works of Sewerage and Sewage Disposal, Footpath Paving, Public Parks, and Recreation Grounds, Street Improvements, New Law Courts, Infectious Diseases Hospital, Mortuary, and other purposes.

The debt of the Borough has therefore been increased through this expenditure, and on 31st March, 1895, it stood as follows:—

	£	s.	d.
Free Public Libraries	1,466	5	10
Law Courts	7,459	3	9
Financial Adjustment with County	1,442	3	2
Consolidation Act	514	1	11
Public Buildings	18,850	13	2
Street Improvements	5,432	8	1
Cemetery	2,039	7	3
Works of Sewerage	106,791	0	11
Footpath Paving	21,736	18	4
Parks and Recreation Grounds	11,829	4	0
Infection Diseases Hospital	2,143	2	1
Mortuary	322	3	6
Stables	788	2	11
	184,718	18	1
Gasworks	178,337	8	2
Total	£363,056	6	3

These figures are after deducting sinking funds in hand accumulated for extinction of the debt.

The general debt of the borough has increased from £74,176 14s. 10d. in 1882 to £184,718 18s. 1d. in 1895, and is now £3 1s. 7d. per head of population, whilst the total debt has increased during the same period from £221,564 0s. 9d. to £363,055 6s. 3d. The aggregate debt is now £6 1s. per head of population.

It must be noted, however, that more than one-half of the debt has been expended upon what may be termed remunerative objects; that is for revenue yielding purposes.

Prior to the year 1889 the Corporation debt was held on mortgages bearing, at what would be characterised in these days of cheap money, high rates of interest, and under the additional inconvenience of having to be redeemed at varying periods. The Corporation, therefore, decided to consolidate the debt, and to issue Redeemable Stock in lieu thereof. In that year, accordingly, a bill was promoted in Parliament, to sanction the consolidation of the debt, and to give power to issue stock.

The present generation of ratepayers have reaped considerable benefits by the consolidation scheme as now carried out and completed. Certain sections of the debt were previously redeemable in 10, 15, and 20 years, whilst others had a period of thirty years, another (gas debt) sixty years to run. Parliament ultimately sanctioned the consolidation, and granted one equated or equal period for the redemption of the debt as it then stood, including the gas debt; and this by actuarial calculation was found to be 41 years. The liquidation therefore being extended over a long period, it follows that the annual requirements to be met out of the rates, being less than formerly, the burdens of the present generation of ratepayers are proportionately lightened and the succeeding generation made to bear its proper and fair share thereof. It would be manifestly unjust for the existing ratepayers to bear the entire cost of improvements in the borough, which are more or less of a permanent character.

Upon the Consolidation Act being passed, the Corporation proceeded to arrange with the various mortgagees for repayment of their mortgages, suitable compensation being awarded in cases where the mortgages were unexpired.

In the latter part of the year 1889 the Corporation made a first issue of £300,000 three per cent. Redeemable Stock to provide moneys for repayment of a section of the mortgages, and to provide moneys also for new capital expenditure and other purposes.

When the remaining unconverted Mortgages were matured, and to provide other moneys also, the Corporation made a further issue of stock in the year 1894 of £131,200, making a total of £431,200. In these amounts are included moneys required for the School Board, Board of Guardians, and Board of Management of the Walsall and West Bromwich District Schools; the Act of Parliament authorising the Corporation to raise moneys required from time to time by the various Boards named.

The town by incorporation has thus been able to raise money at cheaper rates than previously, not only for its own direct requirements, but for the other local authorities in the Borough. This could never have been done by a Board of Improvement Commissioners.

Tho Stock of the West Bromwich Corporation occupies a high place in the list of investments on the London Stock Exchange, being now quoted at £106-107 for every £100 of stock.

The advantages accruing to the Borough by the consolidation of the debt, and in the subsequent issues of stock, have been of considerable extent, and from a financial point of view the saving effected is estimated at about £4,000 per annum.

RATES.

The rates levied in the Borough since the incorporation have been as follows —

	General District s. d.	Poor. s. d.	Total s. d.
1883-4	2 4	3 0	5 4
1884-5	2 2	2 10	5 0
1885-6	2 4	3 0	5 4
1886-7	3 0	3 2	6 2
1887-8	3 0	3 2	6 2
1888-9	3 4	3 4	6 8
1889-90	3 0	2 10	5 10
1890-1	2 10	3 0	5 10
1891-2	2 8	2 6	5 2
1892-3	2 8	3 4	6 0
1893-4	2 8	3 4	6 0
1894-5	2 8	3 4	6 0

The aggregate rates of 6s. in the pound for the year 1895 are made up as follows:—

	s.	d.
Poor	1	$3\frac{1}{2}$
Borough (General Purpose)	0	6
School Board	1	0
Free Library	0	1
Baths	0	$0\frac{1}{3}$
General District and Lighting Rate	2	$7\frac{2}{3}$
Technical Instruction, Overseers Expenses and Police	0	$5\frac{1}{2}$
Total	6	0

The rates levied by the late Board of Commissioners during the last two or three years immediately preceding the incorporation varied from 3s. to 2s. 6d. in the pound. No satisfactory or even equitable comparison can be made with the rates now levied, as against those levied before the incorporation, for the reason that expenditure is now required to be met out of the municipal revenues which was formerly discharged through other sources. Under the Local Government Act, 1888, West Bromwich was constituted a county borough. It continues, however, as heretofore, to regulate the lighting of the borough and the conduct of all sanitary arrangements, with the supervision of lodging houses, etc. But additional and more important powers are conferred upon it. For example, all county or main roads passing through the borough have now to be repaired and maintained by the Corporation, and the building and repairing of all bridges within the boundaries (other than railway and canal bridges) have also by this Act to be done by the Corporation, who have also to defray the cost and expenses of the police and provide for the maintenance of pauper lunatics. These charges were formerly defrayed in part from County funds or Government sources, but from 1st April, 1889, the payments from these sources were discontinued; and as a compensation the Corporation receive the proceeds of the Local Taxation Licenses and a proportion of the Probate Duties. The Corporation have hitherto realised a surplus from the Local Taxation Grants after meeting the additional burdens thrown upon it, and about £3,000 per annum from this source has been applied in direct relief of rates, either the general district rate or borough rate, or both, as circumstances have required.

In all matters except assizes, the borough is now free from county control and the Council have transferred to them all the administrative functions of a county. The borough is also likewise constituted a Quarter Sessions borough.

The Corporation in conjunction with the other county boroughs in Staffordshire, have entered into an agreement with the county of Stafford for the reception of the borough pauper lunatics in the County Asylum at a fixed charge per head; and so long as this agreement is continued or renewed the borough will be spared the expense of building asylums.

The rateable value of property assessed to the Relief of the Poor in 1882 was £157,812, and in 1895 £206,551 10s.

The rateable value of property assessed to the General District Rate in 1882 was £127,577 1s. 3d., and in 1896 £156,216 12s. 6d

The proportions are given in the following tables —

RATEABLE VALUE, 1882.

Description.	At Full Rateable Value.	At Half Rateable Value.	At Quarter Rateable Value.
Houses, Works, etc.	105,262 0 0	,,	,,
Compound Property	,,	36,710 5 0	,,
Land	,,	,,	6,125 15 0
Railways	,,	,,	4,914 0 0
Canals	,,	,,	4,800 0 0
Totals	105,262 0 0	36,710 5 0	15,839 15 0

RATEABLE VALUE, 1895.

Description.	At Full Rateable Value.			At Half Rateable Value.			At Quarter Rateable Value.		
Agricultural Land	,,			,,			5,223	10	0
Railways and Canals	1,514	0	0	,,			21,995	10	0
Corporation and other Public Properties	6,539	0	0	64	0	0	671	5	0
Government Property	7	15	0	,,			,,		
Schools	428	10	0	,,			,,		
Hospitals	140	0	0	8	0	0	,,		
Compound Property	,,			58,763	2	6	,,		
Other Property	111,197	7	6	,,			,,		
Total	119,826	12	6	58,835	2	6	27,889	15	0

LXXIV.—Water Supply and Water-Ways.

The River Tame was somewhat fully dealt with in chap. xxxv, wherein it was indicated that in a very large measure the parish boundaries followed the stream's course. But there is extant a rather quaint seventeenth century record of these *boundary* lines, which is quoted by Mrs Willett (p. 247), and which runs thus: "The outmost boundes of the Parish of West Bromwich are these following: Fromm Brandforde Bridge downewardes the River Tame doth divide that from Halesowen, Rowley, Tipton, Wednesbury, Barre, and Aldrich and Hansworth until that cometh unto Mr Henry Cookes, his land, or Henery Osborne's meadowe, and thence forward the lane leading from Bromwich Forge to Whorston, at or neare Sandwell copey corner, and from thence along a wine Waye slantinge towards a guter wich poynted upon George Alane, his Barne, which stood in the uper cornor of his land towarde Hansworth, part of the barne in West Bromwich and part in Handsworth, as men sayd, and so from thence to the nether end of old Wm. Hunte, his farme called the Street house to a place in Smethwich Lane called Totmons Lowe, and from thence along the hedge rowe which partes Asprs More, in Smethwick, from the land of Thomas Birch, in West Bromwich, to Spane-brooke, and so downe alonge the said Spane-brooke to the river of same at Bromford Bridge aforesaid."

As a source of the parish water supply the Tame has also played a most important part. Then, as to *wells*, allusion has been made to "Sand Well" in Chap. x.; to the "Draw Well" at Dagger Hall in Chap xlviii.; and to the "Hop Yard Well" at Charlemont in Chap. xlix. Another well is, according to Wednesbury tradition, a place of historic import. This is Grigg's Well, at the curve of Coles Lane. Here, it is said, Charles II. when escaping from Bentley Hall, mounted behind Jane Lane, stopped to water their horse.—(See Wednesbury Papers. pp. 81-82). Reeves devotes pp. 5. and 6 to the Tame; and on p. 54 deals with that quarter of the parish known as Lyndon, and where is situated "Lyne Purl," a spring of excellent soft water still flowing freely, but no doubt much contaminated now through the populousness of the neighbourhood. In olden days, when the spring purled through an open country, its pure waters were without doubt a beneficent boon to the sparse population around it; indeed, so beautifully benignant was the "Lyne Purl" that it seems to have inspired more than one local poetaster to sing its praises. One effusion will be found among the papers of the late C. H. Bayley carefully preserved in the Public Library by the zealous librarian, Mr D. Dickinson. [It may not be out of place here to acknowledge the unvarying courtesy and attention of this public official, to whom the writer is much indebted. The rich stores of local information collected in the Free Library by Mr Dickinson, much of it collated and indexed by him, will one day prove invaluable to some abler writer than the present.]

When the wells of the parish were examined some years ago at the instance of the local authority, Lyne Purl was (with may private sources of water supply) condemned on chemical analysis; and by order of the salt authorities it was closed to the public. So strong, however, was popular prejudice in favour of the Lyne water, that the attempted closing led almost to a riot; and at the present time, although a warning notice against the use of the water is attached to the brickwork of the spring, it is to be feared the people entirely disregard it.

At the Government inquiry of 1882 it was stated that the SOUTH STAFFORDSHIRE WATER WORKS CO., who supply this and the surrounding parishes, had been desired to transfer the water supply of West Bromwich to the hands of the Commissioners in bulk, and the Commissioners would then undertake to supply the consumers within the parish area. There were then thirty miles of water mains in the parish, supplying 4,700 houses, or about half the population. Where the wells were pure, the people were still permitted by the Sanitary Authority to use them. The Corporation have not acquired any portion of the Water Works as yet, nor are they at present likely to do so; but a brief review of the inception and origin of this great undertaking may here be useful, as so few public men seem acquainted with that history—except, perhaps, Alderman Richard Williams, of Wednesbury, who was an original shareholder in the concern, and is now a director.

The scheme had its origin in pure philanthropy, being promoted by men who had witnessed and felt the horrors of the cholera period (1848), and who recognised the sufferings of the people always attendant on the lack of a good water supply. Among the promoters—all of them since dead— will be found the names of Charles Forster, Richard Jesson, Sampson Lloyd, James Solly, and Thomas Walker. The area to be supplied included Lichfield, Walsall, Wednesbury, West Bromwich, Bilston, Darlaston, Willenhall (unless supplied by Wolverhampton Waterworks Company), Sedgley, Tipton, and Rowley Regis, all in the county of Stafford, and Dudley and Oldbury, in Worcestershire. The capital was set down as £160,000 in shares of £10, with borrowing powers for £30,000 more. By the Act (1853) the promoters became the first directors, and the "first sod was out" at Lichfield by the late Earl of Dudley, then Lord Ward. Certain works and rights were purchased from the Corporation of Lichfield, and among the numerous other plans for projected works were an aqueduct or main-pipe to a reservoir to be made at Church Hill, Wednesbury; from thence to an intended reservoir in Tipton, near Dudley Port Station; and from thence to a point in the turnpike road "leading from Birmingham through West Bromwich to Dudley," where the said road passes under the Birmingham Canal in the parish of Tipton. Powers were also obtained to buy out the Dudley Waterworks Company, and what with reservations to protect the rights of various landowners, corporations, canal and railway companies, and others possessing large interests in this wide and populous area of operations the undertaking became so gigantic in its financial responsibilities that its credit soon sank to a very low ebb, in fact it is difficult to imagine how the affair would eventually have turned out had not Mr Thomas Walker loaned to the Company, at the instigation of Mr Richard Williams, the sum of £40,000 with which to prosecute the enterprise. For about fifteen years no dividend was earned, and although in these present progressive days it is now paying $5\frac{1}{2}$ per cent. its average rate from the beginning has been only about 2 per cent. Amending Acts have been since promoted and obtained; in 1857 to raise an additional £10,000; in 1864 to augment the capital to £320,000 and to acquire fresh sources of water supply; and in 1866 for the construction of additional works at Burton-on-Trent, at Conygre in Tipton, and at Sedgley. More recent amending Acts have gone on similar lines; while at the same time the interests of the general public have been protected by the insertion of provisos for supplying water at reasonable rates for all necessary domestic and manufacturing purposes; and on behalf of the local authorities for obtaining cheap water for all the public purposes of sanitation, street watering, fire extinction, etc. In fact by those who remember the old methods of supply by the antiquated pail and water-cart, it is contended that the Water Works Company has contributed very largely to the welfare and wealth of the community as well as to its comfort and convenience.

* * * * * * *

Of ARTIFICIAL WATERWAYS within the parish there is a considerable mileage.

The old Birmingham Canal (1768) was $22\frac{5}{8}$ miles in length, commencing at Farmers Bridge and passing through Smethwick, where there is a side cut with three locks rising $19\frac{3}{4}$ feet. From Smethwick the canal continues on one level to Oldbury, Tipton, and Bilston and Wolverhampton to within $1\frac{1}{2}$ miles of Autherley, where it looks down 132ft. by 21 locks into the Staffordshire and Worcester Canal. The Summit level of the canal at Smethwick was originally only one mile in length. and 18 feet higher, and it was supplied with water by means of two steam engines placed at the extremities. Prior, however, to 1787 it was out down to the lower level at a cost of £30, 000.

At a later period Telford improved this canal, shortening the distance from 22 to 14 miles, and doing away with locks between Birmingham and Wolverhampton. The principal branch ran to Wednesbury, $4\frac{1}{2}$ miles, with three locks lowering it 18 feet. But the mines dropped some of this and rendered it of little use.

In 1783 a new Act empowered the extension of the Wednesbury branch from Ryder's Green to Broadwaters Engine, and the making of six collateral cuts. One of these cuts was from "the head of Willingsworth Pool to near the nine-mile stone on the turnpike road leading from Ocker Hill to Wolverhampton"; and another "from Willingsworth Pool tail to Wednesbury Open Field."

West Bromwich is really part of a large island enclosed by canals. The Birmingham Canal, starting from Old Wharf, takes the line of the Stour Valley via Galton Bridge, Spon Lane, and Bromford to Izon's Branch, where the Tipton Canal goes to the left and the other proceeds to Ryder's Green. From this point runs out towards the north numerous dead ends to tap the whole manufacturing district comprising the busy Hill Top and Greet's Green Wards, two of these more distant ends extending to Bald's Hill and Church Lane respectively. From this same point also (Ryder's Green) a direct cut runs to Toll End (on the way to Lea Brook, Broadwaters, Moxley, and Darlaston), from which place strikes out the Tame Valley Canal, skirting West Bromwich at Holloway Bank, Hall Green, and Newton, and running back to Birmingham via Aston, and so forming the artificial Island aforementioned. For other details of the local canal system see HISTORY OF TIPTON, pp. 39 and 40.

LXXV.—LOCAL ADMINISTRATION OF JUSTICE.

Reference to mediæval forms of judicial procedure was made in chapters xii, xiii, and xv, and to manorial jurisdiction in chapter 1.

In the local administration of justice, recent reference has also been made to the wrong and great inconvenience so often inflicted upon the more modern community by the dearth of magistrates. In constituting the Board of Improvement Commissioners it had not always been easy to secure as the complement of its members the three justices resident within the specified limits. The police business had of late years been administered by the county magistrates sitting at West Bromwich every Saturday, in addition to which the Stipendiary Magistrate (of the South Staffordshire Black Country) sat in West Bromwich on alternate Mondays. For more than five years after the incorporation of the municipal borough this inadequacy of magisterial strength continued in West Bromwich. Then a petition was prepared praying the Queen to grant the borough its own independent magistracy.

A separate Commission of the Peace for West Bromwich was granted in 1888, when 18 gentlemen were constituted the first BOROUGH BENCH. To this list 8 names were added in 1892 and 6 more in January 1893.

A grant of QUARTER SESSIONS was made to the borough in 1890, when Mr J. W. Underhill became first Recorder of West Bromwich, and upon his death in July 1892, he was succeeded by Mr R. C. E. Plumptre.

In the meantime, the COUNTY COURT holden at Oldbury was transferred to the larger centre of West Bromwich in April 1889 and till a proper building could be erected, found temporary quarters in a portion of the Market Hall.

West Bromwich had previously possessed no separate County Court, but had formed the principal part of the Oldbury County Court district; therefore, in 1882 it was a legitimate cause for complaint that the former parish with its 57,000 inhabitants was second to Oldbury with its population of only 18,289 in the matter of civil law jurisdiction—the latter still possessing such rights by the survival of an insignificant Small Debts Court.

The fact that West Bromwich had now become possessed of its own magistracy with a Court of Quarter Sessions, and the seat of a County Court for the recovery of small debts, naturally directed the attention of the authorities to the necessity of providing new Law Courts. For this purpose the Town Council secured a site in Lombard Street, and the memorial stone of the new building was laid in July, 1890, by Councillor Heelis, who was chairman of the committee appointed for this special duty.

The architects of the Law Courts were Messrs Wood and Kendrick, and the planning was somewhat unique. As a provincial court of law, it was designed to combine in its accommodation provision to meet all the requirements for the magistrates sitting in Petty Session, the Recorder sitting in Quarter Sessions, the County Court Judge sitting for civil cases, and lastly for use as a Coroner's Court—for West Bromwich has now power to appoint its own separate coroner. The Law Courts in Lombard Street therefore possess some features that are rather novel. They are in the Renascence style, and cost about £5,000. They include offices for the Registrar, waiting cells for prisoners; and every accommodation and convenience for the public service has been thoughtfully and carefully provided.

With regard to POLICE arrangements West Bromwich has not yet thought well to establish a borough force of its own, but for sound economy and real efficiency of working has preferred to continue to avail itself of the county constabulary. The Town Council has therefore contracted with the county authorities for the supply of a sufficient force at a fixed sum per head. The force thus provided consists at present

(1895) of a chief superintendent (that experienced officer Mr Thomas Whitehurst is the present chief). 2 inspectors, 4 sergeants, and 38 constables, 40 all told.

Till 1894 Hill Top, situated within the borough boundaries of West Bromwich, formed part of a subdivision of Wednesbury Police Division. But with the new financial arrangements just recorded, it was necessary to make West Bromwich Police Division and the municipal borough co-terminous in their boundaries. Hill Top was therefore taken away from Barr sub-division of Wednesbury and added to West Bromwich.

About the same time (1894) Handsworth, whose police business had been previously transacted at the old West Bromwich Court, was provided by the county with its own police court and station, and tacked on to Smethwick, the two places making up one police division, and each having its regular sessions of the county magistrates.

In the re-adjustment of the financial relationships between the County Borough of West Bromwich and the Staffordshire County Council, the old police station in High Street passed into the hands of the former authority, but at present the municipality has not quite decided what is to be done with the property.

For the protection of the public against fire the Commissioners had some years ago established a Volunteer FIRE BRIGADE of twelve officers and men, with a steam fire engine, tender, and all necessary appliances. This brigade has since been extended and even more completely equipped by the Town Council.

LXXVI.—LOCAL REFERENCES TO SOME ANCIENT AND NATIONAL TAXES (1291-1890).

How West Bromwich was taxed under feudal government has been shown in chaps. xix. and xxii.; and further allusion to fiscal arrangements in these early times may also be seen in chaps. xvii. and xviii. In the first quoted chapter the contemporary records of the TAXATION OF POPE NICHOLAS in 1291 yielded much useful information, for instance, West Bromwich was then set down as being in the Deanery of Tamworth and Tutbury; also its parish church is described as being appurtenant to the Priory and Convent of Sandwell, and assessed at four pounds, on which was annually forthcoming a tax of one-tenth, or eight shillings. The same return also tells us that West Bromwich was in the *Archdeaconry* of Stafford, and among the *temporalities* of Coventry and Lichfield, and further, that the Abbey of Hales Owen possessed in Bromwich one carucate of land valued at 10 shillings per annum.

At a national taxing some years later a return can be found for Harborne and Smethwick and other surrounding parishes, but none for West Bromwich. This was the NONARUM INQUISITION of 1341, or the finding upon oath by the parishioners of one-ninth of sheep, lamb, fleece, etc., levied for the French and Scottish Wars.

In the reign of Charles II. the overwhelming debts of the King led to the imposition of a HEARTH TAX of 2s. on each hearth, the revenue derived from the tax being settled on that impecunious monarch for his life. To make matters worse, the tax was "farmed," and the poorer householders were often mercilessly distrained upon. In West Bromwich this Hearth Tax yielded for the year 1660 £33 4s. But the 332 hearths on which this was payable included those in Sandwell Hall.

The EXCISE (in 1665) was referred to in chapter xxxii., and manorial *frithsilver* or "peace money" (1649) in chapter xl.

The local incidence of SCUTTAGE has already been recorded in chaps. viii., ix., xvii., xviii., and xx. The LAND TAX introduced by William III. in 1692 seems to have supplanted the three ancient feudal imposts of SCUTTAGE, HYDAGE (an extraordinary tax on each hide of plough lands), and TALLAGE (a toll carved out of the whole of a man's property). The method of raising it was to charge each county a particular sum, according to a valuation of 1692, and assessed upon individuals (their personal and real estates) by commissioners, who generally consisted of the principal landowners.

In 1716 the Collectors of the Land Tax in West Bromwich, as well as the Overseers of the Parish were compelled to seek legal advice as to the recovery of their levies on the manorial estates, then insolvent.

The Vestry in 1721 agreed that two shillings only should be spent at the assessing of the Land Tax.

An assessment made the 2nd May, 1747, for West Bromwich *and Sandwell*, of the monies payable to His Majesty King George II. by a Land Tax, and "assessed by us the subscribers" runs thus:—

	£	s.	d.
Earl of Dartmouth	3	3	9
And for Monk Meadow	0	16	3
(This "meadow" was a school endowment, and this shows clearly that it was in Lord Dartmouth's holding).			
Samuel Clark, Esq	6	11	4
And for Cappers	1	13	0
John Mansell	2	13	6
Joseph Gutteridge	6	14	0
William Smallwood	2	1	9
Edward Osborn...	1	3	4
Mr Turton	1	4	0
Samuel Lowe	1	1	7
Samuel Crowley...	1	4	0
John Silvester	1	3	0
Thomas Twigg	0	19	6
Thomas Wilson...	0	19	2
Jeremiah Wright	0	18	2
Edward Wilks	0	18	0
Richard Hodgetts	0	16	0
Joseph Wright	0	16	2
Edward Whitehouse	0	17	2
James Green	0	16	2
Mrs Abney	0	13	2
Joseph Hill	0	17	2

The above are only the largest sums, the total being about £70.

Till 1798 the Land Tax was an annual tax; afterwards made "perpetual" and "redeemable."

PROPERTY TAX was first levied by Henry VIII. for the French War of 1512. It was strongly opposed by the London merchants, but was afterwards levied at various periods. In 1815 the assessments on the real property of the nation under this Property Tax were £51,900,000; in West Bromwich the annual value of lands and buildings as assessed for same was £13,245.

The WINDOW TAX was enacted in 1695 for the re-coinage of gold. It was increased from time to time for various reasons. A vestry paper preserved at West Bromwich and dated 1763 shows the sum of "9 pence received for windo tax." This tax disappeared in 1851 in favor of an Inhabited House Duty.

Passing allusion was made in chaps. lxxii and lxxiii to the recent (1890) allocation of certain *imperial taxes to local purposes*. West Bromwich as a County Borough now enjoys full control of a revenue derived from Licenses, Probate Duty &c. and applies it to local purposes such as maintenance of Main Roads, Police, &c. which were formerally assisted by the *grant* of parliamentary *aids*.

LXXVII.—From National Taxation to National Defence—West Bromwich During Some National War Times (1640 and 1798).

A perusal of our earlier chapters will clearly disclose the fact that in feudal times the ownership of the land was always charged with the duty and the responsibility of providing the national defences.

From the time of Edward I, however, every parish was bound to keep ready for use a certain amount of armour, and a man (or men, according to the population) properly trained to the use of this armour. The said armour was "viewed" twice a year by the Constable, who reported to the Justices on its condition. The "town's armour" was generally kept in the church. A local record contains the following entry—"Item, the task of West Bromwich, 3s. 8d. armoury, wherewith the parish of West Bromwich was charged for the common armoury, 8th of March, 1596, by John Bowes, Edward Littleton, Edward Aston, Knights, and Thomas, Bagod, Esq. Two corslets with pikes; 1 musket: 1 culeever, 1 archer all furnished with sword, dagger, and girdle." (*Vide* WILLETT, p. 240).

From the SALT COLLECTIONS (vol. xv.) most interesting details are obtainable as to the Staffordshire muster of 1640. In this year Charles I. levied an army to suppress the Scotch Covenanters who had taken up arms against the introduction of an Episcopal form of Church Government into Scotland. Forced to call together the Long Parliament, the King managed to secure grants and loans (Catholic subjects paid sums years in advance for the toleration of their religion), and with these means he levied an army in the usual way through the Lieutenants of Counties.

The muster in Staffordshire was made by Sir Hervey Bagot, Walter Wrottesley, and Thomas Crompton, the Deputy-Lieutenants of Robert Devereux, Earl of Essex, who was then Lord Lieutenant of this County, but is subsequently known to us as the famous Parliamentary General.

The men mustered were the *trained bands*, who had been previously employed in a similar expedition, and an additional body specially levied for this occasion, of 300 impressed men. The cost of their first equipment, and of their maintenance until they reached the rendezvous of the army, was borne by the County, the money being raised by a levy on the Hundreds. This was called "Coat and Conduct Money." On arrival at the rendezvous they there received their arms and were then paid by the King. The pay of 8d. a day was liberal, being equivalent to 2s. a day at the present time; but as it was uncertain the men were often compelled to plunder to obtain food.

In addition to these men there was raised a force of cavalry, procured under an old feudal law of Edward III. (refer back to chap. xviii.) and under which in Elizabeth's reign Staffordshire produced 25 *lancers*, or men at-arms, with horses all completely covered with armour, and 99 *hobelars*, or light-horsemen. At this date (1640) the county produced a force of 69 *cuirassiers*, or lancers, and 31 light-horsemen; the service was evidently popular, as volunteers were always forthcoming when there was fighting in prospect.

The service of the pressed men, on the other hand, was very unpopular. First, the Calvinism of the people often made them sympathise with the Scotch Covenanters;

then they received but little drill—perhaps only while waiting for their clothing, which in the case of Staffordshire men was at Uttoxeter. What with discontent and lack of discipline, insubordination broke out into open mutiny, which the High Constables and the Petty Constables could scarcely suppress; for courts martial were unknown, and the ordinary courts proved ineffective in such cases. Eventually the Staffordshire men, less the rioters, were got to Selby, in Yorkshire, where they were joined on to the rest of the army.

The arms given out consisted of pikes only to the impressed men, while the trained bands were armed partly with pikes and partly with fire-locks, the latter arm then gradually superseding the old wheel-lock musket and rest.

Here are the name's of the men who went from this locality:—

OFFLOW HUNDRED.

	Traine.	*Presse.*
Westbromiene,	Thomas Grove.	William Taylor.
	John Simcoxe.	Simon Affley.
		John Jevon.
		(*Jevon's name crossed out*).
Wedgburey,	George Maydewe.	Richard Wyatt.
	William Paskin.	William Shelnocke.
	Thomas Siluester.	

Perry Barr and Handsworth are grouped as one district, while the name of Thomas Pye from Darlaston is noteworthy.

The Roll then gives:

"The list of the: 50: horses for the Car. of Amun. 14 July, 1640."

The Offlow returns are divided into two divisions, one of which was under the direction of a Wednesbury man, namely:

"Mr Hopkys diaicon.

		li.	s.	d.
Wednesbury.	1 bay nagge baught of Rich. Hawkes, price	5	0	0
eadm.	1 grey nagge baught of John Carter, price	8	0	0
in eadm.	1 sorrel nagge baught of Rich. Tunks, price	5	0	0
West Bromwich.	1 bay gelding baught of Thomas Groves, price	6	10	0

In the same *division* were also a horse purchased from "Rushiall," and one from "Walsall Forren"; *omnes sine condicone*. To go along with these 50 draught horses, 17 carters were impressed "to doe his Majesty's service in the office of Carter, and not to depart from the army without license under pain of death", the two attached to Mr Hopkins' Division were—Thonas Bearesley, Richard Wood.

Among the cavalry probably liable to serve from this locality the following names appear in a list given of the 22 "Trayned Horse" of a few years earlier date:—

						Curiasiers.
Sir Richard Shilton, Kt. ...	...	...	...	...	...	1
Sir Thomas Whorewood, Kt....	...	...	...	...	...	2
Symon Mountford Esq. ...	...	...	...	...	...	1
Humphrey Wyrely, Esq. ...	...	...	...	...	...	1
William Cumberford of Cumberford, Esq....	...	...	...	1
William Cumberford of Tamworth, Esq. ...	...	...	:1
Mrs Lane and her sonne ...	...	...	...	...	...	1

And from a similar list of 9 Hobelars the following names only appear as hailing from this immediate vicinity:—

Light horse.

Mr Pershouse and Mr Stone...	1
Mr Funesby pson of Hansworth	1

At later dates allusion to the same trained forces is to be found in the West Bromwich Churchwardens' Books, as—

"1689. Nov. 4.—Accounted then with William Underhill (the Constable) for 2 levies for the trained shoulders, one at 1d. per £1 and one at 2d."

In 1721, on June 16th, the Vestry resolved that the Wardens might pay for ringing the church bells on certain days of the year, namely May 28, for King George's Birthday; May 29, for the Restoration of King Charles II., August 5 for the King's Proclamation Day, October 20 for Coronation Day; and on November 5 for Gunpowder Plot; yet the loyalty of the Parishioners stopped somewhat cheaply at this, for the resolution goes on to restrain the Constable, "that he be not allowed to give or spend any of the Parishe's money upon the *traine soulders*, or any other persons, upon rejoicing days." The close connection between Church and State in those days is further exemplified by the custom of placing a copy of the King's Arms in all churches, as a sign of his supremacy over the Established Church. The painting of these in West Bromwich Church is recorded in 1716; those recently in Wednesbury Church bore the date 1805.

Coming to the great wars of Napoleon in more modern times, patriotic enthusiasm was aroused in all parts of the country, and in West Bromwich no less than elsewhere. A Vestry Meeting of all the principal inhabitants, the Rev. W. Jesse in the chair passed the following Resolution, on Monday March 12th, 1798.—

"That whereas the French have obstinately rejected every overture for peace, and have openly threatened to invade this country, for the avowed design of overturning the religion, the laws, and the constitution of this Kingdom . . . and to subject Great Britain to the insolent control, to the despotic authority, and barbarous domination of the French Directory. Therefore extraordinary exertions are necessary on our part . . . it is become necessary that all persons of every rank . . . should engage in a general and voluntary contribution in aid of Government for the defence of the country. That a Book be immediately opened in the Vestry to receive contributions. . . . That a Committee be appointed . . . to go from house to house to receive contributions . . . That the following persons be of the Committee:—Rev. William Jesse, Edward Elwell, jun., Thomas Hadley (churchwardens), Joseph Jesson, Richard Jesson, Richard Wright, Thomas Blakemore, Edward Elwell, Isaac Hadley, Samuel Read, and Joseph Barrs."

The resolution, which has been abridged here, is long-winded and grandiloquent, as such productions usually are. But the meeting was evidently very much in earnest, as the subscriptions at once testified on the spot, for the list runs:—

	£	s.	d.
Richard Jesson, J.P....	100	0	0
Joseph Jesson	50	0	0
Edward Elwell	50	0	0
Thomas Blakemore...	100	0	0
(And to cover Assessed Taxes).			
Isaac Hadley...	2	2	0
Joseph Hadley	3	3	0
Edward Elwell, jun.	20	0	0
Samuel Read	1	1	0
Joseph Barrs...	1	1	0
Richard Wright	100	0	0
W. Jesse	20	0	0
Total subscribed...	£447	7	0

No doubt as a stimulus to other parishes all this was ordered to be published in the *Star*, the *Sun*, and the *Birmingham Gazette*.

The residence in the parish of the eminent James Keir, F.R.S., may have had some influence on this military zeal of the parishioners. He had served in the 61st regiment; in 1793 he had written a pamphlet entitled *The Martial Character of Nations*, which would in all likelihood excite a warlike feeling; and later on (1802) he published another pamphlet *Reflections on the Invasion of Great Britain by the French Armies*, etc.—"the meditation of a man of military experience."

The Dartmouth family were conspicuous for the active part they took in all these movements. On Friday, July 6th, 1798, the Lewisham Volunteers, a battalion 360 strong, received new colours from the hands of Lady Dartmouth, in the presence of a crowd, including many distinguished persons. Great ceremony was observed on the occasion, the grounds being kept by the West London Regiment. Then the third Earl of Dartmouth held the colonelcy of Birmingham Loyal Volunteers, till ill-health compelled his resignation in 1807. In 1799 another ceremony of colour presentation had taken place on Barr Beacon, as recorded in chap. xxxviii.

LXXVIII.—West Bromwich Loyal Volunteers, 1798.

Beyond the mere provision of money, West Bromwich soon had also a strong body of men forthcoming to meet the national emergency. But, it may be asked, what was there to warrant all this great national excitement? Certainly the dread of a French invasion was by no means ill-founded at that time although it was probably exaggerated. General Hoche, in 1796, had attempted to land 25,000 Frenchmen in Bantry Bay; but this attempt on Ireland happily failed. The French Republic next threatened an invasion of England, but the North Devon Loyal Volunteers easily prevented a landing at Ilfracombe. At Fishguard in Wales however, a small landing was effected February 23rd, 1797; but the wretched Frenchmen were immediately made prisoners by a body of Militia and Fencibles, under Lord Cawdor.

Napoleon kept England on the alert for some years after this, and in 1803 his armies took possession of Hanover. Between 1798 and 1802 an enthusiastic patriotism raised a force of 300,000 to 410,000 all enrolled in the various Volunteer Associations, and West Bromwich was not behind in furnishing its proper quota. With baggy coat of ample skirts and big pocket-flaps, a military air was further assumed by wearing the pig-tail of seven-inch limit; and this, surmounted by the three-cornered hat then in vogue, gave our grandfathers quite a soldierly appearance.

The original roll of the Bromwich men who joined came into the possession of the present writer a few years ago, and was promptly handed over to the keeping of the town, and is now preserved in the West Bromwich Public Library. The document is in this form:—

A List of the West Bromwich Loyal Association Volunteer Corps sworn before Joseph Amphlett, Esq., Octr, 8th, 1798.

Sworn before Justice Haden, Dec. 2.

Samuel Holden	Thos. Fletcher
John Hatten	Wm. Haines
Joseph Cullwick	Rich. Hawkes
Samuel Mason	John Woodall
Joseph Darby	Edward Fisher
William Holden	James Foxall
John Hunt	Thos. Heartwell

Benjamin Smith
Joseph Fereday
George Bullock
John Harris
John Morris
Rich. Crowley
Thos. Ridge
John Withers
Moses Hall
James Robinson
Thomas Whitehouse
William Fisher
Richard Stamps
Wm. Cartwright
Wm. Crowley
Samuel Ready
Josiah Tonks
Thos. Woodall
Joseph Green
Saml. Assall
James Smith
Wm. Assall
Wm. Phillips
   30

Not Sworn.
Jos. Davis
Jos. Mason
James Parkes
Mesellum Webb
Samuel Sanders
John Sutton
George Sheldon
Josep. Danks
James Bibb
Thos. Simcox
Jos. Lloyd
Paul Bibb
Wm. Whitehouse
Wm. Fisher – *Mr Jesse's arms*
Wm. Watters
Jonah Bissell
Ben. Medley
Elisha Shepherd
Geo. Hill
Thos. Belcher
Ben. Davis
Thos. Throp
Thos. Jesson
   23

Wm. Hill
Saml. Sheldon
Benj. White
Wm. Mallen
Rich. Peters
Wm. Kimberley
Wm. Groom – *right about.*
Wm. Weston
Wm. Hartell
Edwd. Betts
Wm. Lattermour
John Cheshire – *right about.*
John Onions
Charles Throp
Saml. Throp
Wm. Turton
Wm. Jones
James Weston
Daniel Simcox
Isaac Whitehouse
Wm. Chetwin
Roger Hardware
James Hardware
Will Baker
Will Johnson
Thos. Jones
   33
The Band.
Wm. Reeves
John Stokes
Charles Stokes
Wm. Grange
Joseph Buffery
John Holden
John Parkes

———

Not Sworn.
Albt. Jones
Isaiah Danks
Thos. Danks
John Wright
Thos. Jesson

*   *   *   *   *   *   *

The above document shows a total of nearly 100 Volunteers in a place which was but a mere scattered village at that time. The Justice Haden mentioned was the pluralist Vicar of Wednesbury. The reference to "Mr Jesse's arms" may perhaps be an allusion to the Parish Armour mentioned in the previous chapter.

A memorandum in the Church Books, under date 1st September, 1816, states "that the collections from house to house in the parish of West Bromwich (by order of the Prince Regent) for the relief and benefit of the brave men killed, and of the wounded sufferers in the signal victory of Waterloo . . . and other battles of the present campaign" reached a certain amount, and was forwarded to the Waterloo Fund in London by Chas. Townsend, minister.

This terminates the period of the Napoleonic scare.

LXXIX.—West Bromwich Rifle Volunteers (1859–1895).

Thirty-five years ago there was another "French scare." And just as Napoleon I. had called into existence the Loyal Volunteers, so were the modern Rifle Volunteers called into being by the doubts entertained against the pacific intentions of Napoleon III.

West Bromwich was well to the fore again in this great national movement, and in the latter part of 1859 a Corps was formed by Mr Thomas Bagnall, J,P., and drilled at the Police Station with the assistance of Major McKnight, who was then Superintendent of Police. In 1860 came the official recognition of the Corps, when the West Bromwich establishment was to consist of 100 members to be called the "20th Staffordshire Rifle Volunteer Corps," and which was to form part of "The 3rd Administrative Battalion Staffordshire Rifle Volunteers." The command was given to Lieut.-General, the Hon. A. C. Legge as Colonel, and the Battalion Head-Quarters were to be at Handsworth.

The first uniform was of grey, with green facings trimmed with black cord; the belts were of brown leather; and the low-crowned cap had a large horizontal peak, and its flatness was relieved by a green ball at the top.

Enrolment of the first legally constituted members took place at St. George's Hall, Paradise Street, on March 16th, 1860, sworn before Messrs Thomas and John Nock Bagnall. The original officers and men were—

Thomas Bagnall	to be	Captain.
Henry Williams	,, ,,	Lieutenant.
Edwin Hooper	,, ,,	Ensign.
Wm. Jas. Kite	,, ,,	Surgeon.
Benj. Willmore (Rev.)	,, ,,	Chaplain.
Fredk. Ingram	,, ,,	Sergeant-Instructor.

1	Woolley, Thomas, Colour. Sergeant	29	Caddick, Elijah
2	Bayley, Charles Hy.	30	Ault, Thomas
3	Cooksey, John Hudson	31	Woodhouse, John
4	Bright, Fredk. Denny	32	Tarte, John Fredr.
5	Allcock, Egerton	33	Dowdeswell, John Jas.
6	Hartland, Edward	34	Partridge, Thomas
7	Snagle, Wm. Lawrence	35	Martin, Henry
8	Stephens, Wm. Hy.	36	Shelton, Charles
9	Jones, Joseph	37	Wilkins, Henry Rob.
10	Roberts, Samuel	38	Hampton, Thos.

11 Curtis, William
12 Parkes, Samuel
13 Hall, James
14 Colley, Benjamin
15 Wootton, Charles
16 Barrows, Fredk. Welsh
17 Jukes, William
18 Nichols, Geo. Benjm.
19 Bullus, William
20 Butler, Richard
21 Hampton, John
22 Coleman, George
23 Wakeman, Edward
24 Butler, James
25 Sherwell, Geo. Wm
26 Maud, Henry
27 Icke, Saml. Bickley
28 Prince, John Thos.

19 March
56 Fisher, Edwin
57 Homer, William
58 Jevons, John
28 March.
59 Travis, Wm. Thos.
30 March.
60 Millership, Joseph
61 Salter, Thomas
62 White, Samuel
63 Freeman, Edward
64 Foy, John
65 Tyndall, Ed.
April 2nd.
66 Robinson, William
April 4th.
67 Maud, Edward
68 Marsh, Samuel
25 May.
69 Middleton, James
70 Parkes, George
71 Parkes, William
72 Mason, Charles
73 Perry, Charles
74 Woodward, Henry
75 Hughes, John
76 Silvester, John
77 Bessiker, Joseph

39 Hudson, Geo. Allen
40 Fisher, William
41 Siddons, John Robertson
42 Clark, William

43 Farley. Reuben
44 Cottrell, Thos.
45 Moore, Thos.
46 Cooke, Jos.
47 Jones, Thos.
48 Crump, Geo.
49 Cresswell, Thos. Geo.
50 Cotton, Thos. Wm
51 Thompson, Geo.
17 March
52 Ingram, Frederick
53 Kite, Wm. James
54 Hepkins, David
55 Williams, John Wilson
13, 14, 18, 19 June.
78 Bunch, Thomas
79 Williams, Edward
80 Bullock, Ed. Luther
81 Martin, William
21 June.
82 Martin, Thomas
83 Harding, Samuel
84 Pears, Thos.
26 June.
85 Field, William
86 Wakeman, George
87 Tonks, Simeon
88 Dimbylon, Edwin
89 Cashmore, Samuel
90 Robinson, Joseph
1st July.
91 Groom, William
92 Hales, Enoch
93 Troth, Thomas
94 Evans, William
95 Jesson, Henry
96 Bradbury, Samuel
97 Groom, Joseph
98 Hayward, Richd.
99 Savage, John
100 Jackson, Geo.

This was a good start; but like every other human institution the Corps has experienced many vicissitudes. In 1868 sanction was given to increase its strength to 200, when 49 new members were enrolled, chiefly from the New Town and Great Bridge district, where they were drilled on the spot in St. Peter's Schoolroom. At the same time

Mr P. D. Bennett and Ensign Bache were made Lieutenants, and Mr H. L. Brown became Ensign. The average strength of the Corps may be judged by its numbers at three different periods: thus there were

Enrolled in   1860   ...   103 members.
,,   1868   ...   149   ,,
,,   1895   ...   101   ,,

The officers who have had command of the company since its formation—

March, 1860	...	Captain	Thomas Bagnall.
August, 1861	...	,,	H. Williams
February, 1875	...	,,	T. Bache.
December, 1879	...	,,	Frank Caddick.
December, 1891	...	,,	Wm. Hy. Wearing.

The corps was first armed with the muzzle-loading Enfield rifle, which was used till 1870, when the Snider rifle was served out. This was superseded by the arm at present, in use, namely, the Martini-Henry, issued in 1882. The first change of uniform took place in 1875 when the original dress was replaced by one consisting of scarlet tunic with white facings; buff belts were now worn; and for three years longer the chaco was worn, when it was replaced by the helmet now in vogue. In 1890 the corps was provided by public subscription with overcoats and the Slade-Wallace equipment—full campaigning dress.

The designation of the company has not always remained the same. In 1880 it was changed to "E Company, 1st Staffordshire Rifle Volunteers," and some five years later it took its present form, "E Company 1st V.B South Staffordshire Regiment." The employment of the term "Rifle" in the original name implied a force with some pretensions to marksmanship. But one of the most common difficulties to be overcome by the auxiliary forces from the first was the provision of shooting ranges. In this matter West Bromwich was more happily situated than most places. At once, in 1860, Lord Dartmouth granted the use of Sandwell Park as a shooting range for the company. In 1878 the range was enlarged and improved, and thrown open for the County of Stafford Prize Shooting.

The shooting of the West Bromwich Company was always good, and for several years it had the largest percentage of marksmen of any company of the Battalion. Prominent among its shooting members may be mentioned Captain Williams who won several prizes during his captaincy; Major Caddick, who won the St. George's Badge at Wimbledon, and several other good prizes, and last, but not least, Sergeant Amos Adams who has been a member of the company over 32 years, and was in the "Queen's 60" at Wimbledon in 1873, obtained the St. George's Badge in 1879 and in 1892, and won the Battalion Badge in 1879 and again in 1882. His arm is now covered with shooting badges.

In 1865 the Battalion Camps were inaugurated for the Midlands, when West Bromwich Company was among the first to go under canvas in Sandwell Park. This remained the camping ground till 1885, since which higher attempts at army organisation have taken the men farther afield to Aldershot, Strensall, Cannock, and Teddesley Park.

It speaks well for the patriotism and public life of West Bromwich, to observe that in the original roll of Volunteers are to be found such names as those of Alderman Farley, J.P., the present Mayor (No. 43), Alderman Roberts (No. 10), Mr John Hampton (No. 21), Mr Thomas Hampton (No. 38), and other prominent burgesses. Recognition must also be made of the able manner in which the Company's records have been kept by ex-Sergeant Instructor J. M. Carter (1866-1891), and of the courteous manner in which they have been placed at the writer's disposal by Captain Wearing.

LXXX.—Manners, Customs, Sports, and Pastimes.

In Dialetical nomenclature, the name of the town is still "Wess Brammidge." Its natives, in the slang of traducive tradition, are still "Throstles." This nickname is on the same level as that which designates all Londoners as "Cockneys," and which speaks of "Brummagem Buttons," of "Wedgbury Cockers," "Tipton Sharp-shins," etc.: and its derivation may be traced to the sylvan days of West Bromwich, when the parish consisted mainly of heath and wood. But the name "Throstle" was not applied merely because of those pleasant solitudes being the home of that feathered songster the mavis; but because it was the resort of numberless donkeys who browsed upon the open common-lands, and whose discordant bray was thus satirically alluded to under the name of the sweet-voiced thrush. Such was the delicate wit of the natives in the days gone by.

West Bromwich life of olden times seems to have left behind it but few records of those quaint and curious customs, which generally characterised the social history of bygone days. Beyond those given incidentally in the previous chapters, it is not proposed to deal further with them, but to come to those of more modern days.

Dealing with Bull Baiting first, it is difficult to find anecdotes or incidents peculiar to this parish itself. Here is one, however, which occurred at West Bromwich wake many years ago. A bull was to be baited, when one of the sportsmen, in his foolhardy bravado made a bet that he would seize hold of the bull by the nose with his teeth. A wager was laid! and the man, after much manœuvring, at last succeeded, but the animal disliking the proceeding, tossed his head suddenly in the air, and out came all the man's front teeth, and before he could get out of reach the bull rushed at him, knocked him down, and trampled upon him, breaking one of his legs—a punishment which he had sought, if he did not deserve it.

Perhaps this foolhardy individual was trying to emulate the renowned "bullot," Jack Willets, who has been claimed as a West Bromwich man, although it is more probable that he hailed from Moxley. This notorious character had served as a soldier in the Low Countries, after which he led a roving life and is said to have occupied himself in Spain in completing his education in the whole art and mystery of bull-fighting. He flourished in this vicinity about 1743 and was the ring-leader in all the brutal revelry so commonly practised in those days.

Bills to suppress the "sport" were defeated in Parliament in 1800 and in 1802, although a Wolverhampton local Act of 1777 empowered the imposition of a £5 penalty in that parish. In 1811 the Attorney General officially declared that bull baiting on the public highway was indictable as a nuisance. Great efforts were made to influence magistrates and local authorities to put down the abuse. In 1824 we learn from the *Birmingham Gazette* that "two more convictions for bull baiting have recently taken place in this neighbourhood under the Act 'to prevent cruel and improper treatment of cattle.' The first was in the case of W. Walker, of Wednesbury, carter who was convicted in the full penalty of £5 for baiting a bull at Wednesbury Wake, and in default of payment he was committed to Stafford Gaol for one month. The other was in the case of T. Turner, of the same place, labourer, who was convicted in the mitigated penalty of ten shillings and costs for being concerned in the same offence.'

In October of the same year a meeting of the clergy and gentry of the county was held at Wednesbury for the purpose of seeing what could be done to put down bull-baiting by more stringent and systematic efforts than had previously been brought to bear against the sport. As the outcome of the meeting it was finally resolved to form an association, to be called "The South Staffordshire Association for the Suppression of Bull-baiting." An influential committee was appointed, and various rules laid down for carrying out the object aimed at. In the year 1825 a butcher of West Bromwich, named William Bates, was fined £5 and costs, or in default a month's imprisonment, for being concerned as principal in a bull baiting at the wake in that town. Similar convictions took place in all the towns in this part of the country. Still the sport continued, in spite of local efforts. In 1827, at Handsworth, through the activity of the officers of the association, two men named Jones and Thomas were apprehended at a bull-bait near to Little Hockley Pool, at Handsworth Wake, and were fined the full penalties of £5 by Mr Spooner, of Birmingham. In the same year another conviction at West Bromwich led to a long and costly appeal, respecting which a pamphlet was written which bears the following title: "A short authentic account of the late decision on the Bull-baiting Question, in the case of the King against John Hill; with an appendix, containing reports of the speeches of Mr Windham, Mr Canning, and Mr Brougham, in resisting attempts to legislate against the sport. Dudley, 1827." The pamphlet contains much curious matter.

In the last mentioned case at West Bromwich, there were six men convicted under Mr Martin's Act in the November of the said year (1827), when penalties of £5 each were imposed, and the offenders in default of payment were committed to Stafford Gaol. A writ of Habeas Corpus was applied for in the case of one offender, the aforesaid John Hill, and a rule was granted by Lord Tenterden and Mr Justice Bayley. The rule was argued in December of the same year, and Mr Justice Bayley, after conferring with Mr Justice Littledale, made the rule absolute on the grounds that the omission of the "bull" from this Act *was intentional!*

It was probably on the outskirts of the parish that the actual baitings most frequently took place. For instance at the end of Queen's Head Lane, Handsworth, it was said the travellers on the through coaches were sometimes purposely delayed to be entertained with the spectacle of a baiting; while the boundary bridge at Nineveh (a place-name significant of the wickedness of the locality) was a notorious baiting-ground, at which in 1829, it was proposed with artless innocence to welcome the first vicar of Christ Church, by holding a grand exhibition of bull-baiting.

However the law may have regarded the practice of bull-baiting, and whatever may have been the attitude of the public mind *locally*, there can be no doubt that the *nation* at this time stood aghast at the cruelties inflicted on the tortured bulls; and it needed only the scourge of cholera in 1832 to quicken the vulgar mind to the enormity of the thing.

*   *   *   *   *   *   *

In the same way direct references to Cock Fighting in West Bromwich are difficult to find, although there is no doubt it was practised there. But as indirect evidence, here is a ballad—one of the best of its kind—which was written by the learned Charles Rann Kennedy, sometime of West Bromwich, and a descendant of Rev. John Rann once minister of the parish: It is called "The Wedgbury Miner"—

> There was a Wedgbury miner
>   A gamecock rare had he
> Never a better or finer
>   All Staffordshire did see.
>
> This cock while yet but a chicken
>   Would fight with a four-year-old
> The fowls were all panic-stricken
>   At his bearing so gallant and bold

And Boxer he was christened
    His breast was as white as snow
The miner's eyes they glistened
    Whenever he heard him crow.

And out of his hand he fed him
    On barley and cakes and ale
And when to battle he led him
    Was sure he would never fail.

And Boxer's fame was vaunted
    And every stake he won
The neighbours all were daunted
    For he his match had none.

At last, so saith the fable,
    A chap to the miner came,
Whose eyes and face were sable,
    And Nicholas was his name.

Quoth he, "I've a thoroughbred cock, sir,
    Thar never has yet been tried,
And I'll make a match with Boxer
    For fifty guineas aside."

"A match, there's no retreating,
    For fifty guineas aside";
They fixed the day of meeting
    At Wedgebury next Shrovetide.

And now to Wedgebury cocking,
    There posted a motley crew,
From Bilston all came flocking
    And Wolverhampton too.

The tailors, the butchers, the bakers,
    The coalmen from Dudley came down,
The pin and the button makers
    From smoky Brummagem town.

The ring was soon completed,
    The cocks were both brought in, ·
And Nick the miner greeted
    With a nod and half a grin.

The Blackman's cock was meagre
    And spectre-like to view,
Yet he seemed for combat eager,
    And he crowed as loud as two.

When all for the fight was ready,
    They gave the word of command,
Each bird marched bold and steady,
    Out of his master's hand.

And there was no demurring
    They met with pinion and heel,
And fierce was the flapping and spurring,
    And bright the flashing of steel.

Alas! how fleeting is glory
    To fowls as well as men,
Great Boxer, his bosom gory,
    Fell never to rise again.

The miner was mute with wonder,
    He scarce could believe his eyes;
The amazement he was under
    All power of speech defies.

And still he stood for a minute,
    Then off his jacket he threw;
"The devil himself is in it,
    But I'll be revenged on you.'

The Blackman he grew blacker
    Soon as the challenge he heard;
"The devil then be my backer,
    I'll take you at your word."

That voice made all of them nervous,
    Unearthly was the sound;
They whispered "Lord preserve us!"
    But formed a circle round.

The fight not long continued,
    For at the very first blow,
The miner, the iron-sinewed
    Was in the dust laid low.

And all the people assembled
    Turned pale when the sight they saw,
They shivered and quaked and trembled
    And looked at Old Nick with awe.

They looked, and oh, how horrid!
    A change came over his mien,
And horns appeared on his forehead,
    Where none before had been.

There were eyes all red and fiery
    A pestilent Brimstone smell,
And a pigtail curling spiry;
    Sure, 'twas an Imp of Hell!

They leapt up harum-scarum,
    And kicked the benches down,
And fast as legs could tear 'em,
    They scampered out of the town;

The tailors, the butchers, the bakers
    The coalmen in frantic mood,
The pin and the button-makers,
    As if by the devil pursued.

'Tis sure no theme for laughter,
    The miner was left alone,
And what became of him after
    Was never to mortal known.

*   *   *   *   *   *   *

Among the more manly games of modern times CRICKET has always been followed here with zest, and some amount of skill. The West Bromwich clubs, however, high as they have ranked among the other local town elevens, were seldom able to vie with the clubs of Smethwick; a place which has always maintained high rank in the domain of cricket.

Coming to FOOTBALL, a game which took hold of the popular fancy at a somewhat later period, it may be safely asserted that few places have made such a wide reputation in any branch of sport as West Bromwich has in the Football world. About 1873 this game was established very firmly in local estimation at the neighbouring town of Wednesbury, and two prominent clubs rose into fame there. At West Bromwich the cricket clubs commenced to practice and play the newer game under what were known as Association Rules, although a fifteen had and continued to, play the game very successfully according to the older rules of Rugby School. But it was not till the game of football became less the sport of the well-to-do and more the pastime of the working classes, that it took its present hold on popular favour. It was not Salters' Club, nor the Dartmouth Club, which brought West Bromwich football into prominence, but a club of much more humble origin. known as "The Albion." The history of this club and its rapid rise to a position of national importance among the sporting institutions of the country cannot be ignored in these chronicles of the parish of West Bromwich.

It would appear that some working youths, connected with a local cricket club, the bulk of whom were engaged at Messrs Salters' works banded themselves together to play football, and called themselves "The West Bromwich Strollers." This was in the year 1879, and for some time they practised on a piece of open land, and afterwards in Dartmouth Public Park. These youths had to make a collection among themselves to purchase their first football, but diligence and practice soon made them proficient. They next established a weekly subscription of 2d. and an entrance fee of 6d., which entitled subscribers to all the privileges of membership in the newly formed club. In the season of 1880-81 they adopted the name of the Albion, and their cleverness with the ball soon won them great praise from the spectators who began to congregate in the Public Park to watch them. As the team began to defeat all comers, it was realised that there was possibly a great future before it. The players practised assiduously, and by the exertion of their own hands they enclosed a playing-ground, as much to protect their own play from interference as to direct their efforts to the taking of gate money. They succeeded in defeating a club (Nechells F.C.) which had just previously beaten the Dartmouth F.C., hitherto the premier club of West Bromwich, this achievement at once attracted the support and patronage of the town, which was soon transferred to them solely, to the neglect of the Dartmouth eleven. This club presently died out, and was totally superseded by the Albion, who acquired their well-known and centrally situated arena of play, The Four Acres. In 1881 the Albion entered the competition for the Birmingham Football Club; in this series of matches they defeated the Birmingham Calthorpe F.C., Wednesbury Elwells F.C., and Notts Rangers F.C., but were eventually knocked out in the semi-final match by the Wednesbury Old Athletic Club, then the champion combination of the Midlands. Again in 1882-3, in the same competition, they had to succumb to the prowess of these Wednesbury champions. But this season they first encountered the renowned Aston Villa F.C.; it was in the second round of matches for the Staffordshire Cup, and the Albion created some astonishment by making a drawn game; and on replaying the match at Four Acres astonishment gave way to enthusiasm when they defeated the Villa; a feeling which was not diminished when they won the cup outright by defeating the Stoke F.C. in the final. Having made a reputation by winning the county trophy, the Albion next year (1883-4) entered the national competition for the English Cup, but were beaten in the first round by

Wednesbury Town F.C. They obtained a sufficient revenge on the latter place, however, by defeating the Wednesbury Old Athletic in the Birmingham Cup competition, a success quickly followed up by defeating Walsall F.C. in the Staffordshire series; while even the renowned Preston Club also suffered defeat from them. About this time a famous player named Bayliss deserted Wednesbury Old Athletic and joined the Albion Club, this did more than anything could have done at that juncture to establish the fortunes of the game in West Bromwich.

In 1884-5 the English Cup competition saw Albion defeat the Villa F.C. 3 goals to 1 on Four Acres—perhaps a tremendous downpour of rain affected the result; but they succumbed to Blackburn Rovers F.C. in the sixth round, Next season, 1885 6, Albion reached the final in the English Competition for the first time, making a drawn game with the Rovers at Kennington Oval; but when the venue was changed to Derby on the following Saturday they lost by 0 goals to 2. This year the West Bromwich men created a record by reaching the finals for three cups—English, Staffordshire, and Birmingham—making a draw in each whereby they actually played in six "finals." The County and the Birmingham trophies they won. In 1886-7 Albion won a memorable victory over Preston North End F.C. in the semi-final at Nottingham, but failed again to secure the English Cup, which the Villa wrested from them by 2 goals against 0. Next year, 1887-8 at a third attempt, Albion overcoming the formidable Preston club by 2 to 0 in the final, brought the English Challenge Cup to West Bromwich amidst great rejoicing for their opponents had been hitherto considered invincible. In this same season the Albion played at Glasgow for what was really the championship of the world, pitting themselves against Renton F. C., holders of the Scotch Cup, they lost by 1 to 4. In 1888-9 Albion were defeated at Sheffield in the semi-final by Preston North End, losing by 0 to 1 only; next year (1889-90) the Accrington club at the very start knocked out the Albion in the first round. The season 1890-1 saw them reach the semi-final—we are now considering the West Bromwich club as national exponents of the game, engaged in the highest form of competition—but lose their match to Blackbhurn Rovers, by 2 to 3, at Stoke. Next year (1891-2) Albion won the cup a second time by defeating the favourites, Aston Villa, by 3 goals to 0, to say nothing of playing in several other semi finals and finals, Less fortunate next season (1892-3) they were defeated in the first round by Everton F.C. at Liverpool, and again the following year they succumbed on their own ground to the Blackburn Rovers. In 1894-5 they lost the final to Aston Villa by 0 to 1, although they afterwards won the Birmingham Cup, exactly reversing the score with the same antagonists by way of compensation. This is no mean record for any branch of sport.

It may be mentioned that the club has had no better friend than its present president, Councillor G. Salter. It would have been simply impossible for the Albion to have achieved what they have without his assistance. Many of the players have been and are at the present time, engaged at Messrs Salters' works, but they have always been allowed to get off for practice, training, or to play matches whenever required. Among others who have supported the club are Mr H. Jackson, Alderman Heelis, Dr. Rees, Dr. Pitt, Messrs Enoch Wood, J. Roberts and J. Lavender while Messrs Louis Ford, and J. M. Bayliss have been of immense assistance in the arrangement of the club. Amongst Albion club secretaries may be mentioned Messrs T. Homer, T. Smith, T. Foster, L. Ford, W. P. Dix, S. H. Jackson, and the present genial secretary, Mr Clement Keys.

Here it would be out of place to particularise the best players by name: First, because football is a game which depends for its successful playing on the machine-like precision of the team as a whole and not so much upon any individual effort, and secondly, because although the Albion and other great football clubs were originally combinations of native players, in these later days they have largely degenerated into teams of hireling players imported chiefly from the northern counties, or else the northern kingdom. Portrait groups of the winning teams have appeared from time to time in the various London illustrated papers, while every important player and supporter has been sketched and portrayed (more or less truthfully) in many of the sporting newspapers which the phenomenal success of the game has called into existence of late years.

The appearance of the Albion Club in the English final of 1886 marked an epoch; it was the first final of the national competition ever played out of London, and testifies to the growing strength and influence of the provincial clubs as against the older Metropolitan elevens. So influential became the patronage, and so large the crowds of spectators who regularly attended their match meetings, that at last the Albion abandoned the historic Four Acres, and laid out a new ground in Stoney Lane, at a cost of about £650. Further, some four years ago, the club was transformed into a Limited Liability Company, to give it a proper legal status for its somewhat extensive commercial undertakings. The capital of the company was fixed at £1,500, more than half of which has been allotted and taken up. Thus had the dimensions of the institution grown from the small and humble beginnings described; and the Albion and its operations may be taken as typical of the workings of any great provincial football club of these modern times.

*   *   *   *   *   *   *

LAWN TENNIS flourishes in West Bromwich. The Sandwell L.T. Club has a membership of nearly one hundred ladies and gentlemen, and its ground in Beeches Road is replete with every convenience for players. It has no less than eight courts going at a time; there are in addition two ash courts for use in wet weather, and there is also a capital BOWLING green

HOCKEY has its votaries, too. The West Bromwich Club which plays this old-fashioned game is somewhat select: it uses Salters' Cricket ground, and in the Midland Counties League has come out third in the competition.

*   *   *   *   *   *   *

Enlightenment and common-sense are highly exemplified in the public opinion of West Bromwich which allows MUSIC in its PUBLIC PARK on SUNDAY, and also permits the OPENING of the PUBLIC BATHS during certain early hours of the same day of the week.

LXXXI.—BIBLIOGRAPHY OF WEST BROMWICH.

Already in the long course of these chronicles more than forty authorities have been quoted from and named. Local allusions may be further sought in the following works:—

Blome's BRITANNIA	...	...	...	...	...	period 1673
ENGLAND, ILLUSTRATED	...	...	...	...	...	„ 1764
THE TOPOGRAPHER	...	...	...	...	...	„ 1789
Pitts' STAFFORDSHIRE	...	...	...	...	...	„ 1817
Lewis' TOPOGRAPHICAL DICTIONARY		...	...	...	„ 1831
W. Hawkes Smith's BIRMINGHAM AND VICINITY		...	...	„ 1836
White's DIRECTORY	...	...	...	...	...	„ 1855

No attempt has been made to give a succinct account of the rise and progress of the numerous industries of West Bromwich; this would be a task sufficient by itself; but the reader is referred to *Griffiths'* GUIDE TO THE IRON TRADE, published in 1873, pp. 66, 209. 269, etc.

From that voluminous and exhaustive work, *Simms'* BIBLIOTHECA STAFFORDIENSIS may be culled much detailed information about West Bromwich writers and writings, as under the following alphabetical arrangement:—

Bagnall, John Nock, born at West Bromwich. 30th May, 1826. Biographical headings and literary works—the latter comprising "The History of Wednesbury," and three other works.

Bayley, Charles H., born at Warley, 1829: West Bromwich Archæologist—printed with his own private press—his topographical library, sold at London, 18th July, 1883, by Messrs Sotheby, 465 lots, realising £468 13s. 6d: His coins and rare silver realised £40 11s. 6d. on March 19th, 1884.

Creamer, Roland, died at W. B., 1854—obituary reference.

Culwick, James C., b. W. B., 1845—musician, composer &c.

Dean, S. A., born W. B., 1853—obituary reference in 1880.

Dudley and West Bromwich Bank—deed of settlement, 1834.

Dyer, W. H., of W. B., wrote "Papal Policy and English Nonconformists," 1851.

Elton, Rev. Sir Abraam, minister and lecturer at W. B. 1782-90—biographical references.

Foxall, Henry, of W.B., 1758-1823—Wesleyan memoir.

Griffiths, Thomas, a printer of W.B., 1834.

Hodgson, Rev. Robert, Vicar of Christ Church, W.B., 1872-83—biographical and literary references.

Izon, Rev. W. Y. S., born at W.B. 1832—references.

James, Walter, surgeon of W.B.—medical pamphlets 1827 and 1831.

Jesse, Heneage, b. at W.B. 1809—biographical and literary references.

Jesse, Rev. W., b. 1738. Minister of W.B. 1790-1815—biographical.

Jesson, Richard, b. at W.B. 1804—biographical.

Joberns, Rev. C. H, Vicar of Christ Church, W.B. 1883-91—biographical.

Jukes, Rev. Richd., Primitive Methodist Minister in W.B.—list of numerous works including "The Poet of the Million, or Memorials of the Life and Labours of Rev. Richard Jukes."

Keir , James, F.R.S.—biographical headings, and references to the literary works of this eminent man, including his "Life and Writings of Thomas Day" (the author of the popular "Sandford and Mertorn.") This was issued in 1791: he is also to be credited with "A Treatise on the Art of War," the MS. of which was accidentally burnt by the publisher in 1766; an elegy on Gregory Watt. a leaflet oft 1804; and some pamphlets, political and otherwise, and perhaps the translation of scientific works from the French.

Kelk, Rev. Thos., Wesleyan Minister, d. at W.B. 1836—works and memoir.

Kennedy, C. B.—poems, original and translated, W.B., 1857.

Legge—various members of the family—biographical references, with dates, etc.

Lewis, Rev. Lewis, curate in W. B. 1873-5—biographical and literary.

Morris, James Taylor, b. at W. B. 1809—university record.

Murray, David Christi-, and *Murray*, Henry, the brother novelists, both natives of W. B. Justice cannot be done to the eminence of these writers by any casual allusion here, or even by re-printing the list of works given. The former born 1847, has attained a world-wide reputation as a writer of fiction.

Parkes, D. Shrewsbury wrote an "account and view of W. B. Church" in Gentlemen's Mag., March, 1797.

Pearson, John Y. b. at W. B. 1860—university record.

Puckle, Rev. Edwin, b at W. B. 1832—biographical headings.

Rann, Joseph b. at W. B. 1714—biographical headings.

Reynolds, Rev. John buried at W. B. 1727—literary works.

Sanders, Rev. Henry, Curate of West Bromwich, 1752-57. A memoir of him was prefixed to his "History of Shenstone," by Rev. John Butler Sanders, who was born at Wednesbury, 1746.

Shelton, Joseph, born at West Bromwich, 1682—biographical notes. Also of Sir Richard *Shelton*, of West Bromwich.

Simcox, Rev. Josiah, born at West Bromwich—University record, 1662-1665.
Mining Institute Transactions—references to West Bromwich, page 428 of Simms.
Taylor, A.—a printer of West Bromwich—publisher of "Labor Tribune," weekly.
Turton—references to pedigree and various members of the family.
Ward, Henry—married daughter of J. N. Bagnall, of West Bromwich—references to public life, &c.
West Bromwich, q.v.
Weston, Rev. Richard, Curate at Gold Hill, 1873-6—wrote "John Bright and the Curate."
Whorwood and *Whyley* families of West Bromwich—various members referred to.
Willett, Rev. F. and Mrs—biographical notes and literary references.
Willmore, Rev. B. Incumbent of Holy Trinity, West Bromwich, 1858-70—list of works. His son, Mr
 F. W. Willmore, born at West Bromwich, 1848—list of his literary works also.

To this Mr Simms has privately added:—

Hilton, Rev. Richard, was born at Bloxum, Oxon, of poor parents, 1625. His father was named
 Richard. He matriculated at Christ Church, Oxford, 9 April, 1641, and took his B.A. 17
 December 1614, by virtue of the Chancellor's letter; minister of West Bromwich, 30 July, 1648
 till 1662, when he was ejected and became chaplain to Philip Foley, of Prestwood (as
 previously recorded in chapters xxxii. and liv.) He died at Walsall 1706.

Mr Geo. T. Lawley has kindly supplemented these with:—

*An account of the Lectureship in the Parish of West Bromwich, founded by Walter Stanley, Esq,
 in the year 1613, including copies of the Foundation Deed, and of the orders and ordinances
 instituted by Mr Stanley for the endowment and government of his lectureship, &c., &c.*
 Printed by R. Wrightson, Birmingham, and sold by T. Negus, Stamp Office West Bromwich
 1815. 8 vo.
*An Act for dividing, allotting, and inclosing the several open common fields, common pastures and
 waste lands, within the manor and parish of West Bromwich, in the County of Stafford.* 8 vo.
 [Award dated 10th October, 1804].
West Bromwich Health Lectures, by T Underhill, on "Healthy Homes." Dr. Hill on "Fever Traps,"
 H. L. Browne on "Foods," P. Smith on "Nerves," etc.
The Iron Trade, by J. Hogg. W. B. 1869.
A Visible Church and No invisible Members, by Rev. Richard Rymer. W. B. 8 vo. 1861.
A Tribute to the Memory of the Rev. John Smith, Late Missionary to Demerara, by J. Cooper, of W.
 B. 12 mo. 1824.
Sermons, by Rev. Ed. Stillingfleet, M.A., minister of W.B. 8 vo. 1812.

INDEX